BLUES UNLIMITED

Essential Interviews
from the
Original Blues Magazine

MUSIC IN AMERICAN LIFE

A list of books in the series appears at the end of this book.

BLUES UNLIMITED

Essential Interviews from the Original Blues Magazine

Edited by

Bill Greensmith, Mike Rowe, and Mark Camarigg

Foreword by

Tony Russell

University of Illinois Press

Urbana, Chicago, and Springfield

Manufactured in the United States of America
1 2 3 4 5 C P 5 4 3 2 1
∞ This book is printed on acid-free paper.

Library of Congress Cataloging-in-Publication Data
Blues unlimited : essential interviews from the original
blues magazine / edited by Bill Greensmith, Mike Rowe,
and Mark Camarigg; foreword by Tony Russell.
pages cm. — (Music in American life)
Includes bibliographical references and index.
ISBN 978-0-252-03941-6 (hardcover : alk. paper) —
ISBN 978-0-252-08099-9 (pbk. : alk. paper) —
ISBN 978-0-252-09750-8 (e-book)
1. Blues (Music)—History and criticism.
2. Blues musicians—United States—Interviews.
I. Greensmith, Bill, 1949– editor. II. Rowe, Mike, editor.
III. Camarigg, Mark, editor. IV. Russell, Tony, 1946– writer
of supplementary textual content. V. Blues unlimited.
ML3521.B645 2015
781.643092'2—dc23 2015008520

with a book grant from
Figure Foundation

blues the wind uprising

For Simon Napier and Mike Leadbitter,
Blues Unlimited founding editors

CONTENTS

FOREWORD

Tony Russell

In April 1963 the first issue of *Blues Unlimited* emerged like a small green shoot in a near desert. Over the next half century, the blues periodical library would grow to thousands of issues of scores of titles from a dozen or more countries, but at the time, *BU* stood alone on the blues enthusiast's bookshelf, the first magazine to be devoted exclusively to the blues.

A comprehensive blues library today would also include many hundreds of books, but in 1963 that shelf too would have been sparsely occupied. The core items were Samuel B. Charters's *The Country Blues* (1959) and Paul Oliver's *Blues Fell This Morning* (1960), with perhaps *Big Bill Blues* (1955), the story of the blues singer Big Bill Broonzy as told to the Belgian writer Yannick Bruynoghe. (These would be joined later in 1963 by Leroi Jones's *Blues People.*) An avid and well-resourced enthusiast might also have acquired scholarly volumes on African American music such as Howard W. Odum and Guy B. Johnson's *The Negro and His Songs* (1925), Dorothy Scarborough's *On the Trail of Negro Folk-Songs* (1925), and Newman I. White's *American Negro Folk-Songs* (1928). Anyone who had been around long enough to know about it might own Iain Lang's *Background of the Blues,* first published as an essay in the mid-1940s, then as a pamphlet, then expanded into a book. For the serious record collector, there was the French jazz authority Hugues Panassié's *Discographie critique des meilleurs disques de Jazz* (1958), which embraced a number of blues artists, and there were the compilations of label listings that had been occasionally published in the United States since about 1959 under the title *Blues Research.* Still, the shelf was scarcely bowing beneath the weight of works.

The diminutive blues library of 1963 gives some idea of the vastness of the terrain the founders of *BU* were setting out to discover, and how few maps they held at the start of their journey. This is not to say that no one was writing about blues in magazines before *BU* appeared. In Belgium, *Rhythm & Blues Panorama* had been evenhandedly covering jazz, blues, and gospel since February 1960, featuring knowledgeable writing by Bruynoghe, George Adins, Bernard Niquet, and editor Serge Tonneau. Since the 1950s, the world of R&B had been explored by the Frenchman Kurt Mohr at *Jazz Hot* and by the contributors to the Swiss magazine *Jazz Statistics*. Back in the U.K., Max Jones, a staff writer on the weekly music paper *Melody Maker*, though chiefly concerned with jazz matters, had been talking to its readers about blues records since the '40s; he also published a thoughtful essay, "On Blues," in *The PL Yearbook of Jazz 1946*. Paul Oliver had been writing articles and reviewing records in *Jazz Monthly* since the '50s, and there were other contributors to that magazine and its peer *Jazz Journal* who reviewed competently the few blues LPs and EPs that crept onto the U.K. market. Similar notices of blues releases appeared sporadically in other European jazz magazines and in U.S. periodicals like *DownBeat*.

The reason blues was mediated through jazz magazines was twofold: there *were* no blues magazines (and precious few specialist blues writers), and in any case blues was regarded as a sort of relation of jazz: not a poor relation exactly, more an unlettered country cousin. It was thought of as unsophisticated but with a bucolic wit and a down-to-earth outlook—what someone only half-jocularly called "an instinctive lowdown on ontological despair"—that were not only beguiling in themselves but instructively backlit the rise and self-improvement of the urban, and urbane, jazz musician. So the editors of jazz magazines, whether in the U.S., the U.K., or continental Europe, regarded it as a duty to history to give some consideration to the blues and to the tiny body of people who liked it and wanted to know more about it.

But those were people who had typically come to an appreciation of blues through jazz, or through blues artists associated with jazz, like Bessie Smith, or through music poised between blues and jazz, like boogie-woogie, and they generally had a decade or two of listening experience. The founders of *BU* did not belong to that generation. They were in their early twenties, and in their teens they had been drenched by the great cloudburst of '50s American R&B. Their first teachers had been Little Richard, Fats Domino, James Brown, Chuck Berry, and Bo Diddley, and then "hard" bluesmen like Muddy Waters, Howlin' Wolf, Jimmy Reed, and John Lee Hooker—all of them artists who not only were still alive but who also were at, or only just past, the peak of their skills. Consequently, the "museumification" of the blues that permeated its coverage by jazz writers would not be perpetuated in the pages of *BU*. It's true that from the start the magazine did pay some attention to the blues' past, but it revealed to its readers figures like Charley Patton and Booker White—not members of the jazz-blues pantheon, but new and strange gods.

Unaffected by the factionalism that often erupted in the jazz magazines, dividing adherents of the old from proponents of the new, the contributors to *BU* embraced with equal enthusiasm long forgotten figures from the '20s and '30s and working blues musicians of the present. The first issue had articles on the very active Little Junior Parker and the obscure '30s bluesman Bull City Red; the third issue, on Howlin' Wolf, Buddy Guy, and the '30s steel guitarist Casey Bill Weldon; the fourth, on Billy "The Kid" Emerson, who was still making records in Chicago, and Mississippi John Hurt, who had not been in a studio since 1928.

It was cartography on the Mason-Dixon model, with explorers venturing where few, if any, with their concerns had been before, except that now mapmakers were being dispatched not on a single expedition but in every direction to plot the landscape of the blues. It may seem curious that the hub of this project was the southern English seaside town of Bexhill-on-Sea, but, then, Mason and Dixon were Englishmen too.

ACKNOWLEDGMENTS

Through all the various stages Mark Camarigg worked tirelessly to ensure this book came to fruition. The project was started a few years before Mark came on board, but due to the pressure of work, progress had slowed to a crawl. To borrow a well-worn cliché, without his hard work and enthusiasm this book may never have been completed.

Thanks to Diana Napier, who gave her blessing to the project and provided access to Simon's personal papers and photographs.

Many thanks to the contributors to *Blues Unlimited* who over the years selflessly provided interviews, news, reviews, discographical information, and photographs: Herb Abramson, Graham Ackers, Clas Ahlstrand, John Allinson, Billy Boy Arnold, Cary Baker, Dick Bass, Bruce Bastin, Wolfie Baum, Bruce Bromberg, John Broven, Pete Brown, Tony Burke, Stephen Cault, Marcel Chauvard, Dave Clarke, John Cowley, Lou Curtis, Fred Davis, Jimmy Dawkins, Walter De Block, Ed Denson, Jacques Demetre, Bob Eagle, David Evans, John Fahey, Paul Garon, Galen Gart, Karl Gert Zur Heide, Phil Givant, Peter Goldsmith, Robin Gosden, Fred Goulding, Bill Greensmith, Bob Hall, Jeff Hannusch, Paul Harris, David Harrison, Jeff Hatherick, Cedric Hayes, Tim Healey, Gerard Herzhaft, Norbert Hess, Lee Hilderbrand, Andre Hobus, John Holt, Cilla Huggins, Max Jones, Will Jones, Don Kent, Bernard Klatzco, Bob Koester, Kerry Kudlacek, James LaRocca, Steve LaVere, Bob Laughton, Mike Leadbitter, Willie Leiser, Denis Lewis, Don Lindeneau, Pete Lowry, Ken Martin, Neil McBurney, Mack McCormick, Bill Miller, Rick Milne, George Mitchell, Kurt Mohr, Pete Moody, Simon Napier, Frank Nazareth, Richard Noblett, Jim O'Neal, Bengt Olsson,

Paul Oliver, Johnny Otis, Jack Parsons, Neil Patterson, George Paulus, Dave Penny, Sylvia Picher, Wes Race, Charles Radcliff, Stella Reeder, Fred Reif, Clive Richardson, Mike Rowe, Tony Russell, Robert Sacre, Dave Sax, Frank Scott, Doug Seroff, Paul Sheatsley, Dick Shurman, Eddie Shuler, Peter Shertser, Larry Skoog, Neil Slaven, Chris Smith, Francis Smith, Dick Spottswood, Robert Springer, Tom Stagg, Darryl Stolper, Chris Strachwitz, Sandy Sutherland, Steve Tracy, Jeff Titon, Henry Thomas, Ray Topping, Bez Turner, Mike Vernon, Paul Vernon, Henry Vestine, Dave Ward, Gayle Wardlow, Frank Weston, George White, Dave Williams, Valerie Wilmer, Pete Wingfield, Ray Wortley, and Neil Wyatt. Our profound apologies to anyone whose name has been inadvertently omitted.

Mark Camarigg would like to thank Greg Johnson and the staff at the University of Mississippi Department of Archives and Special Collections, John Broven, Dr. David Evans, Bill Greensmith, Ed Komara, Mack McCormick, Laurie Matheson, the North Little Rock History Commission, Jim O'Neal, Dr. Ted Ownby at the Center for the Study of Southern Culture, and especially Rebecca and Owen Camarigg for their constant support and enthusiasm.

Tony Russell would like to thank Alan Balfour and Howard Rye.

INTRODUCTION

Bill Greensmith

Bexhill-on-Sea is a sleepy seaside town in East Sussex on the south coast of England, seemingly populated by old ladies and retired servicemen. I first visited Bexhill as a young boy, with my parents; we intended to spend a week's vacation there. No sunshine and beach for us—it rained endlessly. Bored, damp, and miserable, we soon returned to London. At some later date I discovered that the comedian Spike Milligan was stationed at Bexhill for a period during World War II. He described the town as "an above-ground cemetery," and his wartime experiences there surely account for it being immortalized in some of his scripts for the BBC radio program *The Goon Show.* Such was my skewed perception of Bexhill and the staid and gloomy reputation it enjoyed, deserved or not, during the 1950s.

It was unquestionably the most unlikely of locations for the birthplace of *Blues Unlimited,* the world's first publication devoted solely to the blues. Picking up the magazine for the first time in the 1960s, I can still recall my incredulity upon seeing its address.

Bexhill was home to both Simon Napier and Mike Leadbitter, *Blues Unlimited*'s founding editors. Simon and Mike's friendship began at Bexhill Grammar School in 1955 through a shared interest in rock 'n' roll—and, had they but known it, rhythm and blues, as many artists during this period, such as Joe Turner, Fats Domino, and Chuck Willis, were being marketed and sold as rock 'n' roll. The difference soon became apparent to the pair as they explored labels like London American and Vogue, two of the few domestic outlets for R&B and rock 'n' roll in England at the time. An all-consuming and passionate interest in the blues, in all of its many and varied

Simon Napier and Mike Leadbitter. 38a Sackville Road, Bexhill. (Photo Diana Napier)

forms, quickly followed—and led them in turn to zydeco and Cajun music, at a time when few of us had ever heard those terms.

Weekly record sessions were held at Simon's parents' house. John Broven, a friend and classmate of Mike's, soon joined the pair and was introduced to the records of Jimmy Reed, B. B. King, Elmore James, and Lonesome Sundown, among others. Label listings were pored over, and the trade publications *Billboard* and *Cashbox* were scoured for news and reviews of likely records. Mike and John began writing to many of the companies that regularly advertised in these magazines. Eddie Shuler of Goldband Records in Lake Charles, Louisiana, was one of the first to respond, sending a box of his releases, which included records by Hop Wilson and Juke Boy Bonner. Mike and John had similar success with Paul Glass of both USA and Age Records in Chicago, receiving records by J. B. Lenoir, Homesick James, and Junior Wells. Contact was also established with like-minded enthusiasts, thus setting up a free exchange of information and ideas.

The annual American Folk Blues Festival (AFBF) show, which began in 1962, was a seminal event, exposing many English and European listeners to the blues for the first time. Before that, tours of Britain by blues artists had been few: Lonnie Johnson, Big Bill Broonzy, Josh White, Sonny Terry, and Brownie McGhee were among the earliest. In 1958 bandleader Chris Barber, a longtime selfless supporter of the blues, famously promoted a tour by Muddy Waters and Otis Spann, a monumental event for English blues aficionados. Roosevelt Sykes, Speckled Red, Little Brother Montgomery, Champion Jack Dupree, Memphis Slim, and James Cotton were also early visitors. Some later AFBF shows did garner criticism; there was perceived to be a lack of imagination in the booking of artists. But in reality they were remarkable events, presenting an extraordinary collection of artists on one stage: Sonny Boy Williamson, Muddy Waters, Big Joe Williams, Lonnie Johnson, and others in 1963; Magic Sam, Earl Hooker, Clifton Chenier, Juke Boy Bonner, and others in 1969. Viewing from today's perspective, who would argue with these choices?

In 1963 much of the information that we now take for granted was still to be documented, and a standard blues discography did not yet exist. That blues research was still in its infancy is an understatement, given the meager blues literature described by Tony Russell in his foreword. A magazine devoted exclusively to the subject seemed like a good idea. In April 1963, six months after the first AFBF toured Europe, the first issue of *Blues Unlimited* was published. Its base of operation was the attic of Simon's parents' antique shop at 38A Sackville Road. Subtitled *The Journal of the Blues Appreciation Society* (TBAS), *Blues Unlimited* was a direct outgrowth of that organization. Formed in May 1962, TBAS was based on a similar group created earlier by Max Vreede in Holland; its objective was to collect and disseminate discographical and biographical information, publish sales lists, and function as a lending library.

Issue number 1 contained items by John Broven on Little Junior Parker and Jay Miller (which presaged his book *Record Makers and Breakers* forty-six years later). Paul Oliver contributed an article on Bull City Red; Cedric Hayes produced a discography of the Staple Singers, and Simon an overview of Crown Records, in which he singled out some of the label's more worthwhile issues. A news item reported the death of Mercy Dee Walton, and Mike Leadbitter pleaded for help in compiling label lists of Sun, Bullet, and Hollywood, among others. John and Mike jointly reviewed the current crop of U.S. singles—Hop Wilson on Goldband, Clarence Garlow on Folkstar, new Chess 45s by Muddy Waters and Buddy Guy—and U.K. releases on the recently formed Pye R&B label, including albums by Chuck Berry and Bo Diddley and 45s by Sonny Boy Williamson, Howlin' Wolf, and English harmonica player Cyril Davies. However, "Mr. Davies does not warrant discussion being one of these things we're getting hurled at us from Britain of late." This caustic comment from Simon effectively established the *Blues Unlimited* editorial policy: few blues revivalists were to be included in its pages. An impressive beginning and all for the bargain price of one shilling and sixpence (7½p, or 18 cents).

From the outset it was Simon who undertook the responsibility of physically producing the magazine, typing the pages on stencils and printing them on a Roneotype machine. The pages were then collated and stapled jointly by Simon, Mike, and John. This truly was a hands-on operation. Issue 1 exceeded all expectation: the entire run of 180 copies quickly sold out. Encouraged by its success, Simon cautiously increased the print run to 210 for issue 2, published in June 1963. He continued to increase the print run in increments of 10 and 20 until issue 6 (November 1963), when it jumped to 300. By issue 10 (March 1964), it had further increased to 400, and by issue 13 (July 1964), to 1,000.

Researchers, discographers, and enthusiasts from Europe and the United States soon began to freely contribute articles, interviews, reviews, and information. A discography of B. B. King, compiled by Mike and John with contributions from Wolfie Baum and Marcel Chauvard, appeared in issue 2. "Cajun Corner" made its debut in this issue, followed two issues later by Paul Oliver's "Creoles, Cajuns and Confusion," which added historical context and clarified the terminology. A feature on Howlin' Wolf with an accompanying discography by John Broven, Chauvard, and

Kurt Mohr was the highlight of issue 3, along with the beginning of Cedric Hayes's listing of "Post-War Gospel Records."

The early *BU*s managed to convey a wonderful sense of adventure; the enthusiasm was palpable. The early '60s saw the rediscovery of several artists who had recorded in the '20s and '30s, and *Blues Unlimited* was among the first to report the findings. Issue 4 carried a story by Dick Spottswood about the rediscovery of Mississippi John Hurt and his recording for the first time in thirty-five years. This was soon followed by the rediscovery of Bukka White, reported in issue 7 by John Fahey and Ed Denson. And in issue 15 Bernard Klatzko reported on the search for and rediscovery of Son House, also including a brief interview.

The first major feature on Elmore James appeared in issue 5, following a report of his early death, by Neil Patterson, in the previous issue. With *BU* 5 the subhead *The Journal of the Blues Appreciation Society* was dropped and Mike Leadbitter's name was added as "R&B Editor." With each issue *Blues Unlimited* continued to break new ground, revealing new artists or ones who had been long neglected, while lending support to record companies and to serious projects like Robert Dixon and John Godrich's discography, *Blues & Gospel Records, 1902–1943*, which was published in 1964.

From today's vantage point it is sometimes easy to forget the time and context in which *BU* began operating. Few blues artists had ever been the subject of an article or formal interview before appearing in *BU*. Chess, Vee-Jay, Duke/Peacock, and Excello were active, vital record companies. New 45s by Muddy, Wolf, Sonny Boy, and Jimmy Reed were regularly reviewed. The young Buddy Guy was considered to be in the vanguard of modern blues. Neil Patterson and the indefatigable Pete Welding contributed numerous artist interviews to the early editions of *BU*. Welding, along with Bob Koester and Don Kent, also sent regular tantalizing reports of activities in Chicago—reports that were arguably responsible for inspiring many Europeans to visit that city. Eddie Taylor, Johnny Young, and Big Boy Spires were just a few whose stories appeared in early issues of *BU*. Viewed with hindsight, several of these interviews are less detailed than they would be nowadays. But in the early '60s they were groundbreaking, introducing us to a wide variety of artists, most of whom were unknown to blues fans outside their hometowns.

An editorial in issue 12 announced a price increase: from issue 13 the cover price would rise to a whopping two shillings (10p, or 25 cents). With issue 13 also came the first use of photographs, although they were initially confined to the cover. The magazine now had a smaller typeface and was professionally printed, allowing Simon to retire the Roneo machine. Issue 12 saw the start of *Collectors Classics*, a series of monographs published by *BU*, mostly featuring a single artist and discography. *CC* number 1 was devoted to Muddy Waters. This was soon followed by *Collectors Classics* featuring Chuck Berry, Bo Diddley, John Lee Hooker, Howlin' Wolf, and others. The series ran through the late '60s, eventually being replaced by *BU Booklets*. This series of publications covered a variety of subjects: *Beale Street USA*, *Crowley, Loui-*

Neil Patterson, Simon Napier, John Broven, unknown, Graham Ackers,
Rose and Mike Leadbitter, Anna and Dave Williams, 1964.

siana Blues, From the Bayou: The Story of Goldband Records, and Mike Leadbitter's *Delta Country Blues,* which was to form the basis of a greatly expanded Delta book, a project that unfortunately has remained unpublished.

Another new look for the magazine began with issue 24, when it appeared in A5 size (roughly 6 x 8 inches), a format that lasted until issue 56, when it switched back to A4 (8½ x 11 inches). More photographs were now being used, and the price further increased to four shillings (20p, or 48 cents).

Mike Leadbitter's passion for all things discographical quickly manifested itself in a regular column. "Post-War Discographical Comment" debuted in issue 21, with Mike pondering inaccuracies in the existing Willie Nix discography and issuing a further plea for help in compiling individual artist discographies and label listings. His research, along with that of his co-author Neil Slaven, came to fruition in 1968 with the publication of the discography *Blues Records, 1943–1966.* The primary focus was on the more down-home artists, and some regrettable criticism was leveled at Mike, mainly for the book's typos and for the omission of artists who some thought should have been included. But such comments could not obscure its importance. This was a monumental achievement; just about all the important artists were included, and the book became the foundation of all later work. Further discographical musings were continued in "Rare Post-War Records," a column that first appeared in *BU* issue 57. In attempting to unearth the rarest records of that era, Mike correctly surmised that many postwar items were far scarcer than prewar discs, which often had been produced in much greater quantities.

Ample space was also found in *BU* for blues news and reviews of the AFBF concerts and club dates by Little Walter, Buddy Guy, Jimmy Reed, John Lee Hooker, and other early '60s visitors to England. These occasions provided the *BU* team with an opportunity to conduct short interviews with the artists. For the first couple of years, the magazine would also publish tempting auction lists of records. An early and distressing news item was a plea for help for the great boogie pianist Pete Johnson, who was living alone in Buffalo, New York, in poor health and existing on welfare, all but forgotten. The plights of others were routinely reported, such as Roosevelt Holt's troubles with the judicial system in Mississippi for the crime of selling his 45rpm record without a license, and, following his rediscovery in Los Angeles by Darryl Stolper, the tragic murder of Kid Thomas.

But if one artist was truly championed by *BU* it was Juke Boy Bonner. The first item on Juke Boy appeared in issue 8, when Mike Leadbitter, with Goldband Records' Eddie Shuler, wrote an article titled "The One Man Trio." Throughout the years, Juke Boy was the subject of numerous features and interviews, but none more amazing than the "Help to Save Juke Boy" campaign, which began in issue 44 after Mike's visit to Juke Boy's hometown of Houston, Texas. It had been several years since Juke Boy had recorded, and, with no company seeming to be interested, *BU* made a plea to its readers for each of them to send one dollar toward a fund that would enable him to afford studio time. Each contributor would receive a copy of the record. This well-intentioned ploy resulted in the single "Runnin' Shoes"/"Yakin' in My Plans" (*Blues Unlimited* #101).

The project prompted an interest in Juke Boy, and there soon followed a resurgence of his career: Chris Strachwitz recorded him for Arhoolie Records, and in 1969 he toured Europe with the AFBF. He soon afterward returned to England for an extensive solo tour under the auspices of the National Blues Federation, and at a session in London for Liberty recorded the album *Things Ain't Right,* including "B.U. Blues," in which he recalled his visit to Bexhill. It was a justifiably proud moment for Simon and Mike. However, Juke Boy's newfound European audience did not guarantee him continuing success at home, where his often introspective and topical blues no longer appealed to a fickle local audience, and music jobs became fewer. The title of his song "Struggle Here in Houston" would be sadly prophetic.

A vital part of *BU*'s content was the record reviews. Informative, insightful, and occasionally humorous, they provided an essential service and guide for the magazine's readers, especially those without access to a specialized record store like Dobell's in London's Charing Cross Road or the wonderfully chaotic Dave Carey's Swing Shop in Streatham in south London. *BU* was fortunate in that its revenue was generated by subscriptions and by wholesale sales to specialized outlets and did not depend upon advertising. Thus reviews were not compromised by a sense of loyalty to the advertisers. Reviewers were given a free rein.

Both Simon and Mike reviewed many records. Simon, occasionally using the pseudonym William Bentley, mainly reviewed the prewar items, while Mike, who was never afraid to speak his mind and invite controversy, stayed with the postwar releases. Mike's passion, which led to occasional vicious outbursts of criticism, quickly earned him the moniker "Mike Backbiter." His blunt and acerbic comments were occasionally upsetting to readers, especially when directed at their favorite artists. In his review of Liberty's Rural Blues/Urban Blues series, Mike wrote: "T-Bone Walker fascinates me. I'm always waiting for him to make a mistake and he never does. He is, or was, far too polished for my taste. A brilliant guitarist, but his dexterity is soulless and calculated, leaving me cold." Joe Turner and Roosevelt Sykes didn't fare much better—"their voices grate on my nerves"—a statement few would agree with. The Prestige albums by Billy Boy Arnold and Homesick James both came in for a Leadbitter bashing, and Pete Welding, perhaps justifiably, came to Billy Boy's defense in the following issue.

But Mike was not alone. Rick Milne in issue 41 wrote, "Muddy has a new album out featuring some of the worst intrusions of bursting brass I have ever heard. It's called *Muddy and Brass* or something equally vomit inducing." Tony Russell and Mike Rowe had contributed reviews to the magazine from early on, always knowledgeable and well-reasoned and sometimes revealing wry or irreverent humor. Tony, reviewing the Herwin album *Patton, Sims & Bertha Lee*, stated, "A quarter of the LP is by [Charley] Patton's fiddler Henry Sims, with the eminence playing backup guitar. Now if Patton's voice sounds like the result of a long night on cheap cigars, Sims' fiddle shows us what happened to the box they came in." Mike Rowe, reviewing Rosetta Records' *Boogie Blues-Women Sing & Play Boogie Woogie*, wrote: "The discovery of the Rosetta Stone provided an interpretation of Egyptian hieroglyphics, but modern-day blues scholars will not find the discovery of Rosetta Records so helpful, for the founding mother, Rosetta Reitz, seems to reverse the process and turn known fact into musical hieroglyphics. Admittedly, giving me a feminist album to review is rather like putting Herod in charge of an orphanage, but this sort of nonsense would try any reviewer's patience."

Although more measured and diplomatic than Mike Leadbitter, Simon could be equally forthright and unafraid of taking someone to task. Son House's 1966 Columbia album, recorded following his rediscovery, was much anticipated by the blues community. Simon was particularly vexed by Dick Waterman's sleeve notes, which referred to the Beatles and Rolling Stones while omitting any mention of those who were actually responsible for the rediscovery. In an editorial in issue 30, he characterized the notes as "uninformative," "irresourceful," and "objectionable."

It is interesting to see how our perception of certain artists has changed with the passage of time. Memphis Slim is a perfect case in point. Few artists have recorded more prolifically, and in the early *BU*s he occasionally came in for harsh, and sometimes unjust, criticism. In issue 65 he was the subject of reviews by both John Broven and Simon. John began his review, "Memphis Slim is nobody's favourite," and Simon, "It must be the first L.P. made by Memphis Slim I ever said a good word for." Would Slim still be subject to the same critical gaze today, and reviewers continue to express those sentiments, given some of the releases that currently masquerade as blues? Or was it that we were just spoiled for choice?

The '60s were exciting times and each new release was keenly anticipated. New reissue labels began to proliferate, such as Mike Vernon's Blue Horizon, Mike Rowe's P.W.B., Trevor Huyton's Highway 51, and Robin Gosden and Bruce Bastin's Flyright, all of them making rare and obscure material available to collectors. Chris Strachwitz's labels Blues Classics and Arhoolie were especially admired by Simon, who regularly reviewed their releases, and when he could give one of them only an indifferent review it was obviously troubling to him. Jay Miller's productions for Excello were also firm favorites with the *BU* team, and features on the label and its artists—Lightnin' Slim, Lazy Lester, Lonesome Sundown, and so forth—appeared in the magazine from its earliest days. *Blues Unlimited* undoubtedly helped foster interest in Jay Miller and Excello Records' product, which resulted, from the early '60s onward, in numerous reissue projects—none more exhaustive than the series produced by Bruce Bastin for Flyright, which culminated in a remarkable fifty-five albums of Miller's productions (not counting the numerous CD issues).

Many fact-finding excursions to the United States were undertaken in the late '50s and the '60s. In 1957 Yannick Bruynoghe, author of *Big Bill Blues,* was among the first Europeans to visit the clubs in Chicago. With Big Bill Broonzy acting as his guide, he met and photographed an astounding number of artists. An account of his three-week visit, "Chicago, Home of the Blues," appeared in the 1958 compendium *Just Jazz,* but unfortunately his photographs from that trip were not published for another twenty-five years. *Voyage au Pays du Blues* was the account of a visit by the French blues enthusiasts Jacques Demetre and Marcel Chauvard to New York, Detroit, and Chicago in 1959. First published in the French magazine *Jazz Hot* in 1960 and republished in the U.K. by *Jazz Journal,* their research and the astonishing amount of information they gathered, coupled with their evocative photographs, formed the foundation of much of the blues research that was to follow. Demetre and Chauvard's venture certainly had an impact on the *BU* team. The scene the Frenchmen encountered and photographed—John Lee Hooker and Little Sonny at Joe Von Battle's record store on Detroit's Hastings Street; Elmore James, Muddy Waters, Little Walter, Tampa Red, and many others in Chicago—is today the stuff of fantasy. Then in 1960 Paul Oliver undertook a research trip that took him through several states, interviewing and recording an extraordinary number of artists. The resulting book, *Conversation with the Blues,* is a remarkable and provocative document, considered one of the cornerstones of blues literature.

Blues Unlimited reported on the research trips of the '60s and '70s in features that are rich in imagery, detail, and information. Notable among them were Bruce Bastin's trip to Houston in 1965; Mike Rowe and Frank Scott's 1966 visit to Chicago; Mike Leadbitter's 1967 Texas trip, which led to a series of articles titled "I Know Houston

Can't Be Heaven"; Bruce Bastin and Pete Lowry's various travels, described in "Blues from the Southeast"; and John Broven's visits to Louisiana, recounted in the series "Behind the Sun." In 1970, John, together with Mike Leadbitter and Robin Gosden, visited New Orleans. Interviews were conducted with Huey Smith, Archibald, and a somewhat neglected Professor Longhair, living in abject poverty and reduced to performing odd jobs at a one-stop record distributor. This was before many in New Orleans awoke to the fact that this iconoclastic figure was living on their doorstep and deserving recognition. From the information gathered on these various trips, several books emerged: Mike Rowe's *Chicago Breakdown,* Bruce Bastin's *Crying for the Carolines* and *Red River Blues,* and John Broven's *Walking to New Orleans* and *South to Louisiana*—all seminal works on their subjects and essential to any blues library. *Blues Unlimited* made a brief foray into the book-publishing world with Broven's *Walking to New Orleans* in 1974.

Most issues of *BU* carried an artist interview. Such pieces were rightly considered to be among the magazine's most important features. The notable difference between interviews in the early issues and those in later ones was their length. The first interviews rarely exceeded two pages, but as the magazine's collective expertise grew, greatly helped by the introduction of the cassette recorder, interviews gradually evolved into longer, more in-depth pieces. Questions would be asked about artists' music, their associates and contemporaries, and their social milieu. Some interviewees were gifted storytellers, others more hesitant and guarded. Occasionally more could be learned about an artist from fellow musicians and band members, for they were often positioned to make acute observations. Jimmy Thomas and Red Holloway personified that role: speaking openly, their *BU* interviews are informative, detailed, and witty recollections of their days with Jimmy Reed, Ike Turner, and Lloyd Price.

But while most artists were pleased to discover that people were interested in their careers, and more than willing to impart useful information, there were a few loveable rogues who chose to take liberties with the truth. After all, who would ever know the difference when discussing events that took place years and worlds away? Occasionally some of this misinformation made it to print. The outlandish Doctor Ross interview in issue 28 is, in retrospect, laughable. Big Joe Williams, Homesick James, and Sonny Boy Williamson were all guilty of making extravagant statements. In a feature in issue 8 on Sonny Boy Williamson, based on information collected by John Broven, Sonny Boy claimed to have first recorded not in 1951, the date all the smart money was on, but in 1929. To their credit, both John and Kurt Mohr, in his accompanying discography, questioned the veracity of Sonny Boy's statement. More than forty years later these recordings have yet to surface. Was this pure invention, or was there some substance to his claim? We may never know.

Not everything in *BU* was generated by the regular contributors or the boys in Bexhill. The magazine would occasionally receive pieces from the artists themselves. Chicago guitarist Jimmy Dawkins was the author of several items, as was bandleader

Johnny Otis, who sent interviews with himself and others like Roy Milton, Louis Jordan, and Pee Wee Crayton. Haskell Sadler and O. C. Perkins also sent items. But no matter how diligent the various editors may have been in trying to present accurate information, they didn't always succeed. Issue 84 reported the death of Bukka White. His followers and disciples were no doubt elated when, in issue 85, they learned of his resurrection. White was not the only musician sent to a premature grave: L. C. McKinley was reported dead in issue 14, only to return to the living in issue 18.

Issue 79, published in January 1971, greeted readers with a somewhat less than enthusiastic editorial that bemoaned the state of the blues scene. While obviously delighted by the flood of excellent reissues, Simon asserted, quite prophetically, "Live blues, however, and 'new' blues sessions (as opposed to reissue records) tend to show a steady and general decline. . . . The 'future' is much different to that of 1960. To guess what the next decade will bring is difficult, but a revitalised blues scene is unlikely."

A milestone was reached in 1973 when issue 100 appeared, a sixty-four-page special celebrating ten years of publication. However, major changes were about to take place. From issue 103 Simon stepped down, handing over the sole editorship to Mike. Simon had been the force behind *Blues Unlimited* and had ensured its survival through his business acumen, which he had acquired as a wily antiques dealer. He alone typeset, laid out, and pasted up the pages and handled subscriptions, distribution, and mailing, as well as writing reviews and essays and the occasional sleeve note—a Herculean task he undertook in his spare time. In addition, in July 1971 he had helped Tony Russell launch the magazine *Old Time Music*. After ten years it was time to take a backseat. Issue 103 had a new layout, typesetter, and printer. Under Mike's editorship the content began to feature more R&B–oriented material, and artists who had previously been given little attention were now accorded more space. Record producers and company owners were also sought out, and interviews with Art Rupe of Specialty and Bob Shad of Sittin' in With soon appeared.

By this time Mike was living in London and working as the advertising manager of the magazine *Let It Rock*. He was also heavily involved in numerous album and book projects, most notably the compilation of the first two *Genesis* box sets of Chess material and the Polydor *Juke Blues* series. But by early 1974 he had contracted what at the time was an unknown virus. Somehow he still managed to produce *BU*. An editorial in issue 109 hinted darkly about his illness and apologized for any delays and disruptions to *BU*'s schedule. Tragically, Mike died of meningitis on November 16, 1974, at the age of thirty-two. His knowledge of blues had been encyclopedic and his commitment total.

"Blues Unlimited Carries On," the editorial in issue 112 proudly proclaimed. Simon Napier relinquished his interest in *BU* and a five-person editorial committee assumed ownership, all of whom had been contributors, collaborators, and friends of both Simon and Mike. John Broven and Mike Rowe had been associated with *BU* from the earliest days. Neil Slaven, as well as co-authoring with Mike Leadbitter the first postwar blues discography, had been co-founder with Mike Vernon of *R&B Monthly* and was instrumental in the formation of Blue Horizon Records. Bez Turner had been reviewing records for some time, a job he continued to perform, along with that of subscriptions manager. I had begun making contributions to *BU* about the time Mike took over the editorship. As a photographer I had come into contact with a number of artists and spent a considerable amount of time asking questions while socializing. Foolishly, I had never recorded any of these conversations. It was at Mike Leadbitter's instigation—a mild bollocking, as I recall—that I took my first tentative steps in conducting more formal interviews and serious research. I also assumed the role of photo editor, responsible for the photographic content of the magazine, liaising with Cilla Huggins, our typesetter and layout artist, and the printers, whom we changed several times.

Jackie Wilson and Mike Leadbitter.

The *BU* photographic archive was a treasure trove of unique and extraordinary images. Upon acquiring it, we set about putting it to its best possible use. Our credo was simple: if it's a good image, use it big. No more postage-stamp-size images for us. Strong images were rarely sacrificed to space restrictions, and interviews were often extended to accommodate all the photographs we wanted to use.

Readers' letters are also a staple of most publications, but for years Simon and Mike, for whatever reason, chose not to feature a regular letters page and just published an occasional letter. We quickly rectified this and instituted a letters page, which resulted in some lively and amusing exchanges.

Due to pressures of work, John Broven and Neil Slaven ended their involvement with *BU* in 1976, and for the next ten years the magazine was managed by the team of Greensmith, Rowe, and Turner. If we did not always keep to a regular publishing schedule as Simon had, we did manage to produce what we considered a quality magazine. Mike Rowe and I conducted new research in St. Louis, Missouri, a city whose blues history had long been neglected. There were interviews with Henry Townsend, James Deshay, Tommy Bankhead, and R&B star Fontella Bass; revelatory information on the brothers Aaron and Milton Sparks; and Mike's rediscovery of the pianist Joe Dean, all shedding new light on long forgotten subjects. John Broven contributed a series of interviews, from his 1975 visit to Los Angeles, with Roy Brown, Harold Battiste, Paul Gayten, Joe Jones, and Earl Palmer. As interviews became more detailed and increased in length, they occasionally spanned two or even three issues. Our resolve was to publish solid research while continuing to chart the course that had been established by Simon and Mike.

In 1985 Bez Turner left *BU* to form *Juke Blues* with Cilla Huggins and John Broven. This left Mike Rowe alone to manage the magazine, since by this time I had moved to the United States. Mike, with Tony Russell, carried on for several issues. Issue 148/149 (winter 1987) announced a price increase and bravely looked to the future and a planned "Detroit Special." Sadly, it was not to be. Beset by numerous problems, the magazine ceased publication.

This is not the first retrospective of *Blues Unlimited.* In 1971 Hanover Books published *Nothing but the Blues,* a compendium of interviews and features compiled by Mike Leadbitter from the first fifty issues of *BU.* It was not without fault. Reviewing the book in issue 82, John Broven praised its good points while holding Hanover and ultimately Mike responsible for its shortcomings—in particular, the typos and the lack of an index and a table of contents. Just why the latter was omitted is perplexing, as in 2007, reviewing some of Simon Napier's personal papers, I discovered the missing contents page.

Blues Unlimited was the first to publish many groundbreaking interviews and features. For this retrospective we have chosen, for obvious reasons, not to republish material that has been superseded in more recent publications. Most of the material is reprinted as it first appeared. But it's not often you are given a chance to second-guess yourselves, and we would be remiss if we did not correct known errors. Updated or new introductions, amendments, additional material, and notes have also been added to some interviews.

What is revealing, when reading the old *BU*s at a distance of fifty years, is not so much what the boys in Bexhill did not know, but just how amazingly well informed they were. Today the names of Johnny Shines, Johnny Young, J. B. Lenoir, and Elmore James are familiar, but in England in 1963, or the United States for that matter, who knew?

Simon Napier passed away, quite unexpectedly, on December 1, 1990. Both he and Mike Leadbitter have secure positions in the pantheon of blues journalism. Mike's work was recognized when he was inducted posthumously into the Blues Hall of Fame in Memphis in 2009. Simon's induction is still awaited.

Blues Unlimited was founded by a pair of dedicated enthusiasts and, through a change in ownership, continued to be published by a similarly committed team. Research funded by grants or endowments was never a consideration. Trips to and throughout the United States were funded out of individuals' own pockets and con-

Neil Slaven, Bill Greensmith, Mike Rowe. (Photo Elizabeth Woodcraft)

ducted while on holiday from their day job. Musicians interviewed in London would be bought a pint at the local pub or a cup of tea in one of Joe Lyons's cafés. What was important was an ability to connect with the artist, who, more often than not, would recognize a genuine interest in and affection for his or her music, and this was probably the key to many successful interviews, as well as the start of many lasting friendships. Today *Blues Unlimited* is recognized as the pioneering magazine in blues research.

REGIONAL BLUES

Mike Rowe

The country blues weren't born in the Mississippi Delta, even if that state garners the most acclaim from blues enthusiasts today. The blues developed all through the South and in different ways. For instance, the sound of the Delta—impassioned, emotional vocals, highly rhythmic guitar accompaniment with often bottleneck a major and common ingredient—is so different from the more gentle picked melodies and general tunefulness of the East Coast or Piedmont artists. It's different also from the Texans, whose high, keening vocals and extended guitar lines evince another kind of blues majesty. While all have their gestation on the cotton and sugar plantations and developed from the work songs and hollers about the early 1900s, the sound of the blues developed differently according to the various social and musical factors holding sway in an area—the intense segregation and isolation of the Delta contributing to the harshness of the style, the greater exposure to white Southern music on the East Coast adding a melodic strain, or the greater memories of slave songs in Texas adding a songster element to the genre. Each area often gave rise to a particularly gifted and popular performer who set the standard for the locality—for the East Coast–Piedmont grouping it would be Blind Boy Fuller; for the Mississippi Delta, Charley Patton; and for Texas, Blind Lemon Jefferson, who would be the major influences on the local sound and their followers.

But these blues "regions" are only approximate, and it should be understood that discussion of the "Mississippi blues" is often a kind of shorthand for the Mississippi Delta sound of prime movers Charley Patton, Son House, and Willie Brown. Certainly, Mississippi John Hurt growing up in nearby Avalon would have found little in common with them, while the Tommy Johnson or Ishman Bracey school of Jackson, Mississippi, would have provided stiff competition to the Delta champions. With different styles holding forth in different parts, it would be more meaningful to split Mississippi into various localities, perhaps some even overlapping the state boundaries for each discrete style. Similarly, for the other blues regions, it wasn't only the guitarists who could stamp their sound on an area. In Texas, for example, the Santa Fe school of pianists based in Houston was a remarkable example of a piano culture that was sturdily independent of musical developments in the Northern cities.

Through the '20s and '30s black migration from farm to factory and from south to north and west gradually shaped an urban blues befitting the faster tempo of city life and dwelling with an increasing complexity of instrumentation. But as the music moved north, the host cities sometimes developed, for a time, their own local sound. St. Louis, for example, a halfway point, retained a lot of the country blues flavor and spawned a distinct style of piano blues centered on Roosevelt Sykes, Henry Brown, and the Sparks Brothers, among others. This gentler music making would not last and would be overwhelmed in the '40s by the migrants' race to Chicago and Detroit and the increasing sophistication of the blues sound.

With the onset of World War II this urbanization of the music was accelerated, but the massive increase in migration that followed the traditional routes of the railroads and highways as Delta migrants generally moved to Chicago, East Coast migrants to New York, and Texans and the western states to Los Angeles sparked a last flowering of the regional traditions. These regional factors were gradually subsumed in the northern and western cities as the music moved into the bars and clubs while records and radio broadcasts also helped smooth the idiosyncrasies to some extent. However, the huge migration of the World War II years brought a new audience from the South who would, for a few years, become the market for the new sound of the country blues—electrified and electrifying, a music forged in the steel mills and shipyards and stockyards and auto factories in cities such as Chicago, Los Angeles, and Detroit. Muddy Waters was the inheritor of the Delta blues tradition, and his impassioned vocals and amplified bottleneck guitar set the benchmark for the new Chicago blues, the most striking example of the old-new blues. The West Coast, where a new record industry was built from scratch, played host to black migrants from Texas and the western states and, with T-Bone Walker and Charles Brown in command, fashioned a modern jump blues that was both old and, paradoxically, slick. New York, the host city for Piedmont and seaboard migrants, didn't seem to develop any iconic postwar blues style—maybe the city's jazz history was a limiting factor or the gentle East Coast blues didn't lend so easily to modernizing or electrification.

But there were other, newer regional sounds that grew up where none had existed before, sounds promoted by certain recording studios or the popularity of particular artists. In New Orleans a definite city–jump blues sound emerged, and elsewhere, in

Louisiana, the swamp blues and zydeco, a hybrid of white French Cajun and R&B, were all-conquering. Things moved fast, and it wasn't long before most regional characteristics would be ironed out as radio and records spread the influence of the major and most popular performers, Jimmy Reed and, especially, B. B. King, throughout the blues world.

PART I

CHICAGO

Freddie King

Born on September 3, 1934, in Gilmer, Texas, Freddie King's stature has grown in full measure since his premature death in 1976. Moving to Chicago in the early '50s, King fell into the burgeoning blues scene and learned guitar in the clubs. King's first record, "Country Boy," was a duet with Margaret Whitfield on the small El-Bee label in 1956. He signed with King Records in 1960 and released a succession of hits, many of them catchy up-tempo instrumentals, including "Hide Away," "San-Ho-Zay," and "The Stumble." King relocated to Texas by the mid-sixties, and after appearing at the Texas Pop Festival in 1969, his reputation in the U.S. rock scene grew after recording with rock luminaries Leon Russell and Eric Clapton. Unfortunately, King was not well served on the reissue market until the 1993 Ace *Blues Guitar Hero* compilation and the more recent Bear Family box set, *Taking Care of Business, 1956–1973*, that appeared in 2009, spurring King's induction into the Rock and Roll Hall of Fame in 2012.

In the following interview, author Mike Leadbitter reminds readers of King's Chicago influences on both his guitar and voice. King's sound is best understood in comparison with his Chicago woodshedding influences—namely, Eddie Taylor, Jimmy Rogers, and Robert "Junior" Lockwood. Leadbitter also notes that King's vocal style resembles Buddy Guy more than the smoother style of a T-Bone Walker. This comparison to Chicago performers highlights that the birthplace of an individual is nowhere as impactful as the influences upon an artist in their formative years when applying themselves to the craft.

This interview also marked the end of an era at *Blues Unlimited.* Mike Leadbitter became sole editor of the magazine in 1973 and juggled that job while simultaneously editing a new British music journal, *Let It Rock,* covering jazz, country, and soul. This article appeared in *Blues Unlimited* issue 110 in October 1974 as Leadbitter's last interview published in the magazine. He died just one month later.

—Mark Camarigg

Madison Nite Owl
Freddie King Interview

Mike Leadbitter

Blues Unlimited #110 (Oct./Nov. 1974)

Though somewhat out of favor with his followers at present, 40-year-old Freddie King remains cheerful, taking life as he finds it. As far as he's concerned, he's just a straight blues singer and likes nothing better than reminiscing about the good old Chicago days when there was a blues joint on every corner and men like Elmore James, Muddy Waters, and Eddie Taylor reigned supreme. He might live in Dallas today, but the Windy City has a strong claim on his soul and that's where he learned almost everything he knows about a guitar.

He knows he's good and refuses to let modesty stand in his way when recalling with glee how he would go around "cutting heads" on Sunday afternoons. He once liked nothing better than the chance for a guitar battle, but became notorious for the speed with which he dispatched opponents. This caused lesser men to hurriedly leave the stage as soon as they saw his bulk heave into sight, and legend has it that even Blues Kings paled when he and Earl Hooker entered a club together. Such incidents, however, took place in the early sixties—the chart-busting days—when Freddie, as a musician, was at his peak. The preceding years were as tough for him as they were for anyone else.

Like most of his contemporaries, Freddie King is just a plain old country boy. Born on a farm outside Gilmer, a small town near Longview, Texas, he was raised in a rural environment and his first experience of city life came at the age of 16, when he defied migratory patterns and moved North East rather than West. Shaking with cold, he arrived in Chicago during the December of 1950, clutching a Harmony guitar and wishing he'd never left the South. But he had little choice in the matter: his mother was determined to join her relations in that town.

Freddie's grandmother lived on the West Side and the King family settled there at Bishop Street and Adams. The first thing they all had to do was find work, but big for his age, Freddie had few problems. He just said he was 18 and was quickly hired by a local steel mill. In spite of getting his legs scarred in an accident, he stayed on at the same place for seven years relying on the money earned for the buying of new guitars and other fresh and exciting indulgences. Then, amazed by the amount of music to be heard in his new home, he really fell in love with the blues and at night ran wild, walking the streets to hang out at neighborhood bars though well under age. Wherever there was music you'd find him, and during 1951 he began to polish his technique, borrowing freely from men like Eddie Taylor, Jimmy Rogers, and Robert Jr. Lockwood while developing a pretty unique blues style first learned in Texas. In the habit of really hitting the strings on his acoustic box in an attempt to achieve more volume, he found it difficult to come to terms with electric models and eventually found himself abandoning the softer, mellower, yet amplified approach of his heroes in favor of the harsher more astringent sounds beloved by other youngsters of his age. His became the "new" Chicago blues and he would join the ranks of Magic Sam, Otis Rush, Buddy Guy, Syl Johnson, and so many others, building his reputation alongside theirs. How this all came about is quite fascinating and best left to Freddie to explain.

Freddie King, 1960.

We always kept two or three guitars around our house in Texas all the time. They all played—my mother, my uncles, they all played guitars. Leon King—he got killed in a car wreck when I was 11 years old—he taught me a lot of stuff. I played in church and in school—there was nothing going on in school that I wasn't in. Lots of guys played around there. There was one guy about the same age as my mother. They called him Shorty, Shorty Brown. He was a piano player and every time they give something like a minstrel show in school, they got him to play piano. He and I would play together. He could dance, too, and he's still living in Longview.

I'd always go to Chicago when school was out, after I started high school. My grandmother, my mother's brothers and things, they lived there. So when I finished school, after I was 16, we all just went there. I was playing like Lightnin' Hopkins and Muddy Waters when I got to Chicago, but Jimmy Rogers and Eddie Taylor were different. They really inspired me. I stayed around them all the time. Every time they look up, I'm coming. If I couldn't catch one, I'd catch the other. They'd say, "Don't you ever sleep?" There was a guy in Chicago, identical to T-Bone Walker, L. C. McKinley. He was playing the same stuff and he used to go as "T-Bone Jr.," but, see, I wasn't thinking too much of that, because I wanted to play like those other two cats. That was the style I wanted to play in. Open key of "E" or "A." Those were the only keys I played in then. Those clamps—capos—used to call 'em "cheaters"—I seen where they changed keys with them. So I went and bought me one. Same thing Eddie was doing, I was doing, too.

Eddie was playing at the Kitty Kat on Madison Street then with Willie Foster and Floyd Jones. I'd go in there, but so many people crowded in, the cat told me not to come in anymore as I was under age. His name was Mike, too. But I'd slip through all this crowd anyway and make my way around to the bandstand, where I could sit and just watch Eddie. And then I was at a backyard party once and he brought his whole band down there to jam some numbers. So Eddie was showing me how to play in "E" and I said to him, "Say, man, where you live?" He acted like a fool and gave me his address, and after that I was up his house so much they thought I lived there.

See, after that I worried Jimmy Rogers at the clubs. He was showing me how to use these picks. He was playing with Muddy Waters and in intermission he'd go to walk off and I'd grab him, make him show me this and that. And then there was Robert Jr. Lockwood. I worried him pretty bad, too, but you couldn't really worry Robert Jr. He liked helping people. He loved showing people. Now, this is when I really got into the T-Bone Walker, B. B. King style. Robert had a weird sound like them and I wanted to learn some of that, too. So we got to talking and laughing and he was showing me how to make these chords and Johnny Shines did, too. They said if I could play in the keys they showed me, I could get rid of the clamp—throw the son of a bitch away. They showed me how to play without it. I'd sit up all night practicing, but it was hard for me to do that. But finally, I caught on to it.

I was 17 when I got my first electric guitar, and Willie D. Warren (mistakenly referred to as "Willie Wine" in earlier Freddie King articles) signed for it (acted as guarantor). It was a Kay, but it got stolen and then I turned around and got me another one. A Sunnyland guitar—they're made by Kay too, but that got stolen, too. And I lost my amplifier at the same time. So then, I got me another one. A friend, Lee Edward Brown, signed for me to get it. He worked for the Curtis Candy Company, he didn't play anything. I kept that one for about a year and then I got me a Les Paul (Gibson) and that's when I was playing with Earlee Payton—'56, I started playing with him.

The first guy I ever played with was Sunnyland Charles at a place called Red's Playhall on Madison. He was with a harmonica player named Johnny Dee—really good harmonica player. Charles plays guitar and, really, his was the first electric guitar I played. When I first met him he had some cousins living in the same building as me, and he came in there with his guitar and I said, "Let me see your guitar." He said, "Come go with me," and he taken me to a club called the Spot. It was on Maple and do you know who was playing there? It was Johnnie Temple and Baby Face Leroy. I'd never played electric before, but Charles said, "Get up there and play one." I said, "I'm not good enough to play with those cats, man," but they pulled me up there anyway. A couple of months later I met Charles again and he said, "Hey, man, I'm playing down on Madison there. Why don't you come by?" So I started playing with him. I was 17 years old.

About a block down from where Charles was playing at Red's was the Kitty Kat. I met Sonny Cooper there before I did Sonny Scott. See, I'd go from Red's to the Kitty Kat, and on down the street from there was Ralph's Club, where Memphis Slim was playing, and he had Lee Cooper (guitar) with him. They had a really good band, but on every corner at Damen and Madison there was a band playing. There was the Cedar Club, the Royal Revue—King Kolax was there. And over the other side of the street was the Paris Club, where Danny Overbea was playing. Then I'd go over to Lake Street—go straight across—and there's Elmore James playing over there. Elmore had Johnny Jones's band. There was Ernest Cotton, Boyd Atkins blowing the horns, and then there was Odie Payne. But Odie was working with Jimmy Rogers for a while, and they used Kansas City Red until he came back. Didn't have no car then. I was walking, man, I was always walking. I wasn't frightened of anything. They call it skid row down there, but it was home to me.

After Sunnyland Charles, I was with Sonny Scott (drums) at Red's Playhall. Me, Sonny, and Jimmy Lee Robinson (bass). This was in '52. Then I went to Sonny Cooper (harmonica). There was me, Willie D. Warren (bass guitar), and Jesse (drums). This was at the Kitty Kat, but after it closed up, we moved down the street to the Be Bop Club, which was owned by the same people. So all of us started playing down there. We really didn't have no band then, we was just jamming with each other and stuff. Then I started back to playing with Sonny Scott and Jimmie Lee and we got a good thing together then. This is when I really got into playing lead, 'cause I didn't have a harmonica or anything to help me out. I had to just stand out in front and really keep everything covered up. This is when I really learned to finger and bend and put stuff in there like I'm doing now. I didn't have no help.

I was playing with Scott when I first met Payton. We was playing cocktail parties then, and on Sunday afternoons we'd play at the Stadium Sports Club, right in front of the Chicago Stadium. One band would play there awhile and then another band would get up and play awhile, you know. Payton came in with his band one day, and after I met Payton I started playing with him at the Heatwave, upstairs on State Street. I played with him one night there, on a Tuesday, and on Sunday afternoons we played at the Cotton Club. They had two Cotton Clubs—one on the South Side and one on the North Side, and the owner was Youngblood, a piano player. Count Basie and Joe Williams was there, and they didn't have no blues until we came in. We packed 'em in. So at first I was playing two days with Payton and I had my regular thing with Scott and Jimmy Lee. Then finally I went with Payton (full-time). Smokey Smothers was with him—he joined a little before I came—and he (also) had Mojo Robert Elem (bass) and T. J. McNulty (drums). I guess I played with Payton longer than with anyone else. I was with him about a year.

That lady, Miss Margaret Whitfield, owned the Ricky Show Lounge. She recorded us in '56 and the record was supposed to have been leased to Chess. But there was some trouble with the union along there, so Chess didn't want no part of it and we let (lawyer John) Burton have it. That wasn't me playing guitar on it. No, it was Robert Jr. Lockwood, and Billy Emerson was on piano. The record didn't do a thing on account of the trouble they had, but really it wasn't a very good record, was it? [Note: Freddy is referring to El-Bee 157—"Country Boy"/"That's What You Think"—issued under his name. Margaret Whitfield is also heard on side one, and the other sidemen were Earlee Payton (harp), Mojo Elem and T. (Thomas) J. McNulty.]

Then I went with my own band—I didn't go back to Texas until 1963. Mojo and T. J. came with me from Payton's band, and we played with just the three of us for about a year in '58. But then I got a big band. We got Abb Locke, saxophone player; Hal (Harold) Burrage played piano; and for a while Lil' Mason was singing. And John McCall was another vocalist I had and so was Dee Clarke. We stayed together until I started recording in 1960. We played the Casbah on the West Side and Mel's Hideaway Lounge and the Squeeze Club. Mel's was on Loomis—Magic Sam and all of us used to play there. We also played the Happy Home—that was on the West Side, too—and Willie Mabon and Eddie Boyd also played there. In '58 I just quit work (at the steel mill). I was playing music every night and averaging about $300 to $500 a week after I'd paid the men off. I was charging $500 for a big club dance then, 'cause my band was really popular.

I'd been trying to get with Chess for two or three years (when I signed with Federal), but they wouldn't record me, because they said I sounded too much like B. B. King. But they used me on sessions. Then I'd been knowing Syl Johnson since '56, and he introduced me to Sonny Thompson, who was working for Federal (King's subsidiary). Syl recorded for Federal before me, but they sort of lost interest in him after I came along, and I wasn't very happy about that, 'cause we had been friends a long time. I knew Mack (Thompson), Syl's brother, before I knew Syl. Also Jimmy Johnson is his brother, too. Jimmy has records, too. All three of them used to play together. When I made the first four hits, Syd Nathan (owner of King-Federal) was nowhere around. He was upstairs, but he didn't come down. We got a good sound and Sonny Thompson was a great blues player. The others (on the session), Bill Willis (bass), Philip Paul (drums) and them, was all studio musicians. They lived in Cincinnati.

On August 26, 1960, Freddie went into the King Studios in Cincinnati with Sonny Thompson and cut six titles. Amazingly, three became hits: the haunting "Have You Ever Loved a Woman," superbly sung and played; "See See

Baby"; and the driving "Hideaway," a fine instrumental dedicated to Mel's Hideaway Lounge. The following year, on January 17th and 18th, he returned to Cincinnati again to record two more chartbusters: "I'm Tore Down" was one and "Lonesome Whistle Blues" was the other. An April date then produced "San-Ho-Zay" (San José) and July brought forth "Christmas Tears." When 1961 ended, Freddie had six R&B Top 10 hits under his belt and was the new blues sensation. Such phenomenal success took him straight out of the taverns and onto the one-nighter circuit.

Sonny Thompson put me on one-nighters after "Hideaway," and my first gig, my first stop, was New Orleans. From New Orleans to Texas was my first tour, but going to New Orleans was like going home. Those guys down there were beautiful cats. I checked in a hotel that was owned by a saxophone player with Tommy Ridgely—Mel's Motel. It was two miles out of New Orleans on Shrewsbury Road. Just me and a driver, we drove down from Chicago, and I was very tired when we checked in. The lady there, she said, "Is that your picture there?"—it was an advertisement for the show—and she said, "I think my son is going to play behind you." And the next day, here come all these cats. There's Thomas Ridgely, Ernie K-Doe; there's Al Tousan (Toussaint), Lee Dorsey, Danny White, Earl King, and "Shine," Alvin Robinson. All these cats, man, just ganged up. And I was playing the same show with Thomas Ridgely and Earl King. I played around New Orleans for about three weeks before I went to Texas, and then I played Dallas, Waco, Houston, and San Antonio. And then I said, "Shit, we got more dates, but I'm going home." I had to get a new car when I got back. The one I had was burned out with all that traveling. I was with Shaw Artists then. Shaw had everyone then.

When I left on the next tour, Tyrone Davis was driving for me. I went on a big tour then, there was a whole lot of people. Me, Jimmy Reed, Gladys Knight and the Pips, Smokey and the Miracles, Shep and the Limelites, Chuck Jackson, Bobby Peterson . . . all of us had hot records out. It was called the Dee Clarke Show—he was the main attraction. We traveled in cars—each of us to his own car. We did two numbers each night. That's all we had time for—there were so many of us—and we got $250 a night. I did 50 of those one-nighter tours at $250 a night. There were all Shaw shows. Shaw were making money off us (at the box office), plus getting a percentage (of our earnings).

Unfortunately, as far as the charts were concerned, 1961 was Freddie's first and last big year and the one-nighter circuit rapidly wore him down. Though he continued to record prolifically and saw a flood of albums released, he just couldn't get another hit to keep him in the public's eye. This wasn't his fault, as he continued to come up with excellent, highly commercial material. The blame for his rapid demise rests with the late Syd Nathan. For some obscure reason, Nathan upset some deejays during the mid-sixties and they refused to play his product. This ban became national and had still not been lifted when I visited the company in 1973. Without airplay, all

Freddie King. London, October 9, 1967. (Photo Bill Greensmith)

King artists, even James Brown, suffered and the lunatic situation did more to bring the company to its knees than anything else. Nathan, then a rich man in failing health, died refusing to back down and resolve the matter.

In 1963, Freddie, tired of city life and touring, returned to Texas, buying himself a home in Dallas and settling down with his family. Having completed a mammoth session for Federal in August '64, he stayed away from the studios for over two years and then signed for King itself in September 1966. One date resulted from this final association with Nathan and then he quit to join Atlantic in '68. Lonnie Mack's band and Dallas drummer Frank Charles provided the small combo backup that he was used to for the '66 session, but, regrettably, Atlantic began recording him with a big band and the results weren't so good. A couple of albums and two singles were issued by Cotillion, an Atlantic subsidiary, but little notice was taken, even though Freddie was by then a popular figure in Britain thanks to regular appearances on the pub-club circuit. Dropped by Atlantic in 1969, he eventually landed up with Leon Russell's Shelter label and was marketed B. B. King–superstar fashion for the first time. He refuses to talk about those days, but is very excited about his new RSO contract and seems to enjoy working with Mike Vernon, who at least understands and appreciates him for what he is, and not for what he could be if this, that, and the other were added.

Freddie King's big problem is that he seems doomed to endless comparison with B. B. King. When he first rose to fame it was assumed that he had been vastly influenced by B. B., and writers (including myself) took it for granted that as he'd come from Texas, T-Bone Walker played a significant role in his musical development. No one really looked upon him as someone apart—a Chicago artist, in spite of his background, possessed of an extraordinary ability to churn out fine blues instrumentals or vocal performances of great individuality. Though he performed in the popular style of the day, Freddie was instantly recognizable. If one has to seek influences, then his early vocal work owes more to men like Buddy Guy—"Have You Ever Loved a Woman" being a perfect example—than anyone else, but instrumentally, he's pretty unique. B. B. King's influence, such as it is, is therefore indirect, not direct.

King-Federal released 77 titles by Freddie via singles and albums, and of these, 30 were instrumentals and four were duets with Lulu Reed, Sonny Thompson's wife. To my permanent surprise, none really disappoint, though the instrumentals have an almost predictable monotony at times and the same high standard of 1960 is maintained throughout. Freddie's soft, strained voice is ideally suited to the songs he chose to sing, and his often jaunty approach to 12-bar blues provides a rocking swing missing on many records by his rivals. He also makes the whole guitar work for him, appearing to be as deft with the bass strings as with the treble ones, and comes up with a beautiful, clean, yet funky sound at all times. Next to Jimmy Reed, he was Chicago's most popular export during the sixties, and it's a pity the city had to lose him.

Freddie, a musicians' musician, has long been admired in France, but never really got the attention he deserved from blues enthusiasts at the time when he was really big (this is the first time *BU* has devoted a whole feature to him). Though he influenced several British R&B guitarists of the era (who were of no consequence to those who knew, but obviously more aware), it has only been in recent years that his Federal work has achieved collector status. Oddly enough, the probable reason for this is that he was just too popular, too commercial, too readily available to suit our passion for the obscure. Smokey Smothers, a longtime friend of Freddie's, suffered a similar fate, although he gave us one of the finest blues albums ever and a tremendous, though small, collection of singles. Freddie was dismissed in 22 short lines by *Chicago Breakdown*—poor Smokey only got a name check. It wasn't the author's fault—his main preoccupation was with the dead past, not comparatively recent events or the future, and he gave us what we wanted to read.

Whatever future there is, Freddie will be around to share it. He's still young, in his prime, and has lost none of his creative skill. In fact, his career, such as it is, has hardly begun. He can't be expected to return to square one and rework the initially successful formula, but his output for Shelter indicated that he can survive as an individual even in the midst of a super group. Confused by demands that he be a *today* bluesman, rather than one of yesteryear, he now finds it hard to keep up with very different audiences. Should he play the guitar behind his head and rock the joint with "Hideaway," or should he be cool, yet intense, and do "Woman Across the River"? A difficult choice and in the last couple of years we've all suffered from his mistakes. Perhaps it's just that he's tired of bopping around, sweating profusely, doing the same old jive year in and year out? Perhaps he wants to be known for something new, rather than remembered for something 14 years old? Who can tell? Whatever, he's determined to remain true to himself and keep making music, and that, after all, is more important than anything else.

Notes

Marcel Chauvard and Jacques Demetre, the first people to interview Freddie (1959), provide the following details on artists mentioned in this feature. Between 1957 and

1960, Sunnyland Charles (or Chas) worked with the Globe-Trotters at the Globe Trotter Lounge on Madison. Other members of the trio were Gene Dennis (harp) and Johnny Mae Dunson (drums). Nothing has been heard of him since. Frank "Sonny" Scott plays drums, harp, and guitar. Born at Houston, Texas, on June 21, 1927, he appears to spend his time between Chicago and his hometown, where he once ran the Great Scott label. He claims to have recorded for Duke (unissued titles) and was with Big Jay McNeely's band in June 1959. Sonny Cooper was born on March 8, 1926, in Jackson, Mississippi. He claimed to have recorded for Parrot in 1953 with Freddie, Jimmie Lee Robinson, and Willie Warren and for Chess. Freddie remembers backing him on a Chess session that resulted in "Your Love Is Like a River Boat," a song that remains unissued. In October '59, Cooper was working with Eugene Williams (guitar) and Hayes Winkfield (drums).

Jimmy Walker

Jimmy Walker, born in Memphis, Tennessee, on March 8, 1910, was a veteran of the Chicago blues scene from the rent-party days of the '20s through to the postwar '50s, although it wasn't until 1964 that Jimmy's forceful and hard-hitting boogie piano could be heard on record. An album, *Rough & Ready Piano,* with Erwin Helfer was recorded by Pete Welding for his Testament label (202). Walker recorded again with Helfer, *Blues Boogie Woogie Piano Duets and Solos,* for Flying Fish (001) in 1974. Walker was probably the last of Chicago's rent-party pianists still working when *BU* had a chance to interview him in 1975. Walker remained a mainstay on the Chicago club circuit and, along with pianist Sunnyland Slim, served as an elder statesman on the scene until his death on October 16, 1997.

—Mike Rowe

Jimmy Walker Talking

Mike Rowe

Blues Unlimited #116 (Nov./Dec. 1975)

Well, see, I was born in Memphis. My mother brought me on when I was three years old and I never been back since. Then a Jewish fellow raised me right here,

Jimmy Walker.

see. I left my mother when I was about seven years old and I'd stay with him and he'd always take me back, ya know what I mean, over there to see my mother. At that time my mother lived at 18th and Butterfield. Abe Holtzman was his name. So he sent me to school and I stayed right there at the house. He opened up a delicatessen store down on 30th Street—30th and Indiana. See, back at that time, colored people didn't cross Wabash. And if you crossed Wabash, the police would get you. You wouldn't cross there at all. But, see, me, I was always with him and he was a nice fellow until you made him mad. He'd take me everywhere, and you don't act like you didn't like it, ya know what I mean, 'cause he'd get pretty angry. And I just stayed right on with him. We lived at 53 E. 53rd Street. See, the synagogue was right across the street on the corner of 53rd and Michigan. Before he moved from there, I went back with my mother. I was about seventeen years old then. I started messing around then, trying to play.

This guy—I forgotten what this guy's name is that played for Gloria Swanson. See, now, you're too young to remember any of this. This was a female impersonator. She was the world's greatest female impersonator. She was a man and he didn't wear nothing but women's clothes. He dressed like a woman and he looked like a woman. And this guy was playing piano for him and I was young. I couldn't go in there. Down on 18th Street right off State Street—it was a kind of—it was a storefront, a club they had there. They had two stores and the piano was out right at the front like over to the side. They didn't have no big showcase, ya know, window in there. They had—must have been, oh, I guess maybe 14 or 15 glasses. Just like, you know how they have those section glasses—and one of the glasses was broke, and I would always go around there and mess around with this guy. I always wanted to play. Well, he taken a liking to me and I was running around and, see, sometimes when he wasn't playing, well, I go where he was at and I'd learn, too. Caught on a little bit, then I'd drop back. Then I'd run into another guy by name of Lorenzo Murphy and

I got with him and I got a little tight, and I began to learn a little bit more from him. 'Cause his uncle was a piano player and he learned quite a bit from his uncle Harry, I think, Harry Murphy. Now, he was a old-timer. He plays a lot of blues—he plays blues, but he could play all those popular numbers, too, like "Sam the Accordion Man." Something you don't even hear now, and, ooh, he played quite a few numbers. Well, after a while, ya know what I mean, I had a piano where I could practice more.

House Parties

See, we all used to hang out together. Curtis Jones and Lonnie Johnson, Porkchops (Lee Green), he used to run around, come and hang around us. We'd all just go around, we'd range, like, say, from 39th Street, Federal, and Dearborn all the way on out to 51st Street. In other words, we'd play for parties, see, and this time we'd get about 50 cents a night. We'd play for these house-rent parties. And sometimes you didn't give me but 50 cents. This was alright, but if somebody else give me a dollar or dollar and a half, say, "I'll give you a dollar and a half," ya know what I mean, we're going over here. In other words, like, if you were going to play somewhere, I'll come in (and) I'll help, you see? You wouldn't have to give me anything—we'd all just get together and come on by. Curtis and Roosevelt (Sykes), which, let's see now, Murphy and this guy named Booker—Booker Peebles. Now, you never heard of him, I imagine, but he was pretty good. He played mostly around Cleveland. See, he played here a little bit in Chicago, but he played mostly around Cleveland. Albert Ammons, I knew him pretty well, and what's this other boy's name . . . Art Tatum. See, I knew him pretty well, too. The onliest one I know that did play. I used to run around with him quite a bit when he was playing out here on 61st Street. See, now, one while I was almost playing to a certain extent like him, but I couldn't, ya know what I mean. I couldn't get the feeling, see, that I wanted, so what I did—I want to play like me. I don't try to play like nobody else.

Leroy Carr, he used to be around with us, too. Around here fooling around. He used to sleep on pool tables down here at 43rd and State. Yeah, see, in that time, I was living down at 31st and Wentworth, so, I don't know—when I knew anything he was dead. Pinetop Smith, I know him, too. I never fooled around with Pinetop too much, 'cause he—he was a kinda sarcastic guy, never fool around with him too much. This guy who put out this . . . I forgot the name of this piece, but don't nobody play it—nobody fool with it. Nobody plays it, 'cause it's just kinda tough—it's a tough number—"Cow Cow Blues"! Cow Cow Davenport—yeah, he used to play around 29th and Dearborn between State and Dearborn. A club restaurant—I don't know what that lady's name was. Little ole restaurant right on the corner of the alley. See, back in those days, they didn't have no names.

This guy that made that "44 Blues"—it wasn't Lee Green. No, this guy made "44 Blues" before anybody. He was the one that composed it. We was over at Hop's (Hop Johnson, Curtis Jones's guitarist) house at 45th and Michigan. See, we down in his basement. He lived in the front, see, in other words, just like this was a partition here, ya see. Well, this here was his bedroom, and he had a kind of a kitchen off the side and in here was his piano. And we'd all go in here, ya know what I mean, and sit up here and just play. Different guys come in, I mean, and sit down and play. This guy what made the "44 Blues" keeps coming around—ya know what I mean, I'm trying to call . . . Shoot, Little Brother was probably a little boy back along that time. It was Johnny something, I done forgot now. Hop, he can tell you exactly. Punkin' was the name of this guy that put out the "44 Blues." Punkin', yeah, that's his name. No, that wasn't the guy who got killed at 51st and Federal, because he used to come over there, too, see, and we always used to play at his woman's house up on the second floor. And this guy killed him about his wife. His wife was sitting down beside him and he shot him with a .45. His wife run out the back door, he told him that's why he couldn't keep his wife at home and shoot him with that .45, and he jumped up and ran to the door and fell down the steps. Like the second floor, they run the steps up from the sidewalk right up to the second floor, and people lived on the first floor, they come in on the side here, go under the steps going up. And I can about remember that just as good where the house and everything was and how it was set up. See, the people didn't—they didn't have no whole lot of furniture. See, back in those times things was kinda rough. They didn't have too much furniture—maybe, like a couch. Set a couch up in here and they'd have maybe two or three chairs and a piano, see, and anybody come here.

Clarence (Lofton), he was a pretty nice fellow. Kinda nice about getting around and you playing with him. He liked to fight—liked to drink, see. Before I run into him when we was doing this barn dance out there in Hopkins Park, see, we used to hang out down around 45th and State. Other words, a lady over there used to have a party pretty well every weekend, yeah, and we'd go over there. I forgot what her name was. We all used to go there, 'cause she had a son, see, and he played, too. I don't know, I think her name was Rose and his name was Raymond. I don't know what her second name was. See, what happen, it was kinda like a club outfit, ya know what I mean? It's like you, for instance, you've got a group of people, see, and, uh, you take your group—you bring your group over and you give me a play this week, see. Next week you take your group and my group and we go over and we'll give somebody else a play. This is to help them to get their rent together. See, now, it's about your time, see, for your rent, so they will bring their group and my group and all and come over, ya understand, 'cause whiskey was only 15 cents a half pint. That was moonshine and, ya know, they made money and home brew was a quarter. Home brew is a beer, see. It's made up like beer, but that home brew it was stronger than moonshine—you drink two bottles of it like this and you had it, yes, sir. See, but back in those days, nobody bothered you. You could have $10,000 in your pocket. Just like you come here, you got drunk, take your money off you, and you can drink all you want to, see, and maybe, oh, if you were too drunk, wouldn't let you go home, make you sleep here all night. You get up and you might say, "Well,

I'm going home." Okay, well, you go ahead on home. Somebody'll take you home. You still don't have no money, see, and it may be two days later, three days later, say, "Listen, you tell so-and-so I want to see him." You know you had money when you went there, but you haven't got a quarter. You woke up, you're broke. Well, here, here's all your money, right? Now, they wanted to make the rent money, but they don't want to take nothing from you. See, this is the good part, everybody was nice like that. Womens walk the streets with $50 gold belts around their waist, $25 gold necklace hanging down, walk the streets all night long, nobody bothered 'em. Shoot, you better not try it now!

Bootlegging and the Depression

This was in the '20s and the '30s. Now, see, take like people didn't have no jobs that amount to nothing. You couldn't even buy a job. But me, I had a job working in a drugstore on Elston Avenue. I learned how to read Latin, ya know what I mean, how to fill prescriptions, yeah.

They (house-rent parties) kinda died out, because things began to get a little bit better. People began to go to work a little bit. Well, before the war, see, things began to kinda get better even before Roosevelt's time. I mean people, other words, was making whiskey, 'cause I made some myself, and I used to make as high as $300 a day and I'm not kidding you.

I run into a fellow—real estate. See, what happened, the real estate guy let me stay in a house out on 34th and Vernon to keep the people from tearing them up. Nobody would break out the windows if they see somebody living there, ya know what I mean. And I stayed in there until he rented it, and when he rented it he put me in another place. Well, I stayed on the first floor and I rented out a flat on the second floor. Then this fellow come along that was a bootlegger and he wanted to rent the third floor. Well, I didn't want to let him have it, ya know, but he said, he told me, "Well, I'll tell you what, see, if I can get it I'll let you put a couple of barrels in there." So I put me a couple of barrels in there, and the next thing I know I had these seven barrel vats. These vats was tall. You had to take a six-foot ladder to get up there to drop the sugar in. They'd hold 2,500 lbs. of sugar, see, and I had my stills downstairs. I'm telling you, and I lived right there on the first floor and you walk right in off the street in my house. Shoot, I never had no trouble. And just like we sitting down here now, the police used to come and sit down and do the same thing—sit down and drink. And if you came in for a gallon jug, I take the jug and fill a gallon jug—don't put it in no bag—take it right out here just like you get it. Broad daylight and police ask you, "Where you got that?" "I got that over Walker's." "Well, hurry up and get off the street with it." I tell you—I was a young man. Well, ya know, there was a long time I didn't think that I would work. I didn't have no overalls to go to work in. I had nineteen suits of clothes, twenty-eight pairs of shoes, and just so much shirts and ties and things, and that's the way I stayed. I had six men working for

Jimmy Walker, Homesick James. Chicago, early 1950s.

me and just, like, I'd go out, let's say, for instance, I'd come over your house, I'd get a cab—a yellow cab—and I'd have the cab to wait. And if I'm out on the street walking the street and I see a police, they'd pick me up, take me home. They didn't want me on the street. Shoot, man, I've had it rough and I've had it good. Like, I have ate off a nickel a day—one nickel a day. Lorenzo and I were what you call real stiff buddies. Like, he made a nickel and I make a nickel. He wouldn't spend his nickel and I wouldn't spend my nickel until I saw him. We would go—there was a bakery at 44th and State, and the guy used to have, I guess he must have made it like day-old rolls. Sweet rolls and, ya know, donuts and stuff like that. And he made up a something, like—he call it "Washington Pies," and they was about inch and a half, two inches thick, and he'd cut you off a chunk for a nickel and we'd cut that pie half in two. We'd go to the drugstore. At that time you could get two cigars for a nickel. We don't know whether tomorrow we're going to get a nickel to buy cigars and cakes with, so what we'd do, we'd take one cigar and cut it half in two and we'd smoke half of that cigar, see? Tomorrow we'd have a whole cigar, see. All we'd have to do is buy our cakes tomorrow. (*laughs*) Oh, boy, you talking about rough. We really had it rough, see, and, uh, then this is what happened when we run up on Hop, see. And we all got a nickel or dime, go round and give it to him, ya know what I mean, and he would make up a pot, see. You'd buy five pounds of neck bones for a dime, see, and, uh, if you bought a nickel's worth of white potatoes, you had just more potatoes than you could use at one time. You'd have enough almost to make a meal tomorrow. So this is the way we'd eat then. We'd all go round there and play, eat, and drink—be full. We—we made it. It's been a tough struggle, but I thank God we made it.

The Fifties

The Square Deal on Division Street, Division and Wells, that was my first job. Homesick and I was there. It's on the North Side. Then after I left Homesick and, ya know, I started fooling around. That must have been around '39, early '40s. I gave it up for a while, and then after I left—ya see what happened, I don't know . . . what it seem like to me, I don't know whether I have a different way of playing, whether it's me or feeling I try to put to it, see? In other words, if I don't feel it, you don't feel it. Well, you know what I did? I used to play in church and they said I was playing blues, and I said, well, I just quit. They say they was going to throw me out of church, so I stopped going.

I think if I'm not mistaken the next guy I taken up with was Billy Boy . . . Arnold. See, him and I played out here at the Barrelhouse Lounge—51st and Michigan. We played out there about seven months. See, we went there behind Little Walter. We had Mighty Joe Young and, uh, Robert Whitehead, Billy Boy, and myself—'55. I had people coming in here all the way from Kansas City when we was out on 51st Street, and the guy that had the club, he came down there to 47th Street and he listened to Junior Wells, and meantime he didn't stop to think that this club, 708, this man had the club there way before he had opened there, and he was more established, see? So he told Billy Boy we'll get rid of the piano and we'll get another guitar. So, okay, it's alright, it's alright with me, 'cause I always worked—construction work. See, I was making $550 a week, so when I went there I wasn't looking for no job. So I went on and he said we'll get rid of the piano. Okay, I got people coming in there from Kansas City, St. Louis, Memphis—every week. We start at 10 and at 1 o'clock he'd had to lock the door. And he had two stores bigger than this, and you couldn't get in the first store to get to the bar. So after I, uh, left there, the stuff would begin to fall off, and he'd want to know why they couldn't hold the crowd. So I told him, well, the people come here asking about the piano player. Three or four carloads of people coming in, then they ask, and Billy Boy say he didn't know where I was at. They say, "Well, if he's in Chicago we'll find him." I left there and went to 65th and State, 6500 State. It was a club right on the corner and I went there. I had Johnnie Temple with me, see. And when the people found out I was there, they started loading that up. So Kid (Riviera) told Billy Boy, after the peoples was asking where was I at and they wanted me. So he told Billy Boy to tell me to come back to come out there, ya know what I mean. I could bring my company and I could have a table and I could get my drinks free and everything was free, and every now and then I'd go up and play a number. I shouldn't go up and play no number. I'm making you money and I ain't going to get nothing. No, no, that don't make no sense. So, I didn't go out there the second week. The third week I goes out there, they sitting up playing pinochle! The band just playing and they playing pinochle—nobody in there! I wouldn't bother with it. I just forgot about it, see. Then come along Elmore (James) when he come to Chicago, see, he was living with me then. See, I used to live right on the corner down here. I've been right here between 43rd and 47th Street over forty years. When he moved from me he moved to 4714 S. Evans. His cousin, she used to live about 728, no, 726 E. 45th Street, 'cause I had a store there. His cousin had a room in the back there. Him and I, our first job was at the Tuxedo Lounge. Yeah, that was our first job—left there come to 708. I done forgot now who this other fellow—who else was with us, but, anyway, we left there and went to the Square Deal at Damen and Madison, right on the corner. See, then he started to messing up with my money. Yeah, so I told him, man, you pay him, you pay each one of us our money, see, because here's what happen. He had quite a few people that come in with him, ya know, and they come in and he'd have two or three tables, and what he'd do—he'd go up to the bar, ya understand. He'd get a fifth of whiskey and set it on each table and we'd have to pay for it, see, and we don't even smell it. So I told the man, "Uh-uh, no, not me! Give me what I'm s'posed to get and we won't have no trouble." I had the same trouble with Little Walter when I played with him. See, well, I was going to cut his throat! Shoot, I stopped him right out there on the lake: "Give me mine and I'll get out of here. I'll get me a cab." See, that's me. Don't play with my money! We'd played out here for a dance in Gary, and he thought maybe he figured the whiskey was enough. See, it was a big stage. This was when he came out with "Juke" and we'd been drinking, and, see, each man takes a solo and, ya know what I mean—you got time to go over here and get, ya know, yourself a shot. The man had a fifth sitting here and one sitting there and one sitting over there, see? So you could get up and go and come on back. And this is when we got kinda high. We started playing "Juke," we didn't quit! And the man come up and say, "That's all, fellas, that's all," and started waving his hands like that and, "That's all fellas, cut it down, that's all." And do you know they had to send the police up there to get us? Yeah, we just, ya know what I mean, I guess we just went berserk!

Then I used to broadcast on WLS Sunday afternoons. Forget the name of this guy—about 27th—2710 or 2705 Wentworth, something like that. Because—what's this girl's name—something Davis. Her band used to come in there behind us. Her old man's got a garage at 40th and Cottage Grove now. Tiny Davis! She played down there, too. I done forgotten now who all we had with us, but they had one guy down there who played tenor sax. We'd always have to go get him from out of the street! Yeah, see, the bandstand was almost as high as that piano, and the bar was just about maybe a foot taller, and he walk—he step right off that stand and he'd walk right down that bar get blowing. He'd walk right down that bar and he'd have to get that drink. Walk right down that bar and go on and step right off that stool right on out to the street. And we'd go out there get him, turn him around, and he never stopped walking. Back along the bar right on back on the stand! He was natural crazy, but he could blow! Yeah, that guy could naturally blow.

I never did any recording before. I don't know, I was always afraid of making a mistake. I don't like to make mistakes, see? I do a lot of playing by myself, because I want to get this stuff down pat. I know what it is, see, and it's no need to start off with me with something else, ya know what I mean? I won't accept it. And if there's no feeling with it, I can't get no feeling to it—you can forget it.

I don't ever try to copy no one's style. I want to play like me. I have my own style. See, the thing about me, what I play today I don't have to play it tomorrow. Another thing—I won't play it the same way, because there's something sounds a little different—sounds a little better, and when I play it tomorrow, ya understand, I done heard it. I done already heard it, see, so tomorrow when I play it, I play it a little different."

Louis Myers

A fine vocalist and equally proficient on both guitar and harmonica, Louis Myers was a triple threat. He was held in high esteem by his contemporaries and widely recognized as one of the top accompanists in Chicago. Born in Byhalia, Mississippi, on September 18, 1929, Louis and the rest of the Myers family relocated to Chicago in 1941, a move that was perfectly timed, coinciding as it did with the new emerging Chicago blues scene, one in which Louis was to eventually play a pivotal role.

Throughout his career he played and recorded with a multitude of artists, his reputation secured when he, along with his brother Dave Myers and drummer Fred Below, teamed up with harmonica player Little Walter, who was then at the pinnacle of his creativity. The band was the perfect foil for Walter's innovative style. Rockers like "Off the Wall" and "Tell Me, Mama" to the haunting "Sad Hours" are considered classic Chicago blues.

Willie Dixon, working as a producer for the Abco label, was well aware of Louis Myers's talent, having worked with him at Chess Records, and in 1956 Dixon had him record "Just Whaling" and "Bluesy," a stunning pair of harmonica instrumentals that unfortunately failed to ignite the public interest. A fine session for One-Der-Ful in 1967 remained unissued until its eventual release on the Delmark compilation *Sweet Home Chicago*. Undeterred, Louis continued the life of a working bluesman, occasionally with others like Otis Rush, with whom he also recorded, or, occasionally, Muddy Waters, but more often leading his own band. In the late 1960s, along with his brother Dave and Fred Below, he reformed the Aces. In the early 1970s the Aces toured Europe on several occasions, recording an uneven album in France for Vogue.

An album for Delmark with Myers accompanying Robert Jr. Lockwood fared much better and was followed by a tour of Japan with Lockwood in 1974, which resulted in the Advent album *Blues Live in Japan.* In 1976 BBC Television shot some excellent footage of the Aces at Eddie Shaw's club in Chicago, which was subsequently shown in the documentary *The Devil's Music.* But despite an impressive resume, personal recording opportunities were few. A couple more albums did see the light of day, but the success that should have been his continued to elude him. Louis Myers died in Chicago on September 5, 1994.

—Bill Greensmith

Louis Myers

Bill Greensmith

Blues Unlimited #122 (Nov./Dec. 1976)

You got to be saying something. You got to sound like Louis Myers before I can really feel that you can play a guitar.

—Bobby King

What's In You Gotta Come Out

My father was like a sharecropper. He had land of his own, but it was run by his uncle. He's still got it now, one hundred acres of land, and he was part owner. He inherited it. He's dead now, he died in '60. He played more classic blues than what's going on today, what went on back in his time when I was a baby. He was playing classic guitar, but blues. He was playing around with some cats in Memphis, Tennessee. That was before my knowledge of him doing—I never did know none of the cats that he was playing with. I know my father play mostly for white people back down there. They come and get him and he go stay a week or two weeks sometimes before we see him again, he'd play for like their weddings. My mother played too, they'd play together sometimes. I used to sit on the porch and they'd be sitting up there playing. I imagine he taught her to play.

I can't remember actually when I did start playing. Whenever I'd pick up one of the guitars around the house when I was little, they used to whup me, they used to tear me up. I couldn't keep my hands off the guitar. I loved to look at the tuning pegs and the strings, it was something pretty for me. I used to mess with their guitars; they'd say, "Leave the guitar alone or I'm gonna tear your backside up." That didn't stop me. I had to have a hand on that guitar whenever I could see it. I kept that up and

Louis and Bob Myers. 708 Club, Chicago, mid-1950s.

they whup me until they just gave up whuppin' me. Then my father he just stopped playing around like he used to and started to working more at the house and farming. He borrowed his guitar off to someone and they kept his guitar. I know he let some guy have it. I can't even remember the cat's name. The cat took it off and kept it too long; when he brought it back it was kinda busted. I know him and my father had a little hassle, and he told my father that he had fell off a horse or something and busted the guitar. I know my father told him, "You got drunk and busted it!"

What really inspired me to play as I got up around nine and ten years old was a guy named Willie B. Sesserly and his brother Buncher. Willie B. was the youngest one. He is a good friend of mine right today. He come and hear me play right today. He inspired me to play, really. Because my mother and father they didn't want none of us to play no music no way, but what's in you gotta come out. So Willie B. was a guitar player. He was young, hanging around my father, and that old cat could play better. Willie B. was getting to be a terrible fine guitar player and singer. He could sing. Him and his brother Buncher—he was the one that was tough until Willie B. went away and stayed about a year, a couple of years, and he come back and he was really playing guitar then. He had a harmonica player with him and they both could play. He started to come by the house, he knew the family. We lived not far from one another. He left his guitar over the house because he know I liked to bang on it, and the next day he come back by there, I was so scared he was gonna take it away. He told me, "Say, you can keep the guitar, because I'm gonna be gone for two weeks." And when he got back I think there was only two strings on the guitar. I had done bust them all. But I had learnt how to play something, though, because when he come back he wasn't mad because I broke the strings. He said the strings were old on there anyway. But anyway, he put some strings on the guitar and listened at me bang on it. He said, "You know, you learnt what you learnt on your own, that's good." He tried to show me how to play, and from then on I got very interested in guitar. But, like I said, my father didn't want me to be a musician, and I imagine that's why he whipped me all the time when I touched the guitar. He knew it was in me, but he wanted to stop it right there. He really didn't want me to play the guitar.

Them two brothers, Willie B. and Buncher, they play together, man, they were rough. They played at house frolics. When we were little kids we'd go to other neighbors' houses, might be two miles across the country, you know, like our neighbors and friends, and we'd go around there when we know they gonna have a frolic. Everybody wants to know who's playing there, they say, "Willie B. and Buncher." Well, they were top at that time, they could play, man. You could hear them guitars a country mile, too. Yeah, down there you could. They had them round old guitars, man, they sound so loud and clear. And that's why I started playing. Every so often I learnt a little bit more. I watched Buncher and Willie B. how they played, and just seeing them I know I had to find what they were doing.

My cousin on my father's side, he was a musician. My father's brother—he played guitar, too. His name was Fred Myers, but he died. I guess I was about seven years old. Yeah, they all was musicians on my father's side. I don't know of no musicians on my mother's side.

My brother Bob has been playing for years. See, I always had something to lean on. He used to fool around with the harmonica down there at that time when I was a little boy. He was fooling around with the older boys, everybody down there was playing the harmonica whenever they could get one. And he really could play harmonica. He learnt to play with different names—the cat I done forgotten, but they were very good harmonica players. They hang around, like Sonny Boy and Little Walter, they were tough, but they never did get no . . . Bob was playing harp before he left Mississippi and I was, too. Whenever I could get me a harp, I play that.

Some harp player that we know, he was named Wilhelm. I never will forget him, they call him Wilhelm. He was kind of a shy harp player. He was much older than we was, he was upper teenager cat. I guess he was around about eighteen years old then. I was about seven or eight then. And I know my older brother and Wilhelm they'd be playing all the time, and I used to listen to him, but he was shy. Dark tall cat, he was real shy. Just them two get together you can hear them really playing. Whatever instrument I could get my hands on, if music come out, I was interested in it.

We used to take nails—now, you listen to this. Believe this or not, but this is what we used to do. We used to go out and find cane, tall cane. We call them cane down South, but they call them bamboo poles what they use now, same thing like you use for fishing. Some of them you'd get real large and long joints on them; we cut the joints out of them with the ends of it right on the joint. We'd make a fire and put the nails in the fire and let them get red-hot, and we'd take that and burn holes through them, much as six holes, and we'd make a fife out of it. And sometimes we'd get sounds out of them too, man. They might not be in tune, but we got something out of them! We made whistles out of little small canes. We made all kind of whistles and flutes, anything that made a tune. Yeah, I just loved that music all the time. I still do right now, really. But it's a lot done changed since then.

3948 Indiana

I moved to Chicago when I was eleven years old, the beginning of 1941. I guess we got here around late January. Things started changing, because the war had just got on. I remember real well things were changing, most people leaving farms going into the service. The whole thing, the whole scene back there then was farmers wanting to do a little better. So I guess my father thought that we better move on to Chicago, because my mother had three sisters living in Chicago then.

Coming to the city is really different. You got to get to know the way the city is. I mean, when you come from the country you don't see all the lights, sidewalks, and buildings and things. Yeah, it was really different, but I got to meet musicians. I mean not meet 'em, but just see 'em. They were old musicians, they were old to my time then. But I imagine they wasn't all that old, it was just the time I met 'em, being a boy around eleven years old.

We were living at 3948 Indiana and the first guy playing guitar that I really learnt about was Lonnie Johnson. He was living at 3946½ Indiana in the basement. Yeah, he's sitting on one basement level down there playing on his guitar, and, being the nosey kid that I was, anybody with a guitar, I'm peepin', you know. So I was on the back porch, which I was up on the second floor, and I happen to look down there and I asked my auntie who's that man. She said, "That's Lonnie Johnson, that blues-playing Lonnie Johnson cat." Well, you know, my auntie was a religious woman—church—she didn't believe in no blues, and that's what had me kinda scared of playing then. My father brought an old guitar with him, wasn't no strings on it, but I was gonna put some strings on it and try to play with him. But Lonnie Johnson seem to be a kinda mean man. I know he told me to get away from around there one time. I never did, what you call, get to meet him or shake his hand or "my name is Myers . . ." It's just what you call a next-door-neighbor thing. But I saw him there for about two or three years; all I see him do was go out and in. Some hot days he'd be sitting out on the back in that little basement porch. Sometimes, not often, but every once in a while you might see him out there with his guitar playing. But he was a self-man, a do-it-his-self-man. He didn't play with nobody.

My father was working at some factory. He gave up playing when he left down South, because, like I said, he quit going out, he just did work on the farm and that's all. His guitar laid around till it got busted, tore all up. Then I had to get me a guitar of my own. I think I paid $12 for a little bitty small round old guitar and I kept that for years. I guess I bought that guitar when I was around twelve years old and kept it till I was about seventeen. It was completely demolished itself then, it wasn't no use trying to play it.

I also saw Homesick James. He wasn't going under the name Homesick James then. I don't know what name he was going under, but I know he called himself James. James Williamson? It might have been. Well, I know when I met him I heard Othum, him and Othum Brown. My older brother, Bob, it didn't take him long, 'cause he played harp, and every guitar player wants to see a harp player that could blow any harp. He got around and he knew them. Well, he was playing harp and he always would tell me about a guy named Othum Brown that really play guitar. And I told him I'd be very interested in meeting him. He said, yeah, he want me to meet him, too. But I was a kid—you don't get out to these places, whiskey joints. So one day, one evening I met him and Othum Brown on the street and Homesick James. They both was playing and I got to know Othum, because Othum could really, really play. He was playing on the sidewalk on the street with a cigar box, him and James, and people was gathered around them throwing quarters, nickels, and dimes in the cigar box and they were playing. This was right around where I lived at 39th and Indiana. They were hanging around 39th all the way back down to 31st. They was playing at all these places at night, but whenever they want some money to get them a drink, man, they play right there on the street and get that money. You see them walk off, they got enough money to get them a drink. Othum was pickin' some guitar, mister. I ain't never seen no cat that could pick as much guitar as he was pickin' by himself. He didn't need nobody to play with him, even though Homesick James was playing. They both play, but that Othum could play, now, he could play.

I met Othum Brown back there then, but I never did hang around on Maxwell Street. I never did go down there. I mean those cats had been makin' their little money and things down there for years, you know, but you take the cats around my age bracket, they didn't hang around down there too much. Take, like, Earl Hooker. Now, how I met Earl Hooker, it was like in a little gang fight. We was kids going back and forward to the show, catching the streetcar, jump on the back end of it and ride down to where you going. And I know Hooker, he was running around with a little street gang then and I never did know he played guitar. They jumped us one time on 35th Street, and the next time I saw Hooker he was on the street playing guitar. And, now, he could play, he was around my age bracket. Man, he could play. When I saw him that kinda made me wanna come on out and play on the street, too, but

I never did, because, see, I was always shut in by my peoples or the religion on my auntie's side. Like, we was living in with her and she didn't like blues. This was when I was about fourteen—like, I really wanted to play.

You see, in my neighborhood then, the only cats you could see were the older cats, and they could do what they wanna do. But there I was, a young boy from Mississippi, and all the kids wasn't going for the blues back there then. They was going for swing and stuff like that, and the people didn't like the blues—kinda like the older set. Kids around my age bracket didn't go for that. I used to sit on the porch and play, and the kids used to laugh at me 'cause I was playing the blues, so I quit playing for about four years then. Wasn't no use, my auntie didn't allow me to play and nobody allowed me to play in the house. So I quit and I picked it back up, especially when I saw Earl Hooker. He was playing with another kid named Vincent.[1] He come back to Chicago last year. Now, he can play, too. I don't know his last name, never did. Now he plays jazz. He's one of the best guitar players in Chicago, but don't nobody know it, because he's just come back from Oklahoma in the last year or so, but he used to play around with Hooker on the streets then. Hooker was a terrible young guitar player.

Earl learnt from different cats, you know, same way as myself. Nobody learns to play what they can play by themselves, because it ain't to be done. Only cats that can do that can sit down and write and let other people read it, and then they can play it and then they know this cat invented it. But blues players—they play by feelin'. Like, I hear something Lonnie Johnson did on records, I loved that man. I said I ain't never heard anybody play like this. Lonnie Johnson was in his own bag. A person learns to play from feelin'. The way I gotta hear is how much I can hear and how much it sound to me and how much I can feel it. If it don't stay with me, that's something I'm not gonna learn. But if something stay with me, I can hear somebody do something maybe five months previous to the time I'm gonna do it, eventually I'm gonna do it.

A Good Young Guitar Player

Professional, well, we just eased up into that. Because I had been playing, I started playing for house parties, that's where I met Robert Jr. Lockwood. Some old wine-heads come over and got me to play at their house party. That was terrible, terrible. I don't want to tell nobody about that. That was terrible, man. There I was eighteen years old and I went to this wine-head's building on 39th and State. There was some cats that live in there that heard me play and liked me. They liked the way I was playing for a kid. And he taken me up there and told me he was gonna get some money for me playing, so I go on up there with my guitar. There I am sitting up there playing, and Robert Jr. was there playing when I got there. He play awhile and I play awhile, then we play together. Well, anyway, a wife and a husband got into a disagreement. They come up with big knifes. There I was, you know, I ain't never been through a thing like this. So I got up to get out of there, because when I saw them knives and they were swinging at one another. When I got up and tried to get out of there that's when the woman come grab me. She grab me from behind with the knife, swinging out from behind me at her husband. Her husband in the meantime is swinging at her over me and there I was. Robert Jr. and this other guy that got me there to play told them, "Y'all shouldn't do that, that ain't nothin' but a kid. Y'all turn the kid loose." They were using me for a shield. Every time he cut at her she would push me out there to him, until they told them to stop that, so I got away. That's how I met Robert Jr. I don't know if he's done forgotten, that's been a long time ago. The Pomerange Building, Willie Dixon was living in there, too. This was around about '46, '47, something like that. I think '46. I didn't do no more parties by myself. No. I didn't know nothing about what them people were doing, 'cause I was just as scared as I ever been—them knives, man. Two blades, one coming at you and one coming out from behind you, and I didn't know what to do. I went home and didn't come out the place for nobody.

Amos Milburn sent for me to play guitar in his band. Said they was gonna tutor me into music. I probably would have been a better-off guitar player now had I went with him, but my mother wouldn't about let me go. That was about 1946, something like that. He sent a man first, then he sent a letter. What you'd call a talent scout looking for good young guitar players, and at that time my mother wouldn't let me go. I never will forget that, you know, things like that. You know, the man come there and said, "We'll tutor the boy to become a good musician." Some older musician turned him on, a piano player. I can't think of his name now, but he was living right around the corner from where we were living then. Amos Milburn was makin' records and traveling on the road. I can't think of this piano player's name. He played downtown all the time. He start me tuning up with the piano, 4/40, which I didn't know nothing about, and I learnt how to tune the guitar up to 4/40. He heard me play and he told his friend what a tremendous guitar player I was for such a young boy, and I think he about turned them cats on to me, because he knew all about Amos Milburn and all them cats making records. I was about sixteen.

A man named Mr. Spires, he kept hanging around, like he was interested in me. Arthur Spires. I think Mr. Spires about sixty-five years old now. He got interested in me because, like, I started playing house parties with him, me and Mr. Spires played around a good little while. He recorded for Leonard Chess, "Big Fat Mama."[2] He used to come by and get me all the time. Mr. Spires wasn't what you would call an out-and-out guitar player. He couldn't hold his own, but he could sing real good. But he was trying to learn to play guitar when he got his guitar. But when he heard me play, well, he knew that he could learn with me, because at that time, man, I could really play pretty well. Because anything I hear I could play. I'll find it. A lot goes into playing blues guitar. We play around I guess three or four years. Me and Mr. Spires had it like an incorporated band, me and him. Like he would get the little jobs and things and I would do the playing. Just me and him.

My brother Dave was learning how to play, but he was learning how to play much faster than Mr. Spires, like things that Mr. Spires couldn't learn. Dave would spend a lot of time with me. He'd come around when he'd get off his job, but Mr. Spires, you'd see him maybe two or three times a week. I was playing way before David even picked up a guitar. I didn't even know that he was interested in guitar till he used to say, "I'm gonna go and buy me a guitar." I told him, "If you do, let's get together." So he went and bought him a good guitar, a Gibson. He started learning with me. That didn't stop Mr. Spires. He come and get me and David.

I used to go to the show and Mr. Spires come looking for me one night. He had a party on a Friday night and I went to the show. And incidentally, he had Dave in the car with him. I came home about 10:30 that night and there they sat waiting for me. They were so mad. (*laughs*) Mr. Spires said, "You sure messed up a good night. I had all them girls and things up there, where was you? Me and Dave went there and did the best we could do but . . ." I used to love to go to the show, man. I'd go see me a Western or something like that. You know, my mother would tell me, "Mr. Spires been by here looking for you . . ."

Well, I met Junior Wells. Some of his cousins heard us playing in a building across the street from where he lived. We was playing at some of his relations' house. They was grown girls, they said, "We got a cousin that can play harp pretty good." He was younger than I was. Junior could play. He wasn't playing professionally, but he was playing what he was playing. As you go into music and be more together with one another you come off better. When you're young and got it in you, it'll come out of you. Junior learned how to play pretty well and we started playing together. That time David started pickin' up on guitar better than Mr. Spires was, so when we did get a professional gig, we went on and took the gig, and that's where we cut Mr. Spires out. That was me, Junior, and Dave. We didn't have a drummer for about three or four years.

The Aces

The people started accepting us because we were playing much faster. Our music was mostly up-tempo, and they hear us play and they call us the Little Chicago Devils and wasn't but us three. We were the Three Dukes for a good while. Then we turned ourselves into the Three Aces, then we went to some other name.

Elgin Edmonds, he also took up with me, he liked me. Him and his wife used to take me out fishing, go fishing all the time, because I love to fish, too. He told me one time, "Y'all gonna need a drummer with y'all." Like, we'd sit in with them (Muddy Waters) and Elgin would tell us how we sound with a drummer, but we'd sit up there and pat our feet so heavy till we didn't need no drummer. We had been used to playing by ourselves. We stomp, you know, for the beat. He said, "The way y'all play, y'all don't need no drummer, but y'all do need a drummer so you won't have to be stompin' your feet. I know a boy just out the army. He'd be a good drummer for y'all." And that was Below.

I said, "Well, if you see Below you be sure to tell him." So we got the gig at the Brookmont and he sent Below. Below didn't have a whole set of drums. Elgin let him have the drums, too. So Below come with us, he tried to play with us, but he couldn't. He said, "I can't play with y'all, tonight is my last night." I said, "Man, it's funny you can't learn to play blues, and you say you can play jazz and all be-bop and stuff, it's mighty funny you can't play blues. I can play jazz and you can't even play blues, you know there's something wrong about that." So Below said, "Well, I'll tell you what. I'm gonna try it another two weeks. You talkin' about I can't play no blues and you can play jazz. I'm gonna learn to play the blues." I said, "Well, okay, then." But he had quit. He said he ain't never heard nothing sound like that before. He said, "Man, I can't play that." I could play some jazz by listening, by ear, but that wasn't what I was getting over on. I was freakin' out playing blues.

Shoot. Man, it didn't take Below two weeks to learn, but, see, he had to get in there and create his own beat. You have lots of people who said where I taught Below to play. No, I just showed him the way that a blues had to have a foundation beat to it. He wore out my guitar case. I had an old guitar case; he just beat that till it fell apart and I couldn't put my guitar in it no more. He used my guitar case for a drum, sit there beating it with his hands right there where I was living at. But he invented his beat to go along with the blues; don't nobody learn nobody nothing. A person learns how to get into something, whatever he can fit into his own bag. I tell him all the time, I say, "Below, I read some article where they say Louis Myers taught you how to play the blues. I ain't taught you how to play the blues. I showed you a way to a beat where you had to find a beat so you could play with us, and you had to do that yourself." He said, "Yeah, that's right." I said, "Well, I don't like to see it, because people get the wrong impression. How can I teach you to play blues on a drum?"

We went around and sat in with Muddy Waters when Walter was playing with him, and Walter was planning this thing after his record had come out.[3] He always wanted to play with us, because we was playing faster music; our music was faster than Muddy's and the people's liked to dance with a little speed, jump, or something. And we sat in with Muddy Waters and right away Walter heard us play, man. He said, "God-dog." Walter and Muddy was playing way over there and we went over there on the West Side. That's the first time Walter ever heard us play, and he was completely out of his mind when he heard us play. He was determined to get on the bandstand and play with me, Dave, and Below, see, because Below was a monster drummer. It didn't take Below three months to be a monster drummer in Chicago. Walter heard us play and there was something about us that Walter want to do. See, Junior was playing the harp and we was getting down. He said, "Y'all play fast music." And he got in there and sat in with us one time, boy, and I heard it myself. He said, "Louis, you guys are really playing." But when he left Muddy and come to us, he had his way of playing. You see, Walter had tutored himself in this style of what we was doing and he knew he could play right . . . The kinda stuff that we was playing he was very interested in. I'd be the same way if I heard some dudes out there playing and they sounding and I knew I could fit in. Them the kind of cats I want to play with, somebody that I could learn to play with and learn to fit in with. Nobody don't want to play with nobody they can't play with.

Little Walter

I hired Walter after Junior left and went with Muddy. We cut "Lawdy Lawdy" after Junior done gone with Muddy.[4] Walter called me up and told me that Junior was gonna split. Walter had been back in Chicago for two weeks. They had been gone on the road, everybody know that they out of town. But when I found out Walter was back here in Chicago, because he called me up and said, "You know your boy done split on you," talking about Junior gonna leave the band, Junior hadn't told me nothing about it. See, back there then the union was very strict, the black local. When one cat gonna leave out the band, gonna quit or something, give the proper notice, just like you do the proprietor who own the joint and the man also give you that if he wants to fire you. So Junior hadn't said nothing to me, which he was gonna leave the next two or three days. I asked him, I said, "Junior, when is you leavin' to join Muddy?" That was a surprise to him to know that I knew. He said, "Well, I'm supposed to leave Friday." I said, "Well, okay, then, I just want to know so I can get myself a harp player, because you should have told me." He said, "Well, I didn't know if I want to go with Muddy or not." I said, "Well, that's your business, but I never would have known until you done gone."

Walter had done made "Juke," and the way he was telling me, I think that's why he left Muddy, because he was getting so many requests for "Juke" and he wanted to be on his own. But that wasn't the reason I hired him. I hired Walter because we needed a harp player, and Walter made sure he'd be the first one to know, because otherwise he wouldn't have called me up and told me Junior was leaving. When he did I told him I'm gonna need a harp player with Junior gone and I ain't got no time to find one, because Forrest City Joe was around and we couldn't find him, and he could *really* play. Oh, man, Forrest City Joe was rough! He's the baddest harp player I ever saw. Yeah, ain't nobody as bad as Forrest City Joe. Better than Walter? Oh, yeah, man, yeah. I ain't puttin' none of 'em down, but the fact remains anybody who heard Forrest City Joe knows that he's the baddest harp player that ever lived. He could take them chromatics and play anything that them jazz cats play. He'd take that little harp and you wouldn't believe the things he could play on it.

He'd play the "Tommy Dorsey Boogie" just like that record go with one of them little harps. Nobody could see how he'd do it but him. But he was a wino; he'd play with you a couple of nights, get that money, you wouldn't see him in a month of Sundays. Like I said, I ain't never heard nobody play as much harp as he, no kind of way. That cat could play, never heard nobody play the harp he play. Even when I hired Walter, Walter had to leave for two weeks. He had a show with an all-girl band somewhere traveling across the country. Yeah, he was booked with an all-girl band on a show. He didn't dig that, because he told me when he come back. But we hired Forrest City Joe to play, and he played about two or three days and we didn't see Forrest City Joe no more. But, man, Forrest City Joe was the kind of cat like this: when Walter was playing with us and Forrest City Joe did show back up there, Walter wouldn't let him come near the bandstand. No, sir. I never heard nobody play as much harp as he did.

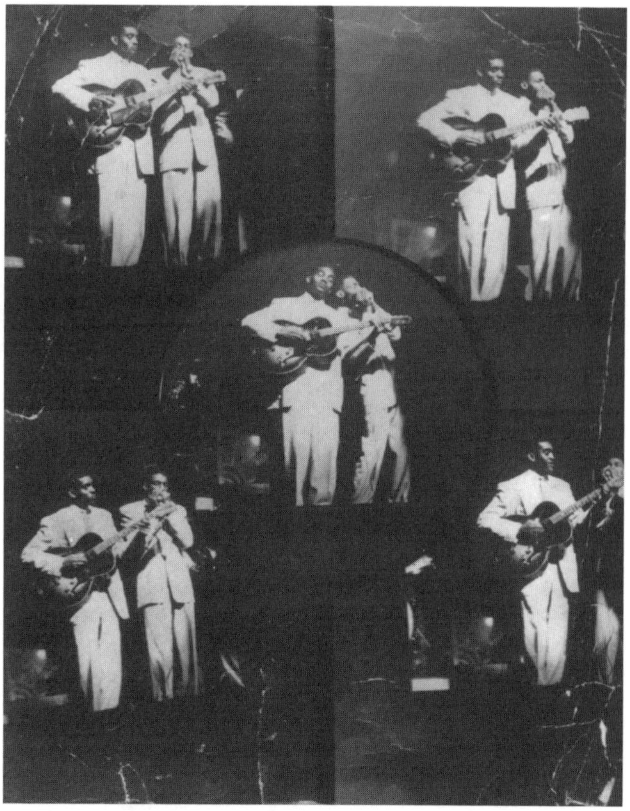

Little Walter and Louis Myers. Apollo Theater, New York, 1952.

Bob (Myers) could really play, man. You wouldn't believe, but he could play just as good as Sonny Boy. But he didn't have the name. Sonny Boy was already out there playing when we were little bitty kids, but they were friends and he started playing around with him. I never did see Sonny Boy, never did see him. My brother used to try and show him to me, but you don't pay things like that no attention. He was playing over there the same place where we got the gig at when I hired Little Walter, the Hollywood. Sonny Boy came down there one evening. My brother tried to tell me, "Why don't you come on down so you can see and hear Sonny Boy?" They was crazy about Sonny Boy then. To me, I didn't think of cats like that, because my thing was playing guitar. I didn't care too much about no harp. But when I did hear his records, I heard what he was saying. That was good enough for me. What he would sing he would play at. And a lot of cats would never be able to duplicate Sonny Boy, not even Forrest City Joe. He'd come very close to the same thing, but not Sonny Boy.

That old Forrest City Joe, he a bad dude on harp, man. He could really play harp. He played piano, too. He was as rough on piano as he was on that harp. Forrest City Joe was a cat like this. He can hear what a cat's saying and duplicate that there. Most of the things I've heard on record he sounds more like Sonny Boy. But if you get down to actual playing, man, if he'd just cut his fooling around and go on and play, like, do his thing, you'd say, now, there's Little Walter sounding like Forrest City Joe. It's just that simple. He'd turn it right back around. You see, if he'd hear somebody do something, it goes in that ear and he'd sound like that, almost. The only difference was that Sonny Boy sing as much as he played. Now, believe me, this cat was a great singer, this Sonny Boy, John Lee Williamson. Yeah, he played them songs, man. He sang 'em and played 'em. You listen at his harp, it'll be saying just what he be saying in the words. But Forrest City Joe, man, come down to harp playing, no kind of way them cats would touch him playing harp.

Little Walter had enough authority playing his instrument to fit in with any band that is playing time, and he could play so strong until he'd dominate. If the band's listening to what he's doing, naturally they gonna make him sound good. We were all playing in the same environment, man, our intentions were the same. If you listen at my guitar playing, man, distinctive sounds and the attitude was there. The little notes that I was pickin'—it's trying to say it's tone. I'm playing tone, and this is what makes the whole world go around in music is tone. He played all different amplifiers. He had a Gibson amplifier and a PA system, two speakers, things like that, whatever he could get his sound over with. Like, to me, Walter studied a way to get himself in on the harp.

But before I knew of Muddy Waters and Little Walter and all them cats, I had heard guys sitting on the corner playing harp out of amplifiers, man. A whole lot of cats playing by themselves, no guitar, now. That was back in '43 and '44. And I think that was before some of them big stars come to Chicago, don't you think? Like I said, I have heard that stuff on the corners, cats with amplifiers. Some of them had little bitty old small amplifiers making that noise out of them with the harp. I know because I used to try and play harp myself, but I wouldn't do it. I used to hear my brother stand on the corner and play harp.

Sad Hours

I cut records with Junior Wells before Walter. I know I made "Hoodoo Man" with Junior Wells. "Mean Old World" and "Sad Hours" was the first record I made with Walter.[5] We had been playing "Sad Hours" down there where we was playing. Junior was with us, we used to play that by ourselves. Junior never tried to play harp on that, though. That was just a number that we liked to play for one particular man, the proprietor, Charles Hallaburg, that was at the Hollywood Rendezvous. He and his wife owned the place then, and this is what he wanted me to play every night. It's something like a—what's that thing's name? (*hums "Blues after Hours"*) Yeah, I guess they call that "Blues after Hours." Every night we had to play that two or three times. When Walter come in, like when I got him with the group after Junior cut out, he come right on it, that's something that he could play on the harp, he could fit the harp in with it. See, 'cause Walter wasn't no slouch on the harp. He could handle the harp, but he didn't go doing anything too obnoxious. He just play what he could handle, like tone. That's all there is about playing harp is tone.

Now, here's a thing that arise at the wrong time. Now, you understand what I'm saying? On the gig we would do it, but when we got down there, when we recorded, Walter wouldn't do it. Dave started playing it and (Leonard) Chess liked it. Chess said, "Hey, y'all play that again, man, do that again." Walter chickened out. Said, "No, no, that's alright." And Chess wants to know why. Now, this makes Chess more interested in it. So anyway, they went on and him and Walter got into a big thing about it. He said, "Man, what you don't want to play a number like that for? That sounds good." Well, Walter had done said, "Well, look, that's one of the men's ideas, I don't want . . ." Now, that's honest as a man could be. I told David myself, I said, "Man, you should keep your ideas." Just the same thing Walter told him. He said, "I've got my numbers, I'm already made, whatever you got keep it to yourself." Chess wanted it and it wasn't Walter's idea, and Walter knew that just like I did. We all knew that. But Chess wanted it. It's a business thing with Chess, which is no more than right. He wanted it because he see that he liked it, somebody else would like it and he could sell many records on it. But that means somebody gonna lose in the deal. So Chess got around there and he talked to Walter, begged Walter, and Walter told him no. But some kinda way Chess convinced David that he'll get the credit for it. But he never did.

Now, you see, Walter didn't want to accept anybody's idea. But he had to play on this when he knows that he could fit in real good. He wasn't gonna just play it out there and let nobody else have it. He wasn't gonna just play on there and do all his thing on there and then say, "Give it to so-and-so." Then, if you look at it you could say this: had Walter had've give it to David, David couldn't play it, because he couldn't play the harmonica part. Chess said, "You're not gonna get by with this number, this number's gonna be played." And in business I would have did the same thing. I don't give a hell who it come from, that's what I want. If I want it, I'm gonna pay for it. I'm gonna get it. That's all there was to it. He just said, "I want that number." And he also told Walter, "You gonna play it, too." And Walter played it.

We never did rehearse. We walked in the studio because we were playing with one another, I know what he's gonna do. See, I'd deal with Walter on his level, what he's capable of playing. If he can play 2, I can play 2/2. You see, because a harp is limited, man. He can't do nothing on a harp that can get away from a guitar player if he can play more than three or four changes. Chess would call you down if things ain't right out there, and they got to be damn near right. Chess was a very funny kind of cat, man. But I'll tell you, when it gets down to that music and that ear, ain't no way you could fool him, and his brother, Phil, was the same. Both of them were what you call good. They had that ear on them, they could hear the blues and stuff like that. They know when it's supposed to be right, and when it ain't right they'd let you cool, try and keep you calm till you come back normally to your thing. He knew what the people wanted and he wanted to sell what the people buying.

It's what a person is producing when he's sounding, whatever number he's doing. Chess had an ear for that, he could detect whether you gonna come through or not, or he's gonna make you come through. I think the sound was something else different, because I know Walter sound good in one studio, and some studios, man, you just couldn't get no sound. I didn't cut that much with Walter. I don't want you to get the wrong impression that I cut a lot with him. I didn't. David cut with him for years after.

Baddest Band in the Land

We toured for years all over the United States playing auditoriums, dance halls, roadhouses, nightclubs. Here we were with amplified music with a different thing altogether. Where I had fun at, after I realized what we were really doing, that the other cats didn't have a chance, some of them bands didn't have a chance. We was playing out of big amplifiers, and they're sitting there playing horns and things with one or two mikes. A ten-, twelve-, or fifteen-piece band, but the peoples had to get up close to hear that. In the meantime, we had big amplifiers, man, and Walter could take one of the things that he was playing out of and sit it way out there, hang it up on the wall somewhere out there. He was using—I think they call them "Macon" PA system, and those things were heavy, man. Do you realize how strong an amplifier is just blowing an instrument out of it? Can you imagine an upright bass gonna sound as loud as an electric bass? You can throw that big upright bass among an electric bass with all them amplifiers, you won't even hear him. You won't even think he's there. In fact, good musicians used to tell me, you're not supposed to hear too much of a bass, you're supposed to feel it. Now, you imagine, we got all amplifiers and here's these cats still playing the old style, just sitting up there playing drive-along-jimmy, no amplifiers. I realized this at the time. Walter, David, Below, and myself, we all knew this. But, now, those cats didn't know, they didn't know until we was up on them. Like we done played and they say, "Man, those cats choppin' us up." We ran into quite a few bands out there with names that didn't have a chance. If they played their set before we played, just call themselves lucky. Because that next set they go back on, them peoples just boo them off the bandstand, wouldn't let them play no more.

I heard a piano player crying one night because he goes to play the piano and there all the notes out of the piano. Piano's done tore up and he's got to play this piano through the night. He's just one, but think about all the rest of them that's been in that same shape. They relying upon the piano for the big chords and things, and they get there and the piano player can't play, because twelve or fourteen of the notes is gone. So they're cooked before they start, right? Anything we play is gonna be heard whether it's right or wrong. How could a small four-piece group do any harm to a big band? All they had to do was look at what we had and look at what they didn't have. We had amplified music. The horn player would stand up there, pull his horn out of its case. We'd always run across some cat that could blow, had volume, that could really get up there, but he was just one in the band. They all got to be choppin' to fool around with us. We would chop them bands. Walter was playing like forty horns, man. His amplifier would sound like that sometimes, put his echo on and God! Music was hittin' the walls and bouncing back to us, bouncing all over the place, and they'd say, "Them cats sound like a giant band and there ain't but four of them." Like, I heard some horn players talking: 'Man, that Little Walter or whatever his name is, he really got a thing going on. Look at the cat, he's got all that volume and them boys, them cats that's playing with him are just something on them guitars and that drummer is outta sight and they got their stuff together."

It was an altogether new different type of stuff that the people was accepting, because we was whippin' it on 'em strong and sure. We was killin' 'em, man. One time I read in a paper that Little Walter was the baddest band in the land and it wasn't but us four. But we had something new and something different. And had we been men among ourselves, we'd been strong right today, still been in a new bag with all the youngsters coming on. We'd still be playing something that the people would be enjoying from now on, but whatever we brought here we wasn't men enough to handle, we wasn't men with ourselves. Everybody had a greedy bag they want to get in. Well, I had to live through that. I never knew what greediness was, I always loved to hear cats play.

But we was playing and getting ourselves together in blues. There's so much stuff we played that didn't get on wax, that is the killing part. Had people had tape recorders back then like today and heard some of the things. Like, say, for instance, you heard Walter on the record. He went there for that one purpose, that was to put something good on record. That wasn't all we played. Like today you got tape recorders, you can follow the performer around and listen to him, listen to what he's got to offer. We played so much stuff, man. When we play our best, like, we beam to ourselves. That's one thing, the greatest stars is facing that one thing, they can't outplay themselves. They mostly do their best with themselves.

I know one Sunday we went up there, 609 West on 47th Street, and Muddy Waters was playing there. It was in the daytime. I met up on Walter someplace and we went over there. Well, Sonny Boy (Rice Miller) was playing there, too. Well, Walter and Sonny Boy, to me they was funny. Like, they never got along, but I imagine they got along, but both of them play harp. Sonny Boy was much older than both of us, and Walter used to wave his hand at him when he see him, and Sonny Boy used to look at Walter real funny, really look at Walter. Well, anyway, Walter said, "Hey, let's go up there and light him up." I said, "Oh, man, I don't feel like foolin' with that old man. You gonna go up and get that old man stirred up. He's gonna blow you right on outta here." Walter said, "Let's go up there and get him." Well, I tell you. Sonny Boy played the way he played—his own trip, the same as Walter did—but, now, to me you couldn't put them both together saying Sonny Boy could overdo Walter with the harp, tricks, and things. Yeah, but, man, Walter could lay down a tone on that harp, he knew that. He whupped that tone on any of them, boy, and didn't even care. He got on up there and stirred Sonny Boy up, and, like I said, Sonny Boy blow Walter right on out, tricked him out is what I mean. He took two or three harps and went through his bag and took the great big harp. He could really put on a show. Well, Walter wasn't that much of a show, but Walter could blow. That's something that he just wanted to do, just tee off with old Sonny Boy to get him—make him go do all them things. But, man, you get on down to nitty-gritty playing, you don't fool around with Walter, because he lay that tone on you. He'd lay back there, you'd see him battin' them eyes, lookin' around at you out the corner of his eye, you might as well turn him a-loose. There ain't nothin' you can do with him 'cause he's gonna be playing tone and come out with some things that make you believe he's sounding a music score. When you hear him you'd say, "How's he do all that on the harp?" I know I heard something, he ain't had no business . . . I heard a way-out horn player saying, "Man, if that cat pick up a horn and get that sound he's getting out of that harp, I'd take my hammer and catch him and do something to him, break every one of his fingers so he . . ." (*laughs*) If you listen at that harp it don't even sound like a harp no more.

We did a gig at the Apollo and they had one of them high-up stages in the back for the drummer, and Below went to hit the drums and the leg slipped off and Below fell. Well, you know, it was a funny thing; the peoples thought that it was in the show, but it wasn't. He went to hit his cymbal way over there and the leg slipped and Below went boom! And the people gave him applause. We laughed about that while we were traveling on the road. Walter said right there, "That Professor got a-loose back there." We called Below "Professor." Walter called him 'Fess. The reason we called him that was because Below was what you'd call more educated than what we were, and he would explain. Back there then he would use his education when it's time to use it. Like when you don't have the appropriate education on some things that's said, Below was always there. He would always speak, put it right. We all named him "Professor."

But we named Little Walter "Little Goola," because he act like a kid. He was a nice cat, but I guess when I left him and the band left him and he got different other cats playing with him, he just changed. This is what I say about blues. It will still change a cat, because he's existing off of that. You see, when a cat's existing off music and he goes and plays with somebody else, he's got to dig his whole personality in order to say what he's got to say, and that's a hard thing to do. Even Walter told me that himself before he died. He said, "Had I been with y'all and treated you guys like men, paid you right, and done the right things, I'd be top man today."

Walter was a nice cat. We was all young and he had a better understanding with us than Junior. See, Junior, to me, didn't have any understanding. But when I hired Walter with us, naturally Walter took over the band, because he had a hot record out on the streets, but we didn't have to change our name. But Walter had so much influence that Dave and Below went on with him in spite of me. The majority won, so I was gone right after he come back talkin' that stuff. So that's why I left him. See, a lot of people don't know why I left him. See, I believed in the right thing. Now, they stayed on with him. Before we left town, going out on an engagement, he used to change the name to the Jukes or Night Caps, things like that, and we already were the Aces. I told the man we should remain the Aces and let it be "Little Walter featuring the Aces" or "The Aces featuring Little Walter" so we wouldn't get lost out here. And they stayed on with Walter and one by one they left Walter. I was with Walter quite two years. Before we hit the road, we had an understanding, but Dave and Below, they left me. I was just one, so the majority won.

We was in the car talking and Walter wasn't saying nothing, because he'd got them together on me. What could I do? But I told them we should keep our name the same and let Little Walter be . . . I said, "You already a star, Walter, you should let us remain the Aces." But he couldn't hear that, and Dave and Below agreed with him, so that was the end of that. I was what you'd call one foot in the door and one foot out anyway, because I don't want to play with anybody that don't want that understanding. Because Walter was a greedy man. He want it all for himself and, like I said, he didn't want to pay right. When a person's that greedy, he ain't got time to do nothing right. And that's the onliest fault I found in him, and that was a big enough fault for me to leave. He didn't want to pay us nothing. I got on to him time after time. I said, "I'm not trying to get into your business or nothing like that, but why should one cat be professional out here? I know one name and you know I know it and you know it. One cat ain't nothing without the other one." "Yeah, but I got a name, I'm Little Walter." I said, "Yeah, that's true, but, you see, we sound good together." I couldn't change Dave and Below's mind, they was older than I was.

When we got to California I saved Walter $900 one night because they were gonna beat him out of his P.C. money.[6] Me and Below heard the cat talking, the cats that ran the show. They were gonna leave Walter out. So we went and hipped Walter, and Walter came and gave me $10! We saved him $900 and his salary that night was only about $300 and something. I said, "Man, you don't like me. Not only you don't like me, you don't like nobody in the band. You don't need me." "What you mean?" I said, "Look, anytime I save a man $900, I figure he should give me more than that. I saved you money that you wasn't about to get and you give me a measly $10. You take your $10 back, you need it more than I do." I told him, "When you get back to Chicago get yourself a guitar player, I'm giving you my notice out here. I don't like to play with nobody that thinks so little of me. I don't want to be around you. We sound beautiful together, but when it comes down to that money, uh-uh."

Biggest Band in Chicago

After I left Walter I had a band with Earl Phillips and Henry Gray, and who else did I have playing down there with me? I had to get rid of Henry Gray, because he drank so much wine until him and Earl Phillips get so drunk they couldn't play. I had to get rid of one so I could keep the other one in line, and I hired Otis Spann. Otis Spann played piano with me before he ever knew Muddy Waters. Now, I don't know where all this come about, but I read something that said Otis Spann was Muddy Waters's brother. Now, I never knew nothing about it. Otis Spann played piano with me, man, for about a year. That's where Muddy got Spann, from me.

Then I had a group with Luther Tucker, Charles Edwards, and Sir Oliver Bibbs on the drums. He used to be one of the old-time Dixieland jazz drummers, one of the best in Chicago. He's an old man. I don't know whatever happened to him. A lot of people remember him from the old school of music. It lasted about a year, I think, then I come up on Otis Rush.

Me, Below, and him had a band from about '56. We quit playing together around '59. I had quit playing with Junior Wells and David at the 708. I quit them at the 708 in about '56 and went with Otis Rush, and wasn't but us three playing together. Then we hired a cat from out of Mississippi named Willie D. Warren. Played guitar, but he had it run down like a bass. He's from Greenwood or Greenville, Mississippi, one of them two. Then we hired a cat named Jerry, played horn, which was Below's friend. Jerry Gibson. And a cat started hanging around wanting to jam with us named Donald Hankins, big cat played baritone. We left this place named Jazzville, a very exclusive jazz club we were playing at on a Sunday evening. We went to the New Castle Rock. We went on the road down South, and after we came back we hired Earl Hooker, that's around '56. We formed the biggest band in Chicago. We had the best band in Chicago. Sometimes other horn players come in and sit in, because at that time me and Otis had the only horn band in Chicago. We'd look around, sometimes we'd have six or seven horns, cats just come in, just wanna jam. We had a swinging band, played nine days a week in Chicago and, you know, there ain't but seven days a week. We played Sunday evening and night, Monday evening and night. We didn't hardly have time off. We played out in Gary and back to Chicago. I've got a picture around here somewhere of myself, Earl Hooker, and B. B. King. B. B. had the pictures made, that was back in '56. He was playing the gig out here at Roberts Show Lounge, and me and Earl Hooker went by there to see him and Hooker got up and played for him. B. B.'s crazy about Earl Hooker, he's crazy about him.

We cut records [for Cobra]. I was on "It Takes Time," "Keep On Loving Me." I cut about four or five records with Otis, I think. Yeah, "All Your Love."[7] "Bluesy" and "Just Whaling," that was the first thing that they put my name on. I did that for Willie Dixon and this Abco cat. We was cuttin' a session for somebody else and he just wanted something different. Dixon come in and said, "I want you to make a couple of numbers on the harp." The band wasn't there. Wasn't nobody there except me, Dave, Eugene Lyon, and Willie Dixon. Eugene Lyon, he was a helluva drummer and a good entertainer, actor, too. Bad dude, boy. He's still around, he's takin' pictures, he's the photo man. He's been doing that ever since he quit playing music. He was a hell-fire drummer. He's playing drums in church now. He made a couple of things with Junior, and also, I think, he made a thing with Elmore James.[8]

Me, Otis, and Below got the job at the 708. We played the 708 till it closed in 1958 and we went back to the New Jazz Castle Rock on a weekend because we gave up on the travel, and we played there until me and Dave got something together. I don't know where we went then. Oh, yeah, we got a job and started playing over there at 63rd and California. We had Bobby Jones, we had a good band then, a rock 'n' roll band, nothing but rock. We played at the 1049 on a weekend, then we went to the place downtown on Rush Street and we played there until '62. We was makin' money then, big money. Playing rock and beautiful tunes, ballads. Only a few times I played a couple of blues by B. B. King, that's all. We had a cat arrange for the band. You had to read the chart.

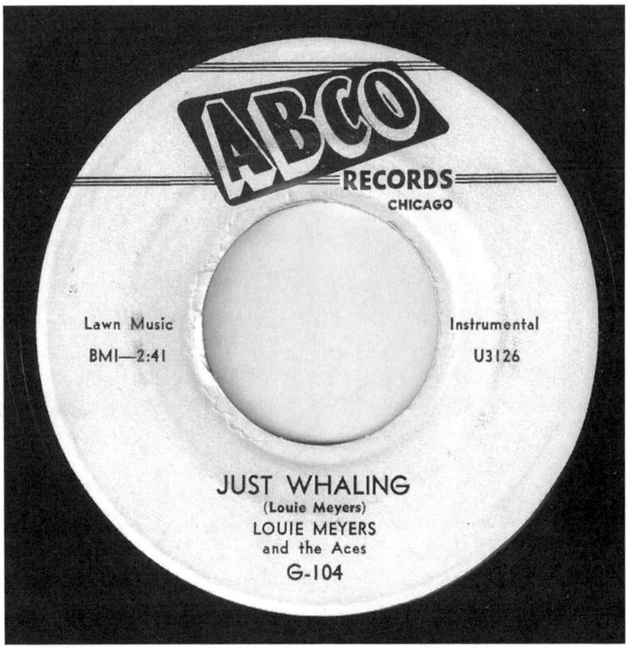

Louis Myers. Abco 104.

I Play for Tone

I recorded one or two of the songs that I did with Otis on the Blue Thumb label in 1969.[9] They ain't too good. That music and them cats out there in California don't know too much. I didn't even like the session. You just can't throw a bunch of musicians together and say this is it. Some cat told me I cut with twenty-nine different artists. He had them wrote on a sheet of paper. I just couldn't believe it and some of them cats I cut with ain't even on it.

I cut with all the blues artists that I know of in Chicago. Chuck Berry, Bo Diddley, Muddy Waters, Little Walter, Junior Wells, Otis Spann, Shakey Jake, you probably ain't heard that about Shakey Jake. One I cut with Shakey, a bad one, boy. It's with me playing harp on and Shakey says it's . . . (*laughs*) But everybody knows it's me on it, the musicians. You see, Shakey don't never set himself up as being a good harp player anyway. I played harp on about four of his things, and we had Otis Spann on piano, it sounds pretty good. I heard that thing when I was playing with Sam Lay back in '67. We was coming from somewhere up in New York. We was riding along in the car and I heard it say "Shakey Jake" and that harp playing on there; even Sam Lay said, "I didn't know Shakey could blow like that." I said, "I didn't either." Then I said, "You know what? When I heard the piano I knew it wasn't Shakey, that was me." Shakey just sing, I played the harp. I made records with so many guys I can't even remember them.[10]

Willie Williams, Louis Myers, Robert Jr. Lockwood, Lefty Dizz, Dave Myers, Bob Myers. Ann Arbor, Michigan, September 1972. (Photo Bill Greensmith)

Have I a favorite guitar player? Yeah, I really do. I mean for the blues, playing a good blues guitar, hard blues, Eddie Taylor, he can play, man. He's underrated. They underestimate a good blues guitar player—when I say blues, I mean *blues.* He can play that and he don't try to play nothing else but the blues. Every time I meet him he's the same Eddie Taylor I met thirty-something years ago. He's playing the blues. I wish I could have a cat like that just to play with. I know he's trying to get him a bag of his own now. He's been out there a long time, longer than I have. He's never got a break. It's one thing that the people will accept you on and they'll keep you right there if you let 'em, it's being a sideman. I know he played with Jimmy Reed around here and made Jimmy Reed, the way I understand it. And I do, because I know Jimmy was hanging around out there where we was playing at. He drink a lot of wine and he was working too, and to me he didn't care too much about playing. But he made a record and got out there and made it big, and he made other good records that the peoples liked, right down to earth.

I was playing at 90th and Mackinaw with my own band and he used to come in there.[11] He hadn't recorded one record and nobody knew Jimmy Reed then. The lady that we were playing for, I think her name was Thelma. She didn't want him to play, because he was a wino, drink wine. I used to say let him come in and play. He come in there a couple of times and play. That cat that he had with him, he was a stone wine-head, but he could play. He could play jazz and different stuff. I don't know whatever happened to that cat. I ain't saw him no more.

Louis Myers. Chicago, April 1974. (Photo Bill Greensmith)

Today I like quite a few harp players. Ain't too many harp players I don't like. Little Walter and some things Sonny Boy did, Rice Miller. I loved some of the things he played. And I also liked Little Pot,[12] but he got killed. I really loved his playing. Both the Sonny Boys I dug. John Lee Williamson had a story that intrigued me. He sings and plays at the same level. And Sonny Boy, with all that wind that he had and cuttin' through with what he had, was alright, too. Little Walter was outstanding because he had the tone locked up. There's no better tone with the harp than Little Walter. The only way you can get anything across, whatever instrument you playing, you got to have that knowledge that tone is the most important thing. Like today I like quite a few young fellows, but ain't nobody playing with them. Yeah, I like all harp players, because being an old retired harp player myself, you can sit down and hear what they intending to do.

Like a lot of people say, "Man, you sound just like Little Walter," or "You sound like this." Any cat that is playing with a tone, because this is where it's at, tone. I ain't playing how much harp a man can play. I ain't playing that, I'm playing tone. I play for tone only. I don't play no harp or riffin' or all that, which can't be done on a harp anyway. I take tone and I could throw myself up against anybody if it comes to a competition thing, and I wouldn't even be worried about 'em, because I know where they're gonna be. I wouldn't care about no harp players living today, none of them, because I ain't gonna be playing what they're playing. They're gonna be up there trying to do something on a harp that ain't to be done in the first place. I'm gonna be playing one kinda way—tone—and you'll see the difference.

Notes

1. Possibly Vincent Durling.
2. "Murmur Low"/"One of These Days," Big Boy Spires, Checker 752.

3. "Juke"/"Can't Hold Out Much Longer," Little Walter, Checker 758.

4. "Lawdy Lawdy"/"'Bout the Break of Day," Junior Wells, States 139.

5. "Hodo Man"/"Junior's Wail," Junior Wells, States 134; "Mean Old World"/"Sad Hours," Little Walter, Checker 764.

6. Percentage money.

7. According to *Blues Records, 1943–1970,* Louis Myers plays on the following Otis Rush Cobra sides: "Love That Woman"/"Jump Sister Bessie," Cobra 5015, and "It Takes Time"/"Checking on My Baby," Cobra 5027. However, the Cobra Records discography is not an exact science and it's possible he is featured on other titles as well.

8. "Just Whaling"/"Bluesy," Louis Meyers, Abco 104. "Eugene Lounge" is listed as the drummer in most discographies. This is probably a mispronunciation of Eugene Lyons.

9. "Coming Home," Chicago Blue Stars, Blue Thumb BST 9.

10. "Respect Me Baby"/"A Hard Road," Shakey Joke [*sic*], The Blues 303.

11. Club Jamboree.

12. Henry Strong.

James Cotton

James Cotton's career as one of postwar blues' preeminent harmonica players can, in retrospect, be viewed as three distinct periods: his early formative years in Mississippi and West Memphis, Arkansas; the twelve-year period he spent in Chicago with the Muddy Waters band; and, finally, upon leaving the Waters band in the mid-1960s, as a successful and highly respected bandleader and recording artist.

James's time in West Memphis, then a thriving hub of blues activity, was spent in the company of Sonny Boy Williamson, Howlin' Wolf, Willie Nix, Willie Love, Junior Parker, and others. As an emerging blues talent, the teenage James Cotton's harmonica playing graced recordings by Willie Nix and Howlin' Wolf, although, inexplicably, he eschewed the harmonica on his own sides for Sun Records in December 1953 and May 1954. "Straighten Up Baby" and "My Baby" (Sun 199) were a pair of confident, but nondescript, blues. However, Sam Phillips, who obviously recognized Cotton's potential, soon scheduled a second session. "Cotton Crop Blues" (Sun 206), which recalls Tampa Red's "Cotton Seed Blues," is an intense tour de force defined by Pat Hare's slashing guitar underpinning Cotton's gruff, brooding vocal. It remains one of the most outstanding recordings of the Memphis postwar era. But sales were almost certainly disappointing and Cotton continued to labor in obscurity until a fortuitous encounter with Muddy Waters, who was in West Memphis scouting a replacement for the recently departed Junior Wells. Cotton immediately joined the band and left for Chicago.

James Cotton further refined his skills while steadily rising to prominence within the Waters band. His powerful yet eloquent playing was featured on numerous recordings when he eventually replaced Little Walter, the harmonica player of choice on Muddy's sessions. In the mid-1960s Cotton embarked on a solo career. His band initially featured the guitarist Luther Tucker before he was replaced by Matt Murphy, a friend from his days in West Memphis. A host of fine albums throughout the years have showcased Cotton's exceptional talent and maintained his reputation as one of postwar blues' outstanding harmonica players. Never quite severing his relationship with Muddy Waters, he often appeared as a special guest on the records of his former boss and continued to perform with him on occasion. In the 1990s he began to suffer health problems, which unfortunately restricted his vocal performance but were not able to silence his wonderful harmonica playing.

—Bill Greensmith

James Cotton

Bill Greensmith

Blues Unlimited #120 (July/Aug. 1976)

I was born in a little place called Tunica, Mississippi, 1935, July 1. My mother used to play the harmonica a little bit; she played things like "The Train" and a thing called "The Hen Cackle," make the harp sound like a chicken, I used to listen at that. I used to hear people sing blues and things, see people playing the guitar, but I never heard them playing it on the harmonica.

Then I heard Sonny Boy, which is Rice Miller. He had this radio show in Helena, Arkansas, KFFA *King Biscuit Time,* and I started listening at that. I was about seven or eight years old. I listened at that for a long time. I heard Sonny Boy play the harp and I tried to play the same thing whatever he was playing. This is what really got me interested in the harp, because I never heard it sound like this before. Then when I started playing like Rice Miller then I came by records by the original Sonny Boy.

My uncle was more into musical things. He knew more of what was happening than my family did. I was like the baby of the family and he liked to have me running around with him. When he found out that I could play a little bit—that sure 'nuff did it, he started carrying me everywhere. [His name was] Wiley Green. He played piano a little bit, not much. He'd just sit down and plonk on it a little bit. So when I started playing harp he used to carry me all the places people go. Maybe one guy would be sitting down playing guitar and he'd say, "I got my boy here, let him play a couple of songs with ya." I was about eight or nine years old, but I'd been listening to Sonny Boy's program for two years. So I went around and played with all the different people that I could sit in and play with.

Then he finally carried me to Helena, Arkansas, to meet Sonny Boy. He knew him enough, he'd been going to see him different places. Carried me there and I started playing with Sonny Boy. Played with Sonny Boy six years. Stayed right in the house with him. My uncle set up somewhere that I could stay with him. I was just living right there on him. My uncle kinda helped it out a little bit. I stayed with Sonny Boy and learned to play all the things that he was playing. Stayed right in the house with him and Mattie.

James Cotton. Chicago, October 1975. (Photo Bill Greensmith)

My mother didn't even know where I was. My uncle know. My mother and father never did know where I was till I come back home. Sonny Boy brought me back home after a couple of years. They found what I was doing and just figured I went away somewhere, my uncle never did tell them. They found out what I was doing, so they liked it alright. So I went back and played with Sonny Boy some more.

[I was] nine years old when I moved in with Sonny Boy, and between the things that I seen him do—like he never did take out that much time to sit down and play the harp with me, but I was around him all the time and I see the things that he did and I hear that all the time. And I got a chance to see other people play.

This is how I met Howlin' Wolf through Sonny Boy, Joe Willie Wilkins, all the little bands around there. Willie Nix, Willie Love, I met all those people right through Sonny Boy. They had little bands, you know. I never knew that there was even that many bands. I thought that there was only one band. (*laughs*)

He was popular then, not record-wise, but from the radio station, as far as the radio station could reach. And he was one of the only guys around doing that that was that good at it. So he had quite a bit of work, always stayed working. I play a couple of songs and sit on his knee, play a couple of songs, then he'd run me off to the car: "Well, it's time for you to go now, you better get out of here." I'd go out to the car and go to sleep.

We played Mississippi and Arkansas juke houses. Somebody lives in a house, maybe two or three rooms. They'd take all the furniture back and put it in one room for this particular day. They'd go out and get some beer and corn liquor, some kinda sandwiches, and Sonny Boy would play there that night.

Joe Willie played the guitar for him. Joe Willie left later and formed his own group. Willie Nix played the drums. And he had this guy called Five by Five, five foot tall and five foot wide—he's a big man, Dudlow. He was playing the piano for us. And that was the group, man. No bass; we wouldn't carry a bass then. If there was a bass it was an upright bass.

Peck [Curtis] played drums for Sonny Boy, then he left and got his own thing. Peck stayed there for, I guess, about a year after I was there, then he split for a while, then he came back. So off and on he was there. He was like a cat always trying to do something for himself. He'd go out and try, sometimes things get bad and he'd be off from work awhile, then he'd get a job back with Sonny Boy."

Did you ever play on the radio with him?

I might have did two or three shows. I never did fool around the radio station that much, because I wasn't up to the really good standard. I wasn't good enough.

The first song I ever played on harp in front of people was "Sitting on Top of the World," "Big Apple Swing," and "I Know She's Gonna Jump and Shout." First three songs I learnt. I used to sit on Sonny Boy's knee—play those three songs, then he'd run me off to the car. When I first went to Sonny Boy he had a 1934 Ford with the door that open backward, like the Lincoln doors open now, with a rack on top of it and "Sonny Boy and his King Biscuit Boys" wrote on the side of it.

Was Robert Junior around?

Oh, yeah, Robert Junior was in and out the band, too. He was the type of cat always tried to get him a band going. He was in the band when I first went there, stayed for four or five months, then he split, then after a while he came back. Guys always trying to get it together.

What kind of guy was Sonny Boy then?

Crazy. He was crazy. Drink a lot of whiskey, had a pretty fast temper. He would fight right away, he'd cut 'cha. He'd get that knife open he'd sure cut 'cha. Crazy guy. But other than that, he was a good man, you know. He had a fast temper, liked to drink, liked to stay out all night long. That's where I get that from, I guess. I tell my wife all the time I'm a country boy. I like to stay out all night long.

Me and him used to go playing, see that the other guys get home. There'd be times we'd ride around till daylight, wouldn't be doing nothing just ride around and talk, come home at daylight. He loved to stay out all night, loved to do that. I think that's where I got started on at that.

What happened when Sonny Boy came north?

Well, Sonny Boy left me with his band. We moved up to West Memphis, Arkansas, and he bought a house. The house got burnt down and I guess him and Mattie started to get along bad and he just left one day.

Sonny Boy Williamson, Robert Jr. Lockwood. Cleveland, Ohio.

We were playing in the Be-Bop Hall on 8th Street in West Memphis. He played the first set, you know, we were all running around getting something to drink and all of that stuff. We didn't know he was gonna leave. So a little bit before the second set started he just came back there. He had a pint of whiskey and me and him sat down to drink that whiskey. This was the first time me and him ever really drink together. I'd get a drink, but I wouldn't drink with him. I give him that much respect, you know. He said, "Well, I'm fixin' to go, you keep the band, I'm gonna leave here. I can't do no good here." That's when he came north. I think he first stopped in Milwaukee. He left me with the band and by me being a young kid and crazy . . . Band stayed together about four or five months then fell apart.

Who was in the band then?

Joe Willie Wilkins, Willie Nix, Willie Love.

Were you on the radio?

We were on a radio station there, KWEM. I kept that show about five months until the band fell apart.

Were you advertising anything?

Well, Sonny Boy had fifteen minutes on the air, some kind of deal he set up with the station, didn't cost him anything. Fifteen minutes every day. He was on from 3 to 3:15. When he left I did it for a while, then the Harts Bread people out of Memphis, Tennessee, heard the show and bought the show for me. I was on for Harts Bread until the band fell apart.

When did the band break up?

1952, '53 something like that. I did quite a few things then, finding gigs where I could get gigs at. Had a job driving a gravel truck. Had a job as a short-order cook. Went back to the farm and did some work on the farm. I did a lot of things. Then Willie Nix started a band and he knew me, so he came to the farm and got me. I worked for him about six or seven months, something like that.

Was this when you cut for Sun with Willie?

Yeah. "Baker Shop Boogie" and "Seems Like a Million Years." I didn't get no credit for that, either. Things like that always happen to me, man. Like I worked with him and I used to sing this thing just to have fun—"Baker Shop Boogie." I didn't think that it would ever get put on a record. So he liked it. He said, "Can I record it?" I said, "Yeah, you can record it." He said, "Won't you give me it?" I said, "You can have it"—just give it to him. I don't think Willie Nix ever wrote a tune in his life.[1]

He was just a country boy, just like me, I guess. Country boy who learnt to play a few licks on the drums and got out there started doing it, crazy like all the rest of the guys. He just got stuck in a bag doing that same thing. Like some people—like I say about the three-change blues, they get stuck in that bag and they get satisfied with that. Willie Nix didn't change as the times changed. He's a good drummer for that blues thing that was going on back then. He was one of the better drummers.

Did you know the Newborns?

Yeah, everybody knew them. They were the greatest musicians around there. Old man Phineas played drums, that whole family were musicians, they were very talented people. They came from Clarksdale, I think, up to Memphis. Yeah, I know Mr. Phineas, Calvin, Little Phineas, all of them. They were the up-to-date musicians around Memphis at this particular time. They were like great musicians there.[2]

Ike Turner?

They made a record with Jackie Brenston called "Rocket 88." It was a big record, big record, man. And that's how I got to know them, right behind that record. Like the record hit. And I found out that they all lived in Memphis and I used to see them playing around, because everybody loved that record. They had a million-seller out there. That's when I first met them, when that record came out.

Jackie split after the record hit?

Yeah, well, he got behind the hit record and he got kinda crazy, figuring he'll go and do it for himself, but he hasn't had another one since! I played in a band with Ike, like one of them bands I played with, Ike was in it. Willie Nix band. Willie Nix playing the drums, Ike piano, and me playing harp. We didn't have a guitar. Played like that for three or four months. Ike was running around scouting different talent and things like that for record companies, tuning pianos, doing everything. Matter of fact, that's how I knew that Sun Record company even existed.

Did Ike get you your deal with Sun?

No, he didn't, but I used to go over there with him all the time. He got Junior Parker this deal with Sun Records. I had a tune that I wrote called "Feelin' Good," and Junior Parker did the record. I didn't get no credit for it, not at all. We used to do this tune, like, at nights when we would go to the clubs. I wouldn't do it on the air. The program was run by requests. People write in to you. I used to get a stack of mail every day for "Feelin' Good." This was the Harts Bread show that I had. It didn't last long, it was a lot of fun while it lasted. I'd get so many letters for it ["Feelin' Good"]. I'd just take the letters and kinda push them aside and never do the song. I'd do it at night when I'd go to the clubs. Then I started to do it on the radio—never should have did that. Next thing I know Junior Parker had it out on record, man. Never got a dime for it, never got no credit for it, never wrote a song like that since![3]

Did you know Willie Kizart?

I heard that name. I'm not for sure, when I see that band [Kings of Rhythm], some of the musicians had split from it then. It wasn't all the original musicians that did "Rocket 88." But I've heard that name before. I know Willie Johnson played the guitar with Howlin' Wolf. You know, that name sounds really familiar—Willie Kizart.

Joe Hill Louis?

The Be-Bop Boy. Oh, yeah, I knew him. He came up from Mississippi, like he came up after I was already in West Memphis. I knew him when he first came there. And he just came there playing by himself and the last time I see him he was playing by himself. He got on the radio station there, he never had nobody play with him. Played the drums, guitar, and the harmonica all at the same time. He just played his own music.

Did you ever meet Elmore James?

I knew Elmore, I did a few gigs with him. Never did do no recording with him. I remember when him and Sonny Boy had out "Dust My Broom." I used to go to gigs with him and play that whenever Sonny Boy wouldn't be with him.

Robert Nighthawk?

Oh, Robert, I knew Robert for a long time, too. Never did play too many gigs with him. I just jammed with him a few times, but I knew him pretty good. Good singer, good guitar player. Sing with a lazy voice, didn't care whether he even open his mouth or not, but when it came out, it came out right.

What was B. B. King like then?

Just a country boy. He played in a little joint on 16th Street. Played Friday, Saturday, Sunday, that was it. Run around, drink around all the rest of the week and have a good time. Get a gig where he could.

There was a lot of good musicians around there that hadn't quite made it yet and it was hard to get a break to do anything. B. B. King was around there, he was just working at this radio station, he didn't have records out. Bobby Bland, Junior Parker, Rufus Thomas, a bunch of musicians there, they'd just get gigs where they could. Really no big advertising, no records out, nothing like that. If you wasn't with a radio station then the people just didn't know you. Because if you had been with one, you could get work.

Did you ever hear of the "In the Groove Boys"?

That's Albert King's band. I never did work with them. I've jammed with them a couple of times. Albert King came up from Mississippi and he stopped in West Memphis. He actually hung around West Memphis with me for about a week or so before he went up to Osceola and put that band together. I think they had a radio show up there, and down in West Memphis where I was I could get their radio show. And they could get mine, like it was on at different times.[4]

Did you ever go up to Osceola and broadcast?

No. I used to go up there and jam with them sometimes at night, playing at the T-99 Club in Osceola.

What kind of band were they?

They were playing a little bit more moderner blues than what I was playing. I was playing the country blues, but by Albert playing guitar and he had horns and everything, that made him a little bit more moderner than what I was. I knew Albert before he started that band, I know him when he started that band. At one time, to tell you the truth, when B. B. King made "3 O'Clock," made a hit record, there was more guitar players come out with the last name King than I've ever heard in my life. Everybody you see was a King. Junior King, B. B. King, Albert King—all of them were Kings. But I know I didn't hear of that many Kings until B. B. King came out with "3 O'Clock."

When did you first meet Matt Murphy?

I met Matt Murphy a long time ago. He was around some during this time. He played with Howlin' Wolf, that was the first band he played with.

Were Matt and his brother playing together?

Floyd came up later. The little band I had brought Floyd up to West Memphis. He lived down at Holly Springs, Mississippi. So Matt was up there first and he played with Howlin' Wolf. Then Matt and Junior Parker played with Wolf and somehow they split and started a group on their own. And then I played with Howlin' Wolf for a while. Then I got a little band and played around for a while then ran into Floyd. Floyd played with me two years or so.

When did you first meet Pat Hare?

Me and Pat Hare just lived around the neighborhood and kind of knowed one another all through the years. Like I knew Pat could play. He just lived with his mother and father. He'd just come out to town on a Saturday, bring his guitar and just sit down and play a little bit. I used to hang around things like that, you know. I used to go jam with him. We used to sit up on the back of a truck and the people would gang up around us. We'd sit there and play couple of hours.

What town did Pat come from?

Parkin, Arkansas.

Didn't he have a group called the Forrest City Blues Boys?

I don't know who owned the group. It was three of them. Jerry Lee Walker [drums], Pat Hare, and what was the other boy's name played piano?[5] They played around for a while. That was the first group Pat was in. Then after that he played with Howlin' Wolf. I got him a job playing with Howlin' Wolf. Then he started playing with Junior Parker and Bobby Bland. Then after I started playing with Muddy, I got him a job playing with Muddy. After ten or twelve years we was back in the same group again. So he played in that group awhile, then he finally split out of that group and started playing with Mojo Buford. That's when he got in trouble up in Minnesota.[6]

Cotton Crop Blues?

That was a little group that I had that didn't stay together too long after Sonny Boy's band fell apart. I ran around for a while, did all kinds of crazy things, then I got a little group together. I cut "Cotton Crop Blues" and "Hold Me in Your Arms" for Sun Records. I cut two records for Sun with that little band of mine, which was four sides. Me and Pat Hare and a boy named Hambone played drums. His name was John [Bowers]. And another fellow from Memphis named Albert played piano on one of the sides. I played drums on "Cotton Crop Blues." There's a couple of the songs I didn't play the harp on, just played the drums.[7] I recorded with Howlin' Wolf, my very first record. I played harp on "Saddle My Pony." Wolf played guitar.[8]

Did you ever meet Sunny Blair?

Sonny Blakes. Is that what you're saying, Sonny Blakes? He was a harmonica player from West Memphis. No, I don't think I knew Sunny Blair.

He played with Sammy Lawhorn sometimes. Bobby King can also remember seeing them?

See, Sammy is from Little Rock. Sammy got around a little bit more than Bobby did, man, like Sammy was playing with a group that kinda moved around a little bit more.

Who was Sammy playing with?

What was this guy's name? They had out this hit record one time, "You Don't Love Me." Willie Cobbs. Sammy's playing guitar on that. So this was the group Sammy was with, so they would move around. That's how I got to know Sammy. The record was one of the last things Sammy did with that group before he split, but he'd been in that band for a long time.

What about Big Walter?

Big Walter is a good harmonica player. I've known him for a long time, he kinda helped me along, too. Not just come up and say play this, play that, but I'd get a chance to hear him, you know. He's been around a long time. I'd get a chance to hear him play and I'd pick up ideas of what he played. Matter of fact, I played in Willie Nix's band with him.

Two harps?

Yeah. We never did get a chance to do no recording. Walter played the lead harp and I played the backup harp.

How long did that last?

Not long. Not long, about a couple of months. Not long. (*laughs*)

It fell apart because of . . . ?

Because of two harp players always run into one another, you know. Walter was always the type of cat he would never stay with a group long. Three or four months and he'd move on—try and do something else, you know. Yeah, that didn't last long. It sound good, but it didn't last long.

Did you know Raymond Hill?

The horn player? Yeah, I know Raymond. Yeah, I've known Raymond a long time, when they did that record ["Rocket 88"]. Raymond was one of the guys that I could communicate with better than anybody in that whole band besides Ike Turner. I got to know Ike really good.

I never really played with Raymond no more than just sitting in and jam with him. I never played on the same show with him, nothing like that. He had a band around St. Louis one time. I think Billy Gayles was in the band. He did a tune called "Tore

Up." I don't know whatever happened to the band, but since then I haven't heard much from Raymond. I knew Albert King and Little Milton before they came to St. Louis. Milton is from Greenville, Mississippi. He used to play with Willie Love.

There's always been a little small circle of us, one right behind the other. Maybe one get a break this year, then maybe have to work the next two years before they get a chance to make a record, but it's always been like that for us. All of us from the South, everybody got a chance to leave the South at a different time, but they end up like all the people I know leave the South. I still know them all now. We all do the same thing.

How did you come to join Muddy?

They was coming up out of Florida, and Junior Wells had split down in Florida somewhere and they still had more dates to do. I don't know what happened to Muddy and Junior, but Junior came back to Chicago, so they didn't have no harp player.

I lived in West Memphis and they had a gig to do in Memphis on a Saturday night. During this time I was driving a dump truck, so I worked to, like, twelve o'clock that Saturday and got off in this little restaurant down on 8th Street. Friend of mine used to play down there—L. D., just sit down and play guitar by himself. I'd go there every Saturday and jam with him.[9] So I went in the place this Saturday and Muddy Waters, Otis Spann, and Elgin Edmondson were in there.[10] I'd never seen Muddy Waters before, you know. I'd heard his records, things like that, so I just went in to play with L. D. When I got in there the first thing L. D. said, "Hey, Muddy Waters is in here, you know." I said, "I don't believe you. Muddy Waters ain't in here, I don't believe that." So I just went up to jam some with L. D. and Muddy Waters come up and started to talk to me, asked me did I want a job. I just looked at him, you know. I almost told him to his face, "I don't believe you're Muddy Waters." He told me that his harp player left and he needed a harp player. This was, like, Saturday evening, so he was working Saturday night over at the Hippodrome in Memphis. He said, "You can start work tonight." I said, "How much you gonna pay me?" So he told me, I said, "Okay, I'll go with you." So, like, Memphis was just six miles from me. I went and got ready still thinking that he wasn't really Muddy Waters. I go and see all the signs up, posters and everything, "Muddy Waters playing here tonight." I went in started playing, because I knew some of his songs, like I'd heard them on record. Went in that night, played that night, and Monday we left coming to Chicago.

When was the next time you saw Sonny Boy?

After I came to Chicago. He left there in '52 or something and I came here last of '54 and we played a gig with Sonny Boy. Played two gigs with Sonny Boy, one in New York and one in Washington, D.C. I don't know how he got to New York. I didn't even know he was playing with us.

Who else was in Muddy's band when you joined?

Otis Spann, Elgin Edmondson, Jimmy Rogers, Bob Hadley, and Muddy Waters. Bob Hadley was a horn player. He never did do no recording with Muddy, just play the gigs with him.

Did you tour a lot?

Well, Muddy was right out there then. He toured the South mostly. That's where he had best sales and things, like Mississippi, Louisiana, Georgia, Florida, and back to Chicago. In Chicago we was working at the 708 Club and Sylvio's, which kept us working all the time. I'll never forget the first time we played New York City. We got booed off the stage. Played the Apollo Theater and got booed off the stage. This was about 1955.

Why were you booed?

They wasn't used to that blues. See we were on the Sarah Vaughan Show with Red Prysock, Al Hibbler, the Moonglows, Chuck Willis, Nappy Brown—and Muddy Waters played more of the Mississippi blues, and they were playing more of a modern . . . And we went out, like we were the opening band. They said, "Boooooo!" They were all hollering at us. I'll never forget that.

What was Muddy's reaction?

Well, he didn't like that. Wasn't nothing he could do about it, the peoples just didn't like us. But after a while, we kept makin' records, kept showing up different places, it was alright all over.

Your style changed a lot from the early days?

You know what happened to me? See, when I came out of Arkansas I played Sonny Boy's style. This was the only style that I knew. I wrote a few things on my own, but it would still come out Sonny Boy's style. Then I came here (to Chicago). (Little) Walter had a whole different thing going with blowing the harmonica and he was right up on top of it. In other words, if you didn't play like Walter or if you didn't play like Junior Wells, around Chicago you wasn't a harp player.

I could play all the blues and stuff, but people didn't respond to me playing like they did those cats. So I started to listen at this. Started to listen, started to study the instrument. This was the first time I really got a chance, you know. I was a musician out there on my own with a good, stable job. I didn't have to quit playing music and go do something else. So I got a chance to study the harp a little bit.

I listened at Walter, Junior Wells, Billy Boy Arnold, all those people and I tried to come up with something just a little bit between all of those cats, with maybe some of the same flavor, but my own style of doing it. So this is what changed me there. They just wasn't playing the same thing here they was playing down there. They had jazzed it up a little bit and it sounded good.

When did you first meet Earlee Payton?

Oh, I been knowing Payton for . . . Payton was one of the better harp blowers around this city when I came here. He had his own band. He had Freddy King playing with him, Mojo was the bass player, and T. J. was the drummer.[11] He had a good group. When I came here Payton was the first harp blower takin' up some time for me. Little Walter and Junior Wells and people like that was really up there then. They didn't have time to fool around with me then, I was just a country boy. And through Payton I seen the way the thing was going and I start to make some moves for myself. I tried to keep it together enough to stay here.

It was like learning to play all over again when I came here, a whole different thing. All the things I had learnt from Sonny Boy, they didn't exist here. So I had to go and learn new things where I could play and be good here. But it was good for me because of all the things that I already knew. I could play like Sonny Boy or play his style, then I learnt what Little Walter and Junior were doing. Then, like, I had all this background, like I knew all these things, and when you know a lot of things then you can kinda take them and do what you want to do with them, which is good for me. But at the time, I didn't think it was good, I thought it was the hardest thing I ever seen.

What was it like recording for Leonard Chess?

Leonard should have been a musician himself instead of having a studio. Leonard knew what he wanted to hear and had a way of getting it out of the musicians. Just a down-to-earth cat. Come out and drink some whiskey, talk about it, cuss one another out, all that kinda thing, just kept it going. He was the type of cat that never got angry, or if he got angry you would never know it. He'd do anything to get what he wanted to get out of the musicians. And he always got it. Come out there, sit down and talk to you—"Well, God damn it, you got to play such and such a thing." And he'd get that in your mind and before you know it, you'd just do it.

I made quite a few records with Muddy. I can't even think of all of 'em. "Walkin' in the Park," "Mojo." I made the second "Mojo" with Muddy, the one that hit. Little Walter made the first one, he had a whole different thing on it. I changed the top of it. Like we kept the bass, kept the bottom, I changed the top. Little Walter played straight, I played chopping licks and was more pushing. That's the one that sold for Muddy.

There also seems like another change in style from when you were recording with Muddy. From about the time you cut that album with Johnny Young. To me you're playing much harder and more aggressively than you ever did with Muddy.[12]

See, well, it's hard to really play what you can play if you work for someone and they know what they wanna hear. I kinda laid back, I didn't ever get in Muddy's way. I just laid back and played with him. I did never try to . . . If it was a song where

I played the solo in it, I'd just play a good solo. I'd never go crazy, because Muddy didn't understand a bunch of that.

Like the first time I played the chromatic with Muddy, he didn't like that. Like he figured nobody could play the chromatic like Walter could. So I went and bought myself a chromatic harp and I was playin' it. Muddy said, "You can't play that harp. I don't even like the way you sound on it, play the other one." So I just had to put the chromatic away! Things like that.

It was funny, you know, like he was used to hearing whatever he knowed and if it was anything new he was scared to stretch out on it. So it taken me awhile before I could really feel like I wasn't playing Walter and I was playing myself. I had to play those solos Walter made for Muddy note for note! That's what Muddy wanted. I had to learn the solos. I had to play them note for note, because this was what Muddy was used to hearing. And if you wasn't playing in his eyesight you wasn't playing or you wasn't playing with him. So that kinda kept me restricted, 'cause I had to play this thing night after night, every night. I couldn't play the things I wanted to play, because I played with him, you know.

Was Chess ever interested in cutting you as a solo artist?

Like I said, man, I've always been known as a good harp player and a hard worker, never had no record to take the weight off me. Like when you get the hit records then that takes some of the weight off you, keeps you from working so hard. You still work hard, but it's appreciated more on account of the hit record. See, I never had that, always had to work hard and just do it from the sweat of my own eyebrow.

Didn't you do something for Cadillac Baby?

I did a lot of recording with Mack Simmons for Cadillac Baby. Never nothing for myself. Most all the stuff Mack did on the Bea and Baby label, I played the harp on it. Mack just sing the stuff. "Jumpin' at Cadillacs" got two harps on it, which that was my tune, too. Mack named it "Jumpin' at Cadillacs." That was my tune, but during that time I was playing with Muddy. I didn't think about trying to record for myself. I'd come up with a tune and play it and somebody would hear it. I'd just give it to 'em.[13]

What about the one for Loma?

Yeah, "Laying in the Weeds" and "Complete This Order." That was the first thing I did when I left Muddy Waters. Just did the two sides.[14]

What about the session with Johnny Young?

Johnny Young really wanted to get a good record out. So the first thing he told me, "You ain't got to worry about me, just play. Play anything you feel, just play." And that's what I did, because there wasn't that restriction there no more. I just put the harmonica where I could fit it in at. I just did it.

Muddy was in the studio when we did it. He thought it was good for Johnny Young, but he's . . . Muddy's one of the best blues singers that I know, but he's set in his ways. He knows what he can sing and he knows what he can't sing, and he don't like to go outside the track. He likes to stay right in his ball game where he knows—which I don't blame him for that. He just likes to do whatever he do and do it good. But when you step on the outside, experimenting with something, he don't want too many parts of it. He said, "Well, that's alright, but not for me."

I loved every minute I played with Muddy, but it was a thing where by me having had a couple of bands before, I'd had the feel of being a bandleader. But as I grew up then I learnt more of the things I had to do. Like I was never able to keep no band together. My one problem, I couldn't keep the fellows together, but as I learnt more things about how to do that and I always wanted my own group. So when I got it together, found I could do that, that was the cause of me to split.

I love Muddy, man. I didn't have a mind playing all of the things whatever he liked, because that could make me . . . I know how to play other things, but I just couldn't do it there. Like I used to get it off by going out and jam, play all the things I want to play. So now I'm just out there. I'm free, I can play anything I wanna play now. So that's better in a way, but I didn't think about it like that at this particular time. But once I was out there I said, shit, I can do anything I wanna do now.

What year did you leave Muddy?

'67, I believe it was.

But you came to England to do a tour for Chris Barber in 1961?

Matter of fact, this was the first tour thing that I ever did like that on my own. This was the first time that I felt really like a good musician. Here I am, started from Mississippi and worked my way over in London—a lot of peoples have never did that, man. I was playing with Chris and his band and they was very nice people, they was very good to me, man, very nice people.

How did he get you for the tour?

Well, they were over here. I guess Muddy Waters had met them whenever he was over there. Matter of fact, Chris and Ottilie stayed with Muddy about a week. We were playing at Smitty's Corner and they used to come down there and listen to the music. We were playing there, like, five nights a week. Chris had his whole band here in Chicago. The whole band came down and played and that blowed my mind, that's the first time I ever heard the group. I said, wow, listen to that music.[15]

So I started talking to Chris and Ottilie and they started telling me about I was a pretty good harp player and that kinda thing. I didn't have any ideas about going overseas and I just said I'd like to go overseas someday and Chris said, "Well, maybe that could be put together." And they did. They got me over there for, like, four weeks, man. It was outta sight. I loved every minute of it.

James Cotton with the Chris Barber Band. Beaulieu Jazz Festival, 1961.
(Photo Val Wilmer)

You cut a couple of records over there?

Yeah, with Alexis Korner, this piano player—what's his name? And Chris played the upright bass.[16]

You had Luther Tucker in one of your bands?

Yeah, well, my first band was Luther Tucker, Bob Anderson, Sam Lay, and Alberto Gianquinto. That was my first band in Chicago. We stayed together for a couple of years and then they started to falling out. Before I know, we had a whole brand-new band again. All the old people that I started with they weren't around no more.

Bob Anderson was the last one to leave the group, then Matt Murphy come with me. I used to build my band up from St. Louis. If I needed a guitar player or drummer, horn player, I'd always go to St. Louis and find one. There's a lot of good musicians down in St. Louis, lot of good musicians, some of them never get out of there or never get recorded.

In between Luther Tucker and Matt Murphy I had a guitar player from St. Louis, name was Charles, I can't think of his last name. He was a good guitarist. And a drummer named Berry Smith. Good drummer, but it's hard for you to get them out of St. Louis.

What's your opinion of your first albums you made for Verve?

I thought that they were good records. I didn't think that the company was behind me at all. The records were put together good, the company didn't do the things they should have did with it. I've always had that. I've never had a hit record, nothing like that, but I stays working pretty much all the time. I never had a record to sell, even get on the charts, I don't think. I've never had a company really go out and work behind me. Like, "James Cotton's really got a good record here, we're gonna really get behind it, see whether . . ." I've never had a company do that for me.

What about your album for Buddah?

Buddah did more than any company that I've ever had. I thought that they gave me more of what I needed than any record company that I've ever been with. I didn't get a hit record there, but they seemed like they were behind it.

Were you on Muddy's *Can't Get No Grindin'* album?

Yeah. Once in a while I still go and record with Muddy.[17]

And were you "Joe Denim" [on Muddy Waters's *Live at Mr. Kelly's*]?

Yeah, that was contract-wise. Muddy was playing at Mr. Kelly's and I was just in town for a couple of days; like I didn't even know he was playing at Mr. Kelly's. I called him up and he said, "I'm recording, why don't you come down and do some recording with me?" So I went and sit in with Muddy, some of the songs I had never heard before. Just went right on the bandstand, didn't rehearse, just went right on the bandstand, just played.[18]

Who's your favorite harp player?

It's hard to say. Like it's a funny thing, and I'm not saying this to be sounding smart either, but when I hear the harmonica players now, they either playing Little Walter or something that I've already laid down. So I don't listen at that anymore. I listen to try and learn more, and I can't learn listening to harp players who play more from the same thing that I play or play the same thing Little Walter play or play the same thing Sonny Boy play. I can't learn anything from that, because I already had did it at one time or another. So me, now, I'm listening to a bunch of horn players. I listen to all the horns and try to figure out parts that I can play.

But my favorite harmonica player, and I guess he always will be, I guess it was because he showed me—Rice Miller. I loved Little Walter because he had a whole different style, but for the bottom of it, really get the feeling out of it, I think Rice Miller was the best harmonica player ever lived.

What horn players are you listening to?

Well, this is something I started a couple of years ago. I listen to John Coltrane, and I really got into Diz (Dizzy Gillespie) and James Moody. Diz plays a lot of things on that trumpet, man. And I've been listening to Junior Walker and the All-Stars for the rough stuff. I can't make my harmonica sound like a horn, but I found that I can pick up some of the things insofar as the advancement of just the three-change blues.

I think if you're a musician you should be able to play anything. A good musician shouldn't be restricted to one kind of music. If he can play he should be able to play blues, rock, jazz, or whatever—should be able to play all of that. Like the average harmonica player, they just play the three changes because the harmonica is not a full keyboard and they don't try to go no further. The average one don't. I've been playing three changes for a long time and I just want to stretch out on it a little bit. I'm always looking for something new, always trying to do something new. Sometimes I make it, sometimes I don't. I'm always trying that. You try it, at least you've tried it, then you know whether you can do it or whether you can't. I'm always doing that. I'm always trying something new and something different.

What kind of amp are you using?

I don't think the amplifier, name brands, got that much to do with it, especially when you play the harmonica. It's within, what you bring out yourself. The amplifier makes it loud, what other people can hear.

Like a bunch of the kids now, kids ask me all over, they come up and see my amp, see what setting I've got on the amp, see what kind of microphone I'm playing through. I guess I was like that, too, when I was coming up. I'd see Sonny Boy's rig and I thought that this had a lot to do with him sounding like he sound, which had nothing to do with it. Whatever he played it put it out loud, that's all it do. You gotta play it—the amplifier won't play it for you. You gotta play it yourself.

Do you play a lot of chromatic now?

Well, I play the chromatic, but I haven't been playing it a whole lot lately. I haven't been doing that much recording with it, but I plan to do that. This is where the horn ideas will come out, because the chromatic is more of a keyboard. And if I can ever get to wind up right, it's a hard scuffle, but if I can get this going, where I can play the scales and things like that. Stevie Wonder has come closer to that than anybody that I know.

Like I told you, I'm always trying something new, so I want to get in that modern bag with playing the chromatic. I'll be able to walk on the bandstand, stand there and play modern tunes with my chromatic. Lay it down then go back to the blues. Then play jazz or whatever, be good at all of that, I don't wanna just half do it, I wanna do it.

Do you practice a lot?

Well, let's say I play the harp a lot. Like I don't practice with the band that much, because we're always working, but I play the harp all the time. I play the harp couple of hours a day.

Sit around the house and play it, or when I'm on the road I sit in the hotel and play it. Sometimes me and Matt get together when we're riding down the highway. He'll get his guitar and we'll sit there and try and get it together like that, have fun while we're doing it. Plus there ain't that uptightness like when we're on the bandstand. There's just the two of us. If we mess it up it don't make no difference, but if it come out good then we've accomplished something.

You tour a lot now playing colleges et cetera?

Like I said, man, I love people and I like to play for people. This is the one thing, I guess, that keep it going, that I love to play for people. It's just a big thrill for me to be doing what I'm doing. I never thought that I would ever do this good at it when I started. I never thought that I would ever be James Cotton just to walk out there and have a band and do it on my own like I've been doing the last ten years.

So this turns me on. This really makes me feel like all the things that I did down through the years were really worth it. I'm not makin' a lot of bread, but it's wonderful just to be doing it. I'm the happiest man in the world when I see people. When I'm working and I get those standing ovation things, everybody standing up smiling, they've forgotten all their troubles, all the things they have to go through with.

In comparison to the things going on in the world today it's worth it to see a few people with smiles on their faces. I feel like the president when I'm standing up there. Just for this second when I see this going on, the president couldn't get a reception like that. This turns me on, man, keeps me doing it.

Any regrets?

No, I don't regret nothing I did in music, nothing. I think it was all worth it. If I hadn't did the things that I did, I wouldn't know the things that I know. It was hard to do. Everything was hard and it's still hard, but I love it, I love every minute of it. If I had to do everything over again, I'd do it. I'd do it right away, wouldn't be no questions asked. I'd just go right to it. Say, "Well, here I go again." Yeah, I loved every minute of it, man.

But I plan to move out of Chicago. I plan to move back to my hometown next year. Gonna go back to West Memphis and open a club. Just be at home, slow down traveling on the road a little bit. Go back to the country. I'm a country boy, I can't live . . . I guess when you get a little bit older everything slows down a little bit. I've been steady at this for about twenty-two years now. Twelve with Muddy and ten for myself. I've turned forty years old; when you think about it, it's kinda hard. I've got two kids, one sixteen and one ten, that I haven't really seen grow up. I think it's time that I spent a little more time with them. Not all the time but more than I have done. So if I can get me a club or something.[19]

I got to be around music. Even if I don't have a group, I gotta have people playing around me where I can go up and jam once in a while. So this is what I'm working for now.

Notes

1. "Baker Shop Boogie"/"Seems Like a Million Years," Willie Nix, Sun 179.

2. Phineas Newborn Sr. was from an area near Jackson, Tennessee. The family moved to Memphis, Tennessee, in the 1930s.

3. "Feeling Good"/"Fussin' and Fightin' Blues," Little Junior's Blue Flames, Sun 187.

4. It is entirely possible that Albert King had been in Mississippi for one reason or another when James met him. But Albert had been living in Osceola, Arkansas, as early as 1938.

5. L. C. Hubert.

6. Following a domestic dispute in December 1963, Pat Hare shot and killed his female companion and a police officer who was called to the scene. Pat was subsequently sentenced to life in prison and died in September 1980. His 1953 recording, "Gonna Murder My Baby," ended up being sadly prophetic.

7. The Sun discography lists the personnel as follows: "Straighten Up Baby"/"My Baby," Sun 199. James Cotton, vcl; Harvey Simmons, Tom Roane, saxes; Billy Love, pno; Pat Hare, gtr; Kenneth Banks, bs; Houston Stokes, dms. Dec. 7, 1953. "Cotton Crop Blues"/"Hold Me in Your Arms," Sun 206. James Cotton, vcl; Mose Vinson, pno; Pat Hare, gtr; John Bowers, dms. May 13 or 14, 1954.

8. "Saddle My Pony"/"Worried All the Time," Howlin' Wolf, Chess 1515.

9. L. D. Beckton (?)

10. Elga Edmonds. Perhaps the most mispronounced/misspelled name in blues history, his name has been the subject of much discussion.

11. Robert "Big Mojo" Elam and T. J. McNulty.

12. Johnny Young's Chicago Blues Band, Arhoolie 1029.

13. "Jumpin' at Cadillac," Little Mack and His Boys, C. J. 607. James Cotton recorded two sides of his own for Bea and Baby that remained unissued until the late 1970s, when they eventually saw the light of day on Red Lightnin' RL 0020, a compilation of Bea and Baby material.

14. "Laying in the Weeds"/"Complete This Order," James Cotton, Loma 2042.

15. Muddy Waters and Otis Spann toured England in October 1958, appearing on the same program as Chris Barber's band.

16. *Chris Barber Presents Jimmy Cotton,* Columbia EP8141 and EP8189. Eight titles were recorded on August 10, 1961. The piano player was Keith Scott.

17. *Can't Get No Grindin',* Muddy Waters, Chess 50023.

18. *Live at Mr. Kelly's,* Muddy Waters, Chess 50012.

19. James Cotton's plans to relocate to West Memphis never materialized. He eventually moved to Austin, Texas.

Red Holloway

The Chicago R&B and jump music scene of the 1940s and '50s happily coexisted alongside the more celebrated and familiar down-home amplified style of Muddy Waters, Howlin' Wolf, and Little Walter. For many years researchers paid this urban genre scant attention, and little information existed on artists such as Jo Jo Adams, Red Saunders, Jump Jackson, Tom Archia, and Lefty Bates. In 1974 Mike Leadbitter, in a column titled "Chicago Flipside," was one of the first people to bemoan the fact that these artists, the clubs they performed in, and the companies who were recording them were largely undocumented. In the following issue Tony Russell began to address the problem in "Blues with Class," but it was more than a decade before information finally began to emerge on many of these artists. Saxophonist Red Holloway was a vital part of this scene.

The clubs these artists performed in were also a little more upscale: the Rumboogie, the Crown Propeller, Club DeLisa, to name but a few. These venues would often feature a floor show: a chorus line, comedian, or some other specialty act, perhaps a shake dancer, along with a blues vocalist. The musicians, versatile and often schooled, were mostly from a jazz background and most had a good working knowledge of the blues. There were of course situations where both scenes interacted. Red Holloway, who played in these clubs for many years, both as a member of the various house bands and occasionally as a featured artist, was unique and, unlike many others, had a foot firmly planted in both camps, touring with many blues artists, including Roosevelt Sykes, Memphis Slim, and Jimmy Reed.

James L. Holloway was born in Helena, Arkansas, on May 31, 1927, and, along with his mother, moved to Chicago at age two. He was for many years an in-demand accompanist and bandleader. As a house musician for Vee-Jay Records during the 1950s, he recorded with artists as diverse as L. C. McKinley, the Spaniels, Pee Wee Crayton, and Baby Face Willett. He also participated in numerous sessions for Chess, Cobra, States, and Club 51 Records, and many others. In late 1958 two sides, "Simple Steps" and "Ala Carte" were issued on Mad Records (1297) by James "Red" Holloway. In 1961 Red moved to New York to join the Lloyd Price Band. But perhaps he was known most famously as a member, along with Joe Dukes and George Benson, of the Brother Jack McDuff Quartet. Red recorded prolifically for Prestige Records, both with McDuff and as a solo artist. The tough organ/tenor records of McDuff's quartet are classics of the genre.

In the late 1960s Red relocated to Los Angeles and for many years led the house band at the Parisian Room; he even made an appearance in the film *Lady Sings the Blues.* Finding himself still much in demand for sessions, he recorded with Charles Brown, B. B. King, Jimmy Witherspoon, Etta James, Eddie "Cleanhead" Vinson, Freddy Robinson, and a host of others, including a couple of singles on his own RH Records and a number of albums as the featured artist. He continued to tour extensively both with bands of his own or along with other people, such as Sonny Stitt.

Few artists are as candid and forthcoming while discussing their personal lives as Red Holloway. Before publication of his fascinating and often hilarious interview in *BU,* I called Red to review some of the information and asked, in view of the personal nature of some of the material, if there was any part of the interview he would like to change. His simple reply was, "Good news or bad news, it's all good news. Use what you want." Red liked the interview and in later years told me that he thought it was the best interview he'd ever given. Red Holloway died on February 25, 2012, in San Luis Obispo, California.

—Bill Greensmith

Red Holloway

Bill Greensmith

Blues Unlimited #117/118 (Jan./Feb./March/April 1976)

Helena, Arkansas. That's about 90 miles from Memphis, Tennessee. Sits right on the Mississippi River. I lived there till I was about 4 years old. You see, my mother was 13 when I was born, and during those years it was a disgrace for a child of that age, especially not being married. My father was 17, and this is very ironic, because my father's mother took him from Helena and brought him here, to Santa Monica, California, to live. And I never saw my father till I was about 20 years old. So it was such a disgrace as far as the small community was concerned till my mother decided to leave and go to Chicago.

Red Holloway, mid-1950s.

My father played violin. My mother played piano and I've been accustomed to a big upright piano. I used to sleep on the piano, especially in Chicago. We had this apartment—well, it wasn't an apartment—it was just one room, really. It was like a one-room kitchenette. You had a stove in the corner and the toilet was down the hall, stuff like that. So we did that part, oh, man, till I got out of high school. The one I stayed at the longest was 215 E. 53rd Street. That's between Indiana and Prairie.

My mother made me take piano, that was a must, you had to play piano. And the way we got this piano, there was a friend and his mother had this piano all these years and he was getting ready to leave town. So he wanted us to keep the piano for him until he could make arrangements to get it. But after some years went by he got killed somehow, so nobody ever claimed the piano. So we kept it. He never had any relatives in Chicago and he had moved to Detroit. In fact my mother still has that same piano right now. So I used to practice. I hated to take piano lessons, but I did for a good twelve years.

My mother used to play for churches. And she'd play a lot of classical, she'd play the "Blue Danube," "The Flower Song," and she had her own version of playing the blues, which was a little unorthodox because of the fact that her blues was like playing for, well, it was a church-type blues, you know. And one of her schoolmates was Roosevelt Sykes, in Helena, 'course he was a little older than she was, but they did go to school. Then this lady gave me this banjo. And I had been trying to play guitar, but I didn't have one. So she gave me the banjo. That was the only instrument other than the piano, and I hated piano. So I just started learning how to play the banjo and I did fairly well.

You wouldn't believe it, I was gonna be a boxer. I used to go to the gym. I was an amateur boxer for about four years. Then I was gonna go in the Golden Gloves.

I must have been 11–12 years old. I was a flyweight. I was weighing 148 pounds.[1] At the time everybody wanted to be like Joe Louis. Joe Louis was everybody's inspiration. Nichols Gym was the popular gym; Ray Robinson used to go round there and train, on 50th and Indiana, in the basement. I used to go down there and watch 'em work out. I had a few fights as a flyweight. I've never been knocked out in my life. In fact I've never had a whippin' in my life from nobody but my mama. But I got hit so damn hard one time, that's what changed my mind about this. I had to decide whether I wanted to be a musician and I think I liked music better, because I stopped one day and was thinking about it.

At that time if you're black you could only be a barber, a waiter, work as a Pullman porter, something like that. You could be a pimp, you could be a lawyer or doctor if you had that kind of money. But most black folk didn't have that kind of money to send a kid to school, so a lot of people were pimps and a lot of them would sell dope. But at that time there wasn't no pushers and stuff. You could buy a reefer and stuff, but that real hard shit, you could get it, but didn't too many people use it. Everybody was smokin' reefers, but really the thing to be in was pimpin'. If you were a pimp, that was the big thing. Everybody looked up to you 'cause you're a pimp.

Like I lived on 53rd, and on 54th and Prairie, which was just around the corner, was this whorehouse. And I knew the lady and my mother knew the lady, so I would run errands. Like I'd go to the store and get liquor and take it back to the whorehouse. I'd steer tricks in there, stuff like that, change sheets, and just do whatever, ya know. Go get cigarettes, all kinds of things. I must have been 13 or 14, somewhere around there. What was so funny, a lot of times I'd run errands for some of the whores and they would want me to take my money out in trade and I'd say, "No, I don't want—you give me my money!" They used to call me James Junior. (*imitates lady's voice*) "James Junior, don't you want to come here and get a little of this good stuff?" I'd say, "No, you just give me my money." They'd give me a dime to go to the store and stuff like that. If I got a quarter, boy, I was really in good shape. 'Cause things were relatively cheap then, you know. But it really was quite an experience. I worked there until, well, until the place finally got busted. I must have worked there about three years.

Sarah had about 5 or 6 whores in there.[2] She did great business, especially on the weekends. Boy, that business was really—it was a 3 and 2—$3 for the trick and $2 for the room. (*laughs*) And, like, I'd get money from the house and I was gettin' money from the tricks. Then a lot of times I'd be on the streets. I'd look at a few dudes and if they look like they had some dough, you know, I'd say, "For a quarter I'll take you where you can have a good time." And I'd take 'em over there. And one time I talked to the policeman. I told him, "For a quarter I'll take you where you can have a good time." He said, "Okay." So I took him over there. But it just so happened, what he did, see, he knew Sarah. And he said, "Listen, don't have this boy out here hustlin' up no tricks for you." At that time in Chicago if you had money you could just about get out of anything. So he said, "It's alright for you to have your tricks, but don't have this kid out there soliciting, because you really gonna get in some trouble." So I had to stop my little hustle. But this was a hustle I started on my own. She didn't have me do it, I just figured I could earn some extra money.

I would play the piano there because I could play boogie-woogie. At that time Meade Lux Lewis, Pete Johnson, and Albert Ammons were really popular and I played good boogie-woogie piano. This was all they needed, I'd make money hand over fist. Dimes, quarters, I would average $3 or $4 a night, which was big dough, because the average worker was making $15 a week. The pimps and hustlers, they were making $40 and $50 a week, which was big money. If you went out on a weekend and spent $5 or $10, boy! You'd really, "Man, so-and-so came over and he spent $10." "$10, goddamn!" This was the latter part of the thirties, just before the war, if I'm not mistaken. Things were very cheap. They had to be before the war, because after the war started everything started getting expensive. People started making a lot of money.

People didn't make big money, but money was plentiful. You could just go out on the street and just hustle, make money. Everybody could make a living. Everybody had some money, people would spend. And the gangsters all during that era, well, Capone, he had had his day and was going through his problems. His brother was the one that was really—Ralph Capone was taking over for Al. There was plenty of policy wheels and plenty of places to play at. Every place you go, on every corner just about, you had a little ole club or something. They had piano players or they may have a trio and there was just plenty entertainment.

I started playing saxophone in 1942, September of '42, and in February of 1943 I was playing with Gene Wright. My inspiration was Lester Young. Well, actually Coleman Hawkins and Lester Young, that's what really impressed me most. I never will forget "Body and Soul" and Lester Young. I just said, "Good night." I just couldn't believe it. I played with Gene Wright's band up until I went in the service in 1946. We played be-bop tunes like the tunes Dizzy Gillespie and Charlie Parker were playing. He'd play blues, but it was a modern blues. Calvin Belcher was the singer and he was a hell of a vocalist.

I went to Du Sable High School. We used to do shows and all kinds of things. We would win the superior rating at band contest all the time. They would put on plays and we would play for it. "Cottontail" and all kinds of tunes; it was quite an affair and was put on every year. And it wasn't no jive music, 'cause Johnny Griffin left this band and went with Lionel Hampton. He was in high school and Lionel Hampton came over as a visitor. Like Duke Ellington came over one time, whenever they would come to the Regal Theater. You see, the band director was a jazz musician and he was with some of the great musical entertainers of that particular period. He knew all the entertainers and he would bring them over and they would speak, stuff like that. It wasn't an amateurish thing. He wouldn't stand for you to play rink-a-tink and you had to practice.

I was going to school and I didn't eat any breakfast one morning. So on my study period I said, "Well, I'll go and eat." I was outside eating when I was supposed to

Red Holloway Army Band, December 1946.
(Holloway is in the front row, second from right.)

be in the study hall. The assistant principal just happened to catch me outside and wanted to know what I was doing. I said I hadn't eaten any breakfast. So he said that's no excuse and took me in the office. They were going to suspend me, then they saw where I had these five deferments and all my best marks were in band. So my mother said, "Well, young man . . ." She took me to the draft board right then and there, that same day. And they took me!

The captain of the band in high school, where I really learned to play, wrote a letter for me to get in the band in the services. But when I got there the sergeant of the regiment I was in tore the letter up. He said, "You're trying to get out of training." But anyway, I took my horn with me and I went over and talked to the band master and he wrote a letter to my C.O. so that I could get in the band. Then we were shipped to another camp and they didn't have a band. It was myself and a drummer that went to this other camp. So I formed a band. I had a jeep and a bus and everything at my disposal. I had a special pass and from three to five in the afternoon we would rehearse. This was all my duties. I had it pretty easy. I really didn't do very much work in the service. I was in the service eleven months and eleven days. I'll never forget that. At the time all married men were supposed to be out of the service by a certain date in '47. So that's how I got out and I got an honorable discharge.

But all in all, I don't regret going to the service. It taught me quite a lesson. It teach you independence, stuff like that. And musically, I always said it. I was never going to be anything but a musician. And all of my wives, before we got married I'd say, "Listen, if you expect me to do something else, forget about it." They always say, "No, I met 'cha as a musician, sure I want 'cha to stay one." But after we get into it, then I'll be gone quite some time, they'd say, "I need a man to stay at home with me at night." So I lost two wives and an outside old lady and six kids later.

After I got out the service I went to the Chicago Conservatory of Music. During that period I was working with Jump Jackson. I worked with him in the '40s couple of weeks here, couple of weeks there, and I worked steady with him in '51. We would go to Peoria for a couple of weeks. But I was going to the conservatory Tuesdays and Thursdays and I was commuting from Peoria, Illinois. I'd go from Peoria to Chicago and get back just in time for the gig. That was a part of my G.I. Bill. It was my intention to be a music teacher but my G.I. Bill ran out. And I didn't have too much money.

What was so funny about when I was in Peoria, like, you know, most musicians would do, you'd have a little ole broad. Now, in order to save rent, me and the saxophone player would get a room together and split the rent. So we had this big double bed, so when you get a broad, well, one would hang out on the street for a while. But, now, if it's going to be an all-night affair, now, after you get through whatever you're doing, what happens is the other would just come on up and either sleep on the big couch or sleep on the floor. But in this case we only had the double bed. So the broad would sleep, like, on the end, I'd sleep in the middle, and the dude would sleep behind me. So when I'd leave to go on to school in Chicago—soon as I'd get back I'd say to the broad, "What's the matter? Looks like you ain't had no sleep." She said, "Soon as you slammed the door the chase started. This fool chased me all around the room. I had to finally walk the streets until you got back, 'cause he said if I don't give up nothin' I couldn't stay!" Boy, it was really funny. There used to be some funny things.

The Flame Show Lounge? Oh, yeah, Dr. Jo Jo. I think he did a thing called "Cabbage Head." "*Whose head is that where my head suppose to be? That ain't no head, that's a cabbage head.*" You know, Jo Jo's in Chicago right now.[3] Oh, he was flamboyant. He was the only cat that would come on stage with tuxedos with full tails. He had red tuxedos, shocking blue, and pink, he was really . . . He'd come out with his hat and cane and stuff singing the blues. Boy, he was really a show. He'd have this cape on and his top hat. Every one of his outfits he'd have a top hat to match. He was a hell of a good vocalist. He was like Wynonie Harris, he had that type of voice, he could really sing. And plus he would go into his little dance. He had a little act together. I was really surprised—well, Jo Jo really wanted to be a pimp. He was pimpin' on the side, too. It was a fluke how he got into the business. He'd go into clubs, like, by him being a leading pimp, you know, they would always say, "Hey, Dr. Jo Jo, hey." He started to wanting to sing 'cause he had a good voice. And he'd go in these clubs and he would sing. That's from what I understand was how he really got started. Then he started writing tunes. And he'd have his Cadillacs and shit, so, like, he always wanted to outdo everybody and everything. He had seven sets of tails made up, capes and shit, blood red, all that kinda shit. He had the shoes and everything to match. When he'd go on stage, boy, you would really have a presentation. And he made everything rhyme, even when he'd introduce another artist.

He made about five or six 78s, but I don't think they released but about two or three of them.[4] I never recorded with him. There was one that got really popular and the others just got released around Chicago. The way they used to do, they'd release them in the city where you were most popular. And if they'd sell good then they'd release them in other major cities. That's what small companies would do. But he made his work after that, he worked everywhere on a lot of the shows at the theaters, Dr. Jo Jo.

The Flame was in this hotel, the Morocco Hotel. Actually the Flame was named the Morocco Lounge, but they changed it around to the Flame Show Lounge. It was like a real long bar and—let's see, what was this cat's name? Nixon! Isn't that funny?—owned the Flame. It was a real intimate thing, a lot of pimps and hustlers used to hang around this place all the time. During that time, this is when Phil and Leonard Chess had the Macomba Lounge right around the corner.

I was with Chess when he first started, when he had Aristocrat. His first company was on 52nd and Cottage Grove, and I lived on 53rd and Drexel, which was right around the corner. He had Gene Ammons and Tom Archia and this blues singer, god damn, Tillman? Last name was Tillman.[5] But anyway, he was one of his artists on Aristocrat. Tom Archia and Gene Ammons used to play at their nightclub all the time. And it's a funny thing how I met Gene Ammons. I knew his father first because of the boogie-woogie piano, and I met him through Roosevelt Sykes. When I met Gene he was just starting to play saxophone. He had a great sound, but he really couldn't play much. And that was another influence because of his sound. I was just amazed that he could get such a big sound. But he wasn't playing anything.

I've been knowing Roosevelt all my life 'cause, like I said, he and my mother went to school together. And naturally we'd have them Friday and Saturday night parties. House-rent parties. You'd sell fish and moonshine and Roosevelt would come over and play piano a lot of times when he was in town. He was on RCA Victor, during that time he wasn't as popular. His records were sellin', but they wasn't really sellin' that well. So he would play house-rent parties, whatever, and that's how I really met him. So when I started playing saxophone, he came by one day and heard me, but I'd been playing with Gene Wright and them.

I went on the road with Roosevelt in 1948. Actually the latter part of '47 until the latter part of '49. There was probably no one you'd probably even know now, because they were just local musicians. David Eagland was the drummer. Chester something was a piano player; he was from Columbus, Ohio. What he would do, he was an act then and he had seven pieces. We would play for maybe an hour, then Roosevelt would come out and do his act. Which, you know, he'd sit down and sing the blues. There's a place called the Rose I remember, the most popular place we played at. The

Rose Room in Dallas, Texas, huge places most of them. We played in Columbus, a place called the Turk Club, they were little dives. But he had a hot record—let's see, what was the name? God damn, I don't remember the name of it, but this record was hot and he was makin' a little money. He still wasn't payin' us that much. (*laughs*) We was makin' $20 a night, which was good money at that time. "Ice Cream Freezer" was one of his tunes. *"My baby's got an ice cream freezer, let me put my milk in her can."*[6] And "I Wanna Do Do" was another. *"I wanna do do do what you want me to, I wanna do do"* and *"My baby's got a hole in her belly and it won't get well, the more you punch it the more it swells."* Oh, man! See a lot of these tunes I sing myself once in a while. I only sing when I have to, not that I care for singing much myself, because I don't have a voice. But a lot of places, they wouldn't hire you unless you could sing. So by me being with these blues players, we'd play the tunes so much you'd remember the lyrics. I used to sing "Ice Cream Freezer" and "Hot Nuts" and people used to like that. Roosevelt had the name of "The Original Honeydripper" before [Joe] Liggins came out with "The Honeydripper." Roosevelt Sykes is the original Honeydripper.

Then I was at the musicians union and I saw this little card that they had where a Nat Towles wanted some musicians in Omaha, Nebraska. So this friend of mine, a trumpet player named Red Higgins, we wrote to Nat Towles and told him we were there; he needed a trumpet player, a saxophone player, and a bass player. So he agreed to pay us $20 a night and he said that he worked no less than four nights a week. So he sent us the fare and we struck out and went to Omaha. This was in 1949, latter part of '49. Anyway, we went to Omaha and started working. What happened, the first two nights he paid us the $20 and the next night he automatically gave us $10 each. I said, "Hey, what's happening here?" He said, "You can see things are bad." I said, "But our agreement is an agreement." He was such a con man till we stayed and each night we was gettin' like $10. Then we'd play cards with him in the day. We'd play tonk and he'd win your money back! Win your $10. So he'd lend you some money, you were actually drawing money on your salary that you haven't got, so invariably you'd wind up staying with him. I stayed in Omaha until 1950, that's where my first kid was born. I couldn't really leave. My wife was pregnant, she going to the doctor and stuff, so I had to stick it out.

Martha Louis, Joe Louis's ex-wife, when she made her debut as a vocalist in 1946, Nat Towles's band was the band behind her. She went out all across the country, but the Regal Theater in Chicago was the first gig they played, but they went all over to New York, Washington, et cetera. Because at the time, Joe Louis being champion and stuff, so his wife naturally was quite an attraction. She was a very attractive woman also and they had packed houses all the time. Of course, I wasn't with the band at that time, but I remember seeing it, 'cause I went to the theater to see her and she had quite a show.

When I came back from Omaha I joined Jump Jackson's band and stayed with him maybe a couple of years, till 1951. We used to go out of town. We used to play in LaSalle, Illinois. We used to play at a place called Martin's Corner in Chicago. That was a blues joint. In fact, Muddy Waters and all them used to play there. There was Art Simms, piano; Fred Clark, saxophone; we didn't have a bass player. Two saxophones, piano, and drums. Me and Fred Clark was doing the singing. Jump wasn't singing. We did like "Red Light," "I Got a Gal," that kinda thing, all of the current rhythm-and-blues tunes of that particular day. And to really make people think that we were hellfire musicians we would throw in a little "Smoke Gets in Your Eyes." (*laughs*) But basically we did just blues, stuff like that, and a lot of gimmick songs like I told you before, "Hot Nuts."

The first recording I done was Al Smith and myself. He had a band and we were in Nashville, Tennessee, and we went to Gallatin, Tennessee, to record. We went to Nashville for about 3 weeks or a month and recorded in a broadcasting studio. Al Smith wasn't any kind of bass player, but nobody never really knew that but the musicians. So we made this recording and the man kept sayin', "Damn, there's something don't sound right." "Broomduster" or something was the name of one of the records, and "Hot-Rod" was on the other side. I don't know who it was we recorded it for, not a popular label, some label from down in that part of the country—oh, shit, I don't remember the name. It had a red label.[7] This was an off-brand label. But I do remember I received a 78 of this recording, but it was quite awhile after. Because what happened, they kept sayin', "Somethin' don't sound right about this record, there's somethin' wrong." We recorded it over and over and over again and there's something still wrong. So the man finally, one of the engineers, they got engineers from other studios, they said, "That bass isn't right, something's wrong with the bass." Then we knew that they'd . . . Well, Al was the leader, you can't tell—we knew what was wrong all the time. We couldn't go and say the bass player's no good and he's the leader. You can't do that. Anyway, the first year they didn't do anything with the recording. There was Norman Simmons, piano; myself; Al on bass; the drummer's name was—oh, hell, I've forgotten the drummer. We had Von Freeman, a saxophone player. We were playing a little blues and a little jazz, but basically it was blues and, well, I wouldn't call it, well, I guess you could call it, "A-Train" is jazz. We were playing tunes of that type and mostly danceable music. We had Charles Gonzales, he changed his name to Bobby Prince. He was the vocalist.

It was a regular show that we had at this particular club. It was an all-white club down in Nashville and the police would follow you home. They didn't want any of them white broads following you home. Some of the waitresses would follow the singer. He was a very nice lookin', he was mixed with Spanish. They'd follow us home 'cause he was riding with us and staying at the same house. So the police would be sure that we went home and they'd hang around to be sure that we didn't leave during the night. Boy, this was really something. We were only supposed to be there two weeks. The lady's husband who hired us at this club had to go out of town for a week or so, and our contract expired while he was gone. So we were really glad to get away from there, because we had to go to this little room when you get off the bandstand. You had all your facilities, your drinks, and whatnot, so we were saying,

"Well, we certainly had a nice stay and we hope sometime we can come back." So his wife said, "Well, you know, Al Smith, George (her husband), he ain't here and he won't be back, but we just don't want 'cha to leave, we want 'cha to stay here, And I think we should have at least two more weeks until George gets back." So Al says, "Well, Miss Roberts, I would like to stay, but actually I got another engagement in Chicago." Because we're trying to get away. She said, "Now lookahere, Al Smith, don't you forget where you at. You ain't there in Chicago." Al said, "Where's the contract?" (*laughs*) We stayed there two more weeks.

Chance Records was before Vee-Jay. Chance was back in '51–'52 and Art Sheridan was the owner of Chance, and Ewart Abner was the administrator, president, or whatever you want to call him. He was running it. The Moonglows and the Flamingos were on Chance and I recorded with them. Chance Records had quite a few artists. Anyway, they did pretty well, but Abner was just spending money pretty fast. And another thing, the distributors wasn't sending the money in. Like if you're big, when the distributors buy something from you, they send you a check. But when you're small, you have to put your stuff on consignment. Then they send you your money, and whatever records they didn't sell, they'd just send 'em back. And a lot of them just wouldn't send you nothin', check or money. You had to get in your car and go and try to collect your money. So that put quite a few companies . . .

There was another company on 63rd Street. I've forgotten the name of it, because they didn't last any time. That was another company that I did a lot of blues on. They lasted maybe a couple of years. Lefty Bates was on a lot of these things.[8] I did a lot on United, too. United, which was Smitty and—damn, what was his name?[9] United was a record company, and there was George and Ernie Leaner, they had United Records Distributors. Now, that's a funny thing about George and Ernie Leaner. You know, I told you I lived over on 53rd and Indiana. Now, right on the corner was a drugstore, and George Leaner used to be the soda jerk at the drugstore. He made up ice cream and all kind of things and that's how I met him. We often talk about that. He never had any idea of ever going into the record distributing thing, but it's just how fate works. How he got into it, he told me he was working packing records at some—I don't even remember the company. Then he found out how easy it was. At that time it was easy to do, because you didn't have a lot of competition to distribute. And then they really got into it heavy.

Now, United Recording Company was a different thing. United Recording Company was on 51st and Cottage Grove. During that time Vee-Jay was on Cottage Grove and Chess was on Cottage Grove. In fact, Chess was across the street from Vee-Jay and United was down on 51st. United, that was their office, they didn't have a studio there. Chess had his studio on the 4700 block on Cottage, and they were building a studio in the back. In fact, I recorded a session for them they never released. Some good material, too, and I sure wish I could get that material back. He paid me but never released the record. Well, what happened, he wanted to get the tunes, a couple of tunes I had for some of his artists. Like I had one called "Hoodoo Man" and he wanted the tune, but I wanted to do it myself. So he kept asking me about it, and finally what happened, he said, "Okay, I'll record ya." He recorded me but never released it. Now, he could have used the material, but I don't think he did. I know Willie Dixon wrote a thing for Muddy Waters called "Hoochie Coochie Man," but I had another fellow record "Hoodoo Man" for me, but this was in the '60s.

You know, one of the things about the Chess brothers, you could always get a job, but you would never get too much money. And they would ration your money out to you. Say, for instance, you could have a hit like Danny Overbea, "40 Cups of Coffee," that kind of thing. I recorded a lot with Danny Overbea and he was a relatively big attraction. And, like, Danny, he'd say, "Man, I need some of my money." So they'd, like, "Just a minute, Danny, now, what's the problem, you need a new car or something?" They had friends, like, just in the 4600 block that owned Chevrolet dealers. You could go to a Cadillac dealer, whatever you wanted. "So you need a car, go down and tell him I . . ." He'd go down buy him a new car or they'd buy him a Cadillac. You get them a Cadillac, then, shit, they'd feel all okay and they'd pay the notes on it, stuff like that. Then they wouldn't ask for the money, you see! The average brother, he'd say, "Yeah, man, look here, that dude's alright. Look here what he's got me, a new Cadillac." And maybe he'd give you $3,000 or $4,000. Maybe you'd suppose to get $50,000 from your earnings. So they give you a $5,000 Cadillac and $3,000 or $4,000 in cash.

Well, basically, there's two ways of looking at it. They were alright. I wouldn't say they were crooks or nothing like that. What would happen, usually, the cats they'd give 'em a lot of money and they'd wind up spendin'. Then they'd come to the record company and borrow more and borrow more and they would never really pay it off. So I guess in the long run the artist did really get all his money. But he got it in dribbles. Now, the way entertainers were spending their money, "I need another $1,000, I need $500." So over a period of a couple of years they would—actually, they were just getting their own money. Now, in my case, they never did that, because I was never really signed with them. But when I needed a station wagon they sent me to one of their buddies and I got a brand-new station wagon. Of course I made the payments, but I didn't have to have any money and stuff like that. So whatever I needed they would see to me getting it.

I tried pimpin' for a while, not because I wanted to, a broad just made me her pimp. She liked me and she was a whore and she just started giving me her money. And she called me, when anybody (would ask), "Red Holloway's my man." Well, I was smart enough. This was in '52, '53, '54. I had my own band then and I was young, had all my hair and my teeth, and I looked fairly decent. And I could play fairly well. So this broad here, in fact I saw her last year. She was young, she was a white broad, she was about at that time 21 or 22, beautiful thing. Dimples and everything, she's from St. Louis. She just asked me out one night in this club I was working, the Club Evergreen. She asked me, "Where is your old lady?" Well, I was married at the time. I said, "Well, what do you mean, my woman or my wife?" She said, "Either

Billy Stepney, Red Holloway, Eddie Ware. Chicago, early 1950s.

one." I said, "My wife is at home, I don't know where my woman is." She said, "Well, I'm your woman for the night." I said, "Oh, you are. What are your qualifications to be my woman?" So this broad gave me $300, she said, "This!" I said, "Yeah, you sure the fuck are my woman, in fact, from now on." Like we went to this hotel and shacked up and we had a talk. There was a friend of mine, his name is Larry Rice, a drummer. He was really pimpin'. He was a good musician, but he was really into pimpin' and I wasn't, because I was mostly interested in music. So she said she had been in his stable, but she really wasn't interested, because he had too many broads and he didn't have time to spend with her. She said that I didn't have to do anything if she got busted, I didn't have to get her out or nothin'. I didn't have to appear at the police station, because at that time the police were really on blacks, especially with white. If you had a black broad, now, that was alright, but if you had a white broad they really would give you problems. So I said, well, I know how to get around that, going to the police station to bail you out. I hired a bail bonds man, 24 hours a day he was on call. And I had a friend of mine who was a lawyer, so I would never have to appear. But during the time that we was together she only got busted twice. She was very careful. I didn't have any real problems. It worked out fine. Then I started leaving town, stuff like that, so we kinda just drifted apart.

The 708 Club. You see, they had a thing, sometimes they would have Muddy Waters and Howlin' Wolf at the same time. This was before they was real popular. I played with a cat by the name of Eddie "Lima Beans" Ware. We had a piano, drums, and saxophone. I can't remember the drummer's name. I would play there when they had like a blues festival at the 708 Club. I would play there with Lima Beans, then I would play with Muddy. Then Howlin' Wolf would come up and do his thing, so it was a real complete show.[10]

Little Willie. Little Willie was a harmonica player, he died around 1956, I guess. What was Little Willie's last name? Shit, that's all I ever knew. Little small black guy, real ugly. He played the hell out of the harmonica. He was just getting popular. I think he had a record out. I don't even know what the name of the tune or anything. He was just beginning to get over as a harp player and he died. Little Willie's stuff was blues, but maybe six or seven months before he died he was becoming very popular and people were getting him for gigs and stuff. I was out of town when he died, so I really don't know what he died of, but it was rather sad 'cause you say, "God damn. Cat just beginning to make it and he cashed in his chips like that." Sure could play harp though.[11]

I remember when Little Walter was playing with Muddy. In fact, when he first came to Chicago, then he got started doing his own thing. You know, Little Walter was a hell of an entertainer, too, you better believe. But he could never keep any musicians. Yeah, shit, he didn't pay them no money. And one thing I'll tell you, that fool wasn't afraid of nothing. Cats would hold guns on him say they gonna shoot him. Shit, he'd walk up and take it away from them, stuff like that. Somebody did shoot him one time, he kept on coming. He said, "You gotta kill me." So the cat turned around and split! Can you imagine a dude running with a gun? Yes, indeedy. Funny things happen in Chicago.

Eddie "Lima Beans" Ware, he was jealous. He was jealous of his entertainers. He really had no reason to be jealous, because he was the one that was popular. He had the hit, well, it was a hit during that particular time.[12] But if, say, for instance, you got better applause than he got for a solo or whatever, you know, he would talk about that all night. He'd say, "If you want to be a star, you get your own band." At first I thought—you know, how cats kid. When I first joined him I thought he was bullshittin' and I didn't really pay it any attention. But the drummer pulled my coat. The cat mentioned it so many times. "Man," I said, "what is this shit?" He said, "He's serious." I said, "Man, you gotta be jokin', serious, because I got a little ole hand for a little ole jive solo." So he said, "Yeah, man, he don't like for you to get too many hands now 'cause he's the star." And he said, "Ain't but room enough for one star in this band." Which was the way he was. And I really didn't think that much of it until he kept talkin' about it. I said, "Well, this cat does have a certain complex." And if he's hittin' on a broad and she digs you, shit. This cat here wouldn't talk, he wouldn't say nothing to you all night long. His piano playing? Shit (*laughs*), oh, boy, his piano playing. Well, I mean, for that particular type of thing that he was doing, I would say it got over for what he was doing. It was really appropriate for the songs he was playing. But I mean basically piano playing, shit, I play better piano.

Danny Overbea, let me tell you. Danny Overbea was a good entertainer, good musician, still is. He's still playing in Chicago.[13] He's a guitar player and singer and he speaks Spanish fluently. He was a good guitar player, he could play. I consider you a player when you can play blues to John Coltrane. I don't put you down just 'cause you play the blues, 'cause there're some blues players who don't play nothing but the blues, but they play the hell out of it and they outplay anybody that you can think of in the blues field. They really play. But "Lima Bean" Ware, shit, nothin'. I'll outplay him any day, and I don't consider myself a piano player. Danny Overbea had something almost as big as "40 Cups of Coffee": "Train, Train, Train." Now, I had the band, it was "Danny Overbea featuring Red Holloway's band." I had Louis Carpenter, piano; Robert "Hindu" Henderson, drums; Hawk Lee, bass. Then I changed piano players and I got Pete Hatch. We would play in halls that hold 1,000 people, nightclubs. Basically we'd play in places that would hold from 250 to over 1,000 people. I think it was "40 Cups of Coffee" or "Train, Train, Train." I was on one or both of them. He had some other things that wasn't as popular. And as usual I've found with record companies, when you start asking for your money they have a habit of putting you on the shelf and letting your contract expire. Like I said, he spoke Spanish fluently. We'd play a lot of Spanish places, too. I wasn't on all his tours, but I done quite a few.

I did something with the Spaniels. There was a deejay by the name of Sam Evans. Sam Evans took the Moonglows, the Spaniels, the Orchids, he had Jimmy Reed. Him and Al Benson got together and put a package show together. We went to about three different theaters in Chicago. This was about '53 or '54, somewhere there, and we went to Gary, Indiana, Milwaukee, and Michigan.

The vocal groups? Woop-dee-dee-woop-woop, wow-woo, they didn't sound like nothin' to me, but I mean, after you play with them awhile they kinda grow on ya. You know what they reminded me of? You have a bunch of youngsters and these youngsters are really trying to learn how to sing. Say, for instance, you have your kids, and to keep them out of mischief you say, "Hey, well, we got a little ole group here and it's just more or less for amusement." Well, that's the way most of these vocal groups sound. Off-key guys, damn. And as far as format, when I say a format, you couldn't have a "Now we're gonna do this course and then after you do the first course, fellas, then we have the lead singer sing this and that, then you go back in the harmony here." Shit, on each course they'd have some different shit. They would sing the words, but the harmony was different all the time. So you couldn't really write an arrangement. You would have to write basically unison for the band and let them sing their own harmonies, 'cause you couldn't give 'em no notes. 'Cause they couldn't remember them, a lot of 'em. Then you'd find the Spaniels, that was a fairly polished group.

To record with? Oh, man, god damn! You'd just get tired of playing the same shit over. You'd do maybe twenty takes, twenty-five takes. God damn, you'd get so sick of that shit. Now, here's what would happen with groups of that type. To cut down on studio time we would rehearse in Al Smith's basement a week, every day from twelve o'clock till six at night, every day the week before. Then we'd go into the studio. Well, we'd know our part. You know, you're doing this basically for a living, so once you get accustomed to playing or reading music, you memorize all that shit. And you'd get tired of going over and over again, then get in the studio and go over . . . ha, ha, man, god damn! So what we would do, we would get ourself a fifth of liquor or something and plenty of sandwiches, and we'd get all soused up at the recording session. That's when we started gettin' hip and started makin' tracks.

The union didn't allow you to make a track for groups, but we just got tired of fucking with it. So we'd make a track, we'd sit there and let them go over and over again with the track. Then when they get through, think they got their part, we'd go in and play the live session. See, at that time, they was only paying $41.25. So if you're makin' tracks, you could do your whole session in an hour, musician-wise. So that means no overtime for the musicians. So in order to make our pay we'd have to be there, and if they keep messing up we'd just have to stay there until they got it right. When the track is over, it's up to the bandleader to make sure the track was cut out. Now, if they used the track, which was illegal, we wouldn't say nothing. Like, we was recordin' all the time for Vee-Jay, so we wouldn't say nothing, because we was gettin' our money from Vee-Jay. We would get paid for overtime that we would do, but didn't have to sit there and play it over and over again. The trumpet players would lose their lip, they playing so many times!

Chuck Berry was at the Stage Lounge when he first came out with "Maybellene," when he made his big hit. And Chuck Berry was gettin' $3,000 a week—$3,000, man, that was a l-o-o-o-t of money. That's what he charged. He had three pieces. In fact, I got the clipping on him, because that's the first time I ever worked with anybody that made that much money. I had the house band and Chuck Berry was the leading attraction. Three grand a week! We didn't charge no admission coming in the door, now, we had to get that money from across the bar. This was before the days of admission other than theaters. But people were coming from all over to hear "Maybellene." And what was so funny about Chuck Berry that first year, Chuck Berry saved $100,000 the first year, but he was sleepin' in his car. He was half eating. He wouldn't stay in hotels or nothing, he was just going the back route on everything, saving that money. So the government asked him how much . . . they want the receipts and stuff for his expenses. So he told the taxman he ain't got none, he slept in his car and shit. So they charged him $48,000 tax. He went out immediately and bought a couple of Cadillacs and shit and he started living first-class. Boy, that was really funny! Yeah, they was some good old days. Didn't make a lot of money, but I was fairly content.

I played with Billie Holiday. I played with her when she was at the Beige Room in the Pershing Hotel, in the basement. In fact, Al Smith had that band, but he wasn't playing bass, he had a bass player. Cadillac Bob had this place at the time. Cadillac Bob was a cat that owned some nightclubs. The reason why they called him that was he always got a new Cadillac every year. Anyway, I was working for Al Smith at the time, he was getting her music straight, he was making all the arrangements, getting all the entertainment and the publicity and makin' all the announcements.

Red Holloway, Louis Blackwell, Candy Rivers, Louis Carpenter, Robert "Hindu" Henderson, Hawk Lee. Leather Glove Lounge, Chicago, 1954.

It was his band but he wasn't playing. This was, like, in her last days, you know, but I'd known her before then.

I played with the Regal Theater house band. Red Saunders had the house band at the Regal Theater for years. You would do three shows a day during the week, four on the weekend. And what would happen is we would play behind the singers, like Arthur Prysock, or whoever. Now, when Nat "King" Cole was on he had his own trio, so we would play the music to bring him on, then his trio would play, then we would play the endings of some of his tunes. We would play fill-in spots on his music and the endings, of course, but he would basically use his trio. A lot of times when they did those production tunes of his that were on record, we would play a lot of the arrangements that were on his original recordings. There were so many of them: Nappy Brown, Gene Ammons, B. B. King, Bobby "Blue" Bland, Junior Parker. Red Saunders was there for many a year. I worked at least three years with him there, maybe even four years. From about '54 up to '57, or something in there. See, like, they didn't have a show every week. They would have a show, like, this week, next week they would have a popular movie. They would have one or two shows a month sometimes, which would run a week each time and those off weeks I would work at clubs.

I would work at the Stage Lounge or the Crown Propeller. In fact, I had the house band there for a long time, even when I was working at the Regal. I would have a cat—in fact, Harold Ashby would fill in for me when I worked the Regal. The shows at Crown Propeller wouldn't start till around ten o'clock, but the band would start playing at nine. So the last show at the Regal would start playing at ten and it was over by eleven. So I would have to have Harold work until I got to the club. It was a very popular club. We had Roy Milton, Arthur Prysock, Roy Hamilton, we had quite a few. They hired whoever was popular at the time. Ben Webster was at the Stage Lounge. You see, the same people owned two clubs. They made the Stage Lounge a jazz club and the Crown Propeller a blues and modern jazz club. We had a girl dancing in a tank. She was doing a thing where she'd get in this big tank and she'd take off all her clothes. Yeah, it was really quite a club.

I recorded with Ivory Joe Hunter in Chicago, January '56.[14] He sent me the fare to come to New York and join his band. I told him I couldn't join him right away, as I had business to take care of. He said keep the fare and join me when you take care of your business. I never did get around to joining him, and each time he would see me he threatened to kick my ass, because I spent the money he sent for the fare! I don't know if you remember "Bacon Fat." His name was Andre something.[15] Well, this was supposed to be Al Smith's thing, but since Al Smith had Jimmy Reed he couldn't go out on it. At that time I had my own band and I was playing various clubs, and when I couldn't get a job, I'd go out with whoever would hire me. So, like, this was one of Al Smith's things and he sent Lefty Bates out on the gig. When Lefty wasn't working I'd hire him and vice-versa, and when both of us wasn't working, Al would always use us in a band that he'd put together. So one way or the other we'd always work with each other. And this was one of those tours where, see, Shaw Artists Corporation, like, they knew all of us because of the record company. Everybody that would come out of the company would go to Shaw Artists. So they knew of the band because we were fairly popular among the entertainers as well as on records. And we would go out with a lot of the artists, especially the branch in Chicago, like Jim Fleming was one of the fellas. He'd call, "Hey, what 'cha doin'? I got so-and-so coming from New York. Can you take a band out with him for a week or a month?" Jim Fleming was head of the Shaw office for Chicago. He knew Lefty, Al, and myself, so he would know who was working and who wasn't. Lefty Bates and I went out behind Andre Williams. And we went out, oh, what was his name? God damn, he doesn't sing anymore, shit. He was a singer, but he act like he was a faggot. I can't even remember the record that he had, it was a hot record. This dude was a little sweetie pie—Darnell! Larry Darnell. Larry Williams was another one of the ones I went out with. We'd go out with a lot of people like that and a lot of the artists on the Vee-Jay label. So that's how Lefty and I got together. We had what you'd call a real vicious circle going in Chicago. There was just a certain amount of musicians that worked all the time, and I just happened to be among that few because of knowing the right people, for one thing. Not that I was such a hellfire musician, but I knew the right people—that's the name of the game.

Memphis Slim? Yeah, we went up to Pennsylvania, down to Nashville, New York state, there's a lot of places that owe us money where we didn't get paid. I saw Memphis Slim in Amsterdam. I was with John Mayall. And I asked him, "Look here, motherfucker, when you gonna pay me some of that money that you owe me from the '50s?" He say, "As soon as they give it to me I'll give it to you!" So I said, "In other words, you're telling me just to forget about it?" He said, "Little brother, you sure catch on fast." 'Course I hadn't seen Slim in years. In fact that's the first time I'd seen him since he's been in Europe. He was a big draw, Memphis Slim. He had records that's been popular for years, but during that particular time that I was with him he didn't have nothing hot out. And the dude kinda skipped out on us that owed us the money. There was a cat named Chink playing drums.[16] His guitar player was "Guitar" Murphy.

Harold Ashby and me used to make all the sessions, because we could read a little bit. We could play blues so we made most of the recording sessions for Vee-Jay and Chess. See, when Harold couldn't make something, then he would say, "Hey, Red, what 'cha doin'?" "Look here, man, they got somethin' going over on Cobra," which was on Roosevelt Road. "You think you can make it?" Eli was a little fat short cat.[17] I tell you somebody that's still popular, singer and guitar player, Otis Rush. I recorded with him. Then there was somebody Sunnyland Slim recorded for.[18] I recorded with Shakey Horton when I was with Cobra. I recorded with him again, too.[19] I think Harold Ashby was on the Shakey Horton session. I may have been on it. But on a couple of them sessions we're both on where they had two tenors, then we would alternate.

Eli had his own studio. You know, his studio was something like this (a small room). He had acoustical tiles in the bottom half of his studio and some in the ceiling, so you'd get a little echo in there. He was building the studio himself, so he never got around to ever really finishing it. He didn't have somebody to come in and put the studio together, he did it himself. And he bought used equipment, that's how he got his sound. He'd maybe put the guitar and drummer on the same track, and I remember I played on a track with the bass player one time. He only had two tracks and one box he would set all his things on. And instead of having a volume control for each line, he had a master volume control. Every two lines he would have a volume control, then a master control for the whole box. So if he wanted to make me soft or the drummer soft, he'd have to turn that one thing that handles the two lines, so invariably I'm soft and the drummer would be soft. The only person that would be on a single line would be the singer.

You'd rehearse there. The only one that we did a lot of rehearsal for was Vee-Jay and Chess. You'd always rehearse a week before you record. But when I'd do something for Cobra, he'd call you up today and you'd be there tomorrow. The session's supposed to start at one o'clock, so you had to be there at ten. Nine or ten o'clock in the morning and you'd run over whatever you were gonna do. Then a lot of times you'd run over the tune and record it then and there. Then you'd sit there and get the next one and record it. So you'd probably be in the studio from nine or ten o'clock to ten o'clock at night, if you had six or eight tunes. And for that you might make $50. But $50 was what you call big dough.

There were so many I recorded with. The Spaniels, the Eldorados, the Dells, the Flamingos, the Orchids. Betty Everett on Vee-Jay. Those things were goin' and coming so fast it's hard for me to really remember. At that time we were called the Chicago All-Stars. We were recording with everybody that would come to Vee-Jay. Harold and I were recording with Vee-Jay, Chess, Cobra, a few on Mercury, Columbia, RCA, but the band that was with Vee-Jay was known as the Chicago All-Stars. But, like, over at Chess, Willie Dixon was doing all the writing, and his thing was the Chicago Blues Band, Chicago Blues Boys, something like that. I was in both bands. I got a chance to record with just about all of them.

Bobby "Blue" Bland and Little Junior Parker, that was in '56, '57 in Chicago. Now, this was for Duke and Peacock. Their musical director, Joe Scott, came to Chicago. What happened is Junior Parker was working with Bobby "Blue" Bland at that time and Don Robey sent them to Chicago, and Joe Scott had wrote all the arrangements and they used the Chicago All-Stars. We recorded down at Universal, took us about a week to do them all. It was all our musicians on it 'cause Junior and Bobby came by themselves. They wanted to get a different sound, because at that time we were putting out quite a few hits, like the Spaniels and Jimmy Reed were doing well. Vee-Jay was doing very well.[20]

Now, here's a thing. A lot of them things we were doing business under the table, shit. You know the $41.25, "Man, give me $30 and hell, shit, don't put my name on it." 'Cause a lot of those times we'd be hard up for money, that's the way a lot of record companies would do, they'd catch you when you're hard up for money. What would happen, see, like when you go to the union, the union take out their little—they would charge 4 percent, which don't sound like a lot of money, but when they get through taking out, withholding, social security, shit, you ain't got nothing out of $41.25. So we'd do a lot of sessions for $30. Well, sometimes we'd do them for $40, supposedly no contract, but they'd put your name on it. But I'd do a whole lot of stuff, man. I'd do, like, $35, and $40 was my going price. They say, "Hey, well, we might as well pay you $41.25 and take out the tax." So I'd say, "Okay, give me 35." Some of them I'd say, "Don't use my name." I used to go in as "Sandusky Red." I've been on many a bootleg session.

I worked in Lefty Bates's band, too. See, what was happening, Lefty Bates he was like the house guitar player for Vee-Jay and Chess. He was on all the sessions that require guitar players. Lefty is a good rhythm guitar player and he plays good solos, too, but after you heard his solos a few times, they kinda all sound alike. But he was a good rhythm guitar, man. He played on a lot of Jimmy Reed stuff. You know, on this "*You got me running, you got me hiding,*" Lefty's playing rhythm guitar on that. And you hear this woman that's singing behind Jimmy, that's Jimmy Reed's wife. Because Jimmy couldn't remember the words, so she's whisperin' the words and she's singing 'em too.

I went on a tour with Jimmy Reed for seven weeks in 1958. We went all down in Florida, Miami, North and South Carolina, and all through Illinois. Al Smith had the band. Let me tell you, Jimmy Reed wasn't supposed to be drinking, you see, and he had a habit. You could walk up to him and say, "Hey, I've got a gallon of good moonshine whiskey." And Jimmy would, "Let me taste it." And if it taste alright he would say, "Okay, I'll give you $5 or $10," or whatever, and he'd buy gallons of this stuff. He'd have four or five gallons of this good moonshine. But during this particular time people were dying of alcohol poisoning, like wood alcohol almost. Well, you know, Jimmy Reed would have epileptic fits when he'd drink too much. So we were trying to get Jimmy to stop drinking, and we told Jimmy a dude had bought some of the liquor from the same cat and he died. And Jimmy Reed had four gallons of it! And as we were going down the highway, he was crying and pouring his whiskey out, he was just crying his ass off. "Boy, y'all sure do treat me bad. Y'all don't want me to drink and I can't do nothin.'"

We were playing in a place in Florida. Jimmy Reed was drunk. I mean, he was really what you'd call drunk, drunk, drunk. We hadn't gotten on the stage yet. We couldn't get him to really act like he was gonna play. And like most of the dances in these halls and stuff, this was for a white audience also, you see, like they would usually have the police or the police chief or somebody of the police come by. So, evidently, the promoter had told the police that Jimmy Reed was drunk and they didn't think they could get him on. So he was just gonna come back and see if he could be of any help. But when Jimmy Reed saw the police and Al Smith said, "Jimmy Reed, the man said that you're drunk and that you wasn't going on and he done called the police and they're gonna put your black ass in jail." And when the police came back there Jimmy Reed got sober as a judge, went out and played his ass off. We stayed on stage for about an hour and fifteen minutes. "Boy," I said, "Isn't that something?" So Al said (to the policeman), "Hey, you wanna job? Just stay with us so we can keep this fucker in line." Boy, that Jimmy Reed's a funny dude.

We had seven pieces. Eddie Taylor was there. Well, Eddie Taylor was Jimmy Reed's accompanist, like he's playing rhythm guitar behind Jimmy. We had Pete Hatch on piano; Phil Thomas, drums; Al on bass. We had a trumpet player—I've forgotten his name, he was from out of Texas—and Von Freeman playing alto. We'd play his riffs, like we was playing counter rhythms to what he was playing. But I mean, basically, his rhythms were all the same thing.

What was so funny, I remember Jimmy Reed was driving. He rented a car and he was drunk—this was in Mississippi. We was supposed to appear in town that night—all the signs was out, he was really hot. So Jimmy ran into some dude's car, ran into his fender. Me and Al Smith were with him and Jimmy wouldn't let nobody drive. So when he ran into this cat's fender, this cat jumped out and said, "You black motherfucker, what the fuck you doin'? I'll kick your ass, you cocksucker, get out that car. You drunk, you motherfucker." And so Al Smith jumped out and said, "Oh, man, don't hit him, don't hit him, man. This is Jimmy Reed and I'm trying to take him home and get him to bed. I'll pay for the fender." He said, "That's Jimmy Reed? God damn, sure is, that nigger's . . . Hey, man, look here!" Somebody else was in his car. "Hey, man, Jimmy Reed just hit my car, god damn, shit." So the other cat was trying to straighten the fender out so that he could turn the wheel. "Man, don't fuck with that god damn fender. Jimmy Reed just hit that. Man, don't worry about the motherfuckin' fender, shit, I've got a man who'll fix it. Don't you worry about it. God damn, man, give me your autograph, Jim." Here's this cat's done put at least $50 worth of damage in his fender.

Jimmy Reed got mad one time with us and he wasn't going to appear. "Fuck it, I ain't goin' that gig. Al Smith, I ain't goin' that gig. You just call Mary Lee and tell her I ain't goin' nowhere. Al Smith, hey, Red, you tell Al Smith kiss my ass." So, like, Al was so used to nursing him. So when gig time come we would always try to find Jimmy, see if he's drunk or whatever, and try and sober him up. So we were lookin' for Jimmy all the day and we ain't found him yet. What had happened, Jimmy had gone to the gig to put some strings on his guitar, and somebody had brought some moonshine or something and Jimmy had got drunk in this little dressing room behind the stage. Well, we didn't think about that. Now it's nine o'clock, we gotta play. We usually play a set then come back with Jimmy Reed. But we're not in the dressing room, we just come from the hotel and go right to the stage. So everybody's lookin' for Jimmy Reed. Al says, "Well, listen, Eddie, where is Jimmy's guitar?" Eddie said, "Well, his guitar should be in the dressing room." So Al's getting ready to make an excuse to the people, 'cause we can't find Jimmy, so he says, "Go and set his guitar and shit up, then if he gets here at least his shit'll be set up." And we'd been lookin' all day, and here's Jimmy stretched out in the back there snoring his ass off. Drunk as a motherfucker. He played that night, too, but he was so . . . he went "*You—got—me—walkin', you—got—me—talkin'*—wh-wh-wh what's them other words?" So the audience would say the other words, 'cause they knew his songs just as well as he did. "Yeah, woo-woo, yeah, every whicha-where, let it roll." (*laughs*)

And one time he had a broad that he was fuckin' and this broad was gonna clip him. She thought that he, well, Al Smith would never let him have over $25 or $30. So she caught herself stealing the money from him. She took his pocketbook, but he just had a lot of papers and shit, and I think he had maybe $20 in his pocketbook. So she split and thought that she had some money. And one of the dudes was coming out the street—this was before we'd even played that night. So one of the dudes, she was whoring and he was gonna trick with her. I think it was Phil Thomas, the drummer. He tricked with her and made the bitch high off some reefer and he stole her money! He stole the whole pocketbook. Then when he gets back to the hotel he finds Jimmy Reed's pocketbook in it. Boy, that was really funny as hell. So Jimmy Reed couldn't find his pocketbook. Well, naturally, when Phil found it, he went to Al with it. He said, "Man, look here. I've just ripped an old bitch off and she must have been to Jimmy's room, 'cause I see she had Jimmy's pocketbook in her pocketbook." So Al went and asked Jimmy—well, he didn't say anything about he had the pocketbook, he just asked him, "Hey, what you been doing today, Jimmy?" "Oh, nothin', Al Smith, I've stayed here all day. I've got me some sleep, had me a nice meal, I ain't doin' nothin'. I been here all day." Al said, "Yeah, Jimmy, I know you had a couple of old broads." "No, I didn't have nobody, I been here all day by myself." Al said, "Oh, come on, Jimmy, knowing you I know you've had some bitch." "No, I've been right here all day, just got me some rest." So Al said, "Well, okay, then, whose pocketbook is this?" "What pocketbook? God damn, where'd you get that at?" "From that bitch that you had up here." "Oh, yeah, I forgot about that!" He was really a funny dude.

And, like, he was always, "I'm not gonna do this. All you motherfuckers, y'all fuckin' on me, y'all takin' my money. Al Smith, you a rotten motherfucker, you takin' my money. You and that Red Holloway, you and that Red motherfucker, I know y'all got my money." We said, "Jimmy, shit, you ain't makin' that much motherfuckin' money." 'Cause what would happen, Jimmy would have to pay us. And I think at that time he was makin', oh, $500 a night, which was good money. I think out of the $500 we maybe was gettin' two of it. We wasn't makin' per man about $25 or $30 a night. I think $30 a night. We was working about six nights a week.

Jimmy Reed would always have something to say. There was never a good day. But he was just funny like this, he never meant nobody no harm. I remember one night somebody pulled a pistol on him. He was drunk, he said, "Motherfucker, you ain't gonna shoot nobody. Shit, you know who I am, motherfucker? My name is Jimmy Weeed, fuck you in your ass." So the cat shot up in the ceiling, pow! And Jimmy, "Man, god damn, I was just playin', man, can't you take a joke, shit. Man, you're gonna kill somebody with that motherfuckin' gun." He got sober as a judge, boy. He was a real nice cat, though. I mean basically he was like a Mr. Jekyll and Mr. Hyde. When he was sober he didn't have nothing to say. He was clear-eyed, he was quiet, he was shy as a motherfucker. But when that sucker get him a drink, boy, it was just like having a gorilla in your house. He could do some dumb shit. I mean he never was mad, but he could do some real silly things.

You see, since Al Smith, no one has really taken the time . . . See Jimmy Reed is a monster. Al Smith used to say, "Well, I'm going to fuck with the monster today, boy. I'm going to see what I can do with the gorilla." At that time, drinking, he was really a pain in the ass, really was. Al was his manager. He knew that this was his bread and butter, so he had to stay on in and make him appear and try to stop him getting drunk and stuff like this. But basically Jimmy is a good cat. He's really a nice person.

We would play for whites and blacks, half and half. Because through Texas, Mississippi, places like that, we'd play for the whites and we'd play for the blacks in the same town. But during that time the whites and the blacks wasn't mixin' too well. So they would have one place in the white area, and then we'd go on the other side of town and play for the blacks. Now, the first integrated thing I remember we ever played was in Fort Worth, Texas, in '58. I did another tour with him in '59.

I'd like to hire him for a week, he could probably do some business. People don't just forget Jimmy Reed. And what was such a drag, out of all these years, Al was finally making it big just before he died. A studio was getting ready to do a movie on all of his entertainers, from the "birth of the blues" like thing. He had just signed a contract and he was getting ready to go pick up $100,000. He died one week and he's supposed to go the next week and pick up the money. He had this thing already set up. He was gonna record all his artists, 'cause I'd got the band together and we was gettin' ready to record. Next thing I know, a friend called me, "I don't know if you know, but Al died." I said, "Al who?" He said, "Al Smith." I said, "You got to be kidding."[21]

I joined Lloyd Price in 1961. I went to New York just to visit, and I was staying in this hotel where Lloyd Price's band were staying and I knew most of the cats in the band. So the bandleader had seen me at the Crown Propeller in Chicago and he said, "Hey, man, we need a saxophone player, you gonna be staying here or what?" So I said, "Well, I've just come to check out and see what's happening." So he said, "Well, look, you wanna job?" I said, "Okay, but I have to go back home first." He said, "Well, I'll tell you what. We ain't going out for two weeks." I think they was paying $200 a week, which wasn't much money, but I wasn't makin' nothing at the time. So I said, "Yeah, alright." So I went and joined Lloyd Price.

He was hot with "Stagger Lee" and "Personality." He had his own show, his own band, and his own forty-one-passenger bus. There were fifteen members in his band. He'd make deals with the theaters. He would go into areas that had big theaters, but didn't have nothing going, he'd rent the whole theater. Then he'd put out all the advertising. He had his own record company, Double L, and, like, they would book up maybe a month. Like one time we had Jackie Wilson with us, Erma Franklin, Chuck Berry, quite a few names. I recorded with him. I can't remember how many damn things I recorded, but I'm on quite a few of his albums.[22]

And what was so funny, we'd get on the bandstand, you'd make an introduction, and if he'd come in off-key he'd say, "Ha-ha-ha, pardon me, folks, the band isn't in tune with me tonight!" And here's what would be funny sometimes. We'd be playing and he'd be looking at the audience, and if somebody hit some wrong notes or something, he'd be singing and smiling at the audience, he'd be laughing and we'd be playing "Stagger Lee." He's singing, "Go Stagger Lee, go Stagger Lee," then he'd turn around, "What the fuck's going on back—go Stagger Lee, go Stagger Lee, you motherfucker, go Stagger Lee." Boy, this cat. Then when we'd be through playing, we'd have a meeting. His manager was like a little gangster, his name was (Harold) Logan. "Lloyd, I'll kick their asses. What's up with you motherfuckers, y'all crazy or sumpin'? Y'all gotta be crazy. What we oughta do is we should take one of you motherfuckers out there and whup your ass real good, that's what ya need. Fuck 'em, they don't need no money, them motherfuckers fuck up that music. Don't give 'em shit. Kiss my ass. Sue me, motherfucker." That's the way . . . that type of shit. Boy, it was really something. But a lot of good musicians came out of his band, and there were a lot of good musicians in that band. Wade Marcus, Gill Ashby, he was the band director. Wade Marcus, he was with Motown as their musical director and staff arranger for years. Yusef Lateef was in that band. Joe Henderson, Earl van Dyke, he was the pianist and organ player; Spider Lindsay was the bass player; Bill Jones was the guitar player, he works with Bobby "Blue" Bland. Shakey what's his name. Tommy Perkson, he's working with Bobby. So you got a lot of cats that came through there.

I'd known Jack McDuff a long time, because we had made Wrigley's Spearmint Gum commercials back in Chicago in '56–'57 and I recorded with McDuff while I was with Lloyd Price. I left Lloyd in '63 and I went with Bill Doggett for about three or four months. While I was with Bill Doggett, in fact, I was here in Los Angeles, I heard this record. I said, "God damn, here's a sucker plays just like me!" But this was the record I made with Jack McDuff, which was "Rock Candy," and it was an immediate hit. So they called me and when I got to Columbus, Georgia, with Bill Doggett and I left him and met McDuff in Chicago. I was with him for about two and a half years. We were based in New York. We went to Europe two or three times, Stockholm, Antibes Jazz Festival, Hamburg. We were in Europe that first time about two and a half months and we were really hot. We had George Benson, too. But as usual, sometimes you get greedy, and when you don't pay your men they ain't goin' to stick with you. We used to argue over money all the time. McDuff just didn't really wanna pay a decent salary. So George said, "Fuck it." He quit, 'course he's come a long way since then.

When I was with Lloyd Price I was on a Gene Ammons session, and I always wanted to be on Prestige because Gene was there and we were great friends. So when I cut with McDuff, he was with Prestige, our producer heard the [Gene Ammons] album and wanted to know who the saxophone player was, so he was the one that contacted me about recording. But I had recorded when I was still with Lloyd Price. I had recorded an album for Motown in Detroit. I had a contract with them, but they didn't want to pay. You got, I think it was $180. They didn't want to pay any money until you got your royalties. Well, naturally, the money comes, when you get paid for a session, the money, whoever is the leader or whoever the session is for, they pay all the expenses. That expense comes against their royalties. So rather than pay you whatever that money was, they say when the royalties come out, then we'll pay. To hell with that. So when I got back to New York from that session in Detroit I had a contract from Prestige awaiting me. Since Motown didn't pay me, I called the union and told them I was with Motown. Signed a contract with them and they didn't pay me and I didn't wanna be with them no way. I wanted to be on Prestige. So the union called Motown and they sent me a release and I got on Prestige. The Motown album was never issued. And I recorded maybe four albums while I was with them. I made a string album. Benny Golson wrote a string album for me, and it was something that the manager decided I should record. I think there may have been one or two tunes that I didn't mind recording, that I wanted to, but the rest of them . . . One of them was "Night with Laura in Sweden"! Ha-ha-ha, oh, man, funny, funny. It got good play, I still get some royalties. The first album was *The Burner,* which did very well.

I moved out here to Los Angeles in '67. I came out here with Lloyd in '62 and I had never been west before. What's happened with me as far as this business is

Red Holloway. Los Angeles, October 1975. (Photo Bill Greensmith)

concerned, I'm still trying to . . . What I'm doing right now is I'm writing material for an album, but I haven't had the chance to really finish anything. This club keeps me so . . . Like, you know, everybody wants to reach their full potential before they die, and I don't think I've reached my peak, because I have never been what you'd call a real popular artist. I've worked with everybody, but I've never had any hits of my own. I've been on quite a few of them. And I know everybody, because I've been playing professionally since 1943. But I've never reached that real peak on my own. I've been with everybody else at their peak. I've been at this club, the Parisian Room, since '69 under my own leadership. I really started there in '67. I handle all the salaries and everything. All the owners do is pay for it. I've been out on the road on my own, but not as a star. I've been to a lot of clubs everywhere with my own band, but I never had a big name, so that's what I'm concentrating on now. I've been fortunate, always made a good living, but with me, money doesn't determine that you're a star. In my book it's your creativity and how the people accept you. If you have talent I'd say you're a star, talent that people like. 'Cause I know some stars, shit, playing-wise, they're the worst musicians I've ever met. But to reach a certain height musically you have to know what you're doing.

Regretted? Yeah, gettin' married. That was the worst thing I could ever have done in my life. 'Cause I went through a lot of money with different wives, lawyers, and shit. If I hadn't gotten married . . . A lot of the things I would do, I had to think of my family, of course, so certain steps I would make for myself I wouldn't do because of the fact that I did have a family. So there were certain times I couldn't go out of town because of my family and my wife. Other than that I can't think of anything I regret. I wish I had spent more time than I did practicing and stuff. I wasted a lot of time those first five or ten years. I wasted a lot of time when I could have done more. But when you're young you have to decide are you gonna chase the pussy or are you gonna practice? And I've got six kids, so I don't have to tell you what I chased. I would like to have just one more kid, though, but I don't wanna get married, though. Fuck that. I don't ever, ever again wanna wife. Shit, no. I'm forty-eight years old and I don't regret nothing.

Notes

1. 147 lbs being the welter weight limit.

2. The madam.

3. "Cabbage Head," parts 1 and 2, "Doc" Jo Jo Adams, Aristocrat 803. [Jo Jo Adams died on February 17, 1988.]

4. Dr. Jo Jo Adams recorded twenty-four sides between 1946 and 1953.

5. Possibly Andrew Tibbs.

6. "Ice Cream Freezer," The Blues Man (Roosevelt Sykes), Specialty 508.

7. "Slidin' Home"("Hot Rod Special")/"Beale St. Stomp" ("Chop Chop Boogie"), Al Smith's Progressive Jazz, Meteor 5013. This pairing was apparently brought from Chance Record in Chicago, where it was recorded. Red is confusing two different sessions.

8. Club 51 Records, 527 E. 63rd Street, Chicago, Illinois.

9. United Records was owned by Leonard Allen. Louis "Lew" Simpkins was an A&R man at United up until his death in May 1953.

10. Red had in his possession a photograph of himself and Eddie Ware and a drummer, whom Billy Boy Arnold identified as Billy Stepney.

11. Red was not quite sure if this was indeed Rhythm Willie, although it does seem to be a strong possibility. Also in his possession was a poster from Club Evergreen dated March 14, 1954. Artists listed are Dr. Jo Jo Adams, Red Holloway, and Willie-Rythm [*sic*] Harmonica, among others. Rhythm Willie apparently died sometime in 1954.

12. "Lima Beans," Eddie Ware, Chess 1461.

13. [Danny Overbea died on May 11, 1994.]

14. According to *Blues Records, 1943–1970,* Ivory Joe Hunter's sessions were all recorded in New York City. However, Atlantic Records was known to record its artists while they were on tour in cities other than New York. T-Bone Walker and Big Joe Turner both recorded in Chicago during their tenure at Atlantic Records.

15. Andre Williams.

16. Probably Chink Evans.

17. Eli Toscano, owner of Cobra Records.

18. "Be Mine Alone"/"Sad and Lonesome," Sunnyland Slim, Club 51 106.

19. "Hard Hearted Woman"/"Back Home to Mama," Big Walter, States 145.

20. "Peaches"/"Pretty Little Doll," Little Junior Parker, Duke 177.

21. Al Smith died on February 7, 1974. [Jimmy Reed died on August 29, 1976.]

22. Red Holloway appears on *This Is My Band,* Lloyd Price. Double L Records, DL2301, an album of instrumentals.

Fred Below

Fred Below was the architect of the Chicago backbeat—a seemingly effortless driving beat that incorporated a definite bounce that was all his own, instantly recognizable on the scores of recordings he made during the 1950s and '60s, a period that is considered the golden age of Chicago blues and R&B. His services were in great demand by both record companies and artists. He was Chess Records' first choice for their sessions and can realistically be considered the house drummer. Muddy Waters, Elmore James, Buddy Guy, and Sonny Boy Williamson are just a few of the artists whose sessions were enhanced by Fred Below's presence. But it is perhaps the Little Walter sessions that are most outstanding. From the beginning, it was obvious that Fred and Little Walter had developed an unquestionable affinity. Fred knew instinctively what Little Walter required musically, which surely gave Walter added confidence while redefining harmonica-based blues. He never sounded better.

Recording sessions comprised only a part of Fred Below's resume. He also spent an extended period playing and touring with Little Walter at the height of his popularity and later went on to join the bands of Otis Rush, Memphis Slim, Buddy Guy, and Birdlegs and Pauline, among others. In the 1960s there were tours of Europe with the American Folk Blues Festival and a tour of Africa with Junior Wells for the U.S. State Department.

The early 1970s found him once more reunited with old friends Louis and Dave Myers, and together they reformed the Aces, the group Little Walter had joined upon leaving Muddy Waters in 1952. This unit worked successfully for several years, recording and touring in both Europe and Japan. In the 1980s Fred's health began to decline, and he died in Chicago on August 14, 1988.

—Bill Greensmith

"Below's the Name, Drummin's the Game"

Bill Greensmith

Blues Unlimited #131/132 (Sept./Dec. 1978)

> I was able to play the beat and put something to it that was a lot different. Because the other drummers around were not—they didn't have as much musical experience as I'd had. My musical experience helped me a lot to really play these blues. I could understand a lot more of it than the other guys that just sit up there and play. I changed it slightly because I had to change it to a way that I could feel it.

Du Sable

My dad's been here since 1919. He and my mother got married in 1919. They were staying in New Jersey and they came here to Chicago and taken up residence here in the city. I was born in Chicago on September 6, 1926.

I really didn't get interested in music until I was in high school, Du Sable High School, and that was back about 1940. I used to go to the movies, the Vendome Theater. I used to go there and see a lot of the bands and then to the Regal Theater. The first one I really noticed was Gene Krupa and people like that. I got interested in it because a few of my friends like Johnny Griffin and Billy Green, they were in bands in Du Sable. Yeah, Red Holloway, he went there, too. In fact, quite a few of the top jazz artists around the country went to Du Sable.

So I got in the band and I didn't play any instruments at all, and I first taken up trombone, but me and the trombone didn't get along. Couldn't do nothing with that. Then I picked up the drum, and I always—well, the beats and things like that—I could remember marches and things. And I said, well, maybe I can learn this instru-

Fred Below. Chicago, September 1972.
(Photo Bill Greensmith)

ment. It turned out that this was the instrument for me, because it was very easy to pick up the beats and learn the music part of it. And I think it was the second year of high school I was in the first band. I was about sixteen years old then. I graduated from Du Sable and went to the army.

Just an Army Boy

I was drafted. It wasn't a matter of wanting to go or not, I was eighteen, at the age, and World War Two was on. I was stationed down in Fort McClellan, Alabama, and that's where I met Lester Young, he was down there. So, like, on the weekends we'd go down to the PX or recreation center and we'd set up a little jam session. Lester Young was in special services there. I couldn't get into special services, I was in the infantry. I went overseas, the South Pacific, Manila, all over the Philippines. I was in two years the first time I came out, December 13, 1946.

When I came back in 1946 I still wasn't able to play in any nightclubs, because I still wasn't twenty-one. I had formed a little group while I was here, but the jobs were just not available, I couldn't play in nightclubs where I would have liked to play. At that time they were very, very strict about twenty-one years old. When they put the sign up said "twenty-one," they meant that.

I went to music school while I was here, Roy C. Knapp School of Percussion, downtown. I took an advanced course in drumming and I graduated from there in 1948. But, see, when I came out the army the first time, I was a staff sergeant, but by me staying out that length of time, when I went back in I lost the stripes. So by me losing the stripes they made me a buck sergeant. So when I re-enlisted I went back in for eighteen months, and I thought maybe the music business will pick up when I get out.

I asked for overseas duty. I said I'd like to go to Europe, and at that particular time you could pick what you want. So I went overseas and was stationed in Mannheim, Germany—427 Army Band. I got special service that time. The 427 Army Band was a very special outfit, because it only played for presidents, generals, big staff, congressmen, senators from the States, things like that, nothing but big staff.

And in Mannheim is where I met Horst Lippmann, you know, Lippmann and Rau.[1] At that time, in 1948, Horst was a promoter. Like, at the weekends, he'd come around to the army camps where they had a band and he'd say he had a job for about four or five pieces. "Say, you think you guys could get together an outfit or something that could come around and play some of these German clubs?" I said, "Sure," you make that little extra money. So every week he and I and a few other guys would go to different towns all over Germany. That was really nice, man.

Back in the USA

I came back to the United States in 1951. When I got home the music scene in Chicago had changed completely. When I left, jazz was the thing, no blues. When I came back, it was just blues. And there was an old friend of mine used to play with Muddy Waters, his name was Elgar Edmonds, he used to play the drums. I'd gone around and tried to find some old friends and I'd run into him. I knew Elgar from back in 1946, we both went to the same drum school downtown. Odie Payne, he went there too. I been knowing Odie Payne since 1946, very good friend of mine, too. So when I come home in 1951 the blues was on the scene. I knew nothing about blues, 'cause I'd never played that type of music. I'd always played dance band, jazz, swing, and stuff.

So Elgar was in touch with Louis and Dave Myers and they had a little group and they didn't have any drummer. So he told them that he knew of a fellow that was a good drummer and that maybe they could use me. So Louis called me up on the phone and told me that they had a job at the Brookmount Hotel. So I came on in and sat down and played with them for the first night, but I just couldn't dig what they were playing, it just wasn't there. Now, they could play it, but not me. So when the gig was over that night I said, "I thank you fellows very much for the job, but I just can't cut it. I don't know what to play, I'm gonna have to quit you." So Dave and Louis said, "Man, you play very good drums. Why don't you just learn to play what we're playing?" I said, "Well, I'm willing to learn if you're willing to teach me." So Dave and Louis took the time and showed me how to play what they were playing, which was the blues. I'd say it took me about a month for me to really catch on and get it to swinging good. Once I got it together then we started getting more jobs, the four of us, Junior Wells, David, Louis, and myself.

Exchange of Harp Players

Little Walter had made this record called "Juke" and the record was hittin' off good. Our group was playing very well and we could play everything Muddy was playing. After Walter's record came out he quit Muddy, and Walter needed a band or some group of musicians that was able to play, that he could play with. What happened was an exchange of harp players. Junior Wells went with Muddy, because Muddy was a big name at that particular time. And you couldn't blame Junior for going with Muddy. Little Walter didn't have no group, so Dave and Louis accepted him into our group.

Now, Walter had the record, we didn't have no record. We was able to play. The record was selling pretty good, and Walter got with Billy Shaw Booking Agency and that was it. We started touring all over the United States. Man, we used to play all through the South; big clubs, things like that, auditoriums, stadiums, ballparks, all over the United States. Some tours lasted a year. Left one year in February, come back next February. We had those long tours. We used to bring a Cadillac and a station wagon and drive those cars up and down the highway and just wear 'em out.

What it was at the particular time we were playing with Walter, we were something new—that is, as far as the entertainment field is concerned. But our type of music had been playing throughout the South for many years, but never on a big scale. When we came out we came out big-scale. And we used to play in some of the places all through the South where the whites and the blacks were not mixing. You couldn't mix, not in the South. So what there was, if it would be in a big place, they'd have the whites upstairs and the blacks on the main floor. And some places we played at they'd have a rope stretched in the middle of the place, blacks on one side, white on the other. We played in one place where they mobbed Nat King Cole. Took him off the stage and he said he was never gonna' play down there anymore. That was down in Birmingham, Alabama.[2]

When we started traveling, going to different places opening up new fields, then we had other musicians from Chicago like Muddy Waters start traveling. See, the Little Walter group started traveling before Muddy and a lot of years before Howlin' Wolf. Howlin' Wolf was in the South. And he was playing in East St. Louis in a nightclub down there. And we passed through the town and stopped by the place he was playing and said, "Man, why don't you come on up to Chicago? There's plenty of work up there." So Howlin' Wolf come on up to Chicago and formed his band. And Elmore James, he was traveling around a lot. I made records with Elmore James. Yeah, I knew him. See, at that time, back in '51, '52, I met all the blues artists.

When our group first started, the first big-time job was the Apollo Theater, New York. The first week we had one of the largest crowds they ever had in the theater, we packed 'em in. It wasn't something that they had never seen, they had never seen nothing on the stage. No harmonica, guitar, and drum group had ever really made it, because this is what you call Southern music, down-home music. So we come up to the big time, which was the Apollo Theater, which was big to us and this was the jumping-off place.

Sunday Night at the London Palladium!

And the people in New York, the booking agent wanted to know what the reaction would be from the people in New York. This was '52 and we had a contract, we were supposed to make a European tour. We had thirty-nine days. As soon as we finished at the Apollo we were supposed to get passports, shots, and everything and the first job was going to be the Palladium in London, England.

It was a big job and they were going to send people with us from the office and everything and the money was great. And Walter didn't want to take it. So the guy says, "Man, if you can get the guy to sign the contract, Walter's just nervous, just scared. He's never been out of the country in his life." And evidently he didn't quite understand what was happening. It was quite a big jump from playing in these little juke joints and things. And he refused. The guy offered me five hundred dollars if I could get him just to sign to say he'd go. And I tried. Five hundred dollars sure looked good.

So instead of that, we came back to Chicago to wrap up some jobs. Walter could have gone to Europe in 1952, he didn't go to Europe till very late.[3] He could have been one of the first people to go to Europe. Our records were selling like hotcakes, couldn't put out one fast enough.

Leonard and Phil Chess

A good thing about Leonard and Phil, there were a couple of incidents that happened that you can say that these cats went all out to help.

One time we were traveling on the road in two cars. Walter was in his car and Robert Jr. and I, and Benny, who was the driver, were in a station wagon. Station wagon broke down. Walter and them were ahead of us. They had gotten to the job and didn't know where we were. We had to get off the highway and get to a filling station to get the station wagon fixed. But the filling station wasn't open and we had to stay there all night and wait for it to open. The mechanic went to another town to get the part, bring it back, and fix it.

Alright, I paid for this out of my own pocket. And I didn't know how to get in touch with Walter, because I didn't know where the next job was. This was someplace down in Texas. I don't know where, but we had to drive about two hundred miles to get to Dallas. When we got to Dallas, I went round to Howard Lewis's place. There was a big club there and he was a booking agent, too. He was one of the promoters of the show but I didn't see him, and so I got in touch with Leonard Chess. My money had run out. I'd paid for the car being fixed and the gas to get to Dallas.

So I called Chicago and talked to Leonard and told him the problem. I told him I couldn't leave there to get to the next job, because I'd no money. I think the next job was in Houston. He said, "Now, here's what you do. You go down to the Star Distributing Company down in Dallas." Evidently they had some dealings with Chess. He said, "You talk to the manager and tell him I sent you. Have him call me here and whatever you want he'll give it to you." So I got three hundred dollars to recover my money and get to the next job. Jumped in the car and went on to Houston. When we got to Houston there's Little Walter and them. Walter said, "I figured you'll be here. I wasn't even worried. I knew if you didn't make the job something had happened but you'll be able to handle it."

Fred Below, Louis Myers, Dave Myers. Chicago, May 1974. (Photo Bill Greensmith)

But when the instruments got burned up, oh, man, that was a heck of a thing. We were supposed to leave that day and Robert Jr. come by the house said, "Below, better go down the club, because it's on fire. I've seen the firemen tearing out the windows." That was down on 39th and Indiana, used to be a club down there called the Hollywood. So we got there and all the front's gone and smoke's coming out, and I look on the bandstand and I see a shell, that's where my drums were. Little Walter's amp was all messed up, Robert Jr.'s case and Tucker's amp, guitar, and stuff. So we didn't have no instruments and we had to leave that day.[4]

So we went down to Chess and told Leonard what happened. He got on the phone and told the promoter what had happened and told him we'll be there the day after tomorrow. We had to go to Dallas that time. So what happened, Leonard gave Walter a blank check and told Walter, "Just fill in the amount, whatever you need."

I went out and pick me out a drum set, everybody got instruments. We spent over two thousand dollars. I worked mine out with Leonard, he said, "I tell you what, you just come back and make some recordings for me and I'll deduct that from the recording sessions."

Most of the Cats Down There Was Professional

At this particular time, that's when I was getting plenty of work. By me playing with Little Walter and the records coming out and I'd be around in Chicago. And guys would say, "I sure like that beat. Hey, Below, I've got a session coming up, do you want to come on and play?" I said, "Well, certainly." But the first records I made were back in 1946. I can't think who the fellas were, some guys from California. They were cut in Chicago at Universal, it was a jazz thing.

Leonard started using me on sessions by me being in the band with Walter. And we were able to get along very well, so I was down there all the time. Leonard and Phil were both very easy to get along with. We were able to communicate very well on music, because if there was a certain little thing that Leonard or Phil might want, they would tell it to me and I would try and put it on the drums. Things that you hear on the records, the idea has come from Leonard or Phil Chess.

But the engineer had to be able to record blues to get a blues sound. They had about three different engineers. One of them was Bill Black—Bill Black or Joe Black—he's a very good engineer.[5] And there was a woman, she was an engineer on some sessions. They had certain engineers all the time. They didn't have the same one, but they all had the same idea and the same knowledge of the blues. Like I said before, blues sound will only come if the engineer knows what he's doing.

There was no difficulty recording there at all. See, the main thing is this: if you're recording the same type of music you get into the trend. So when you set down, you know what you've got to do. You just go right ahead and do it and it doesn't take all day. See, most of the cats down there was professional and everybody know what they wanted to do. When they went into the studio they already know what they're gonna do. Before they go into the studio they've already rehearsed it. So when they get there it's no problem. They say, "Okay, Below, give me a nice beat or shuffle," or whatever type of thing they want, and that was it.

Go Back There and Put Some Shit to It!

The "Little Village" thing? Well, you know, on sessions like that it's a relaxed thing. Everybody is just relaxed and that's the main thing. We'd get a little taste in there and we'd be sitting down and they'd say, "Okay, let's play this thing." And this was one particular tune that never did get right, and I don't know how many—well, you've heard the record and you see how many takes we had. The record never did come out until after Sonny Boy was gone. But this was one thing we really had a lot of fun with.

And you see how the rapport was between Sonny Boy and Leonard. Leonard in the booth and Sonny Boy out there, "Oh, go ahead motherfucker this . . ." and all that shit, you know. This was the closeness of the musicians plus the closeness that Chess had with the artists. These are the only two cats, man, Leonard and Phil, they were just like the godfathers of all the blues musicians in the city of Chicago. 'Cause they gave more start to all the black musicians than any other company.

Sonny Boy was no problem, man. I think we could cut Sonny Boy . . . If Sonny Boy would say, "Below, I got about five tunes, man. I want you to go back there and put some shit to it." And I just jump in there and do my little thing. Robert Jr. and Tucker, they were very good guys, we worked together with Little Walter, so it was an easy thing with Sonny Boy. Sonny Boy had a way of playing that was just terrific, man. Sound and the feeling was just different. And we worked many sessions together and we knew just about the feeling—once Sonny Boy got into it. See, he'd run it over a couple of times, say, "Here's what I want, man. Now you pick up on the beat."

So he'd go and sing the song. He'd got the words down on a paper and he'd sing 'em. So Robert Jr. and Tucker would be sitting there listening, and he'd say, "Okay, come on, let's try one." "Don't cut this motherfucker," that's when he's talking to Leonard. So Leonard say, "Okay, okay." So we'd run the tune down. Tune come out alright. Then he'd say, "Okay, now you can cut." Go ahead and cut the tune, bap! Right over—just like that, first take.

Well, a lot of times, say, for instance, we got some words, maybe the words don't fit him, so he'd change the words around for himself, make them up like that. Another time we got a tune maybe we don't have enough words. You have to make up a verse or two, right there on the spur of the moment. That's the way the cat worked.

Muddy offered me a job many years ago, but, see, Elgar Edmonds was playing with Muddy and I was playing with Walter. Elgar was a very good friend of mine and I would not make the change, for no reason whatsoever. And right today Muddy and I are good friends, but I've never worked with him except on recording sessions. Maybe we've played some jobs together or something, but I've never worked with him as a member of his band.

But years ago there was a problem. And that problem was Muddy didn't use his harmonica player nor his drummer on a couple of his records. So when he played a job the tunes didn't sound the same as the records. So the people started complaining about it, because there was no other harp player that played like Walter. So naturally the harp player he had playing with him couldn't come up to where Little Walter was playing. And Elgar didn't play like me, because I had a different style and Elgar had a style.

So after these couple of incidents happened I stopped making records with Muddy Waters. In fact, I didn't make no more records with Muddy for many years. Some of the first records Muddy came out with and one or two later on I made. But I tried to play in such a way that whoever the drummer was would be able to play what I'm playing. It's a difficult thing, because I can always play myself. But somebody else might not be able to understand what I'm trying to do, and it's a little difficult. So naturally when you heard his band, the band never sound like the record. So Little Walter and I stopped playing with Muddy.

But I tell you what, now, there's many guys I enjoyed recording with. Some are easy to work with, some are not. Muddy Waters—very easy to get along with, because he knows what he wants, give it to him he's satisfied. And I'll tell you one thing, I enjoyed playing with Muddy for one reason. Muddy has one of the best sense of timing, more than any other musician I've ever come across. His timing is just perfect, man, I mean perfect. His words come out, he knows what he's gonna sing and he does it. It seems like he's singing like a drummer should be able to play. Sonny Boy

Williamson very easy. Little Walter very easy guy. Sometimes a little difficult, because a lot of the words never . . . if the words don't rhyme, it don't fit the personality. A lot of guys it's just not it.

Dixon wrote quite a bit of the blues tunes and he arranged, too. He did the whole works. He knew all aspects of the music field, plus he was able to play bass and sing too. He played great blues bass. He used to work with the Big Three Trio. They didn't play much blues. They were able to play anything, and they had one of the great piano players at that time, Baby Doo.[6] Man, you talking about players. Them cats could play anything you wanna name. That's what you call that good stompin' stuff—finger poppin'. And they played all that beautiful stuff.

By Willie Dixon having a thorough knowledge of the music, he was able to put his musical knowledge into the blues and produce things. Same thing as myself, by knowing more about different types of music you're able to put more into it, because, you know, there's more places to go, you understand what I'm saying? Because if you only know one thing, then that's all you can do. But if you know something else, then you've got a chance to move around, to experiment. I recorded for Vee-Jay, Artistic, Cobra, but mainly I recorded for Chess and Chess artists. This had nothing to do with Leonard, because I never had any signed contract saying I wasn't allowed to work for anyone else. It was just that at that particular time, working with Little Walter and with us traveling up and down the highways all the time, I wasn't home regular enough to record with a lot of people.

Memphis Slim

I stayed with Walter up till 1955. At that time I'd been working so long . . . Well, Walter had been getting a lot of feedback, because a lot of jobs he didn't make or something was going on and the band wasn't . . . well, we wasn't getting any better and I thought that it was best if I leave and find another group.

So I left Mothers Day 1955. I could see the handwriting on the wall. Instead of getting better jobs, we were staying in the same trend. We wasn't getting any better and we were getting less jobs. So when I did leave, I took a two-week vacation. Went downtown bought me a brand-new car, went down to Florida and had a ball. Just before I had quit Little Walter we'd toured all through Florida and I'd met a lot of nice people and they said, "Please come back," so I said, "Okay."

When I got back to Chicago I'd had a couple of phone calls from Memphis Slim. So later that evening he phones and said, "Are you working with anyone or have you signed up to go with anybody?" I said, "No, I haven't. I've just come back from vacation and I'm not working with anyone now." He said, "Well, I'd like to have you for a drummer. I'll be back in Chicago in two days. I'll be by your house and give you all the particulars. I have a job working at the Squeeze Club on the West Side. And I have some other jobs that I will tell you about when I get back." I said, "Well, okay."

So I went on and worked with him. I think I stayed with Memphis about a year. Matt Murphy was in the army; we had Jody Williams on guitar, Milton Rector on bass, and a woman saxophone player named Burdette, Burt Davis. Played alto sax, played just like Charlie Parker, beautiful. And this was jazz. See, the way it was set up, when Memphis came on the set he played the blues. When the band was on the set we play the jazz. Jody was playing jazz. He's been a good guitar player for many years. He played blues and jazz.

I recorded with Memphis Slim for Vee-Jay.[7] Like I said, I've played with all the blues guys at one time or another, and I have a very extensive blues knowledge, because I've played with all different types and I'm able to adjust myself very quickly to whatever the situation says.

Otis and Buddy

After I left Memphis Slim I was like a freelance drummer. I played with any group that I felt like I wanted to play with. I've played some with John Lee Hooker. Didn't travel with him, just gigs. What I was trying to do was establish myself as a drummer who's able to adapt himself to all situations.

When I got with Otis Rush we had the first band in the city of Chicago to use electric bass. And this guy Willie he come in and played that bass.[8] First it was Louis Myers, myself, and Otis Rush. And when this guy came in and played that rundown guitar sound like a bass. Oh, man, that turned the blues medium just around a little bit. Because before he came on the scene everybody was using two guitars and no bass. Then we got two saxophone players, Jerry Gibson and Donald Hankins. Then we had a big band sound.

I cut a couple of sides with Otis Rush. I don't know what happened to Eli Toscano, he went out of business, got bankrupt or something.[9] I stayed with Otis about eight or nine months, the band broke up, we had a disagreement over money. When the band broke up we all got with Buddy Guy. I met Buddy when he first came to Chicago. And Buddy was a star way before he started making records. Buddy is a very unique guitar player, he can change styles in the middle of the stream any way he wants.

Birdlegs

I played with Buddy a long while and when I quit Buddy I went to Rockford, Illinois. I stayed there a couple of years, played with Birdlegs Shivers. He was a singer and he had a band, nine pieces. I left Chicago in 1959 to live in Rockford and stayed there till 1962 or 1963.

I met Birdlegs. I was going to the theater up on 63rd Street and who should I see, Birdlegs come along, "How you doing Below?" We had a conversation, he said, "I've got a nice gig playing up in Rockford, I'm supposed to open this weekend. We got three nights, I'd sure like to get you on the gig." I said, "How much you paying?" He said, “Forty dollars a night.” I said, “How much?” I said, “Well, look, I’ve got to give Buddy a notice, I can’t just up and quit, because that would not be fair.” He said, “If you know a bass player and a horn player, I could sure use them, too.” I said, “Same kind of money?” He said, “Same kind.”

So when the weekend came I told Buddy, “Buddy, things ain’t working out right, we ain’t got but two nights here.” We was working at Joliet at that time, “So I’m quitting the band to go up to Rockford.” Buddy said, “Okay, then.”

So at that time the man who owned the place we were playing at let the band go. So Donald Hankins, the baritone player, and Frank Perry, the bass player—he’s dead now—come along with me. When I told them about the job everybody was pleased. They said, “What you say?” I said, “Forty dollars a night.” They said, “Okay, let’s go.” So I called Birdlegs and he said he’d have us picked up. And we got Little Murphy on guitar. You know, Matthew Murphy’s got a brother. Well, his brother came with us, Floyd Murphy. Everybody stayed up there, money was good.

The first two weekends the band played we did tremendous business up there. We worked in the white clubs, we didn’t work no black clubs. We played jazz, rock, blues, everything. Floyd was just like Matthew. Both of them are good, great, they just know everything. Birdlegs sang and also his wife, then we had three other girls to back them up, chorus, like taking off on a Ray Charles thing. And it sold, we had a big show.

There was a big ladies’ dress shop in Rockford that used to give his wife, Pauline, her gowns. In fact, every Friday and Saturday when we played downtown in Rockford, Pauline used to go to the shop and they would dress her out. And she’d be decked out, I mean sharp as a tack from head to toe. So when she was standing up there doing her show it was outta sight. So what happened was the people was diggin’ the gowns and that dress shop was getting the business. The band had tuxedos and dinner jackets and all the things.

We had an organ and piano player, some guy out from St. Louis, name Willie Washington or something like that. Two saxes, guitar, bass, drums, bongo player, and the three girls doing the background chorus. I never cut for Chess at this time. I just stayed up there and we were working every night of the week. Sometimes twice on Sundays and Mondays.

AFBF

I got sick and had to come back to Chicago. I had double pneumonia and I stayed in the hospital six months. I came out in 1964. I was rather weak and the people from Europe, Horst Lippmann, wanted me on the American Folk Blues Festival, but I was unable to go because I was too weak. I played here and there but I didn’t join anyone. I did make some recordings but nothing big. I’ve always made recordings here and there all the time, but the main thing was I wasn’t working with no one in particular.

Fred Below, Jimmy Lee Robinson, Snooky Pryor. Chicago, September 1972. (Photo Bill Greensmith)

After I got my strength back Willie Dixon got in touch with me and said that they were getting another American Folk Blues Festival together and the guy was wondering if I would be able to come this time, and I said I would. So before I went to Europe everybody that was going on the show had to meet over at Chess.

But I enjoyed it, it was great. I was not the star of the show, but the people treated me as well as the stars. They gave me a nice welcome every time I came on the stage, and it seemed like the people were just as anxious to see me as they were the stars. And incidentally, on this show was when I first began to wear the beret. After the first performance in Baden-Baden, Memphis Slim was there. Just like old home week, everybody was there.

That was '65. Sixty-six was something else. In '66, I had two shows in Europe. One was the AFBF, which was four weeks, then we had the Alabama Blues Show, and on that show we had six weeks.

I've been to Africa with Junior Wells. Oh, man, that was a trip. I was playing with Buddy and he had to go to Europe on some sort of guitar show. So the State Department got in touch with me and asked me would I like to go. Lefty Dizz and Woody Williams were on that show. That was ten and a half weeks in Africa.

The main countries the Aces have been going to since the late '60s have been France, Germany, Switzerland, and Spain. In '69 I quit Buddy Guy, because we had gotten back together. But I thought if I could get Dave and Louis together as a unit, if we could get that unit over, maybe we would have a chance to do some recording and make a name for ourselves. And we've been going back and forth to Europe about once a year.

The Japanese thing was entirely different. This was the first time that they had anybody playing our type of blues. Our type of blues is a lot different from big band blues. We got four little jive pieces, and this is strictly down-home blues and that's what we play. And the Japanese people just ate it up.

I've enjoyed my musical career and I've had the opportunity to see a lot of the world. Main thing is I haven't seen it all yet.

Notes

1. Lippmann and Rau promoted the American Folk Blues Festival shows in Europe during the 1960s and early '70s.

2. On April 10, 1956, Nat King Cole appeared at the Municipal Auditorium in Birmingham, Alabama. Cole was touring with an integrated ensemble that included his trio, June Cristy, the Ted Heath Orchestra, and the Four Freshmen. Cole was attacked while on stage by five members of the White Citizens Council of Birmingham.

3. Little Walter first toured England in 1964.

4. The fire at the Hollywood was reported in an April 1954 edition of *Cashbox*.

5. Possibly Stu Black.

6. Leonard "Baby Doo" Caston.

7. Memphis Slim recorded two sessions for Vee-Jay Records. Billy Stepney is listed as the drummer on both sessions. Fred Below did record one session with Memphis Slim for United Records.

8. Willie D. Warren.

9. Eli Toscano was the owner of Cobra Records. Fred Below recorded with Otis Rush for both Cobra and Chess Records.

The Old Swing-Masters

Moody Jones, Floyd Jones, and Snooky Pryor

It would be frustrating to try to pinpoint with any accuracy the birth of the "new" Chicago blues on record. All we know is that the honors properly belong to that group of new Maxwell Street artists who recorded either for Bernard Abrahams or for Chester Scales, a North Side record shop owner. Abrahams's releases by Little Walter, Othum Brown, Johnny Young, and Johnny Williams appeared on his own Ora Nelle label from 831 Maxwell Street while Scales's recordings of Snooky Pryor, Moody Jones, and his cousin Floyd appeared on Planet and Marvel, which may or may not have been operated by Scales or Al Benson.

The year would be 1947 or 1948, probably the latter, for Scales's recordings were later reissued on disc jockey Al Benson's Old Swing-Master label, which started up on January 29, 1949. From other interviews it is apparent that Snooky is convinced that he, along with Floyd and Moody, kicked off Chicago's postwar blues; what is known for certain is that the Scales artists were more immediately successful. Snooky and Moody and Floyd had local hits with their releases, and it was their recordings that really ushered in the new style.

This, then, is the story of the "Old Swing-Masters." Interviews with Moody and Floyd were conducted at the apartment of Rev. Moody Jones and his wife, Willie Mae, on Chicago's North Side and with Snooky Pryor at his son's West Side apartment. I was and still am indebted to all of them for their kindness and the gracious way they answered my questions. It's sad to note that Moody died on March 23, 1988; Floyd, on December 19, 1989; and Snooky, on October 18, 2006.

—Mike Rowe

Moody Jones Interview

Mike Rowe

Blues Unlimited #137/138 (Spring 1980)

"Hottest Thing in Town"

Six foot six and massively built, Moody Jones talks disarmingly of his early blues-singing career, occasionally turning for confirmation to Willie Mae, his charming wife, who enjoyed the reminiscences as much as we did, or his cousin Floyd.

Rev. Moody Jones is perhaps the ideal preacher—a man tolerant, kind, and wise who has seen both sides of life and can talk frankly and laughingly of the earlier foolishness and without a trace of bitterness of a musical career that paid off only in experiences.

Now in his seventies, he was born in Earle, Arkansas, on April 8, 1908. Moody looks back on a life which, though very different from now, was still "a wonderful time."

Moody: So my daddy's name was Henry Jones, my mother's name was Hattie Jones . . . and three children, there were three of us—both, all of 'em's dead but me. They passed on, but that's about the size of it . . . I'm the youngest, yeah. My brother, he was nine years older than me, my sister's three years older than me . . . and there was three more, but I didn't know them. They died before any of us was born, so when it come to knowing the family we didn't get to know them. But we come through this knowing one another. We was very attached, but we had to give it up . . . we had to give it up. Yeah, like Floyd says, I was born down in Earle, Arkansas, Mr. Bob White's place. (*laughs*) In other words, a cotton chopper, yeah.

When I left Arkansas I went to a little place called Wolf Island, Missouri, that's out, I think, that's out from Charleston. And I left there and came to East St. Louis, got with a bunch of fellas around there and began to play with them. We had a little group called All Stars, that was years ago, that's probably back in '27, 1927. We had a group called All Stars. We had some home-made instruments, some instruments we bought. I used to play a tub. I used to play a—a gasoline can, made me a—got me a banjo neck and put it on and played a gasoline can. I played the tub, I can play it better than I can a bass fiddle now. Did you ever see a fella play a tub? It sounds like a bass fiddle, don't it, Floyd? Yeah, I could play it just like I play a bass. Old Fiddler, he used to play a mandolin, see, when I was in East St. Louis. He could play it, too. But I just didn't feel that at that time I was good enough and I didn't bother, and I didn't think there was anything to it anyway. But he was really good. We were playing hillbilly all out there, Western songs, hillbilly and Western. We were out there at that time. No blues. We played a few blues, but we was out there to make a buck and we couldn't get nothing much for the blues at that time, so we learned to play everything. Old Fiddler, he used to come around and hear me play the guitar. He'd tell me, "Say, why didn't you come on and play with me, we going uptown and play some?" Oh, no, I'm not that good! He say, "You don't know how good you are," and he'd go away and I just kept on playing, kept on playing, kept on.

No, I didn't know 'em [other musicians in East St. Louis]. I was working, I didn't fool around with music then. I didn't think it was going to amount to so much at that time, so I wasn't interested. I learnt a little so that I would go out and play with some of the fellas, but I worked. I worked in a flour mill, Hollen Mill and Company down there in East St. Louis, from about 1927 to 1931. I used to bleach flour. Then I worked long time on the Mississippi River on a barge. I had something called a barge line—big, great big steamboats. The sugar would come in from Louisiana, from Mobile, and all them places. We'd unload 'em, put 'em on the dock, load them on the next barges come in, ya know. We did that for four, five years. Finally, I made up in my mind to leave from out of there, do a little running around. That's how I got through, running around, had time to set down to learn.

Before I ever had my hands on a guitar, I said, "I can play this thing." And I believe that I could. The first guitar I ever had, my mother bought it for me for $3 and it was busted up and everything. The neck was broken, cracked all around, but I took the thing and one night—I hadn't hardly had my hands on it, because my daddy was a Baptist preacher and he didn't believe in no guitar—and the first night I had it I played every song that I could sing, but this on one string! Just one string with—I didn't have to say, ya know, what the song was. I said, "I can play this thing and I'm going to add some harmony to it." Then I went to play on two strings. I kept on till I got that harmony where I want. I got three strings there. Then I come to add my bass, back tones, all of it. As I said before, I had an old man. He was a schoolteacher. His name was Walter Hassett. He didn't know but three chords and that was C, G, and—yeah, that's all they was. Now, he didn't know how to send off one to another. Now G7—he used to tell me that was "long G." He said, "That's long G, can you remember that?" I said, "Yessir." He said, "Alright, okay, you work on that chord"—now, that's the only three chords he knew. I took them across the country—I went across the country with them, right. Everything with them chords and I got so I could play in G. I started out playing in E, nothing but E, but I got started playing in G. When I started playing good in G, I switched them chords around, went to play in D then, and I completed—I learned to play in D and then I learned how to play in C. And the hardest thing for me to do was to play a lead in E-flat. That was hard for me to play a lead in E-flat on the guitar, but I worked that out, the whole thing. I sat down, if I could make E-flat and play that out, then I could get in all the other keys. I want to see how far could I go, how much could I make, and I worked on that for months and months . . . how much can I make on these B . . . how many chords I can make, how many minors, how many diminishes, how many seventh chords, how many ninths and all of this. I stayed right there, I wouldn't go out. And

I studied bar chords. They call 'em bar chords—for a year, whole year, nothing but that. I stayed in. I played on the side and studied those chords, and after I completed learning them chords, and then believe it or not, it took me a year to get in time, put 'em in place. Oh, man! Put 'em where they belong and get in time, get back to where you was and go to another place.

I started playing after I come to Chicago, in 1938, I believe. I used to play way back long time ago down South, but it was hitting here and there on the guitar, like I told you one time before. I told you that I played a lot of songs, but I was using the same tune! But I got things straightened out and played everything as it was.

See, what makes it hurt your fingers to learn to play a guitar, it simply because you don't understand how it plays. You gonna press harder than you oughta press. You gonna slide harder than you should, but whenever you get used to it . . . this corn here on my hand for forty years, I guess. My fingers is tough and hands—but when you get used to it, your fingers get tough. I learned the hard way. When I was down South, I used to have to pick. I didn't know what a guitar pick was. I didn't have an electric guitar, so when peoples get to hollerin', we had to play hard at them dances, and all around this part of the thumb be a blister. Yeah! Then I had to learn to play with all of my fingers. I had a pick on this finger and a pick on that finger—that was all of it. I make $2 a night, half a pint of whiskey. (*laughs*) It didn't pay off much in money at that time, but it paid off later because it put me where I could be able to stand anyplace where I wanted to go. Big Bill Broonzy and all of 'em used to say—Muddy Waters and all the rest of 'em used to say, "If I could play like that."

'Cause people used to sit and look at me. They say, "You sure put your heart in it, don't you?" Yeah, whenever I'd do anything, my whole heart went into it. If you heard me, you heard all of me, 'cause I got everything, you see? I used to get up at midnight, think about a song, I'd get up at midnight and play it. I didn't want no light on, because I wanted to go out and play without watching my fingers, ya know? I used to get up in the dark house and my wife say, "What you doing?" I'd say, "I'm going to play this guitar," and get up there and play it, too. And then, you see, when you entertaining, people don't want to look at *this* [*crouches over guitar and shows the top of his head*], and if I'm watching my music that's what they see. They want to look at you and see the expression on your face. And see, ya know, a lot of times people just look at you while you're performing, that do something to 'em. One year I studied nothing but the chords and the next year I studied how to get them in. I learned it and after I got through with that, then I went out, people liked it. Then I began to improve. I began to work on it then, because I wanted something to satisfy the people, eliminate so many sad faces. I used to tell my boys sometime, "Look at the people." Everybody got a distressed look on their faces, everybody in trouble, everybody's worried about something. Somebody's blue, somebody's crying—all this. But wherever we go we kept 'em happy. I'd take the bass fiddle, go out with this, I'd lay it down and play and people laughing at it. I used to whistle like a

Ed Newman, bass; John Henry Barbee, guitar; Moody Jones, guitar; James Kindle, banjo. Chicago, 1942.

mockingbird. I'd get out there and whistle, ya know. Probably they weren't looking at me. I'd whistle like a mockingbird and look down at the bass like I thought it was a bird down there (*laughs*)—wonder where that bird *was*? I'd get down under that bass! So we eliminated a lot of sadness, everything, people glad for us—they was even glad if we decided to get on a streetcar and play a tune or anything.

And then when I met old Tommy Stewart, Stovepipe, and, uh, who else was playing with them guys when I started? Jesse Moore and myself. Jesse was a brother-in-law of mine at that time—they tell me lost his mind. He played a tenor banjo—come down to blues he would just hit in there awhile, ya know, but we had it anyway. But Tommy Stewart, Stovepipe—he was a good dancer, too. I come here and they heard me play a couple of times. I was swift then. And they said to me, "Why don't you come on and go out with us tonight?" I said, "I don't care, I believe I will." I went out with them not planning on making anything, ya know, just to get the swing of the band. Man, I got up there with them fellas and we played together till they went to died out. All up and down Madison Street, out at 63rd and Cicero, also we used to go to the Pitchin' Inn—that's way out across Cicero on Roosevelt Road. They had a place called the Pitchin' Inn and they had some pitchers this tall of beer, ya know. The pitchers would hold a quart of beer and you could get 'em for fifteen cents. And we would go out there and play *all* night long, ya know. Pitchin' Inn—we stayed out there for a year playing at that Pitchin' Inn. There weren't so many colored people out there—if you were out there you had to be a musician. And we made plenty money and plenty tips. The tips amount to more than the original pay, because everybody come in would, after they start to having a good time, and everything outside's quiet, say, "Can you play this song for me?" "Yeah, I can play it, throw your $10." Another fella come along, say, "Give him some more," and they take your box up to the bar, say, "Give 'em something." The tips was real heavy, see? We stayed out there a long time. I played 3241 West Madison, say, about two years—3241 West Madison Street—and fooled around. One of the boys got drunk in the place, and the man said, "Well, you're a good fella, but I'm gonna let all of you go and if you can get anybody else, you come back." So I was away about two weeks and I got another fella to play with me and I carried him back. He played accordion—we called it squeeze-box—he really could play. He was a fella from the West Indies. His name was George and he, after playing one night, looked like he had some kind of spell. I don't know, just—I didn't know him good when I got him, but I guess this is the way *he act.* Man, he got up and stopped playing. He throwed his accordion down and walked up to the bar and told the man, "Give me a drink." He went to hitting on the bar, the man gave him a drink, he got drunk, and the second time I was put out of there. I got put out again. I'll tell you exactly what he told me. Ya see, I had played there two years, and after the first guy made things bad for me he got rid of us and told me if I got somebody else come back, and I got this guy and he made things just as bad for me, and you know what the boss told me? "No more colored people," that's what he said. It hurt me, ya know, but because everyone that I get act that way. So I went by and he had another band in there—a Spanish boy—and everyone was acting nice.

We played whatever they ask for, ya see, but they didn't want any blues till after midnight. They say, "Come on, give us some of those low-down blues. Can't you play something low-down?" I say, "Sure, we can play something low-down." We get on, ya know, they turn the lights down low, have a couple of blue lights over you, couple of red lights, and we go ahead and give 'em the blues then. And you know one place on Madison years ago used to be a tavern up east nearby to Canal Street, used to be a big tavern up there and people would have us play. We'd come in at nine o'clock in the night and start playing and we would play until twelve-thirty. Police didn't allow no more music there after that time of night then, back then in the '30s, but, ya know, what they would do? They had a place they had a trapdoor, and when twelve-thirty or one o'clock come they would open up that trapdoor and we'd go down there. There was just as fine a bar down there as there was upstairs. We go down there and play till day, nobody bothers us. Used to make money like that. People would come in, every time somebody would come in the door the bartender would say, "Listen, we got some boys playing here and I want you to buy them a drink right there." He had Coca-Cola in whiskey bottles, the bartender did, ya know. He had a Old Taylor bottle. He had Old Granddad bottle. He had different kind of brandies, good brandies, ya know, the *bottles,* but everything that was in 'em was Coca-Cola and that was for us, that wasn't for nobody else. And so he would say if anybody wanted to buy us some gin he had a Gordon's gin bottle there full of lemon soda, full of lemon soda. Somebody come back there, say, "I want you to buy my band a drink, whatcha all drinking?" Well, I wants Old Taylor, that's $2 a shot—that's good stuff. He say, "Alright, alright." He pour—he get one of those shot glasses, pour each one of us one of them. Bring it back there and set it to us, ya know. We understood the boss, see—this is what he had us to do. He would tell us that just act like he was saving the money for us. We would give him a portion of it, too. That was back in the '30s. So, man, we take a drink of that Coke, we'd know what it was, ya know. Take a little—say, "Aah." (*laughs*) He was laughing at us, say, "What's the matter, boy? Can't you take it? Can't take that stuff, it's so strong—that's good for you. Give it here. No, I want that drink." (*laughs*) And the boys was drinking it. And after everything was over, when everybody went home, we'd be about the last to get paid, he would pay us out our salary. Then he would go back and get a large jar about that tall and it would be full of money. And he would give it to us, see, that's more for him because nobody would get drunk. We didn't have enough to get drunk. If he give us a pint of whiskey apiece or a fifth we wouldn't want it and he would just take a *little* portion of that money. Sometimes he'd pay us off and give us that money, he call it your B-drinks, B-drinks. I don't think they do that now, but that was years ago. But I tell you, we used to make a lot of money at that.

Somebody come in there, policemens come in there and seeing most of them was Irish, ya know, say, "Can you play a Irish song?" Say, "Yessir." We go ahead and play "Wild Irish Rose," "Irish Washerwoman," that's a jig, ya know, that's pretty fast and everybody love to jump about on that. Yeah, all of those songs. Somebody come in, say, "Can you play any Polish numbers?" We'd play a Polish hop, we'd play "Pennsylvania Polka," or we'd play all kinds of polkas. "Beer Barrel Polka" was in prime then, we'd play that. All those kinds of songs, German songs, Italian songs, Spanish songs. Floyd, you remember "Conchita"? We used to play that song. Somebody asked me what was the name of that song and when I told them the name was so long. I'd be singing that song, boy, and it tickled me so bad I couldn't sing it. That was a mess. You know what the name of that song was? "Conchita Marquitta Lolita Pepita Juanita Lopez"! That was the name of the song! (*laughs*) We were playing mostly for white audiences until we started to recording, ya know. That's why we had a certain place we'd go and play the blues, because we know where they liked them really at. But before it was dawn, everybody loved the blues—white and black. That's what made it so good for us. "Give us some blues"—got some real low-down, we'd give 'em that.

The first piano player that I ever played with in Chicago. He was a fella we called him Black Bill. You ever hear of Black Bill? That was his nickname, Black Bill or something? Say, Floyd, was it Black Bob or Black Bill?

Floyd: Bob!

Moody: Yeah, I remember, Black Bob, yeah. But Black Bob was a piano player and he used to give me a lot of trouble, 'cause he really knew his music and they—if you made one wild note he'd stop right there. Didn't care where you was, he'd stop. Sometime I'd be playing along with him—if I made any kind of wild note there he'd stop playing. Didn't care who was there, didn't care what kind of crowd you have—he'd say, "You didn't do that right!" I wanted him to stop saying that so bad, because I wanted (*laughs*) to be a big musician, too! He'd say, "You didn't do that right now! We'll go over it again." I'd say, "Okay," and we'd go over it again. Yeah, sometimes we'd be rehearsing, he'd do it. Sometimes we'd go in a little old side restaurant we had way on Maxwell Street and be rehearsing there—he'd do it. Sometimes we'd be out playing in a *bar.* We'd be very careful, because he'd stop right there and get you right. He want nothing to go wrong. But after I found out he was doing that, I was really going, because I didn't have anything to do in the daytime but work with my guitar, and I would do it—I'd work with the guitar. Anyway, I played with him a long time. He used to get drunk, too! He—some fellas told him come on, get in the car and go for a ride. He got in the car and when he got through he was in Mississippi!

Me and Robert Nighthawk we played a long time together, and we had another guy called Smitty played with us and we had Smitty played the washboard. Me and Robert Nighthawk played guitar and also I played tenor banjo, see? And I carried guitar and banjo with me. Smitty, he carried the washboard. He played drums, too. Robert Nighthawk, he was a nice fella, but his wife, Ann, I think it was—think it was Ann, ya know, she was a singer for us.[1] She'd sing, dance, roll all over the floor dancing. People throwing money, everything, just throwing that money to her! Well, see, whenever somebody give money we would divide the money, everybody split it up equally—just dollar to you, dollar to me, just keep going till we divide it equally. And if there was more than equal money we spend it. So every time they put down a lot of money she goes to the washroom (*laughs*), pick up all the money and she'd have to go to the washroom! I told her, "Now, listen, if you're gonna rake up all the money and go to the washroom I'm gonna have to go with you!" (*laughs*) Have to go with her because something was happening to the money. When we got through playing we wouldn't have so much money. Out of all the money peoples done throwed us, just a little above our salary what we was getting, see? But some of the money would just disappear!

She played washboard and, well, drums, too, but she had a washboard. Later she mostly played drums a little bit, but she'd get up and dance, that's what made them give us so much money, ya know. She'd get up and dance with a little tight dress on, dress around about her waist. Dollars come flying every whichawhere—I guess she felt she had a right to 'em. That's when they were throwing 'em, when she was dancing. (*laughs*)

Me and Robert played a long time together. We played out on Grand Avenue and Harlem—there was a nightclub out there. We played out there a long time. First part of the night I played a tenor banjo, but after twelve o'clock the man come to me and said, "You'll have to get rid of that thing, because it's penetrating. They can hear it all in the neighborhood and they'll close us down." Then I put it in the case, got the guitar, and Robert Nighthawk—he played harmonica, too, also, ya know—and he played harmonica and I played guitar. Sometimes both of us—each would play our guitars. But that was out on Grand and Harlem. We played out there a long time. And then we used to play out on South Chicago Avenue—that's way out south. Then we used to go over Indiana and play over there. We went all around playing, same thing. Robert was a nice fella to play with. He was kinda serious-minded. He didn't carry on too much foolishness or any clowning—he looked like he was just in his music. I think he was just in his music 'cause he wanted to play like he wanted to play it now. Everybody wasn't gonna play with him, because he wanted to play it *right,* but we didn't have no bad feeling, only about the money walking off!

Floyd: Robert Nighthawk made a many sad blues—he had real soul. I know 'cause just two of 'em, no bass, no horns, no nothing. Then after he and Shorty got together they made a lot of gigs, just them two. Shorty, that was his drummer. He sprung out of a window here a few years back—killed himself.

Moody: But we did quite a few things, foolish things, each one of us. We did things that we would know better than to do now, ya know, but we watched everything, and some money went the wrong way. We want to know where did that money go? But now it wouldn't be like that today, because we could understand it. Maybe we would make a better deal, maybe it would come out better entertaining today. But I tell you, I had a full life of entertaining. I loved it and that's what made it what it was to me, because I loved it. 'Cause if I couldn't get an instrument I'd *make* me one and *play* it! Times fella can make one and can't play it. I'd make me one *and* play it. I just couldn't blow a horn, that's all. I always had it in my mind I wanted to play a saxophone when I was young, ya know, but I never could do nothing with it, no wind. I remember one time I had a trumpet and I give the thing away because I couldn't get it to sound! But, boy, that guitar—when I was fourteen years old my mother bought me one for $3 and I went right on from that night, very night she brought it in the house, I went to playing songs on one string, add another string, add another string—that's the way it started.

I remember one time old John Henry [Barbee] and I were playing. I was out on the streets and all I was just playing a boogie, ya know, and he said he wasn't playing, he was just standing there. One-Leg Sam was playing. He told somebody he was talking about how to play. He said, "I can play right with him just how he's playing." So when we finished the number I said, "I heard John say he can play this right with me." I said, "I wished you had the guitar." Sam said, "He can take mine." And I was playing the boogie in E—it's a good place to play it, ya know, for me and when he sat down I started playing the boogie in E-flat and he couldn't get it. He couldn't play in E-flat. He say, "Wait a minute, wait a minute, where you at?" I said, "I ain't done nothing to the guitar." He said, "Well, this guitar ain't tuned to it." I said, "Oh, yeah, that tuned just right." Sam say, "Yes, it is." And he couldn't play—you know why? If you can only play in one key, anybody can come along and show you up if you get outta that key. But I used to go to the taverns down there, I had the different places where the boys were playing. I'd go around and sit in, ya know, just to be clowning around. Get up there just start playing, say, "Where you want me to play?" I say,

"Anywhere, man, just go ahead, take off." I didn't care where they go, 'cause I'd be right there. Floyd, when we played on the street, we went *out there* to playing, but now people waiting for somebody to come along. And you see one person on the street trying to hit some music, he'll come over there, and another man come to see what is he looking at. And there's two people out there and everybody say, "Well what they doing over here, let's go see." And they didn't have to say that when we were out there, because, boy, when we hit the streets . . .

We used to take long breaks then, man, 'cause we were drinking then, man, we take long breaks. They say, "What time y'all be back?" We say, "Oh, about thirty minutes." In thirty minutes they be there waiting, "Man, where y'all been? Y'all been *too* long now."

Yessir! We had old boy used to hang around us all the time. He was a good crowd drawer, too. He's taller than I—you remember the big fella used to pull all the people in the car? He used to put eight men in an automobile, step on the brakes, and he'd pull it!

Floyd: Yeah. Take a horseshoe and break it—break it with his teeth! He—he'd twist it.

Moody: Yeah, he take a nail and drive it through that table top with his hands, just put that nail in his fingers like this. He used to be out there with us a lot of times, too. He was good, he'd draw a crowd, too. He'd stay around us 'cause we really had a crowd.

One fella where we was—I don't know if you were with us that Sunday when that fella came round, gonna eat a stovepipe! Boy, I'm telling you, people sure taken off with him! He had a joint of stovepipe. He had a piece of stovepipe about that long, rusty; he walked up there where we was playing, throwed it down—boom! It made a lot of noise, everybody looked. He said, "Alright watch, watch," just looking at him, everybody, big crowd, he said, "If I get a lot of money down there I'm gonna *eat* this pipe." He picked it up, throwed it down . . . boom! People just throwing money, throwing money. Get out the way. He got a lot of money down there, he got to raking it together, "Ain't enough money yet. I get enough money down there I'm gonna eat that pipe. Right there, ladies and gentlemen, I don't care about it's rusty." And they throwed dollars and dollars and quarters and quarters. He picked 'em all in. He got all that money—we's playing right in front of a tavern, Goldberg's. He say, "Watch the pipe, I'll be right out." (*laughs*) He went in that tavern (*laughs*)—we didn't see him no more! (*laughs*) He didn't come back out that door, he must have went out the back! (*laughs*) People standing there waiting to see him eat that pipe!

Ya see, people they want to see the unusual, they want to see something unusual. I used to stand and look there was a fella used to come out on the street—he—he had a head, a man's head sitting on his car. He used to charge something like a dollar, but he had it sitting up on his car and the eyes do this—just like everybody's eyes would turn, ya know, just like he was looking at somebody. Wasn't nothing but a head! I used to stand there looking at that thing. I say no use me watching, that he's probably got a battery in that thing. Nobody at all, just a head sitting there. And he be just selling medicine.

Little Walter be out there earlier than we would some mornings. He setting up there with a lead guitarist. He played harmonica on the street sometime. I'd be out there playing. I'd be way up the street, he'd hear my electric guitar, ya know. He'd holler up there, "Do that again. You better not do it again, 'cause I'll do it!"

Floyd: He could pick up quick, too, yes, he did. He sure could.

Moody: He could play that harmonica, ya see. Now, he used to work in a laundry in St. Louis, and when he come to Chicago from down there he brought a mike with him. Now, that wasn't his home, but he—I learned he was working in St. Louis in a laundry and he had somebody's microphone. All of a sudden he got ready to leave from there, he hooked up with some of the boys. That's the way he told me, but I know he told me hisself that he was from the South or somewhere down there.

Johnny Shines and I, we used to play together on the streets and in restaurants. Over there on Maxwell Street, Mary Baker's big restaurant used to be over there. Back in the '40s lady named Mary Baker—she was down on Maxwell and Peoria Street. She had a restaurant down there, and what we'd do when we get through playing at night—I played till two o'clock at night and come in then and go to that restaurant and play till day. Sure, me and Johnny Shines used to play down there till day and go out on the streets. He could play and *sing.* He had a good voice.

Ed Newman, he was my bass player, ya know. We used to play everywhere together. We'd get out there on the streets—no difference, we'd play. I'd play his bass and we'd always put on a show, ya know. I'd put on an act. I'd see a fella playing the bass, "He can't play that thing, let me have it." (*laughs*) Get up and run over there and get it and play right on. Other fella, James Kindle, had the banjo—I'd go over, "Give us the banjo." I'd take it up and play it, ya know, then I had my *own* banjo made out of a can and a neck that I had done found. I could play it good as the other thing, ya know. Then I had my tub, some of them was out there trying to play the tub and I'd play it and they wouldn't know it wasn't a bass! If you heard it and didn't see it you'd think it was a bass fiddle. And so that's the way I'd go from just one thing to another.

Boy, I tell you, I put a whole lot of fellas out there. I learned a whole lot of them guys how to play. Taught 'em, sat up all night, go to work next day. I tell you, Floyd, a long time ago, man, we had everything to work with, but we didn't—people didn't do right, did they?

Floyd: We just didn't have the lift.

Moody: They wouldn't do right then. You can get by with anything now, but I couldn't get by with anything. I had the real thing and you had it too, but we couldn't get by with it then. You know the *first* thing the people went to working on us because we had the hottest thing in town. We had the hottest thing in town. Other fellas was going around copying, playing the records and getting our music, getting our basses off our music and everything.

Floyd: Copying our style and then somebody push them and they was gone and we were still standing there.

Moody: But we made the first record we made when the guy brought it back. He brought the dub back or whatever you call that thing. Ya know, as soon as we made it he brought it back, put it on a little speaker out there, man, and peoples gathering all around, they wanted to buy it. He said, "I ain't even—even waxed it yet." Not yet and they was wanting to buy it. That was the "Stockyard Blues" and "Keep What You Got," "Snooky and Moody's Boogie." They was hot then, but *all* of that—I thinks about that now. All that good hard work, that good hard work, man. You remember how we used to rehearse with them things? If it didn't sound right we didn't put it out. Somebody get an idea in their head now—just hit something and go on out there. Man, we worked hard at that stuff.

They used to ask me, "If a record is released today how is it you can play it tonight?" I say because I studied it—that's my job. I'd just hear a record played once or twice and I'd go in the bar and put money in there and play the thing and hear it. And the people used to try and stump us, ya know. The record released today and they'd come out tonight, "Oh, can you play such a thing?" "Sure, we'll play it." Say, "I don't believe they can play it." "We'll play it." We played it! We play it every time. So they want to know how you do it. You see, when I was a boy and learning to play my guitar we didn't have no light like that. The lamp you light it with a match, a coal-oil lamp, and, uh, something I would want to learn and I just couldn't do it and I would put out all the lights and get up in the dark and play it, because I wanted to be so I could play it without looking at my hands. Put out all the lights and I'd start fooling around, then I'd go to playing. I'd say, "That's it," and never forget it, see? And sometimes way between midnight and day, one or two o'clock in the morning, a song would come to me that I had been thinking about and didn't know how to play it. It would come to me in my sleep. I'd wake up, get my guitar, "I'm going to play that now," and I would have the memory that came to me while I was asleep, ya see. Then I would get up and play it and never forget it. So anything they asked for I would get it. I'd go out, play different places, and when we get through or if we get on intermission, people put money in the box, see, so they could have music. We'd be off on fifteen-minute intermission and whatever they be playing, I'd be listening. The fellas be sitting around there talking, looking at women to talk to, drinking going on and I'd be listening. I say, "Uh, I'll play that." They liked that because they putting money in there to play it, so I'm gonna play it! So sometimes I wouldn't play it that night, but when I'd go in the bar next day, ya know, and I'd put money on it, nickel, sometimes a quarter, I'd play up there and listen at it. Next time we'd go in there and they'd ask for a certain number and I'd play it, and then they would give me the money instead of putting it in there! We'd do that and the fellas would look at me! Well, sometimes I'd get mad and wouldn't go to play one. "Ain't you gonna play?" Say, "I don't feel good." They say, "Come on, you ain't got to do nothing much. We got a special number you play with us." I say, "Okay," so we would make it alright, 'cause I wouldn't get mad.

We went up on the North Side one time—way up north here—and they wanted me to go with them for one reason. And that reason is because we make money. They wanted me to go up there because it was no colored neighborhood, see, and they wanted the kind of songs that the people wanted. They wanted Polish songs, Irish songs. They wanted cowboy songs, they wanted hillbilly songs. We carried Snooky with us with harmonica, Sunnyland Slim, Floyd—they was all there—and sometimes we had never seen them people. They barbecued the whole deal and we had everything we wanted to eat, everything they give us. They brought a fifth of whiskey apiece and set it down by each musician. "This is y'all's." Just drink all they wanta and I wouldn't touch it. I wanted to be *right*. I had had my lesson about drinkin' whiskey, ya know, and ruining your job. So I went and played. We didn't have to play long. We made a big sum of money that night.

[In] '48 or '49—we was cutting up around that time. I'm gonna show Mike (Rowe) how this mark [on the guitar] come here. See that? (*laughs*) I had a pickup on here, electric pickup, ya know, that'll make it sound loud. And I was supposed to been playing, but there was a little ole lady there. There was a little ole lady there and I was courtin' her, ya know. And the little ole lady behind the bar I called myself going with her, too. And so this little ole lady out here, she was talking to me and I leaned over like this talking to her, and a big thick mug hit this back here, and by me having a electric pickup on here it sound like somebody shot me . . . boom! I jumped, put the guitar down, and after I seen nothing had happened, oh, man, I got mad! Then I got up. They had one of these bars where you open it like this and go behind and shut the door. I went up there and opened that bar and somebody done grabbed me and I went back here. And she done come out, said, "Don't you come back here, don't you come back here!" I said, "Well, you done hit my new guitar now," and we headed round there fussin'. When she got ready to go home I went with her, didn't I, Floyd? Weren't you with us sitting there? I went with her and she wasn't talking and I was talking, 'cause I was going to beat her up about my guitar. Got up there and got drunk and went to sleep and she could've beat *me* up. I didn't know what happened. But the next day I went on home and the next day I come back they was looking for me. They sitting up there at the bar—they was buddies! I walked to the tavern where they was—24 Club. I'd cooled off a little bit now, because I didn't want the two girls to go. And I looked at them and they looked at me. I didn't say nothing, they didn't say nothing. So they got up and walked out and I sat down with a drink. Later on we talked about it and that ole girl was scared, too! But, boy, that'll tell you. I sure hated that—24 Club, 24 Club . . . I went there one time looking for my girlfriend, say, "I ain't seen her." I said, "Well, has she been here tonight?" "No, she ain't been here." So, okay, I went everywhere. All the taverns I could, looking for that girl and I couldn't find her nowhere. I called and you know where she was,

Floyd? See, Wes and them living in the rear [of the 24 Club] and those two girls was back there asleep! And I wanted to go back there and they wouldn't let me go back there, 'cause they knew somebody gonna get whupped. Probably been *me* gonna get whupped! Just crazy, but we—we come through it all. I can say it was fun.

Do you know Big Bill Hill? Well, he was having a big show at the 5th Avenue Ballroom one time, see, and he invited me over. It was on 5th Avenue and what?

Willie Mae: 5th Avenue, Madison and . . . California.

Moody: Yeah, and you see what he did, he told me he wanted me to appear on his show, ya know. Just like that. He didn't book me or nothing. He wanted me to appear on his show, told me what night it would be. I told him I'd be there. And I got sick and I couldn't go—he never did have no more use for me. I got sick, stayed sick a long time after that, but when he did see me, man, I was playing on Madison Street one night, at least I wasn't playing, I was over there and I think . . . I don't know . . . I believe Muddy Waters's band, yeah, Little Walter and Muddy Waters was over there at that time, and like they usually do, ya know, when a musician in the house they call him up to play a number? Big Bill Hill was sitting there with his girlfriend, so they got up to the mike said, "Ladies and gentlemen, we have a outstanding guitarist in the house. Mr. Moody Jones, we gonna ask him to come to the bandstand." I got up and went up there. Big Bill Hill got up, took his ole lady out of there until I come down from the bandstand. When I come down he come on back in. That's just how he felt about it, see, 'cause he wanted me to play—to be on his show and I got sick.

Dew Drop Inn, 3609 Wentworth, yeah, they used to have contests out there—a contest between Big Bill and . . . it was just a racket.[2] They used to have contests out there, but, see, reason why I say it was a racket among the musicians—everyone in the tavern, they knew who was going to win in the first place. Now, if they set a time for me to win they wouldn't tell everybody that. They put a contestant up there with me and he know he gonna lose, too, but what they was trying to do was entertain the congregation, see? They had Big Bill up there and, uh, somebody . . . Muddy Waters, I think it was . . . they was the contestants. So Little Walter was one of the judges. Little Walter said to me, "Now, listen, I want you to be a judge, but you remember this one thing: I don't care what happens—Big Bill got to be the winner!" (*laughs*) I said, "Okay," so he went around, told all the judges that, ya know. This was to entertain the people who were coming in buying drinks and everything. So Big Bill, that was his day to win, he wins a fifth of Old Taylor. I think $25 like that he won, and the next time they got together and said who was going to be the winner the next time. That's the way it went, ya know. Everybody know who's gonna win, don't matter how good you can do a thing, the other fella just win if they says so. They just played it like that.

Onliest time I seen Memphis Minnie play here was on 47th Street. She used to play over here on . . . what was it?

Willie Mae: Uh, on 47th? Up there—upstairs in the hall—708 East 47th.

Moody: 708 Club—she used to play there. She brought 'em in, too. She had a crowd then. I tell you what, though, she didn't have nobody get up there and play her guitar. She would play till intermission time, come down and have intermissions, and she'd go back. But where we were we didn't care who played, 'cause nobody gonna beat us anyway. If they beat us at one thing we beat them at another, 'cause we had a band. Her husband, Son, he was onliest fella that knew more about chords than—I mean among us lot. Everybody knows more about—I'm talking about us musicians that knew each other. He was only fella that knew more about them chords than I did. And at one time he felt like I knew more. He told me, "You play. I'm gonna watch you." I used to joke Minnie a lot of times, ya know. I used to tell her, I say, "Minnie, why don't you play guitar and stop playing just one string!" (*laughs*) She looked at me and laughed, but what she was doing she could do it.

What's the guy's name, Willie Mae, played organ with his feet? Earl Dranes. Yeah, you remember him? Earl Dranes was a terrible guy.

Willie Mae: Organist, I guess. Pianist, too, but somehow he get all down in the music so good that he start playing with his feet!

Moody: There was one fella over here on Madison Street I never got acquainted with him, but I seen him a lot of times over there. He called hisself Texas Slim. He wore two artificial guns and, like the cowboys, had on his cowboy hat and high-heel boots.

Floyd: I know a piano player, but I didn't never know nothing but King.

Moody: Oh, yeah—little ole King.

Floyd: Little ole King—was a good piano player.

Moody: That's all we know, King. He was playing when we were around there too, King was—little ole short fella. Yeah.

Floyd: L. B. Lawson.

Moody: He's the one who drove the car and is blind, isn't he?

Floyd: Drove two blocks . . .

Moody: Drove it and he's blind. That's a dangerous man to play with! (*laughs*) We used to play out at Argo. He got mad out there one time—everybody getting out of the way 'cause he might start shooting at us! Like Dixon—the fella they call Arvella Gray—me and him used to play lots together. He was on welfare. He couldn't get his check, his worker kept putting him off. He went down there and shot up the place. Boy! They sent him a check! "Mr. Dixon, don't you come down here no more." Everybody was crawling under the table.

I'll tell you something else, ya see. We didn't hardly ever try to find out nobody's names. For twenty years they just knowed me as "Buddy." Nobody knowed my name. Everybody called me Buddy. Later on it went to Texas Slim and "Slim." Nobody knowed my name was Moody until we came to record. I tell you a lot of fellas we didn't know their real names . . .

Floyd: I think I called you on the record, "Alright, Buddy!" "What you call me Buddy for?"

Moody: Yeah, that's right. We playing "Stockyard Blues"—"Alright, Buddy." When we got home I said, "Buddy? Nobody know Buddy."

Me and Johnnie Mae used to play together.[3] We played on Cermak Road. Yeah, ole Johnnie Mae used to love to play with me, 'cause I could clown, ya know. I never did get tired and I was kinda a comedian. I kept my feet patting, couldn't do it playing, do it anyway. I don't know what that place on Cermak Road was called . . .

Willie Mae: I don't know, it's up in a pocket behind some factories or something, I don't know if it's closer to Blue Island . . .

Moody: Johnnie Mae and all of us used to play at Taylor and Paulina, too, Miss Andrews's place. Wallace had the place first over there, had to give it up and Miss Andrews got it. Floyd, what was that place name where we played—did it have a name or was it just Taylor?

Floyd: Taylor and Paulina.

Moody: I was telling Floyd today, I talked to him on the phone, I said, "Well, I'm gonna tell you something, boy. You all gave me a pretty rough deal. I pushed all you fellas out there, put you where you are, gave you your music. All I got was paid for the session. You fellas draw royalties, all that kind of thing." I'd get the session. I can't sing. I can't sing good enough. I fooled around and lost my voice out there in the open air. I used to play electric guitar and, uh, sing without a mike, see? Sometimes it's loud when you get out there in the air and everybody want to hear you. I was just hollerin' and I had good lungs and fooled around. My voice is tore up. That's what old Joe—Joe Brown said. I called his name. (*laughs*) I had some good blues, ya know, and I wanted to sing 'em. I wanted to make the song, ya understand? 'Cause all the boys was coming in there with a song, they wanted to make the record and I told them I had a song. He said, "What is it?" I said, "Rough Treatment." "Well, I'd have to see what it sound like." Well, my voice had done got bad, ya know, and we sung that and he said, "Oh, that won't go no-how." I said, "Well, why don't you record it?" "No, no, not that." Before I knew anything he done—he had it on tape and Little Hudson recorded it. "Rough Treatment"—my number.

He didn't sing it like it was, ya know, but he got some of the words—or most of the words. He just went out and hollered like he wanted to. I had a kind of South American number I wanted to do for ole Joe Brown, and he didn't act right and I kept it, too. A kind of Latin number, ya know, a Latin beat to it and everything.[4] But still and all he didn't have it as I sung it. They changed it a little bit. They kept the title. They changed it a bit. Because way back I had heard, I had heard the title before. Curtis Jones, Curtis Jones, way back when I was a boy—he sang "Rough Treatment," and I think he the one had the song the "Bedroom Blues."[5] Yeah, but at that time I figured I'd put a little addition to it.

I don't know if I was there when he [Floyd] sang that ["On the Road Again"]. Well, see, because I got my leg broke and Floyd made "Dark Road." I had a cast on my foot up to here and I couldn't sit down. And so I had to play the bass. We went all the way up to the studio and I didn't have the bass with me, and Will let me have his bass and

Moody Jones, 1950s.

I played bass on “Dark Road.” I might be playing on quite a few records and people have never heard of me at all. I played on 'em. We taped many things at home, in different places. Floyd, which one of them records did I play the bass on?

Floyd: “On the Road Again.” You wasn't on “Dark Road.”

Moody: I had planned on going—going out and getting me a big band, but I finally changed my mind when Little Walter made his first record—his first good record, “Juke.” When he made “Juke” he had a old raggedy Hudson car, ya know. I was pretty hotheaded at that time. He said to me, “If this record do good I want you to go on the road with me,” and then before I could say anything he said, “Oh, but you're too crazy about Chicago. You ain't gonna leave here. I'll have to get me somebody else.” And I got hot right there. I said, “Well, you get somebody else.” And so I didn't go with him, but he did get somebody. But fellas told me they couldn't hardly get back home. Put their clothes in the cleaners down South somewhere and they weren't able to get them out, 'cause Walter wouldn't give them no money. But I tell you, when he put out that record he did good.

Floyd: Yeah, that fella was something else.

Moody: Yeah, Walter, too bad . . . all those fellas. Well, I guess everybody ended up different. Surprising thing what a man will do coming through life. He'll pass up a lot of opportunities. It takes a real smart man to think of everything to do—to think the right thing, to make the right decision. But, ya know, after I got old and looked back at it, we didn't get so much out of it as we should have. Could have made a lot of good records, ya know, and put 'em out. Well, I missed one great chance because people I talked with. I had a fellow come from Whiting, Indiana, saw me playing on Maxwell Street over there with a band. He wanted me—he wanted to put me in a big band, see, because he liked the chords I made, and he says, “Why don't you come and let me take you over there to the band?” Say, “I'll show what I'm gonna do.” I said, “Where do you live?” He said, “Whiting, Indiana.” So I say to him—it's on Sunday—I said, "Well, I can't go today, you come here next Sunday and I'll go with you." Sure enough, I thought he was jiving me, he come back the next Sunday. He said, "You going with me today? I tell you, you make orchestra chords and I like that, see, 'cause I've got a big band. I'll put you in. You won't have nothing else to worry about." Then the fellas got around say, "You liable to be trying to fool you or somebody kill you, man, you better stay here." They outtalk me, 'cause they didn't want me to go, ya know. So finally, that was the second time that he was over there, so I said, "Well, you come back next Sunday," *and he come back the next Sunday.* Then I got drunk. I was gonna go that time and I went around to divide the money and the fellas went and got a whole quart of whiskey and we drinked it. Before I know anything it was one o'clock at night. So, you see, I flunked that chance and mostly by listening to other fellas, all of 'em say, "Oh, don't go nowhere with them people, you never seen 'em before. They might take you out and kill you, anything." If I hadn't been thinking like I'm thinking now, ya see, I'd still probably be retired now with a big bank account, big bank roll up there and everything ready to do like Duke Ellington. I did a whole lot of hard work for nothing, and I missed a whole lot of good chances sometimes through not trusting. Sometimes you're afraid to just step on out, ya see, and then by the time you've got ready to step out everything's passed.

See, it takes a real man, takes a thinking man to do that, and some kind of man can see where he made just one, one little wrong step that'll affect him all the way, and then sometime if a man makes the right decision at the right moment, he's got it made from that time on. Just like the prizefighters—they don't have time to make a decision until it's all over. When it's all over he end up broke, he end up sick, end up all knotted up, beat up, and everything. No money, 'cause he haven't got time . . . he young and restless. Me and Floyd Jones used to play *all* night, say, "Ain't you going to bed?" "No!" "Let's go out—go out to . . ." Oh, I remember one morning Sunnyland Slim, Rice Miller, what called himself Sonny Boy Williamson, all of us had been out all night—we had played until the tavern closed. Then we went by Sunnyland's house. We balled over there till day. Say, "Let's go to the Zanzibar over there where Wolf is." Ole Wolf was over there. We went over there. Wolf had us to play some. We got up there and played. Rice Miller was on the harmonica. Ole Rice Miller got hincty, "I'm not gonna play unless you get me some Old Taylor." He wanted Old Taylor—eighty-six proof. Laid his harmonica down, said, "Carry it right there. I want one hundred proof less I won't play." (*laughs*)

Floyd: I can remember the exact words he said, "I don't drink milk. I want whiskey—one hundred proof."

Moody: He can't help it now. Now, you know where the Zanzibar was? I'm gonna show you what a man runs into when he's going through life. Now, we were there drinking, getting drunk, playing the blues, having a good time. We didn't know what was gonna happen later, but I've stood right there where Rice Miller wouldn't accept that whiskey. I have stood right there on that spot and preached. Now, that Zanzibar was taken away and there was a church put there, and I had done quit playing music and I was a preacher. And I told them, I said, "Right here where I'm standing I have played music in here, I've played the blues in here." Now I'm on the other side of life. I want to be a champion just like I was on that side. I strictly had a good time, though. Just crazy, but we—we come through it all. I can say it was fun. Then I met a real sweet wife—I met a real sweet wife after running around. But I tell you it took a whole lot to bring me down to the Lord, because I really—I didn't love nothing but the music and that's all I had in my mind. Now I can't play anymore.

Willie Mae: We met—I think Floyd's brother and my cousin is the cause of us meeting. They set up a blind date.

Moody: Kept telling me, "Come and take my cousin out tonight." I said, "I ain't studying about your cousin." "She's nice." "Who cares how nice she is, I'm tired. I'm going home." Finally, they kept begging me until they got me to go. I went out with 'em that night, and, uh, they put her up in the front seat with me. I used to have a little black car, used to keep it shined all the time. They used to say, "Here come Grand Daddy," when they see that car coming, boy. But, ya see, I took her out and she wouldn't talk to me, see! We went to the tavern where Muddy Waters was playing, 3609 Wentworth. That's the time he told me—he called me to play. He said, "Ladies and gentlemen, we've got an outstanding guitarist in the house. We're gonna ask him to come up and do a number for us, so let's give him a big hand—Mr. Moody Jones." I got up and she wouldn't talk to me. So I went up, Muddy Waters handed me his guitar, he said, "Don't fool with that slide!" So, okay, I played a boogie and I played a blues, and when I come down she wouldn't talk to me. So some little ole girls come in—two of the most cute girls come in and said to me, "Hey, Moody, don't you remember us?" I said, "No." Said, "Don't you remember us from the Hi Hat?" I said, "Oh, yeah!" They said, "Come over here and have a drink with us." And I went over there and, man, she had never talked to me, but you could see her there and so I had a drink with them girls, and I came over there and she liked to talk me to death then! Hi Hat was on Madison Street.

Willie Mae: It was 22-something West Madison.

Moody: I played there a long time, long time and, well, now, I keeps forgetting that guy's name up there. Elmore James was playing up on—that's what I'm talking about, Sylvio's. Uh-huh, I was playing one place, Elmore James was playing at the next place up. That was back in the early '50s.

Now, I didn't quit playing music when we got together. Many times she used to be real angry with me because I wasn't home, but I wasn't doing anything but playing music, and sometimes she'd come out where I was playing music and I'd get her a table. So we went to the Cotton Club. See, on nights when I wasn't playing I'd go round the clubs and have a good time. I had all the nights I wanted to. The Cotton Club's on the North Side—I think it's on Bryan or Wheel something . . .

Willie Mae: On Wheel, I think . . .

Moody: Yeah, right off Clark. It's tore down now. But I told her to get up there on that table and she did just what I told her. We had a line of tables lined up, ya know, just brought the tables together so we could have a party, and she got on that table and walked from one end to the other, stepped on folks' whiskey, about to fall, drunk and everything . . .

Willie Mae: Just clowning! (*laughs*)

Moody: We went to Muskegon Heights. Did you ever know a fella by the name Frank—was it Frank Smith? He was a harmonica player, oh, this is way back in the '50s. I thought it was Frank Smith.[6] I don't know, but he was a real dark fella with a gold tooth in his mouth, and he played harmonica. He called hisself a great blues singer. He just played around with the fellas on the streets like that. But he went everywhere, traveled around. Me and Little Walter would run into him on the street—great harmonica blower and singer, too. I don't think Frank recorded, because he was around the streets all the time. He was a pretty good harmonica player, but he did a lot of hollerin'. He was dark, eyes kinda red, he had a gold tooth in his mouth, and he be out there just hollerin' and blowing that harp. He made a lot of money doing it. He went with us up in Michigan, Muskegon Heights, Michigan, and I think all of us had to sleep in one room, about six of us—all of us. (*laughs*) It was terrible. The whole band and the band's wives, everybody sleeping in one room. He was the only one had no wife. (*laughs*) He was the onliest one didn't have no wife, and we (*laughs*) all got to sleep in one room and everybody who had a wife was watching Frank.

Didn't nobody want to go out get nothing! (*laughs*) Old Frank was around singing to all the women and didn't nobody want to go out to get nothing! Frank was onliest one didn't have no wife. Me and Frank and Sunnyland and, uh, let's see, who was the fourth boy with us? I think there was four of us that night. Anyway, that was a kinda funny thing to me, it tickled me. The next day daylight come, we had to stay there a couple of days and when, ya know, daylight come, people got to going about everywhere and everybody's carrying their wife with them! Frank wasn't carrying nobody. Everybody slept in the same room. Frank say, "I'm gonna stay here and sleep," and wasn't nobody going nowhere except they carried their wife with them. That was the funny thing. They wouldn't take no chances with Frank, 'cause he's too crazy about the women, he was. They weren't leaving their wife with Frank!

Downstairs was a restaurant, but they had us upstairs in a place that wasn't so large. It had a low ceiling. It was a restaurant downstairs and a bar. They had a small place upstairs and that's where they had us playing. And I tell you, it made me sick, because the ceiling was real low and you didn't need my electric guitar then. And we had an electric guitar and, man, the thing was so loud you couldn't hear nothing, and an electric guitar can be real miserable, I'm telling you, in a small place. And everybody wanted to be heard. And a harmonica up there with a mike to it, ya know, and people—I'm kinda sensitive about playing, ya know, because I know all there is to music is time and tune—you ain't got to—it's not loud. Music is not loud in a place like that. Ugly ole place. You say, "Well, let's play mellow in here, we don't need it loud!" And everybody get a little louder, wants somebody to hear him, ya know, and the other fella he'll be playing along, he'll look, he'll leap down there, he'll turn his knob up a little bit, he'll go back to playing. He's not loud enough, you see him turn his guitar up a little bit and he rush back there! But if everybody *toned* down it'd be alright. We had a little low place up there give me a headache. Sometimes you see people sitting all along the bar doing this [*puts hands over ears*] and you know you can't order a drink when it's so loud.

We used to play one place over there at Vi's Lounge. They were playing over there for a long time then Floyd and them got me in with them. So I said, "Let's get back here and play mellow and see what happens." So, okay, and I said, "Now, don't nobody play louder than I'm playing. I'm not gonna drown you out, let's not play so loud." And we getting on alright and everybody said, "That's so nice—this is nice music tonight." And after a while somebody slipped back there and turned the thing up and couldn't nobody hear nobody but me and him. The other would turn it up and then you hear both of them loud. 'Cause I never did like that—be too loud anyway.

There was more fun on the way back from Muskegon Heights.

Moody: Sunnyland Slim tickled me. I think we was up there three or four days playing up there, ya know, and on the way back almost had an accident because everybody telling funny jokes. He was a terrible joker, ya know, and we was almost to have an accident because the driver was laughing. We was hollerin' and laughin' and our eyes was full of water and when we did get 'em cleared and settled down, ya know. There was a man up there waving us down. Radar! He done caught us doing seventy miles per hour and he want to lock us all up. Sunnyland Slim used to have a knot on his head, see. He don't have it anymore. He had it removed—and anytime somebody would get him in a tight place he would feel that knot, ya know. So I said, "No use feeling that knot now! We got to do something to get away from here." The man wouldn't let nobody go. He says, "I wasn't going too fast." Didn't even have a speedometer on the car. The thing was broke so we couldn't tell how fast we were going. So there we was again. Man, we had a terrible time looking miserable!

Moody recalled one of the clubs and the lady who owned it.

Moody: She used to get high every night. She was sitting back there and she get high and give the stuff away and everything. We played there a long time, me and Floyd Jones and Shakey Head Walter . . . and little ole Willie Foster—he used to act so bad! He just get up there and say everything to everybody, just cut up. I'd say, "Boy, you better stop that."

Willie Mae: 'Cause I used to know him when he was in his prime, ya know, and he knew everybody and had a family. He was very nasty.

Moody: I used to have trouble with some of the boys who was playing with me, 'cause drinking did something to 'em, you know. Drinking changes a lot of people. Some people can't contain it, see? I used to drink so much that I couldn't stand up, but I just be having fun, see? But other fellas sometimes—I went to a place on Madison Street where the boys was playing and I just went by to visit that night and they said, "Sit down over there, Moody, you ain't got to go home." I said, "Okay, I'll sit down." I sat down. They brought me a table close to where they were playing, and I sat there and they just kept putting brandy up there and I just kept drinkin'. Wasn't even bothering me. I was just sitting there drinking and when they got ready to go home I couldn't get up!

The favorite drinking story must be when Moody first invited Willie Mae to hear him play.

Moody: On North Wells Street, 876, ah, we'd played, we had been playing over there for quite awhile and the fellas crazy about our music. Peoples was so crazy about what I was doing all of 'em wanted to give me a drink. Everybody see me, "Come over here and drink with us," and so I just tried to drink with everybody, be friendly with everybody, ya know. Everybody'd come along, "Tell the tall guy to come over here." Some of 'em didn't even know me and I'd go over there and take a drink. Finally ended up flopped over my guitar, laying there asleep and they couldn't wake me up. And so the boss saw I was so full of mash they couldn't wake me up. And so the boss saw 'em trying to wake me up. The fellas come around from behind the bar, he said, "Let him alone, don't wake him up. Let him sleep. Let him sleep. When he wakes up he's fired!" (*laughs*) And so they let me sleep, and at two o'clock when it was all over with, the man said, "Let me see, you bought half a pint of whiskey here on credit. I'm taking that out. Here's the rest of your money, don't come back." I said, "What did I do?" He said, "You didn't do anything. That's the reason I'm paying you off and letting you go. Other men playing, you sitting there asleep. You didn't do anything!" Me and Sunnyland Slim and Floyd—we might have had a drummer, too. I forgot who he was.

Willie Mae: I wasn't there. I went home! Brought my sister, my brother, and my sister-in-law—a car full. That was the first time, because they didn't usually go out to play, but they wanted to hear him and he was asleep. They didn't hear him play nothing—not a thing! He leaned over his guitar all the night like that. He didn't play nothing, so they still didn't hear him play!

Moody: Yeah, but I begin to think about that thing, I begin to think. I said, "I'm gonna *stop* drinking." And I would stop drinking for a while and some of the fellas would come along. You ever tried to stop drinking then you don't have to buy anymore—they'll buy it for you! "Oh, come on, man, come on, man, you chicken?" Say, "Yeah." So I started back to drinking. So one time I stopped drinking and we playing on Maxwell Street and some people came from Gary, Indiana, and there was about two hundred people around us on Maxwell, just far as you could see around, and all of 'em liked what we was doing. They was throwing money everywhere and we had two or three cigar boxes of money there. And so one fella said, "What do you drink?" I'm about half drunk, I said, "*Anything.*" He went there and bought a fifth of Old Taylor and brought it out there and give it to me and all. Man, the sun was hot. Really, I didn't intend to do, but I got to drinking that Old Taylor. He said,

"Drink all you want," and you know how some people do when you give something to them and say, "drink all you wanta." Say, "Well, I better load up right here," and when I knew anything, really, I had got drunk *that* time and they done carried me over the street. My bass fiddle player, Ed Newman, he lived over there on Peoria. He lived at 1308 Peoria Street. And another thing, I woke up in his house. I guess it's about three o'clock in the evening when they carry me, probably, but I woke up at his house about one-thirty in the morning. I said, "What am I doing here? Where am I at?" He said, "Well, you got drunk. We had to bring you in." He said, "You ought to be 'shamed, everybody looking at you carried you off the street!" (*laughs*) Then I was '*shamed.* I said, "I'm gonna quit." And I quit. That's one of the things that put me against drinking—especially when you work. There's men who can take a drink at suppertime, a shot, and go to bed. I couldn't do that. If I start drinking it was half a pint, it was a pint, it was a fifth and then, ya see, I know that wasn't a right thing. Anything that can rule you, let it go. That's the way I figured. Some men could rule it and I couldn't. So I let it alone.

What a life! Still we were blessed, because we came through it without hurt. I only got put in jail one time and I never was a criminal, see, but one time my brother got in trouble, and ran off and they couldn't find him. And they felt like I knew where he was and I did not. But they came and picked me up early one Sunday morning, locked me up. "You wanna tell us where your brother is?" "I don't know where he is." They knew me from playing on the streets, so, "I tell you one thing—it gonna be a long time before you play your ole guitar anymore on the streets." They kept me about a week and a half and couldn't find him. My boss called up and they told him, "Tend to your business, 'cause we're gonna tend to this, we don't have to let him go." Boss said, "Book him so he can get out." Said, "No, we can move him from station to station, we don't have to book him." So finally they let me go. For $30 they let me go.

I got songs here now, right now, that I wrote back in the '50s before I quit playing. I never recorded them. I never sang them, never copyrighted them or anything. And then I got me a religious group. See, I stepped across the fence from the other side. I had a Christian group. I'm a minister now. When you put all your—the old folk say, "When you put all your eggs in one basket you can get a basket *full*." So I don't try to do too many things at once. If I'm jack-of-all-trades, I'm good at none, ya see?

Now, if I were going to play the blues, I'd just be honest and say so, just like you, Floyd—you'd be an honest man. And the good part, the blessing about it is because every man should feel free to do what he wants to do. No one has the right to criticize a man for what he wants to do. People have crazy ideas. But you know it's better for a man to work than to steal, and for a musician, a professional, he's working. And if everybody did the same thing, this would be a crazy world. If everybody just played church songs—what you gonna do with the fella don't go to church? What you gonna do with the fella don't even believe? What if everybody played the blues? You couldn't do nothing with that. With the human race—every one of us is different. We may be made like our body, but, now, our mind, there's no two men that has exactly the same mind, the same thoughts, believe in the same things. So this what makes it a great world, for if a person come to church and hear a good sermon, he might say, "Well, I'm going down here now. I done heard a good sermon and enjoyed myself. Now, I'm going down here and hear Floyd and them play something. I wanta hear those blues." What's wrong with that? We got to have variety of things, and you be going to eat, you don't just go in there get you a big piece of meat, eat all of that and say, "I've had my dinner." But you have some meat, some bread, some syrup, some desserts or some pie or some cake—it takes all this to make up a meal. Ain't that right? It [takes] all that to make up a meal, so I'm saying that it takes all of this to make up our world as a whole. If was no musicians, the world's in a bad fix. If there was no church, world's in a bad fix. Because God has fixed it so that every man can have what he want. It's up to that man, every man has the decision, he may change from this to that. Nobody told me to stop playing. Nobody told me to get in church, but I was raised up in church and this was real to me. I came of my own accord. All the fellas said, "Oh, he'll be right back out here next week." I didn't criticize them and don't do it now. But, brother, I'm happy like this and one fella told me—and I was broke then like I am now—one fella told me, "You could make $200 a week." And I said, "Well, I'm not going anyway. I've retired now." So we had a wonderful time.

Moody Jones. Chicago, May 1975. (Photo Bill Greensmith)

Notes

Interview with Moody Jones conducted September 1973, September 1974, and September 1978. Interview with Floyd and Moody Jones conducted September 1973 and September 1974.

1. This is almost certainly Ann Sortier (Amanda Sortier/Porter?), who recorded with Robert Nighthawk for Decca in 1940 and later on her own account for the Chicago label as Ann Sorter McCoy, "Tell It to the O.P.A."(Chicago 101).

2. Moody meant Big Bill Broonzy.

3. Johnnie Mae Dunson.

4. Moody actually auditioned three songs, "Rough Treatment," "Why Should I Worry," and "Please Somebody," on April 28, 1952. All were issued on Flyright's JOB series.

5. Bumble Bee Slim recorded "Rough Treatment" (Vocalion 03637) in 1936. I don't know of a Curtis Jones version. However, Moody's song, apart from the chorus, is different from Slim's and, to be fair, so is Little Hudson's version (JOB 1015) from August 1953.

6. This is presumably the mysterious "Black Frank," recalled by Otis Spann as a harp player who sometimes played with Muddy Waters.

Floyd Jones Interview

Mike Rowe

Blues Unlimited #137/138 (Spring 1980)

Floyd Jones was born in Marianna, Arkansas, July 17, 1917. His father, Robert, and Moody's father, Henry, were brothers, but Floyd didn't meet up with his cousin until the '40s in Chicago. Floyd kept a day job for much of his playing career in Chicago, but never gave up music and in retirement, devoted his whole time to playing the blues.

He got his start when he met Howling Wolf while Floyd was driving a truck for the Nat Phillips plantation near Twist, Arkansas, and Wolf was a semi-professional musician.

Floyd: When did I leave home? In '33. I left with Wolf in 1933. I was living just across from this Twist brothers at the place they call Nat Phillips's farm. So that's where I left from. We went all through Arkansas, Texas, Oklahoma, back around through the low part of Arkansas, then back up through Louisiana, Mississippi. Well, Mississippi is where Wolf was—his home, but he moved around there close around me in 1932. And we was living on the same farm. I started—I played my first dance 4th of July 1933—on Twist brothers . . . forty-two sections of land in one block. Yeah, they did have a farm! And they had a big, what you call boardinghouse—they done had a lot of day workers, a lot of day hands. They had a great big boardinghouse with two stories and then a lot of the different sections had small boardinghouses . . . Twist, Arkansas. I played up there, ya know, off and on. Yeah, still there—all of the older heads are dead, but I think it's only one of the younger fellas are living, but he's got it.

I was singing, uh, "Roll and Tumble" and what I heard, ya know, just like, uh, now, my mother wrote a number way back and, uh, I sung that a few times. Now that, well, she had a title "Overseas Blues" and it was . . . uh, I done forgot this lady made it a long way after then, but she says: *"My mother's dead, papa's across the sea. Ain't got nobody in the world to live and care for me."* Well, now, my mother wrote that in the year I was born, that's fifty-six years ago. Yeah, she played piano, she played bass, she played drums, she played . . . well, it wasn't no bass guitar then, it was just regular and then a fiddle. Well, she played most of them, but she was better on piano—she taught piano. My father didn't play, no, just my mother and her brothers. She had two brothers was musicians. Minnie Bishop was her maiden name, had a brother named Sam Bishop and one named Joe Bishop, but, see, they didn't get to do no recording or nothing back in that time. But they had a jug band way back, ya know, in Arkansas. She was one of the top rally dancers back way in her time, one of the *top.* Then when the Charleston came out she would do the Black Bottom, two-step, all that, see, right along in there. Around Marianna, yeah, Helena, all through Arkansas.

Eddie Taylor and Floyd Jones. Chicago, mid-1950s.

Some of the fellas was never known. There was a fella Lossie Chatman—he never did get to make no numbers or nothing, but he was a good guitar player. He only—he got burned when he was a kid—he only had two fingers on that hand, but he could lead—he could really lead. He played with Wolf a long time . . . sure did. This is still in Arkansas, Phillips—Nat Phillips and, uh, then there was an older man, Tom Foulks, George Foulks and all them fellas I know I imagine is dead now. Tommy Johnson, I saw him, yeah . . . Jim Jackson . . . then there was a fella I done forgotten his last name, but his name was Ted something, he was a good guitar player. He played like Otis Rush with his left hand. He was down around 96 Corner, they call it—that was out from Hughes.

Could you make a living by playing music then, or did you have to work as well?

Floyd: Well, put it this way. It was tough doing 'em both, ya know, and there wasn't much money around, it wasn't much money around. A musician could make a living, he could do better playing than I did working, because if you could take care of what you made, but the average fella, if he playing, if he didn't watch himself he be broke when he got through, ya know. But I know the time this same fellow, James Pettit, was paying me $3 a night, but it wasn't—I was working Saturday and Sunday, and Wednesday I made $2. Well, that's $8 a week. Well, I worked six days for $3.60—sixty cents a day. Well, see, I could beat it and, man, I wouldn't have no food or nothing to pay for if I just worked Wednesdays—then I stayed first one of them places, then the other till time to play. When I came here I made something more, yeah, but it is $7 or $8 what we was making back then.

How did you team up with Wolf?

Floyd: Well, I just seed him around and after he moved on the same farm we were on then I go up to his house and so I'd ask him let me see his guitar. He say, "Be careful, don't break no strings." Then so he had an old guitar, he left along in the spring, and he let me have this guitar. He give it to me and, uh, he come back when I was playing with this Lossie Chatman then—when he come in off the road and, uh, Thanksgiving we played on this Nat Phillips, this fella's place whose name was James Pettit. We played Thanksgiving night, we kept playing in around there till, oh, few days before Christmas and then he was with me when I found my mother—I hadn't saw her in a good while and when I goes back she only lived two weeks. And he left me then and I didn't see him no more until 1934, then we teamed up again. And off and on we worked around, then in '40, last of '41—no, first of '41, I believe, in March—he went to the army and he was over there one year, maybe. Then he come back, we teamed up again. Then in about three months they called him back and he went and stayed awhile, and then he came back and we teamed up again in 1944. And that's when I left from Arkansas and came back August '44. I stayed up here the first of '45 and went back, stayed about a month, then I came back and I've been here ever since.

No, I never did live there (Mississippi). My father was there, oh, few years—now, he and Jim Jackson logged together way back, I don't remember that. But he moved, he brought me to Arkansas. He was around Tutwiler, Mississippi. But I was born in Arkansas, then he went to Mississippi logging and stayed a little while, but I don't remember none of that. Then he went back to Arkansas and me and my brothers was brought up in Arkansas. And, uh, my first time in Chicago was 1933. I come in '33, stayed a couple of months with my aunt, then I went back. Then I come back in 1937, stayed a little while just visiting, then I went back and I originally come here to stay in 1945. Then I been here ever since.

I was living on the South Side—6145 South Aberdeen, my people owned that building there. Then I eventually come to the West Side around Jew Town there for twenty-five years. I just thought I could make more money (in Chicago) and, uh, see, after war-time, ya know, jobs were getting pretty plentiful then and I came and started work. Then I started playing on Maxwell Street and met a lot of the fellas. And so we

Homesick James and Floyd Jones. Chicago, April 1974. (Photo Bill Greensmith)

teamed up and went to playing in . . . what we really used to do, Little Walter and John Henry (Barbee). Well, now, '45, my first gig here, if I can remember correctly, yeah, was with Sunnyland Slim, Little Walter, and Pork Chop. John Henry had it and he went to Kentucky and he got me to play in his place till he come back, we taken two weekends. This was at—it was called Sloppy Joe's, it was Lake and Talman. See, it's tore down now. I know that building ain't there now. And me and Little Walter and them used to go from one tavern to another one and we'd make maybe $10 or $12 a week, and a lot of Sundays I have—we have made high as $30, $35 down on Maxwell Street on Sundays. And I was working in a foundry for about $48 a week.

Yeah, and then I went into the stockyards and I—well, you see, the first job I got was in the foundry. Then I went to Swift's and worked there for a long time. Let's see, when I went to Swift's must have been about '48—first of '48—'cause '45, '46 I was at the American Car Foundry making brake shoes for trains and streetcar shoes. I was a molder.

Floyd remembered an audition at Gatewood's with Johnny Young and a piano player named Pie Face.

Floyd: Gatewood wanted some folks to play. So we went to Gatewood's and so (Big) Bill came down and said, "These fellows can play." So Pie Face said, "I don't play no blues." So I said, "Johnny would." Ya know, he's jumping around so glad to get up there with his mandolin. I said, "Yeah, but you hear what this fella's saying?"

He said, "What did he say?" I said, "He said he don't play no blues. See, he don't play no blues." I said, "What, did you just quit playing?" He didn't say nothing. So Johnny said, "We'll take it, man, we'll take it by ourselves." And I tell you the boy died, Elgin, was drummer, so we started playing—and, uh, then Alfred Erskine.[1]

Al was with Muddy a long time when he died, but he wasn't with Muddy then. He come in, man, and he sat in there and we played the first set and Miss Gatewood give us a pint of whiskey. And so we go back up, then Pie Face wanted to come in. I said, "Man, you don't play no blues." He said, "Oh, well, I'll sit in with y'all." I said, "No, that's okay." And we got Wednesday night there at Miss Gatewood's. She said, "Y'all in the union?" And Al hadn't paid, but he had a permit and Johnny had his card. So she said, "Well, I'll give you all a contract." She first said "indefinitely," then she said, "No, I'm gonna lose on you anyhow. I'll give you a definite contract for three months." Then we start. From then we worked at Sylvio's, then we got the Purple Cat, and then we got to going round and then little later we split up, and then I think we went, let's see, we went to Argo a few nights, then you started working at the Jamboree . . .

Moody: When I started with you.

Floyd: Then we went to the Mill Gate, that was in South Chicago—it wasn't far from the Jamboree. The Jamboree was 90th and Mackinaw and this was 80th, 90th—it was 89th—it was off Mackinaw, because, let's see, Snook made a number about 8910. Yeah, that's right, 8910, that was the Mill Gate.

Moody: Well, Floyd, did they ever know about Richard?

Floyd: Richard Williams?

Moody: Richard who got killed—used to drive his own truck?

Floyd: No, I don't think so. Richard never did recording. He played a lot, around. Richard Williams and Gray-Haired Bill, he was with Baby Face Leroy, Snooky, and me—that's a long time ago.

Moody: Gray-Haired Bill said he was going to play till he died. He did!

Floyd: That's right.

Willie Mae: And who was Gray-Haired Bill? That's who you played with in the basement on 43rd and . . .

Moody: Wentworth. That's how I lost the amplifier. We left amplifier in the place 'cause we were going to go back, we didn't want to carry it home every time, ya know. We weren't going to carry it home every night. So I didn't go back the next night, and when I was back the lady told me that he had come and got the amplifier and I never did get it. Ya know, before I quit playing, Floyd, while I was out there, I tried to get a chance to make "John Henry." So many people had messed it up. Man, I had it, didn't I? I tried to get chance to make that, see, and, oh, my wife saw Big Bill one night—they had him, I think, on TV. That's way back when we stayed over on 45th Street, but anyway he was singing "John Henry." Come closer to it than anybody I ever heard sing it. Except Doc Hopkin.

Floyd: Oh, yeah, Doc could play it.

Moody: Doc Hopkin, he was a white fella with the Prairie Farmers—WLS *years* ago. I remember one night Floyd called me up—I was way over here on the North Side. You remember that night you wanted to play "John Henry" for somebody over here on 90th Street, wasn't it? (*laughs*) You wanted to play "John Henry" and couldn't think of the words. I had 'em. Floyd said, "Tell me on the phone, just tell me what it is on the phone." He went out there and played 'em and made that money, too!

Johnny Young, early 1950s.

Floyd met with Wolf again in '54, with disastrous results.

Floyd: '54, that's when Wolf came here. That's when he first came here. See, I was going to do an audition with him, for the job. His boys he had 'em, but one of the boys was too young. He had to get him in the union and whatnot, and somebody, his parents, had to sign for Wolf to use him, ya know, 'cause he was only eighteen years old, Hubert (Sumlin). So we parked, went in—this is the Rock Bottom, it's on Madison right off Madison on Paulina—and I done lost my guitar, too. He said, "Well, you won't have to use nothing, Mr. Jones, you use our stuff." Then he said, "No, you have to have your guitar." So I went back to get my guitar and they broke in there and stole my amplifiers and everything—they got 'em then.

Floyd and Moody have had a lifetime to digest the savage twists of fate in the Blues world. Their story about Little Willie Foster is an example.

Floyd: Yeah, down there on Maxwell Street some guy stopped me. I didn't know him, so he says, "What you think about that little guy?" I said, "Who's that?" He said, "Willie Foster." I said, "Willie Foster's got a good voice." He say, "Yeah, that's what I'm saying, too." And after a couple of months, ya know, he was working with me. And come up fast, but he fooled around and got hurt. He probably would've made it on up there.

Others didn't even get a chance or anyone to give them a push:

Floyd: Only thing, that nobody don't get you, you stuck, just stay there. Somebody get you and keep pushing you, you got to go.

This was all in the past for Moody, who found his true vocation in the church, but Floyd still played the blues. Did he think he might follow his cousin's example?

Floyd: Really, if you don't believe it, don't do it. If you believe it, do it. Am I right? Don't pretend, I never pretend. "Man, are you going to play the blues?" I'm gonna play on a while longer, I don't know how much longer. They say, "Well come on, play in church. You can make this, you can make that." I say, "No, no I don't feel it." And that's why. I used to—I've done a little playing in church, that's how I know it wasn't right. Because I wasn't feeling it. When I leave church I be looking for me for some whiskey and get drunk, shoot craps, and anything. And I know that ain't right. They say, "Well, you don't got to worry about the other fella." Well, what about wrongdoing and that kinda stuff? And if you don't mean it, it's useless to get in there and pretend it. But mostly, mostly the blues players—the real down soul players come from church. Whatcha bet?

Notes

Interview with Floyd Jones conducted September 1973. Interview with Floyd and Moody Jones conducted September 1973 and September 1974.

1. Alfred "Erskine" has cropped up in other interviews, usually reported as a drummer; whereas in the interview Elgin (Elga) is the drummer, not "Erskine." Homesick James said that "Erskine" accompanied him on his first Chance session but definitely played bass. This suggests that Alfred "Erskine" is Alfred Elkins. Elkins was present at the double JOB session of April 28, 1952, when Moody and Snooky Pryor recorded. It seems more likely that "Erskine" is actually bass player Alfred Elkins and that he is also being confused with drummer Alfred Wallace!

Snooky Pryor Interview

Mike Rowe

Blues Unlimited #137/138 (Spring 1980)

Snooky Pryor, the last of the Old Swing-Master trio, was probably the most successful in material terms. Not, of course, from the music, which he gave up later than Moody in order to get into the building trade. He lived with his wife and family in southern Illinois, spending some of the year on building contracts in Chicago. He also played festivals and made European tours, business permitting, and this combination of activities was certainly more rewarding than a full-time musical career.

Snooky Pryor, late 1940s.

Well, I was born September 15, 1921, which was Lambert, Mississippi, where I was born at. Started playing around the age of eight or nine years old when I decided I wanted to be a musician, crazy about it. My father, he was what you call a minister, a Baptist preacher. Well, in his religion, stuff like that, ya know, he didn't believe in music. Well, I had an uncle and he played music. He played fiddle—violins and all, they called him Tom Harrover, that was his music name, ya know what I mean.[1] And then he had a brother, a cousin also, they called him Will Feather and he played the same instrument.[2] That's the only musicians I know come from my lineage. I heard them play several times at, ya know, little picnics and things back there, but as far as going out to clubs and things when I was small and young, if daddy knew about it he would really give me the works. (*laughs*) I'm named after him. He was named James Pryor, they called him Rev. I. E. Pryor, so my name is James Edward Pryor. He was pastor of a church called, ah, Galilee or something. I don't know. I wasn't much of a church member myself and never have been, ya know. No, no. My mother's name was Willie, Willie Pryor. She died when I was really young. She died in 1939.

Around the little town where we used to live here was a guy there called John Blissett, otherwise they called him Al Bounder, which he was a religious-looking guy. Al Bounder . . . he only could blow one number, but it was real good. (*laughs*) He called it "The Mississippi Drag Line." He was real good with that, and I used to hear him play. It was a little rhythm jump something like a train they called it. But the guy he was really good. He used to keep a crowd around him when he was playin' that. Jimmy Rogers, he know the guy. Jimmy and I grew up around there till I was sixteen years old and I cut out, started on my own. And James Scott, which is one of my favorite musicians, and he instructed me a lot into my music, ya understand, when I was starting out from a kid. This is the one used to steal me out from my father's house, ya know what I mean, to go play house parties. Yeah, he's much older than I am. So he live here in Chicago here somewhere now close around in this neighborhood, so they say, but I haven't seen him. When I was a kid he and Charley they was playing music then, Charley McLellan, even before I thought about playing, yeah. And then somehow or another after I started out in the music and left the South and came up in here and then I started recording, I just surpassed them. He came from Clarksdale when he came here, but he was born around Lambert and Vance, that's right. I bet he'll remember about his mother whipped me about his guitar! I'd get the guitar from behind the door—they used to keep it behind the door. I tried to get it out from behind the door, ya see, I was going to slip it out, ya know, and play it. And just as I opened the door back, the guitar fell out on the floor and kept up a lot of noise and his mother heard it and, boy, did she get me! (*laughs*) This was Lambert.

When I first left I went to Memphis and from there back down in the hill part of Mississippi around in there from where Baby Face Leroy used to live, out there around Grenada and Wynona. And from there I come back up in Arkansas and from Arkansas to Missouri. On the harmonica (*laughs*) I didn't start no work or nothing like that till after I went in the army and came out. That's how I made my living, ya know, when I was a kid. Town to town, house parties and things, and play my harmonica, yeah. Sure, that was rare in those days. Shoot, when you was—back in those days when you could play an instrument then, know what I mean, you were recognized as being real great. And so they was having those house parties, picnics and things, they was looking for people to play and I come along right in the nick of the time this was going on, and so it was really nice for me in those days. Sometime I would run up on guys, ya know what I mean, could play on guitar or some other instrument and we would team up, you understand? One guy I ran up on—called him Cooder Haines—and I run up on him in some parts of Arkansas and after that I never ran into him no more. He was very good on guitar. Cooder Haines, that's what they called him. That's the onliest thing I ever knew. This was around Osceola, Arkansas. Yeah. Then, in Mississippi I played with Tommy McClennan. He and I used to play for house parties. The same Tommy McClennan that made "Bottle Up and Go."

He was a little bitty ole guy. He had a scar right up here on the side of his head. Yeah, I knew him well. He liked to drink, too. And he had a little small wife and they used to fight quite a bit, too! (*laughs*) I forget her name, but he was real small and if you could have seen him in those days you wouldn't have believed this was the guy all this voice was coming from! Oh, I bet the guy didn't weigh over 110 pounds to save his life, if he weighed that much. Little bitty fella, but he really had a voice on him and he wouldn't play his guitar in "natural," ya know what I mean? He always played in what we called back in those days "crossed" and, uh, I don't guess he was able to buy a clamp to go on his guitar, so he used to take a—in order to get it down with the harmonica. In those days I played those fine keys harmonica, and he would take a pencil and a string and tie it across the neck of the guitar he used for a clamp, yeah. This was in Mississippi, around Cleveland, Mississippi. I never found out exactly where he was from, but I know he hung around Cleveland. He and I played around Cleveland and Pace and Boyce, oh, different places. Oh, I messed around with him for quite some time . . . just house parties and things like that. Ya know, what they used to call country break-downs and all that kind of stuff. Yes, he had made "Bottle Up and Go." Yeah, he had made "Bottle Up and Go." Oh, yeah, I used to play with Tony Hollins, too. I been knowing Tony Hollins all my life—ever since I knowed myself I knowed Tony Hollins. Yeah, "Crawling King Snake." He's from Lambert, Mississippi.

All during '36 right on up to '39 and '40, I was just traveling around through different places playing my music, nothing but playing my music, playing my harmonica. In the South, here and all throughout Missouri, all up in where I live at now, where my farm and house is down in southern Illinois. I used to come all up in there. I came to Chicago in '39, then I went back south, stayed there two or three weeks, and then back to Chicago and then the army grabbed me. I was living over here on Erie and Halsted, and Milwaukee Avenue and 647 North Morgan Street right in that neighborhood and then the army. That's where the army caught me. I went in the army and I came out of there in 19 and 45. I was a bugler—still following my music! (*laughs*) Yeah! Yeah, I was a bugler in the army, bugler, messenger, ya understand, and mail clerk. Yeah, I'm the one that blow reveille, wake the boys up. I still stayed with my music! So that's how I created this sound, ya know what I mean, the big sound from the mike, from the army. I did USO shows in the army. I used to go from camp to camp on different islands in the Pacific after they found out I could play harmonica like I did. I used to go to different companies and play harmonica for the soldiers. First sergeant got that set up for me. Just blues. Same thing as I do now—rhythm and blues, like that. Then I played a lot of army songs and things on the harmonica, too. I could even play taps on the harmonica, ya know, "Call to Quarters," the song that you play when the soldiers have to put out the lights and go to bed. So, otherwise, I stayed with my music until after I came back to Rockford, Illinois, at Camp Gretna. Well, I came into Fort Sheridan first and then they sent me out there to Camp Ellis, Illinois, and from Camp Ellis to Camp Gretna, about ninety miles west of Chicago. That's where I was discharged at November 16th, 1945. Came out and grabbed my harps up again, started back out, started back out again.

Even before I got out of uniform, when I come from overseas—well, I, let me see, I came from overseas. I left May 19 and got into Fort Sheridan June 16 and, uh, I stayed in service here until November, from June to November. Well, at the same time, ya see, when I was at Fort Sheridan—that's about thirty miles, maybe not quite that far, north of Chicago, big army camp up there, and I would come down from Fort Sheridan in my uniform. So Sonny Boy—this was in 1945 when I come from overseas—Sonny Boy, he was playing at the Purple Cat. I don't want to get them "Cats" mixed up. They got the Purple Cat and the Kitty Kat, the Purple Cat right there on Madison and Leavitt, somewhere along there. The Kitty Kat was right across the street, about four doors opposite on Madison Street. The Purple Cat was before the

Kitty Kat. Sonny Boy, he was playing at the Purple Cat and this bandstand you had to have a little ladder. This bandstand was way up in the ceiling of the club, so you would have to climb the ladder to get up in the bandstand and so, uh, I had played there several times. Sonny Boy had let me come on his bandstand and play several times. Well, you see, the bartender, they all knew me, because at that time I was in the army, but my wife she was living at 2318 Washington Boulevard. So all of 'em knowed me in that neighborhood and know me through playing my harmonica. I had on my uniform, well, I'd stop on the streets anywhere and play my harmonica, see? (*laughs*) And so all the people knew me up there. And so Sonny Boy had the job playing there and so all the fans they would ask Sonny Boy to let me come up, ya know, and play a number for 'em. And so I started playing and then he had put out a record long time ago called "Apple Tree"—and everybody called me "Apple Tree" because I could play the number, ha ha, better than Sonny Boy. "Looka there, honey, right over by the apple tree," and so the bartender he likeded me, all the waitresses they likeded me, ya know what I mean, and so when I got up there and play, oh, I rocked the house.

So Sonny Boy, he couldn't shake 'em like I could, and then they started giving me too many applause, ya understand, and Sonny Boy he didn't like that. So he came up there and snatched me down off the bandstand. Yeah, told me to get off his bandstand and don't never get back on there, and he didn't let me come back on his bandstand no more. And then after I got out of the army. Now, Sonny Boy the cause that I'm in the union today. He's the cause of I got a musician's union card, yeah. So after I got out the army, he was playing out here in a little club on State Street, 63rd and State, a little club you call the Club Georgia. So he was playing there and a lot of peoples knowed me in there, and so the manager that run the place, ya know, people wanted me to play. But Sonny Boy he didn't want me to play. Otherwise he was the greatest, ya understand, 'cause he had made a lot of records. And so the bartender or the manager of the place Sonny Boy was playing for he got Sonny Boy to let me play a few numbers. So I played a few numbers, got the house rockin' and everything, and the union man came in and Sonny Boy put the union man on me, told him I didn't have a card (*laughs*), told him I didn't have a union card. And so the union man told me if I played music anywhere in any club and he catch me anymore I better have a card. So I went and joined the union after that. This was right back after I got out of the army, around about '46. I had just got out of the army. So I been a union musician ever since. Uh-huh. Oh, me and Sonny Boy used to tussle a lot of times. Me and him had several great battles. But I likeded the guy, he was a nice dude, but he didn't want you to mess—he didn't want you messing with him. See, he wanted to be the king, which he was. (*laughs*) He didn't want you messing with him about his music.

At the time he was playing at the Purple Cat, well, he had Eddie Boyd and I believe Lazy Bill, and I disremember who he had over at the Club Georgia. That's when he turned me into a union man—and what-you-call used to play with him, too—Big

Bill Broonzy used to play with Sonny Boy. I remember all those guys, I used to sit in over there. I used to sit in with Big Bill Broonzy, Memphis Minnie, Son Joe—yeah, I used to play with those guys. East 47th Street at the 708 Club, yeah, me and Memphis Minnie, Sunnyland Slim, and Son Joe, we used to work there at the 708 Club. Big Maceo, I've sat in with Big Maceo, he was playing on Wentworth there, 3609 Wentworth, Dew Drop Inn. Miss King used to own that place. He wasn't with Tampa then. Johnny Jones was with Tampa during this time. I disremember who was playing guitar. John Brim wasn't with him then. John Brim came up after that. Even I have sat in with Lonnie Johnson, oh, I've been around for quite a little while. (*laughs*) Yeah, sat in with Lonnie Johnson and also Johnnie Temple. Yeah, Johnnie Temple, he was a very nice guitar player and very intelligent, too. [We played] up here on Lake Street and this place right below Sylvio's—I forget the name of this place. Not Gatewood's, that's where I used to sit in with Big Bill Broonzy. See, Gatewood's is on one side of the street and this club is on the other side, right below. I know you've heard of Martin's Corner, well, just below Jim Martin's, Gatewood's was on the corner of Western and Lake, I think it was. Yeah, and that's where Big Bill Broonzy would be at all the time. And I went to visit him just before he died. He thought a lot of me, Big Bill did. He was living on Cottage Grove when he died, around about there, 3700 on Cottage Grove.

When I started back out again got my little band and everything here in Chicago. I had a boy by the name of Gray-Haired Bill. Well, first started out was Floyd Jones—yeah, Floyd Jones and I, we bummed around quite a while after I came back from the army. And then from Floyd to Moody, ya understand, because during that time you wasn't getting no bar work or nothing in Chicago then with little bands and things like that. And if you got any work they wouldn't want over one or two pieces. Yeah. And so used to play quite a bit down there on Maxwell, but house parties and things used to be real great here in Chicago, and you could make pretty good money, too, at those kind of places. Oh, my goodness, you'd make all the way from $100 to $150, $200. Yeah, because you see the people, they would sell food and drinks and all this kind of stuff. They really used to have some real nice parties and things . . . here on the North Side, over round Orleans and out here on the West Side, Taylor Street and right off Maxwell on 14th Street, just different places. People used to gamble, ya know what I mean, and have parties and things. And then after I put out that record "Telephone Blues," then I started getting, started spreading a little bit.

Well, the way that happen, I hadn't been too long come out of the service and over here on that street that I speaks about on the record, Sedgwick Street. Well, it was—a guy there named Chester Scales and he was in the record business. He had a record shop and, really, the guy, he really was known and he knew all about the record business and about the distributors. And so I used to hang out round over there, being young and didn't much know what I was doing anyway, because I was just over there gigging we called it then, ya know, little hustle, ya know, playing music. So I was gigging around over there, that was the time I ran into this guy we called him Gray-Haired Bill, which he's dead now—very good guitar player, too. All the musicians they know him. Well, I ran into him and then I liked the way he played and he liked the way that I was playing, ya understand, although I was a little far experienced in music than he was. And so we teamed up and started playing there on Sedgwick Street right by this here record shop, no mikes or anything, just in the open air. And so this guy he came out named Chester Scales, and he asked me what was my name and I told him. He said, "Well, I haven't seen you in this neighborhood long." I told him I had just got discharged out of the army and he asked me would I like to do some recording and I told him, well, I didn't care. I told him, because that was what I'd been looking forward to—making records. He pitched up a big deal and everything. Me, young and not knowing too much about the recording business, you understand, so I told the guy, "Okay." And so he set up a date and everything and he told me he was setting it up on his own label, but when it wind up, Al Benson and a company—I think this company is out in California, Trilon Records—they wind up having the record and the master and everything, although I got paid for the session.[3] But royalties, no, uh-uh, that's out. I only started getting royalties and things until way, way later. Scales was—he was a real genius, if you know what I'm talking about, pretty slick. Yeah, he was my peoples (*laughs*), yeah, but the guy he was real slick, he really knew his business.

He didn't want Gray-Haired Bill to record with me, ya see. Well, that was my hangout over there, ya understand, and then it was a little club right down the street from his record shop and I started playing in this little club. I forget the name—anyway, uh, I built the little club up so and it start to drawing such a bigger crowd there, so Arthur Big Boy Crudup, he came in and played there with me at the same little place right on Sedgwick Street. Then, uh, he heard me and Moody play, ya see, and he likeded Moody and then, uh, Floyd was traveling with us, too, at the time, but I don't know where Floyd was when I got ready to record. I couldn't get up with Floyd, because I wanted him on the session, too. I couldn't find Floyd some kinda way, so Moody and I we went on and did the session, just he and I alone. Yeah, and so it turned out to be pretty good after all.

This may be kinda amazing to you. I wrote the song when I was on New Mill, New Caledonia in the South Pacific, that's when I wrote the song, in the army. And that baby I was talking about I was gonna call up that was my wife, which it is today down in southern Illinois. Yeah, I was gonna call her up on the long distance telephone (*laughs*) and she was right here in Chicago then. That's what that record is based on, so that's how I come by that record. The other side the "Snooky and Moody's Boogie," well, I created that little sound, that little tune when I was in the army, and I used to play over there on Sedgwick Street all the time and the peoples there they went for it, and so that's how I created that song and that's why I put it out 'cause the peoples went for it when I was playing it in the club. I figured if I put it on wax they would go for it then—which they did. And Al Benson, he used to play it all the time here in Chicago on the air. Otherwise, before all these other musicians and Muddy and all the rest of them, there wasn't nobody but Snooky here in Chicago. I had Chicago sewed up once for the blues.

I was the first to amplify the harp. Well, that was after I got out of the army and I went down on State Street. The place ain't there anymore, I never forget it. I will never forget it. I'll never forget the number, 504 State Street, that's where I went and bought me a PA system. None of the musicians had a PA system or nothing like that, 'cause we were going to these little house parties, clubs like that. You were just playing the bare harmonica, you understand, and very few guys had pickups on their guitar then. Some of them had done got these little ole pickup, ya know what I mean? Thing stick right in the hole of the guitar, but they didn't put out too much, so that's why the guys wasn't able to amplify, 'cause at that time they only had a little amplifier, just only carried one guitar. Nobody had a mike under that. Well, by me getting this experience in the army about this hookup and everything, well, I come out of the army with it and I went down on State Street and bought me a PA system and then I bought a mike, too. And then I hooked it up from that, and that's where the big sound started at, here in Chicago. Yeah, I am the one that started it.

The way I got this name Snooky, well, they used to call Jimmy Rogers "Snook." That's a little pet name, ya know what I mean. And after I started playing with Floyd Jones, ya know, during my band and we'd started working together and, uh, at the same time, he had met Jimmy Rogers and he used to call Jimmy Rogers "Snooky." And so after that, he couldn't think of my name, and by me and Jimmy Rogers had been knowing one another ever since kids and we met together in Jew Town one time. Well, I started to calling him by his kid name and Floyd couldn't think of my name and he started to calling me "Snooky." And that's how that got started and then, uh, Chester, this guy that I know that I cut the "Telephone Blues" for, he heard my name being called Snooky and he asked me how I would like to use that on record label. And then by that being my first record, ya know, that I had recorded—Moody was a nice guy, ya understand. I wanted him to be in the limelight and I wanted his name to be on the label. I asked the guy would he print the label up as, ya know, split label, two names—that's in order to give him a name, too. Oh, he said that sounds nice for a music name for me, Snooky, and I've been had the name Snooky ever since. So Floyd started this Snooky and that's how this Snooky got started.

It was back during the time right after I made the "Telephone Blues." [Baby Face] Leroy and Lee Brown, you know this little joint I was telling you about on Sedgwick Street, another joint, oh, it wasn't but four or five doors, a big ole place on Clybourn. Well, Leroy and Lee Brown was playing there. Now, this was back in the '40s, around about '48, '49, something like that, back then. Things was really jumping pretty good then, and so Leroy and I we used to travel around quite a bit. Yeah, used to go from Chicago all through the South, all down in Louisiana, Tennessee. We used to broadcast on radio down there, we used to broadcast in Cleveland.[4] I forget the name of the station. But we were living here in Chicago then and used to go down there on tour, sure did. Baby Face was a great guitar player. He was real great, only one thing was his trouble. Now, he didn't get too drunk to play, but, ya know, for his own good, ya understand, he was just drinking himself into bad health. And he was a nice fellow, real friendly, jolly. He kept you laughing all the time. He was about the funniest guy you'd ever meet. (*laughs*) Floyd and I—we played together for quite some time, too. Eddie [Taylor], he worked with me for a long time.

I can't quite recall now how long it was in between, matter of fact I'll tell you the truth. I forgot the next record I cut after "Telephone Blues," but I know the "Telephone Blues" it went over pretty nice, I know that. It's been so long I done forgot the next time I cut, 'cause after the business started getting so bad it didn't interest me no more. I was only interested in clubs and things, because the records was getting me nothing but a name, ya know?

The way I met Joe Brown through down here on Maxwell. I was in there, my records was selling pretty good, I was in there talking to Bernard, you know the one they call "Fat" down here in Jew Town? Well, he used to be good in the record business here in Chicago and he used to do all the pushing of records and things and, uh, if you weren't in with Al Benson, ya know what I mean, your record didn't hardly get off the ground. And so it happened that my record was on his label so that gave me a good boost. Well, this guy Bernard, well, he's the one handling all these records down in Jew Town there. Well, you see, he was playing these records and things all day long and if he had a pretty good hit, you didn't have to worry about it being sold. And, ya know, Jew Town is just about the heart of Chicago on a Saturday and Sunday, ya know, that's where most of the people be. And so I was in Bernard's place one Sunday morning. Something had went wrong with my PA system, ya know. He used to fix amplifiers, too, so he was working on my PA and he was talking to me about the record I had put out. If you want to know how your record was doing, how it was selling, and how much it was selling, you could go and ask him. He could really put you on, he could tell you what was going on. That's what he was talking to me about as he was fixing my PA system, and Joe Brown happened to come in while Bernard was talking to me. I don't know whether he and Joe had something going or not, but Bernard introduced me to Joe Brown and that's where it started at, ya understand? And he was telling me about he had a label and everything. I didn't know him from Adam. So then, uh, he talked me into recording on his label and come to find out his label wasn't much at that time, but then I didn't know it. And then he told me he was in with Chances—well, you see, I know Art Sheridan, he had a pretty fair label, and so he told me he's supposed to be in with Art Sheridan, also King Record Company. So that's how I met him. Only one thing, he was a hard man to deal with. (*laughs*) From the first beginning, though, he treated me real nice. He started making money, I guess, the way all of 'em go after making money, they gets a little greedy, ya know.

"Boogie Twist," that was on JOB label. Now, that wasn't a bad number, either. That was a pretty good number, "Boogie Twist," and Chess wanted that and Joe wouldn't let him have it. And the reason I didn't go on Chess label years ago, I had my own band. Floyd and Baby Face Leroy and I wanted Homesick James to record with me, and Chess wanted to use his band. He wanted to use Muddy and Jimmy to back me up. I wanted to, ya know, go down with my own band. Well, since he didn't want my own band to back me, well, I told him I wouldn't record for him. And at the same time I don't know what he had against Floyd, he didn't want Floyd, either. After that, Floyd recorded for him, but during the time when they's recordings just like hens' teeth, but recordings was just that scarce back there, and so, uh, I wouldn't record. 'Cause he didn't want me to use my own band. I wanted to use Moody, too. See, at the time, Moody was playing with me. Matter of fact, Moody was a great help. He was a great backer, ya know, behind my music at the time and Chess didn't want him. And I told him if I couldn't record with my own band then skip the whole record business and that's what I did. At that time Chess was down there on 31st and Indiana or 35th and Indiana, down along there somewhere.

See, that's the way lot of those companies was, they was really up tight together. See, now, if they didn't want you to record for them, they'd shut you out everywhere else. Some of them would tie you up on the contract, knowing that they ain't gonna record you, and then they won't release the contract. They tie you up to keep other companies from getting you and they won't record you they own self.

Vee-Jay, well, now, Joe introduced me to them. He said he wasn't doing much business then and he asked me how would I like to record on the Vee-Jay label. I told him it would be alright. Depends, ya know, how they pay, how they handle the record. Well, now, they treated me very nice, they treat me very nice. So he introduced me to Jimmy Bracken. He had me to come into his office and that's when I made "Someone to Love Me," and I think it was "Judgement Day" on the other side. Floyd Jones and, uh, I think Johnny Young was on guitar and Earl Phillips was on drums. Johnny Young, he played mandolin and guitar, too. He played guitar on that session. See, Moody was supposed to play, but Moody he was a guy he was kinda undependable. (*laughs*) Yeah, he just soon as show up as not to show up. He ain't never been too interested in music, but he was a doggone good musician. Hard man to beat.

Johnny Young never did really make it too big, but he was a good musician. Now, he used to do a lot of playing with me. He was a good musician, though, sure was. He strictly stuck by his music, too. Now, he was a man that really loved music.

I played several clubs, ya know. I played the Kitty Kat, the Purple Cat, and this big club used to be on Chicago Avenue, the Ebony Lounge. It's about half a block east of Halsted Street, yeah, so I think it was 744 West Chicago Avenue. I think that was it. Anyway, Bill Hill used to broadcast from there. Yeah, Bill Hill and also Sam Evans, he used to broadcast from there, and I used to broadcast on their program every Sunday at four o'clock. They used to have one hour every Sunday. Me and Floyd and Muddy used to broadcast from there, Muddy Waters. Otherwise, there used to be a lot of celebrities there, but Muddy and I, we was the head of the show. I was playing the harp with Muddy then, yeah, I played harp with Muddy before Walter did. And then I went on my own because I make money. I could make more money, yeah. Otherwise, when Muddy came to Chicago I was going strong, I had a band already. I had a boy by the name of Gray-Haired Bill. Willie Evans, that was his name, but everybody called him Gray-Haired Bill. Well, he wasn't that old, but it was a mystery. I mean his head was really white. He used to work with me at the Jamboree sometimes. His face was young, but, ya know what I mean, his head was white all over. It was a mystery the way he was. And he was a real good guitar player, too. And also a boy named Richard that got killed. Well, Richard was a good guitar player, he got stabbed some kinda way. See, what it was, I had got him, I had to go out of town on a gig. I had to go down to Dyersburg, Tennessee. Homesick James and I had to go down there to do a show, and so Richard was about the best around then, ya know, in Chicago. He had about the best band going in Chicago. And at the time I was going pretty strong and I had a contract out where I was playing at this Club Jamboree and, ya know, it carries a pretty nice crowd. And the manager, which was Ross, he didn't want me to leave and go on tour unless I could put somebody there would draw a crowd. At that time I wasn't working no side jobs or nothing like that then. I was only after music then. Well, you see, then I wanted my job to be secured when I come back, ya know. And so I put Richard in my place to work until I came back. So he had never heard Richard. I got Richard to go out there one night through the week, and Richard he was working and he just only played weekends. I got him to go out there to do an audition. So Ross liked him—my boss he likeded him, so he told me, "Yeah, well, he can keep the club going" until me and Homesick come back. And so he went out there to play and got *killed.* Somebody stabbed him. And Gray-Haired Bill was with him, and they say Gray-Haired Bill tried to kick the guy off him when he was stabbing him. I don't know exactly what year this was, but it was the early '50s. It had to be in the early '50s. And this kid, Willie Mingle, he used to play harmonica for Gray-Haired Bill and Richard, too. Now, he was a pretty good little harp player, too, a guy you call Willie Mingle or Mangle—something like that.[5] Moody, he know him, also Floyd know him. I don't know what happened to him. During the time when I was going pretty strong, ya know, there was a lot of little harp players coming up around here and there, but I used to blow them away. (*laughs*) I don't know if you ever heard of a boy called Gene?[6] He was coming up pretty good. Floyd know him. Then there was a little young kid, well, he should be around forty now, but back in this time he was really young, he was way under me. His name was Sonny Cooper. He was very good with the harmonica, yeah, very good. He told me he was going to record one time. He used to play over here on Madison Street. Yeah, he used to play there. Chuck's Corner they used to call it [at Damen and Madison]. Yeah, I used to know quite a few real harp players. I don't know what happened to 'em—just disappeared. And during this time what I'm talking about, Jimmy Reed wasn't nothing but an amateur then. Yeah, that's all Jimmy Reed was. He used to come up to the bandstand in South Chicago and ask to play a few numbers and I would let him play.

Now, years ago I used to really love music in my young days. I thought there was nothing in the world no better than music back in those days, but now I come to realize it's just another job with me, music. Well, I do know it's an inheritance, I do know that. Who do I think I got it from? Well, I have to be born with it in me, because I never asked nobody since I've been in this world to show me nothing about music. That's right, 'cause nobody have never taught me about music or how to play a harp no way. Now, I heard Sonny Boy's records on the air and played 'em on turntables and things. And this Rice Miller, Sonny Boy Number Two, well, back in 1934, when I was real small and young, he used to come through the South playing his harmonica, and I really think he was the best, ya know, that ever picked up harmonica. He was real good. He was one of my favorites. I don't blow like anybody else. Matter of fact, I don't believe I can. (*laughs*) Yeah, I have my own style. Just about every song I recorded I written most of them all, just about every song I recorded.

Snooky Pryor. Chicago, September 1972.
(Photo Bill Greensmith)

It was a long time before I started messing with a day job. No, I wouldn't do nothing but play music then. Around about '62, ya know what I mean, I really started getting away from it. I remember it just as good. December in '62, that's when I started getting away from it, ya know, 'cause it seemed to be nothing but obstacles during that time, and so I was determined enough not to let anything get me down. I'm still the same way now. I likes to go forward as long as I is going, I don't like to go backward. You don't gain by going backward, you gain by going forward. But I still do some recordings then. I do a few tours and I do a few shows, festivals—if the money's right. If not, I just remain as I am, take it easy. Matter of fact, I ain't got too much to worry about. Father Time is catching up with me. I'm just about made now.

Notes

Interview with Snooky Pryor conducted September 1978.

1. Tom Highroller, according to *Living Blues* 123.
2. Will Fiddler, according to *Living Blues* 123.
3. This is particularly interesting, as Floyd has independently said that "Stockyard Blues" was issued on Trilon. There was definitely a tie-up between Trilon and Old Swing-Master, as some Trilon masters (by Jimmy McCracklin) were issued on Old Swing-Master. But there are no known instances of Old Swing-Master items appearing on Trilon.
4. Cleveland, Mississippi.
5. Willie Mangum, according to *Living Blues* 123.
6. Presumably Gene Dennis (see *Living Blues* 38).

Postscript For Floyd and Moody

Moody Jones died on March 23, 1988, and his cousin Floyd died on December 19, 1989. They leave us with one last story to celebrate their life in Chicago's blues, and although it had to remain untold during their lifetime, it was a story that gave them a lot of laughs for almost forty years. And I think they would like us to enjoy it now.

Moody: Oh, Floyd, don't you remember one time we went out to Sunnyland's house one night? When we had to do some running! Old Wes Brown was shooting at us . . .

Floyd: Oh, man, yeah! (*laughs*)

Moody: Man, that was one of the terriblest times we ever had!

Floyd: Wasn't nobody at that wheel when Wes went to shooting. Old Lucius was down behind—he say the lights have gone. (*laughs*) I said, "Well, start it." He said, "I can't start it." I said, "Well, go somewhere, get on the sidewalk." He went up the sidewalk, didn't he, Moody? He went up the sidewalk.

Moody: Tore up the street sign, that's how he got on the sidewalk with the car, and we went down an alley and met Wes coming that way shooting. And finally, after he done chased us every whichaway he could chase us, shot at us, scared us, everybody getting down in the car, nobody driving . . . and his wife was in the car with us. She say, "Run the red light, I'll pay for it." "What you gonna do if somebody hit us?" "Run the red light and I'll pay. If we don't make it, don't need to pay!" But finally we got out a distance, I said, "Let's go to Sunnyland's house." He was up there asleep. "Come on, man, Wes shooting at us, give us something to fight with." He got up then and got one of those broken-off butcher knives about *that* long! (*laughs*)

Floyd: Now, that's the truth!

Moody: He sat down on the side of the bed, "Ah, sure I got something." He went in the kitchen and got a butcher knife! Now, how we gonna get that close to a man shooting at us?

Floyd: I said, "Man, that fella got *two* pistols!"

Moody: Shall I tell 'em how it started, Floyd?

Floyd: Yeah. Tell 'em all the way.

Moody: See, me and Floyd had been playing for Wes over at his tavern. Floyd had been going with Wes's wife—had been a long time. She's crazy about him, he's crazy about her. Wes is watching and nobody knows it, see? So she went down to somebody's house, me and Floyd was over at the tavern clowning around that night. That's 24 Club—we were playing at the 24 Club on Larrabee. That's where it was—24 Club, wasn't it, Floyd?

Floyd: 1424 North Larrabee.

Moody: So we was clowning, kept wondering where is she at. We didn't see her, she was round to her friend's house. After a while I got a phone call at the tavern. "I want to speak to Moody Jones." I went to the phone. "Is Floyd Jones there?" I said, "Yeah." She said, "Well, y'all come and get me. I'm going out on the West Side. We're gonna drink." So I said, "Okay, okay." So I fooled around and got the word to Floyd, Wes sitting right there. I got the word to Floyd about where she was and everything. She was waiting on me to come and get her. We got Lucius, and, anyway, we finally sneaked out, say, "Well, we'll see ya, Wes." Wes was drinking, he going to bed, he'd closed the tavern. We went around there and got her. She got in the car and we went over to the Foxhole on the West Side. So we got over there to the Foxhole, they sell whiskey there, it was a tavern. But she said, "It ain't no use us buying no whiskey, I'm going back home and get some whiskey out of the tavern." They was living in the rear. She went all the way back there to get some whiskey out of the tavern, to get a fifth of whiskey, and old Wes was looking right at her and she didn't know! (*laughs*) He came out behind her, trailed her, and she didn't know it. She got back over there. We sitting in the front of the Foxhole just drinking that whiskey that she'd done went into the house and got all of us, me and Floyd, Lucius and Sandra—that was her name—just drinking. Ole Wes drove right up beside the car and put a spotlight in it. Somebody said, "Down, Wes!" and everybody went to the floor. When he said, "Down, Wes," *everybody* went to the floor! Lucius there tried to start the car, he got it started and Floyd said, "Go ahead, man, go ahead."

Floyd: He said, "What must I do?" I said, "Go ahead."

Moody: And so after he started off the car, Wes he shot a couple of times. Bang! "Go ahead, man. Go somewhere!" And Lucius went around the corner, driving around the corner and got to a real, rough street—ole Wes was shooting like a cowboy . . . Pow! Pow! And every time he shoot everybody would go down. (*laughs*) So finally we got to an alley, Floyd says, "Go up the alley, go up the alley." And we go up the alley and Wes come in there shooting, pow! Pow! Beating us in that alley. I don't know how a man can make a U-turn in an alley! We got out of that alley, and they had been working on the streets and had the whole street tore up, wasn't nothing smooth but the sidewalk. And Lucius come and slowing and Wes . . . pow! Pow! . . . "Go somewhere, man." "I can't go nowhere." Said, "Yes, you can, go somewhere," and he got up on the sidewalk and driving along, the car just shaking and, well, he got straightened out on the street. Said, "Go ahead." He said, "Red light, red light." "Dat's alright," Wes's wife said, "Dat's alright. Run it and I'll pay for it." "What you gonna do if a car come and kill us?" (*laughs*) So everybody was scared . . . and the sad part about it, after everything cool off—we done run all night and after everything cool off, next morning here come that woman, coming up to Floyd's house talking about, "Is Floyd here?" I said, "Lawd have mercy! (*laughs*) He'll be starting shooting at us again." Floyd said, "You better go home." (*laughs*)

Floyd: But you know the first two or three times he shot, you know what she said? Said, "Lawd have mercy, I'm unarmed." I said, "Man, go ahead, talking about she's unarmed, this cat got *two* pistols. Yeah, his and hers, too."

Moody: Yeah, but after we got everything over with and she come down there the next day—wanted you to carry her to Indiana. I said, "Lawd have mercy!" I was scared to go home. I hadn't been home. I was scared he'd come around there a-shooting.

Floyd: And he asked someone, "One of the fellas had my wife, didn't he?" "Yeah, I don't know which one."

Moody: I explained that it wasn't me first!

Floyd: Yeah, and we was cool. We went back there and played there next Wednesday, ah, that Friday night.

Moody: We went back and played there . . . Floyd had a pistol . . . he had a pistol in his pocket (*laughs*), sitting up there playing with the band, a pistol in his pocket. Oh, Floyd's playing, Snooks blowing . . . "Go on, fella" . . . "Git it, Buddy, git it"—he tell me to git it!

Floyd: Wes sitting out here looking—he looking too and then, uh . . .

Moody: Floyd gonna be bad, "I ain't scared to play for him, I got my gun" . . . ooh (*laughs*)

Floyd: Ole Snook played—what was he playing? "Caldonia"—I guess he must have played it an hour and a half! And I said, "Well, this is the time to hang it up now!"

Moody: When was that? That's back about '49?

Floyd: Uh-huh—'49.

Moody: '48 or '49, we was cutting up around there that time.

Floyd: '48—yeah, that was '48. But don't you put that in no magazine—that cat's still living—no kidding! I tell you!

PART II

DETROIT

Baby Boy Warren

Among the many unsung heroes of Detroit's blues, Baby Boy Warren would rank very highly. Robert H. Warren's blues revealed a consummate craftsman whose attention to lyrics made him stand out among his contemporaries and showed that he learned his trade well from his major influence, Little Buddy Doyle, in Memphis. With unjustly only a local popularity and only one record on a label with more than just local distribution, Blue Lake, Baby Boy resigned himself to steady work in the bars and clubs until the problems of holding a group together became just too much. Then in the '70s he reemerged for a trip to Europe with Boogie Woogie Red in 1972 and appearances at the Ann Arbor Blues Festival the next year, which promised a successful twilight career with a new college and worldwide audience. Sadly, this was only to last a few years, for he died on July 1, 1977. This is his story.

—Mike Rowe

I Was the Baby Boy: Baby Boy Warren Interview

Mike Rowe and Mike Leadbitter

Blues Unlimited #96–98 (Nov. 1972–Jan. 1973)

I never knew what my father looked like . . . See, I was the baby boy and when my father passed they say I was only eight months old. All I can go by is what my older brothers and sisters tell me.

Robert Henry Warren, a large, affable, and articulate man, was born on August 13, 1919, at Lake Providence, Louisiana, the youngest son of Lee and Beulah Warren. He was one of eight children. Around November 1919 the family left Louisiana, moving north to Memphis, and here Lee died of the dropsy in March 1920, leaving "baby boy" to be raised by his widow and the eldest daughter, Hattie, who was then married to a Louis Armstrong. For almost 17 years the Warrens were to live at 620 Mill Street in North Memphis.

Two of my eldest brothers were musicians, but they never did get as far as I did, and become recording artists. But they was very popular in those days for playing parties and all around. So I'll never forget when I was a little boy. I would watch them and my older brother would say, "You better not fool with my guitar," but as soon as his back was turned I'd get a box, can, or chair and I'd (climb up and) get that guitar. Before you know, I could tune a guitar good as he could. It was a gift to me—it was in me to learn how to play a guitar. I must have been between eight and nine years old when I started to play.

I'll never forget when I was twelve years old, there was a fellow who ran an open roadhouse. I was staying with my older brother then and this fellow came and asked my brother, say he would take care of me. He wanted to take me over to play before the audience. And he gave me three or four dollars and a lot of pop. I thought I did a great thing, you know. This fellow's name was Slick Collins. He ran Slick Collins' Road House in Arkansas across the bridge (from Memphis) in West Memphis. I remember when West Memphis was nothing but Johnson's Garage, a little used-car lot, and A. P. Nichols had a little sawmill, and that was just about all there was to West Memphis.

Baby Boy learned much from his brothers, Jack and Willie Warren, both of whom sang and played guitar. Willie was the best, but bone disease affected one of his fingers in 1933, ruining any career he might have had in the future. Through them he was to meet a pianist called Willie "61" Blackwell, who became a lifelong friend. Willie "61" made records in the '30s and is still around

today. And then there was the mysterious "Black Bubba."

We started to playing in Church's Park (later renamed Handy's Park). That's in Memphis right on Beale Street. It's a big park there where all the farmers came. I've started out with myself, Howlin' Wolf, and Robert Jr. Lockwood. And there used to be another boy—this will amaze you—I don't think he ever recorded, but that was the guitar pickinest man I ever seen. They called him "Black Bubble [*sic*]." He was dark. I guess he was the color of my shoe. He was tall and his fingers was about an inch longer than mine. He's the only man I've seen in my life who could play the old "44 Blues" on a guitar and run a bass line at the same time. He's in Chicago now—I forget his real name. And Willie Blackwell—you know how "61" started to learn how to play a guitar? On my older brother's (Jack's) guitar, and I'm the one who used to tune it for him! I was a little bitty fellow when "61" came in—about seven or eight years old. He used to be a piano man.

Baby Boy Warren, early 1950s.

When Baby Boy was old enough, he left school and found himself a day job. He confined his musical activities to the weekends, when he would hang around Church's Park busking or spend seventy cents on a Helena train ticket. At the time, a branch line of the Missouri-Pacific ran through Arkansas to Helena. The journey only took one and one-half hours, and it was worth the time and expense to visit towns like Hughes, Marianna, and Helena, as good money could be earned by a popular musician whether he played alone or with friends. Baby Boy never went into northern Mississippi and had no contact with the older Memphis bluesmen. His circle of friends were all active in Arkansas—men like Sonny Boy (Rice Miller), Wolf, Robert Jr., Johnny Shines, Peck Curtis, Willie Love, and Calvin Frazier.

When I first met Wolf it was around 1938. I'll never forget how we'd go out through Arkansas, around those little country towns in the fall of the year when they'd be gathering in the cotton. We'd hit those little towns on Saturdays—we'd clean up! Make a little money, those guys get to drinking and those women start to braggin' on Howlin' Wolf. Throw him a dollar or two and he'd get down to start slidin' or crawlin'. Wolf used to live at Hughes in the '30s. That's where I met Johnny Shines—he was playing guitar then, too. One of his favorite songs the people used to love to hear him sing was this "Terraplane Blues" that Robert Johnson put out. He could clown and sing with it, get on his knees and all that. He had another song of his own about, *"I'm that old wolf that everybody try to find out why in the world I prowl; say they never gets to see me, but they always hear me when I howl . . ."*

Baby Boy used to make a habit of playing dance halls or roadhouses operated by plantation owners to keep workers happy. He still vividly remembers the drunks, "big-time gamblers," and the women who frequented the "low-life joints." He usually worked from West Memphis to Forrest City and then down to Helena, via Hughes and Marianna, but at various times would try towns in northern Arkansas like Parkin or Blytheville, or visit Caruthersville, over the border in Missouri. He recalled the two main dance halls in Helena, the Busy Bee and one operated by a certain "Bug Mouth," once a bouncer for Memphis gangsters like Red Lawrence or Jim Moorcraft, and famous for the big diamond in his teeth. He also made many appearances at the Little Brown Jug, housed on West Memphis' lively 8th Street and in the capacity as guest only on *King Biscuit Time.* Though he was so involved in the Arkansas blues scene, he still credits Memphis with supplying the major musical influence of his life.

When I was a little kid, the man I most admired was a midget fellow. They called him Little Buddy Doyle. I got most of my style from him. I admired him so much. He had a great big head, and when he walked off with his wife it looked like a mother leading her son someplace. He was just about this tall (*indicates a height of about four feet*). I met him in the park—he went blind before he passed; it must have been about 1958. I know one particular record he made—"Let's Renew Love," that was an original.

The other musician I admired was a woman, Memphis Minnie. I knew her when she come to Memphis and she started playing at the North Memphis Cafe up there on North Main. Proctor, Arkansas—that's where she came (to Memphis) from. She wasn't doing too good when she come to Detroit . . . she stayed in Detroit about three years with some friends of mine. She come from Chicago and I went to see her. She was ageable.

Baby Boy went on to talk of a lasting acquaintanceship with Sonny Boy Williamson.

I first met Sonny Boy and Peck in 1937, out in Helena, Arkansas. Helena—I wasn't just dependent on music, because it wasn't just established enough then for a person to make a straight-out living. It was mostly just weekend entertainment. You could get out, get you ten, fifteen dollars (playing music), and you'd made a lot of money in them days. I used to park cars for the Peabody Hotel for nine dollars a week! Back in those days you could run a whole house for eight, twelve dollars a month!

They used to have some good times around Helena. It used to be a good-time town. Forrest City was a big-time town. They used to have those big dance halls. Sonny Boy would shoot dice, drink whiskey, all kinds of stuff. Around '40 there was Willie Love, Sonny Boy, Peck and Dudlow, Robert Jr.[1] Sonny Boy couldn't get along with anyone too long. He was a hard guy to get along with; that's why Robert Jr. pulled out. Robert Johnson, he married Robert Jr.'s mother. Lockwood's stepfather. This is true. When I met Robert Jr. they was living in Marianna.

Willie Love come out from Greenville. He'd come to visit us in Helena. He even come to see me in Detroit at the Harlem Inn about three months before he got poisoned to death on whiskey. He come to visit and did a couple of shows for me. That's when he had that "Nelson Street Blues." This boy Peck, he used to play drums on the *King Biscuit Hour.* Well, Peck used to play a washboard behind me before he knowed how to hit a drum! He had him a washboard, cowbells, skillets, tin cans—it was very exciting for people to see him hitting all those things!

Sometimes we'd travel (to Helena) on a Friday night to be there on Saturday for those Saturday night dances. We'd all start to jamming together, playing those bells together. Me and Peck and Sonny Boy. Well, I'll tell you why they called Sonny Boy "Footsie." I don't care how much he paid for his shoes or how large he'd got 'em, he still gonna cut 'em. I never seen him with a shoe yet that he didn't cut. I don't care how soft it was, he'd still cut it. That's why they called him "Footsie."[2] He'd wear the big belt with the harmonicas, and when he'd get to blowing he'd have a big bath towel tied round his head . . . he'd perspire so much.

Elmore James, Robert Nighthawk, Pinetop Perkins, and Bobby Parker were just a few of the people that Baby Boy never ever met. He was also unaware that people like Forrest City Joe existed, and it is obvious that they were only "just coming up" when he left the South.

In the South there's a lot of guys who own big plantations; thousands and thousands of acres. They used to have what you call a roadhouse, you know, and we played there. I used to play for this Miller Lumber Company who owned a lot of land in Arkansas. This was out from Hughes; one of the big plantations out there. The people that worked (for the company) got paid daily. They had boardinghouses for them. A fellow called Little Tom Payne was managing it (the plantation) for them.

So this was back in '37, '38. I used to play out there on Saturday night. Only cost me 26 cents to get out there on the little train. He'd pay me for my train ticket, give me a place to sleep, all my drinks was free and food. Then I'd play (on Saturday) . . . and Sunday from 12 to 6 (pm). They'd cut down on Sunday evening at 6:00 to get the fellows to bed; they wanted them up for work Monday morning. And he'd give me a five-dollar bill. You know, I could do almost more with that than I do with seventy-five dollars today.

It was in this same roadhouse that Pete (the houseman) was blown across Baby Boy's lap by a shotgun blast through the window—the act of a drunk who had been ejected earlier. Similar scenes took place most weekends at the plantations and lumber camps. Baby Boy wondered why he was risking his life for a few dollars and in January 1944 moved to Detroit to join the members of his family who were already there. He found work with General Motors, staying with them to this day. However, he still wanted to play music. A meeting with Willie "61" Blackwell started him out.

Willie Blackwell used to come from Flint, and he and I used to go out on Hastings (Street) and we would just go and start walking and people would pay us on the street. And then we'd stop in the bars—the people would know us and have the barman shut the jukebox off, and we'd play so many numbers and they'd pay us. Finally they just set up a little bandstand and we started in the bar. I started up a little combo, 'cause I had a lots of fans.

The local branch of the A.F.M. [American Federation of Musicians] in Detroit, in contrast with those in Chicago or New Orleans, was very active in the forties and fifties. They did all they could to kill off non-union recording sessions, and would stop people playing live music if they were not fully paid-up members. This may explain why the Detroit music scene never really developed at the time. The first time Baby Boy got on stage with a combo he was in trouble. His dues were taken out of the money he was being paid for the gig and he was forced to register his band on the Monday following.

The first band I got was in 1949. That was the start of me recording and playing in an all-union nightclub. George V. Clancy, president of the A.F.M. local, threatened to pull me off the stage if I didn't go down Monday morning and put my whole band in the union. This was at the Brown Derby on John R. and Elliott. I had a fellow called Charley Mills on the piano and a drummer by the name of Curtis Foster. Just a small combo. Charley Mills, that guy could play a lot of piano, but he got sick.

This combo became very popular, attracting attention from local record producer Idessa Malone, who operated a record distributing firm on East Vernor Highway and was owner of the Staff label. Her big artists were Bobbie Caston and Red Miller, both of whom sang in the jazz ballad style that everyone liked then. Idessa also wanted blues.

Idessa Malone, somehow or other, she caught on and she got in touch with me and wanted me to come down to her place. She had a little recording studio down on 604–8 East Vernor Highway. She was going with a fellow who owned a record shop called Sam Taylor—Sam's Record Shop on Hastings.[3] I had several sessions with her and she beat me out of a lot of royalties. Red Miller recorded this number "Bewildered (and Confused)." He did that number for Idessa and I'll tell you what she did for him. This number was making a nationwide hit and she couldn't process it fast enough. Then Gotham Records out of Philadelphia—she sold it to them 'cause they could handle it. And then she turned right around and sold the master number to King Records in Cleveland. They (both) running a lawsuit and sued her. Closed her place down.

Baby Boy stated that his name was changed to Johnny Williams on record labels to prevent him from suing for royalties. Whatever his brush with records and recording wasn't very profitable, but it did help bookings. Mills and Foster stuck with him for five years before things went wrong. Mills got tangled up with a jealous widow and had to quit, and Foster got on dope and ran off with the drum kit. Undaunted, Baby Boy signed Boogie Woogie Red and a drummer called Henry Nickson to take over, duly signing them in at the union. Nickson stayed until his wife started pulling him offstage halfway through a show, and Baby Boy gave up trying to run a regular band. There were too many headaches. He just carried on alone, using pickup combos where necessary:

I signed a recording contract with three companies out of all my career. The rest of them (records) came up on different labels and I don't know how they came about. I signed my first contract with Staff. My second was with Cadet—it used to be Pan-American and Cadet, but Cadet pulled out and the next was Parrot.

Cadet Music was operated by Iz and Harry Liggett (?), who leased many masters to De Luxe in 1952 (the C2 matrix series) before they just vanished. Baby Boy also recorded for them in 1952, but the resultant masters eventually appeared on Sampson and Drummond.

I cut for Cadet at United Sound. I didn't cut that in no small place. Had Johnny Hooks on sax—one of 'em was "Stop Breaking Down." I got messed up and screwed around and, see, my records changed around. I've had some tough luck!

Baby Boy went to the studios for the last time when Al Benson signed him to Parrot. A mammoth session took place at Joe Von Battle Studios, but Benson only issued one record, on Blue Lake, before his company was blackballed by the union and closed down. Battle, left with several masters on hand, issued them himself or leased them to others. Baby Boy, despite spending time in Chicago trying to see Benson, and writing letters to Petrillo, the union boss, never was paid for his work. Feeling disgusted about the whole business, Baby Boy Warren never recorded again.

Well, see, Joe Von Battle cut them, but we was recording in Detroit for Parrot. Al Benson would come to Detroit and when he wanted a master he'd just have Joe send it to him. That's what happened to 'em. I cut "Mattie Mae" in Detroit at Joe's place. I had Sonny Boy on harp, and I was using Washboard Willie on washboard, Calvin Frazier on guitar.[4]

In spite of bad luck with records, Warren was kept busy with live appearances. Among the many clubs he regularly appeared at were Mary's Bar on Hastings; the Casba on Fairey and Russell; the Tavern Lounge at Lafayette and Elmwood, owned by Mrs. Smith, an aunt of Joe Louis; the Rage Show Bar at 14th and Davidson, owned by Joe Green; the Plantation; Sandy's Bar on Pennsylvania and McCullum; the Prince Royal Club on Gresham and McDougall; a forgotten place on the corner of Hastings and Garfield that featured female impersonators; the Flame Show Bar; and the Paradise.

He also played at the Black Velvet, a big club at Mt. Clemens, Michigan, for a long spell, witnessing one of the worst fights of his career when soldiers from a nearby base and regulars battled over women. The struggle left five dead, many wounded, and Baby Boy cowering behind the piano. Another high spot in Baby Boy Warren's career was a booking on the Roy Hamilton Show at Chicago's Trianon, a very big black nightclub on Cottage Grove, when his Blue Lake record was selling quite well. On the show with him were LaVern Baker, Jimmy Reed, Johnny Moore, Big Maybelle, the Spaniels, Eldorados, and Counts. When he wasn't working, Baby Boy would visit the Zanzibar to see Robert Jr. and Little Walter. Walter was not able to play, as he'd just come out of hospital, but a young man in his twenties was sitting in on harp.[5] He was also impressed by the Four Aces, then playing at the 708, with a lineup of three guitars and drums. Then there were the times when Sonny Boy came north to see his old friends.

Sonny Boy was a roamer. He didn't like to stay in one place too long. The first time he come up to Detroit was in 1945. He and another boy—he brought a guitar player with him called Joe Willie (Wilkins). That boy played nice guitar. But he didn't stay long, just a few weeks. They were down there on Lafayette Street, staying with a friend.

Then he came back in the early part of '54. I hired him, gave him a job. He was hunting work and nobody knew anything about him. So he found me—I was playing then for Joe Louis's aunt—the Tavern Lounge. I let him sit in and gave him a few dollars out of my pocket and then everybody started to coming in. They liked the way he was blowin'. Mrs. Smith liked him personally and put his name on the payroll. We had people lined up for two blocks! They had hired policemen on the door to let so many in as they let so many out.

Sonny Boy work with me in '54, then stayed until about the fall of '55. Then we had a little conflict. Sonny Boy's never satisfied. He think you should always do more. So, argue with him, I left the Tavern Lounge from under him and took a new band to the Prince Royal. Before he left Detroit (he lost the job), he had to come to me to apologize and ask for money to buy food. He come back to see me in '64, just before he died. He come to spend a week with me and he say, "You livin' in too nice a place for me," . . . 'cause he liked to use that profane language, you know.

In recent years Baby Boy has concentrated more on looking after his wife, Carrie, and seeing his seven children through school. He has done well at his job, managing to move out to the Detroit suburbs in an attempt to escape the violence and conflict. He continues to do the odd gig. In fact, he had just finished a two-week stint with Calvin Frazier before he came to Europe and he has never lost his interest in music. He is understandably proud of his brief recording career and the way he gave many newcomers a start. John Lee Hooker, Eddie Burns, and Little Sonny are all people who owe something to Baby Boy's benevolence.

Baby Boy Warren. London, May 1972. (Photo Bill Greensmith)

Today he has proved to us that he is still a major bluesman, and we wish him every success in the future. He did all he could to make our very long interview easy, often thinking hard after questions to make sure he had his facts right, and for this we thank him. He added much to our knowledge of the Delta and Detroit.

Notes

1. This was the lineup for the *King Biscuit Show* in 1941.
2. Slitting the sides of shoes to make them more comfortable is an old country habit.
3. This was the address of the Sampson label, which issued one of Baby Boy's recordings.
4. This refers to the JVB version of "Mattie Mae"; Sonny Boy was not present on the Blue Lake recording.
5. Perhaps Henry Strong, a friend of Little Walter.

Big Maceo

Big Maceo (Major Merriweather) was simply the most important blues pianist of the '40s and the greatest influence on Chicago's postwar blues. His legacy can be traced directly through the music of Little Johnny Jones, Henry Gray, and Otis Spann, particularly, but the echoes can be heard through the blues bands of the '50s. Maceo's singing was beautiful; his plaintive smoky-brown voice, soft and sad, seemed at odds with the power of his piano playing, and the combination proved irresistible. "Worried Life Blues," his first record, used the chorus of Sleepy John Estes's "Someday Baby" and propelled Maceo into a recording career of fame, if little fortune. Despite his popularity, little was known about Maceo. The first scant details came in 1955 in Yannick Bruynoghe's groundbreaking biography of Big Bill Broonzy, but it wasn't until 1973 when this writer, acting on a tip from Boogie Woogie Red, sought out his family and acquaintances. With some added information and important corrections to the original *BU* 106 article, this is the authentic story of one of the blues' greatest talents.

This article is based on interviews with Mrs. Rossell Marshall (Hattie Bell Merriweather) and Boogie Woogie Red that I conducted in August 1973. The photographs and extracts from personal correspondence were also supplied by Mrs. Marshall, with further information and photos from Maceo's sister, Mrs. Lucy Kate Brown, and brother, Rev. Roy Merriweather, from 1974. Memories of the Specialty session came from Art Rupe.

—Mike Rowe

Tuff Luck Blues: Big Maceo

Mike Rowe

Blues Unlimited #106 (Feb./March 1974)

According to his common-law wife, Rossell (Hattie Bell) Merriweather, who furnished the details for the death certificate, Big Maceo was born Major Merriweather in Atlanta, Georgia, on March 31, 1905, the son of Kit Merriweather and an unknown mother.[1] Raised in Atlanta itself,[2] he learned to play piano as a youth in the time-honored manner. [As Rossell recalled]: "He started playing just in somebody's home. Started playing for a lady named Roxy and he'd work for her so she'd let him play, ya know."

When, in 1922, the head of the family, Christopher, was hit by a car and died from his injuries, most of the family thought about moving north and following sister Odessa and brother Lee, who'd settled in Detroit. About 1923, Maceo joined Lee and family at 1904 Antietam and kept up his piano playing and learning—his only teacher seemed to be a Mr. Dubois, but the piano lessons probably didn't last long. He was proficient enough to play at house parties: "He went around and played for houses, ya know, where people sell whiskey and stuff like that."

Big Maceo, early 1940s.

Rossell had such a house—upstairs at 980 Alfred Street, between Rivard and Hastings.[3] "And that's where I met him. He used to come to my house all the time and I'd give him money and the rest used to give him whiskey. And I told him don't take no whiskey, don't play yourself cheap. Don't bring no whiskey or no wine, 'cause you soon be a whiskey-head or wine-head

Big Maceo with niece Leola and her daughter Madeline.

and you won't get no place. He didn't know nothing about nothing and he'd have womens just to go around with, but when I got him I put him on records. When I married to him I put him on records. When I married Maceo I was quite a kid.[4] Long before he was working on the WPA, he was the man that walked the track, and when times was bad he was a handyman, when times was good he worked everywhere—he always kept a job. He worked at Fords and he worked all over."[5]

"Maceo" is a childhood corruption of "Major," but the addition of "Big," however, is easier to understand—he was six feet tall and weighed 245 pounds. [Maceo's sister] Kate adds when he played the Arcade Theater between Vernor Highway and Napoleon they billed him as "Big" Maceo. So it was as Big Maceo that he cut his first records, and Rossell recalls: "I sent him to Chicago and when he went to Chicago he met Tampa Red and Big Bill [Broonzy], and Tampa Red found Melrose."

June 20, 1941

Maceo wrote from Tampa's house at 3432 S. State Street:

My dear loving wife,

I arrive in Chicago at 3pm and arrive safely. Baby we will record tuesday Melrose said and dont you worry Just be a good girl because I am a good boy listen baby I reall have mis you it look like I have bin here 2 weeks allready listen darling Mis Tampa and all said just take it easy everything is going to be allright and tampa said it wont be long now So baby Dont think hard of me for not writing more but we are so busy I and Tampa untill I am worn out. So you just be sweet until your husburn come home it is from the one who love you your husburn. M. Merriweather

P. S. Write soon and let me no just how you are getting along your baby M. M.

The trip to Chicago was a gamble and very much a joint family enterprise, according to Kate: "Hattie, she pawned her rings, my sister pawned her rings, I pawned my watch and, ya know, I have quite a few sisters here—Lily Belle, Odessa, Ornice, and myself. It was four of us here . . ." They'd all contributed. That following Tuesday, June 24th, Maceo accompanied Tampa Red on eight sides and recorded six titles under his own name for RCA-Bluebird, including the classic "Worried Life Blues."[6]

Clearly the Bluebird date was a successful debut and Maceo was to become a valuable addition to Lester Melrose's roster of artists. "Melrose was as crazy about them as he could be, because they made his living," commented Rossell.

Maceo was soon in great demand, recording regularly up to the Petrillo (union) recording ban of 1942. There were a further six sides made in December 1941. He again accompanied Tampa on eight sides in February 1942 and another four on July 28th, 1942, the day he cut his own last sides before the studio shutters came down.

He lived with Rossell in Detroit during those years, but made regular trips to Chicago, where he played at the H & T on State Street and at Gatewood's famous joint on the West Side at Lake and S. Campbell. Big Bill Broonzy took Maceo with him to Gatewood's: "The first night we played Big Maceo rocked the house and I didn't have to sing but one or two songs."

In Detroit, "he played all through Black Bottom, but his regular haunts were the Post at Warren Avenue on the West Side; Brown's Bar and the Crystal Bar on Hastings; and a beer garden, El Vido's, at Mack and Russell. Sometimes guys played guitar

Ted's Tavern on Hastings Street.

The Arcade Theatre.

and all kinds of tooty-horns and then he had girls singing—one girl's dead, a girl named Maud."

One evening at El Vido's when Erskine Hawkins was in the house was significant. Kate takes up the story: "Maceo was playing the 'Midnight Blues,' I think it was, and he wrote that on the collar of his shirt and Maceo hadn't recorded it, and Erskine Hawkins . . . he took it away from him just like that. And that was at El Vido's bar. That's where he was at—he was playing so that night and everybody was in uproar . . . and Erskine Hawkins did it just like that. I saw him doing it. I didn't think he could write it all on his cuff. He had a nice cuff (*laughs*), and he just wrote it down like that, and when Maceo heard it, it was what he played. It was his music, and Maceo said, 'That's my record. I played that at El Vido's bar.' And I said, 'Well, you shouldn't have played it 'cause you hadn't recorded it,' ya know. And so he taken that away from him."[7]

Maceo still played house parties and according to Rossell, "Well, he's at my house and I took the kitty, ya know, the kitty-box and I carried it around and when I carried it around they filled that thing so full, and from then on he went to using a kitty-box.[8] I would go around writing everybody's song what couldn't get a turn, 'cause there's so many people there. And I'd go around and ask who want to hear this, who want to hear that. They be hollerin', 'Play so-and-so, Maceo.' Play this, that, and the other. And they'd say, 'Mis Maceo, Mis Maceo, have Big Maceo play my piece,' and I'd go around taking everybody's names, everybody's piece they wanted played, and carry them to him. And he wouldn't play all way through. There was so many people wanted 'Worried Life' he just play it once or twice. And he made money like that. And peoples done paid . . . fifty more people done told him to play 'Worried Life' and he just played it once or twice."

Popularity

Maceo's popularity was such that, inevitably, he inspired a host of imitators—"There used to be a whole lot of Maceos, Maceo Charles and Maceo this-that-and-the-other right here in Detroit." Then there was Robert Merriweather (possibly no relation), who rejoices under the name of Cowboy Bill and was still living in the city, and Bob Merriweather, actually Maceo's brother, Little Maceo (R. Z.), who even "played better

Big Maceo, Rose Allen Broonzy, Big Bill Broonzy, Lil Green, unknown, Lucille Merriweather, Tyrell Dixon.

piano than Big Maceo and he could sing, too. He was six years old and he could play every piece Maceo played. He could play better than Maceo. Maceo he was kinda funny. Bob could have been on records, but Maceo wouldn't put Bob on records and he wouldn't take him to Melrose. He didn't want nobody to get up there with him."

Little Maceo could be seen around the streets of Detroit pushing a cart and dropping in to play at house parties. Sadly, he, too, has passed on, but the Merriweathers were clearly a talented family. There is still a nephew living in Dayton, Ohio, who, again, is alleged to play better piano than Maceo.[9]

But where did Big Maceo get his style? According to Rossell, "He just picked it up hisself. Why, he was a teacher—he taught people. People would come and he would teach 'em how to play. He could play it any way, couldn't he? Play it backward, cross his hands over—he could play a piano. And he really made money."

Boogie Woogie Red remembers Maceo, his idol: "I used to sit right there and look at his mouth when he played the piano, and I have my elbow on the piano. And I wanted to play with him so bad. He took an interest in me, 'cause I was interested in him. See, I was too young to go on the piano, but Maceo say, 'No, look, this is my nephew. Let him get up there.'"

Broonzy would recall, in *Big Bill Blues,* Maceo's grasp of musical theory, and one of the pianists who learned a lot from him was Little Johnnie Jones. Those were the best years: work was plentiful and it seemed as though the good times would continue. Then Maceo returned to Chicago, leaving Rossell in Detroit to look after her house.

In April 1944, Maceo wrote from 2218 W. Washington, where he was staying with Big Bill, to say he'd just got back off the road after a tour of Tennessee and was soon off to Atlanta for two weeks. At the time he was on his own, not working with Tampa, and from May 1944 onward his letters make depressing reading as troubles piled up. Mostly he requested money, which Rossell would send, but apart from unpaid bills were problems with jealous relatives: "Listen Hattie (Rossell) I Don't here from my people anymore But that all wright if they dont care to write me anymore it allwright I will get along . . . I have got my coat stolden since I bin back to Chicago but dont worry about it when I come to Detroit I want my people to know that I aint no tramp."

Things picked up a little when Maceo started back to work, but July found him staying at Tampa's, out of work again, and still worrying about his clothes: "My sister told someone to stop by to see was I ragged and had gone down like they heard."

Maceo wouldn't return to Detroit until he looked the part of the successful bluesman: "I did want to get me a overcoat before I come home listen Baby give me tim to get some of my thing I want to be fix just right."

In August he'd "been kinda sick," but the most harrowing letter came on September 12th, 1944:

> I love you more than the world but I am in a mess I dont need no money or nothing like that and Dont think that I want to keep you in suspense you know Darling I bought me a suit an a few other things and to I bin trying to wait until they start recording . . . am a poter on a train from Chicago to san francisco cal and I cant quit at present . . . whenever I get a chance I am comming home to you and will never leave you again Dont think hard of me Baby for not coming when I tould you I am just in a mess that I will hafter clear up myself But as fare as my welfair and health I am all wright.

The significant phrase is "until they start recording," for the bluesmen were impatient for the ending of the musicians union ban. Many, like Maceo, had to find alternative work, and it doesn't seem to have had the required effect of safeguarding their livelihoods. Petrillo, like a latter-day Canute, failed to stem the tide of "canned music" and by the end of the year the dispute was over.

Tampa had a session in December 1944 and Maceo started recording again in February 1945, accompanying Big Bill Broonzy. Things were to improve, but, sadly, 1945 was to be the last good year.[10]

A few days later, Maceo recorded under his own name and it was obvious that the inactivity of preceding years had not affected his prowess. "Kid Man Blues" was a fine start to a second career, and further sessions in July and October 1945 produced Maceo's "32-20"; the incomparable "Chicago Breakdown," a boogie-woogie solo of immense power; "Winter Time Blues"; and "Big Road Blues."

He then went on the road, but soon rejoined Tampa Red (working at the Flame Club) and recorded with him. He also accompanied Sonny Boy Williamson on one date and backed Tampa again in February 1946, but this was to be the last session.

After less than two years of renewed success, Maceo suffered the cruelest blow of all. During May 1946 he suffered a stroke in Milwaukee and was admitted to the People's Hospital.[11] It was only a matter of a month or so later on December 1, 1946, that Lucille and Maceo's daughter, Sandra Majorette, was born.

Big Maceo ad from *Chicago Defender*, May 25, 1946.

Lucille [his wife], who worked as an elevator operator in a department store, tried to care for Maceo and the new baby, but had to send them to live with Aunt Kate in Detroit.

The resultant paralysis of his right side virtually ended his piano-playing days, though he was to struggle on for some seven years. At home with Kate, Maceo partially recovered and returned to Chicago. He was still popular enough to warrant one further recording session in February 1947 with Eddie Boyd taking over the piano stool, but after that RCA dropped him.

Back in Chicago Maceo's letters to Hattie give an idea of his pitiful existence. March 10, 1948:

> I am as well as you expect But Baby I want you to send me 20 dollars to get me a Ray Lamp . . . the Doctor say I had to have a Ray Lamp.

Back in the hospital in May and trying to get sick pay:

> hattie the company say I would hafter to get my Badge. Before I can get any money. Will you please sin it to me rataway . . . I am in the Hospital in taking treatment . . . I am trying to get well But pleast sind my Badge the ONE with the picture in it.

Then in April '48 came some good fortune in the form of Art Rupe of Specialty, who'd come into town to record Roosevelt Sykes, having been assured by Sykes's manager that the RCA contract had expired. This wasn't so, and Rupe, looking around for other talent, was directed to Maceo, whom he discovered sick in bed. Maceo, desperate for money, struggled up to do the session with Johnnie Jones (who had been under Maceo's wing since about January 1945, soon after his arrival in Chicago and who played piano in a passable imitation of his teacher), Tampa Red, Ransom Knowling, and Odie Payne, and in spite of his physical condition, sang four songs beautifully in that soft, warm, smoky-brown voice.

Poignant

But by May he was again writing to Hattie for $10, and June, after money had been sent, saw the most poignant letter of all: "I got a little job trying to get my hand and legs like they was I am praying for them to get well so I can be Big Maceo again."

September was worse—although there were hopes of his playing again, a department store in Detroit was threatening him with jail over an unpaid bill of $24.30. But at least some of Maceo's prayers must have been answered, for incredibly, he was actually back on the road at the beginning of January 1950. The 18th of that month found him in Bowling Green, Kentucky, on his way to Knoxville, Tennessee, and by February 10 he was in New Orleans.

Back in Chicago in August, it was the same old story, with Maceo finding just enough work to pay his rent until about 1951 or '52, when he teamed up with guitarist John Brim and harmonica player Grace Brim, the husband-and-wife team, and they took off for Detroit, where Maceo cut his last records for Fortune. Another pianist, James Watkins, helped out, playing the right hand while Maceo played the left, and though six sides have now been issued, there are probably others in the can. The session was crude and the results were sad—by no stretch of the imagination was he "Big Maceo again." The recording quality was poor, even by Fortune's standards, and possibly the masters were purchased. Maceo was also recorded extensively at home by a small-time hustler called Keeno, who also worked as a bar photographer. "Keeno came to our house every Sunday," said Rossell, but he later died from a stroke and presumably his recordings are lost forever. Unless, of course, they actually were the Fortune sides.[12]

Maceo's reputation as a blues artist was secure from his first recording, but what was he like as a person? It's clear that he was very popular and much loved by all. Rossell ends by saying: "Everybody liked him—all the policemens—he was a good condition person. He was very nice—he wasn't a person to raise sand, fight, or nothing." He did, of course, drink heavily and she continues: "I think he'd have been well, but he didn't stop drinking—I kept after him about drinking and he could drink an awful lot. Ya know, I couldn't make him live. He tried to put the lights out in Detroit and then he went on to Chicago and tried to put the lights out."

The lights finally did go out, for Big Maceo died on February 26, 1953, at 7:15 a.m., when he suffered a final heart attack at 4706 S. Parkway in Chicago. His body was shipped to Detroit for burial on March 3rd, and until now, his life had been a mystery to us all.

Notes

1. Actually, Ora Merriweather (née Wright). Described as widow of Chris in 1926/7, she was living at 2250 Chestnut.

2. The family lived at Newnan, Georgia, where Maceo was born, and moved to College Park, a suburb of Atlanta.

3. Rossell sold whiskey in Indianapolis from houses on Yandee Street, Lewis, Wandell, and 13th and 15th Streets. Leroy Carr used to play for her. She was still only nineteen when she moved to Detroit.

4. It was about 1935 that Maceo and Rossell got together.

5. Along with the house parties Maceo played the bars like the Silver Grill, [a bar at] Theodore and Hastings, Sam's (an Italian-owned bar) on St. Antoine, the Bluebird, Black Hawk, and the better-known Flame, El Vido on Mack and Russell, Ted's Tavern, [a bar at] Brewster and Hastings, and Dago Hill in Inkster.

6. ["Worried Life" is obviously based on Sleepy John Estes's "Someday Baby Blues," which was issued in 1935, and Maceo must have immediately started playing it or working on it if Kate's recollection is correct. She maintained that the song was the result of a love affair gone disastrously wrong. Zelma Meadows was the lady's name, and Kate tells how terrified they all were as Maceo "walked the street with his pistol—we prayed he'd let her go." To their immense relief, nothing came of it and soon after, Maceo met Rossell.]

7. This would be "After Hours," which Hawkins recorded in 1944.

8. Kate hotly denied that Maceo ever had a "kitty-box" and said that he was always paid by the organizer of the house party. She also denied that Little Maceo ever pushed a cart.

9. Roy Merriweather Jr. is a respected modern jazz pianist.

10. Probably in 1945 Maceo had met Lucille Moultrie in Chicago and they married.

11. The *Chicago Defender,* May 18, 1946, carried an advertisement for a Maceo date at the Flame, but the May 25 paper apologized "to all our friends who were disappointed because Big Maceo was unable to be with us as advertised. He suffered a stroke and is now recuperating at home."

12. *The Blues Discography* lists a final unissued and previously unknown session for Mercury in 1952.

Walter Mitchell

Two long unsolved mysteries involving Detroit blues artists, the whereabouts of both LC Green and Walter Mitchell, were solved in 1986. Regrettably, LC, who had been residing in Pontiac, Michigan, died in August 1985 before anybody had a chance to interview him. However, Walter Mitchell Jr. was then still very much alive and living in Toledo, Ohio.

Standing little more than five feet in height, Walter Mitchell can rightfully lay claim to the name "Little Walter Junior." Born in New Orleans on March 19, 1919, he spent his formative years traveling and meeting an endless stream of musicians, all the while perfecting his craft, before eventually settling in Detroit in 1945.[1]

In 1948 Walter made his recording debut for the Hasting Street–based JVB Records with the eerie-sounding "Pet Milk Blues"/"Stop Messing Around," with Robert Richard playing second harmonica. Two additional sides were earmarked for King Records but inexplicably never saw light of day; a fifth side, the chaotic "Broke and Hungry," was issued in the 1970s.[2] In 1952 Walter and his cousin LC Green traveled to Gallatin, Tennessee, and recorded eight sides for Dot Records. These sides rank among the finest recorded blues from any Detroit artists. The harmonica on the Dot session, previously thought to be Sam Kelly, is indeed Walter. A total of six sides were issued, all credited to LC Green, an unfortunate oversight, as it was Walter Mitchell who handled the vocals on the coupling "Come Back Sugar Mama" and "Little Machine." Walter recorded one last session together for Joe Von Battle, but these recordings remained on the shelf until they were rescued from obscurity and reissued in the 1970s.[3] Subsequent sessions, mainly in the role of accompanist, remain unissued. However, material recorded at a house party in Detroit in 1955, which features Walter leading a small band, were released on T-R-H CD 8001.[4]

It's with thanks to *BU* friend Tim Healy that we finally had a chance to interview Walter, early in 1986. He spoke proudly of his fascinating life, his love of traveling the country, the Detroit blues scene, and his long relationship with his cousin LC Green. Walter Mitchell died in Toledo, Ohio, on January 10, 1990.

—Bill Greensmith

Playing Music Is All I Know: An Interview with Walter Mitchell Jr.

Bill Greensmith

Blues Unlimited #148 (Winter 1987)

I started playing harmonica when I was about four years old. I went to a barrelhouse in the country, in Ferriday, Louisiana, and a guy was playing the harmonica. I told him I could play the drums and they let me play the drums. Then I looked at the guy playing the harmonica and I said, lord, I'm gonna' learn to play harmonica before I die. So my daddy used to whup me, I skipped school and go somewhere where they playing music. And that's where I came from there.

My father was a farmer, sugarcane farmer, and I stayed with him for a while. My mother's brother came and got me and they raised me in Detroit after my mother died. I was about six or seven years old when I came to Detroit. I went to school there and I left Detroit after I got—I hoboed back down there. 'Cause I used to run off, shoot, I left there the last time, run off from home, people hadn't seen me in about six years.

I got me a group in Lake Providence, Louisiana. I was playing with a boy named Little Sam, he played guitar, and a boy called Buck, who played second guitar. William [?] played piano and Robert [?] played drums, and I was blowing harmonica and doing my own singing. Nobody sing but me, that's the only one. So I went on and started playing music all through the country, every weekend I'd go play music. Tallulah, Monroe, Shreveport, Minden—Beaumont, Texas—Pine Bluff, Little Rock, Dumas, Arkansas. Little Walter Junior and His Boogie Blues Boys.

Were you just playing music or were you also working a day job?

Yeah, working in the sawmill, one of them groundhog sawmills that was on the ground. I left there and start working on the railroad. Left there and went to Tallulah working for the Illinois Central. I left there, they had a strike or something, and

Walter Mitchell. Toledo, Ohio, March 1986. (Photo Bill Greensmith)

I came back to McGehee, Arkansas, and I joined some old group playing in the band in McGehee. McGehee almost near Dumas.

You told me earlier that you had met Muddy Waters?

Where did I meet him at? I been and met him a long time ago. He used to play in Dumas, McGehee, all them through there, all in Louisiana. He used to court my oldest sister, who lived in Dumas.

Who were some of the other people you ran into down south?

Yank Rachell, Boy Blue, both of the Sonny Boys. Sonny Boy [John Lee Williamson], he beat Rice Miller playing the harp.

Where did you meet Boy Blue?

Taylor, Arkansas. I ran into Sonny Terry in McGehee, it was a great big boardinghouse and I got me a room there. I was working in the [railroad] roundhouse and on the weekends I'd go where Sonny Terry playing at.

Who was he playing with?

I think he was playing with, what's that boy called? It wasn't Brownie.

Blind Boy Fuller?

No, Blind Boy Fuller always go by himself, he plays guitar and do his own vocals. Anyway Sonny was blowing the harp, so I sit in and they want to take me with them but I didn't go. I met Robert Johnson, I met him in Leland, Mississippi, playing at the—it's in Elizabeth. I lived in Leland, I lived there for a couple of months.

I also met Peetie Wheatstraw in a little place called Sondheimer, Louisiana. Little country—had a big sawmill each side and right over there, they called it the quarter, little shotgun houses. And the man built a big ballroom over there. That's where I met him, he played over there. Sondheimer, Louisiana, that's about 20 miles from Lake Providence going down to Tallulah. He played piano down there. He had some more guys playing, three or four more guys playing. [*looking at* BU *146.*] See that old man, who—Joe Reynolds, yeah.

Did you ever meet him?

One time, that was in Minden, Louisiana. One time played at the Dew Drop Inn, I mess around and got me a little combo, 'cause I was working about five streets over, called Chat 'n' Chew. You go there to drink, when you get hungry you can buy something to chew. Minden, that was out from Shreveport.

LC Green.

You were in the army. Where did you receive your papers?

In Detroit, but I left all my induction papers in the mailbox, every doggone thing. You know where they caught me? Key West, Florida. I'd got a job at the sugarcane mill, and a white guy, boy, he was raggedy—I thought god damn, look at this raggedy motherfucker coming down here. I always call him Cat. I said, "Hey, Cat, you for it this morning?" He said, "Yeah, I'm for it." I said, "Let's get like a bird." See, I'm weighing the sugar, he's taking it off the scale. So Friday he comes sharp, I say, "Hey, Cat!" He pulls that badge out. He said, "We've been looking for you for nine months. What you been catching when you leavin' town?" I said, "Freight train and truck, that's all I did."

Get on the railroad of a night, you hit the ditch, see, when it pick up. Shoot, I'd be on that thing, man, between them bars riding. One foot on this car, other one on that car, one down back down going somewhere, all out in Texas. My uncle used to say, "Boy, you gonna' get killed ridin' them trains like that." I had a cousin standing in the middle of the track to catch a train, don't see how he did it.

Anyway, they brought me back to Monroe, Louisiana. I lay overnight in jail. Next morning, passenger train comes, I got on there, they carried and put me on there. I asked the detective can I call a girl. See, I used to live in Monroe, had a woman that lived there. I said, "Can I make a call?" and I called the girl. I said, "I'm on my way to the army, do you have any whiskey at the house?" She brought me a whole gallon jug of corn whiskey. When I got to the induction station, man, I hadn't turned cold water on me in three days. Shreveport, Louisiana, that's where I got the induction

Robert Richard and Friends. Detroit, mid-1950s.

at, October '41. I was in the 92nd Tanks, I didn't like that. I goofed up, wouldn't do nothing. So they put me on quartermaster, that's about as good as I want, drive a truck. So I drove a truck, then they throwed me right back in the tank unit, I said god damn, what they gonna' do?

I fought the Germans first, then the Japs. We shipped out to England, then to France. I got wounded fighting the Germans. Then I got in special service, that's all I did, play music. I had a bunch of guys who played with me. I was wounded in the foot fighting the Japanese, so that time they said, "You're going back to the States." So after I got where I could walk pretty good I came back to Detroit.

I was discharged January 15, 1945. I didn't work for about six or seven months, then I start working at Ford Motor Company; from there I work for Chrysler, Desoto. Construction, I did that, too.

Did you form a band when you got to Detroit?

Not right off the reel. I had to go around, see, pick up on the guys where they playing, practicing at. So I got some guys, got them all together, I rent me a house myself, and all practicing at my house and that's where all the musicians—Baby Boy Warren. And I named it Little Walter Junior and the Boogie Blues Boys. Well, I went and got my cousin LC [Green], we played a long time together.

Just the two of you?

Yeah, rock the house too!

Where did LC come from?

Minter City, Mississippi. It should be near Greenville. First time I met LC I didn't know he was any relation to me.

Where were some of the places you and LC played?

Detroit and all around Detroit. Little Son at Hastings and 4th; Brown Bar, Watson and Hastings; Lee Sensation at Owen and Russell. We played at Uncle Tom's Cabin on 8 Mile Road. Played at Mount Clemens, Michigan. Flint Bridge Club, played for the Veterans Post there, start at nine till six in the morning. Saginaw, me and Robert Hurd, LC played a big club. Robert Hurd played guitar, Little Al he's drummin', and a boy called Jimmy Williams he's on piano. But they can't sing good, they want me to sing all the time. LC, he sing some now, he help me out. When I want a break I'd let LC carry it on.

Walter Mitchell, JVB.

Do you know who LC learned from?

He just go around like I did, that's what he was doing. Now, these two fingers [index and middle] on each hand growed together, webbed fingers on each hand. They tried to get him to have them split, he said, "No, I was born that way, they can stay that way." That cat can play, man.

Where did you meet Joe Von Battle?

He seed us play on Hastings at Watson bar. It was Watson Street and they named that bar Watson. Joe used to come in there and sit down and look at me playing harp. I hired a boy, Robert Richard, I hired him to sit in when I be gone somewhere, see, 'cause different groups get me and take me out of town. And, shoot, they make a mess of it when I come back, they don't be did nothing, and I got rid of Robert Richard.

Whose idea was it to have more harmonicas on the record?

Joe's. He [Robert Richard] played on there. I didn't want him on there, because I know he'd mess up. That wine, man, I know that boy will mess up. He still screwed up. I like to go by myself, get my thing together, I know where it's coming from.

You were one of the first people to record for Joe?

Yeah, I am the first, I am the first one. Joe said, "Come here, I heard you playing harp down on Vernor Highway, I'm coming down there. I want you to cut one for me." I took my harp and cut it myself. Cut "I Had a Woman She Loving Everyway to Me." I don't know what he did with that.

Robert Richard also recorded and you played harp for him?

Not that date.

You went to Gallatin to cut the sides for Dot?

Me and LC both. Gallatin, Tennessee.

Do you know how the deal with Dot Records came about?

I don't know, man, 'cause LC had the contract and I ain't seen no contract, and I got narn pay out of it. I don't know, LC's sister told me he did get a—

So you didn't get a penny out of it?

No.

Was it through Joe Von Battle that the deal with Dot came about?

No, it was a woman where I was playing at Harry's Bar.

Idessa Malone?

I don't know, I forgot. However, she called Randy [Wood] and Randy sent us our fare there and back. We rode a bus there and back. We spent overnight, there's some more records ain't published.

Where did you record there?

He's got a studio right where he sells records at. Go right through the record shop right on back in the room.

And you sang on a couple of numbers too?

Yeah, let's see, I cut "Sugar Mama," "Something Wrong with My Little Machine." I cut another, "My Home Ain't Here."

"Little Machine" and "Come Back Sugar Mama" were issued under LC's name.

I know it, I know they did.

How many songs did you guys do that day?

Oh, we did about—I don't know, man, we did right smart, half of them ain't come out.

In the middle '50s you cut some stuff live at a house party?

Yeah, that was down on Lafayette in Detroit.

Recorded by Von Battle?

I don't know who cut them, two or three guys had the tape.

Who were you playing with?

All of 'em. Little George [Jackson], [Boogie Woogie] Red. Now, I made two or three records with Baby Boy and I ain't heard none of them. I blow the harp for him. I believe Bobo Jenkins record them, he had a studio right in his house, this was in the '50s. Bobo come and pick me up, got all them guys, car loaded up and go to his house and he had a recording machine there.

Boogie Woogie Red. Detroit, 1950s.

Do you remember Bernie Besman?

Besman, yeah, he stayed in the Bottom, off Lafayette and Dubois at that time.

Did you ever do anything for him?

No.

Did Lee Sensation have any interest in Sensation Records?

Lee don't, it was just a bar selling drinks and dancing. All he do [is] hire bands [to] play in this place, and he pay good too. I played there, I played for Lee, about, gosh, a long time. I had a swinging group, man. I had some guys playing horns, all that kinda stuff. That was a long time ago. I had two sax, two trumpets, one slide [trombone], piano, drums, bass. This was right around in the '50s.

Did you used to play with Washboard Willie?

Yeah, I used to have that group in Detroit. Red, he used to be my piano player. We used to play down there on Russell at the Granary [?], Russell and Alexandrine.

What about Rabbit?

Yeah, Rabbit used to play, we were playing on Vernor Highway, they were playing on Vernor Highway, out from Joe Louis Restaurant across the street.

Playing music is all I know. I played with Little George, I played with Baby Boy. I played with another guy, Left Hand Louis, he played guitar bottom side up. I had a boy here from Mississippi I played with, he got a guitar that got four strings on it, I don't see how he play it, he says, "That's the way I learned."

Do you remember Sonny Boy Williamson playing in Detroit with Baby Boy Warren?

Yeah, and I played on Vernor Highway and Beaumont [?] at the Spot Bar, and I couldn't get down there and get in with 'em. They were playing at Adams and Hastings. I forgot that club name, it's been so long. I played with Bobo, too. I played a whole lot with him.

Charley Mills?

Yeah, ole big Charley Mills, yeah, I played with him. Charley Mills, he could play, but he couldn't handle like Baby Boy Warren could. He and Baby Boy get into it about he got the wrong beat and any doggone thing, and I'd laugh at both of them. "It's my guitar, I play it like I want it, you won't tell me how to play."[5] Me and LC look and laugh at them. Last time I played with Baby Boy Warren was at a great big duplex house.

Did you know Sam Kelly?

Yeah, I know him. I don't know where he come from. I met him in Detroit. Sam Kelly, he's dead, I heard he's dead. He stayed on Forest and Bowman [?] the fourth house this side of Bowman. He played pretty good, I learnt him everything he know. I sure taught him right there in my house.[6] We owned that big hotel called Forest House Hotel.

Do you remember a piano player called Detroit Count?

He must have played more out in Delray. Piano players played more out there than they did downtown Detroit. Boy, you could go out and see the after-hours houses, joints, all out through there, man, shoot. Delray—go out past the army camp and go way on out there in the country. It would be jumping out there, I'm telling you. I used to go out there all the time. Wasn't no fights, no nothing out there. I don't know any names, but I know where you go, though, houses, house parties, and everything. Me and LC would go out there and rake up, man, pay good out there.

John Lee Hooker?

Yeah, you know, John Lee worked with me out at Hinds Farm whole lot of times—that's a place out near the airport in this area [Toledo]. Yeah, he worked with me all the time, I had him working with me out there.

Did you know Playboy Fuller—Rocky Fuller—Louisiana Red?

Now, I know Blind Boy Fuller. Louisiana Red, I knowed him. He didn't stay here, he was probably running around just like I was. Played like Elmore James, I know Elmore James, I know his brother, sure do. I met Elmore in Meridian, Mississippi.

Eddie Burns?

Me and Eddie Burns used to play together with LC, played together down on Lafayette.

Did Eddie play harp or guitar?

He couldn't do too much. He give it to me. I was playing the harp with LC and him and one old boy used to play drums. But we would still practice in that old house down there.

Did you ever run across Grace and John Brim?

Yeah, they were playing in Delray, he was playing at a house party out there and we went out there one night. I played maybe five or six numbers with them. I didn't stay out there long, I had to go home then, 'cause I had been out about two or three nights and hadn't been home.

Henry Smith?

I might have known him.

Clarence Posey?

Do he wear glasses? I knew a Clarence playing piano had some glasses on, sort of stocky cat.

Chuck Smith, played piano?

Chuck, yeah, he passed. Chuck stayed on Erskine and Russell. I didn't play with him, I have been around when he played. When I didn't work I'd go around and see them other guys, sit in with them and like that.

Elder Wilson?

Yes, I heard him play at a house party out in Delray, Michigan. He was a preacher, he's dead now.[7]

Johnny Howard?

I heard him play on West Grand Boulevard for Lee Sensation. I never played with him.

Did you ever see Willie "61" Blackwell?

I ran across him way on the west side of town in Detroit, he was playing way across the railroad. He had a little group playing in there. He from Mississippi.

Harvey Hill?

He stayed on 8 Mile Road. When he get ready to play he had his right foot throwed out. He cuss you out, boy, talk about "Put your god damn foot down, boy," he cuss you out then. I didn't play with him.

Did he play around Detroit much?

Well, when somebody take time, like his brother, his brother Charles, he take him around spots. Otherwise he want to stay around out there on 8 Mile Road. You'd get a whole lot of nickels and things out there, house parties. Let's see, what you call that old place where you go there and eat barbecue? And you could steal all you want if they don't act right. I have stole so much I was afraid to go out there. I sent LC out there and they catch LC. And the old cop, "Which one of you stole Fred Rooney's barbecue?" I said, "That ole LC, he'd steal sweetnin' out of gingerbread and not break the crust." But Fred owed us some money. "Well, I'll pay you guys tomorrow night, I'm busy tonight." I took nine slabs of barbeque and a bucketful of sauce and I got eight loaves of bread. I told LC, "You go in there and keep him company," and I got all the barbecue. Went on down the street and I sell it, 50 cents a sandwich, and got my money, boy.

Sylvester Cotton?

Yeah, I knew him, but since I started living over here I haven't kept up with these people.

Big Maceo?

Maceo? Yeah, I worked with him. I worked with him in Pine Bluff, Arkansas, at the Black Cat place. This was before I went into the army.

Did you run into him in Detroit?

No. I tell you who I run into, Joe Williams. He stayed all night with me, Big Joe Williams, before he died. I was living on John Olive Street [?] in Toledo. Me and that scoundrel high, we sing and played all night.

Did you know him from years back?

Yeah, I met him in Pine Bluff.

Did you work with him?

Yeah. I've met so many people, man, I've forgotten. Wherever I stop at I get me a job for a front, see, keep the peoples off me. Then I go and find me some guys to play music, that's my game. I'd go to a town, like I'd leave here and go to Memphis, hang around Memphis. I'd hang around with some of the guys, musicians.

Who did you meet in Memphis?

B. B. King, Wolf—"I'm de Wolf!" Met Tommy McClennan, I met him on Beale Street in the park, sure was. Me and LC—we playing there.

You know this man, he plays harmonica, that's my first cousin, Little Walter. My mother's sister, they're Jacobs. He's from, ah, I've been there and met some of my people, Areola, Mississippi. I've been right to his house. My daddy was born in Areola and my mother she was born in New Orleans. I don't know how they got together at that time.

Did you ever do any radio shows?

No. Me and LC used to come over here and play, we used to go to bars and play, sure did. I was on TV here in about 1957, a local thing from James Stroller, I was on TV twice.

Who were some of your favorite harmonica players?

Well, I used to like Sonny Boy, Sonny Terry, Boy Blue. Any harmonica player, they can play, but when you know how to cup 'em, some of them let the harp get away from them, mistune, out of time, all that kinda stuff. Can't tell 'em nothing, they know more than you. I tried to learn some of them here, man. I tried to learn someone playing guitar. "Man, I know now." I said, "Well, you go on out there, you gonna' be the last stop of the world." Where I left 'em at, they still there playing the same thing.

Had a group came out of Mississippi, Art Griswold and them. I hired all of them when they first got here, didn't have no job, couldn't get no job. I carried them playing music all in Dayton, Ohio, carried them all up in there, they get up there, they want to fight among themselves. I got rid of them. I hired some more, they want to fight. They slippin' down there gettin' the money unbeknown to me. When it come down to pay-off at night they sittin' down there ballin' over the girls. I got rid of all of them. I call 'em my used-to-be group out of Detroit. We jammed the house when I played on Indiana at the Long Bar in Toledo. When these guys are late coming in, I be done, hired me another guy. Bandleader is something else, man!

Notes

1. There appears to be some discrepancy regarding Walter Mitchell's date and place of birth. According to 1920 census records unearthed by Bob Eagle and Eric LaBlanc and published in their book *Blues: A Regional Experience,* a birth date and place of March 19,

1918, in Pickens, Arkansas, is given. This information is totally at odds with that given by Walter Mitchell. Some credibility must be given to the new information, as the month and day are too much of a coincidence to ignore. While official records have proved a good source of information to researchers, it's perhaps wise to remain somewhat skeptical of data gleaned from census records and death certificates, as the information collected and recorded was occasionally supplied by unreliable informants.

2. The personnel for the session includes Walter Mitchell, vocal/harmonica; Robert Richard, harmonica; Boogie Woogie Red, piano; Little George, bass. "Broke and Hungry," St. George, STG 1002. "Big Stick Candy"/"I Can't Say It," King Records, unissued. Walter Mitchell plays second harmonica on Robert Richard's JVB/King sides.

3. LC Green and Walter Mitchell, "38 Pistol Blues"/"Hastings Street Boogie," JVB Records, late 1940s/early 1950s, reissued on Barrelhouse LP BH012 in 1977.

4. "Watercoast Blues," "Lowdown Dirty Shame," "Shadyland Blues," T-R-H CD 8001, 1998.

5. Charley Mills is usually known as the piano player on Baby Boy Warren's Staff recordings. It's not entirely clear whether Walter is suggesting that he played guitar as well. Despite rumors to the contrary, Mills was still alive in Detroit in 1985.

6. The LC Green/Sam Kelly Von42/3 is another Joe Von Battle two-harmonica opus. The harmonicas are Kelly and Robert Richard, as Walter denied ever recording with Kelly.

7. Despite the suggestion, Walter denied recording with Elder Wilson. [As of December 2014, a 104-year-old Elder Wilson was still living in Detroit.]

LC Green

Mike Rowe

Of all the elusive Detroit bluesmen known only by a name on a record label, one of the most fascinating and exciting was LC Green, an almost total biographical blank.[1] And even his name was misspelled on seven issued sides. Researchers in Detroit had repeatedly asked about him and tried to locate him, but after twenty years of searching only two concrete facts emerged. That he was from Minter City, Mississippi, was first reported by David Evans in an interview with Woodrow Adams while Bobo Jenkins and other Detroit bluesmen thought LC was living in Pontiac, Michigan. All this was known in the '60s and remarkably was all true, but Pontiac, a self-contained community with only amateur blues activity, stubbornly refused to give up its secrets. Not that LC was completely lost, for he was in contact with Walter Mitchell, and the two of them were known to Tim Healy, who had met LC and heard him play guitar on a few occasions. But by the time we got to Walter Mitchell, LC had been dead seven months, with the only new information provided, sadly, by his funeral program. And, again, even that was wrong!

But we were able to piece together a little of LC's story through the kindness of his sister Rebecca: "Yeah, I'm the last of the whole cotton-pickin' bunch!" laughs Rebecca down the phone. "LC was a great blues artist," I try, conversationally. "Yeah, but he never made no records," says Becky. But perhaps we could meet? "Well, what is it you want to know?" Everything! "Well, when he died someone broke in there, stole his guitar and everything. I only got one picture left on the side."

Many phone calls later we arrange to meet at a restaurant in Pontiac, and over several cups of coffee Becky tells me what little she knows. LC—just LC, no Christian names—was born on October 22 (correcting the funeral program), 1921, in Minter City, Mississippi. Their father was Elisha Green and mother, Leler. The parents separated in 1925 and Becky and LC were raised by their father, who remarried in 1929. LC learned to play a toy guitar when he was five years old, but there were no local musicians that Becky remembered to encourage him or form LC's style. I mentioned that Woodrow Adams had first recalled LC, and Becky said so he should have done, as they all grew up together! LC also played harmonica on a rack, which may give a clue to some of the elusive harp accompaniments to his songs, although with Sam Kelly and Walter Mitchell we seem to be well supplied with probables. Incidentally, Becky knew nothing of Walter Mitchell's claim to be a cousin.

That LC was a guitarist was remarkable, considering he had two fingers on each hand joined together. Becky laughs when she tells how he would get mad when she tried to tease him, unkindly threatening to cut the skin between. Before he moved to Pontiac, LC was living with a girl in Memphis, where he played at Riley's Grill, and he never lost his connection with the city, often visiting from Pontiac. On these trips he always took his guitar with him. Indeed, he always took it everywhere he went—so there may still be further reminiscences to be gleaned from Memphis about LC's life. Becky moved to Pontiac in 1937 and LC joined her in the city some time later. She was surprised to learn that he had, in fact, made records, as she only ever knew him to play at house parties or occasionally at the Wayside Inn, and then the Dew Drop Inn on Western Street, Pontiac, and he always played just by himself.

LC worked by day at construction work and played his guitar evenings around at friends' houses. He never married and roomed at various addresses—in 1951 he was living on Lake Street—which accounts for his invisibility to researchers. He used to get together with friends Matilda and Leonard on Pike Street, and Leonard played harp and guitar, too. There was one July 4 when he and Leonard played together in the park as part of the festivities. These public outings were rare, but once Becky, a girl named Wardelle, and LC were at the Mellow Lane Club and Becky sang "Be My Chauffeur." But this was unusual, as LC's rowdy lifestyle and hard drinking (his favorite drink was "White Label") were not to Becky's taste. When the end came, it was no surprise to Becky—"The doctor told him to quit drinking, but he was hardheaded." He died on August 24, 1985.

Notes

1. This interview is previously unpublished.

PART III

ST. LOUIS

Jimmy Thomas

In the early 1970s, Mike Leadbitter told me of meeting Jimmy Thomas, a former vocalist with Ike Turner's Kings of Rhythm, who, improbable as it may seem, was living in West London. Following Mike's death and my own increasing interest in all things Kings of Rhythm, I'd often reflected on his words, but having heard no recent mention of his whereabouts, I'd come to the conclusion that he must have returned to the United States. Imagine my surprise when in 1980 Cilla Huggins obtained the telephone number that led straight to our man, who was living within a stone's throw of the Queens Park Rangers grounds in West London.

Jimmy "Popeye" Thomas was born in Osceola, Arkansas, on January 20, 1939. Raised by his aunt and uncle, he grew up listening to the records of Big Maceo, Tampa Red, Walter Davis, and Sonny Boy Williamson, among others. Osceola in the 1940s and 1950s was a busy and prosperous small Southern town that supported several clubs and juke joints along with a small, but healthy, blues scene. The most popular artist was undoubtedly Albert King, then still known locally as Albert Nelson. While still in his teens Jimmy formed his first band, the Rock and Roll Trays, performing popular R&B and blues, appearing regularly at local venues in and around Osceola.

It was upon Albert King's recommendation that Jimmy traveled to East St. Louis to audition for Ike Turner, joining the popular Kings of Rhythm in early 1958. Closely followed by Tommy Hodge, the pair were replacements for the recently departed Clayton Love. It would also signal the beginning of a gradual shift in Ike Turner's musical direction, one that would take him from his blues base to one that featured an increasing amount of R&B and vocal group material.

The period encompassing the years 1956–1960 was arguably the most creative and inspirational in the Kings of Rhythm's history. Ike Turner, having made the transition from piano to guitar, found a truly unique style that set him apart from all others. A rock-solid band, a succession of outstanding vocalists, and some truly exciting records—in particular, their period with Federal—secured Turner's and the band's reputation.

Apart from a demo recorded in Memphis with the Rock and Roll Trays, Jimmy's first serious foray into the recording studio came when the Kings of Rhythm traveled to Cobra/Artistic Records in Chicago for a marathon session. The band accompanied Otis Rush, Buddy Guy, and Betty Everett, as well as recording numerous sides of their own, mostly featuring the vocal talents of Jackie Brenston and Tommy Hodge. Jimmy was relegated to backing vocalist on a couple of the sides. In recent years he has identified many of the key personnel, subsequently unraveling many previous inconsistencies in the Cobra/Artistic discography. In 1959 he recorded for the Granite City, Illinois–based Stevens Records along with Ike and the band's rhythm section. The wonderfully bizarre "Jack Rabbit" and the storming rocker "Hey-Hey" were issued under the Ike Turner pseudonym Icky Renrut.

Jimmy Thomas was a vocalist with Ike Turner for eight years, during which time he had several records issued under his own name on the Sue, Sonja, and Sputnik labels. He witnessed many significant changes for both Ike and the band. The advent of Tina Turner, their transition from a popular local St. Louis act, through to the early days of the Ike and Tina Turner Revue on the "chitlin' circuit," to their emergence as one of the top R&B acts in the country.

Leaving Ike and Tina in 1966, Jimmy first settled in Los Angeles working local jobs and recording for Mirwood before eventually relocating to London in 1968. In the intervening years there has been an album on Contempo Records and a handful of singles, including his own Osceola Records. Jimmy continues to live and perform in England.

Cilla Huggins and I first met Jimmy one Saturday afternoon in June 1980 for what turned out to be the first of many enlightening and memorable meetings. A gifted storyteller with a remarkably detailed memory and the good-natured patience to answer our unending questions, he approached the task with a great deal of good humor. That initial meeting ran into the early hours of Sunday morning before we finally left, our sides aching from having laughed so much. Jimmy Thomas is a tireless R&B enthusiast. I don't know of many people who would phone you at eight o'clock in the morning to tell you the name of a club that had burned down twenty years previously, the name having just returned to him in a dream! Thanks, Jim.

—Bill Greensmith

Still Hanging Right on in There—Dirty Jim Tells All: Jimmy Thomas Interview

Bill Greensmith and Cilla Huggins

Blues Unlimited #140/141 (Spring/Winter 1981)

I was raised by my uncle and aunt. My mother had me when she was fourteen or something, and my father, I never really knew him, but I knew his family, but, like, he split. He was married, I think, or something like that, when he got my old lady pregnant. She was just a girl. My grandfather was a big black man. My ancestry must be from West Africa, 'cause he looked like them. I've only known the characteristics of the people from West Africa since I've been in England.

This man was a real rich farmer, black farmer in Osceola, Nick Thomas. And there were a lot of sons, lot of boys, and they were real tear-aways, man. Anyway, he got my old lady pregnant, she had me, he split, and my uncle and aunt—my mother's sister and her husband—raised me. And my mother moved to Saginaw, Michigan. So that was my parents. I was still a few months old when my mother moved. I never knew my father, though I knew his brothers and things, my uncles. I was never really interested in him. I don't know where he moved to. I think maybe Detroit, because everybody went up north somewhere. My uncle and aunt, I always knew that they weren't my mother and father. In other words, there was no hiding it or nothing like that. I knew everything, they brought me up very good, told me exactly what was happening.

I don't know a great deal about the history of my family on my mother's side. I know that they were from Greenville, Mississippi, some of them anyway. They had a portrait that used to hang in the house of my great-grandmother. She was a Seminole Indian and I know they come from Mississippi. My mother's name was Ollie Booker.

Any relation to Charley Booker?

I don't know anything about my family on my mother's side. I could have been, but it's something I never did delve into. My mother used to come back once a year, holidays and things, to see me. When I joined Ike and started traveling, played Saginaw, all my folks on my uncle's side, they were all in Saginaw. Saginaw was the place for my folks, so when I went there it was like a homecoming, although I knew nothing about Saginaw. My uncle's name was Isom, Willie Isom; they called him Shag, that was because he had really shaggy hair. And the Isoms they were really great people. That was on my mother's sister's husband's side, who was acting as my father. It was like a homecoming playing Saginaw. It was as if I was playing Osceola, the kind of reception. They nicknamed me Popeye as a kid; that's what they used to call me. I suppose I had tight eyes. If you're short they call you Slim, if you're slim they call you Shorty. My mother lives in California now.

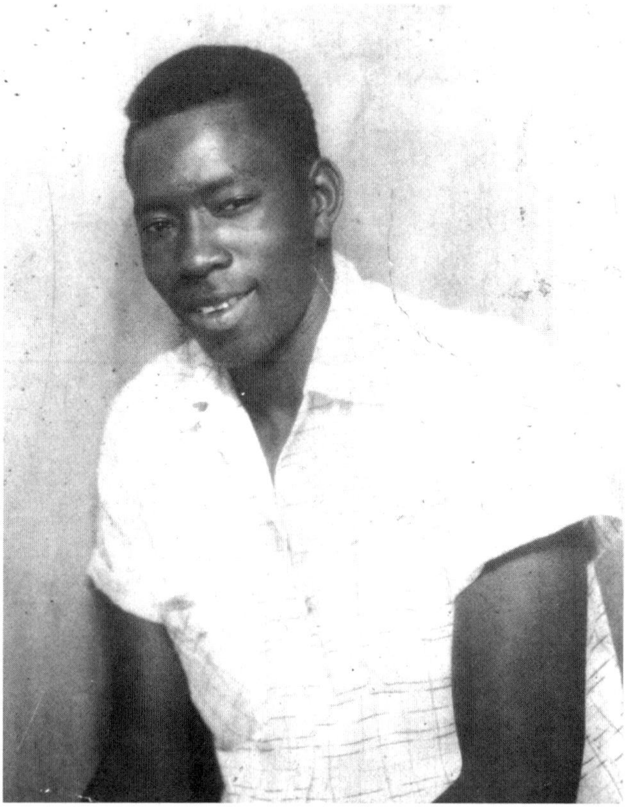

Jimmy Thomas. Osceola, Arkansas, c. 1956. (Photo Stella Reeder)

So what got you interested in music?

Well, shit, let me see now, we would have music classes in school, but, you know, it went in one ear and out the other. What it was, as a little kid I can remember as far back as I can go. My uncle and aunt they were very much, you know, music. What do you call it when somebody supports music? You know, local bands and things. They really dug it. That's how I come to know Albert King and people like that, old blues piano players. They bought a piano and used to have parties and things at the house, Albert and cats would come around, man, and play the piano and guitars.

And I used to sing along with the 78 records, man. They used to have a collection. Wow, if I'd known then like I know now I'd have been a rich man! They had, like, Walter Davis, Big Maceo, they had all them records, man, Tampa Red and all that shit. When I was a little tiny kid, man, I used to listen to them, I used to play 'em. I used to really dig "Going Down Slow" and Walter Davis. I used to like "Detroit Blues" by Tampa Red and all them kind of things. I weren't much more than a toddler, but I could remember the words. I used to learn the words, man, it was great. I used to sing along with the record player.

Although they bought a piano, I wasn't all that interested in learning to play it. I was interested in singing more than anything. I didn't care about playing, although I could pick out tunes. Even at the earliest age I can remember I always wanted to write the songs that I sang. Although I learnt the songs off the records and stuff, I used that as a guide to teach me something new. I would go to the piano, I learnt how to play the piano. I would be trying to pick out new melodies and thinking up new words.

There was a guy—I can't remember his last name, but I can see him in my mind's eye—his name was Lonzo, it was either Lonzo or Alonzo. This guy, man, was one of the baddest piano players that I've ever heard. Reflecting back, maybe he wasn't all that good, but to me—this guy, his fingers were like ballet dancers. Anyway, Lonzo, Albert King, all them guys. Hoss, there was a guy named Hoss, a piano player in Osceola, he was in the time of Alvin somebody.[1] Anyway, Hoss was his rival, they were supposed to be the baddest piano players around Osceola. These guys, man, they used to come around, my old man he bought him a electric guitar, he thought he wanted to be a little novice, you know. Albert taught him a few chords and stuff, but there was nothing serious, it was fun, you know.

Albert Nelson, that's his real name, we used to call him Black Albert. That was his nickname around town. Everybody, "Hey, Black Albert." He used to drive a big trailer truck for a living, for his normal job, hauling seeds, cotton seeds. I was pretty young, but I was a man. I knew what I was doing. Music was a natural thing, it wasn't no thing that I had to struggle to get into or nothing. And there was quite a few guys around school like me, we would just beat on tin pans, anything. You know shoo-wop, Five Royales and people like that came out. The Clovers and all that.

Did you have any gospel experience?

A bit, not a lot. My gospel experience was limited to the local church, which I wasn't forced to go to, which I didn't believe in anyway. I was only there for the chicks. If you didn't go to the church you were left out, you couldn't get any of the chicks, because everybody had to go to church on Sunday. You know choir practices, things like that, so you want to get in the choir, because that's where everybody was, you had more fun. And you get a chance to be away from home sometimes, go and visit other churches. I was never a serious gospel singer, but I always loved gospel groups like the Five Blind Boys, Sam Cooke and the Soul Stirrers, and all them, Mighty Clouds of Joy.

Did you see the In the Groove Boys?

Yeah, I saw the In the Groove Boys playing a lot of times. 'Cause my old man, like a town like that in the South you always get took around to these juke joints and stuff with your old man. They be drinking beer and stuff Sunday afternoon, things like that, dress me up, show me off—loved it. The T-99, that was a little bit later, after I got a little bit older. There were clubs like Distance's place. Distance was a guy who had a club outside of Osceola, one of them juke joints where everybody went.

What was it like there?

Oh, fucking great, man, great. Lovely hamburgers, that's what I remember, I loved hamburgers. Distance had one eye.

I tell you one that was real famous. In your travels did you ever hear of a club called the State Line Club, north of Blytheville? Missouri and Arkansas state line. That's where everybody used to go to get the liquor and stuff, man, oh, it was great. Let's see, there was the State Line Club, there was Distance's, these places were outside [of town]. I can't remember who ran the State Line, but it was a club where all the cats from Memphis and places used to come up [to], like Wolf and all them guys. It was up north of Blytheville, and Blytheville was eighteen miles north of Osceola, and then the State Line was about three miles north of Blytheville. Blytheville is the first town you come to on Highway 61 coming south from St. Louis after you cross the Arkansas state line. Let's see, there's another place I wanted to tell you about, man. This place was out on Highway 40 going west of Osceola. Oh, shit, what was this guy's name? It'll come to me later, these joints outside town where people get in their cars.

Distance was west of town. I got him confused with another club north of town, sort of northwest between Osceola and Luxora called . . . a guy named Black Willie. Now, Black Willie's place was another hot place, man. It burnt down. It burnt down before I even left.

Would this be Willie Bloom's?

No, Willie Bloom's was in town. That was our little teenage hangout. It used to be a grown-up club, but for some reason he turned it over to us. Oh, yeah, shit—Bloom's, man, that was our place. No playing there, it was just a café, just a hangout spot. It wasn't a joint, but I think they used to gamble. They used to have a gambling joint somewhere in the back, back of his house somewhere, but we never knew, we never went in there. We never knew about that place, we were just in the café part.[2]

Yeah, Black Willie's was another party place everybody went there. They used to have ball games out there. Every Sunday was a ball game and there was always some band, either Little Walter [Jefferson] and them, Albert King—somebody would be playing out there all the time.

Did you get name bands out there?

To us they were big names. But Albert, to me, man, he's the epitome of a good man, because he always tried to help us and encourage us in every way.

Let's see, George York's place, that was a café. He also had a hotel that was right on the railroad. And I remember George York had a bald head. He was the first Kojak I'd ever seen, shaved. Real nice man. I remember his wife died when I was real, real little. And his café was right there on the railroad tracks. The In the Groove Boys played there. I mean every joint, all the guys who was around they played in every joint, there was no residencies, everybody moved around, you know, up and down Highway 61, out Highway 40, all the joints. All in between there was loads. There was so many joints down Wilson, Arkansas.

Bootlegger's Alley?

Oh, right, man, Bootlegger's Alley was like a forerunner. This was before the T-99. It survived after the T-99, but the popularity was gone. Bootlegger's Alley was this little area, one joint and a couple of houses, and the joint was owned by a guy they called Bootlegger. And Bootlegger was an ugly cat, man. This cat he had one eye, but a really nice man. I can remember him when I was a kid. They used to gamble there, all the joints would be gambling, pitching dice and shit. Then came the T-99 and everybody started going there. Bootlegger's Alley would have music—now, I'm really going back now, man. I was so small then my uncle would take me around and sit my little ass up on the crap table—a toddler, I suppose.

Albert King with Baby Sister and Louise Reeder outside of T-99, 1953. (Photo Stella Reeder)

What about the T-99?

In the T-99 it was fun. That's the only way you can describe it, fun. M. C. Reeder was the guy that owned it. M. C. was kinda fat, kinda short, wore big hats. Dressed kind of smart all the time, wore string ties and he dabbled in playing saxophone. He was a novice. He dug it, but he was alright. He could honk, he was a honker. Yeah, Jay McNeely, that was his thing. There was one tune he would always want to play when he'd come up on stage and he used to bug us. We liked for him to come up and play with us sometime, because he owned the club for a start, he paid us! "Cornbread," that was his favorite thing and that was it, everybody would be up on they feet, everybody would be clappin' and slappin' . . . It was good fun. M. C., yeah, he was a great guy, man.

He had a beauty shop in the same building—he'd expanded, man. It was a hotel, it was a beauty shop, it was a club, it was everything, gambling joint. But M. C.—well, I don't know if I should say this. Next time you meet somebody from down there you ask them if they know of this. There was a rumor that M. C. was supposed to have three nuts. (*laughing*) I'm telling you, it's true. He was supposed to have three nuts! This is true, he was known for that.

How did this tie in with the beauty shop?

Oh, yeah, the beauty shop. I tell you what it was, here's how it come about, the beauty shop. M. C. added the beauty shop on because he was screwing two sisters, right? He started screwing the older sister, then he started screwing the younger sister, and they were both really fine, man. I'm telling you, to us they were like—Mari-

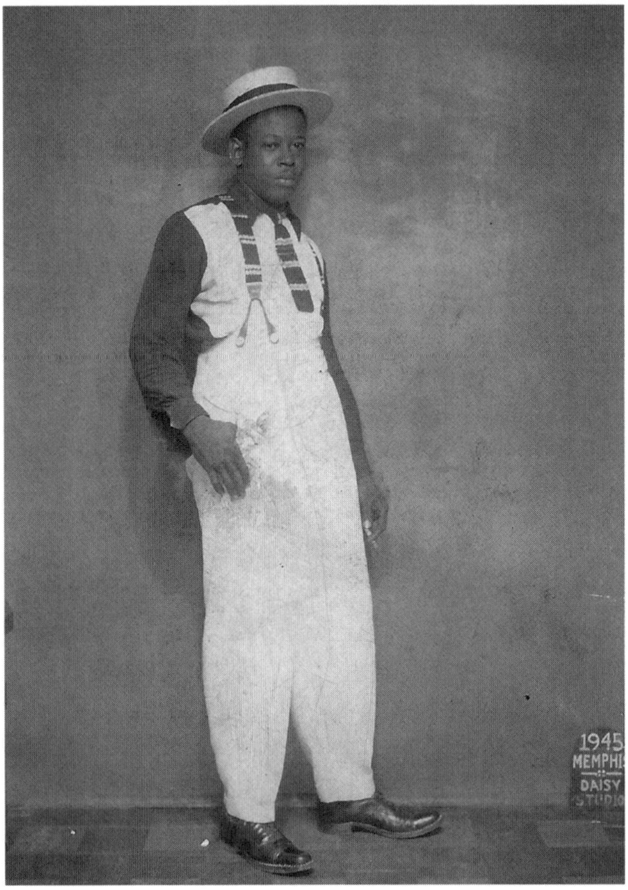

M. C. Reeder. Memphis, Tennessee, c. 1945. (Photo Stella Reeder)

lyn Monroe didn't have nothing on them chicks. I'm sure my memory's pretty accurate on that, they were really beautiful chicks. Black chicks, fair-skin chicks, big tits, everything.

Nobody could believe it. That's probably how he got that reputation of having three nuts. People would kill, man, you know. Chicks would be jealous down there, carry knives, razors, you know what I mean. They would be chasing cats with bricks (*laughs*), you don't cheat. Everybody was cheating, but don't get caught. Your old lady catch you cheating, Jack, you got a real problem.

And nobody could understand it, man, how M. C. had these two chicks. He got the first one and he built the hotel. And he got the second one and he built the beauty shop and both of them was running the beauty shop. There was one called Baby Sister, she was the youngest and he had her as well, and they run that whole complex with M. C. They were sisters and they were beautiful and they knew about the other one. Totally accepted. And we used to be, man . . . we'd have our tongues hanging out. After we grew up a bit, then, they would begin to chase us a bit. M. C. got toppled off his throne after awhile. But that cat was known for that. That's what his whole thing was supposed to have been.

Black Matt?

I'm trying to remember about Black Matt. He was running a café. I'm trying to remember where it was. I don't know what George York's connection was with Black Matt, there was some connection. Black Matt, I know he was supposed to be working for the police, a snitch as they call it. Because everybody—there was whiskey stills and shit, man. People was doing bootleg liquor and stuff, all kinds of stuff was going down. But everybody knew that he was a snitch or whatever, so they accepted him as that. They just knew Black Matt.

Matter of fact, my old man, my uncle Shag knocked his ass off, knocked him out, one punch put him right out. (*laughs*) This was famous around town, man, I'm telling you, this was famous. Because Black Matt pulled a gun on my uncle, in his face. This was out at Distance's club.

I can't remember what it was about, but my uncle he was a really nice-looking guy, he looked like a black Errol Flynn, because he was fair-skinned. He really was a nice—chicks loved him, man, and I think Black Matt was really jealous of him. But he pulled this gun on him and put it in his face and snapped it. He actually pulled the trigger and it snapped, it missed. When I say missed, it didn't fire and it was loaded. It went just like that, man, tried to kill my uncle. And my uncle hit him and there was a crowd, everybody duckin', "Oh my God!" whatever. My uncle didn't give him a second chance, boom, and the cat went down. They used to tell that story a lot. That was famous around town.

So Black Matt wasn't exactly one of my favorite characters back in them days. I mean we didn't have anything against him, and later he apologized and begged my uncle to forgive him and all of that stuff. Because my uncle, everybody liked him, he was a good lad, he was alright. And they knew Black Matt was a snitch anyway, so they cooled it out. But my uncle used to say, "Watch him, man, don't you never have anything to do with that guy."

George York, he was like M. C., he owned a club right on the railroad tracks, located right across from the light plant, the power plant. He was giving the guys work, between him and M. C., because they were the two main joints in town. They had all the connections and everything and they paid the guys, put money up for them. George York also had a hotel in the back of the place, a big hotel right along the railroad tracks.

So the guys would be in town, they weren't earning no money in them days, they probably played for fifty cents. So he was giving them food and shelter and putting money in their pockets, helping them buy their instruments and everything, so he was like a godfather around town, George York. My old man, he was friends with all them guys. I don't know, they were like mentors, they knew him, they knew me and the situation. My uncle was a real good guy. I mean even taking me, his wife's sister's kid. Looking back on it now, he was a really well respected man. Because he was a young guy, all the chicks wanted him and he was hooked up with this lady and not even his own kid, and, man, he was really proud of me all the time.

So that's how I got to know, got help from Albert King, through his respect, you know. Because Albert's a great guy, he always tried to help somebody. Yeah, Black Albert, Big Foot Albert. Yeah, Albert, everybody liked him, too. He'd drive a truck all week hauling them cotton seeds and things, whatever he was hauling, and playing his guitar on weekends. They used to play old Hofners. I remember them big old blond guitars they used to have, electric pickups on them, old Hofners, Epiphones, things like that.

I was so young, man, but the In the Groove Boys were local yokels as far as we were concerned, but to me they were fantastic. Now, them guys, they were old guys. As I grew up in school and me and my boys started to play for real, them guys had been around for ages. And they would sort of help us along, and they would come and play with us sometime, giving us pointers. And they were learning off of us as well, because we were playing another kind of music. In other words, we were doing the shoo-wop stuff, but they were very much just blues. You know, this was after the Midnighters and all them cats came on the scene, because we was into that—WDIA and all that.[3]

Osceola was buzzing Saturday night. Shit, yeah, Osceola was hot. It was tiny, it was small, but, boy, it was hot. I suppose because it was on the road to Memphis. It was one of the obvious places between Memphis and St. Louis. It was even hipper than Cairo and all them places which were bigger towns. Yeah, Osceola was much hipper; matter of fact, Osceola surpassed Blytheville in popularity. Every joint, every café there was gambling. I mean legitimate, supposed to be cafés. You know, in the back or somewhere off the side somewhere there was a little crap house, man, shooting craps.

Arthur Woods, he had a little café. Now, his joint was legit. I mean, they really went there for a meal and things like that, drink beer and listen to the jukebox. Arthur Woods, and his wife's name was Pearl. They were really nice people.

I didn't know too much about Blytheville, but I'll tell you there was Pearl's Grill. That's where all the teenagers hang out, like Bloom's in Osceola, that was the equivalent. There was two clubs in particular, but I can't remember their names for the life of me.

There was another group called the Footstompers or Footwarmers, something like that, somebody and the Footwarmers. They always used to alter around anyway. Sometimes Albert Nelson's band would be the Footwarmers or the In the Groove Boys, they all used to alter around.

There was a rivalry between George York's place and the T-99. Then somebody opened another club called the Club Morocco, which was just a street over from the T-99, and these cats were great rivals. After the Morocco opened up that's when me and my cats were on the scene, just little ole schoolboys. It was very much a novice thing, and we had all the young kids around following us. Sometimes [Eddie] Snow would play with us. Then we had another group that was rivaling us. Me and my group called ourselves the Rock and Roll Trays. I don't know why the hell we called ourselves that. It didn't make no sense, but it just sounded good! We were doing things like "All Shook Up" and stuff like that, which was very much the vogue, and so we had all the little girls and things following us around.

The piano player we called Maestro, Walter Lee. Can't remember what Lee's last name was. Then there was Walter Jefferson, we stole Walter Jefferson from . . . he worked in all them local bands. He was so good everybody wanted him, but he was based up around Cairo, Illinois, a lot. And whenever he was in town he would always stay at the T-99. And they had a ballpark there as well, baseball park out back. Because it was a whole plot of land and it started off just being a club. Then he built a two-story hotel which was just like an army barracks reflecting back. (*laughs*) It was on the north side of town across the railroad tracks. So they had a ballpark out there, and people used to screen off the porch and that was the grandstand. People used to watch the ball game. So Little Walter [Jefferson] joined us. Snow would play with us sometimes, and sometimes Alvin would play with us. Alvin played with Little Walter [Jefferson]. Albert King and all the top local guys that was around. Earl Hooker and all them guys. Now, let's see, who else was around? This guy Hoss. Now, Hoss had long fingers. I remember there was a rivalry between Hoss and Alvin. Now, Alvin could play, he was a real blues and boogie-woogie man. Alvin and Hoss both, they were pretty good musicians, technically speaking. They were always trying to correct people. The people that would come in anywhere, didn't matter about the bars. Them guys would always be trying to show them some discipline and show them about tone. They were always trying to help in that way, although they were very unassuming guys. But they had a great rivalry between them and they were old guys, too.

One thing I remember distinctly about their rivalry was that Alvin had short fingers, short little stubby fingers, but he was fast, man. Hoss used to criticize him, saying that he couldn't play because he had short fingers, "Man, whoever heard of a fucking piano player with short fingers?" I remember Hoss's fingers were really long and slim. This cat could reach a span like that and they used to argue about lengths of fingers, and the guy said, "It ain't never been written nowhere that a cat with short fingers can't play piano." And he said, "Yeah, man, I've never heard of anybody with short fingers being a good piano player." It was always that kind of little rivalry thing, but they were the best of buddies and them guys would alternate in and out of the band.

There was no set pattern of musicians in any particular group, even in Albert King's band. All them guys, I suppose some would leave and some would be working whatever, because everybody had to sort of subsidize their thing. But everybody played in all the clubs, there was no sort of permanent residency for nobody. Everybody just moved around among each other, that's why it was so good. You had a chance to work with all those different guys.

All the musicians sort of drifted between Osceola and Cairo, it was like a permanent gypsyish life for them. I guess they hit all them towns in between, they'd be there.

Lee Taylor, piano player?

Yeah, he was good. He didn't play with us. He was an old cat, he was like Albert King's thing. Let's see, he used to play mostly by himself, I think. I'm not sure, because at that time I was pretty small. He used to come around our house and play. I'm not sure if he played with bands much. I don't think he did, but I'm sure he did play with some bands sometimes, because he was so hot and he was really good, from what I remember. Lee Taylor, this cat was known to be a thief. Yeah, Light-Fingered Lee! No shit. Yeah, everybody knew because he'd been in jail for stealing and shit, but he was honest among his friends.

What kind of stuff would he play?

Oh, boogie-woogie, blues, barrelhouse. He was good, too. He could thump that shit out, boy. Lee Taylor was bad. I knew he was bad, because my old man said so. He used to sound good to me, but my old man knew, he had good taste. That's how I knew about all them blues cats like Maceo, because he had all that kind of shit. That was the records he always bought, Sonny Boy and all them. I grew up on that shit. So if he said Lee Taylor was bad . . . I don't know whatever happened to him, he must have been about thirty or forty then.

But, yeah, Little Walter, he was something else. He'd have a jug of wine sitting by him and he'd sit on a stool with his guitar, and, god, the guy could play, man, I mean really make a guitar talk, make it weep. He was a young guy, but he was older than us, but he fitted in with us better than Snow and them cats, because they were much older. But they all wanted to play with us because we were hot.

Walter Lee played piano, Aubrey Wallace played drums, sometimes we switch around and I'd get on the drums. But we finally got Frank Seals, Son Seals, to play drums, he was the permanent drummer. I didn't know he played guitar until you showed me that picture of him playing guitar. He always used to pick up the guitar and try and play. He was alright, he was learning, but his main thing was a drummer. He was our drummer.

Wilson, Arkansas, was our first out-of-town gig as a band, me and my boys. I remember that, man, we packed up into cars. Shit, I remember we went to Memphis to do a demo. It was some guys, it was Joe Harris, I think he's dead now. He used to work with my uncle, and Joe had lots of brothers. And one of his brothers was named Volley, and they used to live in Toledo, Ohio, and so to us they were slick, man. They came down driving big cars, Big Apple hats and shit, them cats they knew everything to us. They recognized that we were good and being from cities up north, to hear a compliment from them—well, hey, man, we must be pretty good. We must be cookin'.

And them guys, Volley and his partner named Chuck, they decide to manage us. They talked to our parents and things, "We're gonna manage these boys, we're gonna make sure they gonna be alright, they good," this and that. So they started getting us gigs out of town, outside Osceola in little towns like Grider, Wilson, Lepanto. Shit. (*laughing*) Oh, all them little places, man. They even used to get us white gigs. I mean, down there then to play a white gig? Albert King was one of the only guys that was doing white gigs.

White gigs like out in Little River. There's a place called Little River, Arkansas, which was really redneck country, wasn't no niggers out there. Niggers didn't like it around Little River, man, but it was more myth than anything else. It wasn't really as bad as that. But I remember we played Little River and they wanted us there every week. It was really hot. We was smokin', because we was doing all Chuck Berry's stuff—that was my idol, Chuck Berry. I mean, shit, "Maybellene" and things like that used to get audiences standing on tables and chairs.

So Chuck and Volley being our managers were getting us gigs all over the place—white, black, all kind of clubs—and they wanted to take us back up to Ohio. They wanted to take us to Detroit, Cleveland, Toledo, and all up there. We wasn't too sure about that, but we didn't care, man. They was delivering the goods, so we didn't care, man, whatever they say, but going up north, well, I don't know. So Chuck and Volley they decided that they were going to get us to make a record. Now, to us that's what it meant, but in fact it was just a demo. They were going to take the thing and try and do . . . you know, because we knew nothing.

They took us to Memphis, some little ole place down on Beale Street. That was my first encounter with a recording studio and it was a bullshit little studio, but nevertheless to us it was big-time. And, man, we got in there, we saw microphones and things, little booth there. I was the only one that wasn't nervous. To me it was a natural—I was just fascinated by the equipment.

It was called "There's No Need of Crying," and the other side of it was called "Two More Days," and I wrote both the songs. I kept it for a long time. I think I wore it out. They pressed up about twenty-five or thirty of them just so we could give them around to our friends. Each one of us had a few. I was trying to learn to write songs then and they wasn't bad. I modeled "Two More Days" on Frankie Lymon. Oh, man, pride. We was bursting open with pride and we was getting gigs and we was really getting hot, starting fights and things. When I say starting fights, I mean chicks would be clamoring over us and guys want to beat us up! Oh, it was hot, man.

Everybody sang. Everybody played something and sang. I would just sing and I would kick a little drums now and then and I had me a little thing I could play on piano. I had a couple of boogie-woogie things I could play, but we would just swap around. There was no set thing in the band, it was just a good-time thing. We were just doing it having fun, but we knew that—well, some of us knew that it was going to be our profession. I certainly knew that it was gonna be mine, and I think that Son Seals knew it was gonna be his. And Aubrey Wallace, the other boy who sang and played a little drums as well, I think he had an idea that he wanted to be professional. But the rest of the guys got into preaching and all kinds of stuff and getting married. Some of them never got off the ground.

What about Frank Seals?

I'm glad you talked to me about Son Seals. I'm really glad that that's the same guy. His old man was just a character. He had a little café, little greasy-spoon café, and he used to push his little thing around on wheels, selling pig ears and things, pig tails, pig feet, yeah, Son Seals's old man.

Did he have music out there?

No, he was just an old guy, man. He was really a character. I suppose he would be like your typical East Ender who would sell what you call them, snails—winkles and all that. Used to hang out outside all the joints. That's what the old man was and he had a little old greasy-spoon thing that he ran over in Laney Quarters. They called it Laney Quarters, it was shanty houses and shit. Well, they wasn't really shanties, they was alright. The houses were owned by a man named Mr. Laney, he was most of the niggers' landlord in the west side of Osceola. Yeah, Mr. Laney, he owned most of the property.[4]

We was like brothers, man. Shit, that's where it all began with us. Son wasn't on that demo tape. I was sorry too, because I remember he was around. And a lot of the guys—because we was considered a better class of kid, if you like, than Son Seals. I mean, Son Seals—it was real down there, man. (*laughing*) This cat was drinking wine at ten, you know what I mean? He was hanging out! Really, he was. Like he was a real tramp, man, tramp kid. But he was cool, man. We loved him, he was great.

At first we didn't like him. Well, they didn't like him much. Aubrey, Walter Lee, and all them guys, they didn't like him too much. They used to look at him . . . well, Frank used to walk around, his old shirttail hanging out, dusty old hair everywhere, man. He just didn't care. He didn't comb his hair and his eyes all half-mast, but he'd fight, so nobody fuck with him, nobody messed with him, you didn't talk to him wrong. But he was just like that, guys—"You dirty . . ." "Yeah, but I'll kick your ass if you mess with me," so everybody sort of just talked about him and stood off. "You funky, man, you smell, Jack." He'd be beating the drums and shit, "God damn I don't wanna stand—I don't wanna stand by him, man. Why don't you bathe, nigger, wash your nasty ass?"

But, no, he was okay, man. He cleaned up and everything, and one of the reasons why Frank got accepted was because I dug him and my old man dug him too. He used to come over to our place, and we had a nice place. Old man was really clever, he could build anything, do anything. So I was getting support all round, whoever my friends were; if I wanted to bring them home it was cool. And Son Seals started coming around to my place a lot. I was the only one who wanted to associate with the guy and he started to clean up.

We did that demo and he wasn't on it, because they didn't want him on it or something. I can't remember now what the politics were, but Walter Lee played drums. Walter Lee and Aubrey sort of switched around on it, I think. Aubrey, he played drums, really he was a singer, like I said. We all tried. First thing we tried to do as we sang was try to play the drums when we wasn't singing. If it was my turn to sing, you play the drums. Everybody had their little thing and so we just swapped around like that till Son Seals joined the band, and when he joined the band he was the real drummer.

Did he sing as well?

He couldn't sing real good. Now, what was his song? Wait a minute—he had one favorite song, "Jenny Jenny," Little Richard's thing. That was his song and that was about the only song he sang. I don't know, maybe one more. But he was the real drummer and then it started to take the shape of a real band. Then Little Walter joined us and he was the guitar player, he was bad. And Walter Lee started playing the piano. He was the real piano player, and myself was the real singer and Aubrey Wallace also sang. And we had a girl name of Bobbie Clayton. She used to sing with us as well, and we used to do Shirley and Lee tunes and things like that. We used to have a lot of fun. Barbara Jean Clayton, she's probably married with a houseful of babies like the rest of them did. Most of the chicks did that I grew up with.

Robert Lee?

Oh, yeah, a guitar player from Osceola. He was one of the guys from my little group when we would mess around the T-99 and all the little clubs. I don't know if that was his whole name, or was it Robert Lee something? But he was from Osceola and he was at least five years older than me.

When we started playing we were the hottest thing around there. There wasn't no competition. Albert had gone, he'd moved.[5] The only competition we had was from the bands from Memphis, the big bands. I mean we gave them hell, we really did once we found a format, found how to structure things, you know, climaxing shows and things.

People like Bobby Bland, man, we used to be on stage with people like that, whenever they would come to the T-99 and gig. We wouldn't back them, we'd be there, they'd come on and emcee would always, "Hey, listen give our boys a shot, we got our boys here come on and do . . . hey, yeah . . ." So Bobby would get on the mike and say, "Yeah, we got some boys here, little Popeye and his group, the Trays," or whatever we started calling ourselves, all sorts of things. "You know, get them up and do a number." We'd get up and do "All Shook Up" or something. We'd tackle any kind of song, not just rock 'n' roll, anything. And we'd get up and break the house down, blow the roof off the thing!

And guys like Bobby and them, "Hey, these boys is great," and he'd get me up and I'd sing one of his songs like "Don't Want No Woman," which was one of my favorites by him at the time. My voice wasn't strong like his, but I'd be trying to copy him, you know. And shit, man, he'd come and he'd sing with us, he'd start playing the number, get his band back on stage, "Hey, boy, come on and sing this song with me," things like that. We would always blow with them, whoever was around.

Did these guys always bring their own musicians?

Oh, yeah, they had their own bands, B. B., all them guys. T-99 was the place, that's where everybody played. Then the Morocco got hot and that became the T-99's main rival. Because George York's wasn't really big enough to hold the kind of people that them cats drew, but the '9 was big enough.

Howlin' Wolf?

Loved Howlin' Wolf. Wolf used to play a lot at the State Line Club. My old man used to take me up there. In fact, that's where I first saw Howlin' Wolf. He had a whole band, saxophones, he had everything. Them cats come from Memphis, they were professionals to us. They were really big guys. Most of them had horns in them days. Oh, man, he was big shit to us! That just goes to show you how low down the scale we were! We was on the floor, man. But it was great, because them guys they taught us a lot. They liked for us to come around and watch 'em, try to copy them. We never tried to copy no mannerisms, but voices and things. I think that is why I've got a versatile voice now. I can sing in nearly any register. That's because I used to try and sing like Howlin' Wolf and all of 'em, man (*sings "How Many More Years"*). I used to love it, man.

Calvin Newborn and them? We didn't particularly care about Calvin and Phineas Newborn very much. They were verging on jazz a lot, and in them days jazz wasn't really our thing. I mean, I really didn't get into jazz until later.

Junior Parker?

Yeah, Junior Parker, that was another one. Usually wherever Bobby Bland was playing Junior was either—well, I don't know how it was set up, but he was either there by himself or later on he got a band. Now, I don't know if he played like that all around, but when he would come up there it was usually Junior Parker and Bobby Bland. I never knew Junior Parker very much. When I say very much, he would come and maybe get up and do a number at that point. You'd hear about him on the radio, you know, 'cause he was making records, but it wasn't until later when he come into his own right that he meant anything to us. We didn't follow his career very much.

Did you ever see Matt Murphy?

Guitar Murphy? Baddest guitar player ever lived. Yeah, man, yeah! Guitar Murphy, that guy, we used to say he had Highlight on his fingers he was so fast. Highlight was a chemical supposed used to . . . I think it was probably a myth. Suppose if you got a mule or a dog that was kinda sick and you didn't want to put him down, just want him to kind of leave, you didn't have the heart to put him down, you'd just put a drop of Highlight on his ass and he'd run himself to death! That's what it was supposed to be. It must have been some kind of acid stuff, some very hot stuff.

No, Guitar Murphy, this cat, man, his fingers, he used to walk around squeezing a rubber ball all the time, keep his fingers nimble. This guy was bad. I saw Murphy with—let's see . . . I saw him in Chicago later after I joined Ike and them. That's when I got to meet him and got to know him, otherwise he was like a god. But he was just a guitar player that came over with some bands. He was with Bobby Bland. I don't know, I think he came over with Rosco Gordon. Because all them guys was on the higher scale, but all them guys they was just country boys, so they just played, like, whoever had a gig this week somewhere. They all knew each other's numbers, they were all broadcasting together. You never knew who was playing on what half the time, because they all played the same licks anyway.

Yeah, man, I was young then, like from a toddler, but I prided myself on always knowing what was happening with records and things. I really loved it.

Did you ever see Johnny Ace or Earl Forrest?

I never seen Johnny Ace or Earl Forrest live, but Earl Forrest played the T-99. Saxophone players and instrumentalists and things, we never was too much into that, but later when Jimmy Forrest made "Night Train," I remember that. Like, that was a big thing, man. That was like the black national anthem. Anywhere the record played it was like—everybody, "Yeah, do it!"

The same with B. B. King when he first did "3 O'Clock in the Morning." Wow, you'd hear that guitar start, everybody stand up and "Hey!" Beer would be flying. I'm telling you, man, it was great. They'd wear them records out. In the space of a week, less than a week, every jukebox in Osceola had worn out its copy it had. They always had to have a new copy to come in. Yeah, because people just play 'em, man. I mean they just play 'em to death, the jukebox would be smokin'. It would be hot on Saturday night, shit. People drinking that beer, wine and shit, boy, and eating that fish, man. Guitar be singing and B. B. be singing them blues. Yeah, that was great stuff.

But, I mean, in looking back at that stuff sometimes it was like it never happened, it's so far removed. I mean I'm so far removed, it's just amazing. Because them times they will never be again, no way. It's a shame they didn't have videos and stuff like that to capture some of that stuff in them days, because it's really gone. And it's difficult to try and describe it, what it was like, the atmosphere, I mean in those funky clubs, man, juke joints. But you just can't describe it, the smell, everything, the way people act, the language, the whole communication. It was a totally different world and it's amazing.

Did you see any other guitar players that may have come through town, like Robert Nighthawk?

Yeah, Robert Nighthawk, that was another one. Yeah, shit, that's right, because him and Ike they went way back together, because I remember later on after I joined Ike, he used to talk about Robert Nighthawk. He said, "Oh, yeah, I used to see him, he used to come through town sometimes." I don't think I ever saw him.

Boyd Gilmore, Sonny Boy Williamson?

I never see none of them guys, I knew about them.

Adolph Duncan?

Sax player, yeah, I remember him. Adolph was based in Memphis, I think. He was like a really slick guy. He used to wear zoot suits and shit—"Adolph's in town, man." He was one of the pros. Later on I heard he was called Billy, you know listening to WDIA, because he was always on there with them guys, Rosco and all them cats. Yeah, but we knew him as Adolph. He could play. That guy could blow.

Did you know L. V. Parr [guitar]?

L. V. was bad. I remember L. V. I remember he would come to our house sometimes, because he was good friends with my old man.

Did you ever see Ike's band at the time?

No. I never knew anything about Ike Turner until I got to St. Louis. Jackie, because Jackie's record was such a big hit, Jackie Brenston. I didn't see him, but as a matter of fact I bought the record "Rocket 88." Yeah, Jackie Brenston, man, I remember when that record came out, wow! I think the closest Jackie got to us was Memphis or maybe West Memphis. He was pretty big then. In fact, he was so big then till he was like . . .

The band split then?

That's right, they told me about that. It was at that time, I remember, Ike had a little rivalry with Jackie. After Jackie had the hit apparently there was some argument, certain controversy. Because when I joined Ike, Jackie was there and all that. Because Jackie was tight. We was all tight. We used to talk about them days when Jackie had the hit and Ike hated Jackie for that. And Jackie hated Ike because he had to come back and start working for Ike now, whereas he used to be the star. But, now, all them guys when they was working from Clarksdale, around Memphis and that, let's see, they was working with the Wolf and a lot of people. [Willie] Kizart and all them. There was Bad Boy [Willie Sims], Johnny O'Neal he was around there with that set.[6]

But anyway, what happened—Jackie, I can't remember exactly how the song came about, but Jackie got the credit and Ike didn't think he should have. Because every song that came out in them days, it was under the name of someone else, the guy that sang never got the credits, in other words. In them times the way they had their little setup. But Jackie somehow got his name on the record, it was his record "Rocket 88," Jackie Brenston. So the cats was mad, they was pissed off. 'Least Ike was pissed off, because apparently him and Jackie didn't speak to each other for a long time. And then Jackie drank himself damn near to death and came back in to work for Ike in St. Louis later, I remember that.

Big City Four? They broadcast from Forrest City.

No, I never listened to Forrest City.

Jerry Lee Walker was the drummer.

Jerry told me something about that. That's right, he used to tease me a lot. "Fucking Osceola, little ole nigger from Osceola, you ain't shit. Osceola ain't nothing, man." He used to talk about Forrest City, that's right, Jerry Walker. Wow! You just triggered off something there. I never listened to Forrest City radio station, we always listened to Memphis.[7]

KOSE was a white station, wasn't it?

I don't know, because we never listened to it, only when the fellows were broadcasting.

Earl Roberts?

Yeah, he was a disc jockey [on KOSE]. Little cat wore glasses and wore, what you call them little straw hats, you know the kind they show in all them American-type musicals and things? Yeah, a boater. He used to wear one of them and cock it. We call it ace-deuce, cocked to the side. Glasses on, bow tie, real little dandy-like guy, that was Earl Roberts.

There was another radio station in Blytheville called KLCN. They used to also—same guys, Albert and all them.

But radio that's one thing we didn't do. We didn't like KOSE very much. We only liked KOSE for Albert King or Albert Nelson and a few local gospel groups, that's the only time we would listen to KOSE. We listened to Memphis stations. Albert was on once or twice a week. I can't remember anything except it was the In the Groove Boys or something like that, it was no big thing. They did have sponsors, but I can't remember who they were.

Peptikon was B. B. King's one, his first sponsor. When he came on, his little theme song was (*sings*): *"Peptikon sure is good [x 3] / You can get it anywhere in your neighborhood. / Man, I'm really livin'!"* That was B. B.'s first thing. That brought B. B. King on, the Beale Street Blues Boy. They were the only things I really remember as far as advertisements go, bringing on bands. We could get WDIA very clearly, because when I left, shit, it was about fifty-thousand watts then, you could get it in about five states. WDIA was smokin', Rufus Thomas and all them guys. Moohah, he was the Rev. A. C. Williams, but all during the week he was Moohah. Nat D. Williams, that's Booker T. Washington High School. Joe Hill Louis, I think he died or something. Yeah, big fat Ford Nelson played piano, wow. Willa Monroe, she was the Angela Rippon of the black radio. (*laughs*) There was Rufus's little daughter Carla, she came up. Carla Thomas was—well, we wasn't taking her serious. She was alright, but I don't know—to me, I didn't particularly care about Carla Thomas very much. We was more interested in B. B. and them guys. Rosco and all them—they was hot.[8]

I used to hate Joe Hill Louis's music. The reason I didn't like his music was because nothing ever rhymed. If my memory serves me well, this cat used to come on WDIA and his theme song was like this (*sings*): *"The Be-Bop Boy is on the air [x 3]."*

"Tune in at 4 for the little ole show," or something like that, nothing ever rhymed: *"I'll think I'll lay my head down on this railroad track / And let the train cut my head off."* (*laughing*) And I used to want to kick the radio. You fuck, I hated it, at least make it rhyme. Now it would be humorous. If I could listen to it now I could really get off on it, but in them days when I took it serious it was terrible.

Yeah, Bill Harvey, he joined up with B. B. In fact, B. B. went on his first tour with Bill Harvey, I remember, when that was a big thing. B. B. had never flew before and it was his first gig, and he was gonna fly to Houston, Texas. And it was a big thing, they was teasin' him, Rufus Thomas and Moohah, "Yeah, our Beale Street Blues Boy gonna get on the airplane, man, he gonna fly . . ." Yeah, man, and they were playing his records and things. Going to Houston, Texas. Yeah, I remember that real good.

Did you ever listen to Dewey Phillips's *Red Hot 'n' Blue*?

Yeah, WHBQ from Memphis. Yeah, *Red Hot 'n' Blue,* I remember. But there was also another show, *In the Groove.* It was on WMC, it was an NBC national network station, but the local things they slip in between, and I think *In the Groove* came on every afternoon about three-thirty, I think. I can't remember the deejay, but I remember the theme song "In the Groove," it was only on for fifteen minutes and the guy would come on: "Yeah, welcome to *In the Groove.*" I can't remember all the patter, but that was one of the first black music shows that just played black records, just records, as far as I remember. I think it preceded WDIA. I don't remember hearing WDIA until after WMC *In the Groove.*

How did you come to join Ike's band?

What happened, when I finished school I was supposed to went to college in Little Rock. I only stayed a few months, less. I hated it. Couldn't stand the whole thing about college. I was supposed to be studying agriculture and shit like that.

When I came back to Osceola I started working with my uncle and decided, well, I don't know what to do yet, except I know I want to play music, but I don't know where I want to go to play it. I didn't want to go to Memphis and I wanted to get out of the South for a start, and I always thought I would like to go to Los Angeles. But that was all dreams, I'd just got back.

My uncle never objected to me going into music, they were really cool, really was. They tried to tell me, like, hey—because my uncle could turn his hand to anything, like, he built a house. He always tried to tell me, "Wherever you go or whatever you do, just know that you can always work, man, always earn yourself a living. All the things that you done learn from me." And he had a lot of faith in me, I think.

Anyway, I came back and I'd been working about a week, man. One morning, we used to have to get up about five o'clock in the morning, so we could be down at the gig, early start like six. So that morning my old lady was cooking breakfast, me and my old man was up, washing up and everything, the doorbell rang. And who was at the front door 'cept Albert King, five o'clock in the morning with this funny-looking guy. This was Eddie Jones, turn up on our doorstep.

"Hey, Albert, how are you?" this commotion out front. "What's happening, what you doing back? Welcome, what you doing in town?" "I came to getcha, boy," I heard him say that. "I come to get Popeye." I heard all that shit, I thought, what? I dashed out there, "Hey, Albert!" "Hey, boy, you ready?" I said, "What you talking about?" I had overalls on, getting ready to go, man. He said, "This is Eddie Jones, he's a saxophone player, he's with Ike Turner's band and Ike's changing his show and he needs some singers."

To me, Ike Turner was God. I mean, after them hits that we'd heard down there, like, shit, that was really big-time. And incidentally one of my buddies had gone to St. Louis the summer before on holiday and he came back, and he was telling us about the music thing up there and Ike Turner's band was the hottest thing in the land up there. So to us, around Osceola, the name Ike Turner meant that, man, meant God. Because my buddy was a good dancer, man, he knew when something was hot.

So anyway I said, "Really, man?" I thought he was joking. "Me?" "Yeah, shit, you wanna sing, don't 'cha?" I said, "Yeah, sure do, man, damn, but Ike Turner!" Then my old lady started with the questions to Albert, and Albert started explaining and telling them what's happening, this and that. And he's gonna look after me and don't worry. I was supposed to go for a week to try out and see what it was like and that was it. I just packed a few things and jumped in the car with Eddie and Albert and tore up to St. Louis.

Eddie just drove down with Albert for the company. Fuck, man, it was great when I got to St. Louis, man . . . straight to East St. Louis, 3126 Virginia Place.[9] We drove up there. I remember seeing a big Cadillac sitting in the drive. Big old house, fishtails sticking up in the air and shit. I thought, wow, man, this is it, I've made it. I've arrived! Pretty chicks walking up and down the street—I was girl mad. I walked in and there was everybody there, meeting Ike. I remember the first impression I got of him, he looked like Rosco Gordon. He was the cat. So Ike met me and we went downstairs and got around the piano and started playing some songs, run across some things. Soon as I arrived he got out the bed and I sang.

Yeah, let's see, we ran over some songs the first day. I was so scared, nervous. I've never been nervous. I could just sing. I was pretty free about it. But I was nervous, man, I was singing the songs, alright, I was cookin', but I didn't understand nothing about projecting power in the vocal thing, because we didn't have that—we just sang. Anyway, Ike was telling me about things, "Yeah, man, you got a good voice, but I need a strong voice because I've got a big band and these guys are powerful, I'm telling you." I said, "Yeah, I know, I've heard their records." He said, "Well, you've got to sing hard." And so I think it was Jackie, Jackie or Raymond Hill, they said, "Yeah, well, I like him, man. I think we ought to keep him anyway. I think we could use another . . ." Like all them modern group songs and stuff.

So that was a change in Ike's direction musically from just hard-down blues, the Johnny O'Neal–type voice, Billy Gayles and them, what they was doing. So when I came on the scene there was a difference. They started doing things like group numbers. I mean, numbers that were popular, the doo-wop stuff, contemporary music, and it really changed the whole thing, his popularity increased a lot.

Then he hired Tommy Hodge to handle all that old hard stuff that Billy Gayles and them used to sing. Tommy came in a few weeks after me. So that's when they decided instead of getting another Billy Gayles or Clayton Love why don't we have these two guys, because Tommy had a gospel-type voice and my voice was different. I had the modern . . . and I learnt, I started learning from Tommy and the other guys singing that gospel stuff.

Was Tina there then?

No. No, she was around, but she wasn't with Ike. She was living with her mother and stuff in St. Louis, Missouri.

So who was Ike's wife at the time?

Annie Mae. Was it Annie Mae [Wilson] or Audrey [Madison]? I think it was Audrey, because I remember I was fascinated by her beauty. I couldn't believe that cats could get chicks like them. I mean, Annie Mae and Audrey, yeah, man, Ike's old ladies, they would always be them kind of chicks. Like M. C. Reeder's chicks that he had, them sisters, like Marilyn Monroe chicks. Like in them days it was really fashionable for chicks to be like that, good hips, big tits, the curves, and all of them had it, yellow [light-skinned]. Yeah, it was Audrey, the first one I met. Him and Annie Mae had just broken up, she came back later.

Then after that a girl named Lorraine [Taylor], who now lives in Los Angeles. Lorraine is the mother of Ike's boys, the kids he's got now. Sputnik, Ike Jr., and another one, I can't remember his name now. Anyway, she was the mother of them. She came after Annie Mae and Audrey. Then Annie Mae came back at one point. Now, wait a minute, Annie Mae came back, Lorraine was there. I'm telling you, man, like M. C.!

Here's what happened. Now, Annie Mae was smart. I mean she was a clever chick, she really knew how to hustle, man. She knew how to hustle businesswise, she could talk and she was fast and charming. And she was fine. She could get her way with people, you know. She knew how to use her charm and femininity. She really did look great. So she came back in as the business manager. She traveled with us a lot at one point. I can't remember what years they were, but during a certain period in the early '60s. Her and Ike didn't have any kids.

Was Annie Mae actually married to Ike?

I think they was actually married. Because I think he married once or twice, I don't know. It's very difficult, see, because he'd been with a chick before her named Bonnie which I never met. I never knew her. That was in the Mississippi days. I think he married Bonnie. I'm not sure, but I know she was on some early recordings. He used to tell me about Bonnie a lot. And then he met Annie Mae and she was playing piano with the band.

Then Tina come along, who was another hoofer and singer. She was Anna Mae Bullock. What a name, Bullock! We used to call her Bo-lock. Make her mad, man. "Don't call me no goddamn Bo-lock, that ain't my name." Then we started calling her Bo. "What's happening, Bo?" Start a fight, she'd chase us.

But when I first came up, Tina was living in St. Louis and Ike was living in East St. Louis. He had his old ladies and things, and she was just a chick that used to come up and sing. She had a good voice, lot of soul, a lot of heart. But, see, in St. Louis, in them days you weren't supposed to go into joints. I was too young to go into joints and so was she, but the thing was with a guy he could always put his age up. That's what I did, maybe grow a moustache. Ike gave me some suits and shit, fixed me up nice. I looked like a grown-up cat, got a process, hair slick. It looked horrible, I'm sure.

I was about seventeen, because I'd just got out of school. I'd only been away for that summer. I remember Billy Gayles and them had been broken up. Billy broke up with Ike and Clayton Love came in, that's the way it was. They had made "The Big Question" and the reason Clayton was leaving was because he was gonna teach school. He married, his old lady was pregnant or something, and he wanted to settle down and be a schoolteacher, which that's what he was doing. But he was still singing with Ike at the weekends for a while until he got somebody. When I came in that's when he got the idea of changing the whole image of the show by having two singers.[10]

Billy Gayles had another band in St. Louis during the same time. I didn't really meet Billy till after we'd got on the road. Tina had got in the band and we went on the road, done a tour and came back to St. Louis. I had met Billy but I didn't know him real good. He came on the road with us one time for a few weeks, just sort of hanging out, singing with us.

Billy didn't actually play drums with Ike?

No. Not as a drummer. Because I knew him as a singer, and when I found out he was playing drums I was amazed. He was singing and playing drums, I used to go and see his band sometimes. I used to really like them. He was a good drummer as well. He could kick as good as he could sing. That guy was bad and, you know, a drummer that can sing—I don't mean just singing, but you know Billy Gayles what he sing like! That guy, he was magic to watch playing them drums and singing, because he'd be burning on both, and his range—what an amazing guy. And he was so humble. He was such a nice, gentle guy.

That's why Billy and Ike could never . . . He was the kind of guy, you could take advantage of him and that's what Ike did. You know, all them hits and shit that they had.[11] I mean, Ike really took advantage of the guy, and when somebody else—I don't know, his old lady or somebody—told him you should be whatever, apparently that's when they fell out. Billy went on, formed his own band.

Ike Turner's Kings of Rhythm: (back) Jackie Brenston, Raymond Hill, Eddie Jones, Fred Sample, Billy Gayles; (front) Jesse Knight Jr., Ike Turner, Gene Washington, 1956.

Bennie Smith, guitar player with Gayles's band?

Yeah, Bennie Smith with the cockeye. I tell you who he remind me of, he was ugly, really ugly. Bennie remind me of this white actor, Jack Elam, that's the ugliest motherfucker I've ever seen in my life. But he could play, man, he could sure play. This was at the time when Ike was hot around St. Louis. During the time when all the bands was there, Albert, Little Milton, and Billy Gayles had his thing cookin'.

Let's see, who was with Billy? He was at the Moonlight bar and all that shit. Billy played the Moonlight and that thing over on Cass Avenue—what was that called? On Glasgow and Cass, KATZ used to do live broadcast from over there, Dave Dixon and all them before Dave got killed, car accident or something, years after we left.[12]

Billy would sing and play drums with his own band. He could play good and sing good, playing drums didn't inhibit none, he still burn. I think Sam Rhodes was with Billy. I think Lloyd Wallace was on piano. Who else? The horn player who was with Ike at one time, very fair-skinned guy, kind of remind you of Raymond a little bit, Billy Duncan. I can't remember who else was on horn, because I think he had two horns. Gayles cooked, he had a smokin' little outfit there one time, but it didn't last. It's a shame. I presume it's down to the fact that Gayles didn't have nobody doing his business.

A saxophone player called Tyrone Sweet?

Yeah, Tyrone—him and Raymond was good buddies. Tyrone, let's see, I think he was with Billy Gayles, I didn't know him very well.

Like I say, the band was your whole social thing, man. The other guys you'd see and hear them, but I never hung out with them guys, it was always with our boys. We was always running together. But Tyrone, yeah, he was a good horn player, he played kinda like Raymond, really honked, rocked the house, house-shakin' stuff, you know, all outta key and shit. People loved it.

Raymond Hill was there when you joined?

And he dropped off just when we started traveling. He never did go on the road with us. The band started to change around a lot during them times, musician-wise, because some of the guys would go on the road for three months or so, didn't like it, and go back to St. Louis.

So the band when you joined was Raymond Hill, Jackie Brenston, Eddie Jones, Gene Washington, Jesse Knight Jr., Fred Sample, and Ike?

Yeah.

Did Ike ever play piano on stage?

No. But certain times in the night he'd just lay the guitar down, play "After Hours," something like that, and get back on his guitar. But he told me and played me records and things and he said he used to actually play piano—that was his major instrument. He said he hadn't played guitar that long before I got in the band.

That's him on "Rocket 88"!

That's him. He told me that's why him and Jackie fell out. I think that's what prompted Ike to start playing guitar and being a bandleader as opposed to doing it the other way around. Because Jackie got all the glory and everything, and Ike never forgave him for that.

Jackie did go on the road with us at first in 1960 or '61. I just think he got fed up. A lot of the guys we brought from St. Louis didn't stay on the road, because they didn't like the road life. And Jackie was a bit fed up, he'd been on the road a lot of times before he was a baritone player.

He was back to being just a band member?

Baritone player, that's right. The hit was nowhere in sight. He was just a regular cat, he didn't even talk about it unless you mention it. Yeah, he sung, we used to have great fun singing together.

Would Ike let him do "Rocket 88"?

Oh, no. No way, nothing that was a hit, that he had that was a hit, no way. It was incredible that Ike wouldn't allow Jackie to do his hits, people knew about Jackie Brenston, but no way. He was nowhere on the bill. I mean my name was on the bill and who was I? I wasn't shit. But Jackie Brenston's name wasn't on it. That's the kind of thing I was talking about, that jealous thing that went down with him. I don't know how deeply rooted it was, but I know it was pretty deep. They never sort of forgave each other. Each one had their own side of the story, who did the dirty on who. But the kind of things Jackie was singing on the road then was the current hits like Jackie Wilson, "That's Why I Love Her So."

So Tommy Hodge joined the band about the same time as you did?

Yeah. There was about a week in between.

Where did he come from?

I don't know where he came from originally. As far as I know he came from Kinloch, which is a black suburb of St. Louis, it's out by the airport. I think he was born in St. Louis, around that area. He wasn't from down South, he was strictly from the gospel side of things, from the church thing. In fact, I think when he joined us he hadn't actually sung any blues. Oh, man, he was straight outta church. He'd been singing in a gospel group all the time. I think he was with a group called the Smith Jubilee Singers, and he was bad. He was bad, man, he had that gravel.[13]

What was Eddie Jones like?

Hilarious. Oh, man, he was the most humorous guy, that guy would just keep you laughing. He left the band in the early touring days, he didn't come to England, for example. We came over in '66. I think Eddie toured in the early '60s, like when we first went out. He's from East St. Louis. He joined after—this is after Johnny O'Neal and all that stuff broke up.

Even back in them days he was always trying to fly planes and things! (*laughing*) Can you imagine? Eddie Jones always wanted to be a pilot and he was actually flying. He was going taking flying lessons, man, I'm telling you, in East St. Louis! (*laughing*) This cat, man, he knew all about it, he used to be telling us, "Yeah, man, going for my flying today, going flying." Big shit. We thought it was big shit. But in fact we found out that the damn thing that he was flying was like a kite, it was so raggedy. One of them old prop planes, really old ones, the kind where you get out there—Eddie would sit inside, and a guy would get out there and spin the thing. "How the fuck you got the nerve to get in that plane?" We should have guessed it, because Eddie was always the one for . . . If you listened to him talk, this guy, you would think that he's really something.

We'd be at a rehearsal or something and he'd ring up his old lady, "Annie, could you drop the car off today, I've got to go to such and such after rehearsal, ah, drop me the Cadillac off. No, on second thoughts you better put it in, it needs some new brake shoes on the front, drop the Lincoln, I'll have the Lincoln."

He had two or three cars right, big-name cars like that. So if you didn't know him and you never seen the cars you think, wow, who's this cat? He's badder than Ike! Shit, he's badder than the boss, Lincolns and Cadillacs. He's only supposed to be a horn player, you know. But, man, they would be ancient cars, really broken-down bad-looking cars. Buicks—he had a Buick, Cadillac, and a Lincoln, and he was flying planes. So, you know, Eddie was hot shit. He was something, a real character. Crazy guy.

Fred Sample?

Fred Sample, he was an undertaker, man. That's what he always wanted to be. That's why he wouldn't stay on the road. He went at first, made the first trip to California with us, went that far and back. That was it. Went back to—what was the name of that funeral parlor he worked at? Oh, shit, I can't remember now. I think the reason why he was into it so much was because he used to like driving those big old hearses. He used to like it, man, turn the siren on—"Wahhh"—he was crazy. Not a hearse, an ambulance, but they used them the same way, you know, go and pick people up; he loved it, man, I'm telling you. Turning corners on two wheels, siren wide open, he loved all that shit. He used to tell us things about it.

And this cat he was crazy too. When I say crazy, he used to do crazy things. He had a buddy around him all the time, his best buddy name Delarry and he had a big head, too. Delarry just hung out all the time with the band, he was like a roadie or something. Anyway, Fred and Delarry always tried to drive like gangsters everywhere they went, man. Fred had a little Ford, he used to burn that thing up. Eventually Delarry wrecked it on the Eads Bridge. Now, let's see, how did this happen? Delarry took Fred's car without his permission, some shit like that, which he did all the time anyway. Because he had the accident they started a fight.

(*Laughing*) I remember one time—no, fuck, I ain't telling you that. No, man, I can't tell you that. It's a dirty one. I mean it's an evil thing to do to somebody. We didn't do it, I mean we did it but it wasn't our fault, it was Ike's fault, he instigated the shit. He was always instigating shit. Get us in some worse shit, but he always came to the rescue, I must say. One time, man, Ike for some reason had lost a lot of money gambling and he needed some new tires for his Cadillac. So he tells me and Tommy, Fred, and Delarry, you know we'd do anything. Ike said, "Hey, you guys wanna make ten dollars apiece?" Said, "Yeah." "Well, okay, get me some tires for my Cadillac." "Right." "Tell you what. I'll pay you twenty dollars a tire." "Okay, we'll get you five."

So Ike follows us around, we in two cars, I'm driving one. Say, "Hey, man, this is a bit conspicuous driving around." It's like two or three in the morning in two cars, we got to go in neighborhoods where only Cadillacs are. Now, we hit about two cars, got one wheel. Well, they hit, I was driving the getaway car. Tommy was pretty fast, he was strong, kinda big. Oh, Carlson [Oliver] was in on it as well, and Carlson had those three toes, man, he was a big cat.

So anyway, Ike had a buddy who ran a used car lot and his name was Fred Clements, and he was good friends of Ike's because they had done a lot of business. Ike had bought cars from him for the band boys—for Raymond, Fred, all the cats had bought cars through Ike and Fred Clements. Eddie, Buicks and things. They all liked Buicks. They couldn't have a Cadillac, because Ike had the Cadillac. And Fred Clements had a Cadillac, too. And he was well-off. So where he lived was a well-off neighborhood, some Cadillacs around there. We didn't know Fred Clements's car, but Ike knew it. But he didn't tell us.

Anyway, we hit a couple of Cadillacs, got us a couple of wheels, and we hit another one and it was Fred's. Okay, we got about two blocks, man, and there's all the cops in the world. Shit, froze. "Okay, what you boys got in the car?" "Nothing, man." Anyway, open the trunk, Cadillac tires. "We're not criminals, we're musicians, Ike Turner's band." "Really? Hey, Ike Turner's band! Hey, we got 'em." Big scandal, you know, good news, man. Oh, shit. They take us down the police station and Ike come, and somehow—the night sergeant or whoever was the head guy of the precinct—they squashed it. They called Fred Clements up, said, "We got somebody down here," because Ike was with us. Ike had bribed the fucking policeman, the head guy, and it wasn't gonna be reported or nothing.

He called us all over in the corner away from the desk and said, "Okay, boys, here it is, now, look . . ." Ike said, "Fred we're sorry we hit your car." Fred said, "Okay, I know you alright, I know you didn't mean to get me." But I knew, the observer, right? I knew that Ike knew. They squashed that shit. No fines, it never came out in the papers, nothing. But he's good with that shit. He always come to the rescue to get you outta that shit somehow.

They all sound pretty crazy.

Oh, yeah. Motley crew, man, really. It was like watching a film or being on a film set. I wasn't really one of the actors, I didn't think, but looking at it, yeah, I was. It was always fascinating, all those people. It was something to behold, the lifestyles and everything.

It was great, it really was. I never took no sides with none of their disputes or none of their rivalries or anything. I was always trying to patch things up between them all. They would argue about different things, like the thing with Jackie and Ike, for example. Billy Gayles and Ike. All them kind of things. They always carried grudges, they all had done something dirty on each other somewhere down the line. Who was right or wrong, you never could get the straight of it. But I don't know, my closest affinity was with Ike always, because we was close like that.

Jackie and all of them they was all heavy drinkers and they was drinking that really bad shit, boy. That stuff they used to drink you probably wouldn't allow it in your house! Not even to wash the floor. I'm telling you, man, it's really amazing. I'm surprised Raymond's still kicking. I often wondered whatever happened to him.[14]

Did you know Johnny O'Neal?

Not well. Raymond and them's buddies.

Did he used to hang around?

No, because they had their own set. Because when I came in Ike's band, Ike Turner's band was . . . Every band had their own social set, although they was all friends from back home and all that stuff. They used to hang out together sometimes on off nights, certain guys, but very seldom, because they all had their own little social thing. It was like a little club.

Johnny O'Neal's band was called the Hound Dogs, I think. Johnny O'Neal's Hound Dogs. Who was in it? Shit, Bad Boy, Kizart, and who else? I don't know, because I didn't know that band all that well. I only heard them play a couple of times. I just knew them because I went out there one time to that place with Raymond to Firework Station. Raymond and Junior [Jesse Knight], because they was buddies, and some nights when they would be off they would go out there and see if they could poach some of them cats' girls and things. It was that kind of a thing.

What kind of place was it?

Oh, shit, man, funky. Hot. Fun. Total fun. Like the T-99. Fish, hamburgers and fish be smellin', funk be flying. Dance floor in the middle, music be loud and hot.

Raymond and Jackie and them, man, them cats they could put away alcohol, man. Vodka. They used to love vodka. That was their drink. You couldn't smell it, because Ike would fine them if he knew they were drinking. Although he knew they were drinking they would still hide it. Jesse, he could hold his drink pretty good. He try to keep up with them, but he would go to sleep, man, on stage playing! I'm telling you. Look, there was one time, I can't remember the club, but it was outside of East St. Louis. There was some garbage cans in the entrance to the bar right by the stage, the stage was right along side of the bar. Now, there's the garbage cans, where they dump the lemon peels and soda tops and shit.

We was up there playing, Junior on the end, drunk, noddin', playin'. He'd wake up and Ike would be giving him a dirty look, playing his guitar and looking at him. Junior wake up, try to perk up, started laughing, start fucking with somebody in the crowd trying to keep himself awake, anything. Do crazy antics, man, to try and stay awake. Do little monkey dances and things down on the end. Anyway, he knew he was gonna get fined, because he knew Ike had pinned him, but he was still trying to put on a brave face and he couldn't, and he fell asleep again and this time when he woke up he was in the garbage can.

It was funny because we was in the middle of this number and everybody was cookin'. If you could have seen him! And Ike kept looking at him, standing there, dirty look. "Just watch this motherfucker, watch this crazy motherfucker—don't, don't touch him." Fred was gonna try and wake him up, he was still playing, wasn't missing no notes. Then crash! Legs in the air, bass over behind the bar, shit feeding back, everybody falling out laughing. Now, we got to help him up out of the garbage can, put him back on stage. Crazy. He just couldn't handle it. He couldn't keep up with them other guys. But Jackie and them guys, they could drink all night, every night they would do it, they wouldn't miss, not a night. Wake up, start in the afternoon. That's the way it was all the time. You could easily drift off into that kind of thing. It was fun watching it.

What clubs did you play in St. Louis?

There was the Club DeLisa, we had lots of clubs. Ike's residency days were almost over when I joined. He was still playing the Manhattan only sometimes, at weekends or something. When I first joined, the first few months he was still doing the Manhattan in East St. Louis like every weekend. He was playing three gigs a day on a weekend. Do a gig at the Manhattan, maybe a matinee before that. Maybe the Club DeLisa in St. Louis on Vandeventer, between Vandeventer and Washington. Club DeLisa was funky, wasn't nothing high-class, not yet. All this would be from Thursday to Sunday. Monday or Tuesday we would take a day off and Sunday was always payday.

Then over in Madison, Illinois, which is like a suburb of East St. Louis, there was a place called Kingsbury's, which was a real funky joint. Originally it was just a gambling joint, long café, bar, and then they started having bands in there and that was a hot place, used to love it. When we used to get there it was about two in the morning. From two to about six.

So we was constantly packing the . . . you know, we go to one gig, man, unload, everybody grab a piece of shit, stick it on the wall, PA things. In fifteen minutes we'd have the whole thing set up and cook, I mean be ready to burn. You'd think that after sweating and being funky for so long that you'd be really tired and ready to drop. Instead, everybody pile in their cars and shit and, "Okay, see you over the river," and see who can get over there the fastest. It's a wonder we didn't kill ourselves, we used to drive like maniacs through St. Louis, man, across them bridges and things at night. Fuck, it was like madness. We'd be playing gangsters and things, crazy.

Would Ike gamble?

Oh, yeah, he loved to gamble, he'd gamble his ass off. He was pretty good, too. He was alright. He was pretty lucky. He wasn't a guy that studied gambling, you know, where he knew what he was doing. It was really just luck and he was quite lucky. And he usually had enough money where he could sustain long enough if he had a bad streak. If you've got enough money, eventually it's got to turn your way.

The Birdcage?

That was in St. Louis itself. In Brooklyn there was the Paradise Country Club that we used to play at.[15] And about half a mile up the road was this club—I can't remember what it was called now, but it was really a hot club. Everybody just used to say, "Going to Brooklyn, Brooklyn, Illinois." Oh, shit, what was that club, I think it burned down—yeah, the Harlem Club!

The Red Top?

Yeah, the Red Top was in East St. Louis. Pop Stallins, he's an old guy that owned the Red Top. He had a couple of clubs. The Starlight, that was his other club. It was at Firework Station. Benny Sharp and all them cats, Stacy Johnson, Vernon [Guy], and all them used to play there. I used to sing out there, too. Yeah, we used to have a lot of fun at the Red Top, man. That was a hot little spot.

Pop Stallins's son had the band. He had two boys—one was a drummer, one a bass player—had the resident band. We all used to be in that band when we weren't gigging, having fun jamming and stuff.

Do you remember a one-armed trumpet player named Willie who was supposed to have been with Ike?

I remember a one-armed trumpet player, but I can't put it into context as to when and where. He wasn't a member of Ike Turner's band when I was there. I remember this guy, but I can't place him in a particular place.

Piano player with Little Milton, Lloyd Wallace?

Yeah, Lloyd played piano, good piano player. I don't know what Lloyd's doing, he was a very serious musician, he played with Oliver Sain and Little Milton. There was only two bands in St. Louis, Little Milton and Ike Turner, the rest of them were just also-rans, even Albert. Yeah, James Carr, saxophone player, Jerry Walker on drums, Oliver and Fontella Bass later.

But I enjoyed cats like Doc Perry, a bass player I was telling you about. I used to like his band, they played cruder blues. They played the Moonlight, same old places like Albert and the rest of them. Some of them guys' bands I enjoyed more than our band, I suppose, because I knew our band so well. But I knew their bands weren't as good technically, not at that time, anyway. The sound they used to get, the way them cats used to play was different. They maintained that country edge in their blues, whereas we, or when I got in the band, we began to water our thing down. It became a show more, started doing more of the popular commercial stuff.

Doc Perry had the same size band as we had, which was standard in St. Louis in them days, three horns, et cetera. I used to hear them cats at Harlem Club, they used to work out there a lot. It was just outside of East St. Louis going toward Granite City past the Swift Packing Company, Brooklyn, Illinois, that's right.[16]

Did you ever meet Billy Emerson?

Yeah, I met him a few times. I didn't know him. I met him in Chicago, met him in St. Louis. As a matter of fact, I think he came down during those Cobra sessions, came down with us one time back from Chicago to St. Louis. Spent a few days with Ike at Ike's place. Old Big Head Billy Emerson, that's what Ike used to call him.

Moose John?

Yeah, I saw him in Osceola. He used to come through there and hang out, playing bass, Earl Hooker and them. Then I ran into him when I was with Ike, I can't remember where, Chicago, St. Louis, I don't know. When I saw Moose in Osceola he was a clown, a real clown, we dug him. Earl Hooker really influenced Ike more than anybody, I believe it.

Wasn't he living in East St. Louis for a while?

Yeah, that's right, it sure was East St. Louis. That's where I think it was, at Ike's house I met him again. Yeah, Ike used to tease him a lot, tell jokes about what they used to do. Every time they run into each other, anybody Ike knew, they had a lot to talk about, stories. And there was that story about the window situation. They always used to laugh about that. Because there was another story, was it [Ernest] Lane or Ike or both of them? They had to jump out of a window one time naked. Oh, fuck, man, was it Lane or was it Ike? They used to tell this thing and laugh like a motherfucker. There was a married woman involved and one of them or both of them. And the guy was supposed to be at work, a big guy, and they knew him, this cat would kill. He was a bad cat and he come knocking on the door, blam-blam. "Open this motherfucking door." And there was only one thing left but the window. Clothes under the arm, no time to check it out, just jump two stories or something and down through the woods. This was in Mississippi when they were teenagers, things they used to get up to. Ike used to talk about that shit, him and Lane.

Pinetop Perkins?

Pinetop, yeah, I remember he was one of Ike's buddies. He used to talk about him.

Did you have any contact with Chuck Berry when you were in St. Louis?

Well, yeah, we knew Chuck, met him quite a few times. We used to go to his—he had a restaurant. We used to go there sometimes, rap to him and that. It was alright.

I drove him home one night from about 150 miles outside St. Louis, in between Chicago. We'd been up in Chicago recording, in the Cobra days. Driving back home, always liked to drive, man, I just liked them big cars. Cadillacs and things, never liked to sleep in case I missed something. So one night we were coming from Chicago going back to St. Louis on 66. I'm driving, everybody asleep, and I see this bad Cadillac with these fish tails parked on the side. "Ah, it's Chuck Berry's car." So I woke Ike, "Hey, man, it's Chuck." Said, "Pull over, man." It was like three in the morning and they'd been to Joliet or somewhere. They had a gig and—what's the guy's name that's the piano player? Johnnie [Johnson]. He always drank anyway. They was all knocked out.

So we stop, wake them up, "Hey, man, we wiped out." So Ike said, "I'll drive my car, do you want to drive, Chuck?" Chuck said, "Hey, man, you a good driver? You motherfucker, you look—you young-assed punk-assed niggers, you all tear my car up, man." He was really paranoid. He'd made "Maybellene" and all that stuff about cars, and you'd have thought he was a real speed freak, but he was just the opposite, he was so paranoid about speed. This cat, man, said, "Okay, you drive, but don't go over fifty." Now, Route 66 at three o'clock in the morning, you know—shit, man, big trucks and things, varoooom—and you creepin' along!

So I nursed Chuck and them back to sleep, I drove fifty. So finally mouths open and I pushed it on down and I was in St. Louis in like an hour or something like that. Then they woke up saying,"We here! What? Say, man, nigger, you been driving my car at 100 miles an hour." I said, "Yeah, man, but you here, ain't 'cha?" Chuck said, "Well, I say, man, you gotta be bad, because I didn't feel a thing going around no corners, you gotta be ace."

Vocal group called the Trojans, was that one of Art Lassiter's groups?

I don't know. I don't know much about Art's groups except I knew Art and I knew the guys, yeah, they were a proper group. They used to come around sometimes and sing on some of our gigs. But I don't know nothing about the history. They never had a band, not that I know of. I mean, Art used to play a little guitar sometimes.

Was the Rockers Art Lassiter's group?

Well, he was in it. I presume it was his group. Art, Doug, and I forget the other guy, they was brothers.[17]

Raymond Hill told me Luther Ingram was in it?

I don't know, I don't think that's his name. Luther Ingram became a name in his own, this guy never did.[18]

Art came from—I don't know if he was originally, but he was based in Indianapolis. After the song ["Down in the Bottom"] was a hit or something, whatever happened. I know Art was living in that place and Ike sent for him to do this song "Fool in Love." He came down especially for some reason or whether he was just in town visiting or not. But anyway, him and Ike collaborated, and because of Ike's involvement with them before, doing shows and things in town, he was glad to see Art. And he had this song especially for him and all that. And Art didn't turn up for the session, so Tina sung it and that's how Tina was born. That was the birth of her.[19]

Did Eddie Acon have any tie up with Stevens?

Now, that I'm not sure of. Because there was an old guy—like I said, I didn't know nothing about that side of it. Those guys was around and they was the cats.[20]

Ike was doing the recordings?

Yeah, that's right.

They did a version of "Boxtop" which was on Tune Town before the Cobra version, with credits to Ike, Carlson Oliver, and Little Ann.[21]

That's right. Right, now, that's really strange. When Carlson first joined the band, Raymond hadn't left yet. Carlson was just hanging around, he wasn't really on a salary and he took over from Raymond. I think Ike must have sensed something, because Ike was pretty sharp. And Carlson could honk and he honked kinda like Raymond. He was just laying around picking up all of Raymond's licks and learning, I suppose. That's right, because it wasn't long after that before Raymond split. It was right after that that Raymond went back to Mississippi.

Did Raymond ever come back and rejoin?

No, I don't think so, I never remember him coming back.

So he wasn't on any of the Sue things?

No. If he was on anything for Sue it would have to have been something that Ike had recorded and doctored up, you know what I mean. But when we did "Fool in Love" that was all done in St. Louis, but for Sue. "Fool in Love" was done in a studio, not at the house. I can't remember the name of the studio, but I remember the engineer's name was Ed. I can see the studio real clear, but I can't remember the name of it. You probably heard of it, because Milton and a lot of the guys recorded there. It was out in Clayton, which is like a suburb going west.[22]

When Ike was doing that early Sue stuff in that studio he also did Fontella Bass.[23] Now, Raymond was around, I think, at the early stages of that. I think Carlson had just come in on the set. Like I said, I think they were both there and it was a little time later that Raymond left, and I don't mean the next year, but it was a matter of weeks or months. So it is possible that Raymond was on some Sue stuff. Now, what tunes or what I don't know, because most of the tunes and stuff was just rubbish anyway. It was only like "Fool in Love," "Poor Fool," and stuff like that that stuck out, the rest of the stuff was just tracks being filled in.

Fred Green and the Mallards?

The Mallards sound familiar. That sounds like one of them local St. Louis vocal groups, there was loads of them around. Charles Drain and the Imperials.[24] They had to change their name when Little Anthony come along. The Five Du-Tones—they were St. Louis guys originally. They moved to Gary, got that "Shake a Tail Feather" hit. I think they was the Five Du-Tones before they moved. There was a lot of vocal groups around, cookin' ones.

What's this guy's name? Rick Holmes, and this old man had a drugstore, one of

Ike's partners in crime, if you like, when they were doing that shit with Tune Town and all the "Boxtop" shit and all that. He was a black guy, middle-aged, very nice man, and I don't think he knew much about the record business, but he had cake. There was the Tune Town thing and that guy.

And there was another guy that looked after the groups. They had a little rehearsal room, little studio down on Franklin there. It might have been Rick Holmes, the guy we just mentioned. Because there was all these vocal groups hanging around, all day every day, just line 'em up, Jack. I didn't know them guys that well, that was Ike's thing, I was just there then. Yeah, all them little groups be hanging around, I used to see 'em. I used to think what assholes they was just hanging around this funky studio, "shoo-wop-de-wop." They could sing alright, but I looked upon them like bullshit. At the time they were the same age as me, some of them a little older. But my thing I knew was much more heavyweight than what they were doing, because there was so many of them, and I figured they didn't have a hope in hell of anything and there I was with Ike. They was kinda envious a little bit, they gave me a certain kind of respect. "Hey, Jim . . ." "Yeah, motherfucker . . . shit, you can't sing man, get back, got a lot to learn, Jack." (*laughing*) Because I was hanging out with Tommy Hodge and all them bad-assed cats—shit, really heavyweight.

Yet I wasn't doing shit. I was cookin', though, I suppose, for what I was. I had to develop, but I was smokin'. Shit, I'd wipe any of them out. You know I used to wipe Jackie out, Tommy and all of 'em. I used to clean all of them out, it was amazing. Ike used to tease them about it, because they knew, those cats were in front of me. No way I could touch them technically as far as that, but as far as getting across on stage, I used to wipe 'em out, because I was a little young cat, and I suppose there was a certain kind of cuteness about it, the way I would perform. And I would tackle them blues. I'd be singing "3 O'Clock in the Morning" and, shit, I'd sing anything, fuck me. Them chicks would be . . . I'd do B. B.'s "Sweet Sixteen," I'd sing that motherfucker, Jack. There would only be . . . if Gayles drop by I'd back up, don't fuck with Gayles, no way, I don't fuck with him. Because I really admired him too much, but all them other cats, I mean, shit, man, I wipe them out.

But later on when Gayles got back on the road with us, them cats was, "Wow, man, you really developed into a motherfucker, didn't you?" They wouldn't dare fuck with me on stage. And when Tina got in the group, Ike had him two tigers, Jack, he could sic us on anybody. Cats would drop by to sing, you know, from Chicago, you know. Somebody just had a hit like Barrett Strong and all them kind of guys, shit, make 'em look shamed. Yeah, it was great.

But them Tune Town days, them groups, I really thought I was hot shit. Well, to them guys, I was just bullshitting them, I knew I wasn't. It was funny, I used to laugh, plus I'd get to drive the Cadillac and shit. (*laughing*) Oh, what! I was just out of school—that was heavyweight. Big chicks, the chicks you read about in magazines back in Osceola, Jack. I mean, hey, St. Louis, big city and it was just fucking fun, man. That was a fun time. But it was really sad later on. I don't think St. Louis was a shithole then. It might have been, but not as much as, but, man, it just run down to nothing. I hear it's a real shithole now, everybody say so.

There was such good musicians and singers in St. Louis, I mean they really turned out some helluva people. And some people there was just bad, bad, and nobody ever heard of. That was the whole thing, going to gigs and sitting in on cats' gigs, having battles of the bands and stuff.

Seaphus Scott, the Five Masqueraders, Kenneth Churchill, the Lyrics on Joyce. Apparently Joyce was the sister label of Tune Town?

Don't know none of them. That's right, there were some more guys around that were recording for Tune Town that Ike was—I guess he was producing them. And there was a guy named Gabriel, who later became a disc jockey.

What, the "Buzzard Lope"?

That's right and all that. Gabriel, he was a weird guy. I mean he used to dress up like a real angel. Crazy guy, man, good disc jockey, though.

Is he the same guy as the Flock Rocker?

Yeah, that's him. Mitchell Hearns was his real name. Became one of the top deejays in St. Louis after Dave Dixon died. He specialized in blues at one point, then got into mainstream soul music.

Flock Rocker—I wasn't into his music much. We used to really laugh at the cat, he was so absurd. Yeah, man, we would take him around with us sometimes, he come on and do a little spot. Come out in this white robe and this thing around his head with a thing sticking up, makeshift halo, and his trumpet. Everybody would break up, getting drunk, et cetera. But he'd cook, he'd burn.

Roosevelt Marks on Planet Records?

Yeah, Roosevelt Marks lived in L.A. Is he still alive? Now, Planet, that's another story. I'm not sure, but I remember Planet. I think it might have been Ike's label, I don't know for sure. Ike was dabbling and had lots of little bullshit labels.[25] Sony, Prann, Teena, Sonja, I remember Little Milton and them was doing stuff on Bobbin. Ike didn't put nothing out on Bobbin. That was during the time that Milton had "Lonely Man" on Bobbin. I think that was the thing that sorta put them on the map, because it was a local hit.

Was Robert Lyons the manager of KATZ?

That's it. That was the link-up. You know, I told you on the phone I thought there was a connection between Bobbin and the radio station? But I didn't know anything about the politics of the business in them days. I don't know what happened to Robert

Lyons, I didn't know him. He used to come around. I used to see him sometimes, but I didn't know nothing about his business. I think he was a white guy. I know the guy that owned Stevens was white, the Granite City thing. There was a tie-up between Bobbin and Stevens, but I didn't know what it was. As far as I was concerned I thought they were rivals. But I didn't know then like I know now how things can be hooked up. It could have been a sister situation.[26]

Little Bobby Foster?

Yeah, Ike wrote a song, one of his girlfriends, Jane something, wrote a song called "You're So Wonderful." Bobby Foster had a range, a really high falsetto he could go into toward the end of the song. He'd sound like a bird or something. Little girls used to love it. We used to hate it, man. We used to think this cat's squeakin' all over the place, we used to hate it. We used to hate him. He thought he was a little star, I remember that. "Angel of Love," that's it, that was Ike's girlfriend's one. She was a white girl, I remember.[27]

I wasn't at the session, but I can remember they would come around and rehearse before they actually done the record. I think one of them was done on that Ampex. You see, during that Ampex thing that was the beginning of the relationship between Ike and whoever, you know, with the Stevens thing. Because Bobby Foster was one of the artists and I was one of the artists.

Johnny Wright?

Yeah, I remember Johnny Wright, he had a thing on Stevens.[28] I'm trying to remember who the horn player was with Johnny Wright. He had a band like Ike did and I think Ike recorded some stuff with Johnny Wright one time, but I don't know about this recording ("Gotta Have You for Myself").[29] I remember the other side. I remember hearing it, I used to like it. Ike found quite a bit of talent for RPM, he used to tell me about all of that. Ike was a disc jockey, too, he say at some point. He said one of his catchphrase things was, "Anybody want to buy a duck?" Let's see, what he call it? "A dollar two sixty-five." It didn't make no sense, but that was the catchphrase.[30]

I remember doing the Stevens stuff, that was my first time recording apart from the time in Memphis. Junior on bass, Fred Sample on piano. Let me see, was it Gene Washington? No, I think Bootie Lip was on drums then, a guy named John Wings. Gene had quit, he fell out with Ike. But when I first joined he was the original cat. He was one of the original Kings of Rhythm.

This was Bootie Lip's time, I think. He was a good drummer, but he got killed. We called him Bootie Lip because his bottom lip was really fat. He drank lots of wine and clown around, but he was a good drummer. He killed himself in East St. Louis about five o'clock one morning. Ran into the back of a bus that was parked. He'd just dropped some girl off—you know, drunk, slam into the back of a bus. I remember going to his funeral and everything, wiped him out.

Were both of your Stevens things done at the same time?

I'm trying to remember now. No, I think they were two separate things, and I can't remember which was which, because they were all just bullshit, I mean I wasn't really serious. We did one of them in a studio in St. Louis. I can't remember which one it was now, although I can still see the little bullshit studio. It was a little ole thing on Franklin, just where Easton becomes Franklin.

"I Know You Don't Love Me" on Royal American?

That record, there was two versions. The Royal American was done on the Ampex (recorded at Ike's house) during the "Boxtop" sessions. That stuff came out as the forerunner of the Cobra releases of the same things. The two tenor players, that was during the time that Carlson and Raymond both, just before Raymond split the band. The first part of the solo was played by Raymond, second part by Carlson.

And "On My Trail," there was a line in that song where he says, "I'm on your trail, I'll follow you to hell," but he left the "hell" out (on the record). Tommy used to do it live on stage, but he left it out because Ike thought it was a bit dirty, wouldn't get played or whatever.

What about the Cobra deal with Toscano? Was that something Ike sorted out?

Yeah, because I didn't know nothing about it. I was there, but I don't know nothing about the politics of it. We did Betty Everett, it was during the time we did guys that were his own artists, who were already on his label. Like what was his name? Oh, shit, Otis Rush, there was one Otis Rush did.

Ike's band backed . . . ?

Yeah, Willie Dixon came in. On some sessions Odie Payne on drums, I remember that guy, he was the most beautiful drummer with brushes. Fuck, I've never seen anybody play brushes like that guy. Odie, yeah, that's right. Ike's playing guitar and, let's see, who else was there? Otis Rush and somebody else at that time, Buddy Guy. But Buddy, I don't think he was recording for Cobra.

No, he was on Artistic, same thing.

That's right, but he came around. He was over there with the sessions, because they were all buddies from way back. And them cats would all be . . . Whenever we'd be in Chicago recording they'd come around. Junior Wells and who else was there? Shit, I can't remember, maybe it'll come to me later. But all them Cobra guys, I was overwhelmed by them guys, because Otis Rush and them cats was like gods to me. I'd been hearing their records and sitting there in the studio with them! Fuck, it was just mind-boggling.

Did you do anything there?

No. I think we had something in the pipeline. I don't think I actually laid nothing down, or if I did, it wasn't released.[31]

Did you get to meet Eli Toscano?

Eli, the Cobra guy? Yeah, nice guy, but in them days I wasn't really interested in cats like him. They was just around and it was Ike and them doing their politics. He got on with everybody great. I'm sure he was a crook.

He was found in the river.

I'm sure he was a crook. Most of them guys was, they was all crooks, but they was great with the musicians. They was ripping them off left and right, but musicians didn't know no better then. They had their gigs going and they was eating and sleeping, that's all they cared about.[32]

But they made good records?

Oh, man, yes, shit. They really knew their music now. He knew his blues, that's the one thing about all them guys that had them Chicago . . . Like the Chess brothers, I mean, they knew, man, fantastic.

Can you imagine the kind of ground that was being broken in them days when Leonard Chess signed Chuck Berry? People like that, you know, hey . . . And the variety, the diversity, it was great, man, from shoo-wop to the dirtiest blues you could name. After the Cobra thing Betty Everett got signed with Vee-Jay.

Ike knew all them guys, so while we were doing those Cobra sessions we would go out to clubs. Ike used to get up on the stage and I remember one night him and Buddy Guy and Junior Wells. I think it was Buddy and Junior's gig, if I remember correctly. A lot of guys, Otis Rush, bunch of 'em. They showing us around, because it wasn't that often we got up to Chicago. We was usually around St. Louis. Well, the jam was like magic, all them guys was like gods, as far as I was concerned. Since I was a little bitty kid I'd been hearing their records and shit. Harold Burrage, he was another one of the guys who came around. I liked him, liked his voice, that guy—he's a good singer, man.

But Eli, yeah, since you mentioned it, they were gamblers. They lived to that shit, shootin' dice, him and Jake, Shakey Jake. What a name—Shakey Jake!

What about Eli Toscano's right-hand man who got killed?

Tampa, yeah. He was just a guy that showed us around different cafés and things. Eli's right hand. And a few years later when that shit went down he got killed, he was the first one. This was some years later, maybe a year or two. Otis Rush, "Double Trouble"? Yeah, on that session "Double Trouble" he said "millionairies." "Hey, why you say "millionairies," it's "millionaires," Jack. Don't you know how to say that?"

He start to get self-conscious about it. We said, "No, man, keep it like that, it's really nice, don't change it, whatever you do." That was great, it was unique.

Erskine Oglesby?

Yeah, Gayles had two sax players and Erskine was the other guy in Gayles's band. He later joined Ike's band as a baritone player, yeah, that's right, because we got him from out of Gayles's band. He worked with us for a while before we went on the road.

Did he record with you at Cobra?

No, that was Jackie.

So he replaced Jackie?

Yeah, for a while, because Jackie was out of the band for a while and Erskine replaced him. Then Jackie got back in the band, then we went on the road. The first time we went on the road to California, Jackie was with us. I think Erskine didn't want to go on the road, that's why he dropped out. Then we had a nice little variety show, because Erskine could sing, too. He wasn't all that versatile, but he could sing things like "Stagger Lee," all that Lloyd Price stuff. "Stagger Lee" was his favorite song.

Leo Gooden?

Leo Gooden, he's dead now. He died a long time ago. He was a big fat guy, I mean real fat, but he was very rich. He was a black guy, but he was white, very fair skinned—you know how black people is in the States, shades. I don't know where he got his money, but he was a politician of some kind. And he was always into trying to do something with music. He was always trying to promote it in some way.

He opened a club in East St. Louis. I forget what it was called, but a lot of good people played there. Originally it was supposed to be a jazz club, then he graduated over into blues, soul, and R&B. Everybody used to play there and that was one of the most popular clubs around St. Louis area. He used to bring in big-name bands.[33]

There was a club he bought one time called the Bamboo Key Club. Originally it was called the Mambo Club, which was once upon a time owned by gangsters, mafia people. People who used to be in St. Louis, what's his name? Mickey Cohen, he used to own that club. Leo Gooden bought the club.

He was a West Coast figure, though?

Yeah, but he hung out in East St. Louis because East St. Louis used to be the gangsters' thing, because there was a big race track there. The Mambo, it was black like marble—not marble, but that stuff that shines like glass. It was beautifully designed, the shape of it was kinda long, fantastic. So nobody, no niggers ever got a chance to see inside of it until this thing busted open and they put it up for sale and Leo Gooden bought it. Ray Charles, everybody used to come. And he bought another one and sold it to a man named George Quarles.

So Leo, he had a jazz quintet called Leo's Five, though he didn't play. It was in his name because he was the cat. Leo's Five was hot. They used to be all on KATZ, the hottest jazz thing around town, and they had the residency there. Then he started opening up to rhythm-and-blues guys.

He did something with Ike, too. Him and Ike had some stuff going. I don't know if it was ever released or whether Leo just put up some money for Ike to do some trips to Chicago or whatever, but they were very thick at one time on the business scene. I don't know what the hell they were doing. He used to follow us around to a lot of gigs out of town like Springfield and places.

Yeah, strange people, strange lifestyle, even in them days it was all crazy. The lifestyle was crazy, but at that time we thought it was normal. We knew it was kinda crazy, we knew it wasn't like the normal bands that were around. I mean most of the bands were pretty boring and stuff. But I suppose that's why Ike's band had such a reputation. The cats was crazy, man. We get into all kinds of fights.

Oh, man, this was a classic. We all come out the Club DeLisa one night and Carlson Oliver, one of his girlfriends had a car. I think it was a little Nash Rambler. Anyway, she used to follow us around. So the parking lot was across the road. So we all coming out the club with the stuff and we hear, "Ahh—my car's gone!" It's Carlson's girlfriend. "What! Goddamn dirty mother . . . somebody's stole my old lady's car." And while we were all standing there going crazy being flabbergasted, the car passes by. "There goes my car! Some nigger—there it go." "What! Fuck, come on, let's go." So this whole club of people, all the stragglers, groupies, hangers-on, everybody, maybe sixty people in the street, running down the street in the direction the car went. The car had made a right turn up in a little alley. We all know it's the entrance to a school playground and there's a brick wall down there with a tall fence. So we, "Hey, we got him! We got him." So me and Ike is the fastest because we is the lightest, because most of them other cats was pretty big guys.

So there's the car sitting there rocking, lights on, engine still running. The cat done jumped over the fence. So we said, "Went over the fence, come on y'all." Me and Ike hit it and a couple of strides and over. As I looked back, people falling over, it looked like an assault course, we were over in the school playground heading for the next street. Big ole fat Carlson, man, and he only had three toes on one foot anyway. Man, big cats were falling.

Then we see the guy as we turn out into the next street, "There he go." So, man, it was getting funny because as we look back down the street we saw all the gang, the mob. This is like three in the morning and police cars have joined in the race now, somebody called the cops, "Hey, riot, or something." They don't know what's happening, all this shit going on.

So we gaining on this cat. So me and Ike looking at each other side by side. "Fuck, man, we're gonna catch him." "We got him, we got him." We started laughing. So Ike, when this cat gets to laughing it's so infectious, he's got a weird laugh, so we're running and laughing. So Ike says, "What we gonna do?" "We're gonna jump on

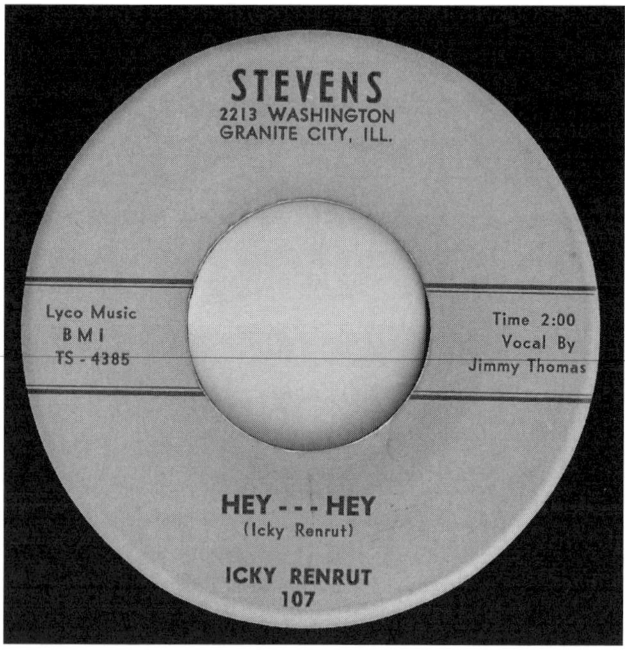

Stevens Records 107.

him." "Wait, I know what to do, don't worry, shut up, don't say anything." He said, "Hey, nigger, stop." I thought, I wonder if he thinks this guy's really gonna stop. I said, "You crazy, man, this cat ain't gonna stop." I'm really falling over laughing. He said, "Nigger, if you don't stop, I'm gonna shoot. I'll count three and if you don't stop, that's it, I'm blowin' your head off." Ike says "One, two, three," and he goes "*Bang!*" This guy, man, he must have thought he really had a gun, you know. He was anticipating getting blown away. He couldn't look around, he didn't have the time. He knew everybody was back there and we was pretty close. And when he said "Bang," listen, you seen cartoons? I've seen some fast guys, Roadrunner and all them cats, man. But this cat on the count of "three" he jumped up about three feet off the ground. He settled back down and never broke the stride, but it looked like smoke jumped out from under this cat's feet. This guy hit another gear. He could have been an Olympic sprinter, Jack, I'm telling you, man. I ain't never seen nobody so fast. He just start disappearing on us. And me and Ike were looking at each other, "Wow, you see that nigger run?" But what a night, man. We used to have all kind of weird things like that happen. That's the way it was. Crazy days.

You told me before that you wouldn't do "Jack Rabbit" on stage. Why was that?

I think it was basically because I didn't like the song that much, so therefore I wasn't nagging Ike to do it. Our repertoire was so full until . . . That song we just did it as a novelty and I don't think either one of us took it very serious. I didn't like it very much and I don't think he cared for it that much. We had fun with it a couple of times.[34]

But "Hey-Hey" was popular?

Yes, that's right. "Hey-Hey" became a little ole classic around St. Louis. I started getting really known from that "Hey-Hey" and "Ho-Ho" shit. I mean kids were really requesting that shit. I remember we used to play a place called Lindy's Hall out in Wellston, in St. Louis. And in them days Ike's band was the only band that was breaking the ice, the white and black thing. And being a black band and playing this stuff that the white kids wanted to hear, it wasn't like Little Milton. Ike's band was doing everything, doing all kinds of shit, especially the rock stuff of that time, like Chuck Berry. I was kicking ass. That was my thing, we began to branch into that.[35]

I remember, man, we got raided in Lindy's Hall because we had such . . . I mean, all the chicks, white chicks, they dug us so much. There was loads of groupies and there was one or two chicks whose parents were somebody, right? So this was really, "How dare you hang around down at that funky Lindy's Hall with them tramps, niggers, and things. What are you doing?"

So they come and got us and marched us out with about thirty or forty groupies and hangers-on and shit, the whole fucking shebang, down to the police station. Let them all go, but really hassling us, searching us for drugs and shit. None of us didn't have any, we were really smart about that shit. Ike knew that he was a target. That his band would be a target because we were breaking ground, he was smart about that. He told us, "Hey, you motherfuckers who smoke, make sure we're out of these clubs, stay clean, because we may get hassled any time."

Then we started getting other places like the Club Imperial and all them. A guy named George Edick had the Club Imperial, which was one of our home places. It was a white club and, man, they loved Ike's band and I was the cat. I was the rock 'n' roll cat. I was Chuck Berry and all that. I mean, we used to get off on all that stuff—the kids did, too. We used to have dancing championships. Ike's band was definitely the heaviest band around, there was no doubt about that. All the kids, black and white, and this club was one of the forerunners of the rock 'n' roll thing in St. Louis. This was before we done any of the "Work Out Fine" hits, before they hit. We were still local.

Did you do any TV shows with them back then?

Yeah, yeah, I did. My first TV show that I remember being in a TV studio, it was funny, man. It was in St. Louis. George Edick had a big hand in this television station and he got a local sponsor to do a program on Ike's band in the club about the rock thing, what's happening. It was like a documentary thing, I suppose. It was kinda documentary, but then it was an entertainment thing, because it was the band, it was us. And he was talking about the club and what was happening within the structure of rock 'n' roll.

Anyway, I had all the youngest side of the people with me and I had to do "Splish Splash." There was no kind of presentation, bam! There was Ike Turner's band. "Whatever you do it's up to y'all." So there was no kind of theatrical thing involved, no props. But me, I'm gonna sing "Splish Splash." The sponsor was Steve Mizerany. He manufactured kitchen appliances—fridges, ranges, washing machines, et cetera, that kinda shit, right? So I said, "Why don't I come out of a bathtub with a towel wrapped around me for real?" So George Edick said, "Shit, man, yeah." That was my stroke of genius, right! "Yeah, shit—hey, boy, look, c'mon, that's pretty good, that's good imagination."

So sure enough they got this bathtub in for me. "Now, it's Ike Turner's band with Little Jimmy Thomas, he's takin' him a bath in so-and-so's bathtub." Whatever the name of the store was, took a sneaky little plug in there and sure enough the camera zoomed in on me—"Splish splash I was takin' a bath . . ." So I come outta this bathtub with a towel around me, so you think I'm gonna be naked or something. So then I open the towel, start dancing around, I got on my jeans and things.

I was great. Fuck, it was the talk of St. Louis for weeks. I couldn't live it down, man. All the black cats were laughing, "Saw you in that bathtub," and they started calling me "Splish Splash." "You gonna 'Splish Splash.'" But it went down great, man. And I saw the tape a couple of weeks afterward. George Edick had a cinema thing in his basement and he was running this thing. He said, "Hey, man," one night after the gig. "Hey, man, y'all wanna see what you did on TV?" Because it was live, everything was live. "Oh, great, yeah." So he got us all down there, sitting back waiting on the program to start. And sure 'nuff, I came up, man, and all through the whole program every song I did I was chewing gum, man. Looking really stupid, chewing gum. When I wasn't singing I'd be chewing gum while the solos and things going on, I'd be dancing away, Jack—chewing.

I was cringing. I was going "Noooo, no. No wonder they were laughing!" It was hilarious, it was so funny. But it was good, it was fucking good and musically it was right, man. It was hot. Because we used to play everything faster than any record was anyway.[36]

Tina Turner?

She was around before me, in fact, but she was just turning up at the gig now and then, she wasn't really singing with the band as such. She had a sister, Aileen, she brought Tina down. She [Tina] was great with me. A lot of the girls and a lot of the guys around St. Louis didn't like her. They thought that she thought that she was hot shit because she was singing with Ike Turner and all the guys, but you know, she was sweet, man, she was nice. Total innocence all the way. I mean, like, sex-wise, total innocence as far as life—she was just an innocent girl. She has always been like that, vulnerable, in fact. She come across like—the big butch chick or something, but no. She wasn't like that at all and she still ain't.

Fontella Bass?

During them days there was so much going on. Ike did record Fontella Bass. Yeah, Fontella and Tina. Fontella could sing, man. She played piano with Little Milton, but not all the time, just when her spot would come up. She wasn't playing as the permanent . . . there was another guy, I think it was Lloyd Wallace. He was Milton's piano player.[37]

During them days that's where the first Ikettes came. These girls worked with Art Lassiter around St. Louis. I think they called themselves the Artettes. The Artettes were

Robbie Montgomery, Frances Hodge, and I think one of Robbie's sisters.[38] Then when they joined Ike, that's when Ike brought Jessie Smith into the band. She was from Alton, Illinois. Anyway, these girls joined, we was already on tour by now. No, that's wrong—wait, we hadn't been on tour yet.

Ike and Tina Turner, c. 1960.

Before the Sue Records?

That's right, just before. Because "Fool in Love" was written for Art Lassiter, which was the Rockers' lead singer. Now, Art didn't turn up for the session or something and Tina sang it and these girls backed her, them three girls I'm telling you about. And, that's right, we went on the road and took them with us. That was the . . . they wasn't Ikettes as such, there wasn't no name. That's when we really got into doing backing vocals. We took them three girls because the record was a hit.[39]

How did the deal with Juggy Murray (Sue Records) come about?

Now, I don't know how that happened or how it came about, I just remember when it did happen. I remember Juggy coming to East St. Louis to Ike's house. And we saw this guy, smart New York nigger, you know, smart cashmere coat and the kind of hats they was wearing in them days, looking like a gangster. And lots and lots of money.

I didn't know anything about the business in them days, just some guy turns up named Juggy Murray and him and Ike were doing some heavy business over this song, this "Fool in Love" thing. I knew about how "Fool in Love" came about, because I was there. But Juggy and Ike got on, made the deal. Ike got lots of money, got a new Cadillac, new station wagon, we hit the road. "Fool in Love" was a smash, it really was everywhere hitting.

So you were still a local band up to the deal with Sue?

Up until "Fool in Love."

But you traveled before, though?

Locally, yeah. Jefferson City, Kansas City, all the places around. We played a lot of places.

At first it was two or three cars. Our first national tour all we had was a Cadillac, an Oldsmobile, and a Pontiac station wagon. Then he bought a long—what you call them things? Like a van, but extended, one of them extended version vans. And it had seats in it and you could put instruments and things on top. And Eddie Jones used to drive it! (*laughing*) And that damn thing, man, it was like an almost bus. Eddie used to wear funny hats and things and used to drive this damn thing and they used to freeze to death. Everybody would always complain, the heater always breaking down. Every time they get it fixed it would always break down. Finally we got more and more popular. Ike, you know, the records start selling so he bought a bus. So then we just had the Cadillac and the bus on the road. Everybody travel in the bus, we travel in the Cadillac. We was supposed to be big-time then, I guess. It was funny, man, but it was great fun, though.

Billy Gayles went to Washington, D.C., with us when we were doing all those theater gigs. He would come up, Ike had him doing a song in the show. This was in '61. Ike would have me introduce him or something. And it was sad to me, because the kids weren't getting off on Billy Gayles. And I knew, shit, I was thinking to myself. It was sad, every night I would have to introduce him, because the kids would be sitting there going, "Groan." And that guy, man, he'd be burning, smoking. I'd think to myself, fuck! And as soon as he'd go off and I'd come on, "Cheer." I'd be singing whatever the current crap was and it just didn't seem right. I felt very sorry for Billy Gayles in that sense, because I had so much respect for that guy. I felt very sorry that he wasn't receiving his proper thing.

But then I was learning. We was on the road and I was a little slicker then, things like that. I knew about showmanship, how to get an audience, and he didn't. He was definitely just a blues man. He was used to singing in them joints. He would just stand there and flat-foot sing, and the kids would want to see you do the Jackie Wilson shit, you know, running across the stage, splits, and all the crap that was going on. He toured with us around Washington, East Coast for about two months. And it was really sad, because Ike was really treating him badly, giving the cat, like, a little pocket money and just paying the hotel bill. It was bad, because Billy was a great man.

Wilson Watson?

Yeah, nice guy. Rich black cat down there in the West Virginia hills, loads of money. He was involved with Lloyd Price and Harold Logan. I think he helped finance . . . He used to book a lot of gigs up and down there.

Hector (?), a piano player?

Oh, that was another guy from St. Louis. He was with us during part of the Washington thing, he didn't stay long, either. Had Hector been working with Billy? I don't know. But this was during the time that Ike got Gayles from St. Louis to join us so he could record him for Wilson Watson. He didn't come with Gayles, he joined us in St. Louis. He didn't stay long, six months something like that, because Ike didn't like the way he played. He would always get drunk a lot.

Were you still based in St. Louis then?

No. We'd moved from St. Louis, but Ike still had his house and whenever we were in that part that would be our base. We would tour from there. Billy left, he taught me so much—him and Tommy Hodge, all them guys—about singing. I used to really listen to them, sing with them. But I knew more about harmonies, so we were learning off each other, but I used to really look up to them guys.

So Ike recorded Billy on that tour?

He did. He made some records in Washington, D.C. That was the purpose of him being with us that few months. Ike was writing some songs for him, for me, some of the girls, and Tina. This was when he was getting his production thing together, his whole package thing for Sue.

Ike was stopping off at various places making tapes and things in studios. We cut some sides in Washington, D.C., on Billy and on this girl named Eloise Carter. Eloise was with Chuck Jackson for a while. Eloise Hester was really her name, she was from Los Angeles, Ike was screwing her. So he had to cut some sides on her. "My Man Rock-Head," some crap, it was really bad.[40]

I don't know what label it was on, I don't know what deals he had with the guy. There was a little fair-skinned guy who was like a little wheeler-dealer record man around Washington. He used to have little offices. I remember we used to go up there and he got the studio equipment and all that stuff together to record.

You know about Jimmy and Jean? Shit, man, that was me and this chick called Wilhelmina, from Washington, D.C. She was another really fine chick who Ike took on as an Ikette, only there was no Ikettes in them days, not yet. But this was the beginning of that whole concept. Eloise was on the road with us and we were backing Tina, plus we had our own spot. It was a revue, it was that kind of thing. I had my spot, Eloise had her spot, Tina was obviously the star, because she had the hit.

When we got to Washington I started messing around with a chick who was one of Jackie Wilson's girlfriends and she introduced Wilhelmina to us. She had a nice voice, but a very soft voice. But she was a nice girl, very gentle girl. So Ike was, like—he was crazy. He was like M. C. [Reeder]. All the chicks in the band had to be his chicks and Wilhelmina was no exception. So anyway, he produced a single of me and her. I think we did two records, in fact, under the name of Jimmy and Jean. I don't remember what label it was on, but it was at the time that they had the Sue contract and there was some fight between . . . Ike was mad with Juggy, so Ike was gonna show Juggy, it was that kind of thing. And, sure enough, Jimmy and Jean's records were selling a little bit.[41]

Who was on drums after Bootie Lip?

This cat Pap. Steeplehead Pap from East St. Louis. He had a steeple-shaped head, man, it was shaped like a half moon on the up. (*laughs*) He played good drums.

Nose [James Norwood] joined after Pap, maybe somebody in between. Oh, yeah, a Washington cat, he was a junkie, but a fucking good drummer. Nose came from Durham, North Carolina, we got him from there. He was in a local band around there. Nose was there about three years, I think, roughly about '63 to '66.

We also picked up a lot of other musicians around Washington during that time, because we hung around Washington a lot. Al "TNT" Tribble, his father was a drummer as well around Washington, he had a residency in some club. But TNT was a really good drummer. He was so funky and had a heavy foot. Drive, shit. And the Kings of Rhythm were known for that driving rhythm.

So the band during that time was TNT on drums, and after him was a guy named Billy something, from Washington, who was a real thin willowy guy who was a good drummer, too. He was basically a jazz drummer so he had technique down pat. He wasn't as driving as TNT, but he was ace. He only played for a few months. We picked up another little drummer out of Memphis one time. I can't remember his name, but we called him Rebop. Good drummer, but I can't remember the guy's name for shit, little short guy. So many people come in and out of that fucking band. Boy, I'll tell you, it's amazing.

There was one little guy we had played drums, little tiny guy, he looked like the guy in the *Mad* magazine. You know the skinny kid on the beach, kick sand in his face, he looked like that one. This cat was like a bag of bones, man, but he could play. His name was Mo. Fuck, I can't remember his name either.

Then we got a big chick named Royster. Vermita Royster, something like that. Gospel chick, used to be in one of them Clara Ward, Marian Anderson, Stars of Faith, or something, she'd sing her ass off. But she, oh, man, I hope none of them hear this shit. (*laughing*) I'll get killed, Jack. But she was built like a football player, big shoulders, big tits, she was strong. And she fancied Mo. And we used to have fun, man. She used to chase his ass through the dressing room. And the cat had a broke back, he fell off a ladder or something and she used to nurse him. He used to hate it. She was big and he was a little bag of bones. I remember that shit, that was funny. This was in the mid-'60s somewhere.

This other boy who was Tina's sister's boyfriend who OD'd—he died somewhere down in Texas. His name was Marvin Warwick, played baritone, really nice cat. I can't remember who the piano player was at that time, but I think it was Leon Blue. Because I know he joined somewhere along the line. Oh, yeah, I know there was a guy from St. Louis. I can see him, his name was Edgar, he was a good little blues pianist.

Jesse Knight Jr. was still with us at that time. He was about five years older than me. Him and Raymond, they were all about the same age. I think Junior was younger than Raymond. He quit the band one time and rejoined again later. When I first joined the band in St. Louis and when we first went out on tour nationally after "Fool in

Ike and Tina Turner Revue. Front row: Bobby John, Jessie Smith, Robbie Montgomery, Vanessa Fields, Thomas "Nose" Norwood, Jimmy Thomas. Standing left to right: Sam Rhodes, Herman Relf, Rayfield Davers, Clifford Solomon, Anthony Chenault, Ernest Lane. Top: Ike and Tina Turner, c. 1963.

Love," Jesse was with us the first time we went out. So for the first year of that tour, I'll say for the first six months, he was with the band, then he left.

Going back to the St. Louis days, I remember this one night we got off—I think it was the Club DeLisa we played. We got some chicks and we was all there. Ike had a big house and a lot of musicians lived there and Junior's room was upstairs. There was a whole bunch of us downstairs in the sitting room with the piano and shit and drinking. Well, Junior was the kind of cat he liked to stir shit. He was a clown. If he came in here, he'd have to start fucking with something, make you laugh. He used to be famous for putting sheets over his head. You know, he'd take a chick to his room and the chick is there to give him some pussy, but before he's gonna do that he's gonna scare the chick, chase her and shit, and the chick would be, "Aaahh!" . . . But he was like that, funny cat.

Anyway, this night, man, wasn't nothing unusual, just Junior chasing a chick down the stairs in his jockey shorts, chick is fully clothed, can't imagine what the fuck. We hear all this noise, "Aaahhh, stay away from me . . ." The chick runs off carrying on a merry little chase through the sitting room, through the living room, back through the kitchen and, shit, running around turning over things with Junior chasing her.

Man, when everything slowed down we're all, "Look, Crow got on his little shorts." He hated that, hated to be called Crow. "Crow, get your ass upstairs and get dressed, Jack. Fuck me, look at him, black-assed Crow." And Junior turned around to go back upstairs and there was these brown shit streaks all up the back of his shorts (*laughing*) where he hadn't wiped his ass too good. I swear, man, we was in stitches. It was so funny because all the chicks was there, everybody was there and the lights was bright. Motherfucker turns around and he's got shit all up the back of his shorts, man. Plus we started calling him Sergeant Starchy after that! (*laughing*) Sergeant Starchy, that motherfucker would chase you. He'd be serious, he'd chase you, man. He'd be ready to fight, on stage, anywhere. Junior—funny cat, boy.

Ike shitted on himself one time on stage, man. Yeah, Eddie Duncan comes into this, man. This was just before my time in East St. Louis. Raymond and them used to tell me about it, they used to laugh about it all the time. Let's see, was Johnny O'Neal with Ike then? I don't know. So Billy Duncan must have played with Ike before Eddie Jones, maybe. Because he sure worked with Ike sometimes.

Anyway, Ike had a bad cold or something and he took some, I don't know if it was Epsom Salts or something. He didn't know what it was, Annie Mae gave it to him. "Ike come on, baby, take this." She could charm the drawers off you. "Come on, baby, if you don't take this that old cold gonna kick your ass." And sure enough she nagged him into taking this shit. Not knowing it's a laxative Ike goes to the gig (*laughs*), you know what happens.

He goes to the gig and I remember the place they told me it happened at, it was a famous landmark after that. Every time we went past it they would always point. Was it the Blue Flame in East St. Louis? Anyway, gig starts to cook, Ike comes on stage, Duncan and them playing, puts on his guitar, tunes up, stomps off the number. I think they said Jackie was singing "Jim Dandy," it was something really hot. "Jim Dandy" was their house rocker, they used to turn the damn club out on that kind of thing. Raymond and them used to walk, the saxes, out through the crowd and all that.

Anyway, Duncan's standing next to Ike on this particular night and suddenly Ike stopped and they kept cookin'. Duncan looks over at Ike and he sees Ike looking funny and easing the guitar off. Nobody don't know nothing yet. He takes the guitar and eases it to the side, slowly, and the band's still cookin'. And suddenly it starts to really stink, boy, and "God damn!" they knew. Everybody knew. All the folks in the front. And as he turned around to lay the guitar down Duncan hit him in the ass with his hand like *plop!* And the only way out of the club was through the crowd. Ike had to walk through that long crowd, walk that fucking gauntlet, Jack, with shit running all down his pants leg, squelching in his shoe tops. And stinking t-e-r-r-i-b-l-e. Man, they told me that, boy. They used to tell that a lot. It was a landmark. That place was famous among the band.

Did they play there again?

No, he became real famous after that. Maybe that's what helped him get famous.

Anyway, we started hanging out around Washington, up there. And that's where this guy joined, Rahoo, played bass. I can't remember what his name was now. Everybody came in the band, I had to have a nickname for. He just looked like a Rahoo to me! He played with us before Sam Rhodes joined, so we had quite a few guys from Washington. That particular band it didn't last all that long. I think Marvin, the guy that died, probably lasted the longest out of that Washington band.

Washington, musically, was very good. There was Billy Stewart and his brother. There was a place called the Spa, a great big old club where all the cats would meet up and jam. Somebody was always hot that was working there. And what's this blues guy, "Trying to Make a Living," Bobby Saxton, met him in Washington, he was pretty hot around there. He was living in Washington at the time. He was one of the permanent fixtures around there.

Jesse and Ike made it up and Jesse started back touring with us again and we went to California that time. That was like '61. Jesse toured California with us. That's when Ike was looking around to buy a place. And I think he toured all around through the country and back a second time and quit somewhere along the line. Then we got Sam Rhodes. That's right, on the way back across, again, St. Louis, one of the bases. Jesse quit, he didn't want to go back on the road.

Sam Rhodes was obviously the next best choice, because he had a similar style. Sam had worked with Billy Gayles and people like that a lot. That's right, Sam was Billy Gayles's bass player before he joined Ike. He had his own little thing going, good band.

Who is the sax player in the photograph in *Blues Unlimited* number 135/136, page 18?

Rasheed Ishmael. His name was Norman Rich, he was from Washington. His adopted Muslim name was Rasheed Ishmael. He was really a nice guy. He wasn't really a staunch Muslim. He tried to be, but being on the road, he was always into things, man, chasing chicks, the whole trip, getting in trouble. And he used to carry the payroll. Ike would give him the money, he was like the band treasurer. And there was a friendly rivalry between him and Eddie Jones. They were both tenor players and they used to really fight hard for which one is gonna get the solos on what songs, you know, things like that.

Slippery Harry?

Oh, yeah, his name was Pat. We picked him up from around Washington—that was during the Wilson Watson days. He was, like, Ike's cat before Rhonda.

Who was Rhonda?

Well, Rhonda was Ike's secretary and she's still Tina's today. She's still working for Tina. She was the chick who done all the—done all the dirty work.[42] So Harry, he come from around Washington.

And Junior was having it off with Harry's old lady. Then Mack Johnson started getting it, Mack started fucking her then. Then everybody—god damn, I hope none of them people don't hear this shit, boy. (*laughing*) I get somebody killed. I can't remember what the fuck happened, but there was a big thing about it. Harry got fired, anyway, him and Ike fell out. Don't nobody stick with Ike too long except a few people.

"Gonna Work Out Fine." How come Mickey and Sylvia were on it and not Ike?

I'll tell you what happened. I know we were at the Apollo and they was on the bill with us. And, you know, they got tight with Ike and Tina and them. And Sylvia's husband—they were doing real good, they had a club, he was a rich guy, rich black man, they had lots of money. Sylvia, she was a great lady, she looked good. We used to go out to their club after the gig. Tina, Ike, myself, couple of the guys maybe. And they got very tight and they got into Mickey and Sylvia's songs, and Ike used to really admire the way Mickey played.

Up in the dressing room one day Sylvia had brought this song in that her and Mickey were writing or had wrote, I can't remember now. But I remember that they had made arrangements to record it and Sylvia was gonna play it instead of Ike playing it. And Mickey doing the talking bits, because Ike was too bashful to talk.

You know, they had the words there and Mickey was telling him. And every time, Ike would crack up laughing or something, he couldn't take it seriously. "Yes, Tina!" breaks up, oh, man, "Cut, cut." So finally Mickey done it. And me and Eloise and this other chick, Wilhelmina, did the background. I sung the top, it was a nice sound having a guy sing the top with two girls, had that little thing, something weird. It was a weird way of life, it was a weird band, really. Always did things kinda strange. Ike may have played piano on it, I guess. I can't remember now, but not very much, he was mostly into the production side of it.

I presume he got credits for all of that as producer, because he was the cat, he actually was in charge. "Work Out Fine" was like Ike and Tina's crossover song. Because before, nationally speaking they hadn't reached a white audience. You know, certain clubs, certain towns, but they started to get radio play on the Top 40 with that record, whereas "Fool in Love" didn't. Nor did "Poor Fool" or none of them others, only the black stations.

What about all those package shows?

Yeah, those East Coast tours, the theater thing. There was the Howard in Washington, the Apollo in New York, the Royal in Baltimore, the "flea pit" as everybody called it, the Uptown in Philly, that was the theater circuit, and the last one was usually Washington, because it was furthest south. Then you start on the one-nighter thing, down through Virginia, North and South Carolina, and all them places.

You did some gigs with Buster Brown?

Yeah. We also done some gigs with Tarheel Slim and Little Ann. Whenever we done gigs like them theater circuits like the East Coast, this was something like '62, '63, somewhere like that. Ernie K-Doe, Buster Brown, all them cats.

Did you ever run across Bobby Robinson?

Yeah, lots of times, used to see him a lot. I don't think Ike had any dealings with him that I know of.

What was Buster Brown like?

I didn't know him, but he was on the show. He was a very quiet old guy, fat, cockeyed. But he was in another world from what I was into. Me and the cats, man, chasing chicks. He was just a nice old cat. He had a nice little set, you know, play his harp, "Fannie Mae," yeah, used to like it. I remember him as being a very pleasant man. Yeah, whoopin' and blowin', he really had a nice style.

We were touring with people like Jerry Butler, Chuck Jackson, no blues people, it was all soul people, R&B thing. The Miracles, Smokey and them, a lot of Motown acts, whoever was hot. There would always be six or seven top name acts touring. The East Coast tour system, it was the normal thing then, the thing to do. Whoever was hot, there was two agencies, Universal and Shaw.

What about Howard Lewis?

Oh, yeah, Howard Lewis, shit! He was outta Dallas. Yeah, he done all of Texas and Oklahoma. Howard Lewis I remember very well. I remember him real good, as a matter of fact, because our bus driver was having it off with his secretary.

She was such a classy chick, man. She used to wear these diamonds and things. Howard was a rich black guy, he was rich, man. I don't know what other line of business he was in outside of promotion, but sometime he wouldn't be on (the road) and he'd send his right-hand boy out there and this lady. The two of them to go around to the gigs with us and get the halls organized and things. And this lady was having it off with Duke, our bus driver. And they was like . . . oh, it was filthy, man! It was great.

And old Duke, let's see, he got . . . Howard Lewis's secretary shot herself trying to shoot Duke. Something happened, really. This was in Oklahoma City, in a motel as we were checking out, something happened. I don't know what, if she pulled a gun on Duke because of some chick or what. But Howard Lewis's right-hand man was in on the whole conspiracy. He knew, but he wouldn't say anything, because he was hanging out with us. I mean, what the hell, he didn't care no ways, he was makin' money. They made up some kind of lie and told Howard Lewis how she got shot. Some kind of accidental thing, she fell down with the gun . . .

There was always funny things happening on tour. We were all in this motel in South Carolina. It was with Chuck Jackson, Ben E. King, the Miracles, there was a lot of groups, and we was partyin' hard in this motel after the gig. And Mack Johnson the trumpet player, who was on Phillip Upchurch's "You Can't Sit Down," he was with us. He was doing the trumpet solo. He was really bad, man. He could really upset a house, blow the roof off, he'd get everybody on their feet, you know, playing that number. He used to use a toilet plunger as a mute! Consequently he pulled a lot of chicks in them joints, they'd follow him. He was a nice-looking dude, but he was a drip.

So we were in the motel partying. So somebody rings up and say come on down to the office, man, something's happened to one of the Ike and Tina boys. So we all made this mad dash to the office. We all pile in the cars and go to an address somewhere, and there's Mack hiding behind a tree, naked. You know, down in South Carolina, three o'clock in the morning. So Ike knocks on this door and we're all on the porch backing him up. So the guy opens the door, say, "Yes?" He looks out and sees all these stars, man. He says, "Well, I caught the nigger in bed with my old lady so I hit him and he ran." So Ike says, "Well, all I want is just give me the nigger's clothes." So he give him the clothes and we split. But there was always something happening, that's the whole point of it. On them tours, man, there was always somebody getting in trouble.

Like this time with Ike and Gorgeous George in Atlanta. Gorgeous George was the guy that was with Hank Ballard and the Midnighters, who were great friends of ours because we toured. This was the original player Gorgeous George. And George was an immaculate dresser, lady killer and all that, but a really great guy. Anyway, we met up in Atlanta in this motel. It had a concrete courtyard and two floors of rooms with their own little patios overlooking the courtyard. And this girl in the group, Eloise Carter, she'd known George from a long time ago, they were great friends. Anyway, Ike was having it off with Eloise and he was very jealous and his nose was wide open for her, man.

He went to the room about three in the morning, he probably thought everyone was asleep. So he crept down, knocked on the door and George was in the room. So Ike starts raising hell and we hear all this commotion and everybody starts peeping out their doors trying to find out the source of this noise. We hear all this cussing, "You motherfucker—god damn." "Well, Ike, hey . . ." We heard the word "Ike" and it was, "Ike's in trouble, let's see what's happening." So we see this little scuffle start up on the thing and Ike slapped Eloise or something and she ran back to the room and, "Fuck you, man . . ."

Okay, now, they get down in the courtyard, George and Ike and Ike's still raising hell. "Nigger, I thought you was my friend—blah blah—don't tell me shit . . ." And George says, "Ike, we don't need to argue and fight, we're grown men. The girl, hey, man, I've been knowing her since . . ." "Don't tell me nothing, nigger . . ." Then Ike swung at George and missed and George—knowing karate, judo, and all these things—he grabbed Ike's hand, did a little spin with him, and Ike's ass went up in the air and, boom, hit that concrete, boy, and bounced. And Ike got up, he still wouldn't stop. George leaned over, tried to tell him, "Hey, calm down, Ike, don't try to do that, be cool, I don't wanna hurt you, man." "You won't hurt me, nigger, what the fuck you . . ." And he swung again and this kept happening. George would take his feet, things like that. Ike was flying up in the air, he was flying all over the place like a dishrag or something.

Jimmy Thomas and Bobby John, 1964.

So anyway, everybody laughing by now. All the band and everybody knew what was happening, they didn't feel sorry for Ike, they thought, serves you right, motherfucker, you think you slick. He never attacked Ike, he just used evasive moves, but he knew so much about the shit till Ike was really raggedy after about the fourth fall. This cat was dusty and bloody. He was wearing a process and his hair was all over the place. His suit was raggedy, trousers torn, one shoe off. (*laughing*)

So George, I suppose, was trying to frighten Ike into submission. He picked up an iron chair, "Okay, motherfucker, you won't stop. Okay, this is it for you, then." There's Ike on the ground, can't even get up. So I ran down and grabbed George and coaxed him on away, cool it out. Ike had black eyes for weeks after, he wore shades. Every time somebody look at him and start laughing he'd want to fight again, it was really funny. Anyway, he learnt karate after that, he became obsessed with learning karate. Him and George became great friends afterward. But there were a lot of things used to happen in them days.

Ike's done some really dangerous things, man. I mean, people passing by shooting in his house and shit. He passing by people's houses and shooting in, he's always been on the border of that kind of stuff.

Yeah, I think it was Lorraine's ex-husband, he took Lorraine from her husband and she was staying over there. One night shots rang out, everybody was in bed. Bullet holes. This was at Virginia Place in East St. Louis. You could see the bullet holes up there. Then he and the guy became great friends. Crazy. Her name was Lorraine Taylor. Her father owned the Taylor Sausage Company. A black sausage maker in St. Louis, can you imagine?

It must have been a lot of fun?

Oh, yeah. I mean people used to think I was Ike. Because they always expect Ike and Tina to be a song thing! And people would often mistake . . . As a matter of fact, I posed for Ike a lot of times. There was a few times he'd have to fly to L.A. or to New York to do some business with the agents and things. Or sometimes he'd be stubborn for some reason and wouldn't come on tour, pissed off or whatever.

A couple of the tours Ike wasn't there, we hired another guitar player to play the licks. And I would do the talking bit for "Gonna Work Out Fine," but nobody ever be there. It was only on a few college gigs where somebody would say, "Are you Ike?" and ask for autographs. Nobody even asked about Ike, people just assumed all the time that I was Ike, except certain places we played so many people knew who Ike was.

And, like, sometimes if I was doing the introductions and things, or if Eddie was doing it, it would usually be one of the guys out of the band or myself would do the introductions, all the rappin' and shit. But nobody ever bothered, because Ike was kinda shy. He was a very shy kind of guy on stage about talking, but he got bolder later on, he wasn't caring about that much of it. But a lot of people really did think I was him, really weird, man. And it was funny posing as him when I had to pose as him. I had to do it because of the contract situation.

If you book Ike and Tina Turner and you pay a certain amount of money to an agent for that act, in Ike's case they had their own agency after a while, that's what you'd expect to be there. Ike and Tina Turner and the Revue. And the Revue consisted of Jimmy Thomas, the Kings of Rhythm, and the Ikettes, and you're in breach of that contract if all these people are not there. And so I had to play that role or otherwise they could have been sued. It happened three or four times, it happened on two tours. There were two tours he actually didn't go out on.

You had someone replace Tina one time when she was pregnant?

Yeah, that's right, Shirley from Detroit. We did a gig in Oakland with her as Tina. That was our first time in California, so nobody knew. She only did one or maybe two gigs. She never became an Ikette, because this was pre-Ikettes.

Bobby John?

We picked him up in L.A. and he was Ike and Tina's valet, looking after the clothes. He was a good singer, but they had no space for him on the show, really, so they just gave him a little spot. He was just a funny guy. He was a good guy to have around, kept the spirit up all the time.

Anyway, we were down in Panama City, Florida, that's right, and we were playing this place in Georgia just across the state line. We was gonna play two towns. That time we were staying in Georgia and Panama City. So we played the first gig. I picked up a chick, the chick followed us to the next gig. We played the first set, I looked up and there she was. So we go outside to get some air, cool off, place packed like sardines, funky, you know. One of the local yokels, man, he was jealous, because she was nice and everything, so he shouted out some obscenities at the chick about her being a groupie and everything. So I, trying to be chivalrous, I wasn't really brave, I was scared shitless, but I'm trying to show that I'm cool. You don't let the lady get insulted that you're with. But there was too many of them, like three or four. If there had been one guy, okay.

The cat jumped off the car and slapped the chick, the chick ran and the guys started attacking me. She tried to help, but couldn't. One of the guys flashed a knife, but I managed to kick the knife. Somehow I kicked him in the right place and he dropped the knife and I hit another guy and he flew, and by that time they'd started to hesitate. Anyway, I didn't stick around, I just started running. As I'm taking off I'm surrounded by cars, so I've got to leap cars. Have you ever tried to leap cars in a dark car lot? Stumbling and falling. But when it's survival and you think guys are behind you with knives and things you really can be pretty good. So, man, I was flying. I was graceful across the hoods and roofs.

So as the guys were chasing me, I don't think that they were too in love with trying to catch me. After that little demonstration they probably thought I was bad, and I was. But there was this one guy that was faster or braver than the other guys, he was closer to me, he was catching up. And by the time he got really near, the crowd came out the joint. So I heard all the yelling and screamin' and shit and gunshots. "Hey, Jimmy, what's happening? There he goes." Pow-pow! So I knew the cavalry had arrived, man. So the other guys were no more 'cept this one guy close to me, so I beat the shit outta him. I had to show something. Bobby John had the gun shooting up in the air. It was always things like that.

I remember one time in Vallejo, California, man, this was supposedly when we'd made it. Forget the St. Louis days, we were on the road. First trip we made to Vallejo everybody warned us before we left out of San Francisco going over to the gig. "Say, man, watch Vallejo. James Brown was over there two weeks ago, man, niggers over there turned it out. They fight over there, man. They turn the dances out. They got a thing going on, it's really violent."

So, well, we took it. Well, okay, something obviously must have provoked it. So we went over, done the gig. We're on stage, it's a big auditorium, tall stage, they didn't have no bouncers, it was a gig. I'd done my bit and I'd introduced Tina. And I'd go up in the dressing room and relax or chase chicks or whatever until the end of Tina's set when I'd come back on, as we had a little finale thing we'd do together. So I'm back in the dressing room and I hear the band break off in the middle of a number, "Fool in Love" or something, and suddenly—shit, you know, started up again. I thought, what the fuck's going on? So I dashed downstairs see what's happening. Some of the cats—Ike had kicked somebody in the face to get them off the stage, trying to grab the girls' legs, go up the girls' legs.

By the time I came down the band had taken off their jackets and were diving off into the crowd, into the front row of them cats, chicks, and everything, Ikettes and Tina and all of them. They had to, the crowd that was doing the naughties, there was a handful of the nasties that we'd been warned about. So anyway, they were leaping off like lemmings and I had to dive off as well, with no understanding of what was going on. It was crazy, man. Total craziness.

Nobody got hurt, we just had a nice dustup. And after the dustup the police came, put them out, take them away, we go back and start the show again, everybody raggedy, we carry on. Oh, it was crazy, man. Yeah, but looking back on it, it was crazy days. It never was normal, but strangely enough it did seem normal. Weird when you think about it, but we thought it was normal.

What was the story involving Bobby John and the band's payroll?

Oh, yeah, in Chattanooga, Tennessee. Yeah, that was really something. It was some kind of con that this guy worked on Bobby. And it was supposed to be an old trick whereby a guy knows you've got a bankroll. I don't know how it really works, but he shows you so many twenties and stuff and the rest of it is just cut up pieces of paper for his bankroll, and he's gonna look after your bankroll and his for some reason.

I don't fucking know what it was about, but anyway, Bobby, like a fool, let him hold his and the guy pissed off. I don't know how it really went, but it was supposed to be a really old silly trick. It was explained to me at the time, but it was too ridiculous to even believe. Crazy.

I bet Ike was pleased.

Oh, boy, I'm telling you, that was fun for days there. Shit. It was really funny.

Where would you play in L.A.?

There was the 5-4 Ballroom, 54th and Broadway. We played all kind of places, shit. In Watts—I can't remember the name of the place in Watts, but we used to play a lot of white places in them days during the surfing times. And we played places like the California Ballroom. I think the 5-4 closed down.

I remember one time at the 5-4 Ballroom. I'd never dropped any reds before. I'd met this groupie and she said, "One won't hurt you." Well, fuck me, I'll try anything once. Well, I dropped one, boy, and I was stoned, not tripping, but very spacey.

It come to the gig and it seemed like I'm burning like never before. Out there on the thing, oh, fuck, man, everything really sounding good. I finished my little bit, applause dies down and I said, "And now, ladies and gentlemen," Ike starts his little theme song, I think it was something like "The Stumble," great, man.

"Yeah, now it's star time, ladies and gentlemen, the young lady you've all been waiting for . . ." You know I'm going through the whole thing, "Fantastic, dynamic, unstoppable . . ." Everything I could think of, man, I'm stalling for time to think of that name. (*laughing*) I just could not for the life of me remember her name. I couldn't call her Ann, that was there, Ann. I thought, fuck, what do we call her? And finally Ike's seen the dilemma and he skipped up by me, "Tina, motherfucker, Tina!"

(*laughing*) I said, "Yeah, Tina Turner, yeah." Boy, I'm telling you, it was funny as hell. I never took another red devil after that, anybody come close to me with a red after that, I ran like a fucking stripped ape, boy.

Did everybody call her Ann?

Yeah. We never used "Tina" on the road. Call her everything, "Bo," never used "Tina" unless you were being funny or something.

We would only be in L.A. three months out of the year, we be touring like nine months. And we would supposed to be, like, resting for three months, rehearsing and getting a new show together and all that. We'd spend about two weeks rehearsing and then we would start touring the West Coast, Arizona, Washington, Northern and Southern California.

When did you first meet Ernest Lane?

I didn't meet Ernest until we got to L.A., but I used to hear Ike talk about Ernest a lot. Ike used to tell us about all his old buddies, Robert Nighthawk. Ike used to tell me about all them cats. But Ernest Lane met up with us in L.A. Ike had been talking about him a long time, but he didn't need no piano player then. Ernest joined the group about the second year that we were based in L.A., second or third. We moved to L.A. about '62 or '63.

Charles McGowan?

Yeah, I knew Charles McGowan, but I didn't know all that much about him. I knew him through Ike, he was one of their buddies. This was in L.A. I didn't know him in St. Louis, but I knew of him. I don't know when he went to L.A., but I met him, Raymond and all that.

Can you remember Billy Gayles coming out to California?

No.

The early live albums, were you on them?

Yeah. On one of them they spelt my name "Jerry" Thomas. Yeah, we did those things down in Dallas, Dallas and Fort Worth.

In Dallas I got to know some of the guys pretty good. Big Bo Thomas and the Twisting Arrows, he used to own a club. He used to have a keyboard player who sang, too. His name was Fred something, he was damn good, as a matter of fact—he could burn. He was the boyfriend of Delores Johnson, she was from Dallas, good singer. She was with Bobby Bland for a while, touring with him as part of his revue.[43]

Ernest Lane recorded in Dallas?

That's it! I remember the song "What Kind of Love Is That You Got," that's what it's called. Now, I don't know if that was ever issued, but I seem to remember . . . I think Ike put it out on his label, one of them—Sonja or Prann.[44] He had a garage full of unsold records on everybody. Things on me. I had one called "The Darkest Hour" which was a nice little record. He had about five or six different labels.[45]

Ike's band was on the session with Lane, the cats, but Ike wasn't there. Let's see, who was on guitar? It was either Herb Sadler or Baby Huey, great big guy, but just like a little kid. That's what we called him, but his name was Odell Stokes, good guitarist, man. It could have been Anthony from St. Louis. A little weedy guy, but he was smokin'—shit hot. It was a good song, I think he done two or three numbers.

Who would cut the live things? Ike?

Yeah, that's right. Mobile stuff. I did "Down in the Valley." Stacy Johnson and Vernon Guy did some tracks on one of them, too.[46]

Where did they join the band from?

From St. Louis. We were already touring, this was one of the times when we just came back through, picked them up. That was about '64 or '65. Vernon was with us a year, less than a year, before we came to England.

Benny Sharp, guitar player [from St. Louis]. He had a group called the Sharpies?

Yeah, yeah.

"I'm So Tired of Being Lonely"?

Yeah, that's right, I don't know what else they made or whether it was only two they done, but they was good. Benny Sharp came on the road with us for a while, because his band didn't last long. He used to work at the Starlight and a couple of other clubs.[47]

I sung with him for a while. Yeah, me and Stacy and Vernon, that's where I met them, this was before the Sharpies. I sung with a couple of bands just messing around. Sometimes there would be so many nights in a week I'd sing with someone else. That lasted about three months or something. I know what it was, I'd got pissed off and I'd left. I can't remember what happened, why I'd got pissed off. We had an argument about something and I said, "Fuck it," and left. I started staying with a chick, big-tittied chick over in St. Louis, little apartment. I hustled around for some gigs. Worked with Benny Sharp, Eugene Neal, done some gigs with Albert King for a few weeks. Then me and Ike made it up.

And the Sharpies came after this?

Yeah, because we'd left St. Louis then. There was a guy named Herbert who was the lead singer on "I'm So Tired of Being Lonely." He was bad, Herbert Reeves.

When they were in the band did they replace the Ikettes?

Yeah, for a while there was just the fellows and maybe one girl. Then we got Ikettes and we had them and Ikettes until Ike sent them all home, fired them all.

Shit, it was a good show, fucking cooking. There was us three fellows and we was fucking hot, Jack. I mean each one was a lead singer, plus as a group. We had a whole part of the show where we done lots of numbers. Break the house up before Tina come on. He had Tina come on sometimes, we would back her, maybe one girl. They was having a lot of problems with girls at the time, and finally we got Venetta [Fields] and Flora Williams, those chicks out of Buffalo. Vernon and them was with us maybe another six months after Venetta and them joined. It always did cook, but to me that was the highlight at that point. Anybody who paid their money to come and see the show got their money's worth.

In them days they never seemed like they could get the success on record that they deserved. Tina and Ike. They were making a little bit of noise, but never no big hits like James Brown and them was getting. Our show was strictly sold on the strength of live performances. The records ticked over and kept us popular. It got pretty big later on after Phil Spector, but it was after that the shit was falling apart anyway.

We was always picking up certain people, adding to the show, making the show varied. Me and Tina would always change routines and stuff, Ike got into it pretty good. He was so rigid at first. He was always trying to change things, but, you know, from where he was coming from musically speaking. That kind of thing we had that he didn't have, so the combination was great. That's why it worked so good. He could deliver anything we could ask for as far as the musical side goes. A lot of times we would create things right on stage. Just be crazy on stage, we used to come on with great routines, man, really funny things, had audiences in the aisles laughing.

I remember one time, man, this was somewhere in Washington. Olympia, Washington, I think it was, yeah. I had on this tight suit, Jack, and it was time to do "Tell the Truth," which we closed the first show with. We started really cookin', the tempo was really hot. It was a decent-sized stage but a lot of wires and things across the stage. You're doing your thing and moving fast and a lot of people doing it, because you got three or four girls as well as me and Tina. So the band kinda step back and they routining as well. It looks great from out in the audience, all that. And me and Tina, man, we used to have these little battles with each other about dancing fast and dancing hard and getting down on stage, "Wow, got you tonight, Jim . . ." Fuck, that night I felt great, felt a little bit *too* great.

My trousers went halfway, I don't mean just a rip down the thing, halfway the whole seam went. So all my ass, everything was gone and I didn't have on no coat, just my shirt. Strobe lights were on, so it was cool and it looked like part of the act. You got to make it look like it was intentional, we meant it! We'd be cracking up laughing, man. And Ike, that cat, he used to laugh, he'd have to lay his guitar—he'd fall over in the corner laughing. But I mean my ass was hanging out and I couldn't quit boogalooin' and nobody noticed, but Ike noticed, Ike noticed it first, he said, "Turn around, Jim, spin, do your famous spin, Jim!" By that time everybody on the stage knew. I went off sideways. Gracefully, sideways.

I mean, like, interrupting each other's songs sometimes, Tina was really great for that shit and Ike was really bad for it. You singing some nice ballad-type thing, lights low, quiet, and Ike would skip up and say something to you in your ear, you know, make you laugh, shit like that. When the show was going it was really good, shame that it broke up. There was never a dull moment.

What happened to Ernest Lane?

I don't know, he just got tired of touring, tired of being on the road, wanted to settle, try to get things organized. He joined the band from L.A., he was already there. Him and Sam Rhodes quit about the same time.[48]

We got another guy after Sam called Ron Johnson from L.A. on bass. Then came different other guys, it started changing a lot then. Al McKay, guitar player. Soko [Richardson] and Lee Miles. Ernest was there a couple of years. I think he joined about '64 or '65, somewhere back there. He was about the same age as Ike.

Eddie Silvers?

Yeah, let's see, Eddie was with us about '61, '62, something like that. Tenor player, he was in Little Willie John's Upsetters.

Who were the band that appeared on *The Big T.N.T. Show* in 1966?

Sam Rhodes, Ernest Lane, Nose, Herb Sadler, and Ike. Herb was a white guy played guitar from Granite City, Illinois.

One of the most embarrassing moments of my life: a couple of years ago I'm sitting up looking at the *Old Grey Whistle Test* and they ran one of the '60s films of Ike and Tina Turner, I remember when we did it. And we did "Tell the Truth," Ray Charles's thing. Me and Tina used to do it. And I came in on the end of the song and my part was real high, the Ray Charles bit, real loud scream and I'd come across the stage on one leg, shit like that.

I was sitting there looking at this thing and suddenly it's Ike and Tina Turner and "Tell the Truth" and I go, oh, fuck, I wonder if they show it all the way through to my bit? And they showed it. Oh, man, I cringed, I ducked. I looked so terrible, so stupid. Oh, what! I said, why couldn't they lose the film or something? Crazy days.[49]

Who else would you tour with?

We did some shows with Jimmy Reed. He had three or four musicians, this was in Oakland, I think. We also did some things with Sonny Boy Williamson and Little Walter. It was really good, because I like Sonny Boy.

Al Benson?

I just didn't like him, he was just a nasty-attituded guy. I stayed out of his way. Because he had such a reputation, he was like God around Chicago. He used to book all them gigs at the Regal Theater, we played the Regal. They had it sewn up, really did. He was a real dictator, man, because he was the hottest deejay.

I've seen him go out and shout at the crowd out in front of the theater. People be queuing up, somebody would be behaving a little bit, you know. He would go out and talk to people like they was fucking dirt, man. Everybody would cringe, like, "Here comes Al Benson, man!" I'd think, shit, I mean, I just couldn't stand it. But I guess he was alright. I was probably, you know—like I said, because I didn't have nothing to do with it. I just didn't like his reputation.

But him and Ike seemed to get on alright. And Ike was the kind of guy, if anybody was shitty or funny or something, he'd know it real quick. So I suppose he was alright, because I don't remember them having no fight. Because Ike was the same kind of guy. Most people, "Oh, fuck, I can't deal with that cat, man." Little Hitler, we used to call him, the Fuhrer. I think Sam Rhodes gave him that name. "Here come the Fuhrer, man, put that joint out quick."

The Apollo Theater?

Man, this was the funniest thing, every Thursday night was amateur night. They used to have this cat who had a big cowboy hat and a pair of red long drawers. This was an ugly cat, man, and some kind of funny shoes and his face painted funny and blanks in his gun. Now, when somebody would mess up, the lights used to flash on and off, all the lights in the building, and a siren would go and pow-pow, the cat with the gun . . .[50]

The emcee would come out, "Well, welcome, ladies and gentlemen, it's amateur night at the Apollo. Let's see what we've got here . . ." They had a little trio on stage doing the backing and this would always be some cats who could play anything. They had to be brilliant because people that would come up—you can imagine, you had to be fast, really quick, to find their keys and stuff.

"So, okay, who's gonna be the first contestant? Let's see, who we got here? This young lady she's gonna sing—what you gonna sing, darling? What's your name?" "My name's Helen," or something like that. "What you gonna sing, Helen?" "I'm gonna sing 'I Know.'" "Helen's gonna sing 'I Know,' brave girl. Alright, let's give her a round of applause, give her some encouragement . . ." This was just a general thing how they would behave.

Then there was this one guy I remember, man. This guy came out after about two or three contestants. "Now we gonna have John, what's your name, boy?" "John Jones." "What you gonna sing, John?" "'Your Precious Love.'" "Alright, John, go and sort the key out with Pete over there on piano." He'd tell a little joke while they sorting it out. "Okay, John's ready. Give him some encouragement, ladies and gentlemen . . ."

The cat, man, the band started, he come in anywhere, musicians trying to find him—all out of tune. Then the fucking lights would start, pow-pow-pow, the guy would be jumping, this clown shooting his gun. Sirens going, audience breaking up with laughter, man. Lights flashing and shit. Shit falls apart. And the emcee would come out when that happens, "Okay, okay." Laughter died down. "Okay, John, you better go back home, practice a little bit more. Right, we'll get on to the next one. Who we got back there . . . ?" The guy with the guns would always be there. Like when you fuck up he gonna come, but from anywhere. He may come from the back of the audience.

Now, after this guy fucked up on "Your Precious Love," they got one of them kind of mikes on stage that come up outta the floor, one of them electric things. So the next contestant's up there trying to sing some shit, she's cookin', going pretty good. Audience got with it a little bit. So after she launches into the thing real good, this guy breaks loose from backstage, the previous guy who fucked up "Your Precious Love." He come out on stage, man, and pushed the chick out the way, "Get out the way, bitch. *Yoourr precious love . . .*" and the band still be cooking on "Mockingbird" or something.

Bang bang, lights be going, "Get him off, get that nigger . . ." Shit going on, man like to start a fight. The emcee comes out and him and another guy grab this guy and they're trying to drag him off stage! Meantime the audience are breaking up. Poor little chick who's trying to sing is scared shitless, she don't know, she thinks it's something she's done wrong. And they drag the cat off. We're still laughing, we're all in the aisles. "Sorry about that, ladies and gentlemen, I don't know who this guy . . . Come on, baby, let's get her back, give her a round of applause, settle her nerves a little bit."

Okay, she launches back in it again. And this motherfucker comes out again, man. He gets loose, they're trying to put him out the thing and this cat broke out from back there again. This time he comes out they stopped it. Bang bang. Emcee comes out, "Hold it, hold it, I've got to get control of this shit." Everybody laughing, poor chick standing there scared shitless again. "Okay, I'll tell you what, since he insists on singing this song, he thinks he's got it so together, let's give him another chance, shall we?" "No, fuck, get the nigger—no, man, let's hear the chick, yeah." "No, wait, we got to be cool. Let's give him a chance or he ain't gonna give us no peace. Alright? Now, man, sing the song."

"*Yoourr precious love . . .*" This cat goes into anything, they can't find him again. The shit starts going again and they still couldn't get this guy off. So what they did, remember the mike comes outta the floor and was controlled remotely from backstage, they lowered it, man. Somebody pushed the thing and the mike started going down. "*. . . Means more to me . . .*" following it on down. The mike disappeared and they drag him off by his heels this time. Oh, man, I'm telling you, this shit would go down, boy, any time those amateur nights at the Apollo, any time you were in for a treat. It was better than any of the shows.

Yeah, they used to have amateur night at the Handy Theatre in Memphis. We played there when we first went on the road. I didn't know much about the Handy except on the radio and stuff. They used to have an amateur night there with Rufus Thomas. That's right, because they televised it, too, it used to be on television—yeah, didn't you know that? Rufus Thomas, little Carla, I remember seeing her on there a lot. The resident comedian was a cat named Robert "Bones" Couch, funny little dude. Him and another guy used to work together. Oh, they was funny. This was when I was still living in Osceola, this would have been in the mid-'50s.

Did you do any national service?

I didn't go to the army through Ike. I was registered in East St. Louis and we was on the road, my paper came. And I had to go and report, took off a couple of days to go. We was in Lubbock, Texas, had to hold up the show. Ike was freakin' out, he didn't want me to go to no fucking army. But luckily the guy who was the recruiting sergeant was a guy who used to come to some of our gigs and he was a great fan. Ike made a call or something. When I got there the guy, "Yeah, yeah, right, man, don't worry, it's cool." Just squashed that shit. Cooled it right on out so I didn't have to go. He used to do things, pull more strings. That cat, man, he could really pull strings.

What about the Phil Spector thing?

Spector was pissed off with America. He had some kind of war going on, the mafia thing, the Top 40 stations, the record industry, the whole thing, there was something happening. I can't remember exactly. Anyway, he was gonna show them they couldn't keep him down, they couldn't stop him.

So he made this record ["River Deep, Mountain High"]—he couldn't get no play. The white stations said it was too black, the black stations said it was too white, so they had him caught, man. So he said, fuck it, I'll release it in England. And he released it over here (in England) and it became a number 2 record. And he said . . . like, that to them.

But toward the end, I started getting really bored, because I started feeling so much more musically and I got tired of doing other people's stuff. And I got tired of being on the road and not being able to record, and that's what I really wanted to do.

I done the road and it was great. It was fun, but I wanted to get serious. On the road, you got to be crazy. You got to be a bit mad or you won't enjoy it, it can be really hard work otherwise. Good days, though. I don't regret none of them days, I tell you that. You're around such crazy people, you learn. (Or) go out like a lot of them did—it's so easy to get into that, drinking and dope.

How did Ike used to treat you?

Oh, I was like his little brother. We was really like that. That's why I watched everybody come and go. I was with them from that time until I left to come over here.

He could put the boot in real good, he could really fire people, fine them and act crazy with them and stuff, oh, yeah, man. I've seen him do people wrong, but he would always have his justification and we believed he was right, me and Tina, that's why we was there all the time. We always would support him, because we felt like what he was doing was bigger than all that other shit.

Me and him never really had no cross wires till one time when I got ready to quit and he fined me because . . . I wasn't really late, though technically he was right, but I was right, too. He fined me twenty dollars. Also, it was a bit of jealousy. Sometime he'd get a bit shitty with me or something. If a chick come in the group and I'd get it and he didn't get it, he'd get a little bit shitty and try and find some fault.

I really didn't believe he was gonna fine me, but, sure enough, when Sunday night came my paycheck was twenty dollars short. I rang him up, man, I said, "Shit, what's the matter, man? Why you fine me?" He said, "You was late the other night." I said, "Okay, I wasn't there in the dressing room when everybody's getting dressed, but when you hit the theme song, I hit the stage." I had been circling around about five minutes trying to find somewhere to park. I just dashed in and I heard them hit the theme song, so I just dashed on stage.

Well, he was fining me because he said I wasn't in the dressing room before he went on. I said "Shit, what difference does that make, man? You wrong, Ike, you wrong, I don't think it's right." I can't remember now how he justified the shit. Anyway, there was a little argument and I wasn't going to argue with him, because I knew you can't win arguments with him anyway, because he's the boss. What's the point? Either you quit or whatever, so I quit. I gave my notice, man, and he thought I was jiving.

Next day he was on the phone, and we must have been on the phone for about four hours just talking and we talked about everything. From way back in the beginning, you know, the shit that I'd been through with him and the shit he'd been through with me. "You know, things are beginning to happen, we need each other, blah blah blah." That wouldn't win. Then he tried to get heavy, 'Well, motherfucker, you know I'll kick your ass, man. You can't fucking just quit like that." And that didn't win. So he said, "Look, come on out and let's talk again before you decide." So I said, "Okay," so we was cool.

They were getting ready to go on another tour, you know, so I said, "I'm not going." I stayed and went to San Francisco and hung out. He was getting ready to come over here on tour and he rang me up from New York. He'd been over here (to England) once and I'd been with him. I'd made a nice impression over here that time. It was the Ike and Tina Turner Revue and I was one of the featured attractions, so he'd sold the tour on the strength of that. Anyway, that's what he told me.

He said, "Man, I'm in New York." I was really surprised, because it's early in the morning. I said, "Shit, Ike, man, what are you doing in New York?" He said, "We're getting ready to go to London, going to England, we leave first thing tomorrow morning. Have you got your passport and everything in order?" I said, "What for?" He said, "I want you to come." I said, "Man, most of my stuff is in Los Angeles. I have to go to

L.A., pack, and then go to New York, and I ain't got my passport anyway. So I have to get a passport." "You can get one in New York." "Man, it's impossible. How can I if you're leaving tomorrow?" Well, shit, a lot had to be done, book flights and things.

He said, "Look, man, I tell you, you gotta do it for me, because I need ya." I said, "Why? It's you and Tina, man, it ain't me. Nobody'll give a fuck whether I'm there or not." "No, man, you don't understand." He told me how it was. So I said, "Okay, hey, man, me and you always." We had that kind of relationship.

This was the second trip. This was after I quit Ike and went back, early '68. I told him, "Okay, man, I'll do this tour with you, but when we get back to L.A. I'm gonna have to leave, because I can't really . . . It's nothing to do with you, it's just that I've had a taste of doing it myself. I want to do things myself, produce myself, write songs and take my career in hand. All the years I've spent with you would be wasted, all the things I've learnt. If I could never put them into good use, what's the point?" And he understood it and he was glad too, he felt proud. He felt like what he taught me hadn't been wasted. About how to be a leader, how to do things, how to get on.

So what did you do after Ike?

As a matter of fact we got us a little thing together called the Goodtimers. Me, Ernest [Lane], Sam [Rhodes], who else, shit? This was '67, when I first split from Ike. Yeah, we got a little thing together and it was going good. Did alright. We had a couple of gigs around town, wasn't nothing, just fun to keep our hand in. Then I split up to San Francisco, me and my chick. We never made no records, it never got that far, just a few gigs.

And the Ikettes left and called themselves the Mirettes. They signed up a contract with Randy Wood, Mirwood Records, so I did a couple of records. The Mirettes had a little hit. I wrote one of the songs on Mirwood. I had two records on that label, "Where There's a Will," "Just Tryin' to Please You," which was one record.[51] The other two sides I don't think were released. That was a nice little time, me and the girls, first little taste of independence, you know.

Next thing I know after I moved to England, President Records bought the masters. Randy Wood came over here, I seen him, and brought the masters over and sold them to President. It became a number 1 soul thing. "Where There's a Will," which was the B-side in America, sold a lot over here.

The last time we spoke you were telling me something about Roy Brown.

Yeah, I remember I did some shows with Roy Brown when I first quit Ike and went to Oakland. In the [Roy Brown] article in *Blues Unlimited* [*BU* 123/124] I noticed he mentioned a guy named Goldberg. Before he went to California a guy named Goldberg, had some guy going around impersonating him.

Well, Goldberg, man, here's something, he calls himself a black Jew. Lives in L.A. and wears a big hat and talks loud. Great character. You either love him or hate him. You hate him at first, probably. And he used to do things like that. If somebody

Jimmy Thomas. London, March 1981. (Photo Bill Greensmith)

hot on the East Coast, which was way away, and ain't likely to get to California, he get some local guy to go around and pose as him. Hell, yeah! This was not too long ago, early '68. Yeah, that guy Goldberg, he used to do all them kind of things. A real crook, man, real crook.

Roy Brown's name was big as shit, "The Fantastic Roy Brown!" This was 1968. Who knew anything about Roy Brown? Up and down California, just little towns and we did a couple of spots in Oakland then we cut it a-loose, man. We had Vernon Garrett on there. Nobody got paid very much except maybe Roy Brown. Him and Goldberg was like that. Goldberg had probably told Roy, "Hey, man, shit, we can still make some money off your name." But nobody was turning up at the gigs, they would be very sparsely populated. Roy Brown was a nice cat, though. The tour lasted about three weeks or a month. You know, hotel bills and things wouldn't be paid, because he was supposed to pay.

It was really interesting to see that in Roy Brown's interview, but he didn't expand on it, I noticed. I thought, oh, wow! Goldberg, it's gonna be good. I bet he's got some really funny stories to tell about this cat, because everybody has, anybody that has been in any kind of contract with this guy.

I remember Ike wanted to jump on him one time, wanted to kick his ass. I don't know what happened, but Goldberg had done something. This was the only guy I knew that would call himself a black Jew.

Did he look Jewish?

Hell, no. He's just a nigger, man. Just a black nigger with a big old cowboy hat.

Why did you come over to England?

I waited to come to that point and England was perfect. Right time and I thought, yeah, fuck, sanity, man, I can really do it here. So I came over. There was the "Beautiful Night" thing, which was released on Parlophone. It was never officially released on that label.[52] Denny Cordell invited me to work with them, to work with the writers' workshop thing. They knew what I wanted to do, get into production, and they just let me go into the studio and do what I wanted. It was great. I'd never been into a studio on my own, my own songs, any musician I chose.

I did a tour with Fontella Bass over here during the time I was doing the Contempo album.[53] I had wrote the songs and I had the album all worked out the way I thought I wanted it. And John Abbey told me he was bringing Fontella over. I said, "Great, man." Just me and Fontella. She had her brother-in-law or something, sax player, he was her musical director. It was a good little tour, thirty days. That was the only tour I did in England on my own.

Anyway, this "Beautiful Night" became a collector's piece up around the Midlands, Wigan, northern soul shit, right, it was one of them. Man, I couldn't believe it, because I forgot about the damn thing. I went up there on this tour with Fontella. I was doing my album tracks, people shouting for "Beautiful Night." And we didn't even know how to play it. It was insane.

That's the only thing I did in England live. Help other people out sometimes for a laugh, make a little money, you know. Did a thing with Elkie Brooks, did a tour with her, only shoo-wops and things. Session work and lots of lead vocals on other people's stuff.

Did you do something on [U.K.] Spark?

Yeah. "No Trouble" was one and "White Dove." I did about three singles on that label.[54]

Tommy Hunt?

He was on Spark. He was with the Flamingos. I knew him in the States, because he did a lot of tours with us, like these East Coast theater things. Him and Chuck Jackson used to have similar voices.

And now?

I've got so many things I'm doing, trying to do. The main thing is trying to get the label going. The label strictly as a vehicle for me. I just want to sell some records right now. Don't want to bust down no chart walls, but I've got the material for it. I'm very confident of what I'm doing musically. You're gonna like some of it, some of it you'll probably hate, but it's fun, it's fun stuff. And it's honest. I haven't done a cop-out. I've never lost my roots.

This is it. The sum total of it. Crazy, but this is it.

Notes

1. Alvin Goldsberry. Piano player and drummer, originally from Clarksdale, Mississippi.

2. Carl Tate/Bob Starr remembered the In the Groove Boys playing at Willie Bloom's club around the late 1940s/early 1950s. By the mid-1950s Bloom no longer featured live music. A small shotgun-style house with a jukebox, it was popular with local teenagers.

It is possible that there were two locations for Willie Bloom's clubs. Bloom was also a piano player, although by the mid-1950s he seemingly confined his activities to private parties. In the early 1970s Willie Bloom recorded an album, *Sweet Man,* for the Jonesboro, Arkansas–based Alley Records, AL222.

3. Radio Station WDIA Memphis, Tennessee.

4. In numerous interviews Son Seals claims his father owned the Dipsy Doodle, a club that regularly featured blues artists. This much repeated statement, continually perpetrated in print, has become an acknowledged and unquestioned fact of blues history. But we only have Son Seals's word for this; others have expressed doubts and have questioned the veracity of Seals's statements. No Osceola resident or musician I've spoken with recalls Son Seals's father ever owning a club or any establishment that featured live entertainment. Jimmy Thomas, a boyhood friend of Son Seals, has claimed all along that Seals's father never owned a club. In this he is supported by M. C. Reeder's daughter, Stella, who also knew Son Seals from childhood. For many years her grandmother lived next door to Son Seals and his father. As the daughter of the owner of the T-99, she was perfectly placed to observe much local blues activity and is quite emphatic in her denial of Seals's recollections. Other Osceola residents have also supported their assertions. Checking Son Seals's claim one last time in 2011, I once again asked Jimmy Thomas if Seals's father ever owned a club in Osceola. His answer was a swift, "Fuck, no!" However, there was, at one time, a Dipsy Doodle in Osceola. As a fifteen-year-old, Ora Lee Swinson recalled going there in 1941 (the year before Son Seals was born). Located in a shotgun house, it was the local teenage hangout, for dancing to a jukebox and drinking Cokes. The Dipsy Doodle was owned by an Ed Johnson and never featured live music.

5. Albert King moved from Osceola, Arkansas, to St. Louis, Missouri, in 1956.

6. Ike Turner, along with various band members, including Willie Kizart, Willie Sims, and Johnny O' Neal, moved their base of operation from Clarksdale, Mississippi, to East St. Louis, Illinois, late in 1954. These musicians did not continue to work with Ike for long, and by the following year Turner had replaced them.

7. Drummer Jerry Walker eventually moved to St. Louis, Missouri, working extensively with Little Milton, Oliver Sain, and leading his own bands.

8. Nat D. Williams was a teacher at Booker T. Washington High School in Memphis, Tennessee. Angela Rippon was a popular BBC Television presenter and news reader.

9. Ike Turner still owned the house on Virginia Place in the early 1980s.

10. Billy Gayles was Johnny O' Neal's replacement as vocalist with the Kings of Rhythm. He in turn was followed by Clayton Love. "The Big Question," Ike Turner and His Orchestra, vocal by Clayton Love, Federal 12304.

11. "I'm Tore Up," Federal 12265, sold well in several areas, appearing at number 2 on the St. Louis *Billboard* chart for July 7, 1956. By the end of July the record had dropped off the charts, reappearing again briefly at number 6 on August 18. Strangely, King/Federal could never seem to decide which side of the record to promote, their advertising often listing "If I Never Had Known You" as the A-side. The situation eventually changed, and "I'm Tore Up" continued to be listed in their *Billboard* advertisements into January 1957.

12. The Dynaflow Inn was at 2840 Cass Avenue, St. Louis, Missouri. Popular KATZ radio disc jockey Dave Dixon died on September 19, 1964, as a result of injuries sustained in an August 28 car crash.

13. The Smith Jubilee Singers were from East St. Louis and recorded for Modern Records among others, although these recordings predate any possible involvement with the group by Tommy Hodge.

14. [Raymond Hill died on April 16, 1996.]

15. There is some confusion with this name. Jimmy is possibly referring to Nick's Country Club, 4201 Trendley, East St. Louis, Illinois.

16. St. Louis bass player and bandleader Doc Perry should not be confused with the East St. Louis harmonica player Doc Terry.

17. The Trojans/Rockers, consisting of Art Lassiter, George Green, Murray Green, and Douglas Martin, recorded for RPM in 1955 and Federal in 1956, accompanied by Ike Turner's Kings of Rhythm.

18. Raymond Hill was confusing the personnel of the Rockers and the Gardenias. Formally a gospel group known as the Alton Crusaders, the Gardenias included Luther Ingram among its members. Accompanied by Ike Turner's Kings of Rhythm, the Gardenias recorded for Federal in 1956. Federal 12284.

19. "Fool in Love," Sue 730.

20. Eddie Acon was a partner in several recording ventures with disc jockey/vocalist/trumpet player Gabriel. Recordings were issued on Joyce, Yvette's, and Tune Town.

21. "Boxtop," Tune Town 501, was recorded at Ike Turner's house, 3126 Virginia Place, East St. Louis, Illinois.

22. Technasonic Studios, 1201 S. Brentwood, Brentwood, Missouri.

23. Ike Turner recorded Fontella Bass in St. Louis, Missouri, in 1963–1964. The recordings were issued on his own Prann and Sonja Records.

24. Charles Drain and the Tabs.

25. Planet Records. The label was owned by Gabriel.

26. Bobbin and Stevens Records were two separate, independent companies. However, the majority of the songs appearing on Stevens were published by Lyco Music, Bobbin Records' publishing company.

27. Bobby Foster, "Angel of Love," Stevens 106. Written by Jane Busung.

28. Johnny Wright, "Gotta Have You for Myself"/"Look at the Chick," Stevens 1001.

29. Johnny Wright, "Suffocate"/"The World Is Yours," RPM 443.

30. Ike Turner claimed to have occasionally worked as a disc jockey at Radio WROX, Clarksdale, Mississippi.

31. Jimmy Thomas is a background vocalist on Betty Everett's "I'll Weep No More," Cobra 5031; "Everyday of My Life," Flyright 589. Jackie Brenston, "You Keep on Worrying Me," Flyright 578.

32. Rumor and speculation abound surrounding the death of Eli Toscana, whose body was pulled from Lake Michigan in 1967. Most attribute his death to a gangland slaying over unpaid gambling debts. There is not, however, any conclusive evidence to substantiate this theory.

33. The Blue Note Club, 4200 Missouri Avenue, East St. Louis, Illinois. Leo Gooden also owned the L.G. record company and Coun-Tree Records.

34. Icky Renrut, "Jack Rabbit," Stevens 104, vocal Jimmy Thomas.

35. Icky Renrut, "Hey-Hey"/"Ho-Ho," Stevens 107, Jimmy Thomas vocal on "Hey-Hey."

36. "Party Time at Club Imperial" recorded c. March 1959. Hosted by Club Imperial

owner George Edick, the show featured Ike Turner's Kings of Rhythm and some of the audience/dancers from the Club Imperial. The show was underwritten by Steve Mizerany, owner of numerous kitchen appliance stores in the St. Louis/East St. Louis area. Mizerany, the self-described "King of High Trade," was himself a St. Louis legend famous for his wonderfully eccentric commercials, his antics on "Party Time" almost stealing the show. Jimmy's memory is at fault on one detail: he emerges not from a bathtub but from a washing machine!

37. Fontella Bass, "Poor Little Fool," Sonja 2006. Rereleased on Vesuvius 1002 as by Fontella Bass and Tina Turner.

38. Robbie Montgomery's sisters were not singers.

39. Robbie Montgomery, Francis Hodge, and Sandy Harrell were the background vocalists on "Fool in Love."

40. Billy Gales [*sic*], "I'm Hurting"/"Dreaming of You," Shock 200. Eloise Carter, "My Man Rockhead"/"I Need You," Sue 742.

41. Jimmy and Jean, "I Want to Marry You"/"I Can't Believe," Sue 743.

42. Rhonda Graam, Ike Turner's secretary starting c. 1963.

43. Delores Johnson was a member of the Ike and Tina Turner Revue c. 1961–1962. In June 1961 Ike recorded her in St. Louis for Bobbin Records' "Give Me Your Love"/"Gotta Find My Baby," Bobbin 132. It is possible that Delores Johnson was no longer with the revue when she recorded "You Can't Have Your Cake" in 1963–1964, Ike and Dee Dee Johnson, Innis 3002.

44. Ernest Lane, "What's That You Got"/"Need My Help," Sony 114.

45. Jimmy Thomas, "The Darkest Hour"/"The Little Cheater," Sputnik 10001.

46. Jimmy Thomas, "Down in the Valley," *The Ike and Tina Turner Show,* Warner LP 1579. Stacy Johnson, "Drown in My Own Tears"; Vernon Guy, "Your Precious Love", *The Ike and Tina Turner Revue Live: Recorded Live at the Club Imperial and the Harlem Club St. Louis,* Kent LP KSD 514.

47. Billed variously as Benny Sharp and the Sharpies, (on Midas Records) or the Sharpies. Four singles were issued on One-derful Records as the Sharpees. Before she became an Ikette, Jessie Smith was also one of Benny Sharp's vocalists. Little Miss Jessie/Benny Sharp, "My Baby Has Gone"/"St. Louis Sunset Twist," Mel-O 102.

48. [Ernest Lane continued to live in Los Angeles, California. In the late 1990s and into the early 2000s, he was once again playing piano in Ike Turner's band. Lane died on July 8, 2012.]

49. *Old Grey Whistle Test* was a BBC Television music program, 1971–1987.

50. Norman Miller, aka Porto Rico, was the master of ceremonies for the Apollo Theater amateur shows.

51. Jimmy Thomas, Mirwood 5522.

52. Jimmy Thomas, "This Beautiful Night"/"Above a Whisper," Parlophone 5773. The record was supposedly withdrawn soon after issue, as Jimmy was signed with Essex Music, not EMI. These sides were issued in the United States on TB Records 101.

53. Jimmy Thomas, *Abyss,* Contempo Records COLP 1002.

54. Jimmy Thomas, "No Trouble"/"Springtime," Spark 1035; "White Dove"/"You Don't Have to Say Goodbye," Spark 1040, released in November 1969 and June 1970 respectively.

Joe Dean

"Joe Dean from Bowling Green" has long been a legendary figure to those enthusiasts lucky enough to have heard his unique record, and both Bowling Green, Ohio, and Bowling Green, Kentucky, as possible hometowns have exercised the imagination of researchers. Interviewed in 1977, Dean was long retired from music and the steel mill and blissfully unaware of the problems of blues researchers. Rev. Joseph Hensky Dean tended the flock at St. John's United Church of Christ on N. Grand and lived quietly on the northeast side of St. Louis, the city where he was born and spent most of his life. A thin, alert, and intelligent man who looked younger than his sixty-nine years, Joe Dean received me with great old-fashioned courtesy and, unlike some bluesmen who turned to the church, was obviously happy to talk about his musical life as he answered questions carefully and painstakingly. Something of a child prodigy, he displayed his musical talent from an early age, and as he told his story with a justifiable pride, it was clear that one lone recording in 1930 was barely the tip of a full professional music career that spanned some twenty-five years.

—Mike Rowe

Joe Dean from Bowling Green

Mike Rowe

Blues Unlimited #127 (Nov./Dec. 1977)

Well, I was born here in the city of St. Louis 1908, April 25th.[1] My mother was named Edna—Edna Goodwin. I derived the name Dean from my father, who was named Andrew Dean, so that made her Edna Dean, ya know. He died in . . . when I was infant. I never knew him, never got a chance to know what he looked like, how he looked. There were no pictures of him, ya know, only what my mother would tell me. I grew up as a fatherless child in a way, but stepfathers, ya know, on and off and . . . well, musical background. Well, it was a gift. I can imagine the Lord gives each one of us a gift, ya know. In my early days I was playing full scale "Chopsticks" at the age of five. My mother's sister owned a piano. My family did not at that particular time and, uh, I used to get on her piano at the age of five and with one finger I'd play "Chopsticks," ya know. It was amazing that I had no coaching. Probably I would have been an outstanding musician now, but my family background was poor. Mother had no money to school me.

Joe Dean.

So I just kept experiencing what my piano playing and after I reached an age about ten or twelve, well, I began to play with both hands. Now, my mother saw that I had the instinct and the gift to play well. She began to buy a piano, which she did and she began to give birthday parties. Her friends and relatives used to come around and they were amazed at a . . . child pianist. In those days they were . . . rare. That was an exception, ya know. And we had oodles of people. The rooms couldn't hardly hold them, because they wanted to hear me and that early age I was mostly a copy box—the old-time Graphophones, ya know, and the old familiar songs. I would hear the records on the Graphophone which we had and I would copy that on the piano. And I . . . I became fluent with it and never read a note in my life, 'cause I never reached that stage and, ah, I begin to get older, ya know, in age, say fifteen or sixteen, the more fluent I became. I kept at it. Oh, I met numerous of older piano players who would sort of tutor me, ya know, show me the scales, see, finger movements. I don't even remember who they were mostly, because they're all dead about now. They were old people. Well, I wouldn't say old then, but they were then, say, around, oh, thirty or forty then and that was, oh, that was real way back before I even got stretched out into music. I was nothing but a lad, ya know.

And a lot of these fellas used to come to my mother's house. At that time we were living 1609 Franklin and that was very early, about 19—oh, I say 1917 or '18. And they would come and play for parties and I would sit there at the piano, watch them how they did it, ya know, and as soon as they would leave I would get right on and I would start, and they would see that I had a gift and they would come back every now and then and show me how to play. And then when I really got up in age, say, eighteen or nineteen, oh, well, I was really stretched out then. Yeah, well, because every, every—at that time they had what you call ah, good-time houses, nightclubs—all sorts of places, ya know, cabarets, stuff like that. And my name began to ring a bell and they would come to my mother's house seeking me, ya know, to play for a night . . . say eight to twelve, something like that and I was about seventeen, eighteen years old. And then, well—I worked in between. Now, this was not a continued thing then, 'cause was no one but me and my mother. And she done a little day work, laundry work, and I had to help be the breadwinner. But in the evenings, at night, I would play for these different places and very soon I found myself I was doing it practically every night!

They were regular—I wouldn't say, ah, clubs or nothing like that. They were just like they give a pajama party, birthday party, Blue Monday parties—that sort. But they'd only be maybe three- or four-roomed house with living quarters. Not a certain club, ya know, but they would always have parties and we'd just go around like that. It was so numerous, ya know, if you were at one certain place or these two certain places over many-year period, then there's no problem that you can memorize this. But if you go to house to house for—we'd be going to three houses in one block—house to house, they'd be next door to each other. Say, 17th and Franklin, 14th and O'Fallon, 23rd and Del Mar, Leffingwell and, well, it's Morgan Street, I'll say then . . . Leffingwell and Morgan and, ooh, boy! They were removed out west. On one, one occasion once we moved out west in about the 4100 block on W. Belle—now, all of these are house parties.

And East St. Louis—oh, many times! 3rd Street (*laughs*)—yeah, I used to play on 3rd Street. At that time I was playing with a friend of mine. He had a house on Carr Street then—2300 on Carr. Every night that we would finish there he had an automobile and he would drive us all over East St. Louis. We'd go down on 3rd Street, but I wasn't professional then. Over there I was just much as a visitor. He just operated a house, but he would take us over there because he wanted to hear me. He wanted to take me with him. He wanted to exploit me in such a way, and we walk into a place there'd be a crowd, he'd say, "I brought my own piano player with me," ya know, and I don't care who would be sitting there, he make 'em get up!

Now, if you want to come up more now, to professional, then I'll have to name these places, because they were at a higher standard than the what you call the good-time houses, ya know. Right, one place I can remember was the Lincoln Garden and they were on Leffingwell and Market Street at that time. And I forget the guy that runs it. I can't think of names, I can't remember names now. And I'll say another one, Liberty Hall. Now, at these places here what I'm naming was mostly on a combo basis. See, I was with a five-piece combo. Yeah. I done solos mostly in the houses, but when it came to the cabarets and nightclubs it was mostly a combo. And I remember one place it was on Page. I can't name that street now, 'cause it was under a viaduct where Waggoner Electric Company was—it was strictly white, strictly white. Well, in those days, these white nightclubs loved, ya know, colored, Negro players. But I soloed out there. Say their nights was Friday, Saturday, and Sunday nights, say, from eight till one—they didn't go over one o'clock in the morning. And then, a broader sense, I played what you call the Chauffeurs Club. That was 3100 on Lawton and Pythian Hall right next to Chauffeurs Club.

Then I can move here from St. Louis, I can go all the way to—before I get back to my records—I can take you down to Memphis, Tennessee. Now, at this point, I done solos. I went to Memphis twice to do solos. And I was so good then I was asked by the manager—what they called the Chicken Shack—it was a pretty well-to-do place, carried a crowd, ya know. They asked me didn't I have instruments, ya know—somebody that—did I know anyone that would have a instrument where we could have a orchestra? Well, ah, not just playing piano. Sure, I knew numerous of them, ya know, like Henry Townsend, he would be with me sometime, and another one was Henry Spaulding. Yeah, he was with me a time or two, and Ike Rodgers, trombone player, he was with me a time or two. Oh, I could name a dozen. So I came back from Memphis to St. Louis and I got in touch with these guys and they all said sure they'd be glad. So I got about four or five of them together and, let's see, our drummer was a boy none of us knew very well. He didn't come up from the ranks, but we, ah, discovered him in a way. He lived in a big flat, but he would come down to a hall that we called—a song was written about it—Old Shanty Town! Oh, I can only remember a few, maybe a couple, I don't know—Sam Board was one, he was a cornet player—and this drummer boy . . . can't think of his name. He was a tall, stout fellow. He was young, about same age I was—about twenty, but I can't recollect who those others were. I think one of them was a clarinet player I know. There was only about four guys. Anyway, I got these guys together.

At that time we had no fancy way to—had no automobiles. We had no transportation and, believe it or not, those that had instruments, ya know, they had to put them in their grips or whatever they had and we hoboed down to Memphis! (*laughs*)

Well, I didn't have any baggage—I had all my baggage up here, in my head! So we went down to this Chicken Shack and we played a whole week there. I think the address was about four or five blocks back from Beale Street, right where the railroad station . . . Poplar Street Station. This was on 15th and Poplar, the Chicken Shack. So they couldn't stay open after one o'clock in the morning and somebody mentioned a place across the tracks—what they call "across the tracks," ya know. Say, "Don't go over there, 'cause it's dangerous." Said, "They'll chop your head off. They'll cut you to pieces over there." I said, "No, they won't." So they wanted to bet us, ya know. "You can't go over there. You guys from across town—you over here. They don't allow us over there." So we taken up the bet. I asked the other guys, "How many want to go with me?" See, if they were going to chicken out—they call it the Chicken Shack, so I put that little gibe in there. I say, "You guys gonna chicken out?" They said, "Oh, we'll go." Okay, we walk from Poplar Street, uh, it was about five blocks across the railroad tracks and then there's a great big row of flats, and this was where you go up a long step—steps lead up on the second floor. And we cross the tracks again, a whole lot of guys was standing downstairs. Boy, they was looking at us real hard, real hard as if to say, "What are you guys doing here?" They didn't know any one of us, ya know—only one guy I knew that went with us he wanted to show us where it was. He said, "I bet you're going to get whupped before this night's over!" We arrived there about two o'clock in the morning—we went upstairs to where the hall was, there was a great big piano sitting in the hall. I sat down, I started playing, and I think I played that record—I had that arrangement before I recorded that record "21 Years Old." It was four or five people and they began to crowd around that piano and they watched me. In about fifteen minutes' time there was about a hundred people in that club and they was all kinda crowded round me. And the guys that was with me with the horn and everything, they never blowed anything! They were—all they was gonna do was have a good time. They just laid their instruments down and just listened to me!

Anyway, I went to Memphis on these occasions, then I came back to St. Louis and got with my mother again. I played around with her at her place, ya know. And some news got out that they needed some piano players in Arkansas, ya know, Argenta, Arkansas. What they call Argenta—well, it's right over a little viaduct—it's right in, might as well say, Little Rock, but you just go over a little viaduct and they call that Argenta. "Arjady" they used to call it—a row of little houses in there. That time I soloed. I went by myself. I didn't take anybody with me.

So I done all of my orchestrations with—here in St. Louis with the Calumet Club, Pythian Hall, Chauffeurs Club, and Lincoln Garden, Liberty Hall, such as that. Now, I finally broke up with them—least or they broke up with me, in other words—the combo did, because they wanted to branch out, and the trouble was that we didn't have an agent, but I knew one fella who did have an agent and he's still making records . . . what did they call him? He had a nickname—if I could call that nickname . . . Roosevelt Sykes, yeah! Okay, Jesse Johnson was an agent then for Brunswick

Recording Company so, now, at that particular time Roosevelt had already engaged Jesse as his agent to record records—Roosevelt taken me over to see Jesse to talk with him to be my agent. But, believe you me, his terms didn't sound quite up to me—the percentage, ya know? And records at that time were very cheap to be made—they didn't pay you very much unless you were a real recording star like those really up there, like Mamie Smith and Bessie Smith—that's where the money was. Little guys like us, the money wasn't there. Jesse wanted fifty percent, ya know, of all the records that I record, so I asked Roosevelt, "Is he getting fifty percent from you?" He said, "Well, he was, but he ain't now." I said, "Well, he won't come down on me any." So I decided to go to Chicago myself.

I rode to Chicago and, uh, Roosevelt Sykes had already told me who to see in Chicago. After I arrived in Chicago I was supposed to see Williams Mayo—Mayo Williams, yeah, he was the head of the recording thing there. And I just walked in there boldly (*laughs*) after I got myself settled in Chicago—just walked in there boldly, I found out where it was, 666 Lake Shore Drive. So I had a quarter change in my pocket and I walked in there boldly and there was Mayo Williams sitting back with his legs crossed at the desk—no one there but me and him. I went in and, "Who are you?" I said, "The Honeydripper sent me." That's what they called Roosevelt Sykes. He said, "Oh, yeah, I know the Honeydripper. What can I do for you?" I said, "Well, he told me that I could record some records up here." "What can you do?" I said, "Well, I play piano." I say, "I'm not much of a singer, but I'll try." He said, "Well, there's the piano." One of them baby grands—oh, man! It sound like I don't know what besides the ones I'd been playing on—I really went to town on them babies, ya know! And I sat down and I played that one song first, and it took him by storm—he didn't ask me to do anything else.

So he got up out of his chair, said, "Oh, man!" I said, "You want me to try . . . ?" He said, "No." So he gave me all the information, said, "We're not ready to record today," but he gave me a time set. I think it was once a month you could record one record, or if you got really into it, you could do it twice a month and so on. He was taken in by that ["21 Years Old"]. I only wasted two—two waxes was all I wasted. The first one he gave me as a playback, so I noticed that my treble on the bass was faster than my right hand, so he said, "Well, you're gonna have to even that up, ya know." And so I was pretty, well—well, I wasn't too polluted, 'cause first thing Mayo gave me was a shot, trying to get my nerve up, courage and everything (*laughs*) and I guess that was real good stuff. I downed that and I was a little woozy there for a while and I got taken away with myself and, boy, that left hand was going (*laughs*) where . . . the right hand couldn't keep up with the left! So he made it play back on the wax and said, "Well, try it over again." And I was pretty well settled then—I broke the nerve, ya know. You do it the first time, you automatically break the nerve if you have to do it again. 'Cause you discovered your mistake . . . So, okay, I ruined two waxes on that and I only ruined one on "Mexico Bound." I ruined one on that and he was satisfied with both, so we got along.

So I had a chance at my mother's house to arrange my music. I wrote the lyrics of both songs, both records, and I played both music—nobody else did that. I was the lyricist on it. I wrote the words and the music. I had been out in Newton, Kansas—not Kansas City, Missouri, now, this is Newton, Kansas, in the state of Kansas, and I was playing for a—I would say a party. I was playing for some people there, I can't remember. Anyway, I was sitting on the railroad tracks getting ready to go play and I always liked trains and I sat on the railroad watching the trains go by. When I went out there on the Missouri-Pacific and it was where the Santa Fe cross the Missouri-Pacific tracks, and the Santa Fe engine was pulling a string of freight cars, and as the train went back about I'd say the third or fourth car from the caboose it had on there initials "M. C." Well, I knew it wasn't Missouri-Pacific, 'cause it goes by "M. P.," but right next to the other side of the car it had "Mexico" spelled out and I knew that the Santa Fe road ran into Mexico, so I said to myself, "This train must be going to Mexico or it's Mexico bound." And right then and there I conceived the idea for that song "Mexico Bound," because that train must have been bound for Mexico. So I went and played for these people at the party. Next day I was by myself, then I practiced on it, got my words together and the music, and I put it together—"Mexico Bound."

I will say, William Mayo [*sic*]—the manager, I'll say, of the Brunswick Recording Company . . . he tutored me a lot of ways on how to make rhymes. So by that he gave me a scroll with different words like "blue" and "new," and you picked one out to match either one that rhymed. So it was a lot of help to me.

William Mayo gave me that title "Joe Dean from Bowling Green"—he thought it would be a good gimmick, a catchy title. We were talking over the situation and he told me that I needed a gimmick—a title of some sort. Well, I couldn't come up with any, ya know—fact of matter I had given him my full name when we had to make papers out, I gave him my full name, Joseph H. Dean. Well, that was too long a name. He say, "Everybody got a gimmick like Pinetop, Honeydripper, and different guys . . . so how about it?" I say, "How about what?" "How about we just label it 'Joe Dean from Bowling Green'?" I said, "Well, I'm not from Bowling Green . . . everybody'll think I'm from Bowling Green!" He say, "Well, it's just a title—it don't mean nothing. Nobody'll sue you and you can't sue nobody." So he did eventually say there was a fellow by the name Joe Dean from Bowling Green, something like that. I say, "Well, suppose we get mixed up?" He say, "Well, I don't think you have to worry about that." So after I asked him, "Well, you think we might get mixed up? Somebody might think he's me and I'm him . . . and piano playing in the music field . . ." He said, "No, this fellow doesn't play piano." So I said, "Okay, let it go at that." So that's how I came by the name of Joe Dean from Bowling Green.

But I had a little ill luck. I didn't like the Brunswick setup either. They wanted to give me a percentage. "All right," he says, "I'll give you two choices: either I can pay you in full for the recording of the records or you get nothing unless it's a hit and then we'll pay you royalties." Oh, boy! Well, ya know, taken back in them years it was almost in Depression times and you're beat for cash, you're beat for money, ya know, so I didn't go along with the royalty deal, but now I wish I had. I think records at that time were about thirty-five dollars a side—yes. See, how much does it come up to now? What they get now? Oh, boy! Well, I sold it for what I could get, but where I made my mistake was he had given me a time set to come back and record again, but something happened at home. My mother became ill and I had to stay there with her and watch—well, I was twenty-one then. I made that song I was exactly twenty-one years old when I made it. That was a sort of a go-ahead kind of thing. I'm already twenty-one so I'm explaining through that song that I'm glad I'm twenty-one, and somebody else hears it and they're glad they're twenty-one. So I was twenty-one years old—my mother taken sick, very ill. I couldn't get back to Chicago to finish my recording and I didn't have any money for a long-distance call, but I could have sent a letter. But I was so distressed until I didn't send him a letter, ya know, but he had my address and he wrote me a letter again, so and when he wrote me that letter why I didn't come on that specific date, then I wrote back and told him the consequences. Oh, well, that kinda tore things apart, 'cause it wasn't long then that she passed away, and I was only about twenty-one years old, twenty-two years old when she passed. But I didn't quit my musical career, now, because of that, but I just didn't go back to record, because I didn't have the means to get back and forth to Chicago, no.

Then I started going out west. I'd been out in Colorado and I was in Newton, Kansas. I played in Newton, Kansas, for about a month and then I've been up to Springfield, Illinois. I played up there for about six months, just one place. It wasn't a nightclub—it wasn't a cabaret, it was sort of a cafeteria downstairs and big hall upstairs, might call it a good-time house, ya know, and the fella run that—he was a pretty good fella. I got my meals three times a day, I got my lodgings—it didn't cost me nothing, and then I made on the average, ya know, I made a lot of tips like that. So I was soloing then. I played a long time for him until I got homesick and then I just up and left Springfield. In Springfield it was strictly colored. Then I had another place that was really white, was in Venice, Illinois, right across the river here, Venice. There was a nightclub there. Somehow or other someone mentioned my name and I think I got a ride. Automobiles was pretty well then, I was getting up maybe twenty-five or thirty years old—so they drove me over to this club to see the boss and it was a lady operating the place, I can't remember their names, either. (*laughs*) Anyway, I played over there with them for about, oh, I'll say about a month and then they decided they were going to close the place. So a musician's life, he just moves from place to place, so that's how I got into really the music. You'll be surprised, though, how often it was—now, mentioning these places, no, it wasn't time in-between. I had worked practically every night playing. I had done that for, oh, fifteen, twenty years, so I was well into it. I played popular music—I played any type of music that were written. Ah, the numbers that I played as my recording was something like . . . one I do remember, "Don't Take My Blue Day Away," and that was done in a blues complex, and the reason I discovered that one because every Monday they call "Blue

Monday"—my mother wouldn't wash, wouldn't iron, wouldn't do anything on, but just have a good time. They call Blue Monday, ya know, after you've been over Saturday, Sunday, you pretty well worn out, ya know, so "Blue Monday" the song that I made then was "Don't Take My Blue Day Away," and I used that in plenty of my halls wherever I would play. And another one, a friend of mine opened a hall by the name of Old Shanty Town and I played that number, oh, I guess about four or five years. It became a trademark, "Old Shanty Town," and he opened his nightclub and he named it Shanty Town and this is where I met this drummer, 'cause he lived in the building that this club was in. The song was about, oh, I don't know, how old it was then when I got hold to it, but anyway, that was our opening. Whenever he would open his club at eight o'clock that would be our opening, ya know. And then I played the number "Blue Heaven," I played a lot of Ethel Waters songs, "Am I Blue?" . . . oh, I couldn't go on, 'cause I had about a two hundred repertoire. By memory about a two hundred repertoire, and a lot of times I would just take it with me as part of a sheet music—no notes on it, just names of particular songs, but I would do this for requests. A lot of places I go and people ask a request for a certain song they wanted to hear and I would look in my repertoire (*laughs*)—I don't know why I did this—say, "Yeah, I got it here," and I started. So that's the way I got in.

Now, getting back to the years with Henry—Henry Townsend, Henry Spaulding, and all these fellas—we would get together just unexpectedly, like. Ya know, I would play at a certain party or something. I'd be playing, then Henry would come in. Henry be playing at a party and I would come in and then we would play together, and then all these other places and fellas were like the same way. Henry Spaulding was a barber by trade. Yeah, eventually, I think, eventually opened his own shop there on Leffingwell and Franklin some years later, and he was a very popular guy with that guitar. The only actual piano players I actually knew were older fellows and then about three or four that came up along the same era that I did. Henry Brown, he came along the same time as I did. Pinetop [Sparks], I knew him, I mean, I knew him real good, ya know? We was friends. We moved around quite a bit from place to place and house to house, and every now and then we'd run into each other unexpectedly, like. Like I said before, someone would hire Pinetop to play for that night and I didn't have no place to play, so I would visit this place there, Pinetop would be there and we would share back and forth, ya know. Give him a rest and I would play. Although he got paid, I'd give him a rest and he'd rest me and a lot of times I'd be playing at a certain place, he'd come in, it'd be the same thing. We'd help each other out that way.

I had places on Morgan Street, so to speak. It was Leffingwell and Morgan and ofttimes Pinetop would come into this place where I would be playing, ya know. There's another—we wouldn't say imposter, but he carries the same name—another Pinetop that they used to call Pinetop, but he played differently than the original Pinetop and there's no way that he compare, compare what he was doing considered to the old Pinetop. At least he tried, he tried to get the finger movements, but it was a lot missing there. The original Pinetop was as steady as I was on that ["21 Years Old"] and nobody could get that style. Nobody could copy that style.

I got "Boogie Woogie" from Pinetop. He and I battled it out there one night—he wanted to see who was the best! (*laughs*) And I came right behind him and everybody just clapped their hands, "Go ahead, Joe, you got him!" We had this little shindig there on Morgan Street where we used to come all the time. We would meet there together and then we'd have it back and forth. And finally he'd start playing the "Boogie Woogie" and by the time he got through his number then, "All right, Joe Dean, I want to hear you," and they say, "Hey, we can't tell these guys apart, who's the best?" (*laughs*) It was fun, it was really fun. And serious, too—in a manner each one of us, we took our music seriously.

One of the s'posed to be greatest at that particular time was a fellow by the name of Starkey. Surprisingly he had only—he had one defect. Now, he was . . . he was so good until what is this lady's name, Louella Miller? They gave a piano recital at Booker Washington Theater, I think that was in the year '29 or somewhere back there, and there was prizes to the winner, ya know. Louella and Starkey was the tops, they topped all the rest of them, ya know. Now, which one of the two would win the prize? And Louella won. But Starkey would have won it, but his defect was he ran his music, his songs together. If, like, if you say, if he starts off on "Stormy Weather," his next song might be "Blue Heaven," ya know, but he do it all in one section. But the judges didn't take that, ya know? And that was his style. Now, he didn't do that ordinarily—wherever he played he would do that—and I'd a little, little head over him as far as people were concerned, and he was considered a really smooth piano player. But wherever he would play or wherever I would approach if I came to that party, he would be there. They would tell him to get up, "Joe Dean is here. We want to hear him." (*laughs*) Now, he didn't get angry or nothing. He would get up and I would sit down and you'd be surprised how people would just gang around me. 'Cause I had a unique style. Those two you heard [the recordings]—that's nothing to what I could really do—I could, oh, ya know, cross hands like that and like mice running over the keys, all kinds of dottios [musical tricks]! It wasn't a—wasn't too much like this fella Starkey. He had—most of his was comic stuff, ya know. He would play comical stuff, he'd jam all his songs into one. He'd hit the natural chords all right. It was interesting to hear him that he didn't have to do it professional-wise. If you sit to listen to him you would enjoy it the way he'd do it, but when it comes to playing for a party or where people had to dance, see, he had to get away from that movement, ya know. People couldn't dance to that movement, no. What his real name was I don't think anyone knew. Even my mother didn't know—she knew him very well. He was one of the old-timers in the music field, yeah.

I stopped playing about somewhere, I'll say in the late '50s, yeah. Oh, all the '40s, in the whole '40s I was still playing. I was still musically inclined in 1940s all the way up to the early '50s, somewhere in there. And when I really quit was way up in the '60s. I just, ya know—boom—I quit altogether and then I wasn't playing at all—I had to work. I had to make a living and I saw no way through a musical career. So I said to myself, the best thing I could do now is look to the future. I've learned from a long time about the city where you are raised or you are born as too much success unless you move out in another area where people probably have heard of you but don't know you. Then you can acquire an agent, and that was my biggest downfall in my musical career, is in getting an agent. And there wasn't any here that I knew of, all except Jesse Johnson, ya know. So the higher agents was in a higher bracket, like Bessie Smith and Mamie Smith and all those. Well, I couldn't reach that high, so I just had to smooth along like I was and I said, "Well, if I try to keep this musical thing going, I'm gonna starve to death." Because it began to get a hold to us. If you could talk to the Honeydripper he'll probably tell you the same thing that I'm going to tell you. It hurt us very much when they brought the, ah . . . machines in, jukeboxes, because there were many taverns that we were able to get work and they began to put these in these taverns. Then nightclubs began to get them. Well, now, where the Honeydripper outdone me, he had an agent in the beginning, where I had to seek one, see? That's why he was so successful, see? So I just strolled along. I said, "Well, I'll get me a regular job and I just can't do my night work if I'm trying to hold a job." What I mean by night work, like, if I work eight hours a day in a steel mill, it'll be foolhardy to go out and play from eight till twelve o'clock and have to get up again at four or five in the morning. So I worked in a steel mill—Granite City Steel—about twenty-three years and I had enough age and enough seniority, enough everything to retire. I think it was '72, 1972. I've been retired now six or seven years.

I would like to talk a little bit about the changeover like I did. And the changing of one's ability or his gift. I say to myself, "Was it the Lord that did it or was I did it myself?" Well, I say this—I felt an uneasiness when I felt that the Lord had called me to be a minister. Well, this hasn't been a long time ago, it's just been a few years back, about say in '71, but it sort of done something to me musically. I never was much hand in playing sacred music, never could, ya know, and all of mine was classical music, jazz and blues and I figured this . . . under the profession that I am now, I can't mix it, ya know? So I say to myself, well, I have to give up one or the other. Which one am I going to give up? Well, I had long given up playing music, so why go back to it now after the Lord has called me? Like I said, I don't know whether it was taken away from me by the Lord or whether I give it up, but I did mention that I didn't think it was right, and then later on as I watch television, quite often you'd be surprised how many musical people, professional like, that are given in a life of Christ. But they still going with the mood. Well, each one of us have our beliefs, ya know, so I say to myself, what's wrong with music, regardless of what kind? Then when I look in my Bible and I study the 66th Psalm, it says, "Make a joyful noise unto the Lord." What's wrong with music? Nothing. It's enjoyable, it soothes the body, it soothes the mind, it soothes the soul regardless of what music it is. But, now, I'd drawn away from it so long—too long, where I couldn't get myself back into the rhythm, you see? Right now I can still make chords. I can still play chords on there, but I forgotten how to get to that A-minor, C-minor which I used to do . . . B-flats, A-flats, ya know. See, that's really digging into music. Which all of that was a gift to me—that I know about. Not no one taught me. Lot of times I say to myself while I'm sitting here and I feel the Lord's talking to me, "Why you sitting here like a goof? If you want to hit a note on the piano, go ahead. So if you want to pick up a guitar, go ahead. You're the one holding yourself back." So it's just that simple. It's just what I don't want to do it, that's why. It's something I just don't want to do. I get no more pleasure out of it, in other words. I can go to a piano and sit down and I don't like what I'm doing myself . . . at this present time, but back then it was a joy, because I had full knowledge of what I was doing. All body, heart, soul, commitment was in it . . . it was a joy. So I . . . I thank God for that. Even though I haven't made a success at recording or orchestrations—I'm not rich from anything. He has given me what every man should be satisfied with, is a home. I can't have any more than that.

Joe Dean Part 2

It was particularly sad to learn of the death of Joe Dean (on June 24, 1981) whom I'd rediscovered in 1977 and interviewed for this magazine (*BU* 127). Despite his entry into the church, Joe was very keen to talk about the old days and his part in the St. Louis piano scene, and he made a very helpful and willing informant. Articulate and intelligent, he was a real pleasure to talk to, and he was sufficiently interested to answer a letter with further questions in 1978. As a result I did a follow-up interview. What follows then as our tribute to a fine person and great, if much neglected musician, is Joe's letter incorporated with the final interview.

> Dear Mr. Rowe
>
> Recieved your letter, with great joy I was very glad to hear from you. In regard, and answer to your questionaire's.
>
> I cannot remember any name's at my mother's house, because they would come and go, and, they were not realy professional.

Like I already said, they would come mostly for the enjoyment. Ah, she—she didn't hire nobody to play. None of them places didn't hire, they just had a piano there and just anybody come in could hit any note at all, well, "There it is, go ahead and play." And they would come in and just for the enjoyment of it sit down, play, play and they be gone and maybe don't see them anymore for a couple of months.

> Sorry, I only ruined one wax on "21 Years Old. We remade it the same day. Recording is a closed session, I never had the chance to meet any others. I was playing for an aged couple, called Mom and Pops: I also stayed as my residence there, the address was 2628 So. La Salle St. I stayed about 7 months, got home sick came back to St. Louis my home.
>
> No I never accompanyed any else on record's.

I never even bothered to go in any of the places around Chicago. See, 'cause all my time was devoted to Mom and Pops—so I couldn't get out at night. They were my boss, they were paying me, so I stayed every night to do for them. And every night was crowded. And they were sorry to see me go. But I had to go—when you got sickness . . . [I played] at nights, ya know? So I had all during the day to get my stuff together and they were the kind of people who never looked over my shoulder to see what I was doing, ya know. They all . . . either they'd be in the backyard (or) they'd be in they room. They'd be in the front and I'd be in on that piano and I'd be there some four or five hours with that one song. I could play any song you could name. I quoted myself about two hundred songs that I knew by heart, but I never even had to spend that much time. I fell in with that song because I was the same age that that song says I was—I was twenty-one years old. And that's when everybody they was going wild on that song, because they was many youngsters who were twenty-one years old at that time. And that was the time just about jukeboxes were coming up and that was knocking a whole lot of piano playing in the head, ya know? It wasn't bothering me too much, because I was in the record business and I was gonna follow it if I didn't have tragedy at home. So anyway, let me get back to Mom and Pop. I played those two numbers. I rehearsed them and rehearsed them. So Honeydripper already gave me the address where to go. See, me and Jesse Johnson got so heated up then, he didn't give me nothing to go by, ya know. But, uh, my buddy did, he gave me the address, told me how to find the place and I was fortunate that they were in the neighborhood—they were only about a couple of miles from the Loop—2628 La Salle—it's not too far from the Loop. And then you have to take the State Street streetcar. Car fare was a dime. That was peanuts, so I got my stuff together, took me five minutes. Once you get off, you cross the Chicago River and just go about three blocks on the other side of the river. And you can see the building to the right before you ever get to it—big, tall building. So I got off the car and I walked all around. I guess it took me half hour before I went in the building, 'cause I never saw such beautiful sight of all them boats, ya know, docked, and I stood there and watched, just looked at them. The boats was swaying and what they call that long ramp they hook 'em on to? Pier, yeah, see I never seen that here in St. Louis. Then I stood down and looked over that lake. Boy, that was fascinating—see nothing but water, and I sometimes say why do people call this a lake? It look more like an ocean. (*laughs*) Oh, that's a mighty big place. I never knew a city could be that big, Chicago.

> Yes, I was very talented, with other varieties of music. In fact, I tried to persuade Mr. Williams to let me record them. But, as he said, I had a contract for recording the blues, so I settled for that. In fact, I was satisfied.

See, I was a writer as much as I was a piano player, 'cause those two sides that I played is all done by me. Written—words, the lyrics, music—nobody helped me. The only thing that helped me any, but I didn't use it, 'cause I already had my layout when Williams gave me, the book of rhymes. See, I already had everything written. But he said eventually, if you need it, ya know, any other time this is a good book to go by, ya know. You can pick a word out and match it so it'll rhyme. Already had my stuff made out when I went to the studio. Let me tell you how this is arranged. When you go to the studio you are in that studio alone. Now, maybe someone recording in another studio—see, those studios are soundproof. Once you get inside there's nothing you hear outside—all the sound is in. Now, anyone could have been recording at the same day at the same time as I was, but I wouldn't know it.

Mayo Williams had pictures of famous artists all around . . . See, we was told . . . if you're not a star, we don't fool with you. He showed me all the pictures of Bessie Smith, Mamie Smith, Clara Smith—all those old-timers back—I mean singers, ya know, that really recorded. Yeah, I used to be among the biggest—I mean, I used to be in their presence. Some I played with, some I didn't. But most of those piano players I knew, they never tried to elevate theirselves. They never dug in to recording and stuff like that.

I met Charlie Creath when I was playing at Jazzland. I met him across the street where they had a joint where they gambled and play cards. He would always be there Monday nights. And one night he came over to Jazzland while me and my group was playing and he asked me, "Why don't you come on the boat sometime?" I said, "Oh, well, when I have time," ya know. So the best thing I did was make up my mind to go on the boat. And when he had his intermission he told everybody, "This is gonna be my intermission, man. You take over." And believe me, buddy, I don't know if they was spellbound, I don't know (*laughs*), but I had more people on the dance floor than Charlie Creath did! Boy, they had 'em lights turned low and I was mostly blues, ya know, but I could play any number and, boy, you talking about a time! They was so thick they was bumping into each other. I only had about a fifteen-minute intermission, but I was proud even to be associated with him . . . a person like Charlie Creath.

Eddie Randall, Eddie Johnson, all them guys—I monkeyed around playing with. Eddie Randall, he out of the business now. He in the undertaker business. He's out on Natural Bridge, him and I came along in that same area. He's an old-time musician."

Mike Rowe: What numbers would you play?

Joe Dean: No specific numbers. Any request somebody wanted to hear. "Dinah" was so popular in those days, "Blue Heaven"—all stuff like that was no problem. See, now we're going back in the early, oh, early '30s—'32 or '33, somewhere along there. See, at that particular time, I was really in the music field. I've done nothing, but that some parts of my life. I used to haul coal, work on the railroad, done odd jobs anyway, but coming into the '30s I was much older and then I really branched out . . . and I forget who that drummer's name was. Did Henry [Brown] ever mention to you a guy named Eddie used to drum for him and, uh, Ike Rodgers? I can't get his last name—he was real light-skinned. He carried Ike. He used to carry Ike all the time. Sam Boyd, he used to muck around like Ike Rodgers every now and then. When we had our combo we used to play at the Livery Hall together and—no, I can't think of the guy's last name to save my life. There's too many Eddies at that time. (*laughs*)

M. R.: Did you know Eddie Miller?

J. D.: I got around to meeting him, but not to . . . like I said a musician's life is all go, go, go. Might be here for a night and you gone somewhere else.

Charlie O'Brien: On the boats, did you tune into Fate Marable?

J. D.: Yeah, yeah.

C. O'B.: How about Armstrong?

J. D.: Henry—I mean Louis. I was unfortunate. I missed Louis's playing. During that period of time I wasn't even in town. Oh, I had gone maybe down in Memphis or Kansas City. I don't think I mentioned Kansas City to you? That came on my mind, too. I used to play at the Orange Blossom, Kansas City. I never will forget the address—704 Independence, Kansas City, Missouri . . . call it the Orange Blossom. And it was a great big hall like Jazzland or some of those places. I was on my own—lone piano player—and I remember a fellow coming in with a clarinet and he helped me out. 'Course he didn't get no pay, though, 'cause he wasn't hired!

M. R.: Did you ever come across a piano player called Jabo Williams?

J. D.: Oh, Jab! Oh, sure! Yeah, Jab used to be down in that area with us. There were two Jabs. There was one Jab who operated a joint on Division Street, and there was another joint on Biddle Street about 1500 and that was where Jabo Williams used to hang out. [He was] oh, kinda slim. I wouldn't say real dark, about medium-brown skin. See, going back that far, uh, that's when we wasn't hardly allowed in the poolroom. But I do remember the poolroom was on the corner of 15th and Biddle and there was another one across the street on Blair and Biddle. But one on 15th and Biddle, they had a pool table and everything there, but they had a piano in there and they ran regular, well, dances. And Jab used to come in there practically every night. And they had a back place where they had another pool table where they play cards, they gamble or shoot dice. This was a great big fellow about the size of that door who operated that place!

> The Calumet Club address is only skechy, but, somewhere in the twenty two hundred block of Market St. on the south side of Market St.
>
> When I was playing across the tracks, that was the name. The address and the street was only the railroad right of way. The house sat back about fifty feet from the Frisco tracks. A rambling two story frame building. It was there, remember? That the title for Mexico Bound Blue's came to me.

I wished for many a day that I would had a real good agent, manager—and I would still be in the field right now. I probably would've wound up now like Eubie Blake—still into it at the age I am. Well, see, uh, what's his name, Johnson, that had that barbecue stand, had that record shop . . . Jesse. If it hadn't been for Jesse I'd have been on my way. See, him and I talked about that, and the Honeydripper, Roosevelt Sykes, he's the one introduced me to Jesse at that time and, like I said, man, he wanted half of what I make, fifty percent. So I called Honeydripper and asked, "How much is he getting off you?" I think he was getting ten or fifteen percent. Now he wants fifty percent. "Think I oughta take it or leave it?" "If I was you, son, no, not for that." Well, Jesse Johnson was the only agent in that field in them days, and even right now the city of St. Louis is bad for all kinds of events to try to get agents and managers, ya know. It's rough here—especially music. It's nothing here.

I wrote the lyrics for a gospel song and that baby hasn't been published yet, 'cause nobody would publish it. Every publisher I went to I had to pay him! (*laughs*) I said, "Look, buddy, I write music I want to make money off it. That's my reason, ya know?" 'Cause I had a fellow in Chicago to—what you call it—complement for me. He wrote the music for it, 'cause, see, I wasn't in gospel music. And I tried to get notes together on gospel songs. I just couldn't do it, 'cause I was too much blues, waltz, popular music, and all stuff like that. So I had the other guy to do the complementing on it. That's when Joe had his music store on Franklin Avenue down there—I had some two hundred copies made. I went down to Joe and talked to him about it and he went back on his shelf. He brought out a stack of songs like that—blew the dust off. He said, "You know who this is singing these songs?" I said, "No." "Mahalia Jackson." He said, "You know how much I'm getting for 'em?" I said, "No." "Fifteen cents apiece." (*laughs*) So he says, "Only thing I can do with yours is stick 'em on the shelf and if anybody comes in and mentions a title or looking for any type of music I might get chance to sell a couple, but the money would be slow." That was way back in '43, about '43 or '44. And I just couldn't cut it. Now, one guy wanted to do it over here on Union Avenue, colored boy he was publishing. And he gave me a better break than any of 'em did, but what he wanted to do—he wanted to change the notes of the song, ya know, the piano notes. So we talked and talked and say, "Well, what's going to be the climax of it? What's in it for me?" He says, "Well, I'll tell you what I'm gonna do. If you agree to change the notes, popularize the song a little bit . . . give me three bucks and I'll be on my way." Yeah, again I'm thinking, I'm paying, I keep paying, I keep paying. I said, "Well, how long is it going to take before it be publicized?" "Well, I don't know how long it's gonna take me to work on it." I said, "No," thought I'd get a better deal. I even went down to Ludwig's and they had a musician there. He ran over that song and when he got through he said, "This is beautiful, really beautiful." He says, "My advice to you would be if you can get you an agent and let him fight your battles. You running all over town or going here and there you gonna have a problem. This song'll go, 'cause it's a hit right off." So this guy who played for Ludwig's said there was nothing wrong with the notes, so the colored guy might've been (*laughs*)—he might've been pulling my leg or might've been trying to figure out something for hisself. So I went around with that song for about a year or more and I just put it down. "The Blessed Name of Jesus"—that was the title. And it was beautiful. I introduced it to the church. The soloist sang it one Sunday and it went over beautiful. But, like I said, nobody here, no agents, no nothing, you just out. So I dunno, I just gave up music. There's a whole lot of peoples now just mixing their religious personalities along with their gifts. There's nothing wrong with music, no, nothing wrong with playing music, or loving music—any type. Well, here I am. I give it up. 'Cause I didn't feel like I would want to sit down and play blues, and somebody got a half pint over here, a case of beer over here and I'm playing the blues to make them happy. They get high, ya know (*laughs*), so I just couldn't see it.

Note

1. According to Bob Eagle's *Blues: A Regional Experience,* Social Security Death Index records list Dean's birth date as April 24, 1908.

Sparks Brothers

In 1932 Victor Records introduced Pinetop and Lindberg, a piano-vocal duo from St. Louis who, with a session of arresting quality, made sufficient impact in the Depression years to be recalled the following year to the Chicago studios, with Pinetop especially in demand as an accompanist. From the company files we learned that pianist Aaron Sparks and his singer brother, Marion, hid behind the intriguing soubriquet, but that was the sum total of information available. It wasn't until 1975, in an interview with their uncle Aaron, that we were able to accord them due recognition for their exceptional, if short, recording career.

—Mike Rowe

Well, Them Two Sparks Brothers They Been Here and Gone: Aaron Cleveland Sparks Interview

Mike Rowe and Charlie O'Brien

Blues Unlimited #144 (Spring 1983)

Pinetop and Lindberg are dead. Whatever the confusions or contradictions in their history—and there are many—at least their passing is certain. "They was all kinfolks. They had two sisters and two brothers—ya know all them folks is dead? All of them—mother, father, they two sisters—whole bunch of them all died and I don't know why, 'cause Marion and Aaron both of 'em ought to be living." Eighty-seven-year-old Aaron Cleveland Sparks pauses thoughtfully in the hot St. Louis afternoon remembering his nephews, pianist Aaron "Pinetop" Sparks and singer Marion "Lindberg" Sparks, and all the rest of the family he has outlived. There is a sturdy independence about Uncle Aaron born of a lifetime's hard work and the kind of pride that comes with extreme old age unbowed by his obvious poor circumstances. The street cries of the children and dogs fill the room of the shabby house on Maffitt Avenue as he recalls Pinetop and Lindberg and their somewhat confusing story.

Aaron and Marion were twins born on May 22nd, 1910, to Ruth and Sullie Gant in Tupelo, Mississippi.[1] There was already an older son, Rufus, and probably two sisters, Jimmie Lee and Mahalia.[2] Soon after the twins were born, Ruth married Carl Sparks, Uncle Aaron's brother, and the boys took the surname of Sparks.

"Piano player Aaron, he learned how to play piano before he could holler and shout," was Uncle Aaron's proud claim. "It was a colored fellow teaching him. He had a joint, ya know, selling bootleg whiskey back in the corner. He just had a crowd there all the time and he just learned to play. His name Arthur Johnson and he been dead so long nobody down there would know him, 'cause he was a old man when he was teaching that boy."

When Carl, Ruth, and the twins moved to St. Louis, probably around 1920, Aaron was to receive some formal musical schooling.

He just learned how to play the blues. After he came in, why, he went to school and they learned him the notes. He just kept getting better and better and got to playing for illegal joints, ya know.

This was about when Henry Townsend ran into him, and he would often accompany Pinetop.

Pinetop was doing a lot of house party playing and, uh, 'cause this was a trend then.

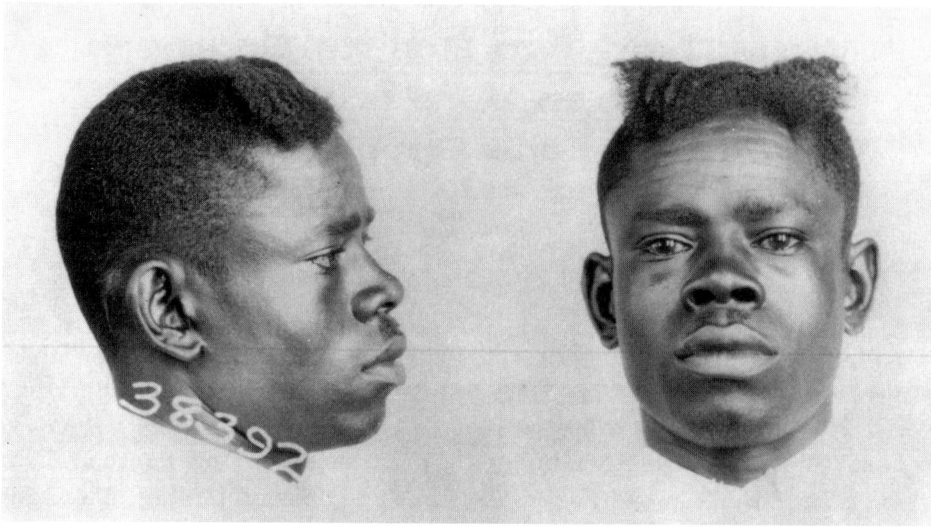

Milton Sparks. St. Louis, 1934.

We would go from house party to house party—give what you call it, rent party—and make some money to pay the rent. We'd go from place to place like that. I mean, it'd be announced at this party before it was over that there would be such and such a place to get their rent paid and Pinetop would play for those kind of parties where they had a piano and I kinda went around him quite a bit.

We'd have jam sessions, ya know. All the musicians was kinda known at that time. We'd have jam sessions. Maybe I'd be playing at some place, and if it was a house party or something there was a limitation on how long we could keep the neighbors up, ya know. So maybe one or two o'clock we'd have to give those people a chance next door to go to sleep, so we would quit, and possibly Pinetop be playing at some other place where they had it in a basement and wasn't no limit at all—all night and all day. So we'd go by there, ya know, and we'd get together and play not as hired groups, but just jamming, as we called it. Mainly house parties or sometimes it would be called some kind of little club. It wasn't officially a club, it would be someplace where it was fairly large enough for people to gather and they would organize and call it a club, ya know. Like the old Charley Houston's house on Lucas. Charley used to have a pretty good size place down there. It was a pretty noted club down there—he had entertainment all the time. I used to play there. I was hired there quite a few times with Sykes. Roosevelt used to play there, Pinetop would play there occasionally. He would use quite a few musicianers.

The house parties were rough, with the music and dancing only secondary to the main attractions of drinking and gambling, and inevitably the participants found themselves on the wrong side of the law. Violation of the Bone Dry Law was an obvious occupational hazard, and Marion was first arrested on July 23,

1928, and Pinetop, November 10, 1928. Marion had further arrests for gambling—November 17 for fighting and December 19, the same year. From this sudden spate of arrests in quick succession it seems likely that 1928 marked the beginning of their musical activities or their appearance in the "life."

When Marion was arrested again on November 16, 1929, he gave his name as Milton Sparks. Whether he decided to change his name in view of his growing police record is conjectural, but from then on, while his family would still call him Marion, Milton was the name by which he was known among his bluesmen peers. Henry Townsend recalls:

Now, at that time Milton wasn't, he wasn't singing. He'd be around, but he wasn't trying to do any vocalist [*sic*] at all and, uh, 'cause Pinetop was the star when it come to singing. And so just out of nowhere Milton decided he was going to sing, and he'd start.

The name "Lindberg" hadn't cropped up before, either. It would not have been uncommon in St. Louis, anyway, after Charles Lindbergh's epic 1927 flight, but Henry suggests it was probably due to Milton's prowess in dancing the Lindberg or Lindy Hop, which itself was named after the famous aviator.

It come along someplace during the time there was a dance—and he was good, a pretty good dancer. And he was probably good at that particular dance. Ya know, it was a kind of swing dance, ya know. I guess it fitted the pattern of the playing and he was very good at that. So I guess they just started to call him Lindy or he started to call himself Lindy or Lindberg or something like that. That's the only thing I could see, because he wasn't called that at first. When I first knew him nobody called him Lindberg, but later years they started to call him Lindberg. He was known as Milton then. Everybody called him by his name.

Of course it might have been made up by the white talent scout who first got the brothers on record. If Aaron was already called Pinetop (as is almost certain), then a *nom de disque* for Milton was obviously called for. [According to Townsend,] Aaron got the name Pinetop because: "He was very good at the number that Smith made. Yeah, he was very good with that number, and as most guys do he just started to call himself Pinetop himself, ya know. So that's how he got that name."

Joe Dean corroborates Townsend's explanation:

I got that ["Boogie Woogie"] from Pinetop—he and I battled it out there one night. He wanted to see who was the best! And I came right behind him and everybody just clapped their hands, "Go ahead, Joe—you got him." We had this little shindig there on Del-Morgan Street where we used to come all the time, we would meet there together. And then we'd share it back and forth, and finally he'd start playing the "boogie-woogie" and by the time he got through his number then, "Alright, Joe Dean, I want to hear you." And then, say, "Hey, we can't tell these guys apart, who's the best." It was fun—it really (was) fun. And serious, too—in a manner each one of us took our music seriously.

It was as Pinetop and Lindberg,[3] then, that their first session was cut in February 1932 when they recorded four sides for Victor in Atlanta, where the company had stopped off to record Blind Willie McTell on the way back from Dallas after recording other St. Louis artists Walter Davis and Stump Johnson with Roosevelt Sykes.

Their first recordings were impressive, as Aaron provided a varied accompaniment to Marion's declamatory vocals. "4 x 11 = 44" was a wonderful boogie with an insistent single-note bass and characteristically "hollow" treble and a great rippling solo passage. Lyrically, the songs all dealt with leaving or changing one's ways, and "East Chicago Blues," with its haunting melody, and the sprightly "Louisiana Bound" were both "leaving" blues. "I Believe I'll Make a Change" is fascinating for being possibly the first version of the later "Dust My Broom" variant. Their opening verse—*"I believe I believe I'll make a change [x 2] / Goin' cut off my gas stove and I'm going back to my range"*—would join the great stock of traditional blues lyrics. The song is also interesting for Marion's introduction of his wife, Janie, whom he was to identify much more explicitly later on: *"I believe I believe I'll go back home [x 2] / Well, this life I'm living won't let Jane be here long."* Pinewood Tom (Josh White) copied the song two years later changing the order of the verses and omitting one, but with only minor variations to the lyrics, and this seems to have been the version that Leroy Carr recorded only days later. Washboard Sam, in 1939, appears to have been the first to copyright it, though.

By the time of their first recordings, Aaron was already an accomplished pianist and he must have been recognized as a valuable accompanist, too, for at their next session, with five pianists participating (Walter Davis, Jesse Bell, Stump Johnson,[4] and Roosevelt Sykes—as Willie Kelly—were the others), Pinetop's ten accompaniments out of nineteen outnumbered even Sykes's. This was a mammoth affair involving no less than thirteen St. Louis artists and thirty-five titles in Chicago, on August 2, 1933, for Bluebird, Victor's cheap label, and Aaron accompanied five artists as well as cutting three sides with Milton as the Sparks Brothers. There was a lot of new talent at this session, including five women singers of no great distinction, and it's tempting to imagine the men had brought along their girlfriends. Whatever, Aaron accompanied Elizabeth Washington, Dorotha Trowbridge, and Tecumseh McDowell, an eighteen-year-old girl from Arkansas and the only one known on the "scene." She'd been arrested the previous year after a fight with her boyfriend, and the following year she was picked up in a swoop on a gambling house at 2248-A Washington with four other women and twenty-eight men.[5] The women singers seemed to be influenced by Alice Moore and sounded not dissimilar, apart from the harsh-voiced Dorotha Trowbridge, whose nasal tones were even more pronounced. Mostly, Pinetop used a simple chorded bass with attractive right-hand work in accompanying them and on the Sparks Brothers' own sides, but his accompaniment to Charlie McFadden's "Friendless Man," with its simple, but majestic, bass and right-hand triplets, was one of his best. On their own sides as well as Aaron's beautiful piano Milton contributed some local color as in "Down on the Levee": *"Down on the levee down by Boot's place [x 2] / Buy me half-pint of liquor find me a roosting place."* Stump Johnson, in *Conversation with the Blues,* talked about the notorious levee joints and Boot's in particular:

And just all around St. Louis down to Boot's on the levee I'd be. And Boot's was one of the most popular places in the city of St. Louis, because all the riverboats would come in there and dock and all the 'ristocratic people would come down there for slummin' and enjoyment. They were very, very tough places, though, and they were shootin' dice and drinkin' whiskey and enjoyin' themselves and it could get kinda rough.

Despite this, other towns were faster, and "Chicago's Too Much for Me" was a not unusual sentiment for artists visiting the city and their first experience of the "fast track." Their other song from the session, "61 Highway," was another that would pass into the common currency of the blues. Sykes had recorded a "Highway 61 Blues" (Champion 16586) the previous year, but this was different in lyric and melody, and it was the Sparks Brothers who coined the now very familiar verse: *"61 Highway, longest highway that I know [x 2] / It runs from New York City down into the Gulf of Mexico."*

1932 or 1933 were hardly the most propitious years to start a recording career, but it's clear that the records were influential on other artists, and recording, anyway, added to the brothers' local reputation. Five feet eleven, 151 pounds, and dark skinned, they were difficult to tell apart, which may have presented problems for the St. Louis Police Department, where they were becoming equally well known. As Uncle Aaron says:

Pinetop, he was a tall dark fellow—both of them was. They was twins. They looked just alike, couldn't hardly tell one from another. You couldn't hardly tell—you meet one over there, then come around here and meet one here, you wouldn't know whether it was him or not. You call him the same thing.

Their personalities were different, though, as Uncle Aaron says again, laughing, of Pinetop, "Oh, yes, he was a nice boy. He was a better boy than Marion was—'cause Marion'd fight in a minute and Pinetop wouldn't."

This is supported by Marion's approximately fifty arrests for peace disturbance, affray, suspect larceny, gambling, and other minor offenses. He'd also acquired, along the way, a further alias of "Marion Smith." For destruction of property in 1930 he served ninety days in the workhouse, and when picked up

Uncle Aaron Sparks. St. Louis, 1977. (Photo Mike Rowe)

with a friend at 23rd and Carr on suspicion in July 1934, they were described: "Both men are well-known police characters and associates of thieves and have been arrested numerous times as suspects." The next month, though, Milton was in Chicago recording for Decca as "Flyin' Lindburg." This was another huge session of mainly St. Louis artists, which had occupied most of the preceding week and weekend. On Friday, August 24, Marion recorded with Peetie Wheatstraw on piano, possibly Bill Lowry on violin, and an unknown clarinetist and guitarist. Interestingly, at this session there were sides by "Tee McDonald" (probably Tecumseh McDowell), "Dorothy Baker" (probably Dorotha Trowbridge), and "Dolly Martin" (probably Tecumseh McDowell, again). The pseudonyms may have been necessary if a Bluebird contract was still in force (although it was a few weeks over a year previously they'd recorded for Bluebird) or they may have hoped to record again for them. In the event, though, for Bluebird's next session of St. Louis talent in July 1935, only Walter Davis and the Sparks Brothers were recalled from the 1933 session. This was to be their last recording date.

It was also the first time Pinetop sang unaccompanied by Milton. Henry Townsend, who was at the session as an accompanist, explains:

> Yeah, Pinetop sang. Milton was supposed to be the singer of the two when the session was drawed up. Pinetop didn't go there to sing at all. He went to play for his brother, Milton. And when we got there, why, just going through measures like musicians carry on, he hummed off a tune or two. So everybody thought he should go ahead and do a number. So he went ahead and did a number. It turned out that his number was the better number after all.

In fact, all of Pinetop's numbers were better than Milton's,[6] and, moreover, with his warm, mellow voice compared to Milton's very nasal tones, he was the more attractive singer of the two. "Tell Her about Me," with its superb melody and wistful vocal, and "Got the Blues about My Baby," a heavier mid-tempo boogie, were his best sides, but incredibly the session produced yet another blues standard. He sang "Every Day I Have the Blues" in a high falsetto, and it's a shock to hear this moving performance for the first time as the song was originally conceived. Milton's songs, two accompanied by Walter Davis and two by Aaron, were more ordinary, but "Grinder Blues" contains an extraordinarily frank tribute to Janie again:

Don't you know I got a little grinder.
She lives in St. Louis, her number is 2721 Stoddard Street.
That little woman grind me to death, boy.
I'm telling you the truth. I don't love nobody but that little woman
her name is Janie (Dubois?)
Hey, man, I feel a verse coming down
Blues I ain't gonna sing these Blues no more [x 2]
I got my mind on Janie, mean I swear I got to go.

While the Ina of "Ina Blues" was probably fictitious, Janie certainly was flesh and blood, for at his 1934 arrest Milton gave Janie as his wife and address of 2721 Stoddard. It was obviously an enduring relationship, too, as the St. Louis city directories list Milton and his wife, Janie, as late as 1947–1948.

In contrast, [according to Aaron Cleveland Sparks], "Aaron didn't have no wife. He just had women. He'd go and stay with this one till she quit him. He'd go and get him another, soon after she quit him—that's the way he lived."

Pinetop fit the traditional romantic stereotype of the blues man—hard drinker, no job, and no steady woman, often in trouble with the law. Aaron lived his life in the joints playing piano and outside of them, he hardly seemed to exist. The joints are shadowy enough, but some of them are remembered. As Joe Dean says:

I had places on Delmar, on Franklin, on Morgan Street, so to speak, but it was farther up than Jefferson. It was on Leffingwell and Morgan, and ofttimes Pinetop would come into this place where I would be playing, ya know. We moved around quite a bit from place to place and house to house, and every now and then we'd run into each other unexpectedly, like. Like I said before, someone would hire Pinetop to play for that night and I didn't have no place to play, so I would visit this place and there Pinetop would be there and we would share, back and forth, ya know. Give him a rest and I would play. Although he got paid, I'd give him a rest and he'd rest me. And a lot of times I'd be playing at a certain place, he'd come in, it'd be the same thing. We'd help each other out that way.

Uncle Aaron, of course, often saw Pinetop play:

Yeah, they had over here on Delmar and, uh, I think it's the 20—right below Jefferson there, they had a joint there. Oh, a great big place, as big as eight rooms and they had dancing and piano playing and sold whiskies in the back and everything. That was way back, you know, when Prohibition was. Dirty Inn, that's what they called it—go down and ask about the Dirty Inn, down by Jefferson and Delmar and everybody around there, all them wineheads will tell you. They done tore it down now and put up a big filling station.

But Uncle Aaron remembered Pinetop playing more out of the city:

He go out there to Bloomington.[7] He played at that place up there—he mostly went every week to someplace to play, but he never played much here, only the Hole in the Wall over on Delmar. That's what it was called, Hole in the Wall, 'cause you went down in the basement. Just below Jefferson. He played out at this place they call Blue Heaven out here in Kinloch. He played there lots. Lindberg never did play nothing, but he sang all the time. He was a good songster. But Pinetop picked up playing piano. And Jimmie Lee sung. Mahalia never did sing.

Henry Townsend remembered Jimmie Lee:

They also had a sister. I don't think she ever done any recording, but she was far beyond in my opinion—she was far beyond Milton or Pinetop for vocalist, and they called her Jimmie Lee. Oh, she had the town sewed up when it come to vocalist. Yeah, she was a great singer, but I don't remember any time if she did any recording.[8]

Their last recording session, July 28, 1935, is also the last glimpse we catch of Pinetop. During his brief recording career he lived at 3139 and 3141 Franklin, and on an arrest in 1932 and two in 1934 he gave his occupation as "musician." Apart from this, the only definite information is that he died long before Milton, but despite intensive searching no death certificate has been found. Aaron never appeared in the city directories, and even the police records are confusing. From the frequency of arrests—eighteen from November 10, 1928, to his last arrest on August 30, 1934—it seems that Pinetop either turned over a new leaf (as Milton certainly did in later years) or, more probably, died soon after, possibly in his late twenties.[9] There is a hint of an early death in both Uncle Aaron's recollections (a suspicion of poisoning) and Henry Townsend's. Thus, Uncle Aaron said:

We all thought he got poisoned, yeah. Because he died just like that—could have had heart trouble, but he was laughing and talking and they hadn't been drinking but two or three . . . They just 'grudged Pinetop of his gift, yeah. Ya know, sometimes people hate you because you wear nice clothes. They'll kill you for it, too. They'll do it. That's just what happened to Pinetop. Pinetop had such a gift the folks walk up and give him ten dollars and he maybe wouldn't know him. He'd had heard him play and perform at these places and that's why he walk up and give him ten dollars. He wouldn't know who he was. But, see, folks, peoples 'grudge you that. They wants that and they ain't done nothing for it. They'll kill you, too.

But Townsend believed that Pinetop just burned himself out in the joints:

'Cause he pushed too hard at it. That's the same problem Pinetop had when he hit his little streak of fame. Why the people—he just a good-hearted guy—"Come on fella, come on." He just followed through night and day, night and day. So after a while, sleep was too far out—he couldn't get it, too far behind, and that was the cause of his death.

After the last session in Chicago, Milton was arrested again the next month, but his subsequent arrest was his most serious brush with the law yet. Possibly he was a bit unlucky. On Sunday, August 23, 1936, Lindberg, dressed up in brown pants and a white shirt with black spots, went to a social function at William Taylor's dance hall at 930 22nd Street. Unfortunately, it's not known what musical entertainment was provided that night, but at eleven o'clock he went into the kitchen and ordered a dime sandwich from Mack Lane, who was in charge of the food. At that point, Edward Randolph, who was president of the club that was organizing the social, came in and Lindberg handed over the dime to him. Lane then asked Randolph for a ticket for the sandwich, but Randolph denied that it had been paid for! Not surprisingly, an argument then started up between Randolph and Lindberg, who, by now, was sitting at a chair eating while Randolph leaned over him repeating, "You never gave me a dime." There was a scuffle and, according to Taylor, Randolph jumped on Lindberg with an open pocketknife and cut him in the chest and leg. Taylor stepped in to separate them, Lindberg ran upstairs, and Randolph left the hall. Half an hour later, Edward Randolph, still armed, returned with his brother Herschel and went to the yard at the rear of the dance hall. Lindberg also came back, still bleeding from the chest wound, and sat at a bench at the side of the hall. Edward Randolph then walked around the counter to Robert Williams, who had been taking tickets at the door until one o'clock, and gave him some tickets from soda sales. As they were checking the tickets, Lindberg got up off the bench, came over, took out his pocketknife, opened it, and stabbed Randolph, who tried to defend himself by lashing out with his feet. Lindberg fled by the side door into Cole Street while Randolph, seriously wounded in the stomach and chest, was helped by his brother out the front door into 22nd Street. Herschel took him to the city hospital in his Ford motor coach and Randolph died an hour later.

Next afternoon at 4 p.m., Lindberg was arrested at 10th and Carr and, suffering from an incised wound of the right leg and stab wound in the left side of his chest, was admitted to the same hospital in a serious condition.

A grand jury indicted Lindberg on September 21 on a charge of manslaughter, and the case was heard on April 16, 1937. After pleading guilty, he was sentenced to six months in the city workhouse. Considering that in 1930 Milton had spent three months in the workhouse for destruction of property, the light

sentence is either an indication of how little concerned the authorities were with black-versus-black assault, or the strong provocation that Lindberg had undoubtedly suffered in this case and the time he'd spent in custody already.

Afterward, Milton still continued to get into trouble with the law, but his arrests were becoming less frequent. Janie was still living up to 1948, but after that nothing is known of her. The twins' mother, Ruth, probably died about 1941 and their stepfather, Carl, who was a junk dealer and had married again, died about 1957. Milton in 1951 was living at 711 Jefferson, which was the Calumet Hotel, where Walter Davis was working at the time as a desk clerk. By now Milton had quieted down, and his last arrest, in 1955, for permitting an unauthorized person to drive, was little more than an echo of his wild past. He married [a woman named] Mary about then and was a reformed character. He even got a job, too—as a construction worker. Uncle Aaron recalls for us:

Pinetop never did have no job. Marion, he didn't start to work none until he married this woman he married, ya know? Then he went to work. He never worked before that. He went back to church and was singing in the choir. (*laughs*) He'd quit singing blues.

Milton never got into trouble again and lived quietly until his death.[10] He was working as a porter at Heckman School in St. Louis when on May 25, 1963, three days after his fifty-third birthday, Milton drove to work as usual and suffered a fatal heart attack. Uncle Aaron has the last word:

Started to working and fell and died right there. But naturally, what I think was the matter with Marion, I think when he was out there singing and going on. I think he drinked too much.

We took our leave of Uncle Aaron with further leads to follow up, but the trail had gone very cold. A couple of brief phone conversations with Milton's, perhaps understandably, hostile widow, Mary, and a fruitless meeting with Uncle Aaron's wife, shed no further light on a rowdy history whose main characters had long died and those left had little interest in or didn't want to be reminded of. And fifty years on, who can blame them?

Notes

1. The year 1910 is in some doubt, Marion having given his birth date as May 22, 1908, and 1909 on other occasions. Aaron's date of birth is not shown, but from his age given on various arrests the year could be 1905, 1906, or 1907! The year 1910 is given on Marion's death certificate.

In 1934 Marion gave "Sullie Sparks" as his father, address unknown, and "Ruth Sparks" as his mother, address 1217 N. 17th Street. There is no suggestion that his stepfather, Carl, was not living with his mother at the time, and Carl was not known by any other name.

It seems probable that Marion was referring to his real father and that Sullie was his name, but he was, of course, Sullie Gant.

Aaron usually gave Tennessee as his state of birth and on other occasions he gave Illinois (East St. Louis). Marion gave Mississippi and specifically, Tupelo, Mississippi, but usually East St. Louis, Illinois, as his birthplace. However, Uncle Aaron's statement that they were born in Tupelo, confirmed by Marion's death certificate, is almost certainly correct.

2. In 1934 Marion listed no sisters and only Rufus Sparks of Percy, Mississippi, as relatives. Rufus was Rufus Gant, but it's hard to know whether the sisters were Gants or Sparkses. Rufus, who attended Marion's funeral in 1963, was then living in Cleveland, Ohio.

3. By the time of the first session Marion had been using the name Milton for at least three years. It's interesting that for the company files he reverted to his real name, Marion.

4. *Blues & Gospel Records* and the *Victor Master Book* are incorrect in listing Stump Johnson as accompanist to Elizabeth Washington's "Riot Call Blues" (Bb 5229). The label states, "Aaron Sparks piano," and this is supported by aural evidence. As far as we know, her Victor issue has not yet been discovered.

5. Among the twenty-eight men arrested were two brothers, Charles Mike and Robert Mike. They could possibly have been the two artists Red and Black Mike whom Big Bill Broonzy describes finding in East St. Louis for Lester Melrose in 1937. But according to *Blues & Gospel Records,* St. Louis Red Mike's real name was John Mac Bailey.

6. Bluebird must have had reservations about their salability anyway, as all of Milton's and a couple of Pinetop's sides were paired for release with, usually, more popular artists; for example, Walter Davis, Memphis Minnie, Tampa Red, Bumble Bee Slim, and Bo Carter. If so, then Bluebird's fears were well founded, for by about March 1937 their only records still in catalogue were 6125 (rev. Walter Davis), 6202 (rev. Memphis Minnie), 6521 (rev. Bumble Bee Slim), and 6529 (rev. Bo Carter), which were obviously issued later anyway, and 5193. This last record might have sold well, but more probably sold so badly that the first pressing was still left in stock and hence was left in the catalogue.

7. Bloomington, Illinois, is where Uncle Aaron assured us we would find a close associate of Pinetop's, a very tall piano player who ran with Pinetop all the time. In the first interview he named him as Arthur Henderson, but he could not recall the name in the second interview.

8. Uncle Aaron, who contradicted himself on some points and was confused on others (not surprisingly, given his advanced age) claimed that Pinetop accompanied Jimmie Lee on record. This seems most unlikely, but there are untraced matrices from the 1933 session, and it does seem strange that Jimmie Lee was not among the "new" women singers who recorded then.

Jimmie Lee's married name was Miller and, according to Mary Sparks, she was last known to be in Fairbanks, Alaska! But in Uncle Aaron's opening paragraph he seems to suggest that she is dead. There was also a cousin Ernestine who ran with Jimmie Lee and the twins.

9. Aaron's police file actually shows twenty arrests, eighteen from 1928 to 1934, with a gap until 1950, and another gap to the last arrest, in 1954. The address given on the

last arrest is actually Uncle Aaron's, and the age, 55, although incorrect, is nearer Uncle Aaron's than Pinetop's. It hasn't been possible to check the address of the 1950 arrest, but the age, given as 52, fits in again with Uncle Aaron's. Further, Mary Sparks, who married Milton sometime between 1949 and 1955, but probably much nearer the latter date, never met Pinetop, who had been dead long before she married Milton. It's likely, then, that these two late arrests refer to Uncle Aaron (who remembered one arrest for a minor offense) and should be discounted. Aaron's pattern of arrests then becomes significant. With no more arrests after 1934, Aaron had either reformed, retired, changed his name, left town, or died. From Uncle Aaron's and Henry Townsend's accounts it seems likely that Pinetop died soon after his last recording session.

10. A note in *Blues & Gospel Records*—"A man named Lindberg Sparks still lives in St. Louis, MO, and claims to be Flyin' Lindbergh [*sic*]"—shows that somebody talked to Milton, probably in the late '50s. Why his claim to be "Flyin' Lindburg" was not taken seriously or why this great opportunity was missed is not clear. We would be very interested to find out who it was who spoke to him.

Fontella Bass

If we were to measure success in terms of record sales, then we would have to place Fontella Bass somewhere near the very top of the St. Louis music hierarchy, because she had one of the biggest-selling records by any St. Louis artist. With its unforgettable bass line intro and Fontella's warm, soulful voice, the 1965 recording of "Rescue Me" is an enduring classic that generated sales in excess of a million copies, earning her a gold record along the way.

An accomplished pianist, Fontella spent her formative years accompanying her grandmother and mother, gospel artist Martha Bass, at numerous church and concert programs. Joining Little Milton's band in 1961 as a pianist, her first recording session was accompanying Milton for the St. Louis–based Bobbin Records. In 1962 Fontella made her debut under her own name, recording four sides for Bobbin Records, "I Don't Hurt Anymore"/"Brand New Love" (Bobbin 134) and "Honey Bee"/"Bad Boy" (Bobbin 140). It's probable that Fontella is also playing on other Bobbin sides by Oliver Sain, the Earthworms, and Leon Patterson. Bobbin Records boasted an outstanding roster of artists, but this did not translate into sales and the company was forced to close its doors in late 1962. Little Milton's contract was sold to Chess Records, who also purchased numerous other Bobbin masters, including the Milton session with Fontella on piano.[1] The following year a dispute between Little Milton and his bandleader, Oliver Sain, resulted in the musicians resigning and reforming as the Oliver Sain Revue. Fontella Bass suddenly found herself, along with Bernard Mosely, as the featured vocalist. In late 1963 she recorded a further two sessions in St. Louis, this time for Ike Turner's labels: "I Love the Man"/"My Good Loving" (Prann

5005) and "This Would Make Me Happy"/"Poor Little Fool" (which also featured Tina Turner) (Sonja 2006).

The differences of opinion between Milton and Oliver Sain were soon resolved, and in 1964 Milton, by this time relocated in Chicago, recommended Oliver, Fontella, and Mosley's replacement, Bobby McClure, to Leonard Chess. Up until this time Fontella's and Oliver's various records had met with little or no success, but the situation soon changed dramatically. Following a request by Leonard Chess, she recorded a duet with Bobby McClure, Oliver Sain's composition "Don't Mess Up a Good Thing" (Checker 1097), in June 1964. Although not released until January 1965, it proved to be an immediate hit and ended the year being voted the number 12 best-selling R&B single. And although their follow-up, "You'll Miss Me"/"Don't Jump" (Checker 1111), didn't meet with quite the same success, it did sell reasonably well. However, following a disagreement with Oliver Sain, Fontella moved to Chicago to pursue a solo career. Around the middle of 1965 Fontella entered the studio to cut what would eventually become her biggest-selling record and the one that will forever be synonymous with her name, "Rescue Me."

Checker 1120 was spotlighted by *Billboard* on September 4, although they singled out the Sain composition "Soul of the Man" as the top side. On September 25 "Rescue Me" entered the Top 40 R&B charts at 37, climbing to number 1 on October 30, simultaneously being on the Hot 100 at 9, eventually climbing to 6. It remained at number 1 for four weeks and for a total of 19 weeks in the Top 40 R&B chart. Its follow-up, "Recovery," entered at 36 on January 29, 1966, though it had lingered in the bottom half of the Top 100 for the previous two weeks. "Recovery" proved not to be as successful as its predecessor, only managing to climb to 13 in the R&B Top 40. The United States was not the only country in which "Rescue Me" established good sales. Entering the English charts at 21 on December 11, it eventually reached 6 on January 1. Fontella made a promotional trip to England and was presented with the gold record on the BBC [television] program *Top of the Pops*.

Fontella toured for some considerable time behind "Rescue Me," but a subsequent album, *The New Look* (Checker 2997), and several more singles could not equal its phenomenal success, and by the end of 1968 a slightly disenchanted Fontella was asking for a release from her contract with Chess. Numerous sessions for Jewel/Paula Records in the early '70s and lone sessions for Epic and Nentu met with very little commercial success. Fontella continued to work as a solo act and also with her husband, Lester Bowie, and the Art Ensemble of Chicago and occasionally recording with them.

In the early 1980s Fontella moved back to St. Louis after a couple of years of living and working in France. She managed to keep a foot in both the rhythm and blues and gospel camps, a rare phenomenon, appearing on shows with Oliver Sain, Martha Bass, and Fontella's brother, David Peaston. A quarter century after its release, "Rescue Me" was given a new lease on life when the song was featured in numerous television and radio commercials. Unfortunately, not being one of the writers, Fontella saw little of the revenue the song generated. Fontella Bass died on December 26, 2012. In this interview Fontella recalls her early years in St. Louis through the 1960s and her involvement with Chess Records.

—Bill Greensmith

Fontella Bass Interview

Bill Greensmith

Blues Unlimited #147 (1986)

I'm assuming your mother was your influence?

Oh, definitely, my grandmother and my mother. My grandmother was a singer also and all of her children were musicians. All of my uncles are musicians, so that's how I got into it. All gospel, they still in the gospel world today.

I was born in St. Louis on Stoddard, 2726 Stoddard, July 3, 1940. I started singing at the age of five. Well, I really wasn't a singer, I was a piano player and I played for my mother at a very early age. At five I was gigging. I was playing all the mortuaries, funeral homes.

I played for Ellis and for Buddy Walton,[2] and that's who paid for my music lessons. I got paid $7 a night. And if I was good I got paid $10. I was very nervous about going into funeral homes, around the dead people, you know, and if my nerves were—"We'll give you $10 if you play." And I'd go for the ten. I'd hold out till they say ten. You know, in 1945, '46, $10 was a lot of money for a five-year-old. And I guess it was big business for the funeral homes. I played at many funerals at an early age, up until I was 12 or 13, until I just said, "No." I didn't want to do it anymore.

Would your mother sing at these funerals?

My grandmother and I, not my mom. My mother was traveling at the time with Clara Ward and Marion Williams and all those. Traveling through Texas on her own, too. So my grandmother kinda raised me, you know, and as I got older then my mother settled in from traveling around the world.

Did you ever go out on tour with your mother?

Oh, sure. I traveled all over the United States with my mother, my grandmother, and myself.

As an act?

Yeah. I played piano, it was like three generations—grandmother, mother, and granddaughter—and we all had different segments. My mother would sing, I'd

Fontella Bass. St. Louis, 1984. (Photo Bill Greensmith)

play piano for everyone, my grandmother and I would sing. And they would take up a collection, like three baskets, and everybody would give to who they thought was the greatest. And my grandmother won every time, every time. Her name was Navada Carter. That's how I left St. Louis, after my grandmother died in 1965. I went to seek the world. She died in January of '65 and by January of '66 I had a gold record.

When did you stop playing with your mother?

I never really ever stopped, believe me. I still do. If she has a program and she needs a piano player, I'll go if I can.[3] After about 13, I started playing for various churches around St. Louis. I was the church organist and pianist. One church I worked for years was Morning Star. The first organ they bought for the church was for myself. I played for so many churches.

What prompted the crossover to rhythm and blues?

Well, being in the church, my grandmother was very hard-cored, you know. They didn't want me to listen to rock on the radio. After I reached high school I would play in school, we would have talent shows. And the first time I got busted was when Ray Charles was in town and they was having a talent show before Ray Charles at the Club Riviera, which was up on Taylor and Delmar, and I played for this group.

I had a schoolteacher friend to ask my mum, could he take me to the show? He knew I was gonna play, so he dropped me off at the club and told me he would pick me up at 12. I was in good hands! So my picture came out in the *Argus* paper because we won, right? And all my mother's church members was calling, "Did you see your daughter's picture in the paper?" There I was on the piano getting down and we won the contest. This had to be in '57, because I graduated from high school in '58, so we're talking about '57, around in that area.

My grandfather and two of my mother's brothers used to go out to all of the blues places like Ned Love's, all over in Illinois, Lakeside, and the Red Top. They would sneak me out the window and I would dress in the car and I would be gone all night till six and seven in the morning. And then they would sneak me back in the house and they did it for years. My mother never told me until about two years ago that she knew.

They'd have me out and they'd send a note up and I'd sing or either I'd go up and I'd play. I was about 16 and I was too young. All I was there for was to sing and dance or play the piano. So my grandfather and my uncles were a great influence on my career, because they just pushed me, I don't care where we went.

I decided to leave St. Louis at one time. I was gonna go on the road with Leon Claxton, that's the Royal American Carnival. And my mother heard about it. Well, I worked the two weeks here in St. Louis with the show and it was paying $175 a week. That was the greatest gig in the world at that time. And my mother came and took me off the train, I mean bodily. I was so embarrassed, because I thought I was grown. She said, "No way." Bip, boom, bam! And I was off the train in two jumps. But you know what? I'm really thankful that she did that to this day.

Well, anyway, Oliver and Milton heard me on the Leon Claxton Show. And I thought I was a little dancer. Leon said—well, one of the girls had got sick on the show and he said, "You been watching the show for a week, do you think you could put on this costume and go out and dance?" I said, "I'm not a dancer." He said, "$550." I said, "I'm a dancer!"

They put me on the back row and they were playing this tune, I never will forget, "Things Ain't What They Used to Be." And you were supposed to go one, two, three, and snatch. The girls were snatching from the front and the back. They went front and I went back. They went back and I went front. I mean, you know, it was all mixed up, but it was a lot of fun. Nobody knew the clumsy girl on the back row who was dancing. But that was the end of my dancing career. I said no, that's not for me.

I was living in the project and Oliver came down and told me who he was and that he heard me on the show. But before I went with Leon Claxton I was working out here at Chain of Rocks, it used to be an amusement park. They used to have a place called the Showboat up on the hill that kinda overlooked the Mississippi. And at that time blacks weren't allowed to go in and sit to listen to the music. And I had my one little special table. Of course, I never sat at it. I was always back in the kitchen, like, "Fix me this, fix me that." I was a great eater. Me and the cooks were great friends. When I felt like really getting boozed up. I'd be in the kitchen and they'd be saying, "It's time for you to go back on." And they used to pass the hat on me, I used to make so much money in tips. I mean, I used to sing "Georgia." It was a piano bar–type club and I would do "Georgia" maybe four or five times a night. Maybe somebody would fall in love with this tune and he'd be crying, "Oh, my wife left me, here's $10, $20, just play it again." It was fun. Anyway, then I got with Oliver and I started playing piano with Little Milton.

Oliver had the band behind Milton?

Yes, he was the band director. As a matter of fact, I wasn't hired as a singer, but as a

Oliver Sain Band, 1962. Left to right: Willie Dotson, Bobby Lunair, Oliver Sain, Jerry Lee Walker, Fontella Bass, Vern Harrell, and Oscar Reynolds

musician. One night Milton decided to get soused and we were there on the gig and everybody waiting for Little Milton and he wasn't there. Oliver said, "Hey, sing." And I've been singing ever since. So it got to be that I would do my little set. Oliver and Milton came from the same hometown—they were just like two brothers. They even married at the same time, they has a double wedding together. They were very close.

So this was 1961 when you joined Milton?
Yeah.

Who was in the band when you joined?
Willie Dotson on bass; Vern Harrell, baritone; Jerry Lee Walker, drums; Larry Protho, trumpet; James Carr, tenor; Oliver Sain, alto; Milton, guitar. Matter of fact, my ex-husband used to play trumpet with us for a while, Lester Bowie.

After Milton it was Phillip Westmoreland on guitar. But before Phillip we had a fellow named Oscar. He played with us for about a year. I'm trying to think of Oscar's last name,[4] because his brother played bass with us when Willie went off on the road with Albert King. He died from exhaustion. We used to call him Blue.

Would you go out on tour with them?
Oh, sure. We used to travel through Mississippi, Louisiana, Arkansas, the whole months of January and February. We couldn't stay in the hotels or use the bathrooms

in the South—we used to have to live with people that we knew. I tell you, the road was rugged. Last stop for the bathroom: Memphis.

Memphis you could get some decent food, because you had your own black soul food restaurants you could go to, decent toilets and hotels you could go to and take a bath, keep yourself clean and get a good meal. And after that, no stop until you get to Greenville. That was Milton's home, him and Oliver. We never did go through Clarksdale at night, we left early enough to go through during the daytime. Because we were a traveling band and that was a hell of a town. And that was Ike Turner's home, that's why Ike is hell! But we're talking about 18 years, not so long ago.

But I've been to Greenwood in the last five years, because my brother is down there. I don't know as an artist what the conditions are like down there as far as travel. But I think when I was trying to deal with "Rescue Me" everything was pretty cool.

My episode down in B. B. King's Club Ebony in Mississippi . . . B. B. owned a club down there. So they had a free-for-all fight before the dance. We were setting up. This was chairs, tables, turn over cowboy-style, and one of the splinters stuck in my leg from a chair over a fellow's back. And there was this black police who was by himself, but he had a gun strapped on him, so he was the police. And these fellows, he was trying to break them up, but they was just fighting all over the club. So this police got a hold to them and all three of them on the floor, so he hollered, "Somebody go and get the police." It was so funny to me. I said, "But you are the police."

There was over two or three hundred people in the club and this was my first awareness of what whites had on blacks in the state of Mississippi. One white cop walked in the club, silence. I'm looking, saying, "Who's breaking this stuff up?" And here comes this one fellow and he's just walking through taking his time and just looking. And even the fellows on the floor, everybody's getting up. This was in '62.

What clubs would you work at in St. Louis?

The Moonlight, that was the big place. Chuck and Al's in Brooklyn, Illinois. Then we worked a club for three years down in Herculaneum, Missouri, this was an all-white club. I used to have to sing for three years, every Friday and Saturday, "Take Your Hands Off Him, He Don't Belong to You." That was my featured number. And after we left there we would come into Chuck and Al's at two in the morning. Two till six, double gig on the weekend. Seven o'clock we were sitting in Crown's Restaurant eating breakfast. We used to play the Harlem Club Blue Mondays, 11 to three. Tuesday, Wednesday, and Thursday—the Moonlight. Sundays we would have dances, the Masonic Hall or the Chase, the Electrician's Hall. We'd double gig the Manhattan Club in East St. Louis.

We got into a lot of incidents with the band, but it didn't happen often. I remember James Carr was dating this lady wrestler. We're all on the bandstand and this fellow had come over to the lady and ask can he sit with her. James is steady playing, steady looking over at the table. The lady finally got up and danced with him and the waitress brought drinks. So on intermission, James, he was just about, "Is this real?"

Oliver Sain Poster, 1963.

and he smacked her, bam! We didn't know the lady was a professional wrestler. Anyway, when you come out of the Manhattan it was a funeral home next door, and you had to go out of the back. This lady was out there and she was just crying. So I went over to her and said, "Sweetheart, it's not worth it." She said, "I know, but I'm gonna wait for him." James came out and she just looked at him, she dropped her conversation with me, she wiped him out. Bim, bam, boom! On the ground! She did a thing on him. He got up and started hauling, he was running. Oh, we never forget that! But this lady, I mean body slam, if you could have seen the look on his face.

Jerry, the drummer, he could spot something in the crowd. He'd be playing the drums, but his eyes would be like a camera through the place. And most places we played in it was one door. We was playing over in East St. Louis at the Cosmopolitan Hall. Jerry picked up on them, he said, "Take down." When he said, "Take down," it was time for the band to find a hiding place, because it's fighting. I'm running off the bandstand and I grab the back of this fellow's coat and I'm running with him, trying to get out the door. But I'm running with the fellow that they trying to shoot! And Oliver would always save me. I felt someone just lift me up and bring me over. And they did shoot him. I don't know if he lived or not, but they did shoot him.

Did you make any of the record dates with Milton for Bobbin?
All of them.

From 1961 onward?
Yeah. That's how I met Bob Lyons, at that time he was the owner of KATZ.[5]

Where did you record the Bobbin things?

We were in an eggshell room down on Grand and Olive. There used to be a big building there, they tore it down about 10 years ago and they used to be upstairs there.[6] It was just a little room, egg crates all around, ceiling and everything, and that's where we did it. Then we went to Chicago for Chess with Milton. That was really big-time.

The things that Ike Turner recorded . . . ?

We did at Technisonic.

The label credits Oliver's band on the Prann sides.

No. It is the band, but we mixed with Ike's band. That's Oliver playing piano, it might be Ike, because he played piano on one of the tunes, too.

Who are the girls on there?

Robbie Montgomery, Venetta Fields, and Jessie Smith, the Ikettes. I forgot about this record. I probably haven't heard it since I recorded it. It's a shame, isn't it? But I was still with Oliver when I recorded these songs.

Did you ever record locally for anybody else?

No. Bobbin was the first in the studio. I remember playing a session with Albert King for Bobbin. One night he needed a piano player and I played on a set for him. That was my first meeting with him other than in the clubs.

Why did Milton and Oliver part?

Well, Milton would get mad at the band and he would fire the whole band. If he got mad at one person he was mad at everybody. And you know, every night it just didn't go well, if you're traveling on the road every night. Milton would get mad at someone, then he'd fire the whole band. And we were tired of it. He did it about three times. So the band just got together and said, "Well, the next time he fires us we're really gonna be fired for good." Sure enough, he did it. So we struck out, did our own thing.

When I was going strong on the road and my husband was playing trumpet with Little Milton, I used to go out and be vocalist. I used to go under the name Sabrina. And Milton would pay me. I'd be traveling on the road with them. I'd go out there and be his female vocalist. I'd go out and do my thing, be background anything, make that money. I wasn't too proud, I didn't mind. I would tell all the artists on Chess, "If you need a background singer, whatever you need, I'm available." And I used to get on a lot of sessions. I got on one of Muddy Waters's sessions doing background.

Every time I played with Milton when he had "We're Gonna Make It" and we were traveling through Texas and Louisiana—we never played that tune all the way through—there was a turnout. Ladies just looked like, when they say, "You may not have a cent to pay the rent"—their purses go upside their husbands or boyfriends or whoever, bam! We never finished that tune on the road. 'Cause they been drinking all night and that was a helluva tune. They was drowning in their sorrows and they was thinking about what he's saying. And I'm telling you, every time Milton sang that song it was a free-for-all, a fight would be over here or over there. The story of everybody's life.

See, when you was in the city it was a different crowd, but, like, going through Texas and those towns, and they be coming from towns 30 and 50 miles around, whooo, they be hanging loose, boy, pocketbooks be flying upside people's heads. And when they got ready to start that tune, everybody be looking, getting ready to run, because they done partied all night and this would be the last number of the night, it's time to go home. And when this record would come on they just couldn't take it. I have several scars on my body from fights trying to get out the way.

Were you still with Oliver when you recorded "Don't Mess Up a Good Thing"?

No. Bobby was with Oliver, but I was not. I moved to Chicago. I left Oliver January 11, 1964.[7] We had a New Year's show with Dick Gregory and Jimmy Smith, New Year's Eve. The night before I had a gig with George Hudson, because I used to do little vocal things away from the band. And this night there was a draft in the place and I went to sing "I Don't Hurt Anymore" and I didn't have a voice. So the band kicked it off again and I could hardly get through the number. So I didn't go to Chuck and Al's that night, I told Oliver I'm going home. We used to double gig on the weekend. We worked at Chuck and Al's for many years.

So the next day I had a gig with somebody else at the Masonic, then we were gonna give our big New Year's Eve thing. Oliver went to bring me home and he said, "Well, you don't have to worry about the gig." Well, that gig was paying big money. He said, "You couldn't make the little $25 last night, you're not gonna make the gig tonight." I said, "Are you serious?" He said, "Yes." I said, "Bye." Slammed the door.

I left on the 11th and moved to Chicago. I was talking to John Burton, that's who brought me to Chess Records. He was the attorney there and that's how I got in there at Chess. He had been talking to me for months, you know, but I hadn't made up my mind to really go. But when that incident went down I said it was now or never. And I was sort of grief-stricken after I lost my grandmother. So I left, I had to get out of St. Louis.

John and I used to get rehearsal rooms downtown in Chicago. He played a little piano. Then Leonard proposed a question to me after I joined up with Chess. He asked me would I record with Bobby McClure and I told him I didn't mind. So I did record with Bobby and we brought out a hit, "Don't Mess Up a Good Thing," "Don't Jump," and "You'll Miss Me." We had those three hits, then I went as a solo artist and my first 45 was "Rescue Me." Then "Recovery" and on and on.

B. B. King, Big Bill Hill, Fontella Bass. Chicago, 1964.

You toured a lot behind those records?

My first professional gig out of St. Louis was the Apollo Theater with "Don't Mess Up a Good Thing," Bobby McClure and myself. This was without Oliver and I had to have music and everything. So it was sort of like my thing and I would pay Bobby to come out on the road and we were making great money. But we were in Washington, D.C., and the split of Bobby and I became over a financial situation. Oliver had a gig for him here in St. Louis and he felt obligated to Oliver, and I can understand that, but at the same time, it was messing up my business on the road, so I had to let Bobby go and I got another Bobby, which his name was Bobby Hutton. So I used him and just paid him a salary to do those numbers with me on the road.

I worked steady for a year behind "Rescue Me," I mean steady. After that, my workload, I slowed it down, I became impregnated! So after three months I went to Bermuda and worked a gig there, I laid over for two weeks after the gig and I just took off from there. Then that's when the big fight came with Leonard and I, and I wanted out with Chess.

I remember one town I played in, Pulaski, Virginia. Never heard of it. They hadn't had entertainment there since Silas Green in 1927! And they had the high school band that played behind me. They had practiced my music and it was the best band that ever played behind me on the road. I couldn't believe it. But my luggage, we had went down on Trailways and my luggage was mixed and it was late on a Saturday and I told this fellow, "I can't go on, I don't have my clothes." He said, "No problem, what you need?" He opened the stores, get on the telephone, "Bob, open your store." No problem. And on the album cover of *Rescue Me,* that's where I got that outfit, out of Pulaski, Virginia. The cap, the boots, the whole outfit. And the guy just came out, he said, "Well, you guys is the first niggers that ever stayed up in the Howard Johnson." I thought I was a big star. We couldn't sleep all night, we was looking at the tree out there, which one they gonna hang us at. This was just me and my husband. I tell ya, first time! I said, "Well, I must be on the town's history books in Pulaski, Virginia." He promoted the thing, but the band was excellent. I was one of the first black females up for a Grammy Award for contemporary, 1965. I don't know how many years the Grammy Awards have been out, but I was nominated, a lot of people don't know that. And at the time not one black was going to the Grammys.

How did you get along with the people at Chess?

Oh, Leonard was great. Max Cooperstein, my buddy, and Phil. You know, we were like one big family and I got a chance to meet a lot of people. At that time I didn't realize that nobody was going in the office but me, jolly old Fontella. They ring the buzzer and I come in every morning and go back and say hello to everybody, and a lot of times I would have lunch with Leonard or Phil or Max or whoever. I met quite a few people just through the office. Leonard was more involved in the radio station, more so than the—and I was always coming in to argue about something, like, "Leonard, what is this?" One day Leonard was so mad at me, after he had his big heart problem, you know, he used to have his little nitro pills. So I was upsetting him this day, he said, "I just don't know about you, Fontella." He took his pillbox and was doing his little pills. "The trouble with you, Fontella, is you just don't trust no one, you don't even trust your mother." I said, "You're right, Leonard. 'Cause I know if I got some money in my purse my mother gonna take it."

Leonard, after we went through our little thing, he did want me to come back, but at that time I'd got off into the commercials and I just wanted to see the world and get off into the new music and that's what I did. '69 is when I left. I asked him for my contract back and I did get that back. And I think it was that June or July, right after I left that March, I read about it in the paper that he had deceased. But I was gonna come back and we was gonna resolve things and do things. But, you know, after the head of anything goes . . . [8]

It really went down the pan?

Well, I'm the one that brought it up. Although they had a lot of catalogue things, it was extensive, but they hadn't had a hit for a while till "Rescue Me" came along and Chess became as hot as a firecracker.

Your mother was also on Chess?

I took her to Chess. I took her there, "Record my mother." And Ralph Bass was handling my mother and she had four albums out on Chess, she did more albums than I did. And I play piano and background on all of them, sure did.

And it was after this that you went to France?

Yeah, and it worked out for me, because every year my mother, brother, and me tour, two or three times a year, it's great.

Notes

1. "I'm Satisfied"/"Someone to Love Me," Checker 1012; "I Need Somebody"/"So Mean to Me," Checker 994.
2. Ellis and Buddy Walton, two St. Louis funeral homes.
3. [Martha Bass died in September 1998.]
4. Oscar Reynolds.
5. Bobbin Records owner Bob Lyons was also the station manager of Radio KATZ in St. Louis.
6. 3903 Olive was one of several addresses for Bobbin Records. According to Oliver Sain, the studio at the Olive location was used only for rehearsals and their sessions were recorded at Technisonic Studios.
7. There is some confusion about this date, as Fontella gives both 1964 and 1965 as the date of her departure for Chicago. St. Louis appearances by her and Oliver Sain were still being advertised in St. Louis in late 1964. There was also a show advertised featuring Fontella and Oliver Sain at the Cosmo Hall, East St. Louis, April 11, 1965.
8. Leonard Chess died on October 16, 1969.

PART IV

MISSISSIPPI

Arthur "Big Boy" Crudup

Despite not picking up the guitar until his early thirties, Arthur "Big Boy" Crudup emerged as one of America's top-selling blues artists after plying his trade on the streets of Chicago. Living in an abandoned packing crate under the 39th Street "L" station, he was signed to Lester Melrose's famed Bluebird label in 1941. His first sides, including "Black Pony," "Death Valley," and "If I Get Lucky," sold well and he eventually produced a number of blues classics. Following his stint with Bluebird, Crudup had RCA sessions in Atlanta, then recorded as Elmer James and Percy Lee Crudup for Trumpet, Ace, and Checker, and in 1962 he produced sides for Bobby Robinson's Fire label. Elvis Presley recorded Crudup's "That's All Right Mama" in 1954 and two others, "My Baby Left Me" and "So Glad You're Mine," in 1956. Unfortunately, Crudup, with little formal education, saw no profits from the success of his songs, and he remains relatively obscure to this day. He died on March 28, 1974, and only after his death did heirs succeed in securing copyrights on his songs.

In this relatively early *BU* interview, author Mike Leadbitter concentrates on a great deal of nonmusical information, and the piece offers illuminating details about the lifestyle of a Mississippi bluesman migrating to Chicago to record and returning to the South to work for a living, whether manning a sawmill or driving a tractor. Indeed, later blues music publications, specifically the American magazine *Living Blues,* aimed to document blues culture, and here Leadbitter's interview provides a template for later journalists. Crudup's frank story reveals the everyday life beyond the lights of the stage or the intimacy of a recording studio. Crudup worked any number of odd jobs in order to raise a family even as he established himself as a bona fide blues act. Crudup also helps place Sonny Boy Williamson II in Belzoni, Mississippi, in the late 1940s and provides rare details of Williamson's life and personality.

—Mark Camarigg

Big Boy Crudup Talks to Mike Leadbitter: Arthur "Big Boy" Crudup Interview

By Mike Leadbitter

Blues Unlimited #75–77 (Sept.–Nov. 1970)

I was born on August 24, 1905, in Forest, Mississippi. Well, when I first started to singin' the blues, why, I reckon I was about, oh, ten years old. I could hear, you know, some what other fellas sung and I would sing that. In a way, practically all my peoples was some kinda musicians. My father was a musician, my mother was a singer, but they never, you know, recorded. Yeah, there was plenty of musicians around (Forest) then. I had a couple of cousins at the time. They played music, but they never did show me nothin'. One of them was named George Hendrix and the other was named Malcolm Banks. I used to sing (in) quartets and I used to sing in the choir.

I lived in Indiana from 1916 until 1926, and the only two singers that I ever seen was Mamie Smith, and I seen Bessie Smith. I was a kid then in Indiana. My family moved there. My mother did 'cause that's the only family I had; my mother and one sister, 'cause my father and my mother was not married. I used to work in the foundries there in Indiana, and, ah, I started in there young . . . 14 years old! In 1926 we moved back to Mississippi. My mother's health went bad and we went back to Mississippi. I farmed, railroaded, used to cut timber, the sawmills and highways, and, ah, all kinds of work. Anythin' that I could get to do. I didn't have much of an education, therefore I had to take what the other fella left.

Well, I reckon I first started to tryin' to play guitar, it was in 1940—no, 1937. That's when I found an old guitar and I started to bangin' on it. I started wi' two strings, then I added the third one and I learnt how to tune the third one, play a little bit with it; then I put the fourth on it, then the fifth, and I played with five strings for a while. And then I put the sixth string on it and I just learnt myself. Nobody showed me nothin'. So I reckon it was just a gift. I never had any teachin', I learnt myself. I just played on my own. After I picked up and finally got where I could make a few chords on it, why, I left Forest and went up in the Mississippi Delta. And you could make a little bit more money by playing at, you know, parties in the Delta than a person could workin' by the day. So I did day work and played for parties on a Saturday night. Well, I went to Silver City and a place they call Paines-Deadman, out from Belzoni. Yeah, well, you see, the place where I was livin', I was livin' on a plantation. That was out in Paines-Deadman, they called it, and a man had a little nightclub out there, and they was playin' records. And, ah, after I came in there, why, then he give me the job playin' on Saturday nights. Ah-ha, for the dance. No, I didn't play with anybody. Well, at the time it was (the popular artists), ah, Tampa Red and, ah, Big Bill, Lonnie Johnson, St. Louis Jimmy, and Memphis Slim. See, they was the ones that I, you know, I didn't know 'em at that time, but them's the one's records was jumpin' big in the South.

Arthur Crudup, early 1940s.

I tell you the reason why that I went to Chicago. I was lookin' for a better job, and so I got there and work was so poor until I couldn't get a job right away, and I would take my guitar on the streets in the afternoon and play for whatever you put in the hat. And that's the way I lived. See, I lived in a pasteboard carton under the railroad tracks for three weeks—nowhere to sleep. And then finally, one afternoon, about 8 o'clock Lester Melrose and one of his singers, Doctor Clayton, they came along and stood and listen at me play and asked me to play for a party. And so I told 'em, yeah, I would. He said, "I'll give you ten dollars," so it didn't take but eleven dollars and forty cents to get me back to the South, see. So I said, "Well, I done made four, five dollars and, ah, get me that ten dollars. I will have somethin' to eat on and catch me a train going back South." So I went, and he carried me to Tampa Red's house and we got over there and they had somethin' to drink, somethin' to eat, and we had a nice time sittin' round talkin', and he wouldn't introduce me to nobody. Then he wanted to know, "Well, you ready to play us a little music?" I said, "Yeah." So I was playin' some of Big Bill's pieces and some of Tampa's, and then I played "I got a coal black mare, how that horse can run." And so then, when they stopped me from playin', he says to me, he says, "How would you like to hear your voice?" I said, "Well, I reckon it would be alright, I don't know, I ain't never heard it back no more than just me singin'," so he played it back. And he said to me then, he says, "Ah, now I'm gonna introduce you to these fellows." Then he came just to introduce me to Tampa and Big Bill and all of them, you know. Then I got nervous, then Tampa said, "Well, there's no need in your gettin' nervous, just go ahead!" He (Melrose) say, "You reckon you can get me up a couple more songs?" I said, "I don't know." Tampa said, "Come on over to my house tomorrow afternoon and I'll help you." So I went over there and he gave me a little instruction on it, you know, how to get my words together, and he told me, "Don't have no fear, 'cause that's the way I done and that's the way the rest of them done." He says, "Nobody perfect," and I just went from there.

Lester Melrose told me, "If the record comes out and it sells, you get a comeback, and if it don't sell too good, why, you won't get no comeback and you'll know it didn't do no good." And so about three months later, why, I got a letter from him. He wanted me to record again and so by that I knowed the record bound to sold. And I done pretty good with them. I wasn't makin' a whole lot of money. I had to record, I had a big family. And I'd go to Chicago to record and go back South and work. That's what I did all the time. Two years ago was my first tour that I ever been on. I was with Bluebird at the time and then, ah, shortly after then Bluebird sold out to RCA, or something like that, but I was transferred from Bluebird to RCA. I stayed in Chicago 14 years, off and on. I say regular, I stayed there from '40 to '45 and then I went back south. And I stayed in the South then until 1950. Then I'd go back and forward and work, stay maybe six months, and then go back home and stay maybe a month and then go back north. Off and on. I stayed in Chicago for 14 years. I was workin' first one job, then another. Firestone Tire and Rubber Company, then Grove Supply and a liquor store.

I never did play music then in the South. I lived in Forest and, ah, Silver City, Mississippi. I was workin' in a sawmill and farmin', and workin' for the city. Just anythin' I could do to make a livin'. See, I had a wife and nine kids to take care of. It's not like a person with a wife and no kids; when all those kids get to cryin' for bread you gonna do somethin', some kind of work. I didn't play much, no more than just a little country dance around there in Forest, because I worked all the time. I had a piano player with me there in Forest. His name was Len, ah, I forget his last name . . . yeah, Len Longmouth. But, now, we never played nothin' but a few pieces together, you know, country dances. Me, him, and Robert Dees, and Percy (Lee), my son. When Robert wasn't with me, my son was with me. He could blow harp, too. That was Percy. He is 37 now, workin' for the city there in Florida. I had known Robert since he was a kid. And I picked him up at a dance and he was trying to blow harp.

I just knowed Elmore [James] in '48. He wasn't exactly playin' on no contract or nothin', but he was playin', you know, country dances just like I was, and me, him, Sonny Boy [Williamson II], we used to play country dances on a Saturday night and maybe a Friday night and a Sunday night. We just didn't have a regular band. Me and him would team up, and if I got a dance at the night, why, I'd get him to play with me, and if he got a dance he'd get me, you see. He was livin' in Belzoni. Him and Sonny Boy, they was livin' in Belzoni and I was livin' in Silver City, which was about, I say five miles apart. I played with Sonny Boy about two months and me and Elmore we played around together for about a year, a year and a half. We both was workin' on the farm.

If Sonny Boy say he never work in his life he's a damn liar. I lived in Mississippi all my life and there's no colored people there that don't work. When I know Sonny Boy in 1948 he was workin'. See, me, him, and Elmore all worked on farms then around Belzoni. Elmore drove a tractor, me, I drove a tractor, and Sonny Boy, he drove a tractor. He didn't play no music but at the weekend. If he wasn't in the fields, he be on the street. No, he did not play at Greenville in the week. I know. In places like Greenville, in them days they didn't 'low colored peoples on the streets after sundown. Sonny Boy had to work! He had an old lady to keep. Elmore had an old lady. I had an old lady and nine kids. On Friday nights and on Saturdays we would play for dances in the country on the plantations. Just me, Elmore, and Sonny Boy. We would get ten dollars and all you could drink and eat. If a man had a club and he hired us, then we would get thirty or forty dollars split between us.

I am an honest man. I have been to the penitentiary, but was for fightin', not for stealin'. I don't mean to say I will not steal, because if you have nothin' and you need somethin' which you can get without too much trouble, you'll steal it. Stealin' ain't against the law. Only when you get caught, that's when the law comes in! I ain't played in Jackson but twice, and one of those times I went to jail. A white man was goin' with a colored girl, and a colored man, he brought her to where I was playin' in a club. The white man came down there and shot at the colored man, but he missed. The colored man parted his hair for him—with a bullet. The police arrested everyone and we all went to jail. Sonny Boy would get too advanced. This white woman in Little Rock, she liked him. And he was in her house taking it easy—he had his shoes off. He'd taken his shirt off and a white man came by. Sonny Boy, he left there runnin'! Me and Elmore was goin' back home in my old car and we ain't seen Sonny Boy. Elmore was sayin', "Where is Sonny Boy?" and I was sayin', "Man, I don't know." My radiator was leakin' and I stop by a ditch to get a little water. Sonny Boy call, "Motherfucker, open the trunk and let me get in!" He was hidin' in the ditch there! So I took him home to Belzoni and he never did go to Little Rock again. He knowed what his life was worth around there.

Sonny Boy was a fine fellow to my suggestion. His real name was Rice Miller. Well, now, I tell you it was a Sonny Boy that was the original and he got killed there in Chicago, in 1948. And after he got killed, then Rice said that him and this boy was cousins and he went under Sonny Boy, (too), but his real name was Rice Miller. I didn't know none of his people and I didn't know but one of Elmore's people. I didn't know where Elmore's native home is, but I met him in Belzoni.

Sonny Boy was doing his *King Biscuit Show* when I knowed him. I could hear Sonny Boy, you know, he used to come on every evening and Sonny Boy would be there in Belzoni! And so it was just a recording they made of him, I think. We would be riding together to a dance and I would turn on my radio and there was Sonny Boy broadcastin' and he was sittin' next to me. I never been on the radio in my life until I was out in California, and here (Britain). It's a very few (musicians) that I know personally on account, ah, you know, I doesn't go to these nightclubs, and the fact is when I'm workin' I try to make all the hours I can. See, I had to pay my way in Chicago and I had to take care of my family back home. I never thought about makin' money by music, other than recording, and I tell you the reason why I didn't. I always thought that I wasn't good enough, that's reason I didn't get to goin'.

Now, I wish I could sit down and play a guitar like Elmore. To tell you the truth, I met a whole lot of peoples playin' guitar and could really play 'most anythin' you wanted, but I have never run into another man could play a bottleneck like Elmore plays it. That's the truth! Once I tried to play like that, bottleneck, but I was makin' chords peoples had never heard before, so I give it up. Elmore told me he had been playing in the same style for 33 years. At the bottleneck. And if he'd—now, that was in '48 that I met him—and if he'd been playin' it 33 years then, why, he knowed every ups and down with that bottleneck. So no man or person gonna pick it up in a few years and think he gonna do it like Elmore, 'cause they can't do it. I don't know what age Sonny Boy was. You know, colored peoples, some of them, they don't tell you their age, they all say, well, I'm here, or somethin' like that. See, they won't just come right out and tell you their age. Sonny Boy told me he had been playin' harp since he was five years old. When he died they say he was 65.

I didn't know Boyd Gilmore or Charley Booker. I never heard tell of Hound Dog Taylor before and he never played with me. I never been in Greenville but twice in my life. Robert Dees is now someplace in Chicago. I would go to Chicago to make records. I went to Atlanta twice. They would send me my bus fare and I would go. See, I was under Melrose at RCA. He was my manager. When I made those records for Chess he was the first to get to me. I made them as "Percy Lee" Crudup. Any extra money I could pick up, see, I needed it. He had a man in Jackson that told him about me. He found me in the field—in the field plowin'. I was living back in Forest then and he took me to record in Jackson—Mrs. McMurry's place. [Lillian McMurray was owner of Trumpet Records.] He had arranged the band himself. I didn't know none of them, nobody but Robert [Dees]. He played harp. I didn't know the drummer.

I cut with Ace before I cut with Mrs. McMurry. I don't know who found me (for Ace). I didn't know the guy. He was an insurance man. He was from Jackson. He was up at the house to collect and heard one of my records and suppose him and this guy was pretty good friends, he 'bout told him. Anyway, one day I was comin' out of the field and he [Vincent] came up and wanted me to record for him. He got the band. Yeah, Robert played harp on that. Didn't know the others; they was just Jackson musicians. Then one time I made, ah, the number I made as Elmer James, "Make a Little Love." Sonny Boy blowed harp. Yeah, well, when she [McMurry] asked me to cut that record, well, Elmore was in Chicago and she couldn't get him back. She had one side and she wanted another side, and so Sonny Boy told her me and

Elmore sounded such alike and that's why I made that record. Sam? That was the bass player. I didn't know him. I was playin' guitar. Well, I suppose she (McMurry) seen where she could make some money off a chump like me. You know, whenever a fella with education sees a fella without education, well, he thinks he can make some fast money, I suppose. I didn't know her personally. Even when the records were selling big I didn't even get any money out of it.

I never drawn a check on my records until it was '62—over 150 dollars out of all the records that was sold. Never over 150 dollars at a period of time that the royalties ended, you know. And the time that I drawed, I think it was '62 or '63, I drawed 1,600 dollars. That was the royalties they hadn't paid me from 1955 up until then. Well, you see, everybody keep asking me why, what do I think about it, them keeping my money. Well, I don't think nothin' about it, because there was more people who made records beside me and that other people cut (i.e., stole). That's right. And at the time Presley cut that number, I didn't hear it until it was on the jukebox, and I wrote my manager, Lester Melrose, and he says, "Yes, I heard it," and I never heard no more. But I do know he was holding the copyright on the songs. He had to collect, because I wrote him about the copyright of that song and he told me, "No," that he was not going to let me have it because of somebody might put me up, would try to get the copyright and would wanna take it away from me. Melrose is dead (now) and Mrs. Melrose is holding the copyrights.

At the time I made some numbers for Bobby Robinson, why, Sonny Boy was in Brooklyn. I had moved from Mississippi in '54 to Virginia, then I moved from there to Florida, and I started to contracting labor in '54 from Florida to Virginia. I'd be six months in Virginia and six months in Florida. Bobby wrote to me in Forest, and my cousins, which is still living there, sent his letter to me in Virginia. I got the letter from Bob wanting me to record and he said Elmore was recording, and so I wrote him back and told him I would and when he answered my letter he sent me the bus fare. The day I got there (New York), Elmore had just bought him a station wagon and him and his band had gone back to Belzoni. Now, that's what Bobby told me, but, now, I never seen Elmore from '54. I saw him over in, no, '53, and I never seen him no more. When I recorded? Uh, yeah, it was in the fall of the year, because I was in Virginia. Ah, my mother died in '61. It was '62. The reason why I say so—I was in Florida when my mother died and I came back to Virginia to bury her. And then I went back and brought my crew back to Virginia. It was in the early part of the fall. The musicians (on the session) was just New York session men. I didn't know any of them! When I finished I went back home. Then I heard that Bobby's company was finished and I heard no more about that record.

I worked up until a year ago and I reckon I would still be workin' every day, which I do do, you know, what I can, but I taken with the arthritis and part of the time the hand here (right) gets stiff. I was still pickin' strawberries, peas then and I just quit. I sold my truck and quit. I run a little juke joint now which my girlfriend is lookin' after while I'm gone. I tell everybody I have come through death, hell, and destruction. My house burned down and now I rent one until I can get the money to build me a new one. Before my mother and my wife died me and my wife had twelve kids to take care of. And then my mother got sick, she had a stroke, and she got disabled to do anythin' and I had to take care of her. There's the doctor's bill for my mother, then, one for my wife, and one for my baby. One thing, whatever was happenin', my family always had meat on the table. Ah, at one time I was gettin' 50 cents a day, but you could come to my house and get a good meal.

Louise Johnson

Since the appearance of this article in *Blues Unlimited,* little additional significant factual information has emerged about Louise Johnson and she largely remains a mystery. Census researcher Bob Eagle recently suggested that Johnson was born about 1908 in Tennessee and possibly lived near Son House in 1940 on the Tate Place at Banks in Mississippi. She has more recently appeared on various reissues focused on Mississippi prewar Delta blues, including the Document and Yazoo labels.

—Mark Camarigg

A Handful of Keys: Louise Johnson Again!

Bob Hall and Richard Noblett

Blues Unlimited #115 (Sept./Oct. 1975)

Very few piano recordings have caused as much controversy as the four sides made by Louise Johnson in May 1930 for Paramount, and as promised in our discussion of Cripple Clarence Lofton (*BU* 113), we are returning to these recordings in this article.

From the collection of John Tefteller and *Blues Images*. Used with permission. www.bluesimages.com.

As is fairly common with female blues artists very little is known about Louise Johnson. She is thought to have been about 28 when she recorded, which places her birth around the turn of the century. She appears to have spent most of her life in the Clarksdale area of Mississippi and was believed to have been from Robinsonville. The pianist John "Red" Williams remembers her in Tunica in the late 1920s. She was a small girl about twenty years old at the time, playing piano in a joint attached to the cotton-oil mill quarters (Olsson 1970, 80). By 1930 she was playing and living on Joe Kirby's plantation near Claxton on Highway 61, Mississippi. Here she seems to have met Willie Brown and, through him, Charley Patton and Son House. She appears, at this time, to have been playing for one Liny Armstrong, presumably a juke owner.

When Art Laibley was traveling through Lula on his way to Texas, he stopped off to get Patton to arrange to go up to Grafton, Wisconsin, to record for Paramount. He left 100 dollars for expenses and another 100 dollars for Wheeler Ford (one of the Delta Big Four) to drive the artists up. Patton went up with Son House and Willie Brown and they picked up Louise Johnson at Joe Kirby's. All the musicians, at this time, stayed around Joe Kirby's largely because they made more corn whiskey on this plantation than anywhere else, and it seems possible that Son House was also living there at this time.

Louise Johnson seems to have been well known by the musicians and was one of Patton's many girlfriends, but just out of Memphis she attached her affections to House after an argument with Patton. At Grafton they all stayed in a small hotel kept by Paramount for their artists. It is here that the story gets a bit confusing, for Son House states that Lemon Jefferson was at the hotel and shared a room with Patton and Brown, but Jefferson was almost certainly dead then. At the recording Louise Johnson was said to be so nervous that she needed the verbal encouragement of House and Brown, although it seems just as likely that they were all drunk.

After the recording session very little is known about Louise, but she seems to have moved to the Clarksdale area, where she continued to play in the juke houses on the plantation in the company of Son House and Willie Brown. Around the early forties she is said to have been going to Memphis, but no trace can be found of her there. It would probably be impossible to trace her now, for she could have married and changed her name or simply stopped playing. In any case, Son House seemed pretty certain that she is dead.[1]

What precisely is the controversy that surrounds this session? It derives from two conflicting statements, one by Clarence Lofton to the effect that he accompanied a female blues singer for Paramount in the twenties and, secondly, one by Son House that Louise Johnson played her own piano accompaniment. Previously we have outlined fairly strong evidence that Lofton was not the pianist. This was based on the keys used during the recordings and on the fact that there is no such thing as an "embryonic" Lofton on record. To our minds there is no doubt that Lofton was not the pianist.

Son House is described by John Fahey as honest, but not possessing a uniformly accurate memory and as freely admitting when he was confused. Son was, however, positive in his identification of Louise Johnson as the pianist. Yet in spite of this it is difficult for many people to believe that Johnson did accompany herself and much argument has been aimed at disproving this.[2] The main objection is the independence of the piano and vocal parts, which is atypical of vocalist/pianists, who normally sing a line and then play an answer phrase on the piano. We concluded: "either Louise Johnson was a quite exceptional performer or we must look elsewhere for her accompanist."

Louise Johnson: vocal. acc. unknown piano.

The simplest way to locate unknown accompanists is to look at surrounding matrices. Two possible pianists present themselves here: Rudy Foster (Pm 12981) and the unknown pianist who accompanied Marie Griffin (Pm 13015). However, neither of these pianists sound in the slightest like the supposed Louise Johnson accompanist. The Rudy Foster sides are believed to be his own piano, but we doubt this and will return to these sides at a later date. In the case of Marie Griffin the pianist plays in a style reminiscent of Cow Cow Davenport but is not as accomplished, and aurally it seems highly improbable that Marie Griffin's accompanist is the Louise Johnson pianist.

Further, in reviewing the hundreds of piano recordings which were made at this time, we have found only two which resemble aurally the Louise Johnson accompaniments, and these were supposedly recorded at a later Paramount session. The artist concerned is the obscure Kingfish Bill Tomlin, and Godrich and Dixon list the session as follows:[3]

KINGFISH BILL TOMLIN: vocal. acc. unk. piano.
Grafton, Wis., c. November 1930.

L-618-2 Dupree Blues — Pm 13057 F
L-619-1 Army Blues — Pm 13034 F
L-620-1 Hot Box — Pm 13034 F♯ (F)
L-621-1 Mean and Unkind Blues — Pm 13057 B (B♭)

(The apparent keys of the recordings are given by each issue number. In those cases where we believe that the apparent key is not the true key, we have given the possible true keys in parentheses.)

There are almost certainly two pianists involved in the Tomlin session, and in view of the key displacement on the last two tracks, probably sides are accompanied by a generally inept pianist who is almost certainly Tomlin himself. It is interesting to note that these two songs are fairly traditional and Tomlin himself sounds [like] an older singer. On "Hot Box" he gives a clue to his origins by referring to "mamlish dog," which would indicate he came from Alabama. What, however, appears to have happened after these two tracks is that Tomlin was replaced by another pianist after "Army Blues," another fairly rare WW I blues, and full of mistakes. "Hot Box" and "Mean and Unkind Blues" are more strictly blues than the previous two titles, and the piano accompaniment is strikingly similar to that on the Louise Johnson records and in the same keys.

A secondary hypothesis in the debate about Louise Johnson's accompanist is the view that there are two pianists on her records (Heath 1970). This view derives from the existence of a jump in the microgroove reissues of "By the Moon and Stars" after the first 12 bars of the vocal. While this break exists on the microgroove reissues, it is not so apparent on the 78 and appears to be merely a change in tempo. Certainly there is no musical evidence whatever to indicate that two pianists were present on the session.

Louise Johnson: vcl. acc. own pno.

Apart from Son House's statements and [the fact] that Louise Johnson is known from elsewhere to have been a pianist, there is internal evidence from the recordings themselves, such as the spoken comments by House and Brown throughout the records. The most important of these for our purposes are as follows:

L-398-1 All Night Long Blues
"Play it long time, Louise" just before the vocal.
"Play it long time, Louise" after the eighth bar of the first verse.
"Play 'em, little mama" just before the verse preceding the piano break.

L-399-2 Long Ways from Home
"Play it long time, Miss Louise" just before the first verse.
"Play 'em, Miss Piano Whupper" during the piano break.

L-419-1 On the Wall (contrary to Godrich and Dixon there are comments on this track)

"Do it a long time, honey" toward the end of the piano break.

There are no comments on "By the Moon and Stars."

Admittedly some of the transcriptions are a bit doubtful. For example, "Louise" could be "Lewis" and "Miss" could be "Mrs." or "Mr.," but overall, we believe the above are accurate.

Conclusions

What conclusions, then, can be drawn from all this discussion? We feel that in view of the evidence, notwithstanding our previous statement, there seems little doubt that Louise ranked as one of the finest blues pianists of all time. An intriguing possibility remains: did Louise Johnson accompany Kingfish Bill Tomlin? We will probably never know. We do know that Son House was invited back by Paramount but didn't go, and so it is not beyond the realms of possibility that Louise Johnson was also invited back and accepted the invitation. There is also evidence (see Discographical Note) that the Louise Johnson session took place not in May but in August, and thus it may be that she and Kingfish Bill Tomlin were recorded at the same time.

Notes

We would like to thank Gayle Dean Wardlow, Francis Smith, John Mastaka, and the John Edwards Memorial Foundation Inc. at the Folklore and Mythology Center, UCLA. Naturally, any error of fact or inference is the responsibility of the authors.

1. The biographical information comes from a variety of sources and only a joint credit is really feasible. We would like to thank Gayle Dean Wardlow, Francis Smith, Steve Calt, and Steve La Vere. Reference was also made to Peris (1967), Fahey (1970), Godrich (1969), and Charters (1967).
2. See, for example, F. Owen with J. Langmead (1965) and R. Heath (1970).
3. [Robert Dixon and John Godrich's *Blues & Gospel Records: 1890–1943* is an exhaustive listing of African American recordings made up to the end of 1943.]

Discographical Note

The dating of Paramount recordings is always problematic, because no company files are known to exist. In the case of the recordings made around the Louise Johnson session, a precise date is imputed because a test pressing dated May 28, 1930, of matrix L-348-2 for issue on Pm 13121 is in the possession of Irene Scruggs. As a result of this, most of the records made around this matrix are dated May 28, which we feel is possibly misleading not least because of the number of recordings made at this time. If we assume that matrices L-312 to L-440 were recorded consecutively, then many days were involved in this session. In addition to this, we feel that the recording-speed fault on the first two Louise Johnson titles indicates a probable known point at which a session would have been terminated. The other two Louise Johnson titles do not display this fault and are undoubtedly a different session.

However, Son House remembers the session as being in *August,* and the only recording from this session which was "advertised," Pm 12990, appears in a dealer's listing for October, which would fit more accurately with an August recording date. The linking of all these sessions seems to result from Wheeler Ford driving the artists up to Grafton. Wheeler Ford was a member of the Delta Big Four, and it is assumed that they recorded at the same time as Johnson, House, etc. It seems equally possible, however, that they did not, for it is obvious that all these people did not go to Grafton in the same car and we are left with the problem of how the other members of the Delta Big Four got to the session. What seems just as likely is that Wheeler Ford was traveling back from Grafton with Laibley or was in his employ and merely took the artists to Grafton.

If we accept an August date for these recordings, it makes it possible that Louise Johnson accompanied Kingfish Bill Tomlin, for there is no reason to accept the November dating of his session. There is, however, a gap of some 200 matrices between the recordings, and this prompts us to ask whether the Paramount L matrix series truly reflects recording order. It seems increasingly likely that this is not so.

References

Charters, S. *The Bluesmen.* Oak, 1967.

Fahey, J. *Charley Patton.* Studio Vista, 1970.

Godrich, J. "Discographical Games People Play." *Storyville* 23 (June/July 1969).

Heath, R. "The Louise Johnson Controversy." *Blues World* 29 (April 1970): 14–15. See also "Blues Forum 205" in *Blues World* 32 (July 1970): 19, and "Blues Forum 252" in *Blues World* 38 (Spring 1971): 12.

Olsson, B. *Memphis Blues.* Studio Vista, 1970.

Owen, F., with J. Langmead. "Where Have All the Loftons Gone?" *Storyville* 2 (December 1965): 11–12.

Peris, N. "Son House Interview—Pt. 1." *78 Quarterly* 1, no. 1 (1967): 59–61.

Discographical Information

Godrich, J., and R.M.W. Dixon. *Blues & Gospel Records, 1902–1942.* Storyville, 1969.

Studies in Jazz Discography 1. Rutgers University, 1971.

Vreede, M. E. *Paramount 12000/13000 Series.* Storyville, 1971.

Louise Johnson—Postscript and Analysis of the Comments

In not so recent years, digital technology has given vintage music restorers a wonderful tool that not only helps them to get the most out of what remains in the grooves but also allows enthusiastic amateurs to easily carry out tasks that would have taken highly skilled engineers weeks to complete. We can now "cut and paste" bits of the music, remove sections, and even rearrange the order.

It did seem possible that the clue to the identity of the piano player could be found in the comments heard during the songs, so (and this to many people may sound like sacrilege) I set about cutting the music out (digitally, not physically) to leave just the comments so that they would be easier to concentrate on—the music being too powerful otherwise.

As I progressed with this heinous crime, what was becoming clear, to my ears at least, was that there are more people around in the background adding comments than just Son House, Charley Patton, and Willie Brown.

Son House is easily recognizable on the two takes of "All Night Long," by his booming rich voice—"Lord let's have a meeting here" or "Louise, you telling," while Willie Brown appears to play only a minor role, and I believe that it's his gruff tones that give out the occasional "Hey, hey", or "Ah, sure now." Charley Patton is perhaps the one who makes the first comment—"Play it long time, honey," and later on, "Play it long time, Louise"—so do we need any more proof than that that Louise is indeed the piano player?

But there is some conflicting evidence as someone in the background chirps in with "I can sit here all night long" and "I can play 'em all night long," or maybe that's "I can stay here all night long," and there appears to be someone else who shouts "wait till my woman comes." Someone else joins in on "Long Ways from Home," but in a more conversational tone. At times he can be heard in the background, talking away almost as though they are talking somebody through something difficult; unfortunately the words are too indistinct to pick out anything that makes sense. It's interesting to note that there is more in the way of background comments on "Long Ways" than on any other track, but Louise can be clearly heard to say, "Now, you can do it a long time, boy," so is that addressed to the piano player? And why does she say, "I'm trying to keep up" on "All Night Long" as if she is indeed struggling to stay with another piano player?

Also the whole session is now thought to be more likely to have taken place in July-August 1930 starting at L-398-1 with Louise Johnson's "All Night Long" and ending with L-433, Charley Patton's "Bird Nest Bound," a total of thirty-five tracks, and that's without outtakes and false starts. Even given the twelve-hour day that Paramount workers were said to have put in during their heyday (which was past by this date), recording one song every twenty minutes would take quite some effort, especially with four artists and both the piano and guitar(s) to set up. It's more likely, then, that there were two separate sessions at least and that Louise started her respective sessions.

This may be the reason why the background comments are few and far between during "On the Wall" and no comments at all on "By the Moon and Stars"—perhaps they had indeed sobered up after a couple of days, or run out of corn whiskey! Certain the piano style seems more confident on the last two tracks.

On balance there is more evidence to suggest that Louise Johnson is the piano player than not, and perhaps the last spoken comment on all of these wonderful recordings is relevant—"play it a long time, honey."

—Dave Williams

PART V

TEXAS

Juke Boy Bonner

Born on March 22, 1932, near Bellville, Texas, Weldon "Juke Boy" Bonner personified the modern bluesman whom writers and staff of *Blues Unlimited* greatly respected. The itinerant bluesman never enjoyed sustained success, but made his mark as an important blues scribe with songs like "I Got My Passport" and "I'm Black and I'm Proud" addressing modern struggles and civil rights issues facing black Americans.

Bob Geddins first recorded Bonner as "Juke Boy Barner" for his Oakland, California–based Irma label in 1957. Bonner later recorded for Goldband in 1960, billed as a "one man trio." These early sides never hit and Bonner's career stumbled when he was hospitalized with severe stomach ulcers in Houston in 1963.

Mike Leadbitter made his first trip to the United States in May 1967 and stayed nearly three months in Houston and Louisiana, a trip that he chronicled in his *BU* article "I Know Houston Can't Be Heaven." A genuine friendship developed between Bonner and Leadbitter, and *Blues Unlimited* readers financed a Juke Boy 45, "Yakin' in My Plans." Juke Boy followed up that gesture with a letter to Leadbitter in *Blues Unlimited* 51 stating, "I've sold about 100 records since they've been out (2 weeks). It is five o'clock in the morning and I'm writing songs (and drinkin' beer). Put portions of this letter in the B.U.—ha ha! OK?"

This activity spurred Bonner's career and he eventually acquired regular gigs and recording dates. Chris Strachwitz's Arhoolie label issued two Juke Boy albums, and in 1969 Bonner visited Europe for the American Folk Blues Festival and an extensive solo tour. He also appeared at the Ann Arbor Blues Festival in 1970. Releases on Liberty and Sonet followed, but, unfortunately, within a few years Bonner, part of a then dying down-home blues tradition, was back in Houston playing for low pay and booking his own gigs. Juke Boy died alone in his apartment on June 29, 1978.

In the following interview, Bonner, both honest and forthright, describes his early days on the West Coast and the difficulty of never quite catching a break. Preceding the interview are Mike Leadbitter's heartfelt liner notes from Bonner's Flyright album, *Juke Boy Bonner: The One Man Trio.*

—Mark Camarigg

Juke Boy Bonner Essay

Mike Leadbitter

Blues Unlimited #111 (Dec./Jan. 1974–1975)

Juke Boy Bonner was a friend of *Blues Unlimited* and maintained a close relationship with Mike Leadbitter and the magazine. Mike wrote many sleeve notes in his time, but it is arguable that his finest was for the first-ever Flyright album, *Juke Boy Bonner* (LP 3501). Juke Boy meant something special to Mike and he was clearly writing from the heart. As the album has been long out of print, we feel it is appropriate to reprint the sleeve note here as a reminder of Mike's underrated literary style.

It is early evening in Houston. The sun is setting and the air is still. On the corner of Pease, just across the railway tracks from Dowling, stands the dejected-looking "Family Inn," looking out on a vista of dusty, dirty roads and listless groups of men and women watching small, grubby children at play. Saturday night is beginning and soon more people will emerge from the tumbledown, wooden houses neighboring the inn to set out for the earnest business of drinking, loving, quarrelling, and, often, fighting. Whether their money is from work or from the welfare, it will be spent this night trying to ease away the sordid reality of ghetto life. Inside the inn the huge freezer is full of canned Jax, Schlitz, and Pearl beer. The morose houseman, S. P., and his wife sit at one of the rough tables surrounding the pool table and wait.

Darkness is creeping when Juke Boy Bonner parks his station wagon on the corner and staggers in with his electric guitar and amplifier. In spite of the intense humidity he is neatly dressed and managing to look clean and fresh. The first of the customers have arrived and the balls on the pool table are clicking gently. Friends turn to greet the resident musician and are answered with a quick smile and a grateful "yes" to the offer of a beer. He is a lean and light-skinned man with handsome regular features. His voice is quiet as he speaks to friends while settling himself in the space provided by the door. By 8 o'clock his equipment is set up and the guitar is tuned to

Mike Leadbitter, Juke Boy Bonner. Houston, Texas, 1967.

satisfaction. It is time for him to put down his beer bottle and begin entertaining anyone who cares to listen.

As the first few notes of the harmonica and guitar ring out in unison, faces begin to look up. One suddenly feels that Saturday night has now really started. People begin to speak loudly and shout for more beer, while the balls on the pool table now connect with violent cracks. Juke Boy has finished a short instrumental warm-up and, swallowing a mouthful of beer, waits for requests. It is still too early and he begins by playing numbers of his own choice. "Can't Hardly Keep from Crying" and "Got No Place to Run" show his mood. His stomach is bothering him and signs of strain show round his eyes. His voice is full of frustration and bitterness, and the harmonica seems alive as it blends with his voice. For a moment he has lost himself, and with a grin he turns to "I Live Where the Action Is." As the solid beat, accentuated by his stomping feet, reaches the ears, broad smiles are in evidence. "Real Quiet Fellow" follows with its Frankie Lee Sims overtones and a drunk begins a slow solo dance on the floor, carefully watching his feet as they shuffle in complex patterns.

Darkness has settled and the light from the inn calls to the crowds outside. The wire door bangs frequently and soon the bluesman is surrounded by a jostling throng. The beer is flowing freely and paper cups appear on the tables, destined to be filled from concealed wine and whiskey bottles. Despite the loud laughter and shouted conversations, Bonner's heavily amplified equipment can still be heard with ease. More people are shuffling on the splintered wooden floor, and the pool players curse

Juke Boy Bonner poster.

as someone collides against the table. Requests pour in. "Dust My Broom," "Man or Mouse," "Meet Me in the Bottom," "You Don't Have to Go," "Things I Used to Do," "Nine Below Zero." No one calls for Juke Boy's own songs, for they have never seen or heard his records, so he picks out the blues favorites and cleverly turns them around to suit himself. Still pleased, the askers bring over beer to help their man oil his throat and begin again.

As the night wears on, one wonders how many songs he knows and can play. He has sung twenty, or is it thirty by now? Perhaps it's more, as it is now 11 o'clock. Bonner is really tired and the effects of drink are showing on the faces around him. He slows the pace and sings "Movin' Back to the Country" to please those dissatisfied with city life; "Can't Let Your Troubles Get You Down" to console everyone, including himself; and "Why Do You Treat Me Like You Do" for all the mistreated "lovers" who have come in alone. Suddenly a girl walks in and sits next to Juke Boy. They smile at each other, and he seems very happy to see her. He bursts into "Goin' Crazy 'bout You" while voices shout advice and encouragement.

Midnight! Only one more hour to go. The crowd's attitude has changed. Many are beginning to stagger home, and others argue or sit quietly looking at their beer. Will S. P. fire his pistol tonight? As you sit watching it is easy to appreciate that at this moment someone close by is being shot or cut (the usual aftermath of Houston's big night). Juke Boy is singing "I Wonder If You Know How It Is" and follows with "Bad Breaks." The old bitterness is rising again as he thinks of lost chances and broken promises. His thoughts turn to Europe, where his only real fans seem to be, and how he has no chance to meet them. "Blues, Blues, Blues" is the finale at 12:55. Five minutes later he wearily packs his guitar away and, with his girlfriend's help, gets his equipment into the wagon. With a final and tired smile he leaves into the morning, knowing that tomorrow night at the same time he will have to go through it all over again. The fifteen dollars he has in his pocket is small consolation.

Juke Boy Bonner Interview

Mike Leadbitter

Blues Unlimited #78–79 (Dec./Jan. 1970–1971)

I have probably spent more time with Weldon than anybody else, but we had never really got down to a really good bull session until the man came to stay a few days with Simon Napier. On the 28th of October of last year, Simon brought him around to my place for the evening and after a quick session in the local pub we settled down to talk. I supplied the food and music and Weldon had the bourbon.

Blues Unlimited: How did you feel when you heard that a guy from England had your records and wanted to write your story?

Juke Boy: I thought some cat was pulling my leg, you know. I forgot all about those recordings I'd put on tape. I was just playing music, so I thought it was some kind of a crank.

BU: You'd really forgotten all those things you'd cut for Irma and Goldband?

JB: Well, I never got anything out of it. Every time I'd go through Lake Charles I'd get the same runaround, you know. I didn't get anything but a new guitar. He'd say, "We've got the record working and it'll be out next week. Just hold on."

BU: Did it sell? I don't think it did.

JB: Well, you got no way of knowing unless you sue somebody and that's not good for your career.

BU: Well, Eddie [Shuler, founder of Goldband Records] did one good thing. He sent a copy of your record to us in England. Here's a letter from Eddie saying, "Glad Juke Boy tore them up over there!"

JB: Man, that Eddie, he's crazy. Best thing he did was put that record on Storyville. The best thing he did in his life. If he ever did a good thing, that was it!

BU: When you were with Bob Geddins over in Oakland were you paid anything for the records you made?

JB: There was, er, with Bob, if anything came of it, he'd tell you. Anyone in Oakland will tell you. If you had anything to do with Geddins and something came of it, he'd see you got your money. He wouldn't pull nothing over your eyes. McCracklin will tell you this.

Juke Boy Bonner, *Blues Unlimited* 45.

BU: Bob Geddins, he's a person no one knows much about here.

JB: He's with Fox now. He's a straight shooter, though. If a record went nationwide or just went through three states, you'd know. There was Lowell Fulson, Jimmy McCracklin, quite a few fellows went to him to record.

BU: Did you know Johnny Fuller? We've just interviewed him.

JB: Yes. I haven't heard from him since I left the coast in '57. He was playing guitar, playing blues and things like "The Haunted House" and all that stuff. I don't know what he's done since then.

BU: What made you go to the coast in '54?

JB: Oh, well, I felt like goin' to California. So I packed up, sold the furniture, and took off. I was married then. Me and the wife, we had two kids, we just took off with the clothes. Keep eating. I don't want to interfere with your meal. It's okay, I'm a slow eater. I got a small stomach. If I eat fast I get sick.

BU: You've got a quarter of your stomach left?

JB: About a half of it. That was ulcers. I was in Ben Taub Hospital in Houston.

BU: When was the operation?

JB: Yeah, that was '63.

BU: What were you doing when you got to the coast?

JB: We stayed in Oakland about a week. My wife had people there. We left and went to Los Angeles for fifteen months, before we really stayed in Oakland . . . in L.A. I was playing on harmonica. Didn't have a guitar at that time. I would just play around the local places; little bars, little bands, in central L.A.

BU: Was it a good scene then?

JB: It was then. I don't know about now. Then there was good happening on the East Side. After me and my wife separated I actually got to going around the clubs and up and down the coast. Then I went sick in Oakland with pneumonia and ended up in Glendale Hospital. When I got out I had to find a job to get some kind of money.

Oh, in Los Angeles, some kind of tie shop and I just worked. I wasn't even playing then. I was broke. One day I went home, got my harmonica, and started walking and playing. I walked from downtown, about 5th or 6th Street, and all the way up to Watts. Then about the 400 block of Central I saw the Jack in the Box club there and Mercy Dee was playing in there with a couple of old guys. A drummer and a bass. So I walked in. I had picked up a few dollars playing on the way. So I told Mercy Dee I was from Texas and he took me to his house, gave me some good advice, gave me a meal, and took up a collection for me, which was pretty good, for when I got back home I was able to pay my rent. He's a nice fellow.

BU: What happened next?

JB: I left Los Angeles and went to Oakland, because there was a lot of money being made in canning there. I worked for Del Monte there and I'd go into town to find the musicians. Go to blues clubs where the music's at, and, er, just anywhere you got a congregation of people swinging.

BU: How did you get to be called "Juke Boy"?

JB: Well, by two friends in Los Angeles. I used to stay with them and we'd ball around together every night. One of these guys would follow me playing guitar, as I was playing guitar and harp then, which is before I went to Oakland. I used to play that harp on the Mercy Dee Show and the Johnny Otis Talent Show. I won a prize on the Johnny Otis Show doing a Jimmy Reed number, and then Jimmy Reed popped up as a special guest and he did a Little Richard thing. That was at the Club Oasis. I didn't have an electric guitar then. I got one of those after I went to Oakland. Anyway, these two guys, we'd go round the juke joints so damn much that they started calling me Juke Boy. I would play along with the music on the jukebox. Little Walter was popular then. I played behind him like that, and, er, Jimmy Rogers, "That's Alright." He was very popular in L.A. Little Walter had "Juke." That was very big in Texas. "Mellow Down Easy" and all that stuff.

BU: Was it playing round these clubs that led you to meet Lafayette Thomas?

JB: Lafayette, oh, yes. He's a great guitar player. He showed B. B. King how to play Lowell Fulson's "3 O'Clock." He took me to McCracklin and Bob Geddins to record. I was playing harp and guitar and I wasn't used to it. The guitar was okay, I just rode along on the bass, but I couldn't get the harp right. Lafayette told me, "Don't worry if you miss a note, I'll cover it up." He played on that record.

BU: I see that on your first record you were called Juke Boy.

JB: Yes, when I left for Oakland I stayed with friends for a few weeks till I got an apartment. Baxter, their name was. They loved music. They had stuff by Redd Foxx,

Juke Boy Bonner. London, November 1969.
(Photo Bill Greensmith)

McCracklin, Jimmy Reed. They were crazy about music. They really started people calling me "Juke Boy," so I just got used to using the name.

BU: When you first started on guitar, what style were you playing?

JB: T-Bone Walker. Yes, I was good at it. At that time I played T-Bone and that was all. He was hot stuff all over the States. I remember the first things he ever made. *"Baby last winter, baby, the snow was on the ground."* Remember that? *"You put me out, baby, and I didn't know where to go."* That was "Got a Break Baby."

BU: What was the first talent show you did?

JB: Trummie Cain's, back in Houston, 1948.

BU: Man, people don't realize how long you've been on the scene. They think you just started a couple of years back.

JB: Man, I've been there a long time. I cut some stuff for Gold Star, but it never came out, 'cause I sounded too much like Lightnin' Hopkins at that time. I cut some stuff for old Fat Atlas on Lyons Avenue and I did some tests for Don Robey. Always the same problem, I sounded too much like Lightnin'. See, I played a lot of guys' music—T-Bone, Muddy, Li'l Son Jackson, Smokey Hogg—I used to play all his stuff. So I was playing what was hot at the time. In the end I had to do something different, get my own style. I had to come over with something new and quit foolin' around.

BU: Who was big when you first came to Houston?

JB: Gatemouth Brown, T-Bone Walker, Lightnin', Charles Brown, Louis Jordan, Roy Brown. They was all great artists. Lightnin' was real popular those days when I was coming up. You heard Brownie McGhee? That "Letter to Lightnin' Hopkins" was a bitch in those days. Then there was Big Bill Broonzy.

BU: Do you know T. V. Slim, J. D. Edwards, Goree Carter?

JB: Goree I know. I played with him a few weeks back at Koret's Smokehouse Lounge. Plays jazz now, he doesn't do blues anymore. The other guys I don't know. See, so many people just give up music. Lots of musicians die, or quit, or just dropped out. They won't touch it again the rest of their life. So it's hard to catch up on them, especially if you act like Hop Wilson. One bad experience ruined him. When I knew Goree, he was just a drummer.

BU: Who got to you first? Skoog? Mack McCormick? When you were "rediscovered"?

JB: Mack came by first and told me a lot of junk.

BU: Did you know that for a few months after we found you were living in Houston, no one would tell us you were found. It was Larry sent me that newspaper story in the end. Then Mack asked us not to print it, as he was saving it for a book he was writing.

JB: Well, you see, Larry was always getting those papers. He was doing a lot of writing at the time, working on the poverty program and all that stuff, so he kept up to date with the Negro newspapers. Skoog's alright. He's selling books now to keep his butt going. Mack came in right before him, it couldn't have been more than a matter of months. He came by one night and wanted me to record and all that stuff. Boom, boom, boom with the hot lines, but Lightnin' had told me about him. I haven't seen him since. Don't know what happened to him. Him and Lightnin' had a big run-in about how Lightnin' went to New York and cut two albums in one day. One for Fire and one for Candid. He got 800 dollars out of one thing, and when one company found the other had beat them on a record, they felt they had been cheated. When Mack went to Lightnin' about the money, Lightnin' wouldn't have none of that bullshit. They parted ways right there.

BU: What do you think of *Blues Unlimited*?

JB: It's good. I like it, I like it very well.

BU: I ask because a lot of people in the States and Canada ask us what we know about the blues as it really is.

JB: Well, there's some people not keeping up with it, who don't know what's happening.

BU: But there's people over here writing about blues and they've never been to America.

JB: There is? They write second-handed? But if you been to America and stayed there you understand it. You get a pretty good picture of it. You got to be broad-minded about the situation. Most musicians are complicated people. They hate a lot of questions that don't make sense. This a fact. A musician will walk off. He's not going to hang around listening to something that doesn't make sense. If you talk shop they like it, but you find it hard if you ask other kind of questions. A blues musician is a complicated person who got enough problems of his own without people asking crazy questions. Musicians all got one thing in common: they likes to drink. A musician's got to be always with the people, and the people always drinking, so they drink, too. You hang around with them you got to relax and enjoy yourself. *Blues Unlimited* is a good magazine. It does more for the blues and people like me than anything else.

BU: Can you think of anyone else your age playing country blues in Texas?
JB: No, I can't think of a one. Sylvester, he's dead now.

BU: Well, I guess you're going to follow Lightnin' to be the last of the great Texas blues singers!

Dr. Hepcat

Albert Lavada Durst, famously known as Dr. Hepcat, born on January 9, 1913, was a barrelhouse pianist and the first black disc jockey in Texas. He learned piano as a young boy and was later influenced by Baby Dotson, Boot Walton, and renowned barrelhouse stylist Robert Shaw. Always keeping busy, Durst recorded two singles for the Uptown label in 1949 and then sides for Don Robey's Peacock label in the early '50s. Notably, Durst made his mark as an enigmatic and influential radio jockey, even publishing a small, fourteen-page booklet, *The Jives of Dr. Hepcat.* Ultimately, Durst's passions changed and he became extensively involved with the Mt. Olive Baptist Church in Austin, eventually becoming an associate minister. He died on October 31, 1995.

In the following interview, Durst discusses his early career and influences. The interview is also significant for providing rare insight and details of a Texas blues scene beyond the more heavily researched Houston area.

—Mark Camarigg

The Jives of Dr. Hepcat: Dr. Hepcat Interview

Mike Rowe

Blues Unlimited #129 (March/April 1978)

"Hey, there chappies, H'lo chicks. You've latched on to Rosewood Ramble with your music recorded. It's a real gone deal that I'm goin' to wheel so stand by while I pad your skulls." The introduction rattled out like a burst of machine-gun fire and, followed by Duke Ellington's "Things Ain't What They Used to Be," was familiar enough to Austin's black population tuned to KVET through the '50s for their favorite disc jockey. For the next hour or two until signing off with Ellington's "Deep Blues," Dr. Hepcat would entertain with R&B records and commercials delivered in the outlandish hep talk of the '40s and early '50s. He might introduce a record with: "Jackson, here's that man again, cool, calm, and a solid wig. He is laying a frantic scream that will strictly pad your skull. Fall in and dig the happenings." Or if advertising a show, he might advise: "Gators, take a knock down to those blow-tops who are upping some real crazy riffs and dropping them on a mellow kick and, chappie, the way they pull their lay hips our ship that they are from the land of razz-ma-tazz."

Today, when ghetto terms have been popularized by the music world and white disc jockeys ape their black counterparts, it's easy to forget that there were pioneers in the art and that the emergence of the black deejay is a very recent phenomenon. Dr. Hepcat was such a pioneer. Not only was he the first black disc jockey in Texas, but he may well have been the first in the whole of the USA. His first broadcast was in the '40s, although the actual year is in doubt. Probably it was before 1949 and it ran for fifteen years, something of a unique record in the annals of black broadcasting history. His piano playing was always secondary to his broadcasting career and only an amateur activity according to this modest and genial man. When we learn that both careers were combined with a day job as sports director of an Austin recreation center, that he published a booklet of his "hep talk" in 1953, and that for the last twelve years he has been a minister of the church, "unique" seems a woefully inadequate word to describe this most fascinating man.

Sitting behind his desk in his office at the Doris Miller Auditorium, the chunky figure looks every bit the blues pianist. But instead of the shouts and laughter of the house party guests, the interview is punctuated by the thud of the basketball on the gym floor outside and the shouts of the young players. There's a natural dignity and a warmth to the man, but, curiously, for one who worked a special kind of magic with the language over the air, in person he seems almost

shy. "Rhythm and blues, that's what I . . . ya know I can't play nothing but boogie-woogies."

Born [Albert] Lavada Durst in Austin, Texas, on January 9, 1913, he learned to play piano when he was young.

Dr. Hepcat, Radio Station KVET.

When I started playing piano blues and boogie-woogies was at an early age—I imagine around twelve years of age—and then I started learning in the church house on the piano I could find. I'd slip in the church house early in the mornings and probably late sometimes through the week and just start pounding out tunes and, strange thing, only thing I could find I found out was eight-beat music. (*laughs*) I sorta liked that type of music. Nobody taught me anything about piano—just by air—we called it "by ear," but it's by air, ya know, the things that we heard. So I sorta was a fan of Pete Johnson, Meade Lux Lewis . . . Albert Ammons, those the guys I used to hear on the radio, ya know, and then sorta it came to me. I just liked that music, ya know, and . . . I had a feeling for it. I liked that type of music and seems like it gets on the inside of me, it works up something, gets something going for me.

I never did play professionally at all. Well, what we said in that time of day we had house-rent parties, they call 'em, see, but it wasn't professionally. But, say, like on Saturday nights, a bunch of us we get together and go to certain houses and they charge ten cents admission and, ah—we play from, say, seven o'clock to one o'clock in the morning for two dollars or dollar and a half (*laughs*), or we had a lot of fun, in other words, see. But that's only as far as I went professionally.

All around Austin—the only thing we would do would probably find a certain place, ya know, that we play at every Saturday night, but there weren't any outstanding ones, ya know? We knew it's gonna be a—we call it a Saturday night supper, Saturday night fish fry, and that's where we were. One was on North Western down here, it's grown up, see, used to be nothing but trees and one or two houses in between that on North Western and a house on East Washington Avenue here. And one on, say, about the 1400 block on East 7th Street and, ah, one down on deep East 7th, what we call "Spanish Town." That's about the area. We found it were better in the houses.

Each house had its own little, ya know, private bars and things, ya know, and little beer and so forth, so we didn't play any of the bars. The bars became popular later on.

Lavada didn't stray too far from Austin, but occasionally he would play out of town.

I stay in the Central Texas area in the small outlying cities like Lockhart, San Marcos, and Taylor—and different places like that, but not too far. I haven't been out of the state, ya know, playing . . . barrelhouse music.

Now and then we'd meet up and jam some, and some of the best piano players that, I mean, way outshine me was at those parties and things. We have one right here in Austin now—he hardly didn't make any records—Robert Shaw. And he and I used to come along together, we play some of the same type of music, you see, but he was a way better piano player than I—than I consider, but, see, we had different touches. And then Robert can play that "Hattie Green," but I play it different, see, but he can play it, see, he can play it and he got a lot of music, he can play well.

In fact, Lavada picked up "Hattie Green" from Shaw "from observing," and, not surprisingly, their repertoires were similar.

Well, I played a, like, in addition to "Pinetop's Boogie Woogie" and "Miss Hattie Green," I played the "Rock Island" and I played the "Piggly Wiggly Blues," and, um, some innovations of my own, boogie-woogie tunes. That's about all. Some mixtures of them all. See, you can play one or two blues tunes—sing a variety of songs to it, ya know. "In the Wee Midnight Hours"—I played that tune and, 'course, you know with one or two tunes you could play all night, sing different songs to it. Kinda like the country music, got two or three chords, but they can sing a whole lot of tunes to it.

Robert Shaw was probably the best known of the Austin pianists, but Durst remembered some of the others.

Uh, let me see—well, Boot Walton. He's now, he plays for church—Boot Walton, and Baby Dotson's passed—he's gone. And, see, Black Tank also passed, deceased. Black Tank, he was from the Houston area, but he came here around Austin. He was a tremendous piano player. He was one of the tops and we called him Black Tank. (*laughs*) Like I say, he's passed now. They were older and I was a kinda kid hanging around the bunch, ya know. But those are about the ones, ya know, that I played around with and the only one surviving in this area is Robert Shaw. And he's pretty good. You know, Robert Shaw and I are about the last of the barrelhouse piano players . . . around in Texas. There might be some other people we've never heard of. Boot Walton, he's still around, but he plays at church music, ya understand. But he was pretty good in those days. Like I said, Baby Dotson, Robert Shaw, Black Tank, yeah, they were the cream of the crop. Make a piano sound different . . . different keys that a polished piano player couldn't reach! Blues keys, ya know. They just caught the sound of a piano box these professional artists can't do. Yeah, it's a different thing altogether, yes, indeed!

Well, a lot of people call it "barrelhouse music," ya know, and I think that's the basics of real good music. Because it has a feeling to it. It has a feeling to it and, uh, certain people, well, they tried to get away from it. They tried to get away from the original, I say, black music, but then you've lost something. You've lost something, you understand? But now they've got to come back to it when you get your basic good music. That's that boogie-woogie and from boogie-woogie, and I'll say eight-beat music, comes all the other music.

Strange thing about it, though, from music, one thing to another, and then I got the job as a disc jockey and because I was pretty good at announcing baseball games out at Disch Field. And I could talk pretty fast, I could spit out those words pretty fast: "Lamp that kitty with the King Kong physique, I most believe he'll put the whammy on that horse skin."

Or after some indifferent play:

"Team B. B.'s manager could stand one more greasing, he's not slick enough. Had two ducks on the pond nobody down and didn't a spike reach the promised land."

The Hepcat's announcing proved as popular as his team, the Austin Black Senators, and brought him to the attention of KVET's owners.

The powers that be at that time said, let's try him as a disc jockey. Strangest thing in that period of time that only thing that a black man could do at a radio station was clean it up! And they took a terrible chance on getting a black man to be a disc jockey. It was a white station, that's all they had. That's all we have now here in Austin is white stations, except they have recently a Latin station. And you can imagine what a crime it was for these white men to sponsor a black deejay in the late '40s, ya know?

Since then a lot of them are famous people now, like I imagine you heard of John Connally, used to be secretary of the treasury and secretary of the navy? Well, he was one of the first owners, and J. J.—Jake Pickle. John Connally, he was the president of the station then, ya see, and I imagine, well, he's one man who believed that everybody should have the right to pursue their happiness if they had the ability. Of course, I evidenced my fear of going on the air then, ya know, because I told him . . . probably my academic qualifications weren't such that I should be over the air, ya know, and he said, "Well, if you want a college professor go out to the university and get one!"

It's not hard to guess at the reaction of KVET's white listeners when the Hepcat first assailed them with: "If you want to be hip to the tip and bop to the top, you get some mad threads that just won't stop." After the shock had worn off the abusive calls came in.

I got a lot of phone calls, "Are you black?" 'Course they used other words. See, the term "black" just came into being. Used to be "negro" or "nigger" (*laughs*), ya know what I mean?

But Lavada and his backers weathered the storm.

When I got on the air things just jelled for me. I used a style that caught on pretty quick being one of the first black disc jockeys, I imagine, in Texas, in this area, and the style I used earned me the name Dr. Hepcat, because I talked different terms, like hepcat terms. Now, the Hepcat's Prayer is:

Now I stash me down to cop a nod
My mellow frame upon the sod
If I should cop a drill before the early bright
I'll lay a spiel on the Head Knock to make everything all right
With that, fly cat, I'll chill my chat
And cop a nod like mad.

You know, terms like that when I'm describing different things that's what caught on, ya know. (*laughs*) That's what I'm talking about, sold sponsors and things like that. So consequently people would tune in to hear that jive, ya know, like a girl we'd call a "fine brown frame." If you want to learn something you "cram your knowledge box." Or if somebody gonna die you "knocking fowl soup" or "going to the skull orchard"—that's going to the graveyard. (*laughs*) And this type of thing, that type of jive.

Dr. Hepcat's liberties with the language kept his sponsors like Grand Prize Beer, RC Hair Pomade, and Thunderbird Wine happy as indeed it did his audience, which eventually spread well beyond East Austin's black neighborhoods. The Hepcat was keeping pretty busy, too—during the day as athletic director of the Doris Miller Auditorium and evenings on the air as well as all the natural spin-offs of a disc jockey career: promoting concerts, public appearances, and even lecture tours of the local high schools. He explains:

I was working here while I was a disc jockey. I had two jobs. See, I used—I'd be on, say, ten o'clock at night till twelve—probably ten till eleven-thirty. Then I had a Saturday morning show, too, every Saturday morning. And I found out I could carry the two together pretty well. You'd have a little conflict sometimes, because in recreation your hours are not stable. See, we stayed open as long as the people were here in the '50s, so there you were. But I'd have to hit that ten o'clock when people expect you to be there. At ten o'clock you must be there! Ya know, 'cause people when they turn that dial they want to hear the Hepcat!

Well, I went from ten till eleven, then from ten till twelve, then back to ten till eleven-thirty and so forth, it varied. Like I said, it was a thrill, and my style, I'd play a record by a certain artist. I'd say, "T'ain't no sin to take off your skin and dance around in your bones!" Ha, ha, ha. And "If you jump a cut in the early bright get you a fine brown thing make everything all right. So knock your stash, cats, fall in the alley and jive like mad." Oh, ya know, you have a whole lot of fun when you get a kick out of doing a job, especially when you doing something you like.

Dr. Hepcat's first record was recorded by Fred Caldwell, owner of the Uptown label and program director at KVET.[1]

Well, I decided I wanted to try to make a record, and then I had a program director who made my first records, ya understand, on the assumption that I could probably make something. 'Course it didn't jell, ya know, because, I imagine, . . . it might could have done better if, I imagine, if the person had pursued it sincerely. If it had had distribution it would have been nice.

The Peacock record is probably even scarcer than the Uptown considering that the Houston label did have some distribution facilities. But it probably came too early in the history of Duke/Peacock Records.

Well, uh, I wrote a spiritual song for a group of boys, Austin boys, called the Bells of Joy. And I wrote a song "Let's Talk about Jesus," and it sold over a million copies, but, listen, me being, ah, sorta sanctimonious in a way, I didn't put my name as the writer. See, I wrote the lyrics to the song, see, but I was afraid that people knowing that I was a rhythm-and-blues disc jockey wouldn't buy it, see? But I was wrong. But I didn't get the money from that, see, but they sold over a million records. The Bells of Joy traveled all over the United States singing that song. I said, well, those are my friends. I said, well, all for one and one for all, but they took it all. (*laughs*) But I dunno, I feel that sometimes things will come to you eventually, but I missed a whole lot of money then. Sure did. Then I had an inroad to Peacock Recording Company. I knew the owner, the president, Don Robey, and his assistant, so it was easy for me to go down and record this record.[2] I didn't make nothing of that either. I imagine about, I believe, fifty dollars recording session, but that was all.

Lavada could only remember the tenor saxophonist Shake Snyder on the session, for despite the credit, the Hepcat Band, it was just a studio group.[3]

They were studio musicians. In other words, he'd call them up when he had a recording session. They were probably musicians around the city, but I imagine Shake Snyder's pretty well known around there if he's not dead now. 'Cause he had to have one of those pipes, ya know, those asthma pipes, whatever it is, ya know, but he could talk. He could play music. He could write it while you were playing it, notes and everything. Ya know, that's extraordinary. He was from the Houston area.

Unusual among Texas pianists, Lavada used a powerful boogie bass, and on a number like "Hattie Green" the effect is dramatic. The Uptown version is up-tempo, beautifully sung and played, while the idiosyncratic "Hepcat's Boogie" is a joy, with Pinetop's calls translated into hep talk with instructions to: *"Knock your statue act / Don't vip or vop / Now stash yourself and / 'Do the bebop.'"* Truly the cat pulling the elephant teeth was a bonnet flipper!

The Peacock version of "Hattie Green" is slower and even more solid than the Uptown. The lyrics are very similar and mainly traditional Texas verses. The

Dr. Hepcat, Uptown Records.

band is very unobtrusive and this, like the reverse, is beautifully recorded. "I Cried Last Night" is an odd blues ballad and very reminiscent of a small group '40s Decca recording. There is an extended guitar solo, but predictably the most noteworthy feature is the rock-solid piano. Both records are rare examples of the authentic piano blues recorded at a time when the jump blues were the sound of the day. Sadly, they didn't sell.

Although he had little success with his recording ventures, Durst's name was sufficiently known for him to promote groups under the Hepcat banner, and he made many such public appearances.

When I became a disc jockey I would get me a little band and go around different places, see, and I wouldn't have to do much, talk a little bit and make an appearance. Just make an appearance and say a few words and let the band play. Well, I used to play some with Johnny Simmons, who's passed now. Johnny Simmons was one of the best musicians in this part of the country. He played piano and, oh, he played all types of tunes and anything you could mention, really. He had a nice little ole band and that's one of the only ones used to go around, used to play for me a lot. They had guitar, drums, and saxophone—let me see—and piano and trombone. As a novelty I'd take over the piano, ya know, and they would kinda back me up, see. We had a boy that sing with us some time. His name was Therau Piper—but lot of those fellows—Johnny's dead. Therau Piper's dead, but some of those fellows around here now that played in that band. But they still playing. See, this Hepcat and his band I'd give—they'd take my name for that party, ya know, but they had their own band. They were pretty good. Like I say, it wasn't too much money at that time, but we enjoyed it. It's a lot of fun. Well, I imagine I done that for two or three years, then I settled down to just being a disc jockey and probably going up to the schools and making little talks and how I got started and so forth and, uh, how to be a disc jockey and what it takes to be a disc jockey and so forth.

In 1953 Dr. Hepcat added a further string to his bow when he became an author and published a fourteen-page booklet on his jive talk.

And I wrote a book, too, called *The Jives of Dr. Hepcat*—on all my jive, ya know. And if I'd had distribution on that and pictures and things it would have sold. Because Memphis, Tennessee, and Alabama, Mississippi—a whole lot of blacks, ya understand, that got real soul, feels that soul, but it—I didn't have any . . . no money, no nothing to distribute it.[4]

Dr. Hepcat. (Photo Mike Rowe)

And then finally I came down to I had to move out to another field. When it's time to change, you know it! Like I say, you got to be able to conform to change. I've got a different outlook and different things, but I maintain that every good and perfect gift come from the Maker, you understand? So that was a gift and so this made me do something else. A lot of times people say when you're called to the ministry that a lot of them say you heard a voice or something, but it's just an inner urge to do something else, ya know. Why so many people commit suicide, they can't go any further, you understand, they can't conform with change. Ya know how every season how the leaves fall off the trees, how during the wintertime the leaves get shed, ya know, because it's change. Those of us who can't conform with change, we die. See you've got to be able to change.

I don't know, a lot of times people ask me would I go back into being a disc jockey again. Well, the answer's no. I couldn't do that again. I've found a real happiness in the ministry. I'm associate minister at the Olivet Baptist Church on the corner of St. Bernard and Cotton, but my home church is Mt. Olive Baptist Church on East 11th Street, but I don't have a church of my own.

Apart from a wistful "Sometimes I say the disc jockeys came a little too soon," with his church and his work at the recreation center, Lavada is well content.

I'm still working, enjoying my work, ya know, helping youngsters, producing some good players. Well, we've had some mighty good boys come through here in the person of "Night Train" Lane. And just recently Hollywood Henderson that played for the Dallas Cowboys and a number of boys have come through here, and we've had some pretty good baseball boys, too. And this is also the home of Willie

Wells. He's, well, he's pretty old now, but he was one of the foremost black baseball players. They're trying to put him in the Hall of Fame, see. We've had some pretty good athletes around here.

And he still plays piano. He doesn't have one at home, but there is a piano at the recreation center.

I still play it. Every now and then I practice up on it, ya know. I don't play as many songs as I used to play, but some of those that I love I play it, because, like I said, every good and perfect gift comes from God and I just keep that gift. Use it. But I don't play it in public no more. Play it for my own entertainment, see, and it gives me satisfaction. And after I get a good feeling from it, put it down for a while.

The questions have dried up and as he looks up from the desk he laughs.

I think I've talked a hole in your clothes!

Perhaps we should take a leaf out of Dr. Hepcat's book to express our appreciation. Dr. Hepcat, you are most monster, righteous, so copasetic, alreet, alroot, and like, this article, all wrote!

Notes

1. The Uptown titles "Hattie Green" and "Hepcat's Boogie" have been reissued on *Midnight Steppers,* Fantastic Voyage CD FVTD 167.

2. There must be some confusion here, for the Bells of Joy recorded "Let's Talk about Jesus" (Peacock 1584) some years *after* Lavada recorded Peacock 1509. Curiously, an earlier Bells of Joy record, "Doing for Jesus," has composer credits to "Lavada Durst" on the 45rpm, at least according to Doug Seroff.

3. This must be the saxophonist listed on a Gatemouth Brown session for Peacock as "Wilmer Shakesliner" (see *Blues Records 1943–1970,* 35).

4. There is a fascinating precedent here, for Dan Burley, a Chicago rent-party pianist and later editor of New York's *Amsterdam News,* frequently devoted articles to the subject and also published *Dan Burley's Original Handbook of Harlem Jive.* Reviewers at the time who doubted if many of the expressions that Burley used were known even to the average Harlemite would have been suitably chastened to find them in common currency throughout America's black ghettos as reported by Durst ten years later in Texas; e.g., Burley's version of the "Hepcat's Prayer" is so very close to the one reported here (see Alan Dundes, ed., *Mother Wit from the Laughing Barrel* [New York: Prentice-Hall, 1973], 215).

Sources

Interview with Lavada Durst, Austin, Texas, September 29, 1977.
Durst, Lavada. *The Jives of Dr. Hepcat,* 1953.
Szilagyi, Pete. "Doctor of the Air Waves," *Free & Easy* 9 (Jan./Feb. 1975): 5.

Albert Collins

Long associated with the stinging snap of the Fender Telecaster guitar, Albert Collins began performing in Houston nightclubs and recorded his first blues instrumental hit, "The Freeze," in 1958. A collection of early singles on TCF Hall, *The Cool Sounds of Albert Collins,* marked his debut album, but it wasn't until 1968 that Collins's career ascended after he recorded a series of albums for Imperial that captured his furious sound.

Collins signed with the Alligator label in 1977 and recorded a series of acclaimed albums that received several Grammy nominations. The guitarist enjoyed continued success into the 80s, eventually winning a Grammy after teaming with Robert Cray and Johnny Copeland on the *Showdown* release in 1985 and even a cameo appearance in the 1987 motion picture *Adventures in Babysitting.* Collins helped usher in a renewed interest in the blues in the late '80s and early '90s and signed to the Virgin subsidiary Point Blank in 1991. He died November 24, 1993, silencing one of the most distinctive guitar sounds in the genre.

The following interview occurred in London on March 16 and 17, 1979, when Collins spoke with *BU* writers Cilla Huggins and Denis Lewis. With the release of his *Ice Pickin* album for Alligator in 1978, his first recording in seven years, Collins visited England and the Continent twice. Although most of his career highlights occurred after this interview, here Collins details his early family life and childhood and the burgeoning Houston R&B scene of the late '50s, including playing in the Third Ward along with Johnny "Guitar" Watson. He also describes his move to Los Angeles, via Kansas City, with the help of Canned Heat's Bob Hite, and his contractual problems with Tumbleweed Records.

—Mark Camarigg

A Long Conversation with Collins

Denis Lewis and Cilla Huggins

Blues Unlimited #135/136 (July/Sept. 1979)

Texas

I was born in a little town called Leona, Texas, in 1932, October 1. I'm Libra. When I was a little kid, you know, my father and mother they worked on, they call—it wasn't a plantation but it was, he was doing farm work, for a man that we lived on his place. Like sharecroppers, right, and they made like a dollar and a half a week which that was nice money in them days. You could buy a lot with a dollar and a half. And after I grew I went to elementary school and when I got to high school I had to quit school to help my family because they kinda got in bad . . . and I got me a job in a service station. I worked to help my family for a while and when they got theirselves together, and they asked me was I going back to school? And I told them no I couldn't make it 'cause I had been out too long. I stayed out of school a couple of years and I said, "There's no sense in me going back to school." So I got as far as the tenth grade and I quit when I had to help my family. I quit in the tenth grade when I was about nineteen, twenty.[1]

I have a sister, she lives in Fort Worth, Texas and I have a brother who lives in Texas also, right out from Houston and I have another brother. I haven't seen him since he was a baby. My father, he's there now, but he's kinda sick. He was a guitar player, but I picked most of my playing up from my uncle. My uncle plays guitar—he's a preacher. He has a big church in Dallas, Texas. His name is Rev. Campbell Collins. I used to play guitar in church when I started out. We called it The Church of God In Christ and I just stayed there too long, you know! (*laughs*)

I used to like to listen to John Lee Hooker and Lightnin' Hopkins, which Lightnin' Hopkins is kin to me, you know. He's in the family on my mother's side. And what happened is when John Lee Hooker had out "Boogie Chillun," that was when I was kinda getting together there. I enjoyed listening to John Lee Hooker's tune because I really admire the man, because when I first started out playing that was what I was playing, like him. You know I wanted to play like him. I was in the country at the particular time, then I moved to Houston, Texas, you know, the big city. We call it the "Big H." I moved to Houston, well—I first went there before I started playing. I went to Houston when I was about nine years old, back and forth like 125-miles range. In the summertime when the school was out I would go back to the country and stayed for the summer with my auntie. And my mother had asthma, which she died from asthma and the climate was too low in Houston. So the little town called Normangee, Texas, that's where my auntie was living at and my mother bought a home up there. See, my auntie raised my mother. She raised up practically all of us, you know, my brothers. She was like a grandmother and a mother, you know, when I went back up there during the summer.

Well, in the first, I was playing piano. I wanted to play piano. I really wasn't interested in guitar. No, I wasn't playing piano in church, I was taking piano lessons. This little town I was telling you about living in—Normangee, Texas—well, it's like thirteen miles from where I was born. I was born in a log cabin. Well, what happened, this lady she had to come from this little town, like thirty-five miles away, and this town was called Bryan, Texas, and she come twice a week. But you know, when it rains in Texas, it floods! During the winter the weather got so bad she come once a week. She used to come like on Mondays and Fridays. So she come on Fridays to teach piano lessons 'cause we didn't have no piano. I didn't have nothing that looked like a piano, the piano was in the school. She come to the school to teach us, you know. It got like where, well, she couldn't come to teach us.

A cousin of mine named Willow Young, he had a Harmony guitar, so he used to let me keep that because I wasn't able to buy no guitar. He let me keep his. So he taught me that tuning I'm playing in 'cause he was playing that. I put one of them little pickups under the strings and started with that for about, I guess, maybe four or five months. Then I bought me an Epiphone with an Alamo amp. I think that's what John Lee Hooker used to use. I think so, Sears Roebuck!

And that's when I ran into Gatemouth Brown, T-Bone Walker, because Gatemouth was living at a little town called Orange, Texas, and he was cutting for Peacock Records, and he was doing a lot of shows with T-Bone Walker and Junior Parker. That's when I went into electric blues. Gatemouth used to use that capo, and I used to have a problem using this finger [*indicates middle finger*] for the, you know, you use this finger for bar and for your different keys. He said, "Try a capo instead of using your finger." I picked that up from Gatemouth Brown, because Gatemouth always uses that style to get the high range of notes. I used to go and see T-Bone Walker, that's what really turned me to the blues. I mean as far as electric blues, I call it electric blues because I used to listen to, like I said, John Lee Hooker and I like that kind of blues. But I wanted to play jazz. But I was living near to T-Bone, 'cause he lived in a town called Conroe, Texas. That's like about sixty-five miles from Houston and he had some relatives lived in. He was kinda raised up around that area and he lived in Houston for a while before he moved to California, and I used to hear him play a lot, you know. I kinda went off into the blues then, but I used to listen to Jimmie Lunceford and Tommy Dorsey. This is where I got my interest in the horns and everything. This was before Freddie King's time, it was in the '50s. I was started out when I was pretty young. Well, actually, I met B. B. King when I was eighteen. That was in Houston, Texas, and he had out the tune called "Three O'Clock in the Morning." That's when I first met B. B.

At this time I was living in the Third Ward in Houston. I was raised up in that ward. Like they say, it's a ghetto, but I lived in the Third Ward off and on since I was nine years old. I went to Blasher High School, elementary school, then I went to Jackie Ace High and I got on the football team for a while. I was on the B team, not the A team! And I got away from that and Johnny Nash was playing in the high school band. Before I cut "The Freeze," before I changed bands, Charles Washington worked with me for a long time. Me and Charles Washington started out together, just me and Charles Washington, nobody else. We used to travel, just me and the drummer, all around Texas. And he played with me for a while, but we didn't cut no records together. He was a drummer and he started out with me.

In 1958 that's when I cut my first record. I cut "The Freeze," an instrumental, in 1958, on the Kangaroo label. We had a dispute about that. See what happened was that . . . okay, I had it first, I put it out first. Fenton Robinson and a guy named David Dean was playing on me, on my tune called "Frosty," and he played "The Freeze" with me. He played with me for, like, four years. So what happened is that they went and re-cut it.[2] Don Robey got mad with me and stopped my record from playing on the air for two weeks because I wouldn't sign no record contract with him. I didn't like him! I don't care you put it out, I didn't like him. He's dead now, I don't care! But I didn't sign with him, I stayed on my own. He tried to make things very awkward, but I had . . . The Kangaroo label had paid the superintendent of KCOH radio, and I played for their grand opening for this radio station, which is still there now. And Don Robey went down and stopped my record from playing for two weeks, and this record company had already paid these people to play my record on the air. So he was fixing to get sued, so they said, well, man, after they found out what had happened, you know, they said, "We can't do this, 'cause Kangaroo Records have done paid this radio station to play this thing." That's the way they had it, when payola was going out at that time.

I played behind a group called the Dolls, an all-girl group. That's how I got my first record. My band was backing them up. It was R&B, you know, we weren't really playing nothing like no disco, but they was singing like the Inspirations. That was on the Kangaroo label. See, that was two schoolteachers, one schoolteacher and this Henry Hayes guy. He's a saxophone player. He used to back me up with my group, because he was a music teacher and this other guy was just a regular schoolteacher. His name was Mel Young. And they were the ones that had the Kangaroo label, including the Great Scott, that when they brought him in. 'Cause the Great Scott was the one that introduced me to doing—they had some studio time left and they said, "Hey, man, those tunes you been playing, why don't you go ahead and play this for the next thirty minutes, you already know it in the band already. Let's see if you can run it down right quick." So I played "Freeze" and "Collins Shuffle." I had Herbert Henderson on drums and I had a left-hand bass player named Bill Johnson and I had Henry Hayes on alto sax and I had Tiny on tenor. We called him Big Tiny. His name was Cleotis Arch. Frank Scott and Mel Young and Henry Hayes were running Kangaroo. Frank Scott, they called him "The Great Scott." He lives in Chicago right now, not the one lives in Los Angeles!

"The Freeze" was first and "De-Frost" was second, on the Great Scott label. "De-Frost" was in 1960. What happened is the Great Scott beat me out of some money, this money-type thing. So he hooked up with, he'd already hooked up with Bill Hall after we did "De-Frost." He got in touch with Bill Hall in Beaumont, Texas, and it's called Hall and Clement. See, him and Jack Clement had this studio in Beaumont, Texas. At first Bill had his part and Jack Clement had his part. So they joined together and that's the reason they called it Hall and Clement. Right down on Pearl Street in Beaumont, Texas. They on Belmont Street now in Nashville, Tennessee. They was producing, like they were producing country and western at first, but Jack, that's what he's still doing now, but he changed over after the Great Scott went down and talked to him about me. I met the Great Scott in Houston, Texas. He come to hear me play. He had heard me for a long time. He used to play with Jimmy Reed, play guitar hisself. He come to Houston. He was handling this kid, Little Frankie Lee. He was handling him, and me and Frankie Lee used to work together, so he asked me about cutting a record.

It was the Great Scott that took me to Bill Hall in Beaumont. They used to have Johnny Preston, "Running Bear," that kind of stuff. They had the Big Bopper, too, "Chantilly Lace." Right along about that particular time it was called Big Bopper Enterprises, 'cause it was named after the Big Bopper after he got killed in the airplane crash. So he went down and made a deal with Bill Hall about pushing this 45, 'cause during that particular time Booker T and the MGs had "Green Onions." And instrumentals were selling in that particular year, 'cause I didn't used to sing. I just played instrumentals and instrumentals always went over big in Texas. Yeah, instrumentals and the Louisiana beat.

Houston was a city of blues and jazz mostly. Lightnin' was playing everywhere. I was fronting then. I used to play behind a lot of musicians that would come into town, like, by themselves. Like I come over here by myself, I'd back 'em up, you know. I had my own group, like I said, I had Big Tiny . . . well, back and forth, me and Johnny "Guitar" Watson had the same musicians. Yeah, Johnny used to play piano for me. Piano is his major instrument. He just picked up guitar. He's a little bit younger than me. I knew his whole family, his mother and all of them.

Clarence Green? Yeah, Clarence, he had his own group all the time. But we used to run into each other every now and then, you know. I know him as a person, but as far as we playing together, no. He had a little group called the Blues for Two, which wasn't but two guitarists and drums. They made a big name for theirselves around there for a while. Albert Reno was on the other guitar. He lives in Austin, Texas, now, last time I seen him. I think he did some session work for other people. He's a pretty good guitar player. Cal Green, yeah, he worked mostly with the Midnighters at different times.

Clarence Holiman? Well, his brother used to play with me before he passed away. Clarence Holiman, he had a brother that played piano. We called him Sweetheart.

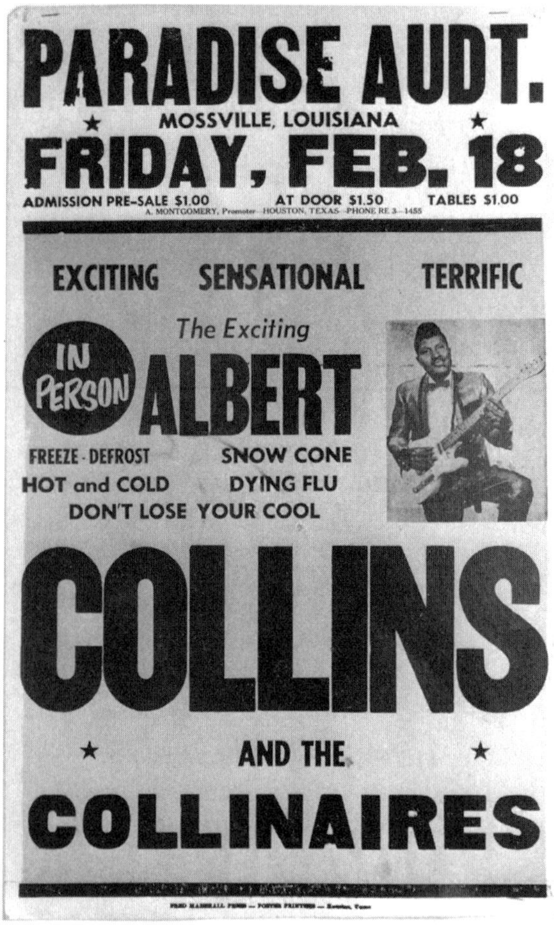

Albert Collins poster, c. 1960.

(*laughs*) Well, he was really sweet, you know, whatever. He drank hisself to death. He died a young man. Clarence Holiman played some things with Bobby Bland, Junior Parker. He's out in Los Angeles now.

Little Joe Washington? Oh, Little Joe! Little Joe stayed right across the street from me. He's hanging out there, he's still playing guitar. Yeah, people used to think he was crazy. Fall all out on the floor, play dead! He had a thing going. He used to do all that kind of stuff, you know. He do everything—play with his toes!

Johnny Copeland? Well, Johnny and a friend of his named Joe Hughes played guitar. They used to play together. They had a group something like the Clarence Green group. And Johnny Copeland put out a tune called "Down on Bended Knees." And he kind of sung like this guy named Nappy Brown. Well, I used to do some shows with Nappy Brown, in Houston, and around the little small towns around Houston, a hundred and two hundred miles radius. Johnny's trying to get something happening for him now. He lives in New York now, but he kinda got away from the music for a while and he's back into it now. He had a nice record one time, "Down on Bended Knees."[3]

Jimmy Nelson? Oh, yeah, "Meet Me with Your Black Dress On." Yeah, I played with him, but I didn't play with him too long. I played with him around Houston, playing little old jobs we were making about six or seven dollars apiece a night. He was working at a steel company. I think he drive a truck for a while, too. He didn't make it really that big. He had a good job, so he just doing records like a hobby. He was—that "Meet Me with Your Black Dress On" was a good seller for him at that time. He went out for a little while, but he didn't stay long. He didn't care too much about traveling. From what I heard he's still in Houston now.[4]

Joe Fritz played with me for a little while, but he used to back up Junior Parker and all of them. He'd blow alto. You ever heard of Joe Scott? He had a good band in Texas one time, he's a trumpet player. I just got his number, he lives right around the corner from my home right now. He's the one that wrote "Further On Up the Road" and all that stuff. He arranged all that stuff for Bobby Bland. Anyway, Joe Fritz stop playing, you know, he always, he do a lot of working on cars. He likes to do that. He's mechanical and he used to do all the sessions and stuff for Robey. So I heard that he's gone back into music and they say he's still really sounding good. I haven't seen him in twelve years!

Bill Harvey? He was a sax player. He used to back up B. B. and a lot of . . . he's dead now. I never worked around him too much. He's been dead a long time. Good saxophone player, too. He had a good band, too. John Roberts, you ever heard of a group called John Roberts and the Hurricanes? Well, he played a lot of stuff around with some of Robey's stuff. Well, I guess he wasn't too big. Archie Bell and the Drells, I hung out around with all them guys. See, we were all raised up together.

The deejay King Bee, yeah he was at KCOH and he helped me out quite a bit on my records. Most disc jockeys—there's a lady jock her name is Gigi. We called her Gigi, her name was Gladys Hill. She helped me out a lot on pushing my records like "Frosty" and "The Freeze," you know, and she passed away not too long ago. She had cancer. She did a lot for a lot of musicians, but I was her pick, you know, because we used to go and do gigs together, because she sang, too. She'd go with me and my band.[5] I had the same guys, Bill Johnson on bass, and Frank Mitchell, a trumpet player, and a blind trumpet player. I had two trumpets and a tenor at one time—I had everything. I always wanted a big band sound. I wants it now!

Johnny Ace/Don Robey

I stayed away from home a whole year once and I didn't even see my house. Yeah, with Piney Brown, that was in '54. I came back home day after Christmas, the day after Johnny Ace killed himself. Stayed on the road a whole year! I enjoyed it. It don't make me no difference. I wasn't living out of a suitcase, I was living out of New Orleans. I stayed in New Orleans six months. I was married then to my first wife. Traveling? I had a wagon, a station wagon. I bought one of those Chrysler limousines. I used to put a trailer behind it. It had three seats in it and my band traveled like that.

Johnny Ace's death? Yeah, a couple of weeks, three weeks before that happened a guy that played in the band with him was telling me, and well, his cousin played with him. This guy wasn't playing, he just said his cousin told him. Say he was driving along one day, Johnny Ace, he just pulled his gun out and starting shooting at road signs, shooting at rabbits. Then he just take one bullet, they say he had been playing with that gun for three weeks. Take the bullet out and point it at you, but he wouldn't pull it. Take it again, spin the chamber, he might put it in his arm like he gonna shoot himself. He did it too many times. He did it the wrong time, because he pointed it at this girl, her name was Shirley. I know her well. I been knowing her a long time, because I used to go to school with her. But anyway, she was there with him that night, because he had been going with her off and on. He spin it around and pointed it at her head and she said, "Oh, don't do that, baby, don't play with no gun like that," and he said, "Oh, I ain't gonna hurt you," and he spin it around like this, "Bam!" He fell over in her lap. She said she kept that skirt she had.

Shirley, yeah, she still alive living in Houston somewhere, I guess. I don't know, it's been a long time since I seen her. If she's still there or done moved somewhere else. But Willie Mae Thornton can tell you where she lives, 'cause Willie Mae go back and forth home all the time, back to Houston. I came in the day after. See, he killed himself on the Christmas Eve. I come on the Christmas. He killed himself on the 24th of December, 1954. I came home Christmas Day to spend Christmas, because I had been gone a whole year and I heard about it. There's a lot of little different stories about that, you see, because, like, one time I talked to Willie Mae about it, she didn't want to talk about it. In other words, cut me off and told me to shut up, you know.

Well, what happened is his contract was gonna be up with Don Robey. See, he had a pretty nice record out at that one time. He had went and said to somebody else and they went back and told Don Robey he wasn't gonna sign with Peacock Records. He was gonna sign with somebody else. I guess under cover somebody was . . . See, Robey he jumped on Gatemouth Brown one time. Gatemouth Brown almost killed him! He jumped on Little Richard, put Little Richard in the hospital. He was fooling around with Robey. He had been working some shows for Don Robey. I played with Little Richard when he had a band called the Tempo Toppers. I took Jimi Hendrix's place when he came to Houston. He had been playing with Little Richard. So Hendrix went with the Drifters. That's when Hendrix was playing the blues then. He went on to those other things later on then. Hendrix was about eighteen or nineteen years old when I met him. He was coming there with Little Richard. So I finished a date with Little Richard, part of his band and part of my band, because a lot of them guys left Little Richard. Because during that time Richard was going through some problems about paying the musicians. You understand what I'm saying? So I went along and did six dates with him and about two months later Don Robey jumped on him, put the man in the hospital, something about contracts or something. I don't know what happened. He'd (Robey) hit you, man, put his gun in your face and say, "You'd better not hit me back!" That's the way he did that kind of thing. He was heavy, a pretty heavy dude. Got mad with me 'cause I wouldn't sign with him. He said, "I'm gonna stop your records from playing!" I said, "I'll tell you one thing, I bet you they're gonna play again." He said, "You smart, ain't you?" I said, "Uhm-uhm." Gatemouth'd like to kill him! He know better than to jump on Gatemouth. Gatemouth's a cowboy. Gatemouth put his boots all over that butt! Every time Gatemouth would hit him, he put his pistol in his face, told him, "Don't you reach in your pockets, I'll blow your brains out!" Gatemouth's crazy! But now that Robey's dead, Evelyn Johnson got everything. Evelyn Johnson, she had the booking agency. She just took over everything.

Well, she used to wear them, you know, the old overalls with the hammer thing, where you hang your hammer on, and rubber boots that come up to here (knee height). Well, she'd fold them down in the summertime. She'd fold them down, you know, it would be 105 degrees, man, she'd be steady walking. She wouldn't walk on the sidewalk every time, she'd walk in the street, where people could see her. With that cap on her head, with beer, and looking mean. You can't upset her, she fight woman or man. Don't make her no different.

Some lady told her one night, say, "You look good, but you need to get out of those boots, man." She slapped that woman. Well, she went to slap her, but the lady ducked, you know, those old rickety tables in one of those old nightclubs, and all the drinks fell over on the floor, and she called her all kinds of names, man. "These my boots! I wear them when I get ready." She don't like you to talk about her boots. You know, Don Robey talked to her one time about going on a show with Bobby Bland and Junior Parker with them boots on. Yeah, she go up on stage with those boots on, with her overalls on. During them particular times when you played clubs you had to kinda look decent, you know. It took them a long time before they could make her put on a dress. She don't wear dresses, I know. I saw her in one dress since I been knowing her! She feels uncomfortable in it. She wears just pants now and a shirt, and her cap. They put her in a dress one time to take a picture. It took two weeks to convince her. "You're a lady. Put a dress on!" I remember that one, but she pulled it right off when she made that picture. I bet she came right out of that dress. She don't like dresses.

We played in Portland, Oregon, together and she ordered a six-pack of Budweiser beer backstage and she say, "Get you a beer, Albert." I said, "Well, okay." So she handed me a beer, 'cause she opened it. So I said, "I can't drink no two beers," 'cause I can't drink too much anyway. I say, "I'll just drink this. Me and my wife will drink it together." So she put something in my beer, man. I just took a little taste. It didn't bother me too much, but it knocked my wife out. She just fell over this way. I said, "What's wrong with you?" She said, "I don't know. I can't walk!" She just went out, and Willie Mae's just sat up there just laughing. I took my wife to the car and some policemen came by and it was during the winter and they saw the steam coming from the engine. So they checked the car and she was laying down in the car. So they woke her up to tell her to crack her glasses, you know, the carbon monoxide would have killed her. When I got back to Los Angeles, maybe about a couple of months later, I saw Willie Mae. One night she came in I was playing at the Troubadour, with Joe Turner, and she started laughing, and she said, "How was that beer?" I said, "I oughta take this chair and go upside . . ." (*laughs*) She always pulling those little funny pranks. She likes to do that. I didn't drink too much of it, but it almost made me not even play my gig! I don't know what she put in there, but it's some kind of stuff they put in your drink and it knocks you out. I don't know what she did! It was funny to her, but it wasn't funny to me, 'cause I didn't know what was wrong with my legs! It might not knock you out. It just make you feel good, 'cause she was probably using it herself.

I left Houston and went to Kansas City, Missouri. I stayed in Kansas City around about three years. That's where I met my wife. That's where my wife's from. I was working out of Kansas City. I worked in Kansas City, but I was working through an agency there that was connected with the Buffalo Booking Agency. They was good friends. I liked Kansas City and I decided I wanted to stay there for a while because my mother had passed away and I didn't want to stay around Houston for no memories. I just got away from everything. That's the reason why I stayed there.

In Houston in 1965, I did the session with Big Walter Price, "The Thunderbird." I played the guitar on the Big Walter "Thunderbird" session. That was at his house, that's all that was, it wasn't no studio. We only recorded a couple of numbers, that's all. I just went over his house one day because he was trying to get a tape to send to Mike Leadbitter. It wasn't no big thing about that and I left. I was in a hurry, too, anyway, 'cause I had to go outta town. You know, Walter, he was trying because me and him were supposed to be coming over here together a long time ago. He knew Mike Leadbitter, and I don't know, somebody screwed up somewhere and we didn't make it. I think Walter messed it up. I got the record at home. I got the tape on it. Dick Shurman, he's the one that gave me the tape, like I'd forgotten about it. He had this tune, Big Walter had this tune "Get to Getting"—"*Take the baby home, pet her and put her to bed.*" I played on that, too. I think he still got the tape. He told me he was going to send it to me. [*sings the song*] It's a kind of weird way he plays it. Yeah, he's something else.[6]

In 1969 I met the Canned Heat in the Third Ward at a place where I was playing called the Ponderosa. I was playing there, just like on Wednesday nights. They was playing at the Music Hall and Bob Hite was looking for me. So he went and found Lightnin' Hopkins and Lightnin' told him where I was playing, 'cause Lightnin' used to come up to hear me every Wednesday night. That's the way it happened. See, Bob come with that beard and that long hair, and I said, "What is this, Jesus?" He come up and asked me and said, "I'm Bob Hite." I'd heard of him but I didn't know he had that beard and that long hair. "Well," he said, "We been looking for you, man, we talked to your cousin Lightnin', told me you were up here." I said, "Yeah." He said, "We're with Imperial Records," and they had called down to Bill Hall, you know, down in Beaumont. Yeah, Bill Hall was looking after me then, that's before they moved to Nashville, Tennessee. So Bob said, "Why don't you try to come out to California, man? We can help you out." So he wrote the liner notes on my first album with Imperial. I wanted to get out of Houston. There wasn't anything happening in Houston. Playing in little small clubs, I got tired of that, man. "Chitlin' circuit" we called it. It was pretty bad for blues, 'cause, you know, trends changes and they was into jazz and that's when this rock stuff came out with the psychedelic.

I was booked at the Fillmore West. I played there with the Who, B. B. King. I played there with Elvin Bishop, Mike Bloomfield, Buddy Miles. I just (1979) come out of a strictly rock 'n' roll club, the Body Shop in Vancouver, Canada, which surprised me.

I got into organ, you know. I been into organ for a long time, because I used to be around Jimmy Smith and Jimmy McGriff. Jimmy Smith used to come to sit in with me all the time when I'd play. He owns a club in the western part of Los Angeles called the Jimmy Smith Club, I think. He's out there now. Last time I played with him was down in San Diego. See, I been around a lot of those guys, you know. I was just learning, trying. I was around Wes Montgomery in the Midwest. I first met Wes Montgomery in Kansas City, Missouri.

Like Ike Turner, he's from St. Louis. I did some, I did "Bold Soul Sister" for him, and I did *The Hunter* album with Tina. Ike was playing piano. That's his instrument, piano. He just picks that guitar, you know, because he'd been on the show. Go on and see the Ike and Tina Turner show, he'd stand out front. He just picked up guitar, like Johnny "Guitar" Watson. Ike felt like he got to a limit when he'd get ready, 'cause he played a certain way and he said, "Man, I want you to put some blues on top of this." He's kinda strict about his music as far as on the bandstand, but I have never worked with him on the bandstand. I wouldn't sit in with him. He's kinda hard, he's very strict about his musicians. My name wasn't mentioned on *The Hunter* album at all, 'cause I was signed with Imperial Records and Ike felt like he might get sued. They put my name on that record as "Al Jackson." But a lot of people knew that was me playing. I didn't get no recognition from that at all, including "Bold Soul Sister." I did it on a Sunday evening. He just paid me for the session, did it in about six hours. Tina already had the material. I just went right on and played in the studio, no overdubbing at all. It was just a straight session. I took the main guitar work all the way through and Ike took the piano.[7]

After *The Hunter* I did a lot of overdubs for Ike in Los Angeles. When I wasn't doing too much, wasn't traveling too much, I'd go out there to Bolic Sounds and do some stuff. He's got a lot of stuff there that I overdubbed that he didn't release. They've got material now. I just went and did overdubs for him. I stayed there three days before I even came outdoors. (*laughs*) I said, "Man, I got to run," and he said, "No, no, no, man, wait, wait. I'll call and get you anything you want." See, Ike is a very funny guy. He's a guy that is self contained, you say? She ask him once for me, go, to come over to London with them. They was coming over here, and he was so into his studio thing. He said, "No, I'm gonna keep Albert here with me, 'cause I want him to stay with me." Well, see, he used to fire—he fired one guy, he was a real nice-looking kid, used to play with James Brown. Played guitar, he was real bad, too, man! I forget that kid's name. I met him in Freeport, Texas, when they played in Freeport, Texas, and he fired that kid the same night, 'cause he went up and got in Tina's face, and Tina said, "Hey, he's a cute little . . ." Ike said, "Hey, man, here's your check!"

After the session work with Ike and Tina, I went back out on the road. I was playing, you know, Pacific Northwest—Portland, Oregon; Seattle, Washington; and Canada. Yeah, I was living in California—Los Angeles. I had my own group—well, I took this guy he played with me, like, seven years. Booker T and the MGs' drummer, they call him Spider. His real name is Larry Daniels, he's from Kansas. We played together in Kansas City, Missouri. He lives in Long Beach, California, now. And I had an Indian kid that played saxophone with me, his name is Sonny Boyan. Very good tenor man, and I had an organ player name Mike, played B3 Hammond, and a bass player named Mike Rosso—he moved to Oregon, and he quit playing. I also played with Howlin' Wolf in Kansas City, Missouri. I played with him at the last gig he played before he died, in Seattle, Washington, a place called Six Stadium. He was on a kidney machine at the end. I played the last gig with Wolf before he passed away. Him and Koko Taylor, and Hubert Sumlin was playing guitar with him.

Recording

I was without a recording contract from the time I did the Tumbleweed. Oh, I'll tell you what happened behind that. See, I was signed with Tumbleweed Records for four years, and Gulf and Western was backing it, and this guy took the money and came over here. Now he's in Seattle, Washington, and the company folded. I called one day and the phone was disconnected and I panicked, you know. So I seeked around and found out that ABC Dunhill had bought all my stuff from Tumbleweed. J. Geils—the group J. Geils—they went with Atlantic Records. So I goes to ABC Dunhill and I tried to get on with them since they had my material and I was two weeks late! Evelyn Johnson from the Buffalo Booking Agency signed Bobby Bland and they already had B. B. King. So the guy turned and said, "Man, I wish you would have been here earlier, but I got enough blues right now." I hung out and hung out, so Dick Shurman got me with Alligator Records. ABC bought everything from Tumbleweed. I've got about four or five tunes that wasn't released. Well, Bill Szymcyk, he didn't produce the album like I wanted, 'cause I asked him to let me be there when he got ready to overdub the reed sections. But I had to go to Canada and they held me there too long, and he [was] trying to hurry up and get his stuff done. Because he had to produce somebody else—he's steady on the road all the time—and we did the overdubbing in Los Angeles. I didn't like that album too much. It sounded too commercial. The singers was one chick and a guy, that's all it was, that's all. They really weren't no singers.

When I'm on the road now in California, I pay my band by the week, weekly salary. But when I was in Texas, I'd give them the money every gig, each night we played. No, they [the musicians] didn't have contracts on recording sessions in them days. All they'd do was pay you for the session and that's it. It was olden days; they've changed all that now. Many times I felt I was being ripped off back then. Yeah, well, people been getting ripped off for a long time. In this kind of business a lot people don't realize how they can get ripped off so bad, because they only want to get on a record. That's what I was doing the first time. The second time I did, when I played "De-Frost." I got with Hall and Clements. I didn't care what happened, that's when—this is a record company, 'cause these other guys only owned little labels anyway, doing nothing—I said, "This here's big enough for me." And then this Great Scott turned around and beat me out of 1,800 dollars. That's a lot of money in them days.

Albert Collins. (Photo Denis Lewis)

Well, see what happened, I had some royalties coming. He went down and collected the royalties, and I didn't know this. So I called down one day, I needed some money, I was buying a house. We did a contract over and he told the man don't come to his office anymore. I didn't get my money. But I always get my own cars. Now, this last album I cut with Tumbleweed, they bought my equipment, like amplifier. But I bought my van, I bought it brand-new. I pay for my own stuff. I don't like no record company to give me anything. I might want to say, "I don't want to cut no more for you, man. I ain't obligated to you!" 'Cause, see, where a lot of musicians make their mistakes, see, you sign a contract and you go out there and buy one of those expensive cars on your contract—you got to sign another one!

Man, when I first met Bruce Iglauer, I like him. You know, a lot of record companies they cut you, they don't care if you're out there, you're on your own. I've had my first Alligator album out now. Next I would like to have a live album. I got a band in Chicago, that's with Larry Burton and Aron Burton. I got Casey Jones on drums and I'm using A. C. Reed. You know, he play with different people. He played with Son Seals, but I'm keeping him with me, you know. He's playing electric saxophone all the time now. I talked to Bruce about me playing with a disco band and seeing how it sounded, run some tracks down. He was kinda interested in it, but you know he like that blues. He say he was excited because all his artists is out of Chicago and, see, Chicago blues and Texas blues are different blues.

I tried to find my directions, because I had my directions. What I wanted, my own creations, because, like I say, I'm listening to those guys. Man, you can play blues so long it all sounds the same. I play a lot of twelve-bar changes, 'cause I wanted a different show from the rest of them guys. I didn't wanna go on the bandstand and just sit there and play, just stand up and play. I like to have the energy! That's another thing I worked on was the energy. You know, I did a show with Albert King, and after you done heard about three or four of his numbers you done heard his whole show. I mean a lot of people say this. I'm not putting him down, 'cause, I mean, I admire the man. He admires me, too. If I deliver my own creation, or whatever you do, you automatically get the respect. If you carry yourself in a respectable way, that's the way I think about it. I wanna keep on going up that ladder. That's what I want, high energy!

Notes

1. Leaving high school in the tenth grade would probably put his age closer to sixteen years old.

2. Fenton and the Castle Rockers, "The Freeze," Duke 190.

3. Johnny Copeland, "Down on Bending Knees" [title printed on original 45], Golden Eagle 101. [Following a revitalized career, Johnny Copeland died on July 3, 1997.]

4. [Jimmy Nelson died on July 30, 2007.]

5. Gladys Hill, "Prison Bound"/"Please Don't Touch My Bowl," Peacock 1618. This is possibly the same artist.

6. Big Walter, "My Tears"/"Houston Ghetto Blues," *The Thunderbird*, Flyright LP527.

7. Ike and Tina Turner, *The Hunter*, Blue Thumb BTS11.

PART VI

WEST COAST

Johnny Otis

This interview was conducted when the Johnny Otis Show appeared on August 1, 1972, at the Aquarius in the old holiday and fishing town of Hastings, some five miles east of Bexhill-on-Sea. Singing, playing piano and vibes, Otis led his band, which included Clifford Solomon (tenor sax), Big Jim Wynn (baritone sax), Gene "Mighty Flea" Connors (trombone and trumpet), Willie "Jitter" Webb (guitar), Jimmy Reed Jr. (bass), and Thomas Norman (drums). The headline act was Marie Adams and the Three Tons of Joy.

Although there was only a short time between arriving at Hastings and going on stage, Johnny insisted on giving an interview. I had long thought about his story, written by the man himself, which was among the best things *BU* had published (nos. 75–78); he was such an intelligent and fascinating man that almost anything he had to say was of interest. Hence we were content to let the interview develop quite freely, discussing different subjects as they arose in the course of conversation.

—John Broven

A Rap with Johnny Otis

Mike Leadbitter, Simon Napier, and John Broven

Blues Unlimited #101 (May 1973)

My First Record

I started my own thing in 1945 after I had formed the Otis–Love Band with Preston Love in Omaha. I made my first record for Otis Rene, who owned the pioneering Excelsior Records. On that date Count Basie loaned Jimmy Rushing as a singer, also two sidemen. I had a nice big band of my own at the time and we were well rehearsed. We did an instrumental with Preston Love and two sides by Jimmy Rushing. I said, "Great, we finished early!" "What do you mean, we finished early?" came the reply. "Three records in four hours." Rene said, "No, four records in three hours." "Oh, shit!" I said. So we hurriedly looked in my music book and found Ray Noble's "Harlem Nocturne," which was really Mickey Mouse music. We did our own arrangement, and although it was done as an afterthought, that was the one that made it.

The West Coast Labels

The main labels were Swing Time [Jack Lauderdale], Aladdin [Eddie and Leo Mesner], Modern/RPM [Jules, Saul, and Joe Bihari], Excelsior [Otis Rene], and Exclusive [Leon Rene]. At the time I was not aware of the Bob Geddins labels, or that the Jimmy McCracklin records I was hearing were made in Oakland. Although I came from Berkeley, which is near Oakland, we concentrated on Los Angeles, where the scene was all happening.

I am sure that people like the Rene brothers or Art Rupe never dreamt their records would smack and crash their way across the country when they first started. "Drifting Blues" by Charles Brown [with Johnny Moore's Three Blazers, Philo/Aladdin, 1946] was the black national anthem for two years. It was all you heard; hits lasted in those days. Things like "The Honeydripper" [Joe Liggins, Exclusive, 1945] and "I Wonder" [Cecil Gant, Gilt-Edge, 1944] were on the jukeboxes all over Central Avenue. At the time, to hear a record you either had to buy it, listen on a jukebox, or maybe see an artist in person. There was not much air exposure. The pressures and competition which cause a record to die quickly today were not the same. The record owners used to work out deals with the jukebox men. The jukebox was a vital outlet, but I was not aware of the details of these deals.

Radio Outlets

Johnny Otis Show poster, 1972.

Radio was to become all important in promoting records, but first it was limited to a few hours a day. The important disc jockeys on the West Coast were Joe Adams and Hunter Hancock. Adams hardly played any blues at first, mainly big band swing. But Hancock was more into folk. His first show was *Harlem Matinee* followed by *Huntin' with Hunter.* Al Jarvis, the first big white deejay in L.A., died two years ago [1970]. He said there was an unwritten law about playing black records—they just were not played. Joe Adams, a young black from Watts, was his assistant, and learnt a lot from Jarvis; he later had his own show on KDAY and acted as announcer when my shows were broadcast from the Club Alabam. Today Adams is Ray Charles's manager. Hunter was on for one hour every Sunday and was the first black program in South California. At first it was mainly big band jazz by Duke Ellington and Count Basie. He took "Harlem Nocturne" and made it into a hit. Later when I had the Barrelhouse club, he played other of my records. Then at last he got music on the air every day and hit a wider audience. Little by little rock 'n' roll was born. Then whites started to trickle into my audience. Way back East the song pluggers used to operate, and they spread to the West Coast when Hunter got going. The magic of airplay . . . and then payola. That's how civilization develops!

Later Johnny was a deejay on KFOX in Long Beach and naturally came across payola firsthand. He didn't like it for the simple reason it would affect the content of his program, "but it was hard when old friends brought along their records and they were bad."

Drifting with Charles Brown

In the late '40s the big artists on the West Coast were T-Bone Walker, Joe Liggins, Johnny Moore and Charles Brown, Roy Milton, and Gerald Wilson, who had a big band like Jimmie Lunceford. Roy Brown was one of the biggest names in the black community in 1948 with "Good Rocking Tonight" [De Luxe], but Charles Brown's "Drifting Blues" was revolutionary, man. I first saw him in 1944 at a talent show when I was drummer in Bardu Ali's band. He was a tall, handsome young man in a light suit and he played "Clair De Lune," of all things, in a black theater. He broke the show up; he followed with "Rhapsody in Blue." He was a schooled musician and had been a music teacher in a black college in the South. Bardu then asked him to play piano in the band. This was long before "Drifting Blues," and I played drums on the session. He did three sides with Johnny Moore and no thought had been given about the fourth song. He was asked if he remembered a Christian gospel number his grandmother used to sing. Charles, who was very much into the Nat Cole Trio thing, didn't think it was sophisticated enough. But it turned out to be the black national anthem for the next two years. People like Floyd Dixon, Little Willie Littlefield, Johnny Otis, and ten thousand others tried to sound like Charles; this was why I hired Mel Walker.

Floyd Dixon? He's doing nothing now. I remember when I was on a ladder painting the Barrelhouse sign. Somebody turned on the PA system, which had an outside speaker to attract people into the club. A kid had wandered in and started to play; he sounded so much like Charles Brown that I thought it was the jukebox. It was Floyd Dixon. He had a nice run with "Dallas Blues" [Modern] and "Call Operator 210" [Aladdin] and other Charles Brown interpretations. Amos Milburn and Ray Charles were also influenced by Brown. Milburn's "Chicken Shack Boogie" [Aladdin] is a thing unto itself, probably one of the greatest records of all time; so much electricity and energy—it's supercharged. I put it on a par with Jerry Lee Lewis's "Whole Lotta Shakin' Goin' On" [Sun] and Ray Charles's live version of "Drown in My Own Tears" [Atlantic].

Struttin' with Duke and Peacock

I first met Don Robey when we took our first tour with the Blues Caravan in Texas. Little Esther was starring. Promotion in Texas was in the hands of two competitors, Carl Lewis and Don Robey. Robey had already started Peacock by then, and he was mainly a dance promoter, promoting different attractions through Texas. Robey asked for about eight different artists to appear on my show, and this was how I found Marie Adams and Willie Mae Thornton. By 1951 Marie had a hit with "I'm Gonna Play the Honky Tonks" [Peacock]. I was featured as talent scout and A&R man, and I did the Little Richard sides for Peacock and later Johnny Ace [for Duke];

"Pledging My Love" was recorded in Houston and "Saving My Love for You" in Los Angeles. [Thornton's] "Hound Dog" was written in full cooperation with Leiber and Stoller and was part of a deal I had with them—the song was not stolen from me.

The Start of Rock 'n' Roll

At first there was so much overlapping. There was more emphasis on rhythm, more animation, less bluesy. Historians point to "Gee" [the Crows] and "Sh-Boom" [the Chords, both 1954] as the beginning of rock 'n' roll. Admittedly, they were the first records that went "pop," but there was a white audience before that. In 1948 the whites used to turn up at the Barrelhouse every Friday night. I don't know why, but it was always a Friday. They ranged from the young up to forty. The accent was far more on rhythm on Friday. Big Jay McNeely was my tenor man, and the crowd went wild when he played on his knees, then on his back, shaking his legs; big fat shake dancer came out singing jump numbers. There was also comedy and burlesque skits. We used to cook Mexican dishes and drink beer and wine.

Country Blues?

We didn't hear or see much in the North, but the country blues singers influenced everyone. I can remember hearing Peetie Wheatstraw, Big Bill, Dr. Clayton. I heard Robert Johnson's "Terraplane Blues" [Vocalion] recently, and although I didn't know the artist or the title then, it was something I remembered from my childhood. The porters who worked on the trains used to bring in records from Chicago and places and would play them on Saturdays or Sundays in the neighborhood. We liked them because they were risqué, you know: "look under your hood," "squeeze your lemon." I didn't record anything like that; I used to aspire to being Count Basie's drummer. We had fun, but didn't take them seriously.

Annie and Her Sexy Ways

At this point, Mike recalled the controversy that arose in 1954 over Hank Ballard's series of "Annie" records for Federal.

A group of people left your country a long time ago and called themselves Puritans. They're still with us. There is nothing as powerful as an idea whose time has come. Rock 'n' roll's time had come, but the public didn't think so. There was a tremendous campaign by the white establishment against the blacks when rock 'n' roll became big. They pointed to the effect of degenerate black lyrics on white youth. It was racism at heart. Not only Basie and Ellington, but "slum" bands like mine and Roy Milton were playing ballrooms and drawing large crowds; whites and blacks were rubbing shoulders together. This is what rancored.

Fats Domino and the Rock 'n' Roll Era

I don't know why, but Lady Dee [Devonia Williams], my piano player, and I had decided we wanted to do the beat of "The Fat Man" [Fats Domino, Imperial, 1949] for about a year before it came out. Then they beat us to it. We didn't know it was good for about another ten million records! We must have first heard it, the beat, from somebody from New Orleans. We were in the Barrelhouse when a man serviced the jukebox and punched the button of one of the new records. We looked at each other and that was that; it's what we'd been thinking about for the past year.

We played with Fats. During the heyday of rock 'n' roll Hal Zeiger and myself were partners in real estate on the West Coast. With our radio and TV shows we had a kind of monopoly on venues. The Little Richards, Chuck Berrys, Fats Dominos would be stars for the night and my band would play the first set. [There was] the Rendezvous Ballroom [Balboa–Newport Beach], the Pacific Ballroom in San Diego, there was another in Santa Barbara [probably the Carrillo Ballroom]; they were all dance halls, no concerts in those days. You couldn't sit the kids down. We would start at 9 p.m. through to 11:30. After a half-hour break, we would come back for a further hour. Everybody was on stage all the time and we used to work to death. It's not so hard today. At first we played in the rough black clubs, although there were a few fine places in Chicago and Los Angeles where people like Count Basie played. We played at the Apollo Theater about ten times; the first time we were second on the bill to Louis Jordan. We became one of the hottest attractions and got a plum holiday week, usually Easter.

Our TV show in L.A. was called the *Johnny Otis Show*. It ran for half an hour every week. We used to have all the rock 'n' roll and R&B stars: Coasters, Drifters, Fats Domino, Ray Charles, Sam Cooke, Moonglows, Little Richard. It was all music and occasionally had comedy with Redd Foxx; the program was sponsored by a local Ford dealer and also a furniture company.

My stay with Capitol? We had a nice relationship, but they weren't geared for R&B; they said themselves that if Atlantic had had "Willie and the Hand Jive" it would have sold twice as many copies. But the studios had a giant, sterile, super-slick atmosphere. I saw the Dick Clarks, Fabians, Avalons, Pat Boones making a dent by watered-down R&B. My Capitol records were contrived to make a hit, although I do like "Willie and the Hand Jive."

Today, Today Blues

Today the picture has not changed much. The radio stations and music is all lily white. The future of black music? If I was an 18-year-old musician or singer, I could tell you. I can see things changing or moving. Folk music is slow-moving, conservative by nature. But why has black music changed so quickly? The black man has always been creative, placing one lay on another. However, when a black artist has created and innovated, white music takes over. Therefore there is added pressure to find something the white man cannot steal.

Johnny Otis. Los Angeles, May 1974. (Photo Bill Greensmith)

It is easy to look back over the past and just remember what was good; you forget all the shit. Maybe we will look back in fifteen years and say Otis Redding, some Wilson Pickett, Aretha [Franklin] was good. Only the good will last. But music must change with a lifestyle because of sociological change. However, it is tragic the way our national treasures have been treated. It is a national disgrace. Joe Turner, a great, great man, a contributor to the culture of America and the world, cannot get a job; Ivory Joe Hunter, Eddie Vinson, Roy Milton . . . it's not fair. A partial answer is the white superstars whose success has been based on black music. If each of them felt a responsibility to take one out, not as a fucking flunky, but talk to the audience it would help. The R&B Hall of Fame? Flopped through lack of interest, and, unlike C&W, the R&B artists are not in a position to help themselves.

I must say that *Blues Unlimited* have been missionaries in the field and I couldn't wait to meet you all.

Roy Brown

As I look now at this feature, I am struck at how generally accurate Roy Brown—the first singer of soul who opened up the New Orleans R&B scene—was in his recollections, with the notable exception of his birth details. I recall that he was enthusiastic, friendly, and always smiling as he told of good times and bad. Of all my published interviews, I would say this one attracted the most positive reaction. It is of personal pride to know that, along with the efforts of Jonas Bernholm at Route 66 Records in Sweden, this interview did much to bring fresh attention to Brown in his twilight years. For this republication, I have edited modestly, corrected a few names, fact-checked where possible, and added a fresh set of footnotes.

—John Broven, 2013

Good Rockin' Tonight: The Roy Brown Story

John Broven

Blues Unlimited #123/124 (Jan./Feb./March/June 1977)

Roy Brown became one of R&B's first stars when his recording of "Good Rockin' Tonight" hit the charts, twice, in 1948 and 1949. In this illuminating interview, conducted in Los Angeles on June 22, 1975, Brown not only told his personal story but also threw much light on the post–World War II black music scene, including the independent record labels, the talent business, and music publishing. Brown described his early days leading up to his time with De Luxe Records, when he became the hottest property in the nation; then came his decline with King, followed by a temporary revival in the rock 'n' roll era with Imperial and his rediscovery in the late 1960s.

Roy Brown.

Well, John, I'm sitting here with your book [*Walking to New Orleans* aka *Rhythm & Blues in New Orleans*] and writings [for *Blues Unlimited*] and I'm a bit flattered, really. It takes me way back, all the old goody goodies, you know.

I was born in (Kinder), Louisiana, September 10, [1920].[1] Most people think I'm older, because my first record was in 1947; I was only 21 then. My mother was a choir director and organist; her name was True Love Brown [née Warren] and she was of Algonquin Indian and Negro extract. My father, Yancy Brown, was a plasterer and bricklayer [born in Opelousas, Louisiana] and we traveled quite a bit in those days. I remember we left New Orleans following my dad's work into a little town called Eunice, Louisiana. I attended elementary school there, a great school, and I had aspirations of becoming a singer. I did most of my singing in the church at that time.

I organized a spiritual quartet when I was only 13, and I recall we were doing some original tunes. I had written the spirituals; I had a knack for writing, I guess. It was a gift. I recall one night we did a thing called "Satan's Chariot Is Rolling By." Man, oh, man, I had about, I guess, six or eight ounces of blackberry wine, and my boys and I we got in the church and we started to sing. We started doing things we'd never done before. The sisters started clapping their hands and patting their feet. They were shouting, "Amen! Amen!" and we had them rolling, you know. I was so very proud, because my mother was there.

When I got home my mother didn't say anything on the way home. We had to walk about a mile and a half back to our residence from the church. When I got home she said, “Okay, so take off your clothes.” I knew what that meant. That meant a whipping, because she didn’t get to me often. But there was a peach tree growing at the front steps and she said, “Get out of your clothes and get me a few limbs.” I said, “Mama, what did I do?” She said, “I’m gonna teach you to jazz up spirituals.” I said, “What do you mean, ‘jazz.’” I didn’t know what she was talking about. She said, “That wasn’t a spiritual you were singing. I don’t know what it was, but it wasn’t a spiritual.” And she just ripped me apart.

But I guess at that day and age I had the rhythm, you know, and I got it from her. She was a singer. I think that was what you might call my inception of doing rhythmic things.

I really believe blues is a natural derivative from spirituals, because I can recall them, I can hear things now. I mean, what catapulted Ray Charles to fame was things other quartets had done in the church; Ray merely substituted lyrics. I recall his “I’ve Got a Woman,” that was a spiritual: “(There’s a Man Going Around Taking Names) It Must Be Jesus.” I used to sing it myself. What I’m saying is there is a very close relationship between spirituals and rhythm and blues and some aspects of jazz, too. But I really believe that the black artist, most of us—the late Dinah Washington, for instance, and I could just go on—we began our singing careers in the church, you know.

Sugarcane Fields, Louisiana

Then I worked in the sugarcane fields. I didn’t hear any blues there, only spirituals. This was out of Eunice. The cane fields were in the neighboring towns, like 25 to 40 miles away: Morgan City, New Iberia, places like that where the farms were. I’d go out there, I’d follow the harvest: I’d do the sugarcane when it was the time for sugarcane; I’d do the rice fields when it was the rice harvest; I’d pick the cotton, chop the cotton, do those things. I was paid about a dollar and a half a day, which was a lot of money at that time. I was very, very thin. My mother used to look at me and cry sometimes, but the doctor said, “There’s nothing wrong with him, he’s gonna be a husky guy.” Anyway, I could hear guys down the fields singing: *“I’m cutting this sugarcane, I’m cutting this sugarcane, I’m cutting this sugarcane, I’m cutting this sugarcane, / For the man, for the man upstairs.”* You know, stuff like that, and I’d hum along with them. But I kept going back to my room, making notes, and putting down things, like little phrases. I’d start rhyming things, then I’d start humming to myself. I was always a little ashamed to be singing the stuff I was getting together around the country because they would kid me, you know. But later all these things became embedded in my subconscious mind, I suppose. They started coming out later, because when I started recording, everything I did, I wrote it myself. So that was the days of harvesting, the farms. It was hard work, but all the other guys were doing it and I didn’t want to be a weakling. I did it too, raw hands sometimes, but it was a living. There was nothing else to do.

Amateur Nights, Los Angeles

My mother died when I was 14, and I didn't want to live anymore, you know. I finished high school in Houston, Texas, and I started to work and I wanted to sing. When I was 17 I journeyed to the West Coast, Los Angeles, and I turned professional fighter for a while. I had 18 pro fights; I won 16, by the way. I was a weight of 143 pounds; I was a welterweight. I could hit, because I came up in the cotton fields and sugarcane fields. I had developed strong arms, but I couldn't stand the sight of blood. It nauseated me. When the opposition discovered this fact, they would give their boys ketchup capsules and if the fight was going my way they'd just bite down on the capsule—let what appeared to be blood trickle down the side of their mouths. I'd just keep away from them, and I'd lose the fight. So my manager said, "Get out of it before you got killed, because it's not for you."

So then I entered an amateur singing contest right here in Los Angeles on Third and Broadway at the Million Dollar Theater. At this time I wasn't singing the blues, mind you. I was imitating [Bing] Crosby; he was my favorite singer, still is. I had two songs: "San Antonio Rose" and a thing called "(I Got Spurs That) Jingle, Jangle, Jingle."[2] Well, I did those two songs and I won first prize.

I was behind with my room rent at a hotel on Main Street. I was paying $2.50 a week and I was six weeks behind. As a matter of fact, they had evicted me. But I would slip up the fire escape and sneak into my room and get up real early in the morning, make up my bed the best way I could, and sneak out down the fire escape again. When I won this first prize—it was $60, man—I made a beeline to the hotdog stand; I set up my boys with hot dogs and chili and root beer. I went to pay my rent and there was a Chinaman in the hotel, he was afraid to take the money. He said, "Where did you get this money, you must have stolen it." So my boy said, "No, man, he won first prize singing." "Him, sing?" Well, I still had some scars from the fight game, you know. Anyway, I paid him off and I bought a couple of secondhand suits. I got a telephone directory and started singing at all the theaters that had amateur nights—and I started winning first, second, and third prizes. This was in Los Angeles in 1945.[3]

Shreveport, Louisiana

After I entered the amateur contests and won a few prizes, I went back to Houston, Texas, to be inducted into the services, but due to my flat feet they rejected me. During the next few days I went around the clubs and a guy from Shreveport came. He wanted an emcee and a singer. I had learned a few more songs, some of Crosby's hit tunes like "Star Dust," "Temptation," "Blue Hawaii," "South Sea Island Magic," stuff like that—crooning, you know. So [the guy] said, "Hey, here's a Negro who sounds white, perhaps you'd be a novelty for my club. Would you like to work for me?" I said, "Sure." He said, "How much money do you want?" I said, "How much do you pay?" I would have been satisfied with about $50 a week. He said, "$125 a week." I said, "Let's go!" I stayed at that club at Shreveport for about nine months. It was called Billy Riley's Palace Park; it was a big ballroom, there was a big ball part. It was away from Texas Street and Fanin, which were downtown. It was my first big real job.

That was my start, that's where I first learned to sing the blues. The first blues song I ever learned was Buddy Johnson and Ella Johnson's "When My Man Comes Home" and Billy Eckstine's "Jelly Jelly."[4] I started singing those songs because the other singers on the show were doing the blues, and the people were throwing their money—dollar bills. [The singers] were making pretty good tips.

[What happened was] my buddy, my drummer, says, "Look, man, you've got a voice. Why don't you sing some blues?" I said, "I don't like the blues, I just won't sing 'em." So he said, "You gotta learn some blues to make some extra money." So then I learned some extra songs and I went from there. My backing was drums, tenor saxophone, guitar, and bass. We used four pieces at that time, the Eddie "Coot" Lewis Combo;[5] they were elderly men, there was nothing more than what they were doing. I was doing "Temptation," "When They Ask about You," "That Lucky Old Sun," that kind of stuff. They were just playing music, that's all. I hadn't developed my shouting or crying style yet, because I was doing a Crosby [act]. This particular club had a big show, reminded me of the vaudeville. We had all kinds of acts and I became a favorite there. I was very happy, you know. We had all types of clientele: whites, blacks. They had me singing the Crosby things and I enjoyed it. It was the biggest club in Shreveport.

Galveston, Texas

I did very well there and later the club burned down. Then I went from Shreveport to Galveston, Texas. I got a job with Joe Coleman's group; they used tenor, guitar, piano, bass, and drums. We played orchestrations, all the hit tunes on the hit parade at that time. I did all the songs: Ink Spots impersonations, I did Frank Sinatra . . . all that stuff, no blues. I stayed there at this particular club for four months. Then I went into a club called the Club Grenada, where I organized a group. The club was run by a woman named Mary Russell; at that time she was the vice queen. She had everyone on the payroll, I can say that now. She had the mayor down on her payroll, the police commissioner; she had houses of prostitution, everything.

We had the top group. As a matter of fact, my group was the first black group on radio in that area; KGBC, I think it was.[6] My theme was "There's No You," a Crosby thing.[7] But I wrote a tune called "Good Rockin' Tonight" and we added a trumpet player to the group; his name was Wilbert Brown, and when we did our radio show he sang "Good Rockin' Tonight." I did all the ballads. One particular day of the broadcast he had an attack of acute indigestion, and "Good Rockin' Tonight" was on the cue sheet, it was on the program. [We were] on the air, he just sat there and toppled over in his chair, but the broadcast had to go on. So then the announcer said, "Here's Roy

Brown and His Melodeers and his new original 'Good Rockin' Tonight.'" The piano player looked at me and I gave him a signal to give me a shuffle rhythm in F and I started singing. Boy, the fellas looked at me; they wanted to laugh, because I started shouting. The announcer, the typist, they all came to the glass screen, they looked in to see who was the new singer. We got telephone calls after the broadcast, "Who was the new singer?" They didn't associate my voice with the falsetto-type thing as compared to my baritone, you see.

At the club that night, they wanted the new singer to sing "Good Rockin' Tonight." So my trumpet player had recovered from his indigestion and said, "Man, I'm not gonna sing it, it's your number." I said, "No," and I wouldn't sing it until the boss made me sing it. So then I stayed there awhile. The other members of the group, besides Wilbert Brown, were—my guitarist's name was Clarence Ward; the drummer's name was Rip Marshall; my pianist, which was a schoolteacher, was Joel Harris;[8] and my bass player was A. D. Adams. We also had a tenor player, Joe Johnson, he was a bad tenor player.

I didn't smoke anything, you see, didn't even drink. I didn't know what whiskey even tasted like until I was about 26 or 27 years of age. That's the truth. I used to drink blackberry wine, because my mother and my aunt used to make it for me. But I remember one particular night, Joel Harris, the pianist, and myself, we were the only ones that didn't smoke pot. A. D. Adams, the bass player; Rip, the drummer; Clarence Ward, the guitarist; little Joe Johnson, they sat up there and all smoked pot. These girls from Mary Russell's house would come in . . . and would say, "Roy sing!" Some of them wanted the Ink Spots stuff, "If I Didn't Care," Frank Sinatra's stuff, "Lovely Way to Spend an Evening"; and I would do all that stuff. We would go upstairs during the intermission; we had a kitty, see. During the intermission the people would give us the money if we gave them the pot. We made money on the kitty because everybody there was into vice. You had your gamblers, your pimps, your prostitutes; you had your bookies; you had everything. They'd come in and in those days if you made $50 that was money; and we used to take away $40 or $50 apiece, each of us, as kitty money. Joel and I had the money, [the others] would have the pot.

So one night we were having a jam session. There was a singer called Paul Love who had a beautiful silvery voice; that guy could sing, he had a voice. So the band said, "Hey, Paul Love's coming, he's coming to knock your head tonight, you better get high, man." I said, "I can take care of business." So they said, "But if you get high, man, you can get in the groove." So I told 'em, "Okay." So I went upstairs. I smoked this stuff, I choked, I coughed, I cried, but I got high, man.

I remember everything I was doing, but I came down the stairs, saw the jukebox, I saw all those beautiful colors; I'd never seen anything so beautiful. I was looking at all these beautiful colors and everybody was cracking up; the word had got around that Roy Brown—they called me Brownie—Brownie was high. I remember going to the bandstand, got to the bandstand, grabbed the mike. I was doing the Ink Spots number “If I Didn’t Care” and my voice sounded so beautiful. You see, we played 40 minutes on and 20 minutes off. I sang “If I Didn’t Care” for the entire 40 minutes. The people were just cracking up. The piano player was looking at me and everybody was smiling; I thought they were enjoying it. It sounded good to me.

In comes Mary Russell. She comes in cussing, “What are you doing up there? Come here!” I came off the bandstand and I said, “How do you do?” She said, “Get that silly grin off your face.” She really liked me, though; I was like a son to her. She slapped my face and said to Bill the bartender, “Take him home.” So Bill said, “I can’t leave.” There was a bunch of sailors in the club. She said, “Brownie, you gotta go home. Call him a cab.” So Bill said, “A cab’s standing just down the street.” It’s about 1:30 in the morning. I didn’t want to leave; I wanted to wait for Paul Love. I’m singing good—well, I thought I was sounding good. She put me out the door. It was 1:30, nothing on the street. I’m afraid to cross the street; I didn’t want no car to hit me. So she came out, took me by the arm, and got a cab. I remember falling asleep across the bed. It was the first time I smoked pot.

We stayed at this Club Grenada a long time until I left there. (*laughs*) If you don’t mind me saying this, I had an affair with my boss’s girlfriend and they caught me. Well, I thought they had, but they didn’t. I left Galveston running, and I went back to New Orleans.

New Orleans

There, I looked in the newspapers and saw two ads; one was advertising Cecil Gant. Do you remember Cecil Gant, “I Wonder”?[9] [The other ad was for] the late Wynonie Harris. Cecil Gant was at the Dew Drop Inn and Wynonie Harris was appearing at Foster’s Rainbow Room.[10] Well, when I was at high school I used to attend the [Houston] Auditorium dances when Wynonie Harris was singing with Lucky Millinder. During my high school days I’d go and hear him, and I’d always say if ever I was going to be a blues singer I’d like to be like that guy. He was flamboyant; he was a good-looking guy, very brash. He was good and he knew it; he just took charge. I liked the style.

When I was in New Orleans I had one suit and there was no bottom in my shoes—I had cardboard. I didn’t even have a bus fare to the club. So I wrote out “Good Rockin’ Tonight” on this brown paper sack and I took it to Wynonie Harris. He took an intermission and I said, “Mr. Harris, can I speak to you?” He said, “Yes, what is it?” I said, “I’ve got a song,” and he said, “Oh, not another one of these songs.” I said, “Yes, I want you to hear it,” and he said, “Don’t bother me, son,” and walked away.

You know, Wynonie Harris, before he’d get on the bandstand, man, he’d walk into a bar and shout, “Here comes Mr. Blues!” Everybody would look and he’d say, “This is Mr. Wynonie Harris, the drinks are on me, get to the bar.” He was wild. He’d jump off the bar and say, “Man, I’ll eat you up!” He was like that. He’d get beat up, but he wouldn’t do those things; he didn’t mean no harm.

Now, you talk about conceited: I thought I was conceited, but this guy . . . he did it in a jokey way. He was billed as Mr. Blues and he was. He and Joe Turner would be on the same stage; he'd make Joe Turner look like a fool. He'd walk up to him and say, "What you gonna sing, fat boy?" Joe Turner couldn't read or write, and Wynonie would say, "Sign this autograph."

I originally wrote "Good Rockin' Tonight" in Galveston. I really don't know what the inspiration of the song was. Words start forming in my mind and melodies. I'm not the type of composer who sits at a piano and finds a chord and what have you. I can read notes, but I can't play. All of my notes are formed in my mind, it's just a talent, I guess. I can't explain it. Anyway, this "Good Rockin' Tonight," it just came to me and I thought it was quite funny because it had Deacon Jones, Elder Brown, and Fanny Brown and all that stuff in it.

When I tried to give this song to Wynonie, I didn't know anything about copyrights. He could have taken the song if he desired to. So he wouldn't take it. During an intermission, the musicians were very jealous of him because he was good-looking guy and he was flamboyant, as I said—and he had all the pretty girls. So they were looking for someone to cut him down. So they said, "Hey, boy, can you sing that song?" I said, "Yes." So I got to the mike, started singing this song, and everyone came around the bandstand. I guess it was different: the voice wasn't that exciting, but the words . . . it was a funny song, a novelty, you see. The guys started clapping their hands, and one guy said, "Hey, man, come with me, I know a guy who will give you a job, perhaps." So he took me down to the Dew Drop Inn, where Cecil Gant was appearing. Cecil Gant had me sing the song, and during his intermission he took me to the telephone, he called De Luxe Records. He called Jules Braun, who owned De Luxe Records [with brother David in Linden, New Jersey]. He woke him up at 2:30 in the morning and had me sing "Good Rockin' Tonight" over the telephone. Jules said, "Hold on to that kid. I'm gonna be down on Wednesday to record Annie Laurie and Paul Gayten. Has he got a place to stay?" I didn't have a place to stay, no food. So he said, "Give him $50, and don't let him out of your sight."

So sure enough, I was very happy. I knew who Cecil Gant was; I idolized those guys. But I was very hurt that Wynonie wouldn't accept it. So Cecil said, "You fool, don't you go around giving songs away, there's a lot of money in publishing." I didn't think much of it. That was on the Monday morning after the Sunday night, so Cecil gave me $50 and gave me a room at the Dew Drop Inn. There were rooms upstairs, and he kept an eye on me, wouldn't let me out of his sight.

Cecil Gant, he was an individual, he was a beautiful man. He's an original. There has never been a Cecil Gant before his time and there never has been one since. A lot of us artists have been imitated, but nobody has been able to imitate Cecil Gant. He sang—he was a heavy drinker, and whenever he sang he was very heavily under the influence—and he did everything from his heart and soul, as if he was pining about something, reminiscing about some sad occasion. He did "Put Another Chair at the Table" and "I Wonder." I remember those things, I was a youngster. He didn't have a sensational voice but he had something in that voice, something catchy, a heart-throbbing thing; he made you feel what he was trying to convey to you. He was terrific, he was beautiful, he was responsible for my career, I can tell you that. If he hadn't made that call to Jules Braun, I probably would have been trying to write for other artists and I wouldn't have gotten started perhaps. He didn't play the piano well, but he played. In other words, he was the kind of piano player for his singing as B. B. King is with his guitar and singing.

The next act was on Monday night. They called it Blue Monday and Cecil had me get up and sing this song. [Herman] Lubinsky from Savoy Records [of Newark, New Jersey] happened to be in the house and he approached me. He said to me, "I'd like to record you," and I was very excited and said, "You would?" He said, "Look, I'm gonna give you $150 right now. I'm at the Jung Hotel." I said, "$150?" We were earning $25 a week. That was a lot of money. He said, "Yes, but I want you to sign a contract; you sit right here and I'll be back." But he didn't come back; he gave me a $100 bill, two 20s and a 10, and he didn't come back.

De Luxe Recording Sessions, 1947–1949

So then Wednesday, Jules Braun came. Cecil Gant got hold of me and Jules Braun said hello to me, took me up to his hotel room, and he talked to me and said, "Look, I want you to get me three more songs. Can you get me three more songs by next week?" I said, "I can get them to you anytime you want." "No," he said, "I want three more good ones." I went back to my hotel room and wrote "Miss Fanny Brown," a thing called "'Long about Midnight" and "Lolly Pop Mama," which was the flip of "Good Rockin' Tonight." So the very same day I called him and said, "Mr. Braun, I have the other three songs." "Oh, no, son," he said. "Not this quick, they gotta be pretty good." I said, "Well, I think they're good." So he said, "Okay, you come down to the studio tomorrow, I'm gonna record Annie Laurie and Paul Gayten."

So, sure enough, they liked the songs, I did them. Now, we had microphone problems. The piano player [probably Walter Daniels] had a mike at his piano, the horns—the reed section and the brass section—needed a microphone. There was only [mono] at that time, no four and eight tracks then, you know. So I got in a stoop, I squatted at the piano and I sang all those songs in this position, while squatting using the piano's mike. I did "Good Rockin' Tonight," "'Long about Midnight," "Miss Fanny Brown," and "Lolly Pop Mama." He liked them and he had me do some more. The band was just a studio band—well, Bob Ogden's band; he was a drummer. They did a very good job, they did the arrangements on "Good Rockin'"—I merely sang the song. They supplied the introduction, it was an all-together thing: the trumpet player [Tony Moret] did the introduction; the tenor player, Earl Barnes, he composed the riffs. It was a good rockin' thing, you know, and, man, I just started singing. The guy said, "Just sing the words," and I did—and I felt real at ease.[11]

On my first recording session, and I didn't know this, but on that session we made the first fadeout record there was ever made. Well, we faded out on "Lolly Pop Mama," and I didn't know that until a lady came out and said Roy Brown made the first fadeout record with "Lolly Pop Mama" in 1947 at J. & M. Studios in New Orleans on [North Rampart Street].[12] It was unintentional. I was singing: "*I got a big fat mama, she calls me her lollipop [x 2], / When she starts to lovin' she never knows when to stop.*" I was singing, "*bye, bye, bye, bye,*" then I really started feeling it and the band started coming in, so they just kept playing. But it was too long, so they had to fade it out; it was too long, but we had just started rocking. The guy said, "Hey, man, I like that," but we didn't do it over. We didn't plan it that way. Wynonie's "Good Rockin' Tonight" was the second fadeout, but Wynonie walked out the studio. The guy said, "I want you to do what Roy Brown and the guys are doing on the end," but Wynonie said, "To hell with Roy Brown, to hell with you," and walked out the studio. So they just had to end it, "*Hoy, hoy, hoy, hoy.*"[13]

We recorded at J. & M. Studio, then later Cosimo's [Recording Studios, on Governor Nicholls Street]. I tried to give "Good Rockin' Tonight" to the guy who owned J. & M. Studios [Cosimo Matassa]; he didn't want to bother with it. I think he just didn't want to take advantage of me. He knew I didn't know what was happening. The studio facilities were very primitive, but let me tell you something. We got a sound out of those studios that we couldn't duplicate. Cosimo, after J. & M., built a small studio; he got a very beautiful sound. Then later he made a lot of money and built a very modern studio [Jazz City Studios on Camp Street]—nothing, no sound.

Blues Twins with Clarence Samuels

Now, at this time I met Clarence Samuels, he was very talented. I think he came from Texas, I don't know [actually Baton Rouge]. But he had a kind of gruff voice, it wasn't a pleasing voice. He could sing, but he didn't play any instrument. He had a strong, powerful singing voice, but it wasn't pleasant to listen to. We were working at the Down Beat club in New Orleans for Freeman Harris; I was getting $4 a night. Clarence Samuels, his wife, and me had a little room: furnishings and a table. We had a piano player and a drummer and we were billed as the Blues Twins. His wife was selling tickets, putting them in a cash register. I never knew how much, they never had printed tickets. I was supposed to get $4 plus a percentage, but I never got the percentage.

So when my "Good Rockin' Tonight" hit the radio, it came out on a Tuesday, the fellas came and picked me up from my room in a pickup truck and took me to Rampart Street. I could hear this sound and they kept looking at me, and I kept looking at them. They said, "Man, don't you hear the record?" I said, "Yeah, it sounds good." I didn't know it was me, I didn't. So we went to the Down Beat club. Boy, everybody was playing the record and then I realized it was me. Man, I stood by that jukebox all afternoon just listening to me sing.

That weekend, you couldn't get in the place. The admission went from 75 cents to $2, then Freeman took over. He said, "I'm gonna pay $8 a night." I said, "Really?" He said, "Clarence, you work for $4." [Samuels] said, "I can't." He said, "Well, I don't need you. This man's got a big record." So Clarence said, "Okay, I'll work." [Freeman Harris] gave me $8 a night. I didn't know what was happening. On the Friday night it was a heck of a thing. When he got ready to pay me he said, "I'm gonna give you an extra $2." I said, "$10?" He said, "Yeah, and you can have that room upstairs, that's your room. I want you to move from Hamilton Street, bring all your things here. You're gonna live with me now." I said, "Thank you, Mr. Freeman." I was getting $10, my own room, I was a big shot—all the girls I need and my blackberry wine.

That Saturday night, the next weekend, a man named Mr. Washington came to me. He said, "Son, you Roy Brown? How'd you like to work for me?" I said, "I got a job." He said, "How much do you make here?" I said, "$10 a night." He said, "I'll pay you $50 a night," and I said, "Yeah, I'm President Truman, too!" He kept following me around, saying, "I'm serious. If you think I'm lying I'll bring your contract 'round to your room. I'll give you a $100 advance and send you down to Parnell's tailors and get you some clothes." I said, "Okay." So I gave him the old address where I used to live on Hamilton Street. The man went there. I didn't plan to be there, there was a cleaners next door, so they called me and said, "Hey, man, there's a man here with some money and a contract, Mr. Washington. He's got a club uptown." I told him to stay there, I'll be right there. So I called a cab and went by there. I went back to my room—the lady had rented it out—and he lay $100 on the bed. He told me he wanted me to sign a contract for $50 a night Friday, Saturday, Sunday; [that is] $150 a week, my room free, my meals free—he had a hotel. And I signed.

Now he sent me down to the photographer to have some pictures made. They put my picture in the *Louisiana Weekly,* put the ad, "Roy Brown appearing." Man, I went up to Freeman's place, the Down Beat, got my clothes, and his wife sent for me: "Somebody wants to see you." I figured it was Freeman, I wanted to get away. So he came and said, "What is this?" He'd got the paper, "What do you mean? You're working for me." I said, "Yeah, but I've signed a contract, the man's paying me $50 a night." "I'll pay you $50 a night." I said, "You didn't pay me $50," and that's how I left the man. That's when I realized there was some money in show business. He was paying me $8 with a $2 bonus and I thought that was something. But that man paid me $50 a night and we just turned back the people. That's when I started to form my band. It was called the Starlight Club, and I had my room upstairs. When I signed with the New York agency [Universal Attractions] that's when we left there with my group, we hit the road. We were together then. We had a lot of fun.

In the meantime this guy came to New Orleans with Dinah Washington. I had "Good Rockin' Tonight" going. I hadn't left to play any dates, this is after Wynonie Harris and I had the Battle of the Blues. He brought Dinah Washington to Foster's Rainbow Room, and Paul Gayten, Annie Laurie, and I were at the Robin Hood, and we just killed them. So this guy, he bribed me, he said, "You come and sing." I said,

"No, I can't do that." He said, "Well, you come and emcee the show." I said I'd do that, so he advertised me in the paper. It said, "Dinah Washington and Roy Brown," and people came over there, too. They made me sing and the guy at the Robin Hood [probably owner Bennett B. Ross] got angry. He gave me a bad time.

So then this guy said to me, "I want to take you to California." I said, "No, man, I'm not going to California." Clarence Samuels, he and I had worked together as the Blues Twins, and he knew my songs and he could sing something like me. So this guy Goldberg takes Clarence Samuels from New Orleans out here to California and passed him off as Roy Brown.[14]

So he gets to the Down Beat club and Simon—I forget this boy's first name[15]—he and I went to high school together in Houston. We worked together because I was singing for a band after the Shreveport thing and he knew me. He went up to this guy at rehearsal and said, "Man, are you Roy Brown?" He said, "Yes," and he said, "You're not Roy Brown. I know Roy. We went to school together." So then they had to pay him to keep him quiet.

When he got to Oakland, California, now, there's a big record store, a chain of them, called Music City.[16] Well, this guy was married to a beautiful girl, and during this time she was coming down to New Orleans and we were seeing each other. The guy found out about it and he could never get hold of me, but he got wind of it. She had gone from Oakland to New Orleans, running around the different places with Roy Brown. So this guy, Clarence Samuels, does a radio show. So this guy and his wife were sitting down having dinner and they said, "We have Roy Brown in the studio." "Well, Roy Brown, how're you doing?" "Well, fine." "Well, you got a big record." "Well, thank you." So he takes his wife by the hand, puts his gun in his belt, and he goes to this radio station KSAN. I'm not sure what it was, but he had to come down the stairs, and when he came down this guy accosted him. He said, "Are you Roy Brown?" "That's right, you heard the new record?" He cocked his gun, then the girl said, "Hey, wait a minute, you're not Roy Brown," This guy said, "No, ma'am, I'm not Roy Brown. Look, I'll show you my driver's license. My name is Clarence Samuels." He looked at him and said, "What you mean parading around as Roy Brown?" He said, "I can explain it." So he looked at the girl; he was about to shoot the guy. So I was glad I didn't go when I discovered that. I was glad.

Hot in the Charts

At that time King had Wynonie Harris, and as I said earlier, he didn't want "Good Rockin' Tonight," he wouldn't touch it. But after I did it and it became a hit, he covered me and for a while he outsold me.[17] He did it on King Records, because King was a big company and Wynonie Harris was a big-name artist. De Luxe was virtually unknown and so was I. In certain areas, especially the East Coast, Wynonie Harris just went haywire with the record, until later I did a little thing called "'Long about Midnight" [no. 1 race, December 1948] and began to get some stature as a singer.

Then my "Good Rockin'" started selling all over again. So it came twice, and once you become a name it's easy to sell records, you become hot. That's what happened to me.

So, sure enough, I started to sing the blues and—would you believe this?—the first 16 releases made the "top four" in rhythm and blues [charts]. In 1949 I had four tunes in the Top 10 simultaneously. I was very happy about that: "'Long about Midnight" was a hit; "Rainy Weather Blues" was a hit; "Rockin' at Midnight" was a follow-up to "Good Rockin'"—that was a hit. "Please Don't Go" was just a fair record. "Boogie at Midnight" was one of my biggest records; it went to the white kids for the first time, the first time I sold to the whites.[18]

Bootlegged

This record I made in Texas [back in 1947], let me tell you about this. This guy railroaded me, he bootlegged me. During the time we were performing on the bandstand, I'd seen these guys around with tape recorders, I thought nothing of it. But the guy [Bill Quinn] had a company called Gold Star, and when De Luxe Records started releasing records on me, I became a star, so to speak. This guy released something on me that sounded terrible.[19] I was on tour and went through some part of Texas and at this service station they were selling records, on Gold Star and Roy Brown. One of my boys brought one out to the car, and my wife [Gertie] said, "Honey, when did you record for this company?" I didn't even know who they were, and I discovered this guy who was in Galveston, Texas, had taped some stuff on me and later on, when I became famous, he released the stuff. I never recorded for him, that's how that happened. He just caught us live, it was very crudely done. But if you're a big name almost anything will sell while you're hot. It's a funny thing. The public is fickle, but once you become a big name they will buy almost anything, and that's how that happened.

"Rainy Weather Blues" on Miltone, let me tell you something about that, man. That was a steal. There was a guy here, his name was Whar Perkins, he was in the bootleg business. You'd be surprised what they were doing to De Luxe, [which] didn't have a wide distribution. When they were doing that stuff I don't think De Luxe Records were even doing the West Coast. My records appeared on the Miltone label, Gold Star, and another label that began with a "J."[20] I never heard of the label before, and I'd have people bring records to me and autograph, I said, "Where'd you get these records from?" I'd buy these records and send them to De Luxe.

A guy would come through and say, "I've got the Roy Brown new record!" The store would say, "I'll have it. Give me 50, give me 20," and he'd say, "You sell 'em, get a dollar for 'em, keep a quarter, give me 75 cents." And they'd sell 'em.

Disc Jockeys

During the '40s it wasn't difficult to get a record promoted, because if you had something saleable—a record with potential sale—disc jockeys at that time, especially rhythm and blues, because they were competing with each other, they wanted to play the new things, because they wanted this recognition from the fans: "Hey, I played this first, I broke this record in this city, this is my thing." If the artist came to that particular city, the record company made sure the artist was on this guy's show. Naturally, if the record artist was willing, he'd put 40 or 50 bucks on the guy, to make sure when he left that record would be played again and his next release would be played.

I had a gimmick: When I went into a certain town sometimes I'd give the disc jockey money just out of gratitude because they were playing my records. Once you become a hit artist you don't have to worry about your records being played. But what I'd do, a lot of disc jockeys are glamour boys, and in a lot of instances there wasn't a lot of money in disc jockeying, except if you were the big boys. Rhythm-and-blues disc jockeys made about 80 or 90 bucks a week, that's all. That's why they were always trying to do little record hops on the side, to help out. What I'm saying is this: I would go to this guy's house, meet his family, I'd go to the corner grocery store and give the man $100, make him give me a receipt, I'd go back to the disc jockey's wife and say, "Listen, for the next four weeks you can buy $25 worth of groceries. Make sure your husband plays that Roy Brown record." Brother, you'd believe me, he was gonna play that record, because every time he sat at the table he was eating some of Roy Brown's food. That was my own idea, and the disc jockeys thanked me for it. I had the wives on my side.

Now, I'm not condemning the South, it's a way of life with those people. Some of my best buddies are the white guys, because they did things and they didn't know why they did it, they were taught that way. What I'm saying, there was a war going out there. The black disc jockeys were competing with the white disc jockeys and a lot of the black disc jockeys. The white kids were listening in when their parents weren't around, they would listen to the black stations. They'd park their cars outside the radio building and listen, they couldn't come in; some would peek through the windows. We'd see them on the outside dancing, but they couldn't come inside—you had cops patrolling the area, no mixing.

B. B. King was a disc jockey [at Radio WDIA] in Memphis, Tennessee, and I went through Memphis in 1949 and I had a thing called "'Fore Day in the Morning." B. B. had a 15-minute show and it was his theme song. He would open his show by singing my "'Fore Day in the Morning." I met him and talked to him, he was such a beautiful human being, he still is; he liked me. I said, "Listen, I heard you today, I was about five or ten miles out of town. You sound good. You should record." So he did and he did a thing called "Three O'Clock in the Morning" [in 1951].

On the Road with the Mighty Mighty Men

Let me say this. I'm very proud of what happened on the road. I recall my very first date at the [War] Memorial Auditorium, Nashville, Tennessee. We had a sellout crowd. I was booked for $400 with a guarantee of 50 percent over $800 [in takings]; I took out over $2,500 that night. I just couldn't believe it. I just didn't think there was that much money for entertainers. But I had "Good Rockin'" going for me, "Lolly Pop Mama"; both sides were going. [De Luxe] had released "'Long about Midnight," which was a sensation for me and they had never seen me or heard of me. They liked the style, I guess I was different; they liked the songs. The people came out to hear me and I went on from there. We set records all over, like, Atlanta, Georgia; Charleston, South Carolina; Indianapolis; Denver, Colorado. I mean, I played every state except North and South Dakota. Anyway, I was very big on the road. There were 31 days in a month and I was doing 25 to 31 one-nighters. My band used to ask me, "Can we get a day off?" It was just how popular the records were.

In the South they roped off the audiences. I can remember when I set attendance records at certain places; they would have the people roped off or the blacks sat upstairs and the whites downstairs or vice versa, that kind of stuff: Louisiana, Georgia, the Carolinas, Texas, Mississippi, Alabama, Kentucky, even. We had to play those places. Where else was there to play? But now things are different, because when I was making hit-selling records, the white kids weren't buying records as they are now. I can recall when they were called "race records" and the whites down South wouldn't even let a black artist's record into their homes. But all that's changed.

In Los Angeles we used to do a regular thing—'50, '51, '53, '54, '55—at Wrigley Field, always used to do it with Nat [King Cole] or Billy Eckstine or somebody like that. I opened the new Richmond [California] Auditorium. The 5-4 Ballroom—it's no longer there—was rather big. It took about 1,400 to 1,600 people and they did big broadcasts from there, too. I remember one night I was doing a [song], they took it off the air, it was too suggestive; Jimmy Nelson used to do the booking there. I also played the Savoy on Central Avenue, and I did some shows for [promoter] Art Laboe; I used to do the Elks Club on Central.

I had a good group, I didn't do it alone. I had a group, my buddies from New Orleans. My star was Leroy Rankins, he was my tenor player. We called him Batman because he flew around with that tenor sax; he walked the tables, he walked the bars, he climbed the rafters. And I had Teddy Riley, the trumpet player—he was my bandleader—he was very good; Frankie Parker was my drummer, he was very good; I had Louis Sargent on alto sax; I had Tommy Shelvin, which is in L.A. now, on bass. I had a kid called Edward Santino on piano; I had guys like Billy Eckstine try to get him away from me, but he wouldn't leave—they offered him all kind of money. We only had six pieces and then later I started using guitar, because at this point I hadn't become as guitar conscious as I am now. My main thing was the tenor sax, that was my main thing. I'd even go for the rhythm, the heavy beat, because I guess I was a bit conceited. I wanted to be heard over everything. I wanted my voice to stand out; you know how youngsters are. I guess people sort of flattered me and built up my ego, and I was conceited, believe me.

Anyway, I had that type of band. I took them through dance routines just like you would a chorus line, all of our hit tunes; the guys had phases they'd go through, certain clothes they wore. Like when we opened a theater like the Fox in Brooklyn, or the Apollo in New York or the Howard in Washington, the Royal in Baltimore, they'd say, "Here's Roy Brown and the Mighty Mighty Men!" and everybody just ran on the stage, just ran out, with a big smile. When they said, "Mighty Mighty Men," nobody in the group except me weighed more than 140 pounds. All of the guys were little; they were nice-looking guys, they were well dressed. If they had a red jacket they had red shoes, if they had a blue jacket they had blue shoes; and when they'd come out we'd go right into one of our hit records. When we started moving, the people started moving with us, and we did that throughout the night; nobody got lazy. When the people left and we came back a second time, they'd say, "Oh, man, this cat was good, I'm gonna be back." That's what does it, you gotta give something good.

I never did anybody else's songs, except if it was a ballad. I used to do Billy Eckstine or Frank Sinatra songs to get loosened up: I used to like "A Cottage for Sale," which Billy Eckstine did, "I Apologize," "Jelly Jelly;" and I used to do "Summertime," Frank Sinatra's "Day by Day" and "A Lovely Way to Spend an Evening." I liked those kinds of things. I did "That Lucky Old Sun," "When They Ask about You"—I'd still like to record that. We used to jive it up and people would be frowning up and say, "I thought you did the blues," but they didn't know I was warming up. Then I'd get into the blues.

You may not believe this, during a night's work I'd sing from 25 to 30 to 40 songs. I can recall when my band would hit, I used to watch the audience. If my band hit and they weren't buying my band, I'd take the mike. If my band hit at nine o'clock and played a set until 9:15 and they weren't moving an audience, I'd sing from 9:15 to 10 o'clock and I would have to change clothes four or five times. I've lost as much as 15 pounds in one night.

But I put it back on; I used to eat like a dog. I remember when I first married my wife [in 1951], the first engagement I took on I had my valet Jesse Johnson order my regular meal: two whole fried chickens, two double orders of French fried potatoes, three bottles of Jax beer. I did a movie for Jax beer once and I started drinking Jax beer. . . . Now, if I eat three pieces of chicken a meal that's a lot, but I'm down from 228 [pounds] to 195.

I bought a brand-new limousine Cadillac for the band, and I bought a brand-new Ford van for the uniforms and instruments. I bought a brand-new station wagon in case they wanted to bring their wives and girlfriends along, and I had a Fleetwood Cadillac for myself. This was all showing off, I guess, because I paid $700 to $800 cash for the limousine in Richmond, Virginia, and I bought the station wagon in New Orleans and I had four drivers. My payroll was $565 a night. I was averaging $1,000 a night, but a lot of people went to commissions.

Battle of the Blues with Roy Milton

The Battle of the Blues, it used to be a popular thing; it could be popular right now. You'd be surprised how many people who know about us guys, who have the records, they would advertise us.

Roy Milton and I used to play the Battle of the Blues for this man [Eli] Weinberg. We'd play 30 or 40 or 50 dates within a six weeks' or two months' period, he and I. Now, Roy Milton had a great organization, he had a great band; his members were just old men, they were immaculate in their uniforms. He had this girl, a hell of a singer with him [Camille Howard], and all of his things were done so smoothly. He had a certain sound; he was a good drummer. We kept together and played these dates. One night he would close the show, the next night I would close the show.

I remember one night we got to Charleston, South Carolina, and Roy [Milton] had a date. It was his night to close the show, and when I say close, we played four hours. If he closed, I opened. I played from 9 to 10, he played from 10 to 11; I played from 12 to 1, he played from 1 to 2. This particular night [his date] was like a goddess. She was tall, about five foot nine, beautiful wavy curly hair; she looked like a Creole, but she wasn't—she had some Indian in her. She had on a long gown. So Roy just came out of the shower, with his robe on, and he and the girl had a drink; they embraced. Now Roy's not too tall, she was looking down on him. It was kinda funny. So I came in, I put on my robe, I said, "Roy?" He said, "Yeah?" I said, "They tell me you wanna talk with me." He said, "Oh, yeah, Roy Brown, I want you to meet my lady." I said, "Roy, this is your daughter?" He said, "How about you let me open tonight?" I said, "No, indeed. There's thousands of people out there tonight, you're the star, you gotta close." I know why he wanted to open, he wanted to get away with this chick, you see. But I wanted him to close and give me the last hour with this lady. He said, "I'll open for you anytime." I said, "No, when we first came, you made it clear to me that on Monday nights on opening, you wanted my band set up because sometimes my band got a bit late, a bunch of youngsters, you know." So, anyway, he went and got the promoter. "No," I said, "it's his turn to close."

New Orleans R&B Talent

I can recall when Fats Domino played with us. We had some dates in Kansas City in [1950], and Fats had started to record, but he hadn't come into his own yet. Something happened to my band coming out of Atlanta, and they were supposed to meet me in Kansas City, but they couldn't. So I hired Fats Domino and a few more guys. We got to Kansas City, I guess, at about two o'clock in the afternoon. We all got rooms, cleaned up, and took a nap. We got ready to go to the auditorium, and Fats Domino couldn't find his shoes and they had stolen his shoes. He wore expensive shoes, his feet were bad. He was such a great fella. So we had to get a guy get out of his bed, open up his store, and buy Fats a pair of shoes. I'll never forget that. That was at the time he'd done a couple of things, but they hadn't hit yet. He was just hanging around New Orleans doing nothing. I gave him some money.

I can also remember some of the other New Orleans artists who started along with me: Lloyd Price, there was this boy they called the Frogman [Henry], Danny White, Smiley Lewis, Paul Gayten, Annie Laurie. I hired Chubby Newsom, she played a lot of dates with me; she upped my attendance because she was such a beautiful girl. I recall Professor Longhair, Dave Bartholomew, quite a few guys; a lot of talent came out of New Orleans. Frankly speaking, the girl who impressed me was Annie Laurie, [she] could really sing.

Hard Luck Blues

But it was all a big thrill. It was something I was very grateful for and I was excited about it. If I went into a bar, into a cafe or post office, people would say, "That's Roy Brown." And the darnedest thing, I'd get into every town—and I hate to say this—it seemed that every seven or eight records was one of my records coming up. This is true, I was just that hot. I guess at that time there were not a lot of great, established rhythm-and-blues artists. There were guys like Joe Turner, Wynonie Harris, T-Bone Walker, those guys were ahead of me, but at that time I had brought something new on to the scene—a new style, a fresh thing—and the youngsters were latching on to it.

I had at this stage, my downfall; this was 1950, when King Records bought out my contract from De Luxe, all my masters; I had no say in the deal.[21] Then they had me sign with Ben Bart of Universal Attractions booking agency, 2 Park Avenue, New York. My personal manager was Jack Pearl, who handled Dinah Washington, Eddie Vinson, all those; and my recording company was Syd Nathan, King Records. Syd and Ben have both died since. But I didn't know my personal manager, the head of the recording company, and the booking agency were brothers-in-law, and, brother, let me tell you something: They cleaned me out. I didn't know what performance royalties were.

When Dave Bartholomew recorded me in 1957 he said, "Roy Brown, you should be a millionaire, but I don't think you are." I said, "No, I'm not a millionaire, I'm barely getting along right now, I had a lot of difficulties." He said, "All the hit records you made, man, you should have money in all the banks around here." I said, "What do you mean?" He said, "The performance royalties, your mechanical rights." I said, "What you talking about?" He looked at me, he said, "You must be crazy, who's your manager?" I said, "Jack Pearl." Then we went to Broadcast Music Incorporated [BMI], and they said they had never paid Roy Brown no performance royalties or writer's royalties, because he never signed a form. My manager had all the forms, he never gave them to me; they were taking all my money.

King were very big, they had their own distributorship, nobody distributed their records. They would rent offices, put their own guys in the distributor offices, they handled nobody's records but their own. They handled King, De Luxe, Bethlehem, and some other labels, but they didn't sell nobody else's records. Syd Nathan, one time, I'm told from reliable sources, had a record company from the back of his car. That's how he started out King Records. He became a multimillionaire; he made his money with the black artists.[22]

When you think about these guys, how they did it, I could tell you things. I don't like to discuss it, what these guys do to you; the artists weren't paid, they weren't compensated for. If you didn't make it on your one-night stands, your personal appearances, you didn't make it. I can recall a certain artist who had the biggest rhythm-and-blues record there was, he was appearing at the Paramount Theatre in New York and he got a royalty check for $500; it should have been something like $2,500. He got a royalty statement for $500, not deductions for what he owed the company. You'd be surprised some of your biggest names don't even read or write; they take advantage of this fact. When you get hep about it, they say he's a bad influence on the rest of them.

"Hard Luck Blues" is still my favorite. Remember that? *"Well, rocks is my pillow, the cold ground is my bed, / the highway is my home so I might as well be dead."* That was my favorite, and "Love Don't Love Nobody": *"Well, talk about love, it's a doggone shame."* James Brown did that, but he didn't sell it. "'Long about Sundown" was a very good one for me. It wasn't a big one, but it was a good one. "Big Town" was a big one; "Bar Room Blues" was big.

When I did "Hard Luck Blues" it was not my band. That was the Jimmy Griffin band from Norfolk, Virginia. They were in Cincinnati at the Mance Hotel and I was not due in for a recording session. But I had played Flint, Michigan, on the same night the late Duke Ellington was at the auditorium. I want you to hear this. I was at the armory, 30 miles away at Saginaw, Michigan. Joe Turner, Lowell Fulson, Pee Wee Crayton were a package. The promoters were fighting each other, but I had never been in the Midwest. A lot of the blacks had migrated from the Southern cities working in the sparkplug factories, the automobile factories. They had never seen Roy Brown, but they had a lot of my records. Would you believe, it was threatening rain, I called a cab to take me to the armory. We got a block from the armory, we couldn't get through, the people were lined up a block square. I said, "I'm Roy Brown, take me downtown, Duke Ellington is here," and he said, "Where you playing?" I said, "The armory," and he said, "This is the armory!" I said, "It can't be," and he said, "Just a moment." He had a spotlight on his cab, he directed the light to a telephone pole. He said, "Is that your picture? This is the armory." I jumped out of the cab, he said, "Hey, what about my fare?" So I came back, gave him $10 and told him to keep the change. When I got to the front entrance, my road manager—he was alcoholic at the time, he wasn't drinking anything—he was astride a big soap box, and the money was pouring in; they had run out of tickets, they had torn the tickets in half then quartered the tickets. Would you believe at 11:30, Duke Ellington came to my dance; about 12:15 Lowell Fulson, Pee Wee Crayton, and Joe Turner from Saginaw, they came to my dance. I went backstage. I cried like a baby, I was so elated, so happy.

So after I went back to the hotel, I gave my manager a $200 bonus, I gave everybody in my band a $100 bonus and I had over $4,000 left from my end on the coffee table at the hotel. I had never made as much in one night before. I started to think about my poor dead mother, how much I could do for her; I'd come into my own, you see. This is before "Hard Luck Blues," early 1950. And I canceled South Bend, Indiana; I canceled Terre Haute, Indiana; I canceled Fort Wayne, Indiana; Muskegon, Michigan. I told my band, my manager, "I'll meet you guys in St. Louis in four days' time." He said, "Where you going?" I said, "I'm going home," but I went to Cincinnati, because the tune "Hard Luck Blues" had formed in the back of my mind and it was lingering on me like a headache.

I took a plane that morning and I flew to Cincinnati. I phoned the record company and told them I was ready to record, but they said, "Hey, you're not due in here. We're recording Tiny Bradshaw and the Griffin Brothers and Margie Day." I said, "I want to record just one song. I gotta record it," and I was drinking—a bottle of scotch in one hand. I was crying, thinking about my mother. I was happy with the money I was making, but I could do so much for her now. My dad left her when I was a child. She was my sole supporter, put me through school and everything. Well, he said, "There's nobody here to record you. Have you got your band here?" I said, "No."

So I went downstairs, where the Griffin Brothers were rehearsing, and I said, "Man, I want to make a record. I'll give each of you men $100; I'll give the two brothers, Buddy Griffin and James Griffin (one was blind) $200 apiece." They said, "Man, we're with you, right now." So they asked if I had my music and I said, "No, you just play what I want you to." Everything I did, I give it them. I'd say, "Play this behind me," and they did. I went into the studio and recorded that one song, didn't hear the playback, and left. Because I was crying, didn't want them to see me crying.[23]

I didn't hear the tune until several months later. I was coming out of Atlanta, and the disc jockey played it three times. He said, "This is Roy Brown's latest, it sounds as if he's crying. He's singing from his heart." It was about my mother. It was my whole life story, how my father drove me from his door, wouldn't accept me. It was about my whole life. It was much longer, but they edited the thing and cut it down. But I wanted to do it and that's what happened to that.

Lucky Millinder did a session on me, he produced the session. On this particular session I did a thing called "The Return of Miss Fanny Brown," which was a sequel to "Miss Fanny Brown," and "Big Town," which was a very big record for me. Another thing called "I've Got the Last Laugh Now," that was a big record for me, and I think I did a thing called "Thanksgiving Day."[24]

Henry Glover was quite a guy. I did a thing called "Boogie at Midnight," it was one of my biggest records with King [De Luxe, 1949]. Henry Glover handled the recording session.

Songs and Royalties

I always selected the songs. They never questioned my ability as a writer, they would say to me, "Hey, you've got some open dates, we want you next month, we've got four days open. The booking agent has four days open, get some material together, rehearse it and go into the studio and record it." Whether it was in Cincinnati, or Philadelphia or Pittsburgh or New York, they never questioned anything I did. I'd just go ahead and do it, and they accepted it. Of course, my first [15] records were [hits], so that established me as a writer of some stature, and they never hassled over songs.

I made my name in '47 through "Good Rockin' Tonight," and I kept this status through '51 with records to "Big Town" [and "Bar Room Blues"]. Let me say this to you: nobody can last forever. I had reached the stage where some of my ideas were becoming what I'd call obsolete. All the other singers had producers, people who'd write for them. My record company, King Records, wouldn't let anybody touch me. They'd say, "No, you write, you record," because they knew if somebody else came up with material, they couldn't handle [the publishing of] that song. All my stuff went into their publishing [company] and they had me covered.

As I said, they wouldn't give me royalties. I hadn't gone through the proper channels. That's what you hire a manager for, to give you 10 percent of your income, to guide you through things. They wouldn't do it, they kept the money for themselves. Nothing I could do about it.

I get my royalties now because Dave Bartholomew, back in 1957, we went to his attorney and called George Miller. He's dead now, but he was vice president of BMI. [Bartholomew] made him send me the proper forms and now the royalties come to my home. I now get royalties from things I did way back in 1947, 1949, '50, '51.

Blackballed

I was looking at your book, those four hit records in 1949, all those royalties I should have had. When an artist would leave one company and go to another, the new company would call the old company and ask what's the most you paid this guy. "I gave him $3,000." You'd better believe it, he'd never get more than $3,000 from his big records and, you know, most of us didn't seem to mind. We just wanted the glory of it. "I'm an artist," you know, to be noticed by people and have all the choice of the girls, the Cadillacs, diamond rings. It's a whole new ball game now; they can't tempt you with that kind of stuff now.

They used to pay $10,000 for a Cadillac and make you pay $15,000. I recall Jack Pearl, my manager at that time, before I went to the union and they revoked his license. He had 10 percent of everything his brothers-in-law had, that's Universal Attractions [Ben Bart] and Syd Nathan, King Records. [The booking agency] included Dinah Washington, the Ravens, Ruth Brown, Bill Doggett, Eddie Vinson, Cootie Williams, all of them. When I spilled the beans to the union, they revoked

[Pearl's] license. They fined his brothers-in-law, made them pay big money, because they had been mistreating [the artists] and that's when they blackballed me. You'd be surprised how powerful certain organizations are. They can hurt you, kill you.

It happened in 1951. I had one of my biggest records, called "Big Town": *"I woke up this morning, I have the blues for big town [x 2], / I'm tired of the country, tired of all the people in the town."* That was a big one for me, but right after that was when I discovered they were robbing me blind. I went to my union and they fined all of them, and that's when they blackballed me. When I took them to the union, they sent letters to all the different promoters around the country that I had become a dope addict, that I had beaten up my wife and kid—I didn't have a kid at that time. I'm not a violent man, I don't even smoke, but that was the word that was out.

They booked me simultaneously in Florida and the Los Angeles area. I used to play from 25 to 30 dates twice a year for Cleo Brown out of Tampa in Florida. I'd play Ocala, West Palm Beach, Miami, Tampa, St. Petersburg, Orlando, all the towns. They booked me out here in California, Oregon, Washington [State], and told them three days before my appearance in Florida that I was in jail: I had beaten up my wife and they'd caught me with dope. When I did go down there a few months later to work the winter dates, [Cleo Brown] only had five dates and I asked him why. He said, "You don't know why? Then start talking to me." I said, "The dates you had me booked in, Mr. Brown, I was on the West Coast. My wife, I called her long distance from New Orleans, she just picked at random six or seven dates; we started matching dates, and the same contracts he had on me I was booked out here." He said, "Well, how can that be?" Then I told him what was happening; they were trying to hurt me—and they did. I became very confused. I was supposed to be a bad actor, that's what happens when you try to fight for yourself.

So I stopped recording, but the records I had done through '47 to '51, I still had name value.[25] So what I'd do, I'd book my own dates. I get out a map and maybe line up 10 or 12 little cities in Mississippi or Alabama or Louisiana, Texas. I'd call the club owner, and I would say, "Listen, I'm Roy Brown, I'd like to cover your territory." He'd say, "I can't buy you, I can't pay you." I said, "You don't have to pay me anything, I'll work for the door. I'll put an admission man on the door, I'll put up all the posters; I'll get the disc jockey 'cause of the radio time, I'll send a man out to promote. You sell your food, your liquor." He couldn't say no, because I would work Monday, Tuesday, Wednesday, Thursday, Friday. I'd charge a small admission, like Mondays through Thursdays I'd charge $1.50 or $1.75. But he couldn't refuse me, because Monday night would become like a Saturday night if he had an artist coming in.

So I would do that and this was how I made it, because I wasn't being booked anymore. This was my livelihood. I had to do this and this kept me going. I'd maybe book these towns in Mississippi for two weeks, and I'd let another week or two go by and set up another area, like maybe Alabama. I never went much further than Alabama, Texas, Louisiana, Mississippi; sometimes I went into Georgia, because Georgia borders Alabama. I did this repeatedly and I kept things going.

Musicians Union

The musicians union caused problems. They'd make you stick to all the rules; they don't give no quarters and don't ask none. The unions are a powerful thing. These guys know this, take advantage of this fact. They'd come around, man, and say, "Let's see your card." "I don't have it, must have left it at home." "Get off that bandstand!" Those kinds of things, [there was] no consideration.

They seemed to envy the musicians, the guys who're making it. I can recall in my hometown, New Orleans, my president used to get on to me: "Why don't you play some dates for us? You play dates for everybody else." I said, "I didn't even know you wanted me to play a date for you. I'll play a date for you, just pick your price." He said, "You gonna charge us?" I said, "Of course I'm gonna charge you." I'd book my own things. So they'd say to me if I booked a dance (I only had a six-piece band): "You gotta have 14 musicians." I'd say, "What do you mean?" "You gotta have another eight guys." "No, man, get them off the bandstand." They'd say, "You gotta pay them." I said, "I'll pay them, but I don't want them on my bandstand." The guys that came, they wanted to play with their chicks and girls. I said, "No, they don't know what we're doing, they don't know our arrangements." "What arrangements?" "My hit records!" They kept pumping me like that, they were angry, you know.

Rock 'n' Roll and Elvis Presley

Then came rock 'n' roll. I believe Elvis Presley, Pat Boone were very active in making this change. I remember Colonel Parker [Presley's manager] making the statement, "I believe the white kids want to hear the black hit records, but I'm gonna have a white boy do it." In other words, if you want to hear "Good Rockin' Tonight" I'm gonna have Elvis Presley do it. A lot of those guys did those things and copied the arrangements note for note, but that way it was accepted. What really happened, when these guys got on television, and do all these dances they had copied us from guys like the Drifters, the Little Richards. But we had never gotten the chance to perform before the white kids, and they thought all these guys, the Elvis Presleys, were original with that stuff. They weren't original. We'd been doing that stuff for years.

Elvis Presley, we used to play for the high sheriff in Tupelo, Mississippi, and my bandleader, my guitar player at the time, Edgar Blanchard, from New Orleans—he's dead now—he loved to drink. It was a dry town and Elvis would come around and Edgar wouldn't let him get on the bandstand. He wanted to sing, but he wouldn't let him. And so he discovered Edgar liked to drink, so he got him a big bottle of moonshine. When I went to the sheriff's house to change my clothes—I used to get drinks because I worked so hard—and Elvis was on the bandstand just playing and singing with them, nobody paying any attention to him, but he followed us: Tupelo, Indianola, Memphis. He went up to Tennessee with us, and on my West Coast tour a few months later Tommy Shelvin, my bass player, said, "Hey, man, there's a hillbilly singing your song ["Good Rockin' Tonight"]." Sure 'nuff, Elvis was singing this song with a hillbilly band, but he never did sell, because he hadn't become Elvis as yet, you know. But that was one of his first recordings [for Sun]. Then Pat Boone did it, Ricky Nelson did it, Wynonie Harris did it.[26]

Imperial Records, 1956–1958

Then 1957 came along and I got back on the beam with "Let the Four Winds Blow" and "Party Doll," and I started working again. Well, what I did, Lew Chudd of Imperial had tried to sign me during the time he signed Fats Domino. He said, "I can break your contract with King Records." I regret the day I didn't sign for him. I didn't know who he was, I didn't trust him. But what really happened, Dave Bartholomew came around to my home in late '56 and said to me, "What are you doing?" I said, "Nothing, just playing a few weekend dates." I was clearing 700 to 800 bucks a week playing the dates by myself, buying my own placards, paying the disc jockeys to advertise and giving him 10 percent of the door to emcee the show. He would talk about it and bring the people in.

So Dave said, "How would you like to record for Imperial?" I said, "Okay," so they signed me to a one-year contract with an open option. "Party Doll" and "Let the Four Winds Blow" were two of the tunes and I did well. I did [most] recordings in New Orleans: "Party Doll," "Let the Four Winds Blow," a thing called "Saturday Night," "Everybody." The group was the same group that backed Fats Domino. You see, a lot of the Fats Domino hits, Fats wasn't even on the recording session. There was a guy called [Edward] Frank, and he played [piano] exactly like Fats Domino, you couldn't tell them apart. They would make the [backing] tracks, and some of the tracks Fats would just go into the studio to dub over the tracks. But this same group, Earl Palmer was in the group at the time, he was still in New Orleans; Lee Allen, all these guys.

"Party Doll" was big [no. 13 R&B, no. 80 pop]. We did 80,000 on that one, then they took it out off the market; it was too suggestive. That was the thing Buddy Knox did and I covered it. "Let the Four Winds Blow" was a million-seller for me [no. 5 R&B, no. 29 pop], oh, yes. I stayed with Imperial just one year, because I had a tax problem at the time. You know, the income tax came down on me. With an artist, if you have trouble with income tax, the Internal Revenue has a right to confiscate the books of the recording company. And no recording company wants you to look at its books, because maybe he's not doing the right thing with his other artists and himself and the Internal Revenue. So they had to let me go. I can understand it, because I was a threat.[27]

Rock 'n' Roll Package Shows

The package shows, this was when I did "Let the Four Winds Blow" in '57. I was master of ceremonies of a package headlined by Mickey and Sylvia; there was Ray

Charles, Larry Williams, Annie Laurie, Nappy Brown, Joe Turner, Etta James, and one or two supporting artists. I made a deal for $1,700 a week as a single, no band. It was a big package. We were playing every night someplace, and the master of ceremonies out of New York, the guy who was going to have the job, he didn't show. So they said to me, "Roy, would you do it?" So I said, "Yes, for another $500." So they said, "Okay." I did it for two weeks, they paid. Then all of a sudden they started reneging. After the second week they didn't pay me my $2,200. I just quit the show in San Antonio, Texas. But I discovered this after I quit: they were selling the show for $3,500 upward and the payroll was only $2,300 a night.

How I discovered this, the road manager had a briefcase similar to mine. One particular night in Charleston, South Carolina, he picked up my briefcase and I picked up his. When I got to my hotel to open my briefcase to get out my scotch—I kept the scotch in the briefcase—it had all these contracts in it. So I started looking through them. Then I discovered what was happening and I said to him next morning, "Hey, man, I got your briefcase." He said, "I know, I know. Did you go through it?" I said, "Yes, I went through it, I know what's happening. I want more money."

The package was out of Universal Attractions. You see, most of these artists, it was really the Weinbergs out of Bluefield, West Virginia. Eli Weinberg, he booked from 30 to 40 dates on one artist. I filled a lot of his dates. He would get a big package together, book the package from the Virginias through Texas, and another promoter would pick it up in Texas through to the West Coast. The West Coast promoter would bring the package out here. What I'm saying is, they paid all the entertainers by the week; they guaranteed them a salary by the week and the payroll was not more than $2,300 a night. But they were selling the package from $3,500 a night and still getting commissions from the people on the show. You had to pay your commission because you were being booked. If you got $400, $500, or $600 a night, whatever you got, you still had to pay your commission. So they were making money all kinds of ways and I discovered this fact. So I wanted a piece of the pie.

"Lonely Teardrops" and Jackie Wilson

At this time, [late] 1958, I recall when Jackie Wilson did "Lonely Teardrops" and I heard him. Louis Jordan and I were appearing at a club in Jacksonville, Florida, and this disc jockey emceed the show. When I got in the hotel room at three o'clock in the morning he was on the airplay with "Lonely Teardrops." He had people calling in who were saying, "Who is this? Who is this? Roy Brown, Roy Brown?" A guy came to my door and said, "I heard your new record, man." I said, "I haven't got a new record, that's a kid called Jackie Wilson." I called King in Cincinnati the following morning, I said, "There's a kid singing identical to me. I want to cover that record, I can sound more like me than he can." But they wouldn't let me do it; they told me to stick to the blues, because they wanted me to write everything so they could take the money—not pay me money.

Berry Gordy wrote "Lonely Teardrops" [with Billy Davis] and tried to give it to me at the Flame Show Bar in Detroit. He said, "Roy Brown, I've got a song for you," because Berry Gordy, Mr. Motown, was playing piano with Maurice King's house band. I said, "Berry, I'm not interested." I didn't say it that blunt, but I just didn't dig it. When I heard Jackie do it, I recognized the song because Berry Gordy wrote the song and I think he also recorded Jackie. Anyway, Jackie got on the Dick Clark show a little later. I was asleep, my wife woke me up, she said, "Honey, Jackie Wilson is on the Dick Clark show." Dick asked [Jackie] who his idol was, he said, "Roy Brown. I can do anything he's ever done and do it better," and he was laughing. I said [*sarcastically*], "Oh, he's paying me a compliment, very good." But I'm very proud of the fact that I seem to have influenced a lot of guys, because I was just a youngster myself when I started out.[28]

Home of the Blues Records, 1960

Then there was Home of the Blues, oh, I forgot, it was such a small thing.[29] I did a few things for Home of the Blues in Memphis in 1960, and I had two things that went well. As a matter of fact, we sold 44,000 copies of "Oh, So Wonderful" in Memphis alone; it wasn't a blues, it was a rhythmic thing with a girl [Mamie Dell] and myself. We also did a thing called "Tired of Being Alone." It sold 27,000 copies in Memphis alone, but they didn't have the distribution outside of Memphis.

What really happened, a guy drove from Memphis to my home in New Orleans. They wanted to buy the [songwriter] rights to "Hard Luck Blues" for Elvis Presley. I said, "No, I don't want to sell."[30] When they got to New Orleans, I was appearing at a club and they contacted me and heard me sing. He said, "Man, you got this same voice all the time, why aren't you recording?" I said, "Well, right now, I'm between recording sessions." So then he got on the telephone and got hold of Ruben Cherry at Home of the Blues in Memphis, and they flew me to Memphis the next day and the third day I was recording.

It was Willie Mitchell's band; he was quite a guy. I can't recall the name of the studio, but it was on Union Street—the same street the WDIA radio studios were on. It was just a small studio, but the same guy we had on my session was Scotty [Moore], who did the early Elvis Presley things. Scotty handled the session.[31]

Door-to-Door Salesman

Then I went out of action for some time and started selling [household utensils for Amway products] out here on the West Coast. I did pretty well, because it was pretty easy to get into the doors, because what I did, I had a gimmick. I had a lot of pictures of me and I rang the doorbell and this woman would come and I'd say, "Ma'am, I'm Roy Brown the recording artist, I'd like to give you an autographed picture." It was always someone over 30 who remembered me. "Oh, are you Roy? Well, come on in."

Some people would buy. I sold encyclopedias also; I did well. Some weeks I'd do a $1,000 commission and, being a recording artist, I guess anybody could do it if they were as big a name as I was. A lot of people don't forget too easily, because they keep playing these records over and over again. Then they say, "I wonder what happened to this guy?" All of a sudden I've come into their homes. I had a ball, man, really, but that's not my bag. Singing is my bag.

Bluesway Records, 1967

The Bluesway thing came about through Lee Magid. A distributor, he died, I attended his funeral and Lee Magid said, "Roy Brown, I've been trying to find you." You see, my problem is I never get around Hollywood, nobody knows where I am. You see, I bought a home in the [San Fernando] Valley away from everything. I'm pretty independent. I guess it's a foolish pride, but I don't get around clubs, around the recording companies, saying, "Hey, I'm Roy Brown," because I got fed up with the record business. I thought everybody was crooks, I'll be honest with you. I just didn't think everybody was on the level, you know. They're still ripping people off right now.

But I attended this funeral and Lee Magid said, "Do you know who I handle?" I said, "No." He said, "I handle Lou Rawls," and I said, "So?" He said, "I'd like to handle you, if you can still sing." I said, "I can still sing." He gave me his office address; I went there in the next couple of days and he had a piano player there. He said, "I want to hear you sing 'Good Rockin' Tonight' again," and I did. I got through just a few bars and he said, "That's enough, I want to do some talking with you." So we sat down and he said, "Can you get me eleven or twelve tunes for an album?" I said, "Yes, when do you want them?" He said, "As soon as you can get them." So I wrote eleven tunes. He got two arrangers—H. B. Barnum and Arthur Wright—I didn't like the arrangements. I said, "Man, this is not Roy Brown. I don't hear that funky sound behind me." He said, "These are proper arrangements," and I said, "For whom? Not for me, maybe for Frank Sinatra, O. C. Smith, or Lou Rawls. I'm a different type of singer."

Anyway, we did it. I forget the guy's name who was head of ABC-Paramount [Larry Newton], but he was away in Europe, there were some youngsters in the recording company. Lee sent in this stuff by Roy Brown, they didn't even know who Roy Brown was. He did the session, they reimbursed him his money. He said, "Are you going to put this through my publishing company?" I said, "Okay." Just before the release they sent an album cover to me to show me what it would be like, and they had a publicity man call me long distance and ask me special things about myself to put in the liner work on the album. Then Larry Newton, I think it is, he came back from Europe and said, "Do you know who this man is? This man is Roy Brown, the recording artist. So this man is a writer, so how in the world could you let him let Lee Magid put all Roy Brown's tunes into his publishing company? We have publishing, too, you know. We want part of the publishing." Lee Magid wouldn't relinquish the publishing, and they didn't release that album [*Hard Times*] until about two years ago [1973]—I did it in 1967. [An] attorney called me and told me they would not release the album, you're with the wrong man. I tried to get away from Lee Magid, but he wouldn't cut me loose; he had me under contract. So my contract expired a short time ago. Now [in 1975] I've just signed with Jimmy Holiday, my producer.

Comeback

Then there was Summit Records. Like I said, a friend of mine, Miles Grayson, I was working out at Orange County, Santa Fe Springs, a little place called the Cat Patch, and he wanted to get into the record business. He didn't know how difficult it was, and I was sort of obligated to the guy, personal reasons. I said, "Okay, I'll do a session," but I knew he didn't know what it was all about. So we named the label Summit Records and I did a few things for him. I did a new version of "Let the Four Winds Blow" and it didn't even get to the radio stations. We didn't promote it, he just wanted to get off into something, you know. We didn't lose much money, but he got hurt some.

When you do a record these days the finished product is nothing. It has to be sold, it has to be promoted. Once upon a time you could take a record to a disc jockey, say, "Hey, man, here's $500, make it a hit," and he'd ride it. But it's not like that anymore. They tell you now, "Wait until it's in the Top 40, then I'll play it." How can you get it into the Top 40 if nobody will play it?

Then came the Monterey Jazz Festival in 1970. Well, it was the Johnny Otis Show; all of the greats were on that, man: Ivory Joe Hunter, Jimmy Rushing, Eddie Vinson, Joe Turner, Little Esther, Roy Milton, and myself. I closed the show and we really did fine.[32] As a matter of fact, this is what really inspired me to come back and produce my own recording sessions, and I did.

I did a thing called "Love for Sale" and Mercury leased it from me. It did quite well for me. I did that on my own label called Friendship Records [in 1971], and I got it started here in Los Angeles, Oakland, New Orleans, Memphis, Birmingham, and Philadelphia. It was really going, then [Mercury] picked it up. This was recorded in L.A. and on this particular session I used Miles Grayson's group—[he's] done a lot of the Little Johnny Taylor stuff. I don't know the names of the [musicians]: I had one guy on guitar, Johnny Jones, he used to play with me for quite a while, because I worked a lot in the clubs in Orange County; I stayed in one club for nearly two years. I paid Grayson to do four sides; he did two songs he wrote and I did two songs I wrote. When he did the songs he wrote, he said the band had to go and left me there with three musicians. I called up a girl to play piano and I kept my guitar player and had five musicians and did "Love for Sale." That turned out to be the hit record.[33] He did the other arranging. I've always arranged my own stuff . . . not putting the notes down, but humming the parts to the different musicians.

All that's behind me now: I've just signed with Jimmy Holiday, and I think he has a working agreement with 20th Century Fox. We're doing an album right now, the greatest thing I've ever done in my life.[34] You'll be one of the first ones to get a copy—you and Charlie Gillett.[35]

Looking Back

But I like to think back, and there were the good years and the bad years. But what I'm saying, poor management has been the downfall of many an artist, whether he's a baseball player, basketball player, football player, fighter, what have you—the managers make the money. It won't happen to me anymore, because right now I have my own publishing company. It's understood that some of these tunes are going to my publishing company.

If I appear at clubs, most people won't believe I'm Roy Brown until I sing. They think I should be older. I'll soon be 50, that's old enough, but by me getting started in 1947 that's way back, but I was only 21 at the time. I'm just very happy about everything, believe me; I've had some hard knocks. This record business is a dirty thing: It can be very good or very terrible.

You know, when I look back in retrospect, I was my worst enemy, because I allowed myself to be taken. But I had nobody advising, everybody was, "Yes, yes, you're right." I had nobody to guide me. But I'm very grateful to have what you might call a second chance, because I can name a lot of the guys who were popular when I was. Of course they're much older, their voices have gone. I'm still here and I'm very grateful. But I want everything to be right. I will never be a problem to anyone, because your attitude changes. I've got a beautiful family: I've been married to the same girl for [24] years come August 18, [1975], my daughter [Connie] is a straight-A student at school. She's a beautiful girl, very popular, just turned 16; she's crazy about her mommy and daddy. I've got a beautiful home, we're doing okay.

What I'm saying is, whoever handles me will have no problems, because there's nothing there to excite me. No glamour, the girls can fall dead if they like, the Cadillacs can go. I drive a new Monte Carlo, my wife drives a Chevron, I'm very happy—and that's it. I want some money and some holdings for my kid. I think God is on my side."

Postscript, 1977

Since this interview, Roy Brown's high hopes with Jimmy Holiday apparently have not materialized. However, he has a new manager, Barry Spinks, and Route 66 Records has just issued an album of his vintage recordings. Even so, I can't help but recall Johnny Otis's classic quote that I used in *Walking to New Orleans,* when he discussed not only Roy Brown but his contemporaries Charles Brown, Roy Milton, Eddie Vinson, and Joe Turner: "These men are national treasures and the way they've been treated is a national disgrace."

Notes

With thanks to Lynn Abbott, Andrew Brown, Stuart Colman, Winfried Freyer, Jeff Hannusch, Jan Kotschack, James La Rocca, Eric LeBlanc, and Darryl Stolper. Also consulted: Les Fancourt and Bob McGrath, *The Blues Discography, 1943–1970* (West Vancouver, Canada: Eyeball Productions, 2006).

1. In his interviews, including this very first one, Roy Brown consistently shaved five years from his age and gave the wrong birthplace. However, he was born on September 10, 1920 (not 1925), in Kinder, Louisiana (not New Orleans) and died in Lakeview Terrace, California, on May 25, 1981 at the age of 60. Birth details confirmed by Brown's marriage certificate dated August 18, 1951.

2. "New San Antonio Rose" was a hit for Bing Crosby in 1941, and "Jingle, Jangle, Jingle" was a hit for Kay Kyser and His Orchestra in 1942.

3. In view of the song years in note 2, it is possible that this amateur show was earlier than 1945.

4. "When My Man Comes Home" was a hit for Buddy and Ella Johnson in 1944; "Jelly Jelly" was recorded by Billy Eckstine with Earl Hines Orchestra in 1940.

5. Eddie "Coot" Lewis was active in the 1930s with his orchestra in Shreveport for dance promoter Isaac "Ike" McKinney (*Jazz Archivist* 22, 2009).

6. Radio KGBC first aired in Galveston on February 1, 1947.

7. "There's No You" was a hit for Jo Stafford in 1945.

8. According to Texas pianist Candy Green, Joel Harris claimed to have written "Good Rockin' Tonight," a fact that Brown vehemently denied.

9. "I Wonder" by Private Cecil Gant (Gilt-Edge) was a massive number 1 race (R&B) hit in 1945, staying on the charts for twenty-eight weeks.

10. The Rainbow Room was located in the Hotel Foster, owned by George Foster.

11. The first De Luxe session was comprised of just "Good Rockin' Tonight" (as "Good Rocking Tonight") and "Lolly Pop Mama" in July 1947. According to Paul Gayten, in an interview with John Broven in Los Angeles on June 15, 1975: "Roy Brown was a spiritual singer, he came to me at the Robin Hood, New Orleans, and he started singing. He could sing the blues great, the pop things great but he didn't have it all together, like bars, because he was a spiritual singer. So he had this song, 'Good Rockin' Tonight.' I sat down with him one night and I said, 'Roy, we're gonna have to do this in 12-bar things.' I showed him everything; he's a beautiful guy, he's here in L.A. He started singing 'Good Rockin' Tonight' and that was it—and I think Al Young recorded him. [Brown] was on De Luxe and he was working on the show with us."

12. Brown is correct: "Lolly Pop Mama" does fade out but very abruptly at 2:20; the full-length acetate master was released by Ace Records (U.K.) in 2005 but lasted only another 10 seconds (on the CD *Good Rockin' Brown*, with other 1947 De Luxe acetates). It is impossible to validate Brown's claim, via a third party, that this was the first fadeout record. Cosimo Matassa's J. & M. Studios was located at 838–40 North Rampart Street, not Tulane Avenue as stated by Brown.

13. Brown is correct again with the fadeout on Wynonie Harris's King recording of "Good Rockin' Tonight." It is another abrupt fade, but it is not possible to say if Harris "walked out" of the studio at that moment.

14. Hit R&B record artist impersonations were rife in this pre-television era.

15. Probably saxophonist Maurice Simon, who was born in Houston in 1929.

16. Almost certainly Brown is referring to Ray Dobard, owner of Music City stores and the Music City label out of Berkeley, California. Both Dobard and his wife, Jeanne, were from New Orleans.

17. Wynonie Harris's "Good Rockin' Tonight" (King 4210) was a Billboard number 1 race hit in a very long chart run of twenty-five weeks.

18. Brown was reasonably accurate in his De Luxe hit record analysis, given a "top of his head" interview situation. The Billboard race and R&B charts indicate he had fifteen hits all told (not 16) from 1948 to 1951. In the early 1948–1949 period, he had three records in the top three: "'Long about Midnight" (no. 1), "Rockin' at Midnight" (no. 2), "Boogie at Midnight" (no. 3). His "Good Rockin' Tonight," as Brown indicated, made the charts twice: number 13 in June 1948 and number 11 in April 1949. Other race/R&B chart hits in this time frame were "'Fore Day in the Morning" (no. 6), "Rainy Weather Blues" (no. 5), "Miss Fanny Brown" (no. 8), and "Please Don't Go" (no. 9).

19. The Gold Star release "Deep Sea Diver"/"Bye Baby Bye" was recorded in Galveston, Texas, in 1947 and was Brown's first. At that time Bill Quinn would not have had a tape recorder, so it is almost certain that these were authorized studio recordings featuring Brown's club band. Interestingly, Brown rerecorded "Deep Sea Diver" in the same year for De Luxe, but the acetate was unreleased until it appeared on a 2005 Ace (U.K.) CD.

20. Outside of De Luxe, the early part of the Roy Brown discography does not show any releases other than on Gold Star (one) and Miltone (two), and certainly nothing on a label starting with a "J."

21. For more on the King–De Luxe buyout in 1951, also the King branch network, see *Record Makers and Breakers* by John Broven (University of Illinois Press, 2009).

22. In the later King–De Luxe period, 1950–1951, the R&B chart hits were "Hard Luck Blues" (no. 1), "Love Don't Love Nobody" (no. 2), "'Long about Sundown" (no. 8), "Cadillac Baby" (no. 6), "Big Town" (no. 8), and "Bar Room Blues" (no. 6). All of these recordings are included in the 1991 Charly CD, *Blues DeLuxe.*

23. "Hard Luck Blues" was recorded, with the Griffin Brothers, on April 19, 1950. Despite Brown's comments, he did record three other tracks that day: "Cadillac Baby," "New Rebecca," and "Sweet Peach." There are no sessions by either Tiny Bradshaw or the Griffin Brothers and Margie Day (who soon signed for Dot) listed in the King logs for that day.

24. On January 16, 1951, Brown did record "Big Town" and "I've Got the Last Laugh Now." However, the other two sides recorded that day were "Good Rockin' Man" and "Wrong Woman Blues." There is no sign of "Thanksgiving Day" in Brown's De Luxe discography.

25. Although Brown had every cause to forget his time at King, he did in fact record for the label in 1952 through 1955, with another two sessions in 1959 but without any hits. A cross-section of recordings from this later King period can be found in the 1993 Ace (U.K.) CD *Mighty, Mighty Man!*

26. In 2012 the BMI song register showed "Good Rockin' Tonight" as composed by Roy Brown, with publishing by Brown Angel Music Publishing and Trio Music, indicating that Brown's heirs were benefiting from the song's considerable earnings.

27. The Imperial period lasted from September 26, 1956, through March 6, 1958. After recording in New Orleans during the first year, Brown had a one-off session in 1958 in Los Angeles with rockers Johnny and Dorsey Burnette. All told, there were twenty Imperial sides that appeared on a 1995 U.S. Capitol CD, *Roy Brown: The Complete Capitol Recordings.*

28. Of the many artists influenced by Roy Brown were notables such as Johnny Ace, Bobby Bland, James Brown, B. B. King, Little Milton, Little Richard, and Clyde McPhatter.

29. Home of the Blues, owned by Ruben Cherry and Celia Camp, was based at their record shop at 107 Beale St., Memphis, Tennessee, from 1960 to 1962. Although the label produced no hits, it had a strong artist lineup with Brown, including Dave Dixon (also from New Orleans), Willie Mitchell, the 5 Royales, Larry Birdsong, and Billy Riley. Interestingly, Brown did not mention the best of his four Home of the Blues singles: "Rocking All the Time."

Before signing for Home of the Blues, Brown hit a low point (not discussed in our interview) when he "was arrested by the FBI in February 1960 for defrauding a promoter out of $200 by impersonating B. B. King over the phone and trying to get him to wire him money in New Orleans." (Jeff Hannusch, *I Hear You Knockin': The Sound of New Orleans Rhythm and Blues* [Ville Platte, LA: Swallow Books, 1985.]) This incident was confirmed in a story headed "Nab Rocknroll Singer as Con" in the St. Louis *Argus*, on February 26, 1960, which noted, "If found guilty, he faces a possible fine of $1,000 or five years in prison" (courtesy Bill Greensmith). As well, Brown told Jonas Bernholm of Sweden that he "never completely cleared up his tax situation and served time in a federal prison." (Notes to *Saturday Nite* LP, Mr R&B Records, 1982).

30. This interesting incident implies that Elvis Presley was contemplating recording "Hard Luck Blues." At this stage of his post-Army career, Presley, through New York publisher Freddy Bienstock of Hill & Range Music, had enough clout to demand a large percentage of writer and publishing credits to record a song. If Brown and publisher Blue Ridge Music, associated with King Records, rejected the Presley offer, as Brown indicated, it was probably to their detriment. The intermediary is not known.

31. From Brown's description the session could have been recorded at Sam Phillips's Sun Studio at 706 Union Avenue. However, about the time of the Home of the Blues sessions, Phillips was in the process of opening his new Sam Phillips Studios at 639 Madison Avenue (near Union), where Scotty Moore was appointed as a salaried studio manager and chief cutting engineer in June 1960. (Colin Escott with Martin Hawkins, *Good Rockin' Tonight: Sun Records and the Birth of Rock 'n' Roll* [New York. St. Martin's Press, 1991.]) The new Phillips studio is the more likely location.

32. Brown's "Good Rockin' Tonight" was included in the Epic LP *The Johnny Otis Show Live at Monterey!* but was not recorded live.

33. "Love for Sale" did seem to make some noise but never charted nationally pop or R&B, even when on Mercury.

34. The 20th Century Fox deal never materialized, but the 1975 LP may have appeared on Brown's Friendship label in 1978. In the period from 1962 until his death in 1981, Brown also recorded for DRA, Connie (named after Brown's daughter), Chess (unissued), Gert

(named after Brown's wife), Tru-Love (named after his mother), AMFPR, Faith (another Brown label), Solid Smoke, and Intermedia. As well, there were the important Route 66 and Mr R&B LP reissues by Sweden's Jonas Bernholm from 1977 onward; the first album, *Laughing but Crying: Legendary Recordings, 1947–1959*, led to Brown's successful European tour in 1978.

35. Brown admired Charlie Gillett after the respected English author and broadcaster wrote about the 1970 Monterey Jazz Festival appearance in glowing terms.

PART VII

RECORD MEN

Henry Glover

When this interview with Henry Glover by a sixteen-year-old Steve Tracy was first published in three installments in December-March 1972, it was the first extensive discussion with Glover that had ever appeared in print. *BU* was always interested in exploring more than the lives of truly great but barely functional blues singers from the 1920s and 1930s and the related valuable history behind them, as the "moldy figs" would have it. The focus on King Records was a valuable impetus to many further reissue programs and subsequent research dealing with more contemporary styles of blues. Besides King's own repeated reissues on the King and Gusto labels—the earliest already under way when the following interview was done—reissues by Jonas "Mr. R&B" Bernholm on Route 66, Saxophonograph, Dr. Horse, and Jukebox Lil, and programs on Charly, and Ace followed, along with other scattered but important releases on Time-Life, Rhino, Westside, and Proper, and a massive Freddie King set on Bear Family. When Jon Hartley Fox's *King of the Queen City: The Story of King Records* was published in 2009, Fox gratefully acknowledged the importance of Tracy's interview and research in the book's preface.

In recent years there has been a concerted effort in Cincinnati, Ohio, to recognize the contributions of King Records and to preserve the site on which the company stood. With a board of directors that includes Honorary Chair Bootsy Collins and legendary King drummer Philip Paul and associations with the city of Cincinnati, Xavier University, and the Evanston Community Council, the campaign for King Studios has generated a development budget and has collected over one million dollars to date in its quest to establish a nonprofit educational and recording facility (for more information, or to contribute, contact info@kingstudios.org). The organization has also sponsored video-recorded educational events such as the "King Records Roundtable," featuring Dr. Steven C. Tracy of the University of Massachusetts Amherst, Philip Paul, Otis Williams, Dr. Christine Anderson of Xavier University, and Dr. David Purcell of Kent State University. Tracy incorporated elements of his interview with Glover into a chapter on King blues and R&B in *Going to Cincinnati: A History of the Blues in the Queen City* (University of Illinois Press, 1993). Although *BU* often eschewed what it called the "cold, dead, clammy hand of academia," its contributions are recognized by music, American studies, and African American studies departments that seek authoritative information in the fields of blues and R&B.

After Henry Glover left King, he produced LPs for Muddy Waters (Grammy winner), Paul Butterfield, and Levon Helm, and helped arrange horn charts that were used in the Band's concert and film, *The Last Waltz.* He was honored by the National Academy of Recording Arts and Sciences and inducted into the Alabama Jazz Hall of Fame in 1986. Henry Glover died in St. Albans, New York, on April 7, 1991. Of the major musicians about whom he spoke in the interview, Freddie King died in 1976; Roy Brown on May 25, 1981; Bull Moose Jackson on July 31, 1989; Sonny Thompson on August 11, 1989; Bill Doggett on November 13, 1996; John Lee Hooker on June 21, 2001; and Lula Reed on June 21, 2008.

—Steve Tracy

King of the Blues: The Story of a Record Label Henry Glover Interview

Steve Tracy

Blues Unlimited #88/89 (Jan./March 1972)

I interviewed Mr. Glover in a place very familiar to him: King Record Studios in Cincinnati, the place where he had his first job with the company. Times are hectic these days for him. When I met with him he was looking over some masters and getting ready to fly back to New York. He rushed in, finishing off his lunch, remarking that he's "been running late for the past five years!"

Well, Steve, I'm giving you this information. My name is Henry Glover. I am now vice president with Starday-King Records. I am a resident of St. Albans, New York, which is about sixteen miles from New York City proper. I've lived there for seventeen years—eight years before that I lived in Manhattan with the family. I was associated for some time with King Records; now known as the Starday-King Records Complex. Syd Nathan gave me a job back in the early '40s as his artist and repertoire director, and I was perhaps the second black man to ever have an executive position with an independent record company in the United States.

The first was a gentleman called by the name of Mayo Williams. He was connected with Decca Records. He was responsible for some of the very early blues discoveries. He had quite an active catalogue at Decca with blues artists.

I finished college in '43. Did graduate work in Lane University between '43 and '44 and went with a band called Buddy Johnson. After Buddy Johnson I played with Tiny Bradshaw, an artist I later picked and recorded for King—about eight or nine years later. He was dead and I brought him back to life again. I did the same in the case of Lucky Millinder. He came up with a couple of hits between "I'm Waiting Just for You" and some of the others. I came through Cincinnati with the Millinder orchestra and Syd Nathan came to see Millinder and I about making some records. Millinder couldn't do anything himself,[1] because he had to live up to the terms of his agreement with Decca. He did let Bull Moose Jackson, Panama Francis, Sam "The Man" Taylor record, and later the saxophonist by the name of Burnie Peacock. Out of all of us in the band, Bull Moose Jackson happened to be the lucky one to come up with the hits!

Bull Moose Jackson was the first successful rhythm and blues artist King Records had. Of course, in those days we referred to them as race artists. Trade magazines listed them, and, ah, had them in this special category—race records. Bull Moose was a saxophonist with Lucky Millinder's band, with whom I was very friendly. Dear friend of mine, and that was the arranger and first trumpet player with the orchestra. We first met Syd Nathan in the hotel where he came and said he was forming a record company. I had a record company and he wanted some sides. The early sides on many of the R&B artists were cut in a studio downtown called the Herzog. I don't know whether they're still there or not. Bull Moose Jackson's first side with King was what they called in those days, and what we still refer to as, a "cover." Joe Liggins had a song out by the name of "The Honeydripper," and we tried to duplicate it as close as possible.[2] His band was known as "Bull Moose Jackson and the Buffalo Bearcats," a name given him by Lucky Millinder, with whom he was playing at the time. His first very big hit was a thing called "I Love You, Yes I Do" that I wrote. After that we had a succession of big sellers, "All My Love Belongs to You," "I Can't Go On Without You," "Bowlegged Woman," "Little Girl Don't Cry," and he has a couple of things that were in sort of double entendre, like "Big Ten Inch Record" . . . As his popularity waned, of course, he had lesser records than the ones that I've referred to previously.

My duties at King in the early days were general. I did quite a few things. Syd was a very brave man. He was in the midst of building equipment. He and I designed the original echo chamber, and it was at King that one of the very first was used. We duplicated the system in our early mixing setup at the King Studio and it's still

Bernie Pearlman, unknown, Earl Bostic, Syd Nathan, Henry Glover.

existing. My duties were not inhibited only to the blues and R&B. I did many of the country and western artists like Moon Mullican. I did all of Moon's early recordings and Grandpa Jones. I recorded Cowboy Copas and the York Brothers. The Everly Brothers copied their style. Let's see, Boyd Bennett was one of the original rock groups. When I came with the company, he, like Ivory Joe Hunter and Lonnie Johnson, had hits out. Moon Mullican's country hit (and in those days just like they said "race records," they called the country records "hillbilly"), Moon Mullican had a thing out called "Jole Blonde," which was in the Louisiana dialect that Hank Williams made famous. Immediately after that we had a thing that Moon and I wrote together called "I'll Send My Ship Along at Today's Funeral," a country standard, it's in our catalogue.

As I said, I worked with Syd on many projects in the early days of the record company. Naturally, him putting together a pressing, printing, studio distribution complex, there were many things that you could do and you at the same time learn. I moved to Cincinnati in 1949 and stayed until 1950 in order to learn the basics of the recording setup—a rare opportunity not only for a black man but also for a white. I was taught the basic fundamentals of the business of music and the studio mechanics and such. So, as I said, it wasn't a matter of my experience with Syd or the company which is being tied down to the musical end. I've received great knowledge of the business end as well as the complicated copyright situation, licensing and publishing, which I'm still at.

Fortunately, I had a fairly decent education and I protected all of my songs with copyrights, and I own 50 percent of every song this company has ever recorded by any artist. I recorded and wrote for a company called J & C and in their catalogue are big hits like "Fever," "Twist," and "Drown in My Own Tears." I am at present waiting on the renewal term contracts so I can put them in trust for my children.

John Lee Hooker, with whom I had the pleasure of recording—conducting recording sessions—was very unique. He was extemporaneous in his creativity. He wrote songs as he played and his foot was his rhythm, and I believe that my amplifying of my recording—I put the microphone on his foot to pick up the sound of him patting his foot as he played—had a lot to do with the influence of this four beat that they use today. Of course with him trying to compose a song, play the guitar, and pat his foot all at the same time, it wasn't always the best rhythm you ever heard, but at least he would try his best to do it. My early experience of recording him, I used a 4 by 8¾" plywood board on the floor. He sat by that and put a microphone on the sound of his foot. We had very good sides by John Lee. I would say some of his . . . perhaps examples of his best. However, he, like others, was very poor and would jump at any chance to record for any record company that made an offer. Many companies had duplications of John Lee Hooker sides, because he would record for anyone with a dollar bill at the time. I don't think he has to do that now, because I understand he is still living and he's doing a great job. He is legend among the blues buffs and other people.

Robert Henry was a kid from Dayton who wandered into the office one day and made an audition for me. He was, he had to be unique for me to even think of recording him. He played the piano, the guitar, and the mouth harp and sang all at the same time. Not all at the same time, but he complemented himself with one or the other and such. One song that he had in particular, that I liked very much because it related to me, my knowledge of the old traditional, what we called country-folk blues. It sounded so authentic that that was my reason for recording him. I think the title of it was "Something Is Goin' Wrong with My Lovin' Machine." Some of his lyrics and expressions were so typical of the old authentic blues singers that down through the South years ago you'd see walking the street, playing for a nickel or a dime . . . sometimes they'd dance also.

Detroit Count? I don't know too much about him. I never recorded him, so I'd rather not go into that too much, but I do know he had a band and he would come in from Detroit to record. I don't know whatever happened to him—whether he became great. When I came with King Records, as the recording director in the late '40s, Lonnie Johnson was a blues singer-guitarist. I had known him for many years, because he had been in Detroit, singing in different clubs. One in particular was a club that the famous Joe Louis Sparks owned, called "The Three Sixes." Lonnie was what you would call a table troubadour and he would go from table to table playing and singing. There was another very fine artist at the same club at the same time, Bobbie Caston. Had a very fine version of—what was the tune? "God Bless the Child (That Has His Own)," and a couple others. They associated her styling with that of Billie Holiday, and they say she may have had some influence on Billie Holiday . . . Back to Lonnie . . . when I came with King Records, Lonnie had moved to Cincinnati and he lived over in Rockdale, where he had purchased a house—I don't know the exact address; it's near Reading Road. In fact, I was passing there the other day and it is one of the better-kept residences in that particular area. Lonnie had a big song at the time, "Tomorrow Night," and several others, but none racked up sales like his "Tomorrow Night."

I also recorded Roy Brown. We inherited Roy with a deal from a purchase of De Luxe Records, which was a Linden, New Jersey, corporation owned by several brothers—Jules and Dave Braun. I understand now that Dave Braund is very wealthy because he has gone into a lot of operations, as he did when the independent record business was in its infancy. He took advantage of that, and I understand that he had a lot to do with the origin of the slot-car track for kids, those little automated machines. He is a very brave man. He had several artists on the label with Roy Brown.[3] There was Annie Laurie, Paul Gayten, sides by the famous Billy Eckstine and his band, and the jazz artists like Benny Carter. However, we had more success with Roy Brown than with any others. Roy happened to be the composer of "Good Rockin' Tonight," the very big song that was instrumental in the success of Elvis Presley. Roy had recorded the song himself, but Wynonie Harris's version of it became the big hit that gave Presley the idea to record it. Presley copied many of the vocal gymnastics of Wynonie Harris as well as the physical gyrations, and he was lucky to pick up the one tune and make it a very big hit. We were restricted with our possibilities of promoting this song into realms beyond where we had it (i.e., the "R&B" market), because it was considered filth. They had a definition in those days of the word "rock" meaning the sex act, rather than having it known as "a good time" as they did later.

Roy Brown, however, did come up with very big records. Like many artists that had a series of things in those days, he sang songs about "Fanny," "Fanny Mae." Many songs now refer to "Fanny Mae." I think this particular origin of the name is in black folklore. They always refer to the hind parts as the "fanny." It was a sort of tongue-in-cheek description of a woman and perhaps how she looked—her shape or something. He constantly sang songs about "I want my Fanny Brown" and different things. Roy also had a very big boogie record called "Boogie at Midnight" that I wrote with him. We recorded it in New Orleans. The city of New Orleans had quite a bit to do with some of the early rhythm-and-blues artists. The Biharis from the coast with their different artists would come in to New Orleans and record various blues talents, and Roy Brown, Paul Gayten, Dave Bartholomew, and some of the others were instrumental in getting these artists together for these independent manufacturers. I will say that if Roy had been a guitarist, he would be as popular today as

B. B. King, because in those days Roy was bigger than B. B. King and people said that B. B. sounded like Roy Brown. But today you play some of the old records by Roy Brown and you'll say he sounds like B. B. King. He had one very soulful record titled "Hard Luck Blues" that had a tremendous lyric on it. I can't see why maybe some of the rock groups today who have gone back that far didn't pick up such a copyright and redo it, because it was so great. Some of the lines in it are fantastic—*"Rocks is my pillow"* and *"Cold, cold ground is my bed . . ."*

Again, I refer to the case of Robert Henry, how authentic these people were in that day, linking that era to the past that I knew something about, the early blues singers. I mentioned earlier, also, that Lonnie Johnson was a legend then. He was quite an old man when he died. I will say that Roy Brown was one of the finest soulful blues singers that I had the pleasure of working with and he is still living. I saw him a couple of years ago. He's in California. He still sounds good to me, and, I don't know, any day I may go and record him.

Jack Dupree is one of my very—well, one of my favorites, also. Well, I can say that about all of them. I say some of my best friends sang the blues. Jack and I were very close—he and his wife, Lucille, who he's written a couple of songs about. In those days we had her name in quite a few of them. In those days many of his songs were directed lyric-wise to her. Jack was an ex-fighter and his early name was Champ Jack Dupree. I understand he wasn't much of a fighter. He was a better piano player and blues singer. We made many records with Jack, but didn't have anything very big with him until a record was brought into my office recorded already by the name of "Walking the Blues." "Walking the Blues" was one of the very first basic, hard country-blues things that went into the pop market, if not the very first.

The content and message was so timely, because, I think that particular year, whatever year it was released, was one of the hottest summers we ever have had.[4] Of course the narration, the talking part, in "Walking the Blues" was Jack's story of walking along with a guy on a hot summer day, and he's telling him to slow down until he gets to thinking and he starts talking. Now, I don't know if "Tongue-Tied Blues" came before or after "Walking the Blues," but it was also another big record with Jack, but it didn't go into the pop market. In the black folklore they usually refer to speech impediments as a lisp or tongue-tied or tied-tongue and that was, of course, a person who had this particular impediment. Jack made a comedy thing or routine out of it. It was very successful on a couple of records, "Tongue-Tied Blues," "Stuttering Blues," and it was always referring to him telling his mother-in-law off, or talking about his wife or talking to her or such. He's a truly great artist.

Country Paul is an artist I found in New York City. His real name was Paul Howard.[5] He was a very sickly young man at the time. I would say he was in his early twenties when I recorded him, and in a couple of years he passed. However, we do have quite a few masters on Country Paul and we just released some with Ralph Willis.

Ralph Willis was one of the early greats, also. He was a guitarist. He played blues—the FM stations are picking this thing up now, Country Paul and Ralph Willis. We call it "Faded Picture Blues." His big record was "Your Picture Done Faded, You Left Hangin' on the Wall." I would say Paul died maybe around 1954.

The artist of all artists, ha-ha, Willie John. I didn't consider Willie John in the category of some of the artists I have just referred to, because he was in a class all to himself. He was a really, truly great singer. I would say that blues came so natural to him that he was just a master at that, and no one living during that day could touch him. He had some of the greatest blues gymnastics and voice gyration that you could ever dream of a person having. He was a typical rhythm and blues artist, egoistical. He, of course, became involved in drinking and some of the other vices that go along with the business. It seems as though some of those artists are the ones that perform better. The very nice artists don't make it. Willie John was a headache . . . I think his whole short life explained the same. He was involved with a murder and he served time and he died in prison—to commemorate that particular thing, we have an album out now called *Free at Last.* Both the artists and our art department came up with such a very fine cover, because they had the jail door open and it seems as though, like, whatever the hereafter was for him, his miserable soul was free.

He was going on to wherever guys like Willie John would go. I think his success was just written for him in the cards, like they say. Willie John came into my office, was brought in by a personal manager by the name of Allen. I heard Willie John at 5 o'clock, and I was so impressed with him that at 8 o'clock I had musicians in the studio in New York City and I recorded him. "All Around the World" had just been released that day for the first time and I heard it coming into work. I picked the record up, covered it, and changed the arrangement completely, realized what should have been in that record! At the same session I recorded "Need Your Love So Bad," which was also a big hit with Willie. After that we had many hit sides until we had the monster of them all with "Fever." I don't think, even with the pop versions of it today, it's very hard to top Willie John's rendition of "Fever," or the sound that we got on the musical track in our studio here in Cincinnati, where it was recorded. The bass is so prominent that it sounded like, in those days, a Fender bass. We were able to get all this, what we call modulation, on the record and made it quite effective. It had a lot to do with the sales, because it was a very big record.

Ivory Joe Hunter I knew, because, just as Lonnie Johnson, when I came with the company as a regular employee, Ivory Joe had a hit on the label called "Don't Fall in Love with Me." He had several others. We did a R&B version, which was perhaps the first of an R&B artist doing a country song. We did "Jealous Heart" with Ivory Joe and it was a very big hit. Peculiar to that record also, we had a jazz saxophonist, Eddie "Lockjaw" Davis, play the introduction.

Shortly thereafter we lost Ivory Joe, too, but we had many hits with him. We had a thing called "Waiting in Vain" and "Guess Who?" We had a special sound coming from Ivory Joe Hunter, and I would always make arrangements to catch the Ellington Band and use the men from the band to play behind Ivory Joe, so all of his records had the sound . . . Russell Procope, who's a very fine alto saxophonist, played some

Wynonie Harris, c. 1950.

of the leads. We had Ray Nance backup on some. We had Sonny Greer. We've used Tyree Glenn, many of the Ellington musicians. We lost the contract to MGM in 1950, and that's when he came in with this very big song called "When I Lost My Baby, I Almost Lost My Mind."

Wynonie Harris, without a doubt, is one of the greatest blues shouters. Sometimes you have to make distinctions between the sounds and types of blues singers. Now, Wynonie Harris was not a true blues singer, because he couldn't do all those tricks that Roy Brown or Willie John could do with their voices. However, he could do a shout, a blues shout.

Wynonie passed, I think, a year or two ago. He had songs that bordered on those that were selling in the popular market. We took country things and put them in R&B—like we had one called "Good Morning Judge"—it was an old country song, written by Louis Innis. We had another one with him that was very big called "Bloodshot Eyes," written by Hank Penny. Hank led a western band in Hollywood. We recorded it with him first, but it didn't sell. So we recorded it with Wynonie and it sold. Some of Wynonie's early songs were dealing with black life, Negro life; "Grandma Plays the Numbers" and themes relative to black life . . . he too used the word "fanny" quite a lot, because he covered a lot of Roy Brown's songs. They had sort of a friendly feud going with each other because they were both popular at the same time. I do recall in Columbus, Ohio, or someplace, they jumped up on each other's Cadillacs and banged the hoods off. The two of them, at the time, were making enough money to buy new ones the next day. They both are really great blues singers.

Earl (Connelly) King walked into my office for an audition. His name was Earl King. I think our first records were put out under the name of Earl Connelly, but we felt that the name Connelly was a little hard and you didn't have it right on your tongue, so we started to put "Connelly" in parentheses until we dropped it completely. It became just Earl King. His very big record was "Don't Take It So Hard." He was a very good blues singer based in the church, with which there is, of course, a very close tie. The line of demarcation is so thin that you can almost say that they are the same when it comes down to the soul part of a hymn. Earl was an artist like this. I had another artist at the time that was of the same class. A girl by the name of Lula Reed. I had many big hits with her.

There were not many unusual things happened at recording sessions, because I had a manner about me whereas that it was business and I conducted it as a business. There were musicians in those days who gave me more respect than they did other recording people, because I had a good musical knowledge that they respected. I was of a certain character that they were given respect by me and they gave me respect, also. I didn't allow drinking in the studio. Of course, today it's just so opposite. When you go in the studios everybody's smoking pot—every day, ha ha! In those days we ran a pretty tight ship to keep people as straight as possible at the studio. I felt that the creative mind sober was greater than when it was soaked with alcohol, or any of the other type of stimulants I hear about today. I guess that's why I place more value on some of the things created years ago. Today you run into the studio and you are taking a chance on the law of averages. It's not working out too much. It's taking the overall picture of the profit of music and trying to get something with an artist. To get an artist started just don't happen like it did before. No one is concentrating like we did in those days. So when you say a session, as I remember it, I can perhaps recall every session that I ever did—can almost name the musicians on the date. I even kept a format going whereas I would only use a certain sound for one artist and never duplicate in connection with another.

I find that that is one of the evils of today's recording. Too many producers feel that they can go into a studio with the same number, the same men on every artist, and create good records. They don't, because it's a oneness that goes along with the continual use of musicians and you cannot get away from it. It really puts the overall sound, the image of your recorded product, in a rut.

I remember, I can recall the first date that I did for Syd, for the company as an employee, as the recording director (1949). It was with Todd Rhodes, a piano player from Detroit. He had had a couple of records like "Page Boy Shuffle," but I came in and did a couple of instrumentals, "Teardrops," "Pot Likker." I was impressed with Todd's band because he had a couple of very fine musicians in it. This band read and, of course, I was just out of a band that read, and I could get more out of it than I could some of the others.

Country Paul would come into New York and I would record him at a studio called Rose. I think Tom Rose is still living. He was the son of the old man during the time we were on Broadway and 52nd Street. Country Paul was, like I said, sickly and he was very conscientious, however. He gave out with whatever he could do for you. 'Course, during the same time I had the idea going about the foot. Also, I had a microphone on a board or something and many of the record engineers in those days would laugh at some of the requests that I would make regarding something for him to pat his foot on, because it just wasn't being done. However, they would get it for me. As I was saying, one of the tunes that he did is his description of looking out the window on Broadway. Some of his lines that he sang that were sort of extemporaneous. He said, like, *"Look at that old boy sittin' in the street"* . . . just something to say. Whatever came up to him when he was playing. Of course today even James Brown uses that where he has a good instrumental thing and he has some talking that he will do along with it, to carry the interest on, you know, regarding the music and the beat.

I have many friends, and if they would wander into a club someplace and some of them would hear a group singing or an artist, they would call me and say I should go by there. That was the way Joe Tex was brought to me. I was in Miami for a convention and someone said I should go to a club called 12 of Hearts and listen to these two guys sing. I didn't know it was Sammy and Dave [Sam & Dave of Stax records fame]. Of course I had them with Roulette, not with King. The gentleman who just walked in was with Otis Williams and the Charms. I heard the Charms [for the] first time outside my window in the Mance [Hotel] in Cincinnati. They serenaded out the window for about four or five weeks, and finally (*laughs*) Henry Stone came to town and heard about that. I was so busy doing other things that I didn't have a chance to record them. He signed them up on a label called Chart and I recorded them for him. The very first record they did was a big hit; it was "Hearts of Stone."

I recall that night in the studio I used the same gimmick that I did in the case of Willie John. I had just heard about a record that had come out in California that was a hit. I can't even think of the group's name, but it was a thing called "Hearts of Stone." I had the record into Cincinnati so fast no one ever heard of the other group. We got the record out on the street before they ever got it distributed. Of course, the Charms had the big hit on "Hearts of Stone."

Every artist that I ever recorded had to be a favorite, otherwise I didn't record him. All of them were my favorites. We had various labels, of course. We had King . . . Federal . . . De Luxe, and even earlier, before we had King, we had Queen. There was a jazz label called Bethlehem. That was about all Syd was working with in those days. Later, of course, there came some others. Henry Stone had a label called Crystal, which later became De Luxe. We had some gospel labels. We had Glory and a couple of others. It was a matter of just printing the label for a record that was a hit. In those days all it had to do was just be a hit. We didn't care what label it carried.

Of course, I think I told you how I found talent. You know, someone would call it to my attention and I would pick it up. Sign it up myself. I had a batch of contracts in my briefcase at all times, which I don't do now. We pay lawyers who ponder over them for six or seven months and that's why we lose them. In those days you would just get a contract out of your briefcase and get it signed. If you got an artist, you recorded the next day. Today if you want an artist, you have to go through all the courts and the families and everything else (*laughs*), and it's best just not to fool with them.

King's plans for the future? Well, it's to continue to be in business. I am vice president of the company now, and of course we are aiming in the direction of audiovisual product (videotape). There are certain things about that that I wouldn't want to make any disclosures about, but we will be very big in the direction of audiovisual. We have physical plant facilities that will accommodate any area that we like to go into. It's a must. It's here. There's no need of people saying it's around the corner, because it is here. We have built at Nashville in the Starday studio, a very fine board that is compatible to the new quadraphonic sound, and we will be doing quad cutting here in Cincinnati and Nashville. We have a very fine engineer, Dave Harrison, in Nashville that built a board with the help of a genius down in Florida by the name of Geep Harnett. Many of our electronics that we have in both studios were purchased from Geep. We are also acting as distributor for his products. He is even going into manufacturing of tape decks and equipment to go with tapes that is made by Ampex and some of the other companies.

We have given big interest to the company going pop. Whether you go into what we call middle-of-the-road, whether you go into underground, whether you go into acid music, there is just so many different categories that it's hard and maybe not right for me to describe it as such, but I still believe it's going back to nothing but white music or black music. People who are black are going to buy black music. Many of the black artists ridicule white radio stations for not playing their product in order for them to get in the pop field. However, on many of the black stations you never hear any white records. I can't take sides with either case. I'm in the middle. I do believe it will always remain as it has in the past, where black people will buy black records and white people will buy white records. It is unfortunate that some of the mechanics of big publishing and the conglomerate domination of the business has caused certain black artists to have a different taste of what they record and such. In many cases there have been criticisms of the people in the black industry that are related to music or to the industry.

[There is] criticism about the black artist having to record Beatles' songs or other famous white writers' songs in order to get them played on the air. I heard the very comical description of that, saying that a girl like Aretha Franklin shouldn't be singing a tune like "Eleanor Rigby," because it doesn't have anything to do with the perpetuation of the black scene or black life or some of the other things that these people are striving for. Many black writers in New York are coming under these things because they have dominated the music business of their people for many years. The pop market, or, like, you might as well refer to it as the white, have taken the stronger things from it and used it over into their business.

But they weren't forced on it. I mean they didn't force their music on the white artist, but some of the writers, they feel that "Hey, Jude" is being forced on a guy like Wilson Pickett, because it's not his type of thing to be doing. I heard various descriptions of why the black writer, black producer is not at his very best today, because they don't know how to go for his message or material. They don't know what to write about. Years ago there were pains, agonies, trials and tribulations that were very easy to describe and write about. Today any rock group that you hear on the radio has explained the black man's problem in such an eloquent way that it isn't necessary for the black man to sit down and tell it. Just this morning I heard a thing called "Southern Whiteman" by Neil somebody ["Southern Man" by Neil Young]. Anyway, the rock artists have taken the problem of the black man and part of his music and he is protesting. Whereas before the black man just sang about it. It wasn't complaining, it was just part of his living.

Other very fine descriptions of what has happened in music is that I have seen kids from white affluent families become the very best country blues guitarists, and to the blacks it's a lost art. One in particular, John Hammond at Columbia Records, is an heir to the Hammond Organ people and he has a son who plays the countriest, funkiest black blues that I've ever heard in my life.

Another comical expression that I've heard is that the rock artists are white artists taking dope and absorbing themselves into the problems of those things that have been a matter of course for the black man. Someone said, like, the guy has to go on a trip to play that kind of music or get those kind of ideas. The black man has been on a trip all his life with his trials and tribulations.

I don't know what I just said has to do with, but I get wound up when I start talking. It's just things I hear and it may be interesting if you want to copy this off and read it.

Notes

1. In 1945 Lucky Millinder was under contract to Decca; however, several vocalists and musicians associated with his show-band recorded under their own names for Nathan. Millinder did not officially join King until 1950.

2. "The Honeydripper" was the first Queen/King release (no. 4100). Benjamin Jackson was born at Cleveland, Ohio, in 1919 and formed his own band in Buffalo after working with Freddie Webster. He joined Millinder in 1945 as tenor player and occasional vocalist.

3. Roy Brown, from New Orleans, joined De Luxe in 1947. He became one of the most successful and influential singers of the forties. De Luxe was based in Linden.

4. "Walking the Blues" was a 1955 hit and a cover of the same song by Willie Dixon on Checker.

5. "Country Paul" was actually Carolina Slim. His real name was Eddie Harris. Maybe Mr. Glover has confused him with a King hillbilly artist called Paul Howard.

Ralph Bass

Mike Leadbitter was among the first researchers to recognize the importance of the pioneering record men and their role in the development of rhythm and blues. In an early issue of *BU* he urged fellow researchers to interview the company owners, A&R men, and record producers, realizing they were a long neglected resource and a potential wealth of information. Steve Tracy's interview with Henry Glover was one of the earliest to appear in *BU,* and upon Mike's assuming sole editorship, features appeared on Art Rupe, Bob Shad, and Stan Lewis that documented their beginning and involvement in the independent record business that began to flourish in the mid-1940s.

There were no course studies or existing rules on how to enter the rough-and-tumble independent record business, a world populated by idiosyncratic Runyon-like characters that Ralph Bass joined in 1944. In a long career Bass worked for some of the biggest and best companies specializing in rhythm and blues: Black and White, Savoy, King/Federal, and Chess Records, producing such legendary artists as T-Bone Walker, Little Esther Phillips, Johnny Otis, Hank Ballard, the Dominoes, Little Willie Littlefield, and James Brown, to name but a few.

Whether or not by design, Ralph Bass granted few interviews. Norbert Hess interviewed him twice while Bass was working for Chess Records. The first interview, conducted in 1973, focused on his involvement with Johnny Otis and Little Esther. Speaking with complete candor on the genesis of Little Esther's "Double Crossing Blues," he offers us a rare and humorous perspective on discovering and recording a new talent and the hazards he encountered promoting a hit record. A second interview two years later covered the broader aspects of his fascinating career.

In later years Ralph Bass hinted at the possibility of a biography, but that project never materialized. Thankfully we have Norbert Hess's compelling interview. Ralph Bass died on March 5, 1997.

—Bill Greensmith

I Didn't Give a Damn if Whites Bought It! Ralph Bass Interview

Norbert Hess

Blues Unlimited #119 (May-June 1976)

I have visited and interviewed Ralph Bass twice in his office at the Chess Building in Chicago, 320 East 21st Street. The first time, unfortunately, my tape recorder broke during the interview without my notice, and the second time, Ralph was involved with visitors and recording and was not concentrating too much on my researching questions. By the time you read this, I am again in the States and I hope to get more information from this interesting man. When I set up a date with Ralph in September 1973, I mentioned I'd be mostly interested in Ralph's connection with Johnny Otis, Little Esther, and both Savoy and Federal Records. When I arrived at his office on the fifth floor of the Chess Building, I first asked him how he became interested in music at all. I was so impressed by his enthusiastic impromptu story that I just let him tell it.

No, I'd rather not do that, I'd rather just stick to Johnny. (*laughs*) I'll preface it by a short thing about Johnny (Otis). I was a producer of nothing but jazz. I was recording Dizzy Gillespie and Charlie Parker and Wardell Gray and Dexter Gordon and all the jazz greats. Erroll Garner, I did all the early hits for Erroll Garner. I was such a jazz fanatic that if I heard a commercial record I would break it. One day, by accident, I recorded one of the biggest pop hits of the country, "Open the Door, Richard," and I said, "Is this [the] kind of shit that makes money?" Because I was spending all this man's money on all this jazz shit and it wasn't selling. So then I got very interested in R&B. We called it "race music" then, and I'd heard of Johnny. Johnny used to have a band that used to play at the Club Alabam in L.A. on Central Avenue. So I contacted him, how and when I just don't remember. I know he had a club with Bardu Ali, who is now Redd Foxx's manager, place called the Barrelhouse out in Watts. I signed

Ralph Bass. PS Recording Studios, Chicago, 1977. (Photo Norbert Hess)

Johnny to a contract, doing commercial things. There was a group called the Robins and which I had signed to the company I was working for, Savoy Records. I was A&R man for Savoy and we had brought . . . there was a little girl, Little Esther, Esther Phillips now. She was thirteen years old and I remember Johnny and I were in the midst of recording the Robins at a studio in L.A. called Radio Recorder, and Esther came down and Johnny said, "Let's audition her." And I said, "Okay," and at the end of the session I took part of the group and I used the bass voice in the group, Bobby Nunn. And just fuckin' around we did one thing by Jesse Mae Robinson called "Double Crossing Blues." Johnny had reworked the song, he had an act at the club, comedian act, they did a thing about the "lady bear," which was very funny. I didn't understand it at first, being strictly au fait, well, jazz au fait. I'd never heard the expression about "lady bear," and I used to go in the club and say, "What the fuck are you laughing about?" every time they get about the "lady bear" till Johnny told me what "lady bear" was. "A 'lady bear' is an ugly, black broad, who can't get a man because she's so ugly. She'll hit you on top of the head and drag you away (*laughs*), very aggressive." He used the gimmick line in the song and changed the lyric. He gave the song to Esther and we recorded with Bobby. Herman Lubinsky, who was a nasty motherfucker—he's a good record man, a great record man, but he's a cheap motherfucker, that's why he's a millionaire, I guess. I sent the dubs to Herman Lubinsky in Newark and I said, "Send me $10 for the girl who didn't go to school, pay her bus fare," and all that shit. He wrote me and said, "What the hell are you runnin' out there, an office for schoolchildren? I don't pay no damn guy $10 to hear a little thirteen-year-old kid sing!" Well, of course, in those days thirteen-year-old kids were unheard of. Especially Esther, who never sounded like a thirteen-year-old kid. There was another girl at that time who was very popular, but she had a childish approach to a song. I just sent the dub on, no title, no information, no nothing. We were hoping that one of the things that Johnny had done with the Robins was gonna be a hit. Anyway, about four o'clock in the morning I get a call from Newark, New Jersey, from Herman Lubinsky. "Who's that little girl you recorded and sent me?" he said. "She's gonna be the biggest thing in the country, sign her, get her to sign contracts now," I said. "What in the hell are you talkin' about, man?" Then he told me a story about the disc jockey Bill Cook in Newark.

There was a disc jockey who came into Herman's office—he had a big show. In fact, Bill was Roy Hamilton's manager later on in life and Bill was the biggest thing in Newark. Bill came into Herman's office and said, "Herman, there ain't a damn thing that's sellin', nothing big. Do you have anything new that I can listen to? Maybe you got something that might mean something?" Herman said, "Well, my California man sent me some shit, just a pile of shit." So he listened to the things and all of a sudden he come running back, very excited, in Herman's office. He said, "Man, who is this? Goddamn, this is great, what's the name of this thing? This thing is going to be a smash hit!" Herman got all excited and Bill said, "I'm gonna put it on the air. What's the name of the thing?" Herman said, "I don't know. We didn't put any title on it, just that dubbing." He put it on the air and, sure enough, the board lit up. And he had a contest. Herman couldn't wait for me to tell him what the title was. He had a contest and he said "Double Crossing Blues." That's a funny thing, because everybody got double-crossed on this record.

After the phone call I drove my car, must have been four o'clock in the morning. Johnny lived out in Watts, knocked on the door. Phyllis, his wife, got up and I said, "Get Johnny up, Phyllis!" Johnny had just gone to bed after playing at the Barrelhouse. I said, "Wake up Johnny, we got a smash hit!" He said, "Man, I heard that shit before." (*laughs*) I said, "No, man, we got a smash hit!" He said, "What, the thing with the Robins?" I said, "No, man, the thing with Esther!" (*laughs*) He said, "You got to be kidding, that piece of shit?" He got the dub out and put it on the record player, shaking his head. He couldn't believe it. He said, "Of all the goddamn things I've ever done in my life, this piece of shit has to be it!" I said, "Well, Johnny, now, we both know that the things we dig ourselves never necessarily mean that the public out there will dig 'em. It's just whatever is a combination of lyric. Esther, she sounds so much like Dinah Washington." Her mama was a domestic, worked out in Pasadena. We got in the car. I had some contracts with me. We went out to where her mama worked and had her sign the contracts.

What happened, we now had a smash record and Johnny knew, being a musician, that any success he would have would be through Little Esther. Who the hell wants to hear a goddamn drummer—what the hell does it mean? But Esther, he managed Esther. First of all, we didn't have no money. I didn't have no money, Johnny didn't have no money. We know we had to get some bread and front [money] to get a bus to go on tour. We went to a man named Harold Oxley, who had a booking office on the West Coast. There were very few booking offices that booked nothing but soul talent, black talent. So Harold started booking us, but we needed money for a bus. I said, "Johnny, what we'll do is make enough money on these dates on the West Coast to be able to get us a bus." There was a cat named Ed Fishman, who was managing the Robins. The Robins were the group. We used their bass voice, Bobby Nunn, to sing with Esther "Double Crossing Blues." Johnny said, "This motherfucker, Ed Fishman, is a thief and a crook. He's gonna fuck us out, fuck us up!" I said, "No, we'll be careful." So, sure enough, Ed Fishman wanted to stop the record, because he said it was the Robins' record, not Esther's record, because Bobby was on it. So I said, "I'll tell you what. We'll give you part of the thing. We'll give you Esther, but we need some time." We were gonna fuck Ed Fishman, but we couldn't do it now. We had to play these dates to get enough money. Well, he gave us a release saying the Robins don't claim the record, which meant that Johnny could make enough bread off the record to be able to do what he wanted to do. When Ed Fishman found out we double-crossed him and signed Esther to Harold Oxley, he dedicated to fuck us up.

I never will forget, we had to play three one-nighters, one in Bakersfield and one in Redwood City, and then we had to play the big dates, Oakland and San Francisco. I went up ahead to promote the record—it was unbelievable how big this record was. There was a promoter there—he and his wife were the promoter—I can't think of their name. I laid the promotion out in front. There was a cat named Jumpin' George Oxford, a white boy who had the only soul program in that area, and I had made arrangements for her [Esther] to be in this show. He had a very great friend of his who was a great basketball player who had a show in Oakland, Don Barksdale. I also had a personal appearance for Esther set up with the biggest record shop in San Francisco. Anyway, I get a phone call the day before the one-nighter in San Francisco from the local promoter in San Francisco, saying, "How old is Esther?" I said, "She's thirteen." He said, "I got a call from the police department saying because of her age she couldn't perform. She can't perform in a place where booze is served." California had a real rough law about minors because of the Jackie Coogan thing, where Jackie Coogan's mama fucked him out of a lot of money and because of a lot of child actors, minor actors in California, making a lot of money, so they had these laws. I said, "Good God almighty, Ed Fishman probably called the police department and said, 'Hey, you know there's gonna be a thirteen-year-old girl gonna appear on a show where booze is gonna be dispensed,'" and all that bullshit. I remember walking the fuckin' streets at night trying to figure out a way. I couldn't get hold of Johnny, he was performing, en route . . . where the hell was Johnny? Then an idea came to me. I got on the phone. There was a girl named Mickey Champion who sounded a little bit like Dinah, but who could imitate any singer you could think of. I got hold of Mickey and told her, "Call Oxley, Johnny's booking agent, and he'll give you the bread. Get a plane and come right up here, I'll meet you." Johnny didn't know anything was happening, 'cause I couldn't reach him. I was gonna have Mickey be Esther. I was gonna substitute her.

Meanwhile, I had to cover myself up, so I called the promoter and said, "Who are the police authorities?" He said, "The Juvenile Department." I said, "I'd like to meet with them, give me their number and their names and we'll meet." I met with them the next afternoon and they read the riot act to me about minors performing. I tried to give them a sob story. "This little girl had no money and this is her big break," and all that shit, and that wouldn't work. Finally, an idea came to me. I said, "How does the law read? Will you read me the exact law?" They said, "No one under eighteen could perform while intoxicating beverages were dispensed with." I said, "Beautiful, I'll tell 'em to just close up the fucking bar while she's singing." (*laughs*) Only says "while alcoholic beverages were being dispensed with," that was the loophole! They said, "Okay, but she can only sing till ten o'clock, because that's the law." I said, "Okay." Well, Mickey came up and Johnny came in about the same time. I told Johnny the whole story, and Johnny said, "Oh, shit, that'll fuck us all up!" I said, "No, Johnny!" and I told him what the plan was. We got Esther in her room and her sister, who had been traveling with her. I told her, "You got to get yourself back to L.A., 'cause you can't be seen here." I told her what we were going to do and she started to cry. I said, "No, baby, don't worry about a thing, this is only in California. Unless we get over these two goddamn dates we got up here, which will buy us the bus to be able to perform all the one-nighters we got, we won't be able to work." So we put a veil on her to cover her face up and got her ass out. (*laughs*) We took her to the bus station and sent her ass on to L.A. Meanwhile, one of the cats we had hired to take Bobby's place to sing the male part to "Double Crossing Blues." Mel Walker, his name was. We got a record player and we got the two of them in a room and we got them rehearsing all fuckin' night "Double Crossing Blues," so that Mickey sounded exactly like Esther. And we got the fuckin' short dresses—Mickey was, like, twenty-one, she had two children and we put the fucking short dress on her all night long, that's what she did.

Next day we had a deejay thing with Jumpin' George in Oakland. (*chuckling*) Johnny and I were cueing Mickey in on Esther's life in case whatever questions are asked. I said, "Look, baby, if you can't answer the questions, you must keep your mouth shut and I'll answer it for you or Johnny will answer it." So the three of us went down there, Johnny like this (*pantomimes and laughs*)—he's scared to death. He ain't never done no shit like this. We got to the station and the deejay is asking all these questions. "How does it feel for a young girl?" and that bullshit. Every time he'd ask her a question that she couldn't answer, Johnny or I would bust in and answer the question and we got over that hurdle. Now, the next was a personal appearance at this record shop. God damn, we got a block and a half away and there were the police. Shit, the arrest squad! There must have been five thousand kids there with their mamas, all there to see Esther. Johnny said, (*laughs*) "I ain't goin' through there, we gonna get killed. We got to get killed, you can't fool those kids." (*breaks up for a moment*) I said, "Johnny, it's either now or never, baby. Either we get through this or we're dead." We finally plowed through this crowd and it was just a small record shop and you could hear the voices sayin', "Hey, where's Esther?" "Shit, if that's Esther, my mama is my grandma." We could hear this rumble, "Where's Esther?" We were back in this booth and there was a wall, and we thought for sure these people were gonna take this wall in on us. So I finally got an idea to quiet them, because we knew

Johnny Otis.

damn well there was gonna be a riot. I said, "Have you got a record player and a microphone?" "Play the fuckin' record," and I says to Walker, "You and Mickey get up there and sing this fucking song, sing it here!" They played the record and then Walker and Mickey started singing the damn thing and the kids said, "Well, maybe it don't look like Esther, but she got to be. Sounds just like her, got to be her." We passed that motherfucking test. (*laughs*) Poor Johnny was almost in a state of shock. He was scared to death some shit was gonna happen.

Now, something happened with one of the trumpet players, Lee Graves. He decided he was gonna go home because he didn't dig what was happenin', or something was going on. So I'm down [at] the bus station looking for him, bring his ass back. You must remember that Johnny's band was the first entertaining band. He decided the band wasn't just going to sit down and play or stand up and play. They were going to perform, and he had an act, all kinds of things goin'—he had a gimmick. You must remember that Johnny had played the Apollo Theater. He'd seen Pigmeat Markham work and Moms Mabley work, the great black comedy acts work, and he had incorporated a lot of this shit in the band, so that they did skits. Some of the skits Pigmeat did and so forth, whatever he'd seen. The cats in the band sang, they all moved. It was the first entertaining band in the country. In fact, James Brown copied all his shit from Johnny's band, because Ben Bard—later on, not too soon after that—Ben Bard booked Johnny's band. I had to get Johnny away from Harold Oxley for reasons, other reasons. Later on I gave James Brown to Ben Bard and Ben became the manager—that's another long story. When James formed his band remembering Johnny's band, I had James do the same damn thing with his shit. A very entertaining band, everybody had to do something—okay, now getting back to the story. So I went to get Graves, who had an integral part in many of the things that Johnny was featuring in the band. By the time I got back to the hall it was after ten o'clock and here's the promoter, man, was he worried. He said,

"God damn, they're gonna put us all in jail, shit!" It was after ten o'clock and they didn't close the bar down while Mickey was singing. Johnny wasn't there. I said, "Where's the man?" They said, "There he is!" Here comes the lieutenant, same cat I'd talked to. I had a special license he'd given me to perform providing the bars were closed and she didn't sing after ten o'clock. You know, what the fuck, ain't nobody get to a dance till after ten o'clock! I said, "Come here, I want to talk to you 'real quiet' . . . the girl up there singing is not Little Esther. That girl up there is over twenty-one. I decided not to play Esther, because most of these people come here after ten o'clock at night." You must remember it was more of an adult crowd than the type of audience that goes to see a show today. I said, "So I pulled her understudy in, but if anybody ever finds out that little girl is not Little Esther, there'll be a riot here!" And the place was jam-packed. There were wall-to-wall people and they had a police broad searchin' all the women coming up for weapons and they had a policeman searching all the cats. "There'll be a riot here. You'll need the whole damn police force to put this fuckin' riot down. If you want to go backstage and be very quiet about it, Mickey will prove her name is Mickey Champion and she's over twenty-one. She's got her driver's license and the whole bit, okay?" I wasn't gonna take a chance putting this little girl on, you know. I sent her home. That was the truth. He went back there and satisfied himself that it wasn't Little Esther; it was Mickey Champion. Johnny was sweating! (*breaks up for a moment*)

Little Esther Phillips.

Everything was cool. My only thing was if there was anybody in that audience who was from L.A. and knew Little Esther, 'cause Esther had worked all around Watts. She made all these amateur shows. She'd been doing some work around there because of the popularity of the record at that time. I was just hoping that nobody knew her. Well, sure enough, about twelve o'clock here come two dudes: "Hey, baby, you the manager? Where's Little Esther?" I said, "Man, what are you talkin' about?"

He said, "Where's Little Esther? That broad up there ain't Little Esther. We are from L.A., we know who Little Esther is!" I said, "Come here, baby, she was here." I was hoping he wasn't here at ten o'clock. I said, "She was here," and I took out the special license, the one from the police department that let Esther sing till ten o'clock. "See," and I showed him the fucking license. I said, "Man, we don't want her to go to jail, she's only thirteen. Be cool about it!" I talked 'em out of the damn shit, give 'em a few bucks. (*laughs*) Everything was beautiful except getting the fuck out.

As I was paying the damn hotel bill—George Washington Hotel, I think, some black hotel in San Francisco. As I was checkin' out, in came a phone call for me, said, "This is the *San Francisco Chronicle.* We were just told you pulled the biggest hoax in show business." I said, "What's this?" They said, "You had a little girl you were advertising as Little Esther and she didn't appear." I said, "If you print one line about that fuckin' story, we'll sue you for everything you got! That was Little Esther up there last night! We'll sue the shit out of you!" "Man," I said, "Johnny, let's get the fuck out of here before everybody finds out what's happening." I said, "Let's go and see Don Barksdale," the basketball player, who had a show, was a big man in the Bay Area and went to school with Johnny. We drove to his house and told him the whole story. He said, "You mean you lied to me, your buddy?" "We had to!" He said, "Don't worry about it. I'll cool the newspaper."

I tell you this story about Johnny's early career. If we hadn't done that, God knows how the fuck we'd have made all these—we didn't have no money—where we'd have got the bread to get the bus, to make it possible for everything that happened to Johnny. There are many other stories connected with Johnny and what we had to do. I think Johnny's biggest thing was in being able to handle people. He has a kind of a charisma about him that attracts people to him and they believe him. When they leave him they'll curse the shit out of him. They'll think he's stealing the ass off them. I don't think Johnny ever did that, knowingly. They'll talk about him like a dog behind his back and they'll blame everybody else, including me, for what happened, but when they get with Johnny they love him. There's a thing about Johnny. He's a natural leader-type thing. He has everybody believing in him while they are with him, but when they're away from him, something else. But *with* him, very loyal. He has tremendous talent, because he went through a lot of shit.

We both went through a similar lot of shit. He married a black woman, I married a black woman. Johnny was married to a black woman way before I was, and so for all purpose and intent I think Johnny was black. Nobody knew Johnny as a white boy. Johnny was Greek.

The other story about Johnny being white and being in black music was . . . we played Biloxi, Mississippi, a one-nighter, and I had Little Esther in New Orleans. It was during Lent period. In Lent period you don't play in New Orleans, nothing happens in that period. I was in New Orleans and we were taping a show we had to do at the auditorium, a one-nighter we had to do, and we were taping a show with one of the deejays down there. In getting Esther back to Biloxi we were late getting there. I got to the club—no club, it was shit. There were all these warehouses that were boarded up with wooden windows.

The promoter came on out and says, "Hey, is Johnny Otis white or black?" I said, "Who want to know?" He said, "The police, man, we all goin' to jail." In the South a white musician couldn't play with the blacks. There was a city ordinance about that kind of shit. I said, "Tell them to come over, I'll talk to them." "We all goin' to jail," he said. Poor Johnny, man. I look at the bandstand, everybody's looking over to see what's gonna happen, 'cause down there they put your ass in jail for . . . Here come the police with his nightstick. He be hittin' his leg with the nightstick and a toothpick in his mouth. He ready to hit somebody. He said, "What are you doin' down here, who are you?" I said, "Is it against the law to protect my money? I own this band, I'm down here protectin' my money." "Well, what's that white boy doing up on the bandstand?" he says. I said, "What white boy? I don't see no white boy!" I'm trying to think what to tell this fuckin' cat. "I don't see no white boy!" He said, "You're from the North. Down here we can always tell these niggers . . ." and he started telling me all this shit about how they can tell niggers and he got to some fingernail bullshit. I ain't never heard of no bullshit they can tell by fingernails. While he was talking an idea came to me. I said, "Wait a minute, man. You want to give that dark boy a whole lot of credit?" He said, "For what?" I said, "Well, his great gran'mama is black and he ain't ashamed of being black. Just suppose someone like that came down to your hometown, eat in your restaurant, stayed in your best hotels, then I hit him on top of the head and married your women." "Shit!" he said. "He don't want to do that, he's black, his great grandmammy black, he's black!" So the police took the hat off his head and scratched his head and said, "Come to think of it, there must be two, three millions down here just like that, passin'!" (*breaks up for a moment*)

The sequel to the story is that now he thinks Johnny is black, dig? 'Cause we used to put dark makeup powder on Johnny and dye his hair real black. The sequel to this story is, after this tour, I had to get back to my gig with Savoy Records. 'Cause when Johnny asked me to come with him, he said, "I can't trust nobody. Ralph, would you come and manage my band? Take care of the bread and everything. I was on that road for four months. I lost all this weight, man." (*laughs*) I had to get back to my gig, so I said, "Who you want to take care of the band?" He says, "Earle Warren." Earle Warren was the straw boss for Basie, played alto sax for Basie, and Johnny and Earle were very tight. I said, "Okay." Now, Earle could "pass." He looked like a Mexican.

Meeting Ralph again in April 1975, I heard a big part of the rest of his career: Born Ralph Basso on May 1, 1911, in New York City to a German mother and an Italian father, Ralph learned to play violin in school but soon became interested in jazz records. By 1944, an accident to his hand ended his career

as a musician and he became a disc jockey and lecturer with a growing interest in race music. He noticed that the black market wanted records that the major companies were not supplying. Ralph, who was already in Los Angeles, started to produce some race records himself and sent acetates to several independent companies offering his services. Only Black & White of Cleveland, Ohio, answered, and Paul Reiner, head of the company, asked him to arrange further sessions. Here, I have to quote briefly from an early *BU* (#79, page 10):

> Ralph went to the local Musicians Union on Central Avenue to find out who were the best musicians. He was told to contact Sammy Franklin, then popular in the clubs. He signed Franklin and went to Radio Recorders, then the only independent studio in L.A., but they were booked up, so he hired a studio in a radio station. He had half an hour before Reiner arrived, so he explained to the engineer that he hadn't the faintest idea about cutting records and asked for a quick briefing. Then he rumpled his hair, rolled up his shirt-sleeves and generally "mussed" himself up. As Reiner walked in, Ralph was rushing around and shouting instructions with great authority. Impressed, Reiner soon left, telling an aide, "the guy looks like he knows what he's doing." This is how Ralph became a producer.

That was in 1944. I started for that company. I produced T-Bone Walker. "Bobby Sox Baby" was a smash hit, Lena Horne, Phil Moore, a lot of jazz acts. Earl Spencer, the big band Stan Kenton bought the book from. Some square bands, like Henry King, Jan Garber, society bands. A great Mexican named Chino Ortez sold big to the Mexicans. I was the first one to record Essy Morales, the great flute player, who died many years ago. Also Ivie Anderson. Jack McVea—"Open the Door, Richard!", the first million-seller I produced. It was the one that changed me. I was recording all this heavy jazz shit in L.A., including Charlie Mingus. I did "Bird" (Charlie Parker) and "Diz" (Dizzy Gillespie) with Slim Gaillard and it wouldn't sell. Then I was doing a blues date on Raymond Tarren, McVea's drummer. We were doin' eight sides to fulfill a contract and they all sounded alike. I said, "Let's do something different!" and we came up with "Open the Door, Richard!" It changed my whole concept. Been on a commercial kick, I've done some jazz things since, but only commercial jazz. Sammy Franklin was the first band I ever recorded, "The Honeydripper." I copied Joe Liggins. Portrait was my own label, with Erroll Garner on it. My own company—that was during Savoy. I had a label called Bop (before Savoy). I had the original "Chase" with Wardell Gray and Dexter Gordon, recorded live. I knew I had the first jazz hit on my hands, but I didn't have money to finance the pressing. I was in Chicago seeing my distributor, Monroe Passis, who was originally a branch manager for King Records in Chicago, but opened up his own distributing company. While I was in his office, Herman Lubinsky called up because Monroe was handling Savoy. Lubinsky offered to help when he heard my needs. I went to New York, as I was going to do a deal with Al Green to handle "The Chase." Al was an alcoholic and had gone missing and nobody could find him. As my money ran low I called Herman Lubinsky in desperation and that's when we made a deal. I talked to Freddy Mendelsohn, who's running Savoy now, and they are gonna rerelease those things I did on that label. Herman suggested I go on a salary and be his man on the West Coast, and that's how I got with Savoy. That was 1948. I stayed three years until 1951.

By now Savoy has been bought by Arista Records of New York, but there are plans to reissue several albums and 78s later this year, among them Brownie McGhee, Johnny Otis, Little Esther, and several other blues, jazz, and gospel acts. In 1948 Ralph tried another deal with Al Green as he looked for a distributor for his Erroll Garner recordings, to be issued on his Bop label. Again he contacted Lubinsky, who agreed to do the Bop/Garner distribution, but he double-crossed Ralph and issued them on Savoy. Lubinsky did cut four sides by Garner. When Garner got to the studio he found the elevator broken down and had to walk up twenty flights. When he arrived exhausted, Lubinsky wanted him to play boogie-woogie! Garner refused and cut "Laura," "Penthouse Serenade," plus two others. He vowed never to cut for Lubinsky again. All the sides Ralph cut with Garner were "one take" items, cut on three-minute shellac discs. On each take, after two and a half minutes, Ralph would signal Garner he had thirty seconds to wind it up.

Ralph was the West Coast A&R man for Savoy and spent only a little time in New York, where he recorded Lucky Thompson, Linda Hopkins, and Brownie McGhee and Sonny Terry for the company. He was responsible for almost all of the Robins', Johnny Otis's, and Little Esther's records. He met Otis at his Barrelhouse in Watts.

The Barrelhouse, a hundred people, with a dance floor in the middle, the bar . . . Bardu Ali and his wife, Tila, used to be in charge of the thing. Johnny's only thing was the goddamn band—that was his part of the thing. Johnny hired the acts and played the music there. There was a place right next to the Barrelhouse, and that's where Johnny got all his fuckin' ideas. It was a storefront church. At intermission time Johnny and I would go out and stand in front of this old storefront church and steal all the fucking tunes played inside! (*breaks up for a moment*) That's true! That's where Johnny got a lot of his ideas, from the old storefront church. The Barrelhouse was a local club, most of the people who went to the Barrelhouse were from that area—it didn't draw any Hollywood figures. Nobody would "slum" out there, it was too rough. I remember bringing Herman Lubinsky into the club. Herman, I don't know why little cats always like carrying a lot of money on 'em, I don't know why. There's something about small cats, short cats with power, I don't dig. I think it's because of the fact that they know they've been very short as a child and they want to get even with the world. Like all them motherfuckin' dictators we've ever had, everybody in life that was a bad guy, was always a short cat. (*laughs*) It's a remarkable thing. Lubinsky was short and fat, puffing on a cigar, had them diamonds on his hands, and always carried a couple of thousand dollars in his pocket. When we got finished he went to pay the bill in the Barrelhouse and he flashed all that fucking money—shit! Johnny came over and said, "Johnny, get us out of here, man!" Johnny had to get two or three cats to get us out of the club. (*laughs*) It wasn't a bad place, but you don't flash money like that in a ghetto club. The Barrelhouse was a ghetto club. Johnny had a lot of good talent that performed there, local talent, of course, no "names"—he couldn't afford "names." Esther never sang there. She couldn't work in a club in California, she was only thirteen. I think they sneaked her in a couple of times. There wasn't much you could really say about the Barrelhouse except that was where Johnny got all his ideas from first and worked his thing up, the blues thing, the blues kick—got his band together.

After the Robins left and later split into the Robins and the Coasters, three members of the band took over the vocal group part as the Blue Notes (Lee Graves, Donald Johnson, Walter Henry). Ninety percent of the Savoys were recorded at Radio Recorders. Esther's Federal sides were done in Cincinnati. I think there were only two independent studios in Los Angeles at the time. There was one studio on Western Boulevard, but they were crazy. They wanted royalties on every record, on top of paying them for the use of the studio. I told them, "Kiss my ass!" (*laughs*) So we were all using Radio Recorders. Capitol was using Radio Recorders, too. It made it difficult for studio time. You had to book it two or three weeks in advance, minimum.

On some of the Savoy discs Bass is credited as co-author of the songs.

Yes, Johnny and I would write half the night, when we had the time. We'd be in the streets of Los Angeles, two or three o'clock in the morning, shooting ideas at each other. I was a gimmick writer, the gimmick line, that was my forte. I could think of the gimmick line, that was the whole song, the basic idea. "Work with Me, Annie" was my gimmick, but my name is not even on the song (credited). A lot of times I didn't put my name on things, as I figured I already had the publishing rights. Later on in life I learned. I believe if a cat makes a genuine contribution to a song, he should be listed as one of the writers.

Ralph also traveled for a while with the Johnny Otis caravan.

Just the first four months; after that I went back to my gig. I became an "instant road manager," because Johnny couldn't find anybody he could trust. I became a pretty good road manager. (*laughs*) While the band would be playing a gig, I'd be working on the bus, trying to put it together, but we never missed a gig, outside of one time—they made the gig, but without instruments or Esther. Redd Lyte was driving the panel truck and put it into a full spin and turned it over several times. We had instruments all over the place. I buried Mario Delagarde's bass fiddle there. Redd Lyte was arrested because he couldn't find his driver's license, as he'd lost his wallet when the truck was turning over. Lee Graves, Esther, and Redd Lyte were in our group, so they missed the gig. The rest of them played it. Mel Walker and Johnny probably sang the whole thing. (*laughs*) We showed up a day or two later;

we had to jump from Shreveport to Oklahoma City. That's how we were booked—one-nighters, four or five hundred miles apart, with no sleep. Half the time we never stayed there, just kept driving, tryin' to make our gig, sleep in the car. No bed of roses. Actually, it was illegal to jump more than two hundred miles a day. The band, they was all nice cats, we didn't have any problems. Some problems with Lee Graves, that's about the only one we'd have a problem with. Lee would get high on the bus. I remember one night goin' through Oklahoma, Lee and the valet got high on the bus. I didn't give a damn, personally, but in the Deep South they were rough if they caught you with the shit. You got five, ten years in jail, then they'd confiscate the damn bus. I made a rule that nobody would smoke the shit in the bus. I knew they were smokin' the shit, so I stopped the bus and put 'em off, took their shit, and left them in the middle of the highway. It was dark. We got their luggage out and said, "Go home, you cats, fuck it!" We hadn't intended to leave them, just scare the shit out of them. We drove about a mile down the road and pulled over and waited. Then I said, "Okay, let's go back and pick 'em up. I think that'll teach them a lesson!" (*laughs*) There was very few problems after that. Some rules I laid down for the good of all of us, not for one or two. We had to think of survival, and in the fifties, survival was the name of the game.

Later, Earle Warren, Preston Love, and "Papa" Hess traveled with the band as road managers, respectively. In 1951 Ralph Bass moved from Savoy to King Records.

Federal was owned by Syd Nathan, head of King. It was a subsidiary created for me. All my productions went on to the Federal label. Esther was signed under contract to Savoy, and when I went with King I knew that the contract was no good, because here in California you had the Jackie Coogan law. The contract had to be approved, number one, by the courts, and the court would have to set up a guardian for her. Her Savoy contract was never handled that way. It was just a contract signed by her and then by her mama, which was not legal in the state of California and I knew it.

That's how I got her to King. I went to California and we hired an attorney, who did it properly. Went through the courts and the contract was declared null and void, and she went with me to King. Johnny never came with me to King or Federal. Syd gave me that label, Federal, because I had a production deal with him. To keep it straight, every record that came out on Federal, I got a production credit for. All my acts were on Federal, which was even James Brown later on. Johnny never came with me. He got fucked up with Don Robey down at Peacock, and he gave him all that black-white shit down there and Johnny double-crossed me, really, instead of signing with me. He was supposed to sign with me; he signed with little Don Robey. Robey gave him a big story and then he got fucked out of that big song they did with Big Mama Thornton, "Hound Dog." Johnny never was with King or Federal. He played behind Esther on all the things I did with Esther. We never did get a hit with Esther again, not a smash hit.

Little Esther recorded thirty-two titles for Federal in the period from January 1951 to March 1953. In fact, all of these were produced by Ralph, but the last four songs were not backed by members of the Johnny Otis Orchestra. On most of the others the entire Otis group, without the leader, played the tunes and they were released as "Little Esther with Orchestra," or under the pseudonym of Earle Warren. The Dominoes dueled with Esther on two numbers before they became stars under their own name. Bass combined Esther also with Little Willie Littlefield and Bobby Nunn on several other songs.

Just a chance thing, nothing pre-planned. They just happened to be in town. Leiber and Stoller wrote some of the songs for Esther, like "The Storm" and "Saturday Night Daddy." "The Storm," they wrote it on the date in the studio. We were having trouble getting a sound effect of rain, so I put the mike in the urinal and flushed it and got a giant sound like rain. That was one of the most famous stories that went around King Records, how I got that sound effect.

Ralph produced an endless list of rhythm-and-blues artists for Federal, like the Dominoes, the Midnighters, Hank Ballard, Smokey Hogg, Preston Love, Hemy Hill, John Lee, Roy Byrd, Dorothy Ellis, the Royales, Pete Lewis, Jimmy Nolen, Jimmy Witherspoon, Big Jay McNeely, Little Willie Littlefield, Young John Watson (nowadays Johnny "Guitar" Watson), and others, with such hits as "K. C. Loving," "So Fine," "Every Beat of My Heart"—well, there are so many. Johnny's band was used on many as the house band.

Most of the others don't stand out in my mind, 'cause nothing ever happened to them. You only remember the ones that are important to you. I recorded thousands of sides I don't even remember.

I asked Ralph if he had any problems with censorship on such catchy lyrics as "Work with Me, Annie," "60 Minute Man," or "Saturday Night Daddy" (by a then fifteen-year-old Little Esther).

The first censorship record came along with "Annie." "60 Minute Man" was the next thing jocks wouldn't play. [Actually, "60 Minute Man" came first.] "Annie" was the first one that little kids started buying and bringing home. We never made that record for kids, but for adults, black adults. The funny thing about whites, if they talk about sex in their own language, it's cute—like that famous song "Makin' Whoopee" that Eddie Cantor did. It was a great song, but what the hell was he talkin' about? He was fuckin' the broad and they had a baby and that was from "Makin' Whoopee." That's cute. But as soon as you say something that the white doesn't understand, like "Work with Me, Annie," there's tremendous sex connotations. Actually, those days we used the word "work" for everything by musicians, people in the show business—"Work with it!" relating to a dance routine or a great solo. It was a general word, it didn't just mean sex. We used it in the song as an adult humorous word. It was funny, but it was called to our attention, it was a dirty expression, it should be banned. That was not a "kiss of death" for the record (*laughs*), it was a boon. We sold close to a million on that and "60 Minute Man." Those things we did then are tame compared to words used today. I wasn't aiming at a teenage market, just a general market, kids from eighteen and up. We didn't have no twelve-, thirteen-year-old kids listening to our records, and of course, the blues were done for black adults. We didn't even have whites in mind. I didn't give a damn if whites bought it—if they did, groovy!

Ralph has many stories to tell, for example, about the Dominoes.

I was in New York and I was running the New York office with Henry Glover. Syd Nathan owned that building. On the top floor was a publisher, who is today one of the big publishers in the country. Harold Arnstein, who is probably one of the best copyright attorneys in the country, had the penthouse. Someone called me up and said they would like me to audition an air check of a group that one of those big amateur shows on radio—this was 1951. It was the first act they ever recorded for King Records, for Federal. This cat came in with the air check, which was "Goodnight Irene," which was a pop song at that time. I said I couldn't use it, as it was neither fish nor fowl. It was not black enough to sound black or white enough to sound white, and I didn't dig the kid who was singin' lead. Trying to be a Broadway tenor singer, Broadway musical. Billy Ward called me up to see what I thought of it, and he was so insistent that I told him to bring the whole group down to audition in person. When I heard Clyde McPhatter sing, I said, "There's your lead singer!" When I heard Bill Brown sing bass, he was the nearest thing to Ricky of the Ravens. I said, "There's your two leads!" He said, "What kind of material are you looking for?" I said, "The Orioles," who were very popular. He said, "That kinda shit? I can write those all day!" That was Billy Ward, who was a vocal coach with Rose Marse, who had backed them, an office on Broadway to coach vocal groups. He had no concept of rhythm and blues. He didn't know what rhythm and blues was. Being a vocal coach, the Broadway show–type of material appealed to him. I played him some Orioles things, and he came back later with the group and some of that kind of material, and that's when I signed them on. The first thing I did was "Do Something for Me" at Bell Studios on 8th Avenue, and I said, "Wow! That's it!"

Or about the Platters:

I produced the first ones, the ones for Federal. I first met Tony [Williams] at the amateur show at the Club Alabam, Hunter Hancock's show. He didn't sound like a blues singer, but he impressed me. He didn't even win third prize. He impressed me so much—to me, he was a modern Bill Kenny [of the Ink Spots]. I took him in my office that night and signed him. He lived in Jersey at the time and he brought his family back to L.A. I told him I couldn't sell singles. "Let me put a quartet with you," and I put a quartet called the Platters with him. I told them, "This is your new lead singer. Do you want to record for us, or don't you?" That's how I did it. I didn't have the time to rehearse them, and we did one session and nothin' happened with it. I was in my office at King, in L.A. one day, and I overheard someone come in and ask for some Platters records. I came out of my office to find out what his interest was. It was Buck Ram, and he was interested to see if I planned any further recordings. It turned out he was their manager and a vocal coach. I told him I knew of Tony's talent and if he worked on the group, I'd do further records. He spent time on them. We did another session and it sold fairly well on the West Coast only. When they came in to do the next session, they came in two and a half hours late. We only had half an hour left at Radio Recorders. We had time to do only one take and that was "Only You." Buck said, "We'll do it over again, it won't cost anything. Be damned I'm paying all these musicians and it will go into overtime." At the time the Platters were doing background work for King and they wanted $50 a side. Syd Nathan got mad and said, "I can get any amount of groups to do 'Doo Wop' all over the place for $10 a side!" Buck Ram got upset and asked for the Platters' release, which Syd gave. Bob Shad was in town at the time for Mercury. He picked up the Platters and they re-did "Only You" for Mercury. The only difference in the Mercury version was that they lowered the key; they used the same arrangement. We sued them and they "settled," 'cause you're not supposed to record the same song within five years. I made a deal between Federal and Mercury, whereas we got part of the money. They left us and got their first million-seller (*laughs*) and I had it in the can!

Ralph Bass also discovered James Brown.

Getting him was like a James Bond story. I found him down in Georgia. I heard a dub and it was so different that it knocked me out, cleaned me. I said, "Where can I find him?" I was in Atlanta, Georgia, at the time. It wasn't called James Brown; it was a group named the Famous Flames. So a disc jockey and I drove down to Macon, Georgia, from Atlanta in a pouring rainstorm, pouring like crazy, and I found out that James had a manager named Clint Brandly, who had a nightclub and was the local promoter. James was out on parole to Brandly at the time. See, James had a very hard young life. James was a "society outcast." Since Macon was such a Jim Crow town, I was told to meet Brandly by parking my car in front of a barbershop which was right across the street from a railroad station and when the Venetian blinds went up and down, to come on in. And I did. And I looked at Brandly and the cat said, "Yeah, I got a contract from Leonard Chess in my hand. I was waiting for Leonard Chess." Well, Leonard Chess was on his way, 'cause Leonard always said to me, "I'll never forgive you, 'cause you beat me to James Brown." That was one thing Leonard always kept saying to me. Now, he was on his way, but, see, in those days, airplanes—if the weather was halfway bad, they couldn't come in. They had no radar and all that jive they have today and so he was grounded. Well, anyway, I gave the cat $200 and I said, "Do you want to sign right now?" He says, "You got a deal. I'll call the whole group in to sign the papers." I don't know James Brown from a hole in the ground, and I went to the club that night and I saw him do his show, crawling on his stomach and saying, "Please, please, please,"—he must have said "Please" for about ten minutes. I almost got fired for doing the record. After I collected my $200 that I paid out and paid for the expenses, I went back to St. Louis and King sent some people looking for me to tell me I was fired. I called the old man up and asked Syd what's wrong. He says, "Man, you cut the worst piece of shit I ever heard in my life!" I said, "What are you talkin' about?" He says, "Man, this man sounds like he's stoned on the record, all he's saying is one word!" I said, "Oh, you mean 'Please'?" He says, "Yeah, all he's saying is 'Please, please, please, please, please.'" I says, "Well, I'll tell you what, put the record out in Atlanta, Georgia, and if it doesn't sell, baby, don't fire me, I quit. I'll walk clear all over the country to show you how bad this record is." Well, the rest is history. Who knew then that James would be what he is today? He was a country kid then; he used to call me "Mr. Ralph." He was so brow-beaten with that shit down there. I says, "Well, man, don't call me no 'Mr. Ralph.' Either call me 'Mr. Bass,' or call me 'Ralph,' but don't call me no 'Mr. Ralph!'"

Ralph Bass still collects a pretty good amount of money from the ARMO publishing company that he co-owned with Syd Nathan on a fifty-fifty basis, and many hits are signed to this company. ARMO is named after the first initials of members of Ralph's family. Except for Earl Bostic, he never produced for King, and left Federal in 1958. Federal continued for about six years, issuing many 45s by Freddie King and sides by Bobby King, Eddie Clearwater, and Smokey Smothers among others, but some, like James Brown, went to the mother company, King. In 1960 Johnny Otis became the A&R man on the West Coast for King Records, while Ralph became a producer for the Chess/Checker/Cadet/Argo company in Chicago, where he still works. Bass, described by Peter Guralnick as a "flamboyant, jive-talking hep-cat with a bulbous red nose and a penchant for colourful, slightly dated hip-talk," has produced almost all the big names of the Chess stable, such as Muddy Waters, Bo Diddley, Howlin' Wolf, Etta James, Sonny Boy Williamson, Ramsey Lewis, Moms Mabley, and Pigmeat Markham. Now he feels he's more or less a "watchdog" of the blues and is getting disappointed that his time of two-track recordings and blues is over—especially since Chess was recently sold for a mere $950,000 to the All Platinum Company and most of the old big names are dead or leaving the Chess family.

INDEX

Bill Greensmith is a photographer from England now living in St. Louis; producer of CDs for Red Lightnin', Ace, and Rhino Records and consultant for numerous record companies; former co-editor of *Blues Unlimited* (1974–87); and former host of a weekly blues program on KDHX, St. Louis (1989–94).

Mike Rowe is a longtime blues broadcaster, reviewer, writer, and compiler and the author of *Chicago Blues*.

Mark Camarigg is publications manager and former assistant editor for *Living Blues Magazine* and chairs the Study of Southern Cultures annual Blues Symposium at the University of Mississippi.

Music in American Life

Only a Miner: Studies in Recorded Coal-Mining Songs *Archie Green*
Great Day Coming: Folk Music and the American Left *R. Serge Denisoff*
John Philip Sousa: A Descriptive Catalog of His Works *Paul E. Bierley*
The Hell-Bound Train: A Cowboy Songbook *Glenn Ohrlin*
Oh, Didn't He Ramble: The Life Story of Lee Collins, as Told to Mary Collins *Edited by Frank J. Gillis and John W. Miner*
American Labor Songs of the Nineteenth Century *Philip S. Foner*
Stars of Country Music: Uncle Dave Macon to Johnny Rodriguez *Edited by Bill C. Malone and Judith McCulloh*
Git Along, Little Dogies: Songs and Songmakers of the American West *John I. White*
A Texas-Mexican *Cancionero*: Folksongs of the Lower Border *Américo Paredes*
San Antonio Rose: The Life and Music of Bob Wills *Charles R. Townsend*
Early Downhome Blues: A Musical and Cultural Analysis *Jeff Todd Titon*
An Ives Celebration: Papers and Panels of the Charles Ives Centennial Festival-Conference *Edited by H. Wiley Hitchcock and Vivian Perlis*
Sinful Tunes and Spirituals: Black Folk Music to the Civil War *Dena J. Epstein*
Joe Scott, the Woodsman-Songmaker *Edward D. Ives*
Jimmie Rodgers: The Life and Times of America's Blue Yodeler *Nolan Porterfield*
Early American Music Engraving and Printing: A History of Music Publishing in America from 1787 to 1825, with Commentary on Earlier and Later Practices *Richard J. Wolfe*
Sing a Sad Song: The Life of Hank Williams *Roger M. Williams*
Long Steel Rail: The Railroad in American Folksong *Norm Cohen*
Resources of American Music History: A Directory of Source Materials from Colonial Times to World War II *D. W. Krummel, Jean Geil, Doris J. Dyen, and Deane L. Root*
Tenement Songs: The Popular Music of the Jewish Immigrants *Mark Slobin*
Ozark Folksongs *Vance Randolph; edited and abridged by Norm Cohen*
Oscar Sonneck and American Music *Edited by William Lichtenwanger*
Bluegrass Breakdown: The Making of the Old Southern Sound *Robert Cantwell*
Bluegrass: A History *Neil V. Rosenberg*
Music at the White House: A History of the American Spirit *Elise K. Kirk*
Red River Blues: The Blues Tradition in the Southeast *Bruce Bastin*
Good Friends and Bad Enemies: Robert Winslow Gordon and the Study of American Folksong *Debora Kodish*
Fiddlin' Georgia Crazy: Fiddlin' John Carson, His Real World, and the World of His Songs *Gene Wiggins*
America's Music: From the Pilgrims to the Present (rev. 3d ed.) *Gilbert Chase*
Secular Music in Colonial Annapolis: The Tuesday Club, 1745–56 *John Barry Talley*
Bibliographical Handbook of American Music *D. W. Krummel*
Goin' to Kansas City *Nathan W. Pearson, Jr.*
"Susanna," "Jeanie," and "The Old Folks at Home": The Songs of Stephen C. Foster from His Time to Ours (2d ed.) *William W. Austin*
Songprints: The Musical Experience of Five Shoshone Women *Judith Vander*
"Happy in the Service of the Lord": Afro-American Gospel Quartets in Memphis *Kip Lornell*
Paul Hindemith in the United States *Luther Noss*
"My Song Is My Weapon": People's Songs, American Communism, and the Politics of Culture, 1930–50 *Robbie Lieberman*

Chosen Voices: The Story of the American Cantorate *Mark Slobin*
Theodore Thomas: America's Conductor and Builder of Orchestras, 1835–1905 *Ezra Schabas*
"The Whorehouse Bells Were Ringing" and Other Songs Cowboys Sing *Collected and Edited by Guy Logsdon*
Crazeology: The Autobiography of a Chicago Jazzman *Bud Freeman, as Told to Robert Wolf*
Discoursing Sweet Music: Brass Bands and Community Life in Turn-of-the-Century Pennsylvania *Kenneth Kreitner*
Mormonism and Music: A History *Michael Hicks*
Voices of the Jazz Age: Profiles of Eight Vintage Jazzmen *Chip Deffaa*
Pickin' on Peachtree: A History of Country Music in Atlanta, Georgia *Wayne W. Daniel*
Bitter Music: Collected Journals, Essays, Introductions, and Librettos *Harry Partch; edited by Thomas McGeary*
Ethnic Music on Records: A Discography of Ethnic Recordings Produced in the United States, 1893 to 1942 *Richard K. Spottswood*
Downhome Blues Lyrics: An Anthology from the Post–World War II Era *Jeff Todd Titon*
Ellington: The Early Years *Mark Tucker*
Chicago Soul *Robert Pruter*
That Half-Barbaric Twang: The Banjo in American Popular Culture *Karen Linn*
Hot Man: The Life of Art Hodes *Art Hodes and Chadwick Hansen*
The Erotic Muse: American Bawdy Songs (2d ed.) *Ed Cray*
Barrio Rhythm: Mexican American Music in Los Angeles *Steven Loza*
The Creation of Jazz: Music, Race, and Culture in Urban America *Burton W. Peretti*
Charles Martin Loeffler: A Life Apart in Music *Ellen Knight*
Club Date Musicians: Playing the New York Party Circuit *Bruce A. MacLeod*
Opera on the Road: Traveling Opera Troupes in the United States, 1825–60 *Katherine K. Preston*
The Stonemans: An Appalachian Family and the Music That Shaped Their Lives *Ivan M. Tribe*
Transforming Tradition: Folk Music Revivals Examined *Edited by Neil V. Rosenberg*
The Crooked Stovepipe: Athapaskan Fiddle Music and Square Dancing in Northeast Alaska and Northwest Canada *Craig Mishler*
Traveling the High Way Home: Ralph Stanley and the World of Traditional Bluegrass Music *John Wright*
Carl Ruggles: Composer, Painter, and Storyteller *Marilyn Ziffrin*
Never without a Song: The Years and Songs of Jennie Devlin, 1865–1952 *Katharine D. Newman*
The Hank Snow Story *Hank Snow, with Jack Ownbey and Bob Burris*
Milton Brown and the Founding of Western Swing *Cary Ginell, with special assistance from Roy Lee Brown*
Santiago de Murcia's "Códice Saldívar No. 4": A Treasury of Secular Guitar Music from Baroque Mexico *Craig H. Russell*
The Sound of the Dove: Singing in Appalachian Primitive Baptist Churches *Beverly Bush Patterson*
Heartland Excursions: Ethnomusicological Reflections on Schools of Music *Bruno Nettl*
Doowop: The Chicago Scene *Robert Pruter*
Blue Rhythms: Six Lives in Rhythm and Blues *Chip Deffaa*
Shoshone Ghost Dance Religion: Poetry Songs and Great Basin Context *Judith Vander*

Go Cat Go! Rockabilly Music and Its Makers *Craig Morrison*
'Twas Only an Irishman's Dream: The Image of Ireland and the Irish in American Popular Song Lyrics, 1800–1920 *William H. A. Williams*
Democracy at the Opera: Music, Theater, and Culture in New York City, 1815–60 *Karen Ahlquist*
Fred Waring and the Pennsylvanians *Virginia Waring*
Woody, Cisco, and Me: Seamen Three in the Merchant Marine *Jim Longhi*
Behind the Burnt Cork Mask: Early Blackface Minstrelsy and Antebellum American Popular Culture *William J. Mahar*
Going to Cincinnati: A History of the Blues in the Queen City *Steven C. Tracy*
Pistol Packin' Mama: Aunt Molly Jackson and the Politics of Folksong *Shelly Romalis*
Sixties Rock: Garage, Psychedelic, and Other Satisfactions *Michael Hicks*
The Late Great Johnny Ace and the Transition from R&B to Rock 'n' Roll *James M. Salem*
Tito Puente and the Making of Latin Music *Steven Loza*
Juilliard: A History *Andrea Olmstead*
Understanding Charles Seeger, Pioneer in American Musicology *Edited by Bell Yung and Helen Rees*
Mountains of Music: West Virginia Traditional Music from *Goldenseal* *Edited by John Lilly*
Alice Tully: An Intimate Portrait *Albert Fuller*
A Blues Life *Henry Townsend, as told to Bill Greensmith*
Long Steel Rail: The Railroad in American Folksong (2d ed.) *Norm Cohen*
The Golden Age of Gospel *Text by Horace Clarence Boyer; photography by Lloyd Yearwood*
Aaron Copland: The Life and Work of an Uncommon Man *Howard Pollack*
Louis Moreau Gottschalk *S. Frederick Starr*
Race, Rock, and Elvis *Michael T. Bertrand*
Theremin: Ether Music and Espionage *Albert Glinsky*
Poetry and Violence: The Ballad Tradition of Mexico's Costa Chica *John H. McDowell*
The Bill Monroe Reader *Edited by Tom Ewing*
Music in Lubavitcher Life *Ellen Koskoff*
Zarzuela: Spanish Operetta, American Stage *Janet L. Sturman*
Bluegrass Odyssey: A Documentary in Pictures and Words, 1966–86 *Carl Fleischhauer and Neil V. Rosenberg*
That Old-Time Rock & Roll: A Chronicle of an Era, 1954–63 *Richard Aquila*
Labor's Troubadour *Joe Glazer*
American Opera *Elise K. Kirk*
Don't Get above Your Raisin': Country Music and the Southern Working Class *Bill C. Malone*
John Alden Carpenter: A Chicago Composer *Howard Pollack*
Heartbeat of the People: Music and Dance of the Northern Pow-wow *Tara Browner*
My Lord, What a Morning: An Autobiography *Marian Anderson*
Marian Anderson: A Singer's Journey *Allan Keiler*
Charles Ives Remembered: An Oral History *Vivian Perlis*
Henry Cowell, Bohemian *Michael Hicks*
Rap Music and Street Consciousness *Cheryl L. Keyes*
Louis Prima *Garry Boulard*

Marian McPartland's Jazz World: All in Good Time *Marian McPartland*
Robert Johnson: Lost and Found *Barry Lee Pearson and Bill McCulloch*
Bound for America: Three British Composers *Nicholas Temperley*
Lost Sounds: Blacks and the Birth of the Recording Industry, 1890–1919 *Tim Brooks*
Burn, Baby! BURN! The Autobiography of Magnificent Montague *Magnificent Montague with Bob Baker*
Way Up North in Dixie: A Black Family's Claim to the Confederate Anthem *Howard L. Sacks and Judith Rose Sacks*
The Bluegrass Reader *Edited by Thomas Goldsmith*
Colin McPhee: Composer in Two Worlds *Carol J. Oja*
Robert Johnson, Mythmaking, and Contemporary American Culture *Patricia R. Schroeder*
Composing a World: Lou Harrison, Musical Wayfarer *Leta E. Miller and Fredric Lieberman*
Fritz Reiner, Maestro and Martinet *Kenneth Morgan*
That Toddlin' Town: Chicago's White Dance Bands and Orchestras, 1900–1950 *Charles A. Sengstock Jr.*
Dewey and Elvis: The Life and Times of a Rock 'n' Roll Deejay *Louis Cantor*
Come Hither to Go Yonder: Playing Bluegrass with Bill Monroe *Bob Black*
Chicago Blues: Portraits and Stories *David Whiteis*
The Incredible Band of John Philip Sousa *Paul E. Bierley*
"Maximum Clarity" and Other Writings on Music *Ben Johnston, edited by Bob Gilmore*
Staging Tradition: John Lair and Sarah Gertrude Knott *Michael Ann Williams*
Homegrown Music: Discovering Bluegrass *Stephanie P. Ledgin*
Tales of a Theatrical Guru *Danny Newman*
The Music of Bill Monroe *Neil V. Rosenberg and Charles K. Wolfe*
Pressing On: The Roni Stoneman Story *Roni Stoneman, as told to Ellen Wright*
Together Let Us Sweetly Live *Jonathan C. David, with photographs by Richard Holloway*
Live Fast, Love Hard: The Faron Young Story *Diane Diekman*
Air Castle of the South: WSM Radio and the Making of Music City *Craig P. Havighurst*
Traveling Home: Sacred Harp Singing and American Pluralism *Kiri Miller*
Where Did Our Love Go? The Rise and Fall of the Motown Sound *Nelson George*
Lonesome Cowgirls and Honky-Tonk Angels: The Women of Barn Dance Radio *Kristine M. McCusker*
California Polyphony: Ethnic Voices, Musical Crossroads *Mina Yang*
The Never-Ending Revival: Rounder Records and the Folk Alliance *Michael F. Scully*
Sing It Pretty: A Memoir *Bess Lomax Hawes*
Working Girl Blues: The Life and Music of Hazel Dickens *Hazel Dickens and Bill C. Malone*
Charles Ives Reconsidered *Gayle Sherwood Magee*
The Hayloft Gang: The Story of the National Barn Dance *Edited by Chad Berry*
Country Music Humorists and Comedians *Loyal Jones*
Record Makers and Breakers: Voices of the Independent Rock 'n' Roll Pioneers *John Broven*
Music of the First Nations: Tradition and Innovation in Native North America *Edited by Tara Browner*
Cafe Society: The Wrong Place for the Right People *Barney Josephson, with Terry Trilling-Josephson*

George Gershwin: An Intimate Portrait *Walter Rimler*
Life Flows On in Endless Song: Folk Songs and American History *Robert V. Wells*
I Feel a Song Coming On: The Life of Jimmy McHugh *Alyn Shipton*
King of the Queen City: The Story of King Records *Jon Hartley Fox*
Long Lost Blues: Popular Blues in America, 1850–1920 *Peter C. Muir*
Hard Luck Blues: Roots Music Photographs from the Great Depression *Rich Remsberg*
Restless Giant: The Life and Times of Jean Aberbach and Hill and Range Songs *Bar Biszick-Lockwood*
Champagne Charlie and Pretty Jemima: Variety Theater in the Nineteenth Century *Gillian M. Rodger*
Sacred Steel: Inside an African American Steel Guitar Tradition *Robert L. Stone*
Gone to the Country: The New Lost City Ramblers and the Folk Music Revival *Ray Allen*
The Makers of the Sacred Harp *David Warren Steel with Richard H. Hulan*
Woody Guthrie, American Radical *Will Kaufman*
George Szell: A Life of Music *Michael Charry*
Bean Blossom: The Brown County Jamboree and Bill Monroe's Bluegrass Festivals *Thomas A. Adler*
Crowe on the Banjo: The Music Life of J. D. Crowe *Marty Godbey*
Twentieth Century Drifter: The Life of Marty Robbins *Diane Diekman*
Henry Mancini: Reinventing Film Music *John Caps*
The Beautiful Music All Around Us: Field Recordings and the American Experience *Stephen Wade*
Then Sings My Soul: The Culture of Southern Gospel Music *Douglas Harrison*
The Accordion in the Americas: Klezmer, Polka, Tango, Zydeco, and More! *Edited by Helena Simonett*
Bluegrass Bluesman: A Memoir *Josh Graves, edited by Fred Bartenstein*
One Woman in a Hundred: Edna Phillips and the Philadelphia Orchestra *Mary Sue Welsh*
The Great Orchestrator: Arthur Judson and American Arts Management *James M. Doering*
Charles Ives in the Mirror: American Histories of an Iconic Composer *David C. Paul*
Southern Soul-Blues *David Whiteis*
Sweet Air: Modernism, Regionalism, and American Popular Song *Edward P. Comentale*
Pretty Good for a Girl: Women in Bluegrass *Murphy Hicks Henry*
Sweet Dreams: The World of Patsy Cline *Warren R. Hofstra*
William Sidney Mount and the Creolization of American Culture *Christopher J. Smith*
Bird: The Life and Music of Charlie Parker *Chuck Haddix*
Making the March King: John Philip Sousa's Washington Years, 1854–1893 *Patrick Warfield*
In It for the Long Run *Jim Rooney*
Pioneers of the Blues Revival *Steve Cushing*
Roots of the Revival: American and British Folk Music in the 1950s *Ronald D. Cohen and Rachel Clare Donaldson*
Blues All Day Long: The Jimmy Rogers Story *Wayne Everett Goins*
Yankee Twang: Country and Western Music in New England *Clifford R. Murphy*
The Music of the Stanley Brothers *Gary B. Reid*
Hawaiian Music in Motion: Mariners, Missionaries, and Minstrels *James Revell Carr*

Sounds of the New Deal: The Federal Music Project in the West *Peter Gough*
The Mormon Tabernacle Choir: A Biography *Michael Hicks*
The Man That Got Away: The Life and Songs of Harold Arlen *Walter Rimler*
A City Called Heaven: Chicago and the Birth of Gospel Music *Robert M. Marovich*
Blues Unlimited: Essential Interviews from the Original Blues Magazine
Edited by Bill Greensmith, Mike Rowe, and Mark Camarigg

The University of Illinois Press
is a founding member of the
Association of American University Presses.

Designed by Jim Proefrock
Composed in 11/14 Minion Pro
with Eurostile and Avenir display
at the University of Illinois Press
Manufactured by Cushing-Malloy, Inc.

University of Illinois Press
1325 South Oak Street
Champaign, IL 61820-6903
www.press.uillinois.edu